ECONOMIC DEVELOPMENT OF THE UNITED STATES

THE IRWIN SERIES IN ECONOMICS

Consulting Editor
LLOYD G. REYNOLDS
Yale University

AMES *Soviet Economic Processes*

ANDERSON, GITLOW, & DIAMOND (eds.) *General Economics: A Book of Readings* rev. ed.

BALASSA *The Theory of Economic Integration*

BEAL & WICKERSHAM *The Practice of Collective Bargaining* 3d ed.

BLAUG *Economic Theory in Retrospect* rev. ed.

BORNSTEIN (ed.) *Comparative Economic Systems: Models and Cases* rev. ed.

BORNSTEIN & FUSFELD (eds.) *The Soviet Economy: A Book of Readings* rev. ed.

BUCHANAN *The Public Finances* rev. ed.

CARTTER *Theory of Wages and Employment*

CARTTER & MARSHALL *Labor Economics: Wages, Employment, and Trade Unionism*

DAVIDSON, SMITH, & WILEY *Economics: An Analytical Approach* rev. ed.

DAVIS, HUGHES, & MCDOUGALL *American Economic History: The Development of a National Economy* 3d ed.

DOLL, RHODES, & WEST *Economics of Agricultural Production, Markets, and Policy*

DRUMMOND *The Canadian Economy: Organization and Development*

DUE *Government Finance: Economics of the Public Sector* 4th ed.

DUE & CLOWER *Intermediate Economic Analysis* 5th ed.

FELLNER *Probability and Profit: A Study of Economic Behavior along Bayesian Lines*

FERGUSON *Microeconomic Theory* rev. ed.

GAMBS & KOMISAR *Economics and Man* 3d ed.
GORDON *The Investment Financing and Valuation of the Corporation*
GRAMPP & WEILER (eds.) *Economic Policy: Readings in Political Economy* 3d ed.
GROSSMAN, HANSEN, HENDRIKSEN, MCALLISTER, OKUDA, & WOLMAN (eds.) *Readings in Current Economics* rev. ed.
GUTHRIE *Statistical Methods in Economics*
GUTHRIE & WALLACE *Economics* 4th ed.
HAGEN *The Economics of Development*
HARRISS *The American Economy: Principles, Practices, and Policies* 6th ed.
HERBER *Modern Public Finance*
HIGGINS *United Nations and U.S. Foreign Economic Policy*
JOME *Principles of Money and Banking*
KINDLEBERGER *International Economics* 4th ed.
KUHLMAN & SKINNER *The Economic System* rev. ed.
LEE *Macroeconomics: Fluctuations, Growth, and Stability* 4th ed.
LLOYD *Microeconomic Analysis*
LOCKLIN *Economics of Transportation* 6th ed.
MEYERS *Economics of Labor Relations*
PEGRUM *Public Regulation of Business* rev. ed.
PEGRUM *Transportation: Economics and Public Policy* rev. ed.
PETERSON & GRAY *Economic Development of the United States*
PHILLIPS *The Economics of Regulation: Theory and Practice in the Transportation and Public Utility Industries*
REYNOLDS *Economics: A General Introduction* 3d ed.
RIMA *Development of Economic Analysis*
SCITOVSKY *Welfare and Competition: The Economics of a Fully Employed Economy*
SIEGEL *Aggregate Economics and Public Policy* rev. ed.
SIRKIN *Introduction to Macroeconomic Theory* rev. ed.
SMITH & TEIGEN (eds.) *Readings in Money, National Income, and Stabilization Policy*
SNIDER *Introduction to International Economics* 4th ed.
SPENCER *Managerial Economics: Text, Problems, and Short Cases* 3d ed.
VANEK *International Trade: Theory and Economic Policy*
WILCOX *Public Policies toward Business* 3d ed.

ECONOMIC DEVELOPMENT OF THE UNITED STATES

JOHN M. PETERSON, Ph.D.
Professor of Economics
University of Arkansas

RALPH GRAY, Ph.D.
Associate Professor of Economics
DePauw University

1969

RICHARD D. IRWIN, INC., Homewood, Illinois
IRWIN-DORSEY LIMITED, Georgetown, Ontario

First Printing, March, 1969

Library of Congress Catalog Card No. 69–17159

Printed in the United States of America

PREFACE

Our purpose is to present a brief version of the American economy's growth story. Although for the most part our account is presented in laymen's language, the point of view is very much that of the economist. This orientation emphasizes quantitative measurements and the changing geographical, technological, and institutional conditions that influence human material progress.

The remarkably different rates of growth and levels of economic attainment that we find in the world today explain the intense interest of both the economist and the layman in the subject of economic growth. Why does the United States have a standard of living so far above any other nation? How did our historically rapid rate of economic growth start? How was it sustained? Will it continue? These are some of the questions that this book introduces at the outset and keeps in focus throughout.

It is not our purpose to relate everything that occurred in the American economy between the first colonial landing and today. Rather we wish to explain how the economy grew and to demonstrate the effects of growth upon economic life. In accordance with this limited objective the text is shorter than the comprehensive textbooks on American economic history. However, a relatively heavy reliance upon graphs and tables has added to page length. We have opted for brevity in the text in order to avoid the mass of details that would cause a loss of perspective about the overall processes of growth and change in the system. Thus topics related to growth are given lengthy treatment while some standard topics in American economic history texts are omitted or given only brief mention. For example, wartime conditions, early unionism, and social reform movements are described but only as they are relevant to the growth process.

The book is divided into four parts, each dealing with a traditional period of American history. This division permits emphasis upon four phases of American development: preparation for growth, the start of rapid growth, transformation into a modern economy, and the strains of continuing rapid technological change in the contemporary economy. This organization also permits dealing with colonial origins and the between-war years, 1860 to 1920, which are often slighted in the shorter textbooks on American economic history. Part I reviews the various economic, political, and social developments that set the stage for rapid growth in the late colonial and subsequent periods. Each of the subsequent sections begins with a summary of overall growth data, then analyzes changes by sector in the same sequence as the decades in which they were most important. This unified treatment of the economy within short periods avoids the disconnected treatment of particular sectors covering the whole length of American history—an organization common in shorter textbooks.

The framework of the text is built of the concepts of economic theory. Essential terms, therefore, are introduced gradually and are explained at their first point of use. Brief explanations of economic principles are woven into the exposition wherever necessary to focus on key relationships. Yet the emphasis is on the use of theoretical tools to tell the growth story and not on a technical discussion of the tools themselves. Several appendixes are included, not as afterthoughts, but because the material is best treated as a unit which makes review of the immediately preceding chapter and reading of subsequent chapters more meaningful. In the same spirit, we avoid preliminary definitions, argumentative digressions, and self-conscious introspection about the limitations of our present state of economic knowledge.

Economic data are presented graphically wherever possible, and the reader is instructed on how to read graphs. All graphs and tables are essential parts of the story, and the text refers directly to the specific points brought out by the graphs and tables. The visual aids along with the text headings are selected to aid the reader's grasp of the story of the text as it unfolds. Detailed facts presented in the text also are marshalled as supporting or illustrative material to the sequence of main ideas. The study questions at the end of each chapter enable the reader to check his understanding of the main ideas rather than cross-examine him on factual details.

Varied uses of this book are possible. It was developed and tested as the sole textbook for a college of business administration course on American economic history that is required of freshmen students prior to their taking the principles course. We hope that foreign students and adults concerned with economic development problems will find it a succinct account of the American growth experience. We also hope that it can serve as a reference book for high school teachers and their students.

On the other hand, more advanced courses in American economic history can use this book as a core text, an organizing device, to be supplemented by library readings and/or research paper assignments.

It has been used in this way by one of the authors. Also, several books of readings are available to supplement the text in standard upper division courses.

We want to express our gratitude to Paul W. Milam for insisting on this book and to Winthrop Rockefeller for initiating the series of events that led to bringing the second author into this effort. An intellectual debt is owed to the scholars who have examined in detail the record of American economic growth and, thus, made a book of this sort possible. Chief among those upon whom we relied are the research staff of the National Bureau of Economic Research and Douglas C. North. Professor North's work had an extensive influence upon our treatment of international trade and payments, regional changes, and agricultural development. We also thank students and graduate instructors for their comments, LaVerne Peterson for her long hours of typing and mimeographing, and Sally Gray for her patience and counsel and, especially, for preparing the index.

February, 1969

J. M. P.
R. G.

TABLE OF CONTENTS

INTRODUCTION

PART I. PREPARATION FOR GROWTH: 1492–1783

PART II. START OF NATIONAL GROWTH: 1783–1860

PART III. SUSTAINED RAPID GROWTH: 1860–1920

INDEX

Introduction

Chapter 1 INTRODUCTION

The United States is the envy of the world in its remarkably high level of production in relation to population. Yet many of the mid-20th century problems of the United States stem from the Nation's rate of economic growth—the rate at which production of goods and services has increased.

In domestic affairs the growth rate has been criticized as both too rapid and not rapid enough. Too rapid a rate of growth is seen as the cause of certain strains of adjustment—the technological displacement of skilled workers and the depression of particular industries and areas. On the other hand, too slow a rate of growth has been charged as the cause of the persistently high unemployment in the late 1950's. In the 1960's, the public became concerned that perhaps the economy is not able to expand jobs fast enough to keep up with the increased numbers of youth seeking their first jobs. More recently price inflation, largely associated with the war in Vietnam, has plagued the nation because spending has grown faster than the ability to produce.

In foreign affairs the nation has been faced with a dual problem of accelerating its own growth rate to keep ahead of rival industrial nations and of helping poor nations get started on their own path of rapid growth. After recovering from World War II, Russia and other European nations have continued to grow faster than the United States and to provide more competition in world markets. America's example of lagging growth threatens to convince some of the poor nations to look to Communist nations for leadership as to the path of rapid progress. The poor nations also are seeking material assistance and advice on how to raise their own production rapidly. Not only have there been no quick ways to mount the path of rapid national expansion, but also advisors often have found the problems of initiating rapid growth in the underdeveloped nations strange and baffling.

These problems have stimulated new interest in the growth experience of the United States. If we understood our own history better, it is hoped that we might be a little wiser in dealing with our own growth problems and giving guidance to other nations. This does not mean that past experience can be repeated or applied as an exact guide in the future. Nor can we transfer unaltered lessons from our past to nations with radically different social and economic conditions. Also study of just one nation's experience is not enough. Yet study of the past is the main way that we can discover the forces controlling our growth and that of other nations. Knowledge about these forces is still limited, but there is a growing body of new information and new interpretations about America's growth. The intelligent citizen today needs to gain some acquaintance with these new ways of looking at our past.

A good starting place for our inquiry into the U.S. growth experience is provided by two startling contrasts. The first is the wide disparity in average income levels between the industrial nations and the poor nations today. The second is the wide disparity in income levels between industrial nations today and the income levels those nations enjoyed 100 to 200 years ago. In the long sweep of the history of mankind, the present era of modern industrial production is both brief and phenomenal. America's experience is but the leading example of something new in the experience of man.

CONTRASTS IN INCOME

It is no great surprise to most Americans to learn that their Nation has the highest consumption level of any nation in the world. It long has been taken for granted that the United States is the first ranking industrial nation of the world. What is hard to realize, especially if one has not traveled abroad, is how far ahead of other industrial nations our incomes are and how appallingly low are incomes in the poor nations. The clothing, automobiles, homes, personal possessions, and incomes that Americans take for granted seem fabulous to other peoples who view American movies and see American tourists. It is difficult for Americans to realize, for example, that with only 6 percent of the world's population, they have over half of the world's telephones and automobiles.

Income Differences

In order for international comparisons to be more than impressionistic, we need a summary measure of economic welfare. That measure is income. For families, it is customary to use annual money income as a measure of the welfare level or ability to buy and to consume of a group of persons. Savings or accumulated wealth, of course, provide a temporary means of increasing consumption, but, over time, income provides the continuing means of consumption. Income, in turn, is derived from what is earned in production, and the total production of goods and services provides the basic means of consumption in a whole nation.

In a complex, high-income economy the link between income and production is not as clear-cut as one would prefer. Not all production leads to income payments to individuals, and not all income is consumed. Some output must be used to maintain the productive ability of buildings and equipment, some is invested in expanding productive capacity, and still other production is diverted to government use. To account for the relationships between income and production, in recent decades economists have developed a comprehensive system of measures called the ***national income accounts.*** These are used to sum up the total value of a nation's production and income payments for each year.

The income accounts are summarized briefly in the next paragraph and in the appendix to this chapter. Both are worthy of careful study since the study of economic growth relies heavily upon being able to use these measures for analysis and comparison.

It will be helpful to distinguish two general measures of total production and income. ***Gross national product*** (GNP) is the total money value of all goods and services produced during the year in a nation. This measure requires records and estimates of the total quantities of all types of items produced. These quantities are multiplied by the prices of each item, and the resulting money values are added together. Some of this total production must be used to repair and replace the value of worn-out buildings and equipment; so the sum remaining after deducting depreciation is called ***net national product*** (NNP). Since prices are raised slightly by adding sales taxes, deduction of these taxes leaves the ***national income*** received by business firms and individuals. To get ***personal income*** we also must deduct the part of profits retained by business firms, and we must both subtract and add back certain payments to and from governments (profits taxes, social security taxes, pensions, and interest on debt) which do not arise from current production. Personal income, then, is equal to the total of income payments to individuals—in the form of wages and salaries, rent, interest, dividends, earnings of self-employed persons, and pensions.

In order to make international comparisons more meaningful, let us start with family income comparisons in this country, a measure that is roughly comparable to personal income and may seem more familiar. How widely do family incomes vary within the United States? In the 1960 census, interviewers visiting each home obtained reports that showed the median family income was $6,845. (Median means that half of the families received more and half received less than the figure cited.) Suppose we rank all families by income level and divide them into five equal groups. The one fifth of the families with the highest ranking incomes averaged $15,588, or more than double the national median. The one fifth of the families with the lowest ranking incomes averaged $1,576, or a little less than one fourth of the national median.

What do we mean, then, when referring to the "poor" in this country? The term "poverty" frequently has been applied to family incomes below $3,000, but this is rather arbitrary. It is about the dividing line between the lowest fifth of families and those above, but it was close to the national median of a few decades earlier. Some account needs to be taken of the number of persons in a family. If families averaged between three and four persons in the lowest fifth of all families, then their average income came to about $400 to $500 per person. It is significant that then the smallest social security pension (for a single woman over 62 years of age) was $32 a month, or $384 a year. It would seem, therefore, that one fourth of the national median family income represents about the socially acceptable minimum standard of living.

We must turn to state averages for some figure more comparable to that of a poor nation. Because of variations in family size, a convenient single figure of comparison is provided by dividing total personal income payments by the population in the area. Personal income per capita in the United States in 1960 was $2,223. The state of Delaware had the highest per capita personal income—$3,013—about one third above the national average. The state of Mississippi had the lowest per capita personal income—$1,173—not quite one half of the national average.

How do these income differences within our country compare with international differences? For these comparisons, the more inclusive measure, GNP, is more readily available; we can divide this by the total population to get GNP per capita. In 1960, GNP per capita in the United States was $2,792.

Compared to the other industrial nations, the United States was far above the others in GNP per capita. The second ranking nation was our neighbor, Canada, with about two thirds of our average. Next came

Australia and New Zealand. Most European nations were below one half of the U.S. average. Even England, the earliest industrial nation in history, had only about one half of the U.S. average, or an income about equal to that of our lowest income state. (See 1–1.)

Among the underdeveloped nations of the world, GNP per capita levels are below one fourth of the U.S. average. In fact, United Nations publications have used an income level below one fourth of that of the

1–1. Developed and Underdeveloped Nations

Source: United Nations, *Yearbook of National Account Statistics, 1962* (New York: International Publications Service, 1963).

United States as a definition of "underdeveloped." Most of the land area and the bulk of the population of the world is in these nations. Since one fourth of the national average is regarded as a "poverty" level within the United States, these nations are indeed "poor" as a whole.

There are wide differences among the underdeveloped nations. For some of the poorest nations, the GNP per capita is below one twentieth of the U.S. average. As national averages, this means most of the people are below this. Because many of the lowest income nations also are heavily populated, it has been estimated that roughly half of the people in the world during 1960 lived on an income of below $100 a year, less than $2 a week.

Natural Resource Differences

How do we account for these national income differences? More important, what made the United States not only the first ranking nation in income but also in a class by itself far outstripping all other high-income nations? This is a difficult question for which there is no easy answer. And contrary to widely accepted notions, differences in natural resources are not by themselves a rich source of insights about income differences.

Natural resources undoubtedly are important to the attainment of high-income level, or at least they make it easier to achieve. Yet, they are not the only important condition for a high income, nor do differences in resource endowments provide a satisfactory explanation for all national differences in income levels.

Among the very poor nations, for example, there are some which have very meager resources, such as Libya with its desert lands. There are some, such as Java, that are very densely populated. On the other hand, some very poor nations, such as India, have very fertile lands and a variety of resources, and many of the nations of Africa and South America are poor but not at all crowded—much of the fertile land is still uncultivated.

Among the higher income nations also are found examples of nations which are limited in resources and crowded. Israel, for example, has resources similar to those of its Arab nation neighbors, but has a remarkably high income. Switzerland, the Netherlands, and Denmark are examples of small and relatively crowded European nations with very high incomes.

From an economic standpoint national boundaries, of course, may be somewhat arbitrary, for many small nations are able to attain high-income levels by active trading relations with neighboring regions. So perhaps a comparison of the basic resources of the various continents of the world would be more meaningful. If we separate North America from Latin America at the Rio Grande, separate Africa from Asia at the Suez, and treat the national boundaries of the U.S.S.R. as separating it from Europe and Asia, we have five large continents of comparable size and two small ones—Europe and Oceania (comprised of Australia and New Zealand).

In terms of its land resources, North America does not appear to be unusually favored. With about 14 percent of the world land area, it has a little less than this share of wasteland, about the same share of pastureland, and a little more than this share of forest and arable land.

Europe seems most favored in terms of a minimum of wasteland and a much greater share of arable land. Asia also benefits from having much more than its share of arable land, although it has much more than its share of wasteland and low shares of pasture and forest lands. The U.S.S.R. has more than its share of arable land and forest land but less of pastureland. Both Africa and Latin America are low on arable land but long on forest and pasturelands. Oceania is long only on pasture. (See 1–2.)

1–2. COMPARISON OF RESOURCES BY CONTINENT

	Land Area		*Population*	*Natural Resource Potentials*			
Continents	*Total (Million Acres)*	*Arable (Million Acres)*	*(Million)*	*Iron Ore (Billion Metric Tons)*	*Coal (Billion Metric Tons)*	*Petroleum (Million bbl.)*	*Water Power (Million hp.)*
World Totals	33,381	3,030	2,400	293.4	6,266	95,208	750.3
			Percent of World Totals				
North America	14.0%	17.9%	6.9%	25.6%	48.9%	28.8%	13.8%
Latin America	17.2	6.9	6.7	12.4	...	12.5	11.4
Europe	3.6	12.0	16.5	8.6	10.2	0.7	11.5
U.S.S.R.	16.5	18.3	8.0	3.7	19.1	5.9	10.7
Asia	19.9	28.2	53.0	8.9	17.6	51.9	13.1
Africa	22.5	15.2	8.3	40.7	3.3	0.2	36.5
Oceania	6.3	1.5	0.5	0.1	0.9	...	2.8

SOURCE: W. S. Woytinsky and E. E. Woytinski, *World Population and Production* (New York: The Twentieth Century Fund, 1953), Table 215, p. 471.

In terms of population distribution, of course, these land shares appear more unequal. If shares of arable land are taken as most significant, then Europe and Latin America have about the same share as their proportion of world population. Asia is crowded with 53 percent of the population and only 28 percent of arable lands. North America has more than double the share of arable land than its share of population, but Oceania, U.S.S.R., and Africa also are favored quite similarly. Population density, of course, is accumulated historically, and it may reflect the success of a peoples in achieving a balance of population in relation to productive resources rather than simply a deficiency in resources.

North America appears somewhat favored in mineral resources, although this is difficult to measure. In terms of all kinds of metallic and nonmetallic minerals (except fuels), the United States alone produces roughly one fourth of the world output. Of course, output often reflects more the level of utilization of resources than the initial resource advantage—periods of shortage spur exploration. However, in iron ore reserves, for which some estimates by continent are available, North America is somewhat favored with about one fourth of the world total, compared to only 14 percent of the land area. However, the outstanding concentration, 41 percent of the world reserves, is in Africa; both Africa and Europe have about twice the proportion of the world's iron ore reserves as their share of total land. The other continents have less than their land shares.

The world's coal reserves appear to lie in two belts around the world at about the same latitude. It is in coal that North America may have been most favored historically, because a coal and iron combination was important in the early development of a steel industry complex. According to the estimates in the World Power Conference in 1948, North America had close to half of the proven and probable coal reserves of the world. While the extent to which such reserves are known may reflect the extent of active use in production, there is no doubt that North America's share is unusually large. The other continents in the Northern Hemisphere also share this advantage, for Europe, the U.S.S.R., and Asia have large shares. Europe has more than double its share relative to land area. In the Southern Hemisphere the same climate zones lie near the southern tips of South America, Africa and Oceania—where some coal also is found.

Petroleum reserves also seem concentrated in a few zones, and North America is one of the favored continents with more than one fourth of the proven reserves. Latin America has about its share, while over half of the world total is in Asia—concentrated in the Middle East and the southeast Asian islands. The U.S.S.R. has substantial reserves, but Europe, Oceania, and Africa all together have less than 1 percent of the total.

This distribution of the major energy resources, however, is somewhat offset by the distribution of waterpower potential. Africa, which is short of coal and oil, has over one third of the world's waterpower potential. The other continents have very similar amounts. In relation to their land areas, North America has an average share, Europe has much more than its share, while the others have somewhat less than their shares.

These comparisons, of course, are very crude. For many resources, only limited data are available and the extent of potential reserves is unknown and undiscovered. Much also depends on the location of resources and their closeness to cheap water transportation, an important resource in itself. Also, the market demands for particular resources and the knowledge of how to use them is constantly changing and determining what may be considered valuable. But what is known about resources does not suggest any easy explanation for income differences among nations.

Man-Made Differences

To account for the wide differences in incomes among nations, we must account for a variety of differences that have resulted from human behavior. Population is one of the most significant differences in this category. A high-population density means a high ratio of people to scarce natural resources, and this may be a handicap to achieving a high ratio of production to population. A fast rate of population increase also intensifies the problem and makes it difficult for production increases to keep pace. Rapid increase in population usually means a higher proportion of children in the population. Thus, there is a greater burden of supporting and educating more children per working adult. The higher income nations usually are less densely settled (except in cities), have slower population increases, and have a larger proportion of the population of working age.

Another major difference between high-income and low-income nations is the productivity of the workers. An overall measure of this, of course, is the value of total production per worker, which is very similar to the measure of GNP per capita. There are various other illustrations, however, of the ways in which American workers produce more than most workers elsewhere. In farming, for example, production is not only greater per worker, but frequently in terms of yield per acre as well. Russia has not been able to equal the corn yields of the Iowa farmers. Some of the Far Eastern nations specializing in rice and soybeans—such as Burma, Thailand and China—cannot match the yields in Louisiana and Arkansas. In manufacturing, data are not as readily available, but American exports are able to compete with foreign goods made by workers paid much lower wages because much less American labor time is required.

Not all of this difference in labor productivity is due to differences in quality of workers, but at least some of it is. Poor health, a characteristic of poor countries, obviously affects the ability of workers to produce. Until recently, a large part of the population of some of these countries was affected by malaria and other debilitating diseases. Insufficient food also can affect worker energy. Illiteracy and lack of skills also prevents the rapid adoption of improved methods. For example, in the

United States it is estimated that the rising average education level of the work force is responsible for perhaps two fifths of the increased productivity in the past three decades. Thus, it is not surprising that measures of health and education vary among nations in a similar manner as income levels. (See 1–3.)

1–3. SELECTED MEASURES RELATED TO GNP PER CAPITA

Selected Nations	*Population Percent Increase Yearly*	*Infant Deaths per 1,000 Births*	*Literacy Percent of Adults over 10 Years*	*Percent of Workers in Agriculture*	*Gross Investment as Percent of GNP, Yearly*
Over $750					
U.S.	1.6%	27	98%	12%	18.7%
France	1.6	42	97	36	15.5
United Kingdom	.5	26	98	5	15.9
W. Germany	na	43	na	23	26.0
$300 to $750					
Israel	14.0	39	75	15	25.3
Austria	.4	48	97	33	23.8
Italy	.9	53	na	40	21.6
Argentina	2.0	62	86	23	19.0
$150 to $300					
Turkey	3.0	na	35	75	12.6
Brazil	2.4	107	48	68	17.7
Philippines	1.9	109	62	71	8.4
Mexico	2.8	81	55	58	10.9
Below $150					
Egypt	2.5	127	25	75	5.0
Indonesia	1.6	200	55	71	6.0
India	1.3	119	18	70	10.0
Pakistan	1.1	125	14	80	5.1

na: not available.

SOURCE: U.S. Senate, Document 52, *Foreign Aid Program* (Washington, D.C.: U.S. Government Printing Office, 1957), pp. 242–43.

Another important difference among nations is the kind of work its people are primarily engaged in. In the poor nations, people are principally agricultural. As a nation gains a higher income level, however, fewer of its workers farm and more are engaged in a wide variety of nonfarm occupations. While productivity in farming tends to be higher in higher income countries, productivity and incomes almost always are even higher in nonfarm work. Thus, the shift of population to higher income work accompanies the higher average incomes.

A very important difference among nations is the amount of tools and power that the worker has to help him do his work. Adequate data are not available for comparisons of the quantity of tools used; however, we know they are provided through saving and investment, and the higher income nations currently save and invest a higher percentage of their national income than do most poor nations. Also, the total consumption of energy per person varies widely among nations, and energy consumption is a rough measure of the amount of power used in production as well as consumption.

Finally, there are wide differences between the high-income and low-income nations in their knowledge of production methods and their ability to organize production. In the poor nations much production is still conducted by obsolete methods for lack of skilled workers and engineers able to use new methods, lack of university teachers to train the engineers, and lack of research institutions and scientists to adapt methods to local conditions. Furthermore, few managers have experience with large-scale business organization; and there are inadequate business services, financial institutions, or marketing channels to enable large-scale production to be carried out in a modern fashion. In contrast, Germany and Japan, with many of their factories destroyed during World War II were able to rebuild rapidly because of their technical know-how, organizing abilities, and institutions. Thus, many of the underdeveloped nations are not ready for industrialization. They do not have the attitudes, knowledge, and organization needed to make use of the financial aid and advice that is available from other countries.

Apart from chiefly economic institutional differences that make some nations grow while others languish, there are a host of man-made social and political differences that cause productivity to differ. Where government is looked upon as a servant of the people and the economic system in general, growth rates tend to exceed those in nations where government is regarded as an agency to be manipulated for the profit of a ruling establishment. In a similar vein the attitude of those who rule, whether by majority consent or out of sheer power, has much to do with whether the economic factors we have cited above are conducive to growth. For example in our South in the days of King Cotton, the ruling class saw little reason to spend heavily in the public sector for education or other purposes. As a result the transition to a nonagricultural economic base has been slow and painful.

HISTORICAL CONTRASTS

These wide differences among nations have raised baffling problems for the administrators of foreign aid programs. One of the difficulties is that the advanced nations themselves have had very little recent experience under conditions that even resemble the very primitive conditions found abroad. Individually, we do not remember what it was like to begin development from a low level. It requires a study of the history of the economic development of the advanced nations.

Unfortunately, the available historical data on national income do not go back very far. In only a handful of advanced nations are income estimates available for a century or a century and a half ago. Even that long ago per capita incomes in these countries were three to six times higher than in the very poorest countries today. To find somewhat comparable levels in Western Europe, one has to look before the time of Columbus. The late Middle Ages was the last time that a European traveler, Marco Polo, was able to find in China a state of economic development on a par with that in Europe.

A broad review of historical information, however, very clearly indicates a sharp contrast in our productive ability between the present and our past, not more than a century or two ago. In the past century alone, the advanced industrial nations have raised their income per capita three to six times. And while the periods for which we have data were periods of remarkably rapid and steady growth, it is apparent that this rapid growth did not begin much earlier. If we simply extend the known trend lines backwards, they would appear to start from zero between one and two centuries ago, which we know is not possible. Our best historical information suggests that growth began slowly over several centuries and then began a rapid climb very recently. Furthermore, this rapid growth was limited geographically to the countries of Western Europe and their European-settled colonies.

Population Explosion

Some idea of the rather sudden change in human productive powers that has occurred in history is provided by estimates of world population changes through the centuries. Realizing that most of human existence on earth has involved a struggle for survival, we can attribute a long-term rise in population to an increased ability to produce food and other essentials and to combat disease and other sources of early death. Life itself has existed on earth only a half billion of the roughly 3 billion years since the earth was formed. Man has existed an even smaller fraction of this period, perhaps 1.75 million years.

From an economic point of view, the history of mankind may be classified into three eras, separated by two great revolutions in the methods of production. The first and longest period of time may be called the ***food-gathering*** or ***hunting era.*** In this first period, men lived by hunting, fishing, and gathering fruits and nuts. At first men were predatory and killed and ate each other as well as other animals. Food supply was uncertain; human life was miserable and short. Some improvement was made through the intelligent contrivance of wooden and stone tools and the control of fire. The population was small and scattered. It has been estimated that a maximum density of 2.5 persons per square mile on favorable terrain was about all that the plant and animal life could support. So, by 7000 B.C. the world population could not have exceeded 20 million, and it may have been as small as one tenth of that. But, suppose we arbitrarily select 10 million as the estimated population in 7000 B.C.

The second period, or ***agricultural era,*** of mankind began with a revolution in methods of obtaining food. When mankind learned how to plant seeds and to herd domesticated animals, he made his food supply more stable and raised his standard of consumption. About the earliest known farm village was excavated near Jericho in Palestine. Geiger counters, which can show the age of radioactive carbon in materials fabricated by man, date the farm implements in that village at about 7000 B.C., while hunting implements found in the same area were about 800 years older. With better means of production and more food, population began to grow until the area became crowded or approached the agricultural limits of human support. There is some archeological evidence that techniques of farming gradually spread from the Near East to the rest of the world. As one travels into Europe, Africa, India, and China, the oldest discovered agricultural settlements tend to become more recent. This spread of farming techniques permitted a gradual growth in world population. In the broad fertile valleys of the Nile, the Tigris-Euphrates, the Ganges, and the Yangtse, farming populations were more concentrated and urban centers of civilization developed. Man's knowledge of tools and methods gradually improved and became more varied. Yet the contrast in standards of living could not have been very great between the beginning of recorded history in Egypt about 2000 B.C. and, say, that of medieval Europe about 1000 A.D. The world population has been estimated at about 200 million at the time of Christ, and close to half a billion around 1650 A.D.

The modern period, or ***industrial era,*** is very recent. It may be regarded as beginning with a gradual conversion to scientific attitudes and business organization during the Renaissance and Commercial Revolution which took place in Europe between the 12th and 17th centuries. Or, it may be dated from the Industrial Revolution occurring in the last half of the 18th century. The latter is more useful in giving a more specific dating, and it is widely used as indicating the start of rapid economic growth and the introduction of a cluster of industrial inventions. So, we may select 1750 as a convenient starting date. In the modern age, major changes occurred in farming that enabled farmers to support more people in nonfarm activities. But the major changes have been characterized by mankind's use of nonhuman sources of energy,

1–4. World Population Explosion

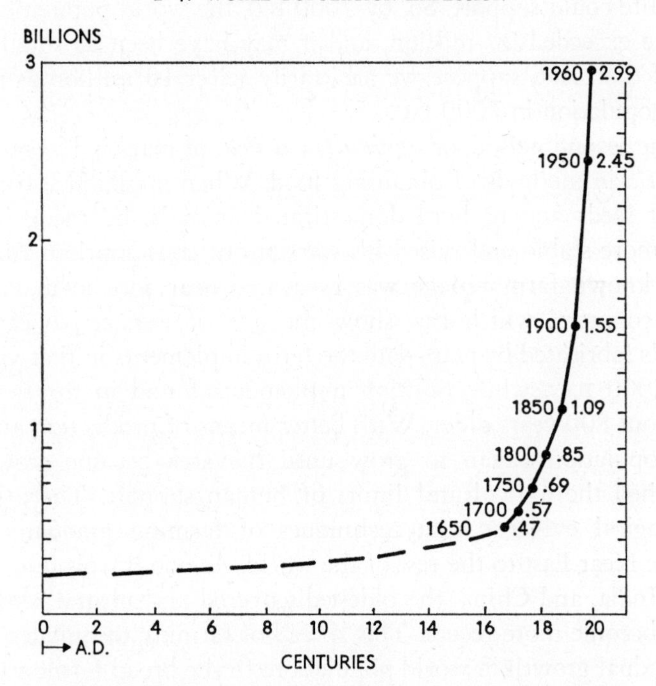

Source: UN Population Division, *The Past and Future Population of the World and Its Continents*, World Population Conference, 1954, Paper No. 243 (New York, 1954).

vast accumulations of machine tools, and rapidly increasing scientific knowledge to produce a vast new variety of goods and services. The result has been a rise in human standards of living undreamed of in all previous history. In the advanced industrial nations, problems of famine and disease have been virtually eliminated.

The result of this revolution in human productive powers has been a very sudden and rapid rise in world population. In terms of trends over all of history, it seems like an "explosion" in numbers. (See 1–4.) It took 16 centuries after the time of Christ to double the world population. In one century prior to 1750, population increased 50 percent, which added as many people as were added in the previous 16 centuries. In the next century and a half, world population doubled. It took only one century to double again and only the first six decades of this century to double once more. It may take only the last four decades of this century to achieve another doubling.

During the 18th and 19th centuries most of this rapid increase was centered in Europe and European-settled colonies. The leading European and North American nations went through a "population cycle" of adjustment. Initially, both birthrates and death rates were high, with some fluctuations in deaths due to wars, famines and plagues; so population increased slowly. In the early expansion stage, death rates fell rapidly due to improved agriculture, sanitation, and medicine. In the late expansion stage, birthrates also fell rapidly for a variety of reasons: less child labor, more female employment, higher education costs and postponed marriages, and birth controls. So population increases slowed down until the present stage, in which both birth and death rates are low, although fluctuating somewhat with wars and depressions.

In recent decades, however, population increases have rather suddenly become very high in the poor nations. Extension of modern public health and medical services to other continents has rather suddenly reduced death rates in the poor nations. In spite of efforts to develop these nations, production cannot possibly be increased as rapidly. So, what has popularly been termed the "population explosion" has been occurring in a few decades in the poor nations rather than over two centuries as in the now advanced nations. In some of the poor nations, population has outrun production so that per capita incomes today may be lower than in 1900.

The Great Transformation

Besides total population growth, there are other rough measures of the sudden historic change in human productive powers. One is provided by estimates of the proportion of the working population engaged in nonagricultural activities. The importance of this measure lies in the fact that as food supplies become more plentiful and easier to obtain, more labor time is available for production of other goods and services.

In a hunting society, of course, virtually everyone is engaged in some activity related directly to obtaining food and clothing. In an agricultural society, some surplus above bare necessities is produced; this releases some people for other activities—such as for trading, government, defense, and religious activities. For example, the Great

Wall of China and the pyramids of Egypt were built with surplus labor in an agricultural society. In a modern industrial society, even more surplus over subsistence needs is produced, and even more of the workers are engaged in other activities. For the world as a whole, in 1750 about 20 percent of the population probably was working outside of agriculture. By 1950, about 40 percent of the world's working population was in nonfarm work. In the most advanced industrial nations, the

1–5. Shift to Nonfarm Work, Selected Nations

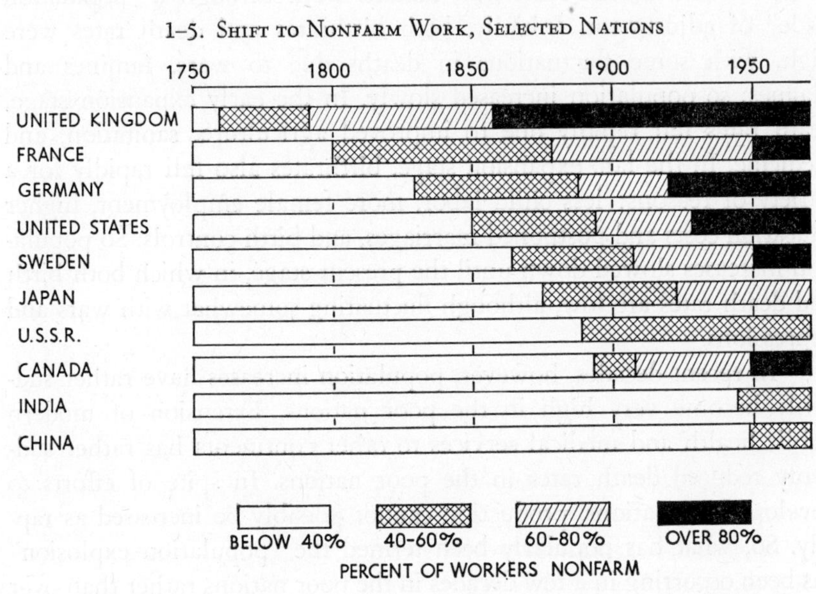

Source: Carlo Cipolla, *The Economic History of World Population* (Baltimore: Penguin Books, Inc., 1962), p. 25.

historical transition has been much greater, for the proportion of workers in agriculture may fall below 10 percent.

The increasing proportion of the work force engaged in nonfarm activities, in fact, provides a rough index of the historical progress of economic development within the leading nations and of the approximate time sequence in which different nations began to become rapidly industrialized. The pace of change and the levels reached in different nations, of course, varied with the natural resource advantages for specializing in the export of agricultural or other products. So this is only an approximate indicator of development. (See 1–5.)

The Industrial Revolution first occurred in England and then spread to Western Europe and North America. Near the end of the

19th century, Japan, Russia, and Canada began to industrialize. The proportion of the work force in nonfarm activities reached 60 percent in each country in about the same time sequence; each nation increased its nonfarm percentage over time.

A more refined measure would be the change in the distribution of workers among various occupations and industrial groups. In fact, it is in this broader sense that we use the term "industrial development" rather than in the popular sense of "more factory jobs." The percentage of workers in manufacturing, in fact, may rise to no more than 30 or 40 percent in advanced nations. What has happened in most advanced nations is a gradual shift among three broad types of activities. The ***primary*** or extractive industries—farming, fishing, forestry, and mining—have most of the employment initially. Then, the proportion of workers increases most rapidly in the ***secondary*** or, for the most part, goods-producing industries—manufacturing, construction, and transportation. Finally, goods-producing activities decline in importance and there is a rising proportion of workers in ***tertiary*** or services industries—trade, personal and business services, finance, medicine, government, education, and entertainment.

It seems that as human productivity increases in the most essential and basic industries, people do not choose to spend all of the surplus for the same type of production. They use their expanded opportunities to consume a greater variety of products. Parents, for example, may place a top priority on saving for their children's educational needs once they are properly fed and clothed. Thus, both rising productivity and changing consumer priorities are behind the changing distribution of the work force.

The historic transformation of production also has taken place in the tools and inanimate energy which the worker has to assist him in production. It is commonly observed that we are living in a "machine age," and nearly all productive activity in advanced nations is largely carried out with the aid of mechanical equipment of many types. What is most significant, however, is use of nonhuman energy sources to run the machines, as well as provide heat and light for mankind. For most of his existence on Earth, man has depended upon human and animal muscle power to do his work. The lever, the wheel, and other mechanical contrivances provided only minor extensions of his power. Then in the Middle Ages the water and windmills provided the first important usage of nonanimate power. With the burning of fuels to drive steam engines or internal combustion motors, and with the conversion of waterpower (as well as other engine power) to electricity, man has vastly increased his powers to conquer his environment and produce to satisfy his desires.

An index of man's rapid progress in production, therefore, is provided by measures of world consumption per capita of various sources of energy—wood, coal, oil, and water. In the last century, the per capita use of energy of all sorts has more than tripled! While most of the increased energy came initially from coal, oil and gas have recently become almost as important. Use of waterpower has increased; atomic energy, solar power, and other energy sources may be common in the future. (See 1–6.)

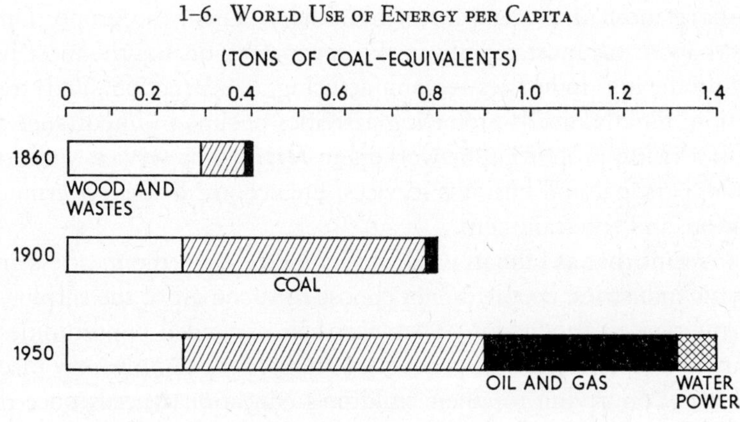

1–6. World Use of Energy per Capita

Source: United Nations *World Energy Supplies in Selected Years, 1929–50* (New York, 1952).

The transformation of production has occurred not only in the types of work done and in the tools and energy used, but also in the organization of production. Large tools and use of energy have required large-sized human organizations. More and more people have become "employees" working under someone else's supervision. Production organizations the world over have become larger, involving more people in each coordinated unit. Workers also have become more specialized and interdependent. No longer does each family take care of its own production of food, clothing, and household items. No longer do the customs and ceremonies of the tribe organize and coordinate the extent of cooperation among peoples. Today, through specialization and market exchange, people have become more dependent upon other people and organized for cooperation in a very complex manner. Rapid transportation and international trade have brought the Japanese factory worker, the Arkansas cotton farmer, and the Liberian iron miner into an invisible network of cooperation and interdependence—an interdependence that has raised the incomes of all who participate.

STUDY OF ECONOMIC GROWTH

Since World War II, scholars have been very much concerned with these two great contrasts. Why and how did a few nations in Western Europe and North America start and maintain such a rapid economic growth that their incomes far exceed any experienced in other parts of the world? What are the forces that influence the starting and sustaining of rapid growth in a nation? As already indicated, knowledge still is very limited on this subject, but the questioning and studying process is well under way. The nonscholar can gain a better understanding of the past growth experience of the United States by knowing something about the scholar's concepts and approach.

A Reinterpretation of the Past

Study of the past is Man's main source of guidance in dealing with current problems. Much of social science involves comparisons of a variety of recent experience to determine the interrelations of events and the consequences of particular actions.

History, as a field of study, aims to provide a narrative record and interpretation of the more important events and facts in human experience as far back as possible. While attempting to consider all important aspects of human events, written history must necessarily be selective of the great mass of details available. So it always must interpret what happened. For early periods of time, there were few records made that provided numerical data on economic activities, and the early historians also made little attempt to interpret events in the same quantitative terms that are considered important today. Each generation of historians, indeed, has interpreted past events in terms of its concepts and understanding of relationships in nature and in human society. Some reinterpretation of history, therefore, is made necessary by new concepts and new quantitative information about past events.

Economic history arose as one specialized kind of selection of facts about the past—a concentration on the economic aspects of human activities. Early historians merely concentrated on political and military events. As later historians began to try to take into account the widest possible range of political, economic and cultural events, they began to rely more and more on specialized studies. Economic history became a special field as economics developed as a major field of social science.

Economics may be defined as the study of how society is organized to solve the problem of achieving the most satisfaction of unlimited human wants with the use of scarce resources. The economic problem may be viewed either as an effort to ***maximize*** the beneficial ends achieved by the use of given means of production or as an effort to attain given ends by ***economizing*** the use of scarce and costly productive means. Nature never has been too bountiful in providing all of the resources needed to satisfy human needs. Throughout most of human existence on Earth, nearly all of man's time and effort has been required merely to provide for basic physical needs—a bare subsistence. Only in recent centuries have some of the world's people experienced a remarkable increase in their capacity to produce the goods and services they desire. Even with this increase in production, human appetites for more and different goods and services have grown also. So the economic problem always remains with us. In terms of all human aspirations—economic, political, religious, cultural, and scientific—there always appears to be more to be done than we have the means and time to accomplish.

The ***study of economic growth*** is a newly emerging specialized field of study that combines both economic history and certain new concepts and theories of economics. Economic history traditionally has dealt with a broad range of descriptive details about economic conditions and events—consumption standards, modes of production, inventions, means of transportation, financial institutions, and so forth. The study of economic growth concentrates on long-term trends, on certain aggregate measures, and on the interrelations of major parts of the productive activities of a nation. This new approach to studying the past is influenced by the current practice of economists of looking at all economic activities in a nation as one interrelated system—often referred to as "the national economy." New data are developed to extend the national income accounts to previous periods in history. New concepts and theories are suggested as to how key measures of productive activity and various forms of organization may be interrelated in a complex sequence of changes over time.

Measures and Concepts of Growth

To understand this new approach to the study of both current economic progress and the past growth experience of nations, it is important to identify the main aggregative measures used, and to distinguish carefully certain terms. In any new field, certain common words may be used with a new or special meaning, and many people may continue to use quite different words loosely and interchangeably. This leads to much confusion.

By now, it should be clear that the study of economic growth is very much concerned with some measure of the total economic activity in a nation and with some measure of the resulting economic welfare of people. For the former, we already have introduced the measure gross national product as representing the money value of all types of production in a nation during the year. For the latter, we have spoken of income per person, or more broadly of GNP per capita. Essentially, we will consider the ratio of the total production to the total population to reflect a nation's capacity to produce the material means needed to satisfy human wants.

To deal with changes in these measures over time, we need to distinguish between two terms. The first is that of ***economic expansion,*** or what some authors call extensive growth. This merely refers to an increase in the total production and income. Accompanying this increase in production may be the growing value of other measures, such as an increase in total population. Since many parts of an economy may increase in unison, they may be used to represent the expansion of the economy when a good measure of total production is not available. Estimates of population increase, for example, have been used to reflect expanding production in past historical eras for which no production measures are available.

It also should be noted at this point that we are referring to continuing increases over long periods of time. In this kind of study, we are concerned with secular trends rather than with temporary and erratic changes.

The second term is ***economic growth*** or intensive growth. This means an increase in production per person—an increase in the ratio of production to population which makes possible higher income and living standards. When both production and population are increasing, the production must increase faster in order for their ratio to increase. The term "economic growth" is applied to any positive increase in the ratio although a decrease might be referred to as "negative growth."

Unless otherwise noted the "rate of growth" refers to the percentage change in the ratio. This provides a means of comparing the growth of nations of different size and of the same nation at different periods in time. As already noted, the ratio of production to population is an indicator of average welfare in a nation, although it does not indicate how incomes are distributed among persons nor how wisely resources are being used to serve human needs. It also reflects the average productivity of the people as producers, although it does not indicate the proportion working nor their hours and efficiency.

The significance of the distinction between these two terms is that not all expansion involves growth in the sense of progress in average income levels. If population rises as fast as production, there simply are more people with about the same means of satisfying their wants. Likewise, a nation may expand by spreading more people over more land and thus achieve no higher production per person. If population outruns production, there actually may be expansion but a negative economic growth. Or production conceivably might remain the same while population decreased (say, through migration), so that there was no expansion but there was economic growth. Usually economic growth has been accompanied by expansion and aided by it; but one does not require the other, and the two may differ in their rates of change.

A third term should also be distinguished, and that is ***economic development.*** This is not a measure. Rather, it is a complex process of changes in the methods and organization of production. Economic development is a difficult-to-identify set of conditions and events which tend to bring about those changing relationships over a period of time; and the changes may occur both in technical methods of production and in the social organization of productive activity.

The significance of the distinction in these terms may be clarified with an analogy to living organisms. In the life of a plant or animal, growth involves more than simply getting bigger—that is, expansion. Growth of living organisms involves changes in the proportions and relations of the parts to the whole, while the whole expands. In fact, the sequence of changes in the parts and in their functioning within the whole permits or causes the expansion of the whole organism. Growth to maturity implies not only more size, but also more capacity to function. A man is not merely larger than a child; he is more able to serve himself and others. This analogy with growth in living organisms undoubtedly lies behind its widespread use in connection with rising production in nations.

However, we must be careful not to let our choice of words dominate our thinking about this subject. We do not know when (or even if) growth ever reaches "maturity" and stops in the history of a nation. Also, we do not know whether different nations or different historical periods belong to the same species—that is, we do not know whether they will grow in the same patterns and be determined by the same causes. Our terminology merely helps us keep clear what changes we are referring to—changes in total production, changes in production per person, or changes in methods and organization that influence production.

Elements of Production

The goods and services produced are considered by economists to provide the end products immediately available for use by people to satisfy their desires. The act of satisfying desires is called ***consumption,*** and it is assumed to use up or destroy the goods and services. The more durable goods, of course, may be used or consumed over longer periods of time. Most of economic analysis is concerned with the use of scarce resources to create or produce goods and services. To use the analogy of a machine, we may say that resources are put in at one end and goods and services are created and put out by the machine's "production process" at the other end. From this analogy is derived the common terminology, ***inputs*** (resources) and ***outputs*** (total production of goods and services). Economists view the production process broadly in terms of the following main elements: inputs, technology (or known methods), management and social organization, and output.

Among the inputs of production, the economist includes more than just the ***natural resources***—such as lands, minerals, plants, water, fish, animals, and other raw materials that may be collected from the earth in their natural state. It takes labor to collect natural resources, reshape them, and transport them to where they can be useful in satisfying wants. So the people engaged in production, and the knowledge and skills they possess personally, are the ***human resources*** of production. But that is not all. The results of past labors and past use of raw materials may be withheld from consumption (saved) and used to produce tools (invested) or provide other goods used in further production. These are ***accumulated resources*** which are just as essential to most forms of production as the labor and materials currently introduced. Traditionally, economists have referred to these three types of resources—natural, human, and accumulated—by the symbolic terms ***land, labor,*** and ***capital.*** The word "capital" in this basic resource sense must not be confused with a sum of money or the bookkeeping terminology used to refer to the assets of a business firm. Still another traditional term used in referring to land, labor and capital, is "the factors of production."

The main reason that economists always have been concerned with the quantities of productive resources is because most products can be produced by different methods using different proportions (or ratios) of resources. A greater proportion of capital, for example, provides the same workers more tools, which enables labor and capital together to produce more products. While all resources are scarce relative to human wants, the particular resources which are relatively most scarce may have greater value in production. They need to be used more sparingly in the present and expanded if possible in the future. The economic problem, therefore, always has been viewed as a matter of combining resources most efficiently to obtain the greatest possible number of products of the types most desired by consumers.

1–7. Elements of Production

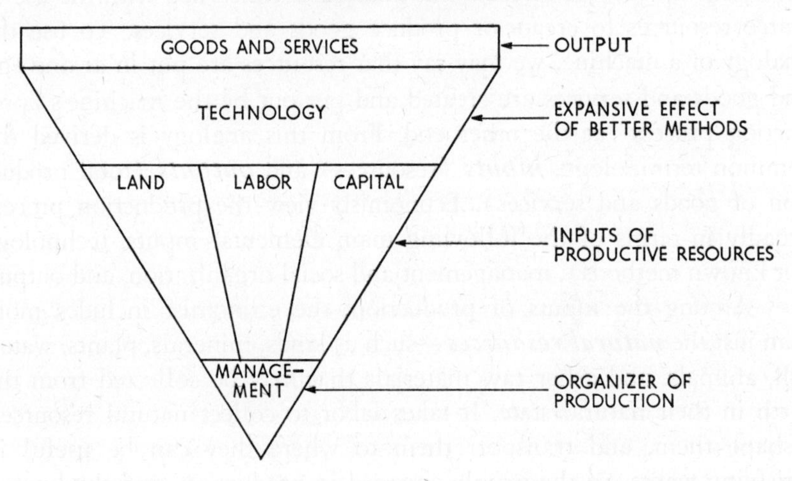

Economists in the past, however, may have been overly preoccupied with just the quantities and ratios of productive resources. The Industrial Revolution has involved sweeping changes in methods and organization of production. An invention changing the know technology or methods of an industry also changed the possible proportions for combining resources, stretched the scarce inputs, and raised the resulting output.

The production process also requires effective ***management*** of each production unit and efficient ***social organization*** of all production in the economy. The "manager" of a production unit must decide on the products to be made, determine the methods to be used, hire the productive resources, and ensure that everything flows smoothly. The social organization of the economy also determines the types of production units, the development of improved methods, the allocation of resources, and the quantities and distribution of products.

A schematic diagram may be helpful in picturing the roles of these ***elements of production.*** This scheme may be imagined as applying to a particular production unit (say, a business firm), or more abstractly to the total productive activities of a nation. Imagine the production process as a spinning top. At the fulcrum on the bottom is the manager (or the social organization) that organizes and holds together the whole process. The manager hires or purchases the three productive resources—land, labor and capital—which sit on top. He combines them in the most efficient proportions to achieve the greatest possible production of goods and services. The technology shows how wide the top can be. Now expansion (and perhaps growth) is possible if one or more of several things happens: if management does a more efficient job, if the quantity (or quality) of resources is increased, or if the known methods are improved. The study of economic development and growth, therefore, systematically looks for changes in these elements of production in an economy. (See 1–7.)

Organization of the Economy

Man is a social animal, and in his economic productive activities (as in other activities) his behavior is much affected by the forms of social organization used. At one extreme the individual may work alone or in a small family or large kinship unit of production. At the other extreme, all individuals may be organized into production teams by government organizations. In between there are various types of cooperative associations, such as the business firm. The various types of units of production also may be relatively isolated and independent from each other, or closely cooperating and dependent on each other. Under various forms of organization, the nature of the cooperation is influenced by social attitudes, customs, and laws.

Broadly speaking, there are three major principles by which economic production in a country may be organized. All three may be used in varying degrees in the same economy, but we may roughly classify countries as having one or another dominant type of organizing principle.

First, there is organization by ***tradition.*** Under this principle, all decisions as to methods of production, choice of products, choice of occupations, and distribution of rewards are determined by custom, tradition, or religious practices. In both primitive and old agricultural societies that developed slowly over the centuries, this principle of organization predominates. Past experience with methods of doing things has been imbedded in the social customs and habits of thought of the people. The rules are handed down from parents to children. Custom dictates everything that an individual is supposed to do, and social criticism and discipline are exercised over those who would try to change the social order.

Second, there is organization by ***command.*** This is the principle of using physical force to coerce people to do what some central authority decides should be done. Whether the source of authority is military or political, the principle is one of deciding for others what changes should be made in the existing or customary organization of production. In all societies some things may be decided centrally or collectively by setting a rule that individuals must follow—for example, conscription for military service, the payment of taxes, public health and sanitation practices, and so forth. But in some countries, particularly where there is dictatorship, a large part of the productive activities of the multitude of the people may be determined by general rules or by arbitrary decisions of a few officials or a ruling class. This may be a short-cut method for the government—as in Communist China—to make a rapid break with traditional customs and introduce new methods of production. But it also involves sacrifices of individual freedom, preferences, and standards of consumption. In some democratic societies, there also may be attempts to plan and direct the productive activities of the masses while leaving considerable freedom and initiative to the individual to adjust to the centrally determined decisions.

Third, there is organization by ***markets.*** This is the principle of leaving decisions on production and consumption up to the choices of each individual, while the organization of social cooperation is determined by the outcome of a multitude of interactions of individuals in the process of voluntarily exchanging goods and services. The process is described by the word "market," which originally described a central place in a town where people gathered to sell their surplus farm goods for other goods. With the development of transportation and communication over long distances, exchange activities extended far beyond towns to involve people in different nations. So economists use the term "market" to refer to any related exchange activities in a similar class of goods or services. Some free exchange, of course, occurs in all societies; but a "market economy" may be an appropriate label for a country in which the major part of all production decisions is determined by individual free choices in exchange activities.

In the study of economic development and growth, therefore, the economist attempts to determine the way production decisions are made. He must consider the form of government, the forms of cooperative association, the laws, and the social customs and attitudes. To understand our own national experience, we must not take these matters for granted.

One social mechanism that is important to all highly complex societies and especially to a market economy is the use of money as a common medium of reward and exchange. We have indicated that the measure of total production is a sum of money values determined by multiplying prices times quantities of goods. A price is simply a ratio of the amount of money exchanged for each unit of a good. The study of growth, therefore, must be concerned with two kinds of changes in prices. First, there are simultaneous changes in all prices in roughly the same direction and relative amounts. This reflects a general change in the value or "purchasing power" of money itself. We speak of this as a change in the general or average price level. Second, there are differential changes in the prices of different goods. These reflect shifts in the ratios at which one good may be exchanged for others. These may be referred to as changes in the price structure or in market prices.

The Development Process

Since economic development is a complex process of changes in methods and organization of production, the study of development is concerned with certain evidences of this change. As already indicated, the great transformation of production that occurred in modern industrial society involved a shift in the proportion of workers in nonfarm activities. The study of development, therefore, gives major attention to different ***sectors*** of the economy—especially farming, trade, transportation, and manufacturing. As production organization becomes more complex, attention also must be given to more detailed industry breakdowns of economic activity.

As a market economy develops, there is an increasing degree of ***specialization*** and division of labor in production. Study, therefore, must be directed to export activities and the extent of trading and market relations. The effects of specialization and market size also are related to the size of production units and the changes in production methods that are made possible.

As production organization becomes more complex, more attention must be given to the interrelations and sequence of changes. One aspect of these interrelations is the role played by industries and government activities that directly serve a wide range of other activities. Investment in the facilities of these industries and government agencies sometimes are referred to as ***social overhead capital.*** More will be said about this term later, but examples are found in the providing of various forms of transportation—the building of ports, highways, canals, railroads, and airports—and various utility services—electric power, gas, water, and sewerage works. Another aspect of these interrelations is the extent to which one export industry gives rise to or is supplanted by a ***diversity of industries.*** Also, some industries may benefit others by their purchases or by their close association in location.

Finally, the study of development must be concerned with changes in ***management*** and ***technology.*** The quality and efficiency of organization is more intangible and difficult to assess; but the study of development must be concerned with such subjects as education, the encouragement of invention, and the initiative and skill of managers.

1–8. Illustrative Stages of Growth

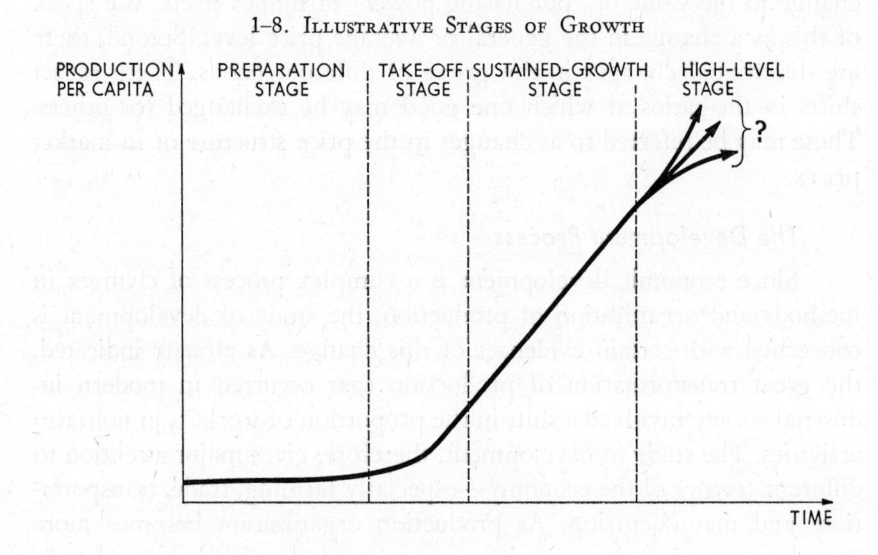

Throughout all discussions of growth and development there runs the notion that different conditions may be more important at different times. Development may not be a uniform process over time. It may proceed from one stage to another. If we plot the trend line of a nation's growth in per capita income, we find that it typically starts out rather slowly, then increases rapidly for an extended period, and finally at a high level of development may slow down, continue as before, or accelerate in some unusual cases. Some conditions may be important throughout all phases of such a trend line, while some might be more critical at the beginning or at the start of more rapid increases. (See 1–8.)

Professor W. W. Rostow has proposed a theory of stages of growth. As a predictive theory of history for all nations it has been optimistically misleading. Accordingly we will not rely upon Rostow's stages of growth as a statement of how an economy must grow or as an explanation of the development process. However, Rostow's stages comprise a useful classification and description device which brings with it a widely used and convenient terminology for organizing discussion of growth. The traditional historian's method of dividing American history into four periods separated by major wars also fits this classification of stages.

In this book the organization of chapters will follow the traditional historical periods but using the terminology of stages of growth. Rostow lists his five stages as follows: the traditional society, the transition, the takeoff, the sustained drive to maturity, and the age of high-level mass consumption.

In Part I, the Colonial period of American history is presented as being in the second stage, the transition from a traditional society to a market society. In Part II, the Pre-Civil War Period of our national history is presented as including the takeoff stage. (Rostow uses the analogy of an airplane gradually gaining speed then suddenly taking off when he describes the sudden upturn in rate of economic growth that occurred in this country just prior to the Civil War.) In Part III, the Post-Civil War period is presented as the stage of sustained growth in which America rose to industrial leadership in the world. In Part IV, the modern period since World War I is presented as America's present stage of high-level mass consumption, which is full of both promise and adjustment problems.

APPENDIX TO CHAPTER 1 ON NATIONAL ACCOUNTS

The national income accounts are a systematic way of summing up the total goods and services and total income produced during a year. It is useful to have this system because the transactions between different organizations are complex, and the records from different sources might be duplicating and confusing. The figures are published each year by the U. S. Department of Commerce.

It should be noted that the figures arise out of market sales. Production by an individual for his own use—such as sewing a dress or carving wooden bookends—would not be counted because there was no sale. Also, the quantities of goods and services are valued by money prices, for there is no other way to add up diverse items, such as automobiles, cotton, potatoes, and taxi rides.

There are two sides to every sale. Someone's expenditures become someone else's income. Thus the total value of production can be accounted for from the expenditures side and the income side. The expenditures are made by consumers, government, private investors, and foreign purchasers.

The income side is complicated by three considerations. First, we ordinarily don't consider receipts as "income" until all costs are paid, including the cost of replacing worn-out capital (which may be estimated as a capital consumption allowance or "depreciation"). Second,

1–9. 1960 National Income Accounts
(billions)

Expenditures Side		Income Side	
Gross national product	$504.4	*Gross national product*	$ 504.4
Personal consumption expenditures	328.9	less: depreciation	− 43.1
Government purchases	100.1	*Net national product*	461.3
Gross private investment	72.4	less: indirect business taxes	− 45.6
Net foreign purchases (exports less imports)	3.0	business transfer payments	− 1.8
		plus: statistical discrepancies	3.1
		National income	417.0
National income by types:		less: social insurance contributions	− 20.7
Corporate profits	$ 45.1	profits taxes	− 22.3
(profits taxes 22.3)		retained profits	− 8.7
(retained profits 8.7)		plus: business transfer payments	1.8
(dividends	14.1)	government transfer payments	27.3
Interest	18.4	government interest	7.8
Rent	11.7	*Personal income*	402.2
Proprietors' income	48.1	less: personal taxes	− 50.4
Wages and salaries	293.7	*Disposable personal income*	351.8

certain taxes added onto the price of goods usually are not considered income payments for productive services. Third, national income is not received entirely by individuals. Some is held by corporations and some is transferred to government. Individuals also receive some income payments that do not arise out of their current production services. So the national income accounts summarize several steps of adjustment of total production value to arrive at personal incomes. The figures for 1960 are shown in 1–9.

STUDY QUESTIONS

1. What summary measures of human welfare may be used to compare groups of people in different places and different periods in history? What is a "poor" family? a "poor" nation?
2. If we try to explain the causes of income differences among nations, why are natural resources only a partial answer? What measures of man-made differences help explain income differences? Why?
3. What basic changes occurred in man's relation to physical environment that broadly divides his past into three great eras? Why has population increase recently become a problem?
4. In the absence of historical income data, what other measures suggest the increase in human productive powers in past periods? How or why do these measures suggest a "transformation" in the methods and organization of human productive activity?
5. Why is there any need to rewrite history? What is economics? In what way is the study of economic growth a different approach to study of the past?
6. Why is it important to distinguish between economic expansion and economic growth? Explain this statement: "economic growth is only the score, economic development is the game."
7. Why do economists pay special attention to the three basic types of resources? Why are the other elements of production important?
8. What does it mean to say America has a "market economy?" How are prices important to the study of the American economy?
9. In what ways should the ideas of economic development as a process help us organize our study of America's past?

PART I

Preparation for Growth: 1492–1783

Chapter 2 RISE OF A MARKET ECONOMY

To understand the beginnings of the economy of the United States, it is essential to grasp three facts about its origins. First, its eastern coast was settled initially as a European pioneer colony. Second, its colonial culture and institutions were influenced by the advanced stages of European tradition from a medieval traditional economy to a modern market economy. Third, its national status was begun with a well-developed market economy at the start of the Industrial era in world history.

The fact that the most advanced industrial nation today had a colonial origin should be of considerable interest to underdeveloped nations which recently have won their own freedom from colonial status. We must be careful, however, not to try to draw easy lessons or parallels, for we started with advantages these nations may not have. The Thirteen American Colonies—as well as Canada, Australia, and New Zealand—were pioneer colonies in which the small, scattered native populations were pushed aside. In spite of Indian wars, there was no significant problem of adjusting dual societies or of transforming native cultures. The pioneers brought European culture and economic institutions with them and started at a very advanced level of development.

Europe was in the late stages of a transition when the American colonies were settled. The traditional economy of medieval Europe already was breaking down and a market economy was emerging. Many of the older institutions, however, lingered on as impediments to Europe's development. In the American colonies most of the features of the new society were established to begin with. There was no struggle to overthrow a ruling class nor to make over institutions. This new start was also influenced by the pioneering conditions in the colonies. The natural opportunities and obstacles attracted the most adventurous individuals and forced them to be self-reliant and adaptive.

The new nation that was formed began with a fully developed market economy at a time when the Industrial Revolution was in its first stages. This meant that we started at an advanced stage of development with a high degree of readiness to begin our industrialization and rapid growth. Per capita income in America already was about that of England and probably was matched by few other places in the world. We were an agricultural nation highly specialized in export crops and a trading nation actively engaged in world commerce. We had the institutions, leadership, skills, and wealth needed to launch our own development.

The modern industrial era was first launched in the environment of the newly emerging market economy. It is important, therefore, to understand the nature of a market economy and how it came into being. No one invented it. It arose gradually out of the activities of many Europeans even before national governments were formed and before anyone quite understood it. Economists merely began to describe how it worked and gave it a name—"capitalism."

The term capitalism may be misleading, for capitalism may be defined narrowly as an economy characterized by private ownership of the resources of production. Private or individual ownership of most resources, however, has been the practice of most societies during most of world history. Outside of the family unit, collective ownership has been more the exception than the common human practice. "Capital," as accumulated resources or tools of production, also is needed in all nations regardless of how production is organized.

It is the degree to which market exchange organizes production that distinguishes our national economy. We inherited this system from Europe, and it flourished in Europe during several centuries prior to the American Revolution. In a sense, this means that the time of Columbus is a better starting date for the study of our origins than is the first Virginia settlement.

EUROPE'S TRADITIONAL ECONOMY

Under the Roman Empire a fairly high standard of living had been achieved in the Mediterranean area and much of Europe. Under the security of the Roman troops, a wide area of trade and law had enabled considerable cooperation through exchange to flourish. With the end of the Western Roman Empire in 476, under the invasion of Germanic tribes and the Huns, European society became more fragmented and went into a decline. The following period often is referred to as the Dark Ages or Middle Ages. This "medieval" period in Europe covered about a thousand years, until about 1453 when the Eastern Roman Empire ended and Constantinople fell under the control of Muslim armies. It was during this period that Europe developed its characteristic traditional economy.

Medieval Hierarchy

Medieval European society was highly fragmented politically and economically, but it had common characteristics and a thread of unity in its religion and social attitudes. Europe as a whole was organized loosely into one overall federation with two rival pinnacles of power. One hierarchy was the church with the Pope at its head. The other was the "Empire," a tradition of leadership that began in 800 when Charlemagne was crowned emperor.

The medieval hierarchy of political organization is referred to as a "feudal" system, and this term is still used to refer to any social power structure with similar characteristics today. The main characteristic is that of a hierarchy in which the real powers and the independence of decision are held by some middle layer of numerous and semi-independent leaders. The emperor, kings, and dukes derived their power solely from the sworn loyalty of the middle layer of barons and princes (heads of principalities). These were the personal leaders of small armies of knights and foot soldiers. Each knight was economically supported by an estate of farmlands, perhaps captured in battle and granted to him by the leader of his army. The baron-leader also had his own estates, but he was in close communication with his knights on their nearby estates. The small army was disciplined and had common interests as a unit of mutual defense against marauding bands or neighboring armies. This was not often true, however, of the larger political units. The kings depended on the barons to voluntarily contribute soldiers or to join a loose coalition army. Among the kings there was constant jockeying for power over territories and much forming and reforming of coalitions. The emperor seldom exercised more than nominal authority and seldom over more than a large part of Europe. All rulers were supported mostly by estates under their own management and only partly on levies of economic contributions from their subordinate barons.

The Catholic Church had a hierarchy of its own and asserted at least nominal authority over the political hierarchy. Having been established as the state religion under the Roman Empire, the church assumed the authority under the chaotic conditions of the Middle Ages to appoint emperors and kings. Because of an accumulation of religious offerings and gifts by both individuals and rulers, the church accumulated wealth and estates of its own. At times it controlled some armies and ruled some territories. It frequently was involved in struggles between kings and in rivalry for power with the emperor. In addition to its religious influence over the people, it was able to wield considerable power because of the divisive conflicts between kings and barons.

Below these two upper classes of noblemen and churchmen were the townspeople (the burghers or bourgeoisie). Like the noblemen's castles, the towns were walled and fortified for defense. In the town was a central marketplace for trade, merchants' stores, craftsmen's shops, often a town residence of a nobleman, and a cathedral and other church buildings. The merchants and craftsmen were a small middle class, but they were little higher in status than the soldiers and supervisors of the noblemen's estates. In the lower classes were the apprentices, the servants, and the peasants who made up the vast bulk of the population.

Static Customs and Other Worldly Religion

Throughout medieval Europe similar customs and religious attitudes prevailed. Custom ruled all behavior because conditions and knowledge were static. While the nobles occasionally fought battles to protect or expand their power, production and daily living went on year after year with no change. A person's social status and occupation were inherited from parents, who also passed on the skills and methods learned in the past. These methods were accepted as the only ones or the best ones, and changes were feared. Persons of one social status or one position in the heirarchy owed certain services, contributions of specific goods, and obedience to persons of a higher rank, but a few customary rights as well as duties were recognized. Customary prices and wages were expected to be paid, although usually in goods rather than money.

Religious attitudes pervaded all customs. Christianity had gained supremacy over the pagan superstitions of the tribal peoples that settled down to agrarian living in Europe, and it provided a more orderly view of the universe and a more moralistic code of conduct. Yet Christianity in medieval times provided a pessimistic, fatalistic view. Conditions of living, in fact, were mean and uncertain. Undernourishment and famine regularly took a heavy toll among the peasants, and even the upper classes were not immune to risks of sudden death from disease or war. Christianity provided only the hope that after death there might be a more pleasant existence in eternity. The threat of eternal punishment reinforced civilized standards of moral conduct. The mystery and uncertainty of events were explained as a divinely determined plan that provided unpleasant tests of the moral merit of an individual during his temporary lifetime.

Religious attitudes were hostile to trade and market exchange activities. The customary wages and prices were sanctioned as the only ethical ones, as the "fair wage" and "just price." This made some sense, of course, in a basically unchanging economy periodically threatened by local famines and shortages due to bad weather and poor transportation. Religion urged charity to meet individual misfortunes and emergencies. Prices were not expected to function as incentives to adjust to changing conditions. Lending also was regarded as an act of charity, and the charging of interest, called "usury," was regarded as a sin. Preoccupation with monetary gains and the accumulation of wealth (or even an emphasis on consumption and pleasure) were condemned as immoral, as worshipping material rather than spiritual goals. Medieval Christianity, therefore, was hostile to "business," and it provided little encouragement for individuals to strive for greater productivity, to experiment with new methods, or to introduce change.

Subsistence Agriculture

In the Middle Ages over 90 percent of the working population was engaged in agriculture. The basic unit of production organization was the farm estate, or "manor." The manor was owned and ruled usually by a nobleman or "lord." He might be a knight, a baron, or king; each was supported by his own lands. The wealthier nobleman might have several estates. Some manors also were owned and ruled by the church. The products of the manor barely supported the lord, his servants, his soldiers, and the peasants, and there was little surplus to meet the levies of the kings and the church. Each manor, or local group of manors near a town, attempted to be self-sufficient, and this self-sufficiency was partly responsible for the bare subsistence living standards (as will be explained at the end of this chapter).

In appearance, the manor was a small village in the midst of some cleared land and forests. There would be a cluster of huts, perhaps a blacksmith shop or a grist mill, and a manor house or castle for the lord or his supervisor. Attached to each hut was a small garden and perhaps a fenced yard for fowl and livestock. Stretching out away from the village would be two or more open and unfenced fields for crops or pasture. In addition, there usually were some nearby untilled lands used for pasture and some forested lands. (See 2–1 for a schematic view of a medieval manor.)

The methods of farming were very primitive, so the production per worker was very low. At first a two-field rotation system was common, with one idle and used for pasture while the other was sowed in some grain. Later, considerable improvement resulted from a three-field system, with rotation of wheat or rye with barley, oats, or peas, and with the third year for idleness or pasture. The worker holdings were very small, with the fields divided into long narrow strips representing what a single ox-pulled plow could cover in a single day without too many turnarounds. The peasant might hold several separate strips in different fields and also was responsible for working strips owned by the

2–1. A Medieval Manor

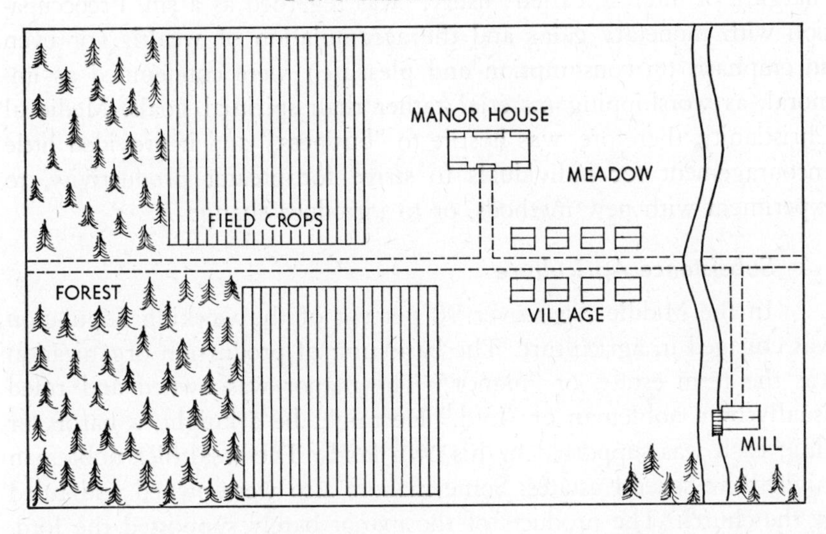

lord. No fertilizer was used. The use of horses for pulling wagons and plows became more common only after the invention of the horse collar. Cattle were turned loose in open pasture without any selection or breeding. There was a shortage of hay and fodder, so most livestock was slaughtered and salted or smoked in the fall.

Most peasants were serfs permanently tied to a particular estate with a status equal to that of a slave. It had been discovered in late Roman times that farm workers on large estates would work more diligently if they were assigned their own land and shared in the crops. As the North European tribes settled down to farming, the farm worker usually fell under the protection of some lord and his soldiers in exchange for a regular share of his output and permanent submission to his control. Regulations soon bound him to the land so that he could not leave, and he might have to get permission or pay a fee to marry or to inherit a landholding. He was obligated to work the lord's land or share his crops and perhaps to work in the manor house as a servant. He also owed the church its tithes. The lord also might monopolize and charge fees for services of the flour mill, oven, winepress, leather tannery, and blacksmith shop. Still, the serf usually had some customary rights to work certain strips, to use certain tools of the lord, and to keep his own garden and household property. Some landless serfs might be virtually squatters with no rights, and some free peasants owned their land with minimal tax obligations. Conditions, of course, varied widely in different parts of Europe and in different centuries.

Though the agriculture of the medieval period appears inefficient and unnecessarily ritualistic to us, agricultural organization in the Middle Ages served to provide a floor against famine. However, its communal allocation of resources hampered individual experimentation and, thus, slowed the growth of productivity. During the late Middle Ages, though, agricultural organization slowly evolved as adaptations were forced upon it as whole regions moved away from local self-sufficiency to specialized production for commercial markets.

Handicrafts and Trade

A limited amount of handcraft manufacture and trade was carried on in the walled towns. Both the craftsmen and the merchants were organized into associations called "guilds." Leaders of the various guilds usually formed the town council. Political leaders often left the towns alone or even granted them self-rule and monopoly rights over their particular crafts and trades. It was convenient for the rulers to let the guilds determine their own rules and administer the towns; but more important, they wished to encourage the production and trade which yielded them additional revenues in taxes. Assistance of the towns also was frequendly sought to provide soldiers and to lend money to finance wars.

The craftsmen actually were small business operators as much as were the small merchants. The master craftsmen—shoemakers, tailors, etc.—owned their own shops, tools and materials, although they might contract for work on the buyer's materials. If their sales were large enough, they might hire one or more journeymen, who had not yet saved enough money to start their own shops. Young boys also worked several years as apprentices to learn to become a journeymen. They received little more than board and room and were bound by contract to obey the master craftsman.

Other town dwellers were soldiers, servants, or casual laborers for menial tasks. Even for the poorest worker, however, the towns were islands of freedom; for usually a peasant who found refuge there for over a year became free of obligations to a manor lord.

In regulating their own trade or craft, the guilds frequently became rather restrictive and monopolistic, although usually their regulations positively supported free market exchange, at least for their own members. In small local markets, supply was usually too plentiful. If too many craftsmen or outside sellers entered the market, the prices might be lowered. Thus, restrictions were placed on the number of apprentices that could be trained and the length of their training. Furthermore, to prevent overproduction, hours were limited. In fact, the shops which had family quarters in back, often were required to have open shutters in front so the people passing on the street could see that the rules were being obeyed inside. Rules also were directed, however, against monopoly or harmful practices by any guild member. Forestalling and engrossing, efforts to buy up foods or raw material supplies before they reached the market in order to create scarcity and hold up the price, were forbidden. Standards of quality and fair weights were upheld by inspection. Laws of contract and credit were developed and disputes were settled by courts. The restrictive nature of town laws and guild rules was implicitly based upon the assumption of slowly growing markets and thus the notion that expansion of one firm was achieved only at the expense of other firms.

COMMERCIAL REVOLUTION

It was the rise of commercial activity in the towns that was the main source of breakdown of Europe's traditional society. Increased trade gradually increased the power of broader political units, the national kingdoms. It helped to revise attitudes toward nature and encouraged efforts to improve methods of production. It shifted the social organization of production toward that of a market economy.

Rise of Trade and Business

Trade had never completely stopped in the Middle Ages, but in the 12th and 13th centuries it gradually began to flourish throughout Europe. This was due partly to the series of Crusades which occurred over this 200-year period, to the reduced neighborhood warfare which accompanied the rising political stability, and to the growth in population which followed. In fighting the Turks, Western European nobility became acquainted with and acquired a taste for the spices, silks, dyes, drugs, jewels, and other luxury goods from the Far East. Trade links to India and China were established primarily by the Italians, largely via water routes through Constantinople, although a smaller overland trade was carried on through Russia. From Italian ports, overland routes were established through the Alps to Germany and the Scandinavian countries and through France to Holland and England. Later shipping was increased between the Baltic Sea, the English Channel, and the Mediterranean Sea.

To purchase the luxury goods and other scarce items, people in some areas began to produce a surplus of certain types of goods for export. England had much grassland suitable for sheep grazing; so it became a major exporter of wool. The Scandinavian countries exported iron, copper, furs, timber, and tars. From the Baltic and North Atlantic areas came herring and salt. Various cities in France began to manufacture cloth, armor, and other craft articles.

To carry on this trade, some merchants usually had to travel in ships and overland caravans, and they would gather at annual fairs in several of the northern countries to exchange their goods. These fairs were great temporary marketplaces and were regulated by the merchants themselves. As goods began to move more frequently and regularly, some of the fairs became permanent and cities grew up around them. Port cities also flourished as international marketplaces.

In carrying out this trade, many of the modern forms of business organization were developed. The large merchants were engaged in a wholesale and long-distance shipping business. The typical form of large business was the family partnership, which kept together as a loosely related unit as the family grew and prospered. Temporary associations, however, frequently were formed for a particular ship's voyage or even a convoy for mutual defense. In such cases, many different merchants would share in the financing and share similarly in the final results, if the ship were lost or if it returned with large profits. These were an early form of what later became "joint-stock companies," in which many people might purchase shares in a venture as co-owners. Another way of sharing risks developed into an insurance agreement, whereby the payment of a premium fee in advance by an owner (or shareowner) would enable him to recover all or part of his loss from an insurer in case the ship were lost at sea.

The large merchant also became an investor in a large variety of production activities. In the cloth trades, the "put-out" system of manufacture involved a merchant supplying materials to craftsmen who worked in their own shops or homes and brought back the finished materials for which they were then paid by the merchant. Some merchants also became partners in large mining organizations and other production activities requiring considerable numbers of workers and much capital. Usually, however, they diversified as they grew larger and they invested in a great variety of activities—including city real estate speculations, construction, and development of large farms for export products. Frequently only the larger merchant had large enough accumulations of money, could afford to take large risks with part of his wealth, and had the imagination and information necessary to see the opportunities.

Both accounting and credit practices also developed with the rising trade. Large businesses, transactions over long periods and with distant places, and a multiplicity of goods and activities required the development of accurate and meaningful record keeping. Double-entry bookkeeping was developed as a vital tool to business operations. Banking developed from merely a matter of deposit accounts—or safekeeping of gold and silver—into a lending activity. Written notes enabled agents of a merchant to withdraw money from his deposits; soon written notes enabled another merchant to collect payment by drawing upon his deposit. Bills of exchange also became a written agreement to receive shipped goods in exchange for a promise to pay after a period of delay. Although at first interest was regarded as prohibited by church rules, the interest soon was disguised, since the bills of exchange easily could be written for somewhat larger payments than the value of the goods initially received. A large wholesale merchant usually extended short-term loans (delayed payments) on goods shipped or materials furnished to small merchants and craftsmen. A deposit bank, or any business with large balances and diversified operations, could lend out part of their reserve funds without expecting all claims against their funds to come in at once. Thus, lending bank practices were gradually developed.

Breakdown of Feudalism

In the 14th and 15th centuries, a number of troubles shook the organization of European society. In 1348, a terrible plague, called the Black Death, killed many people—from one tenth to one quarter of the population in some areas. Also, England and France became involved in the Hundred Years War. The resulting manpower shortages, along with some peasant rebellions, soon disrupted some of the class privileges and customs. A great split occurred in the church, and for a while it had two popes. Subsequently, a number of reform movements were directed at the church. In 1453, Constantinople fell to the Turks, and with this the remnants of the Eastern Roman Empire finally ended. Many historians date this as the end of the Middle Ages.

During these two centuries there also occurred a revival of interest in arts and learning, which historians have called the Renaissance. Men of wealth supported artistic and scholarly activities. There was a beginning of scientific inquiry and an effort to improve the practical arts of production. Among other inventions introduced were the printing press, gunpowder, and new navigation instruments.

Near the beginning of the 16th century, in a new spirit of inquiry and discovery, Europeans began to explore the oceans. Blocked off from land routes to the Far East via Constantinople, a search began for a water route. In 1492, Columbus chanced upon America, and in 1498 John Cabot similarly found Laborador. Vasco da Gama reached India in the same year, and Magellan circled the globe in 1522. So, within a single generation, the Europeans had "discovered" the other continents and established colonial outposts on all of them.

The beginning of the 16th century also saw the beginning of the Protestant Reformation that was to break up the domination of the church and change religious attitudes toward business. The printing press led to a wider reading of the Bible and a questioning of church authority. Luther nailed his radical theses to a church door in 1517. In the 1530's, King Henry VIII broke with the Pope and established the Church of England. For over a hundred years in Europe there was a series of religious wars between Protestants and Catholics.

As feudalism broke down the nation-states rose and the beginnings of economic development could be observed as the preconditions for rapid growth were gradually fulfilled. Trade among European nations, including North Africa and Asia Minor, increased as the beginnings of national specialization got underway. In part this trade expansion was made possible by the emergence of the financial institutions that are required for a high degree of specialization and trade among nations—in this era commercial banks emerged as vital links in international trade providing for the first time many of the banking services that today's merchants take for granted.

The system that replaced feudalism was, of course, the first stage of the market system we know today. Land, labor, and capital emerged as separate factors of production; as the serfs won their freedom, the guilds declined, the putting-out system rose as a forerunner of the factory system, and the mills that had been built adopted new techniques. Europe and its trading satellites were truly undergoing a transformation that provided the basis for an economic revolution in later years.

The last claim to being emperor of Europe also ended in 1555 when Charles V abdicated and divided his lands between two successors. For several previous centuries, various national kingdoms had gained strength—in England, France, Portugal, and elsewhere; no emperor could claim to control them. Trade and industry had provided the kings with an important source of tax revenues with which to buy cannons and ships and to support armies of their own. Merchants also loaned kings large sums of money in times of war in exchange for special favors and monopoly privileges. So the kings became less dependent upon the voluntary support of barons. As large kingdoms came to have more permanent boundaries with less constant warring between small principalities, people became more conscious of national ties. The new national kingdoms developed their own bureaucracy to administer tax collections and exercised closer control over local conditions.

Production for Market

The discoveries and colonization of the 16th century rapidly expanded European trade. Trade, in turn, not only disrupted the political and religious order of feudal society, but also it began to reorganize production activity. The independent subsistence agricultural units began to be supplanted by specialized production for exchange in markets. When only a small part of production was for exchange locally, it was possible to barter (or swap) one product or service for another. As a larger part of production became traded and as the goods exchanged moved over greater distances, money became increasingly the medium of exchange. People sold goods or services for money; then money was used to buy a wide variety of things.

The Spanish colonies in South America greatly facilitated the expansion in trade by expanding the supply of money even more rapidly. The weight of gold or silver (minted into coins) was the common unit of money exchanged in trade. In 1500, Europe had been somewhat short of gold and silver. In the next century and a half, it is estimated that Spain's gold and silver imports more than tripled the total supply of money in Europe.

The increase in money supply was accompanied by a long period of price inflation—a general rise in most prices—nearly everywhere in Europe. In England, for example, it is estimated that between 1500 and

1600 the general price level more than tripled. This would have required a continuing rate of increase of only 2 to 3 percent per year, and that may not seem very fast compared to some inflations experienced in modern times. However, people in the Middle Ages had been accustomed to long periods of stable production and prices. These continuous price increases soon confounded all of their expectations as to "just prices" and "fair wages." Many things were blamed: bad crops, heavy taxes, high wages, and so forth. (See 2–2.)

2–2. Gold Inflow and Prices

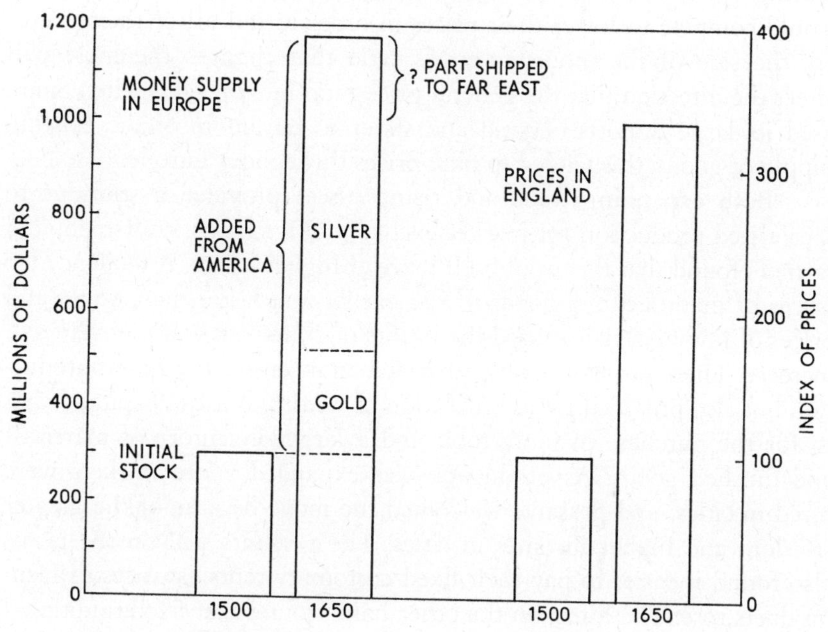

Source: Earl J. Hamilton, *American Treasure and the Price Revolution in Spain* (Cambridge, Mass.: Harvard University Press, 1934).

A better explanation for the price increase was provided by what is now known as "the quantity theory of money." This explanation was offered in 1568 in one of the first books on economics (in Jean Bodin's *Reply to the Paradoxes of M. Malestroit*). The theory most simply put is that, given the volume of production to be exchanged, the general price level will change by whatever proportion the volume of money changes. If the quantity of production were changing at the same time that the supply of money was changing, then the change in the ratio of money to goods would be vital in determining what prices did. This is because a price is simply a ratio of exchange of money for goods. For example, if $10 exchanges for 10 units of a good, then the price is $1 per unit.

If twice as much money were suddenly put into the hands of all buyers in a market without any change in the number of goods produced for sale, the buyers would tend to bid up the prices to about double their previous level. Conversely, if the supply of goods was suddenly doubled with the same amount of money in buyers' hands, the prices would tend to be cut in half—for buyers would not be able or willing to buy the increased supply unless prices fell, and the sellers would compete to lower their prices in order to sell all of their goods. So, the side of the money-to-goods ratio that changes the most will affect the direction that the general price ratio moves. Thus when Spain used its large imports of gold and silver to buy more of the existing supply of goods, this tended to raise prices throughout Europe.

Both expanding trade and rising prices provided a stimulus to specialized production for market exchange. Merchants, craftsmen, and farmers found that they could sell more at higher prices. A tendency for prices of manufactured goods to rise earlier and faster than wages and prices of raw materials caused the profits of craftsmen and merchants to increase. These profits not only provided an incentive to expand production but also provided an accumulation of wealth to use as capital—that is, for the purchase of more tools and a larger inventory of materials and finished goods. As production was expanded, more workers were hired in cities; and peasants welcomed the move because of the greater freedom and higher incomes in cities. The peasants still on the farms also found it easier to pay their fixed customary rents as prices of farm products rose. The lords, on the other hand, found that fixed traditional rents purchased less goods at the higher prices. They, in turn, tried to protect their incomes by increasing their acreage of cultivation or by improving methods. Sometimes wealthy merchants rented idle lands and put them to use producing farm products for market.

Late in the 16th and throughout the 17th century, therefore, there was a rapid increase in specialized production for market, and with this change came many improvements in production methods. In mining and manufacturing, various improvements in methods and products were introduced as production was enlarged. In agriculture, idle lands were cleared and drained, and new and old lands were fenced in—"enclosed"—in order to protect crops from animals or to develop pure breeds of improved livestock. New crops were introduced and new methods of crop rotation and plowing were soon used.

England's Woolen Industry

Wool exports were the basis for the early development of England's trade and for its first major manufacturing industry. A merchant class got its initial start handling exports of wool to the Lowlands, France, and the Baltic countries. Then some merchants began to hire workers and produce woolen cloth in London. London expanded as a major trading, shipping, and financial center. Woolen cloth and other goods were mainly produced in small craft shops, which were organized into guilds.

In the 16th century, expanding European markets and rising prices had two types of effects on England's woolen industry. First, farm production of wool was greatly expanded by devoting more pasturelands to sheep raising. Henry VIII's seizure of church lands provided some of the new pasture. Much idle land was cleared or brought into use. Other ways for the lord of a manor to get land for sheep raising were to consolidate his strips of land into one field, to buy up the holdings of peasants, or to take over the open pastureland which previously had been available for the common use of all peasants. Since the sheep lands usually were fenced in to minimize herd-tending, these various measures have been called by historians the "enclosure movement." Both expansion and reorganization of land use were involved. Since less labor was required to herd sheep than to tend crops, some peasants were displaced by the reorganization. This may explain the problems with numerous vagrants in Elizabethan times. Poor Laws were enacted in an attempt to levy local taxes to support the poor and put them to work.

As a second effect, the woolen cloth merchants sought to expand woolen manufactures quickly without the restrictions of the London guilds. They began to move their production locations into rural areas to use the displaced farm workers and peasant families under the put-out or "cottage" system. Woolen textiles were made in a series of steps, each step by a separate type of craftsman. The wool had to be cleaned, carded, and spun into yarn. The yarn was woven into cloth; then the cloth was fulled, burled, and dyed. A clothier merchant, therefore, would buy the wool and send it out to neighboring cottages to be prepared and spun, mainly by women and children. When they brought him the yarn, he paid them. Then he hired weavers to weave it into cloth on his looms, either in their homes or in his shop. After paying the weavers for the finished cloth, he took it to a fulling mill and then brought it home to be cut, stretched, and sent to market. Only upon final sale did he get back the money he had paid out, plus a return for his efforts.

The town workers in the textile guilds fought the movement of industry into the rural areas. In 1555, they persuaded parliament to pass the Weavers Act, which limited the number of looms a clothier could own, the men he could hire, and the weavers' apprenticeship period. Enforcement, however, was difficult, and the law soon was disregarded. In making woolen cloth, most of the clothiers were fairly small businessmen, anyway, and depended upon wool brokers and merchants to bring them materials and sell their products. It was in making woolen worsted cloth that the master comber frequently became a very large merchant. Since the long-haired sheep were raised best in northern England, worsted textile making became concentrated more in that region. Gradually the worsted merchants became more skillful in designing their patterns and dyes to appeal to customers and gained an increasing share of the European markets. As demand expanded and shifted more to worsteds, production became even more concentrated in England's northern industrial towns.

Shipping, Colonies, and Diversified Industries

Along with its expanding woolen exports, England was able to develop a thriving shipping industry. Some merchants carried on trading ventures with all parts of Europe, some attempted colonial ventures, and some even engaged in piracy against Spanish ships. Queen Elizabeth encouraged all of these activities as well as shipbuilding. After the defeat of the Spanish Armada in 1588, England rose to the position of a major naval power. Early in the 17th century, England began to develop colonies in North America, and the East India Company was chartered with the exclusive privilege of developing a heavy trade with India.

Several industries developed in connection with the new consumer products made possible by colonial imports. New beverages—coffee, tea, and cocoa—soon became very popular and with them came an increased demand for sugar. Crude sugar, or molasses, was imported from the West Indies and refined in England. Rum also was made from molasses, and it competed with brandy in European markets. In England, the main drink of the common people soon became beer brewed from locally grown hops. The British tavern became an important social institution, and along with beer drinking, the smoking of tobacco became popular. This created demands for American tobacco plantations, but the tobacco processing was done in England.

A rapid expansion of shipbuilding, the construction in growing cities, and the burning of firewood soon created a shortage of fuel in 17th-century England. Outcroppings of coal, however, were readily available in northern England, and over half of English ships soon were engaged in the coastal trade, mostly carrying coal. Not only did English consumers turn to coal for heating and cooking, but many industries began to use it as a fuel. For example, with the lumber shortage, there was a shift to the use of stones and bricks in construction, and the baking of bricks in kilns required coal. The widespread use of coal stoves required more iron for gratings. The rapid construction of more houses also required more window glass, and more glass was demanded for bottles, lanterns, and cheap glassware.

A rising demand for salt by the fishing industry, as well as for preserving foods generally, led to a demand for large iron and copper kettles for boiling sea water to make salt. The textile industry also required dyes, and this led to building of alum and copperas, i.e., ferrous sulfate, factories which used large kettles. Discoveries of zinc ores in England permitted the development of manufacture of brasswares—brass is an alloy of copper and zinc. Government encouragement of the manufacture of gunpowder brought the development of saltpeter mills, and the making of cannon required large ironworks. A great variety of iron products, of course, was required in shipbuilding, construction, stovemaking, and other industries.

Along with the rising demand for consumer products and some heavy industry products, there gradually developed more skilled crafts. Brown wrapping paper, for example, first was produced in England. Later, with the rise in the printing industry, the French skills of making fine white paper were introduced. Protestant refugees sometimes brought skills and knowledge of special industry techniques with them to England. The development of silk textiles, for example, was made possible by skilled immigrants.

Altogether, then, English manufacturing underwent a rapid and diversified development in the 16th and 17th centuries. The period between 1540 and 1640, in fact, has been called the "earlier industrial revolution." It was in this period that the North American colonies initially were being settled.

COLONIAL OUTPOSTS IN NORTH AMERICA

Motives for Colonizing

European explorations and colonizing efforts in the 16th and 17th centuries were motivated primarily by desires for economic gains. An initial objective was to find a cheap ocean route for trade with the Far

East. Hopes for quick riches were stimulated by Spain's discoveries of gold treasures and silver mines in South America. It also appeared that new products and fertile soils provided profit opportunities through developing production in the New World. National governments, anxious to build up their own power through exclusive claims to trade and colonies, participated in some of the exploration costs. But the costs of settlement and development of production were left primarily to private financing.

The types of colonial settlement varied with the area and nation involved. In the Far East, trading posts were mostly established at the ports of densely populated countries. In South America, the Spanish conquered an agricultural native population and put them to work in mines and on plantations. In North America, where the natives were scattered and nomadic, the French established only a few port cities and inland fur trading posts. Only in the English colonies did large numbers of Europeans settle and simply push back the native peoples.

The earliest English colonies were established by chartered joint-stock companies with the hope of making a profit. The initial failures of Sir Humphrey Gilbert and Sir Walter Raleigh in the 1580's to establish colonies in Newfoundland and the Carolinas demonstrated that large and long-term financial investments and a hardy group of permanent agricultural settlers were needed. In 1607, the Virginia Company of London succeeded in establishing the first permanent colony at Jamestown. In 1620, the first New England colony was established by the Plymouth Company, which was a combined venture of merchants and a community of Puritans seeking freedom from religious persecution. In 1630, the Massachusetts Bay Company established a colony and then moved its headquarters to the colony, giving it a form of self-government. A large number of settlers then came to this colony, and some moved on to establish colonies in neighboring Rhode Island, Connecticut, and New Hampshire. Early Dutch and Swedish companies also established colonies in New York and New Jersey, but they were not heavily settled and later fell under English control. In spite of success in establishing settlements, these early joint-stock company ventures were not profitable.

The other colonies were established by land grants from the Stuart kings to favored noblemen. In these proprietary colonies, an unsuccessful attempt was made to transfer the feudal system of land estates to the New World. The proprietors made personal investments to encourage settlement and to establish production on some of their own farms. They expected to profit mostly from sale of land, rents on land granted to others (called "quitrents"), and duties on trade. Usually, however, the land had to be given free in order to encourage early settlers, and later the quitrents were resisted and were poorly collected.

The last of the Thirteen Colonies that later became one of the United States was Georgia, established in 1732 over a century after colonizing had begun. Throughout the Colonial period (until 1776), the settlement was limited geographically to the coastal edge of the North American continent. Initial settlement was in natural harbors and along partly open river valleys. Further farmlands had to be

2–3. Colonial Settled Areas

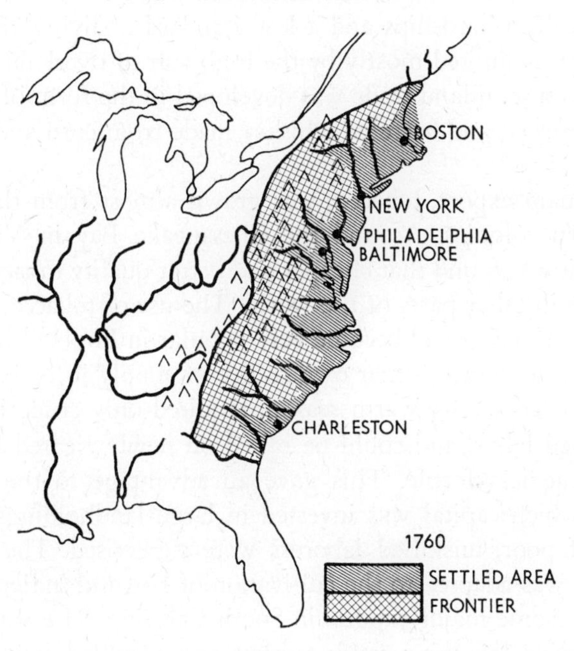

laboriously cleared of trees for the lands were heavily forested. Movement inland was limited by the stopping of river transportation at the "fall line," where rapids or falls marked the foothills of the Appalachian Mountains, the main barrier to later penetration of the continent. Nearly all transportation and communication was by water, along the rivers to the coast and over the ocean to Europe. A little coastal trade occurred between the colonies, but very little roadbuilding was done to link the colonies by land. (See 2–3.)

Export Specialization

From the beginning an effort was made to find suitable products for export to England. Not only was it important to find an income to justify the flow of initial investment funds from England, but also the colonists were not completely self-sufficient and required manufactured goods. Even the trapper, for example, who traveled far inland and was isolated for months, needed guns, ammunition, and goods to trade with the Indians. Of course, the abundance of natural resources provided the means for considerable self-sufficiency. Forests provided the building materials and part of the tools. A wide variety of crops and livestock could be raised, and these could be supplemented with game and fish. Corn was perhaps the chief crop and was grown everywhere. Yet only the backwoods pioneer families attempted to be nearly self-sufficient, for this involved hardships and a low standard of living. The frontier production was limited mostly by the high cost of overland transportation; but even so, inland trade was developed in the form of furs, cattle driven to market, and barreled whiskey made from corn and carried by mule.

The main export, tobacco, was grown almost from the outset in the southern colonies. Around the Chesapeake Bay in Virginia and Maryland, it was found that cheaper and better quality tobacco could be grown than in other parts of the world. The use of tobacco, introduced from South America, had become very popular in England; the English were pleased to develop their own source of supply in North America. Tobacco needed a long warm season, required only crude implements and unskilled labor, and could be raised on newly cleared land as old fields became less fertile. This gave an advantage to the plantation system in which capital was invested in large landholdings and large numbers of poor, unskilled laborers were supervised. The plantation system also was adapted to the cultivation of rice and indigo, which by 1700 had become major exports in South Carolina. Rice was grown in swamplands or low-lying fields subject to controlled irrigation from tidewater rivers. It also required a warm climate and much tending by unskilled labor. Indigo was a complementary crop which could use the labor in different seasonal peaks; production was fostered by British subsidies to supply dyes to the English textile industries.

The middle colonies—Pennsylvania, New Jersey, and New York—also had a main export crop, wheat, which was raised on fairly large farms. Most of the product was processed locally into flour before exporting. Considerable livestock and salted meats also were exported.

The New England farms, however, were predominantly small and produced only for local town markets. The main exports were drawn from the resources of the ocean and forests—in order of importance, they were codfish, whale oil, and ship timbers. Some meat products also were exported.

An active shipbuilding industry developed in New England, and many New Englanders became sailors, ship captains, and world traders. Other manufacturing firms throughout the colonies were primarily engaged in processing raw materials: sawmills and grist mills everywhere, flour mills in the middle colonies, processing of naval stores in the South, and small ironworks in many locations.

Maryland became a large exporter of iron, but wrought iron and iron products were sold locally. Other manufactures were strictly for domestic consumption. Most farm families and the plantations relied heavily upon household manufactures. Late in the Colonial period some production of shoes and clothing was organized by large merchants under the putting-out system. A few skilled artisans did handcraft production in small shops in the large port cities.

Merchants served as middlemen in carrying out the exchange of goods in this predominantly agricultural and export economy. Traveling peddlers sold to backwoods pioneer families. The general store sold everything and bought everything in the small village. At the port-cities, export-import merchants managed a wholesale business, and commission agents purchased crops for British merchants and ordered goods for colonial planters. Shipmasters managed to find opportunities throughout the Atlantic area for disposing of exports and picking up imports. Since there usually was a shortage of coins in the English colonies, a considerable part of this trade was conducted by barter and credit.

Organizing and Expanding Production

In view of the suitability of natural resources for this wide variety of exports, it might seem that investors should have had no trouble getting a quick profit on colonizing ventures. However, they faced the necessity of producing with a combination of resources—labor and capital, as well as land. America's characteristic production problem from the beginning was the scarcity of labor and capital to combine with plentiful natural resources. At first this depended on how rapidly labor and capital migrated from England, although later expansion depended more on American birthrates and savings.

There were four main ways that the labor supply was brought to the Colonies. First, groups of settlers obtained land grants and settled in organized villages, primarily in New England. Usually these were religious minority communities that migrated with their own capital. Second, individuals with their own capital obtained land grants under the "headright" system, whereby a specified acreage of land (usually 50 acres), was promised for each person landed in the colonies. Small independent farmers came with just enough capital to establish their own family farms. More wealthy individuals brought servants or financed the transport of others and thereby obtained the land for each person he brought.

Third, many penniless laborers were brought as ***indentured servants.*** The indenture was simply a contract whereby the person's ocean fare was paid, he was promised food and lodging, and he might also receive a small payment or some land upon termination of the contract period. In return, he promised to labor without pay under the discipline of a master for a period of time, which might be from two to seven years. This enabled the large landowner to "buy" his labor supply by purchasing indentures from ship captains. The captains, in turn, would use labor recruiters in England. Under the Head Right System of the middle and southern colonies, anyone who could prove to have paid passage for someone to the New World was given a certain number of acres. Thus the indentured servant system was a source of both labor and land.

Not all of the recruits were voluntary, for recruiters sometimes resorted to kidnapping. Also, at times, English prison populations were reduced by shipping the inmates to the colonies for sale as indentured servants. Not all of these were undesirable criminal types; imprisonment for debts and religious or political reasons was not uncommon. The Georgia colony, in fact, was founded as an outlet for people in debtors prison. It is estimated that one half of all European immigrants to the Colonies was indentured.

The fourth source of outside labor supply was Negro slaves from Africa. First brought to Virginia in Dutch ships in 1619, the slaves did not begin displacing indentured servants for most of the plantation labor supply until around 1700. Some slaves were used in all of the colonies, but mostly for city work in the North. On the southern plantations, slaves soon were found to be advantageous because of the longer period of time over which they could be used, even though their initial price was higher. In warmer climates it also was possible to keep slaves working a greater part of the year. The type of crops grown also permitted large numbers of unskilled slaves to be supervised by one overseer.

The amount of free labor for hire always was very scarce. As soon as they had finished their indenture service, most farm workers went to the frontier to start their own farms. Most skilled workers soon owned their own shops. Because of this expectation of starting their own shops, as well as because of the small number of workers and their closeness to their employers, a "working-class" consciousness and the organization of guilds or unions had little opportunity to develop in the colonies. While only scattered examples of wage rates are available, most historians agree that wage rates were higher in the American colonies than in England. This is consistent with our expectation from economic theory. If in one place labor is very scarce in relation to capital and land, then labor will command a higher wage than in areas in which it is less scarce compared with other inputs. (This is merely one illustration of a general rule with respect to rates of pay and relative scarcity of inputs.)

The relative scarcity of capital also was a problem, especially since business and financial institutions were not yet developed to facilitate the investment by many small English investors in distant enterprises. In spite of some use of joint-stock companies in trade and colonizing ventures, most business was conducted by individuals and partnerships. Capital usually had to accompany the labor that migrated to the colonies; without the institution of the indenture contract, much of the migration of labor and capital would not have been possible. Many farmers, craftsmen, boatbuilders, fishermen, and merchants, of course, brought their own capital with them. The opportunities for making a profit obviously were expected to be large, and many expected to return with their fortunes made, although they often ended up staying to build even larger fortunes. Another source of capital was the amount of credit extended by British merchants. As their trade with the colonies expanded, the amount of loans on goods shipped and the amount of advances on crops increased. One of the paradoxes of the rapidly growing colonies was that many of the wealthiest men in the colonies were heavily in debt. This was partly a result of a tendency for some planters to attempt to live luxuriously and maintain an elaborate country house, even though tobacco prices might fall drastically in some years. More important, however, was the strain of attempting to expand rapidly and the extensive speculation in land that most merchants and planters engaged in. Profits were plowed back into expansions of inventories and the purchase of new lands in the expectation of more production and higher land prices as the Colonies became more settled.

By the end of the Colonial period, most of the expansion in capital probably was provided by the colonists themselves. The Colonies provided an opportunity not only for a man to acquire ownership of land but also for a man to build up his own farm or business capital. New England trading merchants accumulated wealth at sea that they later found opportunities for investing at home. On the farm and in farm-related businesses, much of the capital investment involved the use of labor and native resources to clear fields, construct buildings, and make wooden tools, wagons, and furniture.

Population: Evidence of Growth

In a similar manner, the colonial labor supply soon was reproducing itself. In spite of continued rapid immigration, by the 18th century the population growth each decade was more dependent upon domestic birthrates than upon new immigrants. The total population after 1700 increased at a steady percentage rate that doubled the numbers every 20 to 25 years. (See 2–4.)

2–4. Colonial Population Trend

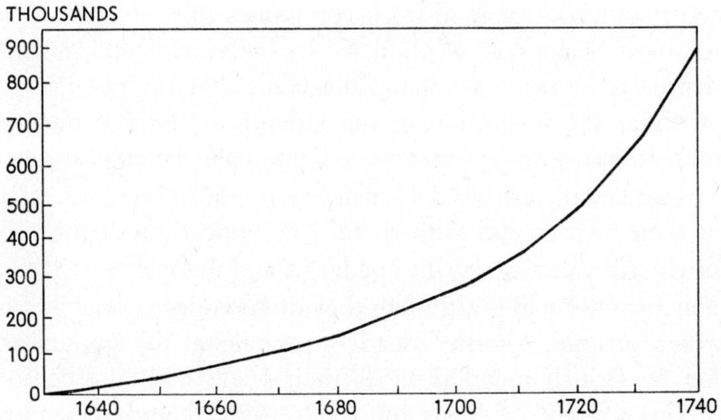

Source: U.S. Department of Commerce, *Historical Statistics of the United States* (Washington, D.C.: U.S. Government Printing Office, 1960), p. 756.

Although data are not now available, birthrates may have been unusually high. Benjamin Franklin thought that Americans married earlier and had more children per family than did the population in England. Death rates, especially among younger people, also may have been low compared to Europe, although high by modern standards. At any rate, one indication of a high rate of reproduction and population increase is a high proportion of the population of pre-working age. Records of the first U.S. census in 1790 show more children under 16 than adults over 16.

As we have indicated for long periods of prior history, this rapid rate of population growth may be taken as evidence of high levels of production per capita. From all indications the American colonist was living well. Food was abundant and varied. The people were relatively healthy for those times. Production in the Colonies was expanding as rapidly as population could grow, and the habits of saving and plowing back investments to expand production were important factors in this rapid growth.

THE THEORY OF MARKETS

In the 17th century, most of Europe was well on the way to establishing an international market economy. This was the century in which America initially was settled. The American colonial economy was based on agricultural, forest, and fishing exports, and its merchants were actively engaged in world commerce. This initial start with a market economy was important to the rapid development and growth of the new nation. It is important at this point, therefore, to understand how a market economy works.

The market system has been difficult for many people to understand. To begin with, it does not seem like a system at all. It operates without conscious direction, and it is difficult to view as a whole. Therefore, it often seems chaotic and irrational. It was not founded or invented by anyone; rather it developed gradually and is constantly changing. Thus it is hard to define and pin down. It appears to depend upon isolated and selfish actions of individuals; so, it appears to be unrelated to standards of social ethics.

It is is important, therefore, to begin by grasping certain fundamentals in a simplified theoretical form. Some of the complexities will be revealed later in the course of presenting the history of national development.

Market exchange must be viewed first as a voluntary means of achieving cooperation and specialization in production. Second, the direction of production is guided by price signals that result from a multitude of individual decisions and actions. And third, social values and controls are imposed impersonally through the competiton of many buyers and sellers.

These functions of cooperation, direction, and control are achieved in other ways by a command economy and by a traditional economy. The advantages of the market system lie in its attempt to provide the maximum possible satisfaction of individual consumer preferences with the greatest possible freedom of individual choice by producers as well as consumers. This is a combination of social goals highly valued in Western European culture, which evidences both Christian concern with individual welfare and humanistic concern with individual freedom for self-development. Of course, the unmodified market system does not guarantee that incomes will be distributed equally among families and individuals or according to any other particular concept of justice. Our assertion that it is conducive to maximizing consumer satisfactions assumes a given distribution of income and ability to earn income. When the market system fails to produce an income distribution pattern that the society feels is acceptable, political mechanisms are put in operation to correct the situation. We shall discuss such mechanisms later in the text. At this point we should consider the operation of markets as organizing forces within the economy.

Cooperation through Exchange

Any form of exchange or trading of goods between individuals is essentially a form of economic cooperation. In the first place, it is voluntary. Both parties enter into an agreed-upon arrangement by their own choice, or they may choose to refrain from doing so. Secondly, the exchange becomes a form of interdependence. The widening of trading relations means a greater dependence on others and less self-reliance. But something is gained. Cooperation means both giving assistance and receiving assistance in a way that means accomplishing more together than can be done alone. The reasons for this explain why attempts to be self-sufficient usually result in low incomes. There are three basic ways in which an individual (or community) gains through exchange. Let us forget money and consider the basic form of exchange, that of barter—the swap of certain goods held by one person for other goods held by another person.

First, other goods may be obtained which one wants but does not have and cannot produce. This represents an absolute gain. For example, if England could not produce tobacco, it could obtain this product by exchanging woolen textiles for tobacco grown in Virginia.

Second, one may have a superior ability to produce certain goods so that more of other goods can be obtained through exchange than by producing them oneself. This is an absolute advantage over others in producing certain goods. For example, assume that northern England alone could produce a long-haired type of sheep that had superior wool for worsteds and that the same region could produce all other goods as efficiently as elsewhere. North Countrymen would be able to obtain the greatest amount of other goods by specializing in sheep production and trading wool for other goods because their wool output could command a premium "price" in exchange for other goods.

Third, one may produce nothing in a way that is superior to others, but one may produce some goods almost as well as others can, and some goods very poorly compared with others. In this situation one gains from concentrating on producing goods for which one has the least disadvantage and buying from others goods for which one has the greatest disadvantage. For example, the New England colonies may have been able to produce neither meat products nor wool for delivery in England as well as England could produce them for itself; but because the disadvantage was less in meat products than in wool products, it paid New England to concentrate on exporting meat products and not wool. The same principle applied in reverse for England which had a superiority in both products. It was better off in concentrating its fields in products for which it had the greatest advantage. This principle (of concentrating on goods with the greatest advantage or least disadvantage) is called the "law of comparative advantage," and its logic underlies the patterns of national specialization and division of labor in foreign trade.

A voluntary exchange, therefore, is mutually beneficial. Both parties to an exchange gain by improving on their initial position. Why, then, is market exchange frequently viewed with suspicion, as though one side were likely to exploit the other? One reason may be that the two parties do not start out with equal advantages, and people may resent this. England, for example, may have been more productive in both wool and meat products. The land may have been more fertile and the incomes of its people higher. Exchange is not an equalizing procedure. Only charity, progressive taxation, or expropriation may do that. Exchange only improves each party's absolute position.

Another reason may be that one party may be misinformed, accidentally or deliberately, about his alternatives. The advantage of a particular exchange must be compared to a person's real alternatives. If there is a better exchange offer from a third party, the advantage from a proposed trade will be a second-best choice. Or, if one is misinformed about the qualities of the goods obtained—for example, when a horse is claimed to be younger than it really is—the trade may not be a real gain. So, uncertainty about alternatives or fear of misinformation may cause a person to be suspicious when he is offered a "trade." Exploitation can be involved only when one party attempts unfairly to restrict the alternatives or information of another.

The alternatives to an exchange are determined independently of the exchange and tend to narrow the range of discretion (or indeterminacy) of the "bargain." Left to themselves, the two parties may find that there is some range of variation in the exchange ratio of their two goods at which both still may gain. Neither is willing to exchange for less than a minimum amount of the other good (the amount at which the exchange represents no gain for him). Between the two limits, there is some common gain to be divided. The question is how the common gain is to be divided. Left to themselves the two parties can only haggle or bargain. The alternatives of trading with a third or fourth party, however, raise each party's minimum terms. Multiple buyers and sellers, therefore, provide a socially determined standard by which each party judges what is a "fair" bargain.

Now, let us reintroduce money, which is called a "medium of exchange." To find various individuals with whom we could make exactly the best exchange of our goods for the variety of desired goods would be extremely difficult. If we can trade for money and then trade money for goods, the efficiency and convenience of exchange is greatly facilitated. The principles of exchange advantage remain the same. Money merely is an intermediate good and a temporary storage of trading value. It provides a convenient common measure of the general trading value of each good, for that value is expressed as a "price," a ratio of exchange of money for a unit of that good.

Greater Production by Specialization

Before discussing prices, one further advantage of exchange needs to be noted. It permits specialization in production which in turn permits greater production to be achieved with the same resources—that is, greater productivity. By concentrating on producing one product, a person (or firm) can increase his productivity in three ways in addition to the aforementioned gains from using superior abilities or a comparative advantage. First, one may ***learn*** better methods or improve skill through repetition and concentrated attention. Second, one may ***waste less time shifting*** from one type of work to another—from getting ready to use tools, handling materials, and putting away tools. And third, one may gain ***economies of large scale*** from use of advantageous tools or equipment that have a large minimum output size and cost—such as a blast furnace.

These advantages sometimes have been referred to as the gains from "division of labor." The advantages apply to the specialization of business firms in one type of product and also to the specialization of each worker within a firm in one phase of making a product. To avoid confusion, the term "specialization" will be used to apply to the products made by a firm, and the term "division of labor" will be used to apply to the worker tasks performed within a firm in making a product.

The significance of all this is that per capita production and consumption standards can be raised by enlarging the extent of social cooperation. This can be done in a command or traditional society if a larger and larger number of people and resources can be closely coordinated. In a market economy, it occurs through enlarging the market and extending trade. The rise of trade in Europe, therefore, provided a means of raising productivity and living standards in the 16th and 17th centuries.

Production Directed by Price Signals

The next thing to realize about market exchange is that the social cooperation is not erratic and chaotic; it is coordinated by prices which act as signals guiding the decisions of individuals. The price of a good, of course, results from the choices of individuals. If it becomes more scarce, less of it may be exchanged for other goods—its price goes up. If people's desire for it lessens (say, due to a new substitute good), less of other goods may be offered in exchange for it—its price falls. The price of a good, once determined in the market, then becomes a signal to individuals adjusting their further actions.

Price signals in a market economy help perform certain general ***economic functions*** that must be accomplished in any type of economy. Any economy must "decide" in some way (*a*) its priorities as to the types and quantities of goods to be produced, (*b*) the most efficient methods of using resources in this production, (*c*) the incentives and rewards to be used in achieving this efficient use of resources, and (*d*) the rationing of consumption in relation to the available production. Let us examine each of these in detail.

Prices Show What Consumers Want Produced. A market economy relies upon voluntary choices by individuals and is guided by the combined value priorities of all individual consumers. It is assumed that the consumer himself knows best what he wants. He shows his preferences by his actions when he allocates his limited expenditures so as to purchase goods that will have the greatest combined value to him. The choices of many individual consumers interact with the relative scarcity of goods to determine prices, and prices in turn direct production. Therefore, we say that a market economy is guided by the principle of "consumer sovereignty," for the consumer is like a king with the sole right to choose for himself what he wants. Consumer choices set the social value priorities that ultimately regulate production. Note, though, that it is only assumed, not guaranteed, that the consumer knows best what he wants—consumer ignorance or misleading claims of sellers reduce the consumer's sovereignty.

Prices Show Which Methods Are Efficient. "Efficiency" is a measure (or ratio) of the value of results compared to the value of means used. In a market economy the value of results is determined by the price of a product times the quantity produced, and the value of means used is determined by the prices of resources times the quantities used. The accounts of a business firm tend to reflect these as revenues and costs. The greater the difference, revenues minus costs, the greater the profit and also the greater the measure of efficiency of the firm.

Prices and profits indicate the directions of adjustments in resource allocations that would be most socially beneficial. The most profitable industries are those in which more output and investment are socially needed. The most profitable firms are those which should be given more resources to manage. A rise in the price of one resource indicates the need for finding methods of economizing on that resource and using more of other resources with it in achieving the same production. Higher prices for the same resource in certain industries or areas indicates where resource owners should direct the use of more of this resource. Ultimately, the costs of production for one good reflect how much the resources used are valued by consumers in alternative uses, in making other goods. (This is known as the "opportunity cost" principle.)

Prices Provide Incentives for Efficiency. The prices of resources and the profits of business determine the income rewards to individuals for participating in production. In general, the value contributed to production is the principle upon which incomes are distributed in a market economy. If people produced only for their own consumption, it would be obvious that they could consume only what they had produced. In all forms of social cooperation, however, measures of individual contributions are needed, as are incentives to induce the individual to make his maximum contribution. In a market economy, prices provide an objective, socially determined measure of the value of an individual's contribution. Simultaneously, the price times the quantity of an individual's resources determines his income reward and thus his incentive.

Changes in conditions constantly are occurring in the world, but few people like to adjust. Changes in prices, therefore, provide changes in the incentives and thus encourage individuals to adjust their decisions on resource uses. Firms are encouraged to invest and expand where profits are greatest, and workers are encouraged to move to the industry or area where wages are greatest.

Uncertainty about the future constantly affects people's choices and the rewards actually realized. When social demand for a product suddenly rises, the firms already producing it receive a windfall increase in profit from the rise in price on their existing goods. Yet the increased profit provides an incentive for expansion in production. Likewise, when expanding production increases the demand for workers, a rising wage rate provides the workers already there a windfall increase in wage income. If people only knew in advance where the increases would occur, they could adjust in time to receive these gains. Unanticipated changes, however, also may involve losses. Since most costs of production are contracted for in advance, it usually is the residual profit receiver who takes the greatest risks of unexpected loss. The possibility of receiving the greatest unexpected gains provides his incentive for this extra risk-taking. The man who undertakes the residual profit-receiving risks of a business, frequently is called the "entrepreneur," a French word for enterpriser or one who undertakes to do something.

Prices Ration Consumption. Prices also provide important incentives to the consumer to restrict and redirect his consumption choices. At any moment there rarely is enough production of goods to satisfy all wants; so consumption constantly needs to be restricted to the available supply of goods. Prices automatically restrict how much of all goods a person can consume with his limited income rewards (although he may temporarily use his accumulated wealth to buy more). At the same time, changing prices of particular goods encourage him to be more sparing and nonwasteful in consuming goods that have become more scarce. By requiring a greater sacrifice in order to consume a very scarce good, the limited supply is conserved for the free choice of everyone and especially of those to whom it is most valuable.

Prices also provide incentives for general restriction of consumption to less than current production (saving) in order to put goods to use in expanding future production (investing). Interest, the price of borrowed money, is a reward for saving and also a part of the cost of using capital resources in a particular form of production. (The other part of the "cost" is the average profit expected which barely provides an incentive that offsets the risks of loss.)

Social Control via Competition

Another important aspect of market exchange is the way competition among a number of sellers or buyers provides the alternatives individuals can choose among. We have seen that while each person benefits from voluntary exchange, his alternatives determine the relative advantage he gains. Likewise, consumer choice has meaning only where there is a choice, at least potentially. And workers seeking to get the most income from their labors fare better when several employers offer alternative work opportunities. The rivalry among firms to expand their own sales and to minimize their costs in order to make a profit is what provides alternatives to consumers and resource owners alike. Each firm, therefore, is limited in its prices and is spurred in seeking better methods by the actions of rival firms.

Unfortunately, competiton is not viewed in the same light by firms as by the consumer or resource owner. The firms simply would like to make a profit and not necessarily by improving methods or expanding. If a single firm can control the sole source of supply, or if a small group of firms can agree to act jointly, to "monopolize" (act like one seller), larger profits can be obtained by restricting production and selling fewer goods at higher prices. As we noted earlier, frequently in the European trade centers public regulations had to be enforced to prevent a large merchant from buying up (engrossing) or stopping (forestalling) the supply of a good to a town market. On the other hand, as we have discussed, guilds frequently used public regulations to prevent entry of new sellers and restrict production in order to hold up prices. Large merchants frequently sought to monopolize a trade, and kings frequently granted and enforced such monopolies. Nevertheless, with many towns and nations in rivalry, with a rapidly expanding trade, and with methods rapidly changing, it was difficult for a few suppliers to exercise complete monopoly power for very long. The point to be noted is that while ideal competitive conditions seldom existed, active rivalry among firms was an important element in the successful development of the European market economy.

Ultimately, the social value of a market economy depends upon maintaining some competition among firms. It is competition that forces profit-seeking to expand production of consumer-desired goods and introduce cost-reducing methods of production. Thus, competition is the social discipline or control that is exercised over profit-seeking firms. The slogan "free enterprise," which is so highly valued in America, refers not to a new "divine right" of businessmen to do as they please; rather, it refers to the freedom of rival firms to enter or expand in any field of production free from monopolistic restraints from government or private sources.

APPENDIX TO CHAPTER 2 ON RATIO CHARTS AND INDEX NUMBERS

The study of economic growth requires frequent reference to rates of increase in various types of data. Ratio charts and index numbers provide two of the helpful ways that number series can be presented so that ***percentage*** rates of change can be observed and compared most easily. A little time invested by the student in studying this appendix will prove very valuable in understanding the various comparisons and analyses of economic data series that we will present throughout the succeeding chapters.

2–5 uses a ***ratio scale*** (as the vertical measure) to present the same data on colonial population increase as are presented on an arithmetic scale in 2–4. The usefulness of plotting data on a ratio scale graph is that the slope of the trend line indicated by the numbers

2–5. Colonial Population

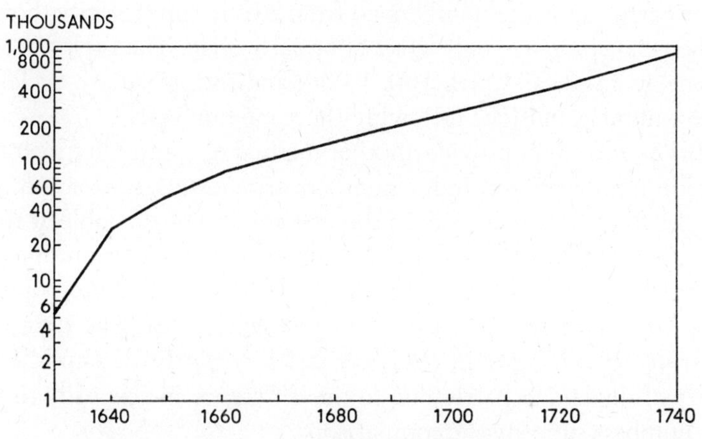

Source: U.S. Department of Commerce, *Historical Statistics of the United States* (Washington, D.C.: U.S. Government Printing Office, 1960), p. 756.

automatically represents the percentage rate of change. The ***steeper*** the trend line, the ***faster*** the rate of change (or the higher the percentage increase). By comparing the slopes of the trend line at two different periods of time, we can compare rates of change in the different periods. Or, by comparing slopes of two different trend lines in the same period, we can determine which trend is faster.

In 2–4, population appears to start out with slow increases and then begins to increase more rapidly. Actually this is a half-truth. In absolute terms, the increases are small in size at first and later get larger. The slope of the line on the ratio scale in 2–5, however, reveals that population grew at a very rapid percentage rate between 1630 and 1640, at a slower rate between 1640 and 1660, and at a still slower (but steady) rate after 1660. About the same rate of increase (a doubling every 20–25 years) continued with very little change for the next two centuries—until after 1860.

The ratio scale is a logarithmic scale. The series of numbers in 2–4 could have been converted into logarithms by looking up the numbers in a logarithm table in a mathematics book. Logarithms then could have been plotted on the arithmetic (ordinary) scale in 2–4, and the result would have been a curve, identical with the one in 2–5. The same result is achieved more easily, however, by plotting the original series of numbers on a sheet of graph paper (called semilog paper), which has the space intervals varied in accordance with logarithms. A ratio scale (or semilog graph) is quickly identified by the rapidly narrowing spaces between successive intervals of numbers. The spaces start wide and get narrower as the numbers go from two to nine. Notice, however, that the ratio chart is evenly spaced for each cycle. The cycles all begin with one, as follows: 1, 10, 100, 1,000, and so forth. Each cycle has a different number of digits following the same numeral.

Index numbers provide another method of comparing the rates of change in number series. Index numbers are most useful for comparing two series for the same period. In the first column of the table at the end of this appendix are presented the colonial total population figures for alternate decades. In the second column are presented Negro population figures (mostly imported slaves) on the same dates. The difficulty in comparing the changes in the two series is partly due to the large number of digits and partly due to the difference in size of both series. Index numbers simplify the comparisons.

To convert the first column into index numbers (shown in column 3), a base year is selected, in this case 1700, and the index number 100 is assigned to this year. For each other year (say, 1680), the number for that year (151,507) is divided by the number for the base year (250,888) and multiplied by 100 (to move the decimal two places to the right). The result is the index number (60). This computation is repeated for every other number in the series. The same base year is used for the series on Negro population; and each number in that series is divided by the number 27,817 in the base year. This provides a second index number series shown in the fourth column.

With both series of numbers expressed as index numbers with a common base year, it is possible to compare quickly which series grows faster between any other year and the base year. For the year 1720, the index number (159) minus the base year index (100) shows a 59 percent increase in total population since 1700; and there was a 147 percent increase in Negro population. From 1700 to 1740 the index numbers show increases of 261 percent and 439 percent. For the two decades prior to the base year, it is quickly seen that total population increased over 3 times, while Negro population increased almost 10 times. From 1680 to 1700 the total increased by two-thirds, while Negroes quadrupled. The percentage change is not as easy to compare between other years not including the base year, such as from 1720 to 1740, but still easier than working with the raw data.

	Number of Persons		*Indexes*	
Year	*Total*	*Negro*	*Total*	*Negro*
1660	75,058	2,920	30	11
1680	151,507	6,971	60	25
1700	250,888	27,817	100	100
1720	466,185	68,839	159	247
1740	905,563	150,024	361	539

One final word of warning: the size of index numbers in two different series does ***not*** reflect their ***comparative size in the original numbers.*** In 1740, for example, the Negro index is larger than the total index, although Negro population was smaller than total population. Each index number, it must be remembered, merely shows a comparison with the base year number in the same series of numbers.

STUDY QUESTIONS

1. Why begin the study of America's economic development with conditions in Europe as far back as Columbus? Later, when our Nation was formed, what advantages did we have that some poor new nations lack today?
2. In medieval Europe, why was the political organization weak and decentralized? How did custom and religion handicap progress? What was the basic production unit? Why was productivity low? Why were towns semi-independent?
3. Why did the rise in trade gradually break up the traditional order? Why did gold imports raise prices? How did the rise in trade and prices reorganize production?
4. Specifically in England, how did trade lead to agricultural specialization and to the start of manufacturing? What resources encouraged further trade, and how did this stimulate further manufacturing?
5. How was the colonization of North America affected by England's trade

expansion? In what different ways did the southern, middle, and northern colonies specialize in exports to England and Europe?

6. How did the expanding colonies obtain labor supply? How did labor scarcity affect wages? How was capital needed to expand production? How was capital obtained?
7. Why do people exchange goods (trade) at all? Why don't they gain equally? Why does specialization (in producing for exchange) raise productivity?
8. In a market economy how do price signals guide people's free choices so that the basic social decisions necessary in any economy are made?
9. In a market economy how do the free choices of individuals provide discipline and social control over individuals?

Chapter 3
POLITICAL FOUNDATIONS

The American Colonies inherited more than the market economy from England. They also inherited political conditions, institutions and policies that favored economic growth within a market economy. Their colonial experience reinforced this inheritance, and the American Revolution was more like a family quarrel than a break with family tradition. The new nation was launched with an aversion to central government powers that primarily grew out of general experience rather than a more narrowly defined set of views about economic policy.

Certain basic political conditions necessary to growth under any kind of economic system were present in both England and America. First, there were long periods of ***peace*** and internal order. Security from violence is a prerequisite to cooperation in production and to accumulation of capital resources. Local banditry and civil disorders disrupt organized production, and major wars exhaust or destroy resources. Specialization and large production units require close contacts with large markets. While ocean trade with other nations is very helpful in starting growth, wars and trade restrictions tend to hamper development of a high degree of economic organization. Second, nations with large populations and diversified resources in one political unit have an advantage in sustaining their own growth. Third, a stable system of law and courts was developed early in England and was passed on to America. Cooperation in production is based upon common understandings as to rights and obligations, and these must be enforceable or subject to adjudication if resort to violence is to be avoided.

Political institutions and traditions especially favorable to a market economy also were developed in England and passed on to America. Freedom of the individual was protected by ***civil liberties*** upheld in independent courts. A constitutional tradition restrained government officials to limited powers to rule under the law. And most of the laws were made by ***elected legislatures.*** Under such a political system a wide scope may be given to individual freedom of choice and initiative, and the necessary functions of government may be directed to serve a wide diversity of individual interests with the broadest basis of voluntary consent. None of this is to say that there was no unrest in Colonial America; the Colonies were treated as such with the nature of political, economic, and legal relationships between England and America being determined primarily by the British.

Finally, the economic policies of government in England and America probably were helpful to growth under a market system. For one thing, ***economic objectives,*** rather than missionary religious zeal or military ambitions for conquest, were dominant in government. For another, only a ***minimum of governmental control*** was exercised over private economic activity. In large part this was due to the weaknesses of the administrative powers of government and to the popular opposition to central authority. Initially, England sought by direct action and control of private activities to encourage national economic development, although government controls never were as extensive in England as in other parts of Europe, and they later became progressively less restrictive. The United States started with a popular support for general restriction of the powers of government, mostly for political reasons. So it was largely by default rather than by design that economic decisions were left largely to private markets.

INHERITANCE FROM ENGLAND

During the American Colonial period, Europe was embroiled in almost constant wars over religion, national boundaries, and colonial empire. Absolute monarchy was the typical form of national government, and mercantilism the predominant economic policy of governments. These were political aspects of the transition from a traditional to a market economy. England tended to be farther along in its transition stages, and it was from England that America received its political foundations. A chronological view of America's Old World ties is shown in 3–1.

Nationalism

Several large nation-states emerged from the Middle Ages as the new form of political organization in Europe. A loose collection of small principalities in Italy, Austria, and Germany long remained in the central European "empire"; but strong national kingdoms arose all

3–1. A Chronology of America's European Background

European Events	Centuries	American Events
Renaissance	15th	1492 Columbus discovers America
1517 Reformation starts 1524 Church of England Religious wars in Europe Gold imports; inflation England expands trade; sheep raising, enclosures; textiles 1588 Spanish Armada defeated	16th	
England develops industries 1642 Civil War in England Cromwell; Navigation Acts 1660 Stuart kings restored; Whig and Tory parties 1688 Glorious Revolution, Bill of Rights, Cabinet 1689 King William's War	17th	1607 Virginia Colony founded 1620 Plymouth Colony founded
1702 Queen Anne's War Agricultural improvements, population rise 1745 King George's War 1754 Seven Years' War Industrial Revolution 1776 Smith, *Wealth of Nations* 1789 French Revolution 1793 Napoleonic Wars start	18th	1732 Georgia Colony founded (last) 1754 French and Indian War 1775 War of Independence 1776 Declaration of Independence 1789 Constitution ratified
1815 Napoleonic Wars end	19th	1812 War with England

around it in Spain, France, Sweden, and Russia. The kings were able to suppress the local powers of provincial barons with the aid of large armies of mercenary soldiers and with the aid of a large bureaucracy of tax collectors and central government officials. As communications improved, people began to become conscious of their identification with a nation due to common ties of language and culture, a dominant religion, and the experience of bitter national wars.

The new nations, however, were regarded by the kings as their personal domains. Strong kingdoms were established by force of arms, either in repressing local barons or repelling foreign invaders. After gaining power over an opposing group, the kings insisted on absolute and unquestioned authority to rule as they pleased. Whether they were ordained by the church or not, they justified their rule as a "divine right" inherited by birth. Councils of nobles and merchants were consulted or solicited for support in times of need, but they were ignored or disbanded most of the time. Trade and industry were regarded merely as sources of tax revenues and supplies for their armies. Colonies were sought as sources of riches and power for the kings.

The new nations were almost constantly engaged in major or minor wars. Religious controversy was a major source of the conflict. The Protestant Reformation had swept through most of northern Europe. At first the Emperor and the church had tried to suppress it in Central Europe, but after a series of wars the German princes gained the right to determine the religion in their own provinces. France fought internal wars at the end of the 16th century and late in the 17th century before finally suppressing a strong Protestant minority, the Huguenots. The Lowlands became divided as the Protestant Dutch fought for their freedom from Catholic Spain. The religious controversies then were mingled with wars over royal succession, struggles for enlargement of national boundaries, and naval battles for possession of colonies or trading posts. There were many intrigues and alliances to stop strong nations from expanding, to restore a religion's dominance or freedom in a territory, or to establish a royal family's power and marital ties with other lands.

England, as an island nation, was favored by its geographic isolation from Europe. With most of its population concentrated in the broad flatlands of the southeast, it achieved national unity more easily. Wales, Ireland and Scotland were less populated and more rural, and they came fairly readily, if not enthusiastically, under the control of the English kings. Starting with a less rigid feudal structure and weaker provincial barons, the Tudor kings were able to establish strong control at the beginning of the 16th century. Building up a strong navy under Queen Elizabeth, England staved off the only major invasion threat by defeating the Spanish Armada; then, England's naval supremacy was established in the 17th century by a series of naval battles with the Dutch and the French. Yet very limited commitments of soldiers and resources were made to land warfare on the European continent.

England also was favored with comparatively little religious strife. The Church of England was established at first to serve political purposes and the beliefs were little changed. Then, Protestantism grew stronger in England and there were continual demands for reform. At first, the beliefs and practices of the Church of England were fairly ambiguous and allowed considerable diversity of local practice. Edward VI and Queen Elizabeth were tolerant of a wide diversity of opinion as long as their own control of the hierarchy of the church was not challenged. An attempt by the Tudor queen Mary to restore Catholicism, however, aroused internal controversies. Under later Stuart kings, fears of Catholic suppression of other minorities were mingled with fears of outside intervention by Catholic kings from Spain and France. For a short interval under Cromwell, a small Puritan minority suppressed the freedom of other groups. Following the Stuarts considerable personal freedom was allowed, although public office was denied to both Catholics and Protestant Nonconformist sects. In the 18th century, however, the religious struggles had subsided, and there was increasing tolerance of a diversity of individual beliefs.

As noted earlier, the period from 1540 to 1640 in England was marked by rapid industrial growth. This was a period of internal peace and rapid rise in naval supremacy. It was a period when England began to establish its colonies and build up world trade. A few of the colonists settling in America were refugees seeking greater religious freedom. Yet because most of the colonists were from England, they still thought of themselves as being members of the English nation.

Democracy

England was developing a limited monarchy form of democratic government at the same time that it became a strong nation. To some extent this trend was rooted in traditions from earlier centuries of individual legal rights and parliamentary representation in tax matters. As the role of central governments expanded during the Middle Ages in response to kings' desires for greater military, political and economic power, the old revenue sources, primarily from the royal estates, became inadequate and taxation became necessary. As such questions as the kinds of taxes to raise and the distribution of the tax burden had to be solved, the conflict for control between the monarchy and parliament became an important factor in the development of political democracy in England.

As early as 1215, a revolt had forced King John to sign the Magna Charta which recognized ancient rights and liberties, including the individual right to trial by jury and the need for consent by a council of noblemen to any new taxes. The term "parliament" (from the French verb *parler,* "to talk") was applied to earlier councils that advised the king and presented petitions; but the Model parliament in 1295 first set the example of being selected to represent all classes of freeholders and all parts of the country. In the next century it was divided into two houses, with the higher nobles and clergy sitting in the House of Lords, and the smaller landowners and merchants sitting in the House of Commons. The kings, however, retained traditional powers and sources of revenues and could disband parliament and fail to call it into session for long periods. So the actual influence of parliament varied with the strength of the king and his need for new revenues in time of war.

The powers of the English kings were limited more effectively and permanently after two successive revolutions in the mid-17th century, during the period when the American colonies were being established. The revolts broke out because of a combination of religious and economic issues involving individual freedom and representative legislation. The people were alarmed by royal alliances with the Catholic kings of Spain and France and by stricter enforcement of older beliefs and ceremonies in the Church of England.

Parliament also resisted the attempts by kings to raise revenues arbitrarily through imposing their own taxes and making royal grants of monopoly privileges to a favored few. By this time, a large middle class of professional men and merchants had become influential and many of them had become owners of small land estates as well. While the upper nobility were few and weak, the knights and the squires (or landowning gentlemen) were numerous and dominated parliament. So, in 1642 the Civil War was fought to depose King Charles I. The various revolting groups could not agree, however, on religious issues. For over a decade Cromwell ruled as a military dictator, and a small minority sect of Puritans was dominant. After Cromwell died, parliament, in 1660, invited Charles II to restore royal rule. Again, however, Charles II and his son James II aroused religious fears through appointing Catholic officials and making secret agreements with Catholic France. They also attempted to assert royal powers over those of parliament. So, in the Glorious Revolution of 1688, parliament invited William of Orange and his English Wife, Mary, to come over from Holland to take the throne.

With these events, England was the first major nation to undergo revolution limiting the power of rulers and establishing the beginnings of democratic government. These events occurred more than a hundred years before the American and French revolutions. The English revolution was milder and less set back by dictatorship than the later one in France, where the monarchy had become more absolute; but the immediate changes in form of government did not go as far or as rapidly toward democracy as those in the American Revolution.

What England passed on to America was a set of developing political ideas as well as the example of revolution. The parliament dissolved by King Charles I in 1628 had drawn up a Petition of Right which denied the king's power to resort to martial law in peacetime, to billeting of soldiers in private homes, to arbitrary imprisonment without trial, and to taxation without act of parliament. When resummoned in 1640, parliament demanded that its meetings be held regularly, that it not be dissolved at the king's will, and that it have power to impeach the king's officials. After Cromwell, when the king was restored, Charles II had to agree to most of these conditions, although he did not entirely live up to them. When William was given the throne he had to sign the Bill of Rights (1689) which affirmed the citizen's rights of petition, habeas corpus, bearing of arms, and freedom of speech.

Two political parties, the Whig and Tory parties, had arisen under Charles II; and parliament gained the power under later kings to approve the king's cabinet of chief administrative officers headed by a prime minister. In 1690, John Locke wrote his *Treatises on Government* which spread the ideas of limited powers of government. He attacked the idea of divine right of kings and argued that men were born free and equal. Government was viewed as determined not by a natural order of classes but a social order of agreed-upon laws binding both rulers and subjects. The individuals were held to have a right to liberty and property; and revolt was justified if these rights were violated.

In those times only men owning property were regarded as capable of participating in the responsibilities of self-government. So parliament represented a small proportion of the total population. Once ideas are let loose in the world, however, they tend to spread and influence action. Eventually, after the Industrial Revolution expanded the middle class and raised the earnings of workers, parliament passed successive reform bills over several generations extending the right to vote to lower income groups and equalizing the proportional representation of rural and urban districts.

Mercantilism

The economic policies of most European nations during the American Colonial period were very similar in goals, ideas, and methods. The particular practices were developed gradually and applied in varying degrees at different times and places. Some written arguments were made supporting particular laws or advocating particular measures, but generally there was no one written body of ideas. Historians have coined the term "mercantilism" to describe these characteristic economic policies of European national governments during the three centuries from 1500 to 1800.

If the varied lot of policies that constituted mercantilism can be meaningfully fenced in by one definition the following serves as at least a descriptive definition of mercantilism: mercantilism was an economic policy, calling for a great deal of government intervention in economic affairs, which was directed toward increasing a nation's wealth, power, and self-sufficiency in a period of intense international rivalry, and whose principal tactic was to encourage exports in return for gold.

The main goal of mercantilism was national power. Primarily this meant the power to make war. For the kings and ruling classes who regarded the nation as their own domain, power also meant wealth for themselves. Little consideration was given to the economic welfare of the bulk of the people as individuals. The national government was not oriented toward consumer choice and individual values. In the thinking of those times, there was little realization of the possibilities of improving methods of production to raise the productivity and living standards of workers. Economic progress was still a strange idea. In a world of fixed opportunities, the way to "get ahead" was through seizing an increased share of available resources and wealth. Thus, the objective of national governments was economic expansion rather than economic growth.

The three main ideas of mercantilism may be summed up under the terms ***bullionism, self-sufficiency,*** and ***colonialism.*** The first idea, bullionism, was that national power and wealth depended upon the stores of money metals in the government treasury, or in the hands of wealthy ruling classes. A well-stocked treasury could be used to buy supplies and hire troops in time of war. Essential to the idea of bullionism was the additional idea that money metals, or national wealth, could be accumulated by a "favorable balance of trade." This refers to an excess of the value of exported goods over the value of imported goods. The difference in payments was expected to result in an inflow of money metals. By selling more to other nations than it purchases from them, a nation receives a greater share of the world's money. Another subsidiary idea to bullionism was that if a nation carried imported and exported goods in its own citizens' ships, it would pay other nations less money for freight carrying charges. Thus, shipping was regarded as serving like an export industry in bringing in more money. Under the idea of bullionism, therefore, the policies of mercantilism aimed to encourage expansion of export industries and shipping industries and discourage imports and the use of ships of other nations.

The second idea, self-sufficiency, was that a nation should produce as much as possible of its own needs for goods, especially essential goods, the supply of which might be cut off in time of war. Greater self-sufficiency was believed to reduce imports and thereby increase the favorable balance of trade. This belief was contradicted by the principle of comparative advantage in trade which suggests that more might be gained by concentrating on increased exports of those goods that a nation's resources are better adapted to producing. Yet the more prevalent opposite notion, that trade consists of gaining at the disadvantage of someone else, led to a desire to depend less on others for imports. The danger of being cut off from supplies during time of war or by retaliatory trade restrictions, of course, does provide a justification for seeking some self-sufficiency. Under mercantilism, the emphasis simply was placed upon self-sufficiency as being nationally beneficial without considering the costs of foregoing cheaper imports or the degree of damage from being cut off. Under the idea of self-sufficiency, the policies of mercantilism aimed to protect inefficient national industries from lower cost imported goods by such measures as taxes on imports (tariffs), subsidies to national industries, or complete banning of the import of foreign goods. Consumers, of course, paid higher prices for the nationally produced goods.

The third idea, colonialism, was that colonial production and trade should be organized to serve the needs of the home country. Colonies were sought as sources of raw material supplies that were not available or were scarce within the national boundaries. Colonial trading posts also were a means of increasing the favorable balance of trade. Spain showed how colonies could be a direct source of imports of money metals from South American mines; but the production of sugar in the West Indies islands was an equally desirable source of wealth, for the sugar could be sold to other nations to enhance the balance of trade. The Portuguese and Dutch showed that Far Eastern trading posts could be very valuable souces of unique goods which could be traded for much money in Europe. To protect colonies, of course, it was important to have a strong navy, and national ships were needed to carry the raw materials. It also was expected that colonies would serve national policy by trading only with the mother country and buying the products or goods manufactured by the mother country. It was not regarded as in the interest of the home country or its protected industries for the colony to develop its own manufacturing or its own self-sufficiency. The colony was regarded solely as an instrument of national power and welfare and was not expected to have objectives of its own.

It should be noted that mercantilism tended to place its emphasis upon certain favored industries as strategic to national development. One was shipping and the other manufacturing. To some extent domestic agriculture was protected by tariffs to maintain a minimum self-sufficiency in food supplies. Manufacturing, however, was given the most emphasis. Manufacture of arms, munitions and ships, of course, was directly important to a nation's war-making power. Manufactured goods also were viewed as the main means to increase exports and obtain a favorable balance of trade. In an agricultural age, when most areas provided nearly all of their own food, trade in manufactured goods especially reflected the greater specialization in production and higher living standards of the expanding market economy. With a general improvement in agricultural production in the 17th century, there also was considerable surplus of labor in Europe. Thus, labor services seemed low in cost; and the way to national wealth seemed to lie in using idle workers to manufacture more goods. Trading a surplus of labor services (embodied in manufacturing goods or used in shipping) for rare raw materials and additional stores of money metals seemed to be the way to build up the power and apparent wealth of the nation.

The main methods of mercantilism relied upon direct government action or the command principle, although considerable use also was made of indirect action through providing positive and negative incentives to influence private decisions. The assumptions behind this approach seemed to be that whatever was commanded to happen would happen and that little else might be accomplished in the absence of government decisions and actions. These assumptions, of course, reflected a lack of understanding of how market exchange directs private production decisions through price signals as well as a lack of understanding of the complex requirements of overall economic development.

The two most direct methods of mercantilism involved (1) the establishment of government agencies to carry out certain activities and (2) the passage of regulatory laws telling individuals what they must do or what they must not do. The former involved the hiring of workers by the government and directing their activities in state production enterprises. When cannons or naval ships were needed, it seemed to be an obvious method for the government to hire its own workers to build them in government arsenals or government shipyards. Governments sometimes supplied ships, supplies, or soldiers for missions of exploration. The passage of regulatory laws also seemed to be an obvious method. The import of some foreign goods or the outmigration of critically skilled artisans simply would be forbidden. Merchants could be required to use ships of national citizens. These regulatory laws can be regarded as extreme forms of negative incentives, because the threat of punishment can be persuasive.

The indirect methods of mercantilism, however, were to provide specific rewards or monetary penalties as additional incentives to guide actvities of private individuals. If more production of some product were desired, a bounty could be paid per unit of production, or a bonus could be paid for quantities over some minimum. Prizes and special honors could be awarded for unusual quality or initiative in making discoveries. The monopoly privilege was a special kind of reward incentive. Essentially, it forbade others to participate in certain types of production or trade in order to reward a chosen group with the exclusive privilege of profits from that field. If the risks of loss were a great barrier to those undertaking a new task, the monopoly privilege might offer them greater chance of large profits as a reward if they succeeded. One advantage to the government of the monopoly grant was that it required no direct commitment of finances or risk of loss by the government itself. Also, the government did not have to provide the management or personnel to carry out the venture. It merely offered an exclusive privilege to induce someone else to organize a new production activity. Finally, negative penalties could be used as a method to guide individual actions. Tariffs often were collected on imported goods mainly to discourage their import or discourage their purchase by consumers. But, tariffs aside, mercantilism usually made little use of negative incentives other than to apply legal prohibitions enforced by punishments.

England had begun to develop mercantile policies early in the 17th century as the American colonies were being settled. The policies were not as extreme as those of Spain and France, especially in their administration and application, and the personal goals of the king were less important. Yet similar policies were adopted as serving to strengthen national power and to build up home industries. Not until the middle of the 18th century were these policies widely criticized as not best serving national interests.

COLONIAL EXPERIENCE

Special conditions in the American colonies brought the traditions of monarchy and mercantilism into sharp conflict with the new ideals of freedom and democracy. The Americans had had a long period of colonial experience with individual liberty, self-government, and freedom of trade. They long had been left alone without enforcement of regulations by the mother country. So when the attempt was made in the middle of the 18th century to apply stricter enforcement of mercantilist regulations, the American Revolution was precipitated. At this point it may be useful for the reader to review the chronology presented in 3–1.

Independent Pioneers

The independent character of the people who came to settle the colonies was such as to suggest that they would resist restrictions on their freedom. About 60 percent of the white American colonists in 1776 were English and another 18 percent were Scotch and Irish. Only 15 percent all together were German, Dutch, Swedish, and French; and the origin of the remaining 7 percent is not known. As we have noted, many came to New England and the middle colonies seeking freedom from religious oppression. They had fled from restrictions on freedom to think and live as they pleased. About half of the immigrants had been penniless and had come as indentured servants seeking to work their way to a better opportunity for themselves and their children. Even in the southern colonies, the small farmers greatly outnumbered the large plantation owners. They became owners of farmland, labored hard and sacrificed to build up their own capital, and raised large families. For them America had provided an opportunity to break away from a rigid class society and to improve their income status by their own efforts.

The frontier conditions in the colonies developed a hardiness and self-reliance in all who settled on the fringes of existing settlements. While resources were favorable, there were initial hardships to endure. Much labor was required to clear land and build buildings. Most of the necessities had to be raised locally and manufactured in the home or village. The pioneer was a resourceful jack-of-all-trades—he farmed, he built, he hunted, and he made things for himself and his neighbors. In small iron shops, the Americans became great improvisors and mechanics. Of course his heritage included a readily imported technology, but his genius lay in adapting that technology to frontier conditions in which labor, private capital, and social overhead were scarce compared with England.

The pioneer also was accustomed to providing his own defense. Nearly everyone was armed for hunting; and they all had learned to fight alone or in small groups against the Indians. In the wars with the French and Indians, the colonists learned that they could expect little help from England; and they also learned that European troops were not suited to fighting in forested country where small bands with mobility and concealment could wreck havoc on massed columns of

3–2. Population, 1740–1800

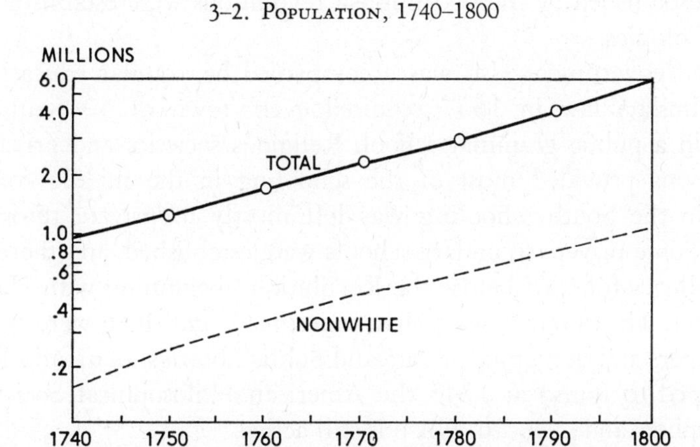

Source: U.S. Department of Commerce, *Historical Statistics of the United States* (Washington, D.C.: U.S. Government Printing Office, 1960), pp. 7, 9, 756.

troops. The American colonists also demonstrated that an armed citizenry could be more vigorous fighters than hired professional soldiers.

Even after frontier conditions had ended in the long-settled parts of the colonies, the frontier continued to be important to the economy. Population continued to mount rapidly, and the older settlements became more crowded. New immigrants and new generations sought new, cheap lands to settle. Land prices rose, and most men of wealth constantly speculated on rising land values by purchasing new lands in the West. A rising population also meant expanding markets for merchants and small manufacturers. While production estimates are not available for the Colonial period, the trade statistics show a rapidly rising volume of imports and exports. Both the settler and the merchant alike viewed the frontier as a source of expanding economic opportunity. (See 3–2.)

Self-Government

The long experience the Colonies had had with participation in government also prepared them to assume control over their own affairs. The chartered colonies in New England had been started as privately governed ventures, and many of the New England towns had started as self-governing communities. The first American representative assembly started in Virginia in 1619; and while most colonies became royal provinces after 1660, all of the colonies had legislatures in which members of the lower house were elected. English common law and courts were established, and the British traditions of personal liberty firmly established by the two English revolutions were established also in the Colonies.

Self-government also was accompanied by popular education. A Massachusetts law in 1647 required every town of 50 families to maintain a public grammar school. Religious societies and private organizations provided most of the schooling in the middle colonies, while in the South schooling was left mostly to private tutors and clergy. Some private secondary schools were established, and there were nine colleges founded before the Revolution (beginning with Harvard in 1636). Thus literacy was fairly widespread, and there were over 50 newspapers and numerous private and public libraries. Benjamin Franklin helped to found in 1743 the American Philosophical Society for philosophers and scientists which is still active.

The colonial legislatures were quite active in exercising and attempting to expand their authority. Since they were expected to levy taxes and duties to support the salaries of the governors and their customs officials, there were frequent quarrels over salaries and expenditures. The Anglo-French conflicts raised the prestige of these assemblies; for England had to turn to the colonies to enlist militia, procure local supplies for British troops, and find additional ways to raise revenues to carry out military operations. Colonial leaders commanded militia and advised England on the conduct of frontier wars.

In peacetime, government expenditures were very small. The chief form of tax in the northern colonies was the property tax, but the poll tax and various excise taxes were relied on more in the southern colonies. Import duties, or tariffs, also were widely used as sources of revenue. There was very little social legislation; the poor were put to work and orphans often were sold as indentured servants.

The colonial legislatures were influenced by mercantilist thinking in their own economic policies of self-development. Some regulations were placed on industry, especially to standardize the packaging and quality of export staples, such as tobacco and flour, and thus to protect the reputation of colonial goods with European customers. To encourage some lines of production, offers were made of bounties, prizes, subsidies, land grants, and tax remissions. While some early use had been made of monopoly grants, Massachusetts declared monopolies illegal in 1641. A number of colonies prohibited or placed a tax on the export of commodities needed by local industry. Attempts were made to levy import duties, or tariffs, in order to favor local industries as well as to collect revenues; but in 1724 Britain banned any colonial duties on the goods of English merchants.

One of the chief economic problems of concern to the colonial legislatures was a shortage of money. Because more was imported from England than was sold to England, British money did not stay long in the colonies. Trade with the West Indies, and some piracy against the trading ships of hostile European countries, brought miscellaneous coins to the colonies, chiefly Spanish; but the weights of coins were not very standardized. Until the English government overruled them, the legislatures had tried various measures to keep money in the colonies—placing a higher official value on coins in the colonies than in England, minting coins in a lighter weight, and even prohibiting the export of coins. Land banks were chartered in some colonies with power to issue paper notes that were secured by real estate mortgages. In 1741, the private land bank companies were discontinued by a retroactive extension of the South Sea Bubble Act of 1720. Then most colonial legislatures began to issue paper money, and some government-owned banks issued paper money. Excessive volumes of notes issued in some of the colonies resulted in drastic depreciation in the value of these notes. Since payment of debts with these notes hurt English merchants, they got parliament to restrict the issue of paper in the New England colonies in 1751, and the restriction was extended to all colonies in 1764.

In these various efforts of the colonial legislatures to influence their own economic affairs, they did not evidence any hostility to the ideas of mercantilist policy as instruments in their own hands. But they did run into increasing British mercantile restrictions on what they could do politically or economically. When industries developed in the Colonies that might compete with industries in England, home pressures on parliament resulted in bans on the export of these colonial goods to England—the Woolen Act of 1699 and the Hat Act of 1732 are examples. In 1755, Maryland alone produced about one seventh of the British production of iron, and the colonies exported much iron to

England. Later restrictions were placed on the production and export of manufactured iron products. However, the regulations upon iron products manufacturing were largely ineffective.

Freedom of Trade

The merchants and shipowners of the American colonies had become very practised at worldwide trade, and their prosperity depended upon multinational trading relations inconsistent with a trade limited to the mother country. This arose out of the way that the northern colonies were able to find markets for their exports and pay for their imports. A lack of balance of trade with England was behind much of the colonial scarcity of money. The southern colonies did not have much difficulty because nearly all of their exports were made to England, and these balanced their imports. Trade with the West Indies also was pretty well balanced. An excess of exports to Europe provided the money to import slaves from Africa. (See 3–3.)

3–3. Colonial Trade, by Areas, 1769

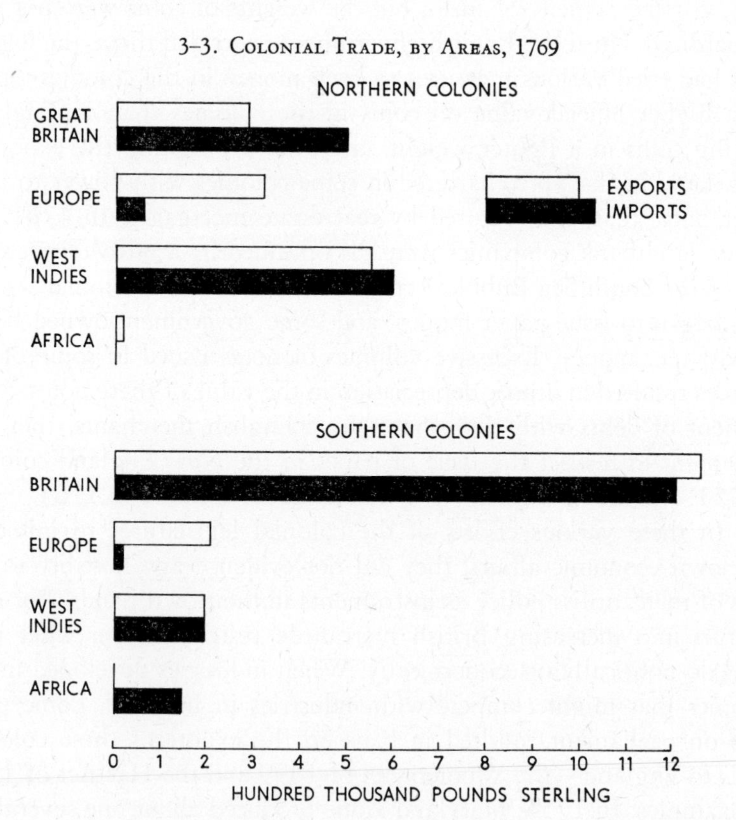

Source: U.S. Department of Commerce, *Historical Statistics of the United States* (Washington, D.C.: U.S. Government Printing Office, 1960), p. 758.

The northern colonies, however, had to depend more upon trade with other areas in order to pay for their excess of imports from England. While their ships and lumber were highly demanded in England, Europe provided a better market for their fish, wheat, and meats. The West Indies plantations specializing in sugar production for export to Europe also provided a market for food supplies for their slaves. Thus, the northern merchants and trading ships had built up considerable trade with other areas.

Usually a ship could maintain full cargoes going and coming, as well as obtain the money to pay for the goods brought back by traveling

3–4. Triangular Trade Routes

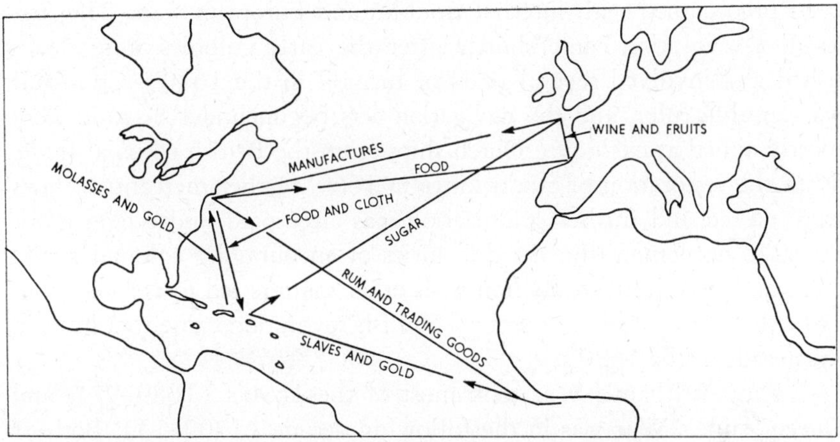

Source: U.S. Department of Commerce, *Historical Statistics of the United States* (Washington, D.C.: U.S. Government Printing Office, 1960), p. 758.

one or more well-established ***triangular trade routes.*** For example, the export of food to southern Europe might result in carrying wine and fruits to England and then returning to New York with English manufactured goods. Or, by carrying food and cloth to the West Indies and then sugar to England, the money also could be obtained to return from England with a full load of manufactured imports. One of the most profitable triangular trade routes was to carry rum and trading goods to Africa, exchange them for Negro slaves and gold to be taken to the West Indies, and then bring back molasses (unprocessed sugar for use in making more rum), and a profit in gold. (See 3–4.)

The ocean-carrying trade itself was an important industry to the northern colonies, and the shipowners always had been resourceful in finding profitable opportunities for trade almost anywhere, but especially in the West Indies colonies of various countries. Sometimes, when England was engaged in hositilities with some country, American ships might engage in piracy against the enemy merchant ships.

Enforcement of Controls

Much of the Yankee trade with European colonies was in violation of the laws of other nations as well as with British laws. The application of English mercantile regulations to the American colonies was bound to cause a conflict in interests and wills. Furthermore, for most of their history, the American colonies had been neglected by England; so greater enforcement of existing regulations precipitated the final crisis.

During nearly every decade of the Colonial period, England had been preoccupied with internal troubles and European wars. The first English revolution came shortly after the early colonies were established and involved several years of turmoil in the 1640's. Cromwell was an able ruler, and the navigation acts begun under his rule were mostly aimed at excluding Dutch ships from the British colonial trade. With the restoration of Stuart kings in 1660, further mercantilist laws were passed and further colonization was attempted under land grant favors to noblemen. But the difficulties of encouraging colonial settlement and British preoccupation with other matters led to very lax control over the colonies. The second English revolution came to a head in the decade of the 1680's.

King William's War took most of the 1690's (1689–97), and Queen Anne's War was in the following decade (1702–13). Both of these wars involved armed clashes between the French and English colonists in North America; and for the next 30 years of peace, the French and English were rivals in establishing forts, arranging alliances with Indian tribes, and developing colonial trade in the West Indies. King George's War occurred briefly in the 1740's (1745–48); then the French and Indian War lasted from 1754 to 1763. Known as the Seven Years' War in Europe, it was fought also in Asia and finally established England's superiority over France and its allies in naval power and colonial possessions.

Immediately after the French and Indian Wars, England began to pay more attention to colonial affairs and attempted to enforce its mercantilist policies. In part, the crisis was precipitated by a temporary attempt by King George III (who came to the throne in 1760) to assert more autocratic royal powers. Parliament also was concerned about strengthening the enforcement of colonial policies favoring the merchants and industrialists in the home country.

A general tightening of the enforcement of trade regulations was one source of tension. While England long had had laws regulating colonial trade, there always had been difficulty in enforcing them. The Navigation Act of 1651 required that goods entering English ports be carried by ships of the exporting nation or British ships. Since colonials were included as British subjects, they benefitted from this regulation aimed at excluding Dutch traders.

Other early regulations, however, required that certain enumerated colonial products could be exported only to England and that European imports to the colonies must be brought first to English ports. These regulations tended to deny much of the direct colonial trade with other countries and foreign colonies. In spite of customs officials and special admiralty courts established in the colonial ports, the colonial merchants managed to evade these regulations and were openly defiant of them. They especially objected, therefore, when regulations were more rigorously enforced and when writs of assistance (search warrants) were used to locate illegal shipments.

Parliament also launched a program of raising more revenues from the American colonies to help pay British war debts. In 1764, the Sugar Act imposed high duties on imports from foreign ports. This was taken by the colonists as a mere indication of a host of more restrictive policies that the British would pursue in the future. The following year the Stamp Act placed a tax on documents and newspapers, and the Quartering Act compelled the colonists to support British troops in the area. The Townshend Acts of 1767 imposed import duties on a number of products. Due to colonial boycotts, protests and mob actions, these duties were removed in 1770. The colonists again were inflamed, however, by the Tea Act of 1773, which gave the British East India Company a monopoly on export of tea to America where it was subject to a small tax. When a Boston crowd dumped a shipment of tea into the harbor, parliament passed a series of measures of punishment, called by the colonists the "Intolerable Acts."

To the further alarm of the colonists, the Quebec Act of 1773 annexed to the Province of Quebec all of the lands west of the Alleghenies and north of the Ohio River. While a British proclamation in 1763 had reserved all of the lands west of the Alleghenies for the use of Indian tribes, this had been ignored by the settlers. But to extend the Canadian province into this territory threatened the westward expansion, and each of the colonies had claims to land in the West. This combination of the western land issue with the issues of taxes and trade tended to unite both the poor western settlers and the merchants in the port cities in opposition to British policy. As a final stroke, parliament answered the petitions of the First Continental Congress with the Restraining Act of 1775, which added regulations intended to destroy finally New England's trade with other areas.

Thus, the American Revolution was not an uprising of a poor and long-oppressed peoples. It was a crisis of economic and political relations between a semi-independent province and a distant central government that attempted to restrict the freedoms that long had been enjoyed.

FORMATION OF A NATION

The formation of 13 separate colonies into one nation was not accomplished solely by the fighting of the Revolutinary War. Certain problems of economic and political disunity were experienced before a strong national government was formed. An understanding of America's economic development as well as its political history requires an understanding of the limited federal powers and limited economic policies with which the Nation was launched.

Problems of Disunity

After the outbreak of fighting in 1775 and the Declaration of Independence in 1776, a seven-year period of warfare and blockade passed before England finally recognized American independence (in 1783). During the war, the 13 states had been very loosely united militarily and politically. The Continental Congress served as little more than a steering committee for the war. In 1781 the separate states finally ratified the Articles of Confederation (drafted in 1777). After the war, a number of problems of disunity plagued this confederation of states and led in 1787 to the drafting of a constitution for a stronger federal union.

A paramount problem was the need for stronger national defense. The war itself had been won partly because Britain was not able to ignore dangers elsewhere and concentrate enough military force in America. The alliance with France had brought decisive land and naval forces to help win the final victory. The Continental Congress had had to rely upon the states to raise and assign militia to a national army. The states were very unequal and irregular in their support.

The new nation continued to find itself without adequate powers to raise and support a national army and navy. The security and economic development of western lands also was threatened by European colonial powers. In the North, England refused to abandon its fur trading posts along the southern shores of the Great Lakes and was encouraging Indian hostilities against American pioneer settlements. Many American loyalists had found refuge in Canada, and there was the danger that their hostility might lead to future conflicts. In the South, Spain held Florida and was fomenting trouble with the Indians. Spain also held the Gulf Coast and New Orleans; and for a time the export of western goods was restricted.

Congress also found it difficult to establish trade agreements on favorable terms with European countries. Several signed treaties, but only Sweden and Russia provided reciprocal commercial privileges. The most serious problem was with England. American ships now found themselves outside of the British Empire and even more restricted by the old Navigation Acts. Import duties and port charges hurt American exports and shipping, and a flood of postwar British imports caused considerable outflow of money and a shortage of coins in America. In attempts to retaliate and bring Britain to terms, the state legislatures began to place tariffs on British goods; but the different levels of state tariffs only caused British ships to seek the ports with the lowest duties.

Congress continued to find itself heavily in debt and had no power to raise its own revenues. During the Revolutionary War the states had been reluctant to tax heavily or to supply Congress with enough funds. Both Congress and the states had incurred large debts and had issued much paper money. There was little confidence in the ability of the Continental Congress to redeem its paper money, so it traded for much less than its face value. This led to the expression "not worth a Continental."

The combination of a shortage of goods and a large supply of newly issued money had caused a severe inflation of the general price level during the war. Most prices, even in coin, more than doubled. (See 3–5.)

After the war, the economy stagnated in a severe depression. Shipping continued to be crippled and exports to England were low. Prices had fallen drastically after the war. This caused many people to incur losses, but it especially pressed heavily upon people who had incurred debt during the war when prices were high. Attempts to foreclose on mortgage and imprison debtors brought about Shay's Rebellion among farmers in Massachusetts. After Britain's large flood of imports were sold on credit immediately after the war, there was considerable concern among merchants about maintaining debt-paying habits in the private economy.

Finally, the states were involved in quarrels and rivalry. They not only found themselves in competition for foreign shipping, which hampered the raising of tariffs, but also they attempted to place duties upon the interstate shipment of goods. Fortunately, the settlement of conflicting claims to western land was reached when Maryland had refused to sign the Articles of Confederation until other states agreed to cede their western lands to federal ownership. This made possible the ordinances of 1784, 1785, and 1787 which provided for the national government

3–5. Wholesale Price Index, 1749–1800

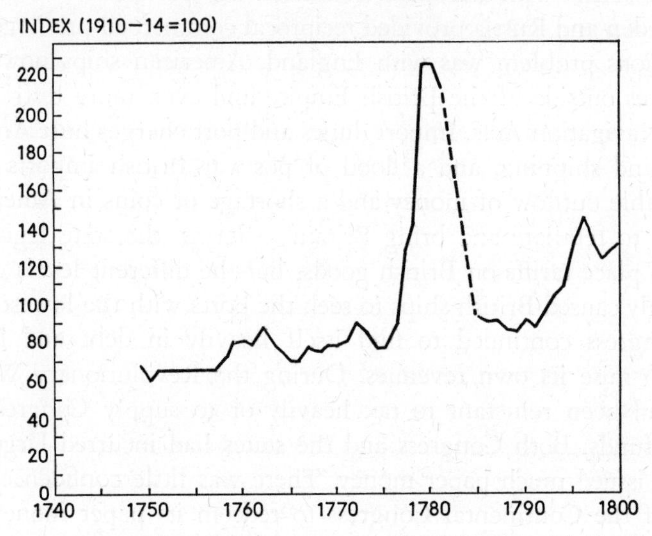

Source: U.S. Department of Commerce, *Historical Statistics of the United States* (Washington, D.C.: U.S. Government Printing Office, 1960), p. 116.

to survey and sell western lands and for the eventual organization of new western states.

In spite of the postwar depression and looseness of the confederation, important gains were made during the period. America's overseas trade expanded greatly, manufacturing grew, and agricultural output increased. What is more, the confederation constituted the groundwork on which the federal government was to be built.

Federal Powers

The Constitution of the United States was drafted at the Philadelphia Convention of 1787 and was ratified by enough states in 1788. It was declared in effect when the new government took office in March of 1789. It provided the national government with independent executive and judicial branches, as well as a legislature divided into two houses. This meant a national government with an elaborate checks-and-balances system of divided central powers. During the first session of Congress the first 10 amendments to the Constitution also were ratified to remedy the oversight of not providing a "bill of rights." It must be kept in mind that each of the states was initially independent; and the Constitution granted to the central government only the bare minimum of powers needed to overcome the previous problems of disunity. Fortunately, the wording and amendement procedure was flexible enough so that later changes could be made by a gradual process of evolution.

Of fundamental importance to later economic development was the uniting of the 13 separate states into one nation. This internal unity made possible the later creation of a large internal market, so important to specialization, large-scale production, and high productivity. One of the important powers granted to the federal government, therefore, was the power to regulate foreign and interstate commerce. It also was given the power to control a national army and navy and to supervise foreign relations. The power to levy taxes to raise its own revenues was essential to make the other powers effective and give the federal government some independence.

The federal government also was given a few other powers that were important to its economic functions. The power to incur debts and issue and regulate money rounded out its fiscal powers. Specific provision was made for regulation of bankruptcy, the issuance of patents, and the establishment of post offices and post roads. Two catchall clauses that provided a basis for later expansion of powers—in addition to the power to regulate interstate commerce—were the "general welfare" clause and the "necessary and proper" clause.

Initial Economic Policies

The way that the new government used its constitutional powers inevitably was to set precedents for later economic development of the Nation. The main economic policies were few, and they arose out of the problems that had been experienced in establishing the Nation. These policies were determined under the leadership of President Washington and the men who later became identified as leaders of the Federalist party. Alexander Hamilton, as the first Secretary of the Treasury, was responsible for drafting and presenting the reports and legislation that embodied these policies.

The first set of economic policies established three sources of federal revenues. A need for independent tax revenues had been one of the main weaknesses of the Continental Congress. One of the first acts of Congress, therefore, was to pass the Tariff Act of 1789, which provided a source of revenues through low ***duties on imports.***

Alexander Hamilton also recommended two other sources of federal government revenues. One was the rapid ***sale of lands*** in the western territories. Unfortunately for the small settlers, the Land Ordinance of 1785 provided for sale of land in minimum size units of 640 acres. This meant small settlers had to buy from land speculating intermediaries. For a new government with little administrative structure, however, this may have provided a quick and efficient way to transfer land to settlers and obtain government revenues. The other source of revenue proposed by Hamilton and adopted by Congress was the levying of ***excise taxes*** on domestic production, mainly on whiskey. One of Hamilton's purposes in levying domestic taxes was to display federal authority, and in the "Whiskey Rebellion" of 1794 that authority had to be enforced with troops. But it also may be regarded as a test of responsible democratic government when the people recognize the necessity of paying the cost of government by levying taxes on themselves.

A second main policy area of the new government was to establish a national currency system with a stable value. The Amrican people had experienced the demoralizing effects of rapid inflation due to the inability of the Continental Congress and the unwillingness of the colonial legislatures to levy wartime taxes to support their armies. Instead, there had been an excessive resort to the printing of paper money and to borrowing. The ***Mint Act of 1792*** adopted Hamilton's recommendation that both gold and silver coins be issued; but Hamilton's major proposal, also adopted, was the chartering of the Bank of the United States (1791). One fifth of the capital was subscribed by the government and the rest was private. The bank acted as a depository for government funds and could lend to the government. The bank also was authorized to issue its own paper money notes, backed partly by gold and silver but mostly by government bonds. This established a fairly sound system of paper money. It also established a large central bank institution which could exercise a restraining influence on the inflationary issue of notes by state banks (because it could refuse to accept notes of doubtful value in handling the transactions of the government). In spite of this, there was a considerable rise of prices in the first two decades during the life of the first Bank of the United States (1791–1811).

A third main policy of the new government, again under Hamilton's recommendation, was the issue of new bonds in order to pay off all war debts. The federal government promised to pay all of the state debts incurred during the Revolution, as well as the debts incurred by the Continental Congress. The payment of debts, of course, is fundamental to the maintenance of long-term agreements with investors. By indicating a willingness to pay all debts and by setting about to use an orderly procedure of applying tax revenues for this purpose, Hamilton won the confidence of foreign governments, foreign investors, and private citizens in the credit and good faith of the new government. This act of good faith simultaneously enabled him to sell new bonds to replace the old debts and to provide for a gradual paying off of these new bonds with current revenues. This kind of credit policy was to help federal borrowing in the future. It also helped the state governments establish more sound finance policies and later to borrow large amounts to build roads and canals. Indirectly, it helped establish the confidence of foreign investors in the economic environment for private business ventures in the new and expanding economy. So the main economic significance of these policies was not merely that it solved problems for the government officials, rather it prepared the way for large flows of foreign capital that were needed to help build the economy.

Still another policy recommendation by Hamilton was not acted upon—the deliberate fostering of new manufacturing industries in America. In particular, Hamilton's famous *Report on Manufactures* proposed higher tariffs on imported manufactured goods and subsidies to new industries. This represented a continuation of a mercantilist type of policy thinking that was common to his times. The Revenue Act of 1792, however, failed to raise the rates as high as he recommended. Congress apparently was not willing at that time to consider any economic policies that did more than provide the minimum functions of the new central government. The tariffs enacted merely provided needed revenues. About one third of the early federal budgets was required to pay interest and gradually retire the large debt, and over half was required for defense. Initially, no federal programs were undertaken either to regulate the private economy or to undertake direct government expenditures for investment or production, although, Congress did enact patent legislation. For the time being, at least, the American people simply were wary of central government actions beyond the minimum needs of providing for defense and for a sound money.

EMERGING IDEAS

The beginnings of the American economy were shaped by the conditions that existed in North America and the background of political institutions and ideas that prevailed in England. The ideas about government economic policy which were widely accepted at the time were those of mercantilism. While there had been resistance to England's mercantilist restrictions as they applied to American colonies, there had been no hesitation on the part of colonial legislatures to adopt mercantile policies to further their own development. In their later history Americans continued to be pragmatic about requesting any government action that appeared to be successful in meeting problems. The people were more practical minded than theoretical.

Nevertheless, at the time of the American Revolution, some new ideas about government economic policy were emerging in France and England. These ideas were critical of mercantilism and favored less government regulation of economic activities. Although probably not widely influential in America until after the Civil War, these ideas were consistent with the limited economic policies of American government from its beginning. They are mentioned here, since this is the period when they were first discussed. Also, it rounds out the discussion of the transition of Europe from a traditional economy to a market economy to examine the government economic policy ideas that soon were proposed as an alternative to mercantilism. The distinction must be kept in mind, however, that the ideas emerging in discussion were not actually influencing policy until much later in history.

Leave Markets Alone

Beginning in the late 17th century, a number of "liberal" writers in both England and France had been critical of mercantilism. In their view government should be liberal rather than restrictive in its economic policy. They saw that a profusion of taxes, duties, and regulations could be a hindrance to production and exchange. Monopolies could be granted and maintained as political favors rather than as necessary incentives to risk-taking. Each traditional craft and trade might use regulations to resist change and improvements in methods. These criticisms of mercantilism culminated in the 1750's in a group of writings by Frenchmen who became known as the ***Physiocrats.***

The Physiocrats popularized the policy slogans of *laissez-faire* and *laissez-passer*—that is, let things alone, let them take their course. This meant that governments should cease trying to command or direct production. It was based partly on a better appreciation of the workings of markets—an idea that individuals driven by self-interested motives but guided by market prices and competition would bring about socially desired production. It was not necessary for government to command things to happen. Furthermore, things might work better without government interference. The Physiocrats based their analysis of a market economy on the importance of agriculture and land as the sole source of surplus production. Accordingly, they recommended taxes predominantly on agriculture. France, of course, was a major agricultural country, and much of the land owned by the nobility and church was virtually untaxed.

In 1776, the same year as the Declaration of Independence, an Englishman, Adam Smith, published his book *The Wealth of Nations.* Smith, who was influenced by several English writers before him as well as by the Physiocrats, advocated a similar policy of leaving the market alone. He argued that if each member of society were free to pursue his self-interests, a harmonious and socially beneficial economic order would result, as if guided by an "invisible hand." Smith did not agree with the Physiocrats that only agriculture was the source of production. He stressed the importance of labor, which was able to produce more through specialization in exchange and the division of labor within the firm. And Smith stressed the importance of capital in providing labor with more productive tools. The accumulation of capital thus became a source of cumulative expansion and economic growth. Smith, of course, was influenced by the industrial progress and rapid expansion of England in his time (as we shall see in the next chapter).

Freedom of Trade

Both the Physiocrats and Adam Smith argued for government policies tending toward more freedom of trade. They rejected the mercantile idea that national wealth consisted of money in its treasury and emphasized the production of goods as the real source of wealth. Accordingly, they viewed trade as an exchange of goods. To them the objective of exporting products was to obtain useful and needed goods, not merely to obtain money (which is valuable only if it can be exchanged for goods eventually). Trade was an extension of organized cooperation and specialization to a larger market, and both importing and exporting nations would gain by the exchange of goods.

The various liberal writers were, of course, influenced by the concept of comparative advantage in their advocacy of free trade among nations. They recognized that free trade would allow nations to reap the mutual benefits of specialization and exchange that are sacrificed by a policy of self-sufficiency. Smith and others also recognized that persistent attempts to sell more than was purchased might be self-defeating. An excess of exports could not forever bring an inflow of gold, because other nations would run out of money!

The quantity theory of money suggested how market adjustments might be made to balance exports and imports under a free trade policy. It would come about through effects on price levels in both nations. If nation X had an export surplus and received gold from nation Y, this would increase the money supply in nation X. An increase in money supply would tend to raise the general price level in nation X. The opposite would happen in nation Y, a reduced money supply and lower prices. With lower prices in Y than in X, it would be harder for X merchants to sell more goods as exports to Y. So nation X's export surplus soon would be wiped out by a decline in its exports and an increase in its imports. The adjustment would come about automatically by effects of money supply on general prices and effects of prices on individual decisions of merchants.

The national interest, in terms of all producers and all consumers, is sacrificed, therefore, in any tariff policies intended to protect or favor the interests of any particular group of producers. Raise the tariff on woolen textile imports to keep the price high for a nation's textile industries: the result is not only higher prices for consumers of woolen textile goods, but also reduced wool imports will lead to reduced exports by other industries—that is, lower incomes for producers in industries other than woolen textiles.

Political Economy

The writings of the Physiocrats and of Adam Smith were confused and ambiguous on many points. They were imperfect and oversimplified in many respects. But they were the beginnings of the application of the methods of science to economic matters. They were the first systematic theories about the causes and effects of economic events.

In the realm of science, it is not the origins of ideas that make them valid or useful. It is how well they work, how well they explain some of the systematic relationships involved in human events. Not many of the relationships may be understood at first, and the initial explanations may be imperfect. Theories, therefore, are not simply right or wrong—they usually are only partly right. But theories can evolve and be modified to improve their effectiveness. It is not very useful, therefore, to categorize economic theories by their origins or age. We do not simply discard an idea because it came from an agricultural viewpoint or was an "18th-century notion." Thus, the formation of the ideas of laissez-faire was influenced by the 18th-century doctrine of natural law, but the validity of the analysis of the workings of a market may be independent of the philosophy that colored the first attempts to make the analysis.

Mixed in with the scientific content of economic writings, however, is usually considerable expression of opinion or choice on public policy issues. Thus, Adam Smith not only developed some useful theoretical analysis, he also expressed a policy point of view. A policy is less subject to empirical testing and logical proof than is a scientific theory. It expresses value preferences about what is regarded as "good," and it relies partly on faith as to what methods will result in the most "good."

The early economists called their subject "political economy" or writings about public policy. While most economists try to distinguish some aspects of their studies as contributing to the scientific knowledge of economics, they usually recognize that a large part of their work still lies in the area of "policy" discussion and debate.

The ideas of mercantilism and laissez-faire, therefore, need to be understood as an aid to historical perspective. They were policy points of view that arose out of the conditions of particular historical periods; and they influenced the policies of governments in later periods. Some elements of these ideas are essential parts of modern economic theory and will prove useful in analyzing the economic growth and development of our Nation. No attempt will be made, however, to evaluate the precise validity or argue the full merits of such ideas in the modern setting.

APPENDIX TO CHAPTER 3 ON COMPOSITE PRICE INDEXES

It frequently is useful in discussions of economic growth to refer to changes in the general level of prices of all goods. It is not difficult to understand the notion of some average change in all prices, even though particular prices change in varying degrees. What is not immediately realized, however, is that the measurement of such general changes may be difficult or not very meaningful unless the relative importance of each good is specified and held constant in computing the average price change. What is required is the computation of a "weighted average" of all price changes—that is, a "composite price index." Common examples of composite price indexes are the *Whole-*

sale Price Index and the *Consumer Price Index* of the U.S. Bureau of Labor Statistics.

Let us construct a hypothetical example of how a composite price index may be computed. There are different methods used, but here we will be concerned only to understand the general idea of how the importance of goods must be used as "weights" before the different prices are averaged together. Suppose we wished to construct a composite index of food prices for American colonial exports and that there were only two foods, wheat and rum. Assume the following hypothetical price and quantity data for two periods of time:

	Year	
	1750	*1760*
Wheat quantity (bushels)	75,000	105,000
Wheat price	$4.55	$5.11
Rum quantity (gallons)	25,000	30,000
Rum price	$2.53	$3.54

Now, can we average the prices of different foods and then compute the change in average prices? No, we can't; they are in different units of measurement—bushels and gallons. What we are trying to do is ***average the changes*** in prices. We could do this using price indexes for each type of food price separately and then average the changes in their indexes. If we select 1750 as the index base year, we can set each price for that year as equal to 100. For each food, the price index for the next period is the price for that period divided by the base year price and multiplied by 100. (See Appendix to Chapter 2 on Ratio Charts and Index Numbers.) This gives us these price indexes:

	Year	
	1760	*1770*
Wheat price index	100	112
Rum price index	100	140

The indexes show that the wheat price has risen 12 percent while the rum price has risen 40 percent.

What is the average price change? If we total the two indexes and divide by 2, we get an average of the two indexes in 1770 equal to 126. (The base year index remains 100 regardless of method of averaging.)

This is commonly called an "unweighted average," but more accurately it might be referred to as an "equally weighted average," for both index numbers are treated as equally important. By this average, the general food price level appears to have risen 26 percent.

How do we measure the relative importance of wheat and rum in making up a composite price index? There are various alternatives, and the one we select depends a lot on the particular problem we are considering. For example, we can select the total sales value of each product sold—the price times the quantity of each product. In 1750 our example indicates that the total sales value of wheat ($4.55 × 75,000 = $331,250) was about five times larger than the total sales value of rum ($2.53 × 25,000 = $63,250). The total value is an appropriate measure of importance when we are considering national income or consumer spending. Alternatively, we might want to use physical quantities as a measure of importance—say, when the physical cargo space is an important consideration. In our example, however, let us use total sales value as the measure of importance or weight.

How do we use the weights in making up the composite price index? We could use the sales figures, but to reduce the example to the simplest terms, let us simply use their ratio, 5 to 1. The sum of these two weights is 6. Now, a weighted average is obtained simply by multiplying each price index by its weight, summing the results, and dividing that sum by the total of the weights, as shown in the following for both years:

	Year					
	1750			*1760*		
	Weight ×	*Price Index* =	*Weighted Index*	*Weight* ×	*Price Index* =	*Weighted Index*
Wheat	5	100	500	5	112	560
Rum	1	100	100	1	140	140
	6		600 ÷ 6 = 100	6		700 ÷ 6 = 117

The result that we now have for the second period (the base period index of 100 again is not changed by averaging methods) is an index of 117, which shows that weighted average change in prices was an increase of 17 percent.

In this example, the weighted average price change (+17 percent) is smaller than the unweighted average price change (+26 percent) simply because the price change for wheat was smaller and because wheat was five times as important in total food sales in the base year.

In order to understand the meaning of composite price indexes, we need to be aware of the following two important assumptions. First, the computation requires the selection of some measure of importance to provide the weights for the composite index. Different weights can produce quite different results. The selection involves some judgment as to what is most appropriate for the particular purpose in using the index. Second, the same weights are used for all years of comparison. This is because the purpose of the index is to show price changes alone. This kind of comparison, therefore, requires an assumption that the importance of the different foods (in this case their sales) remains the same (or at least that they do not change in ratio to each other). Actually, we know that this assumption seldom is valid. But usually when we use price indexes, we want to compare the price changes alone with the sales changes looked at separately. (A more serious difficulty is when the types of food or their quality actually changes, but this is still another problem of economic measurement of change.)

STUDY QUESTIONS

1. In any type of economy, what political conditions are essential to economic growth? In a market system, what political institutions and policies are favorable to economic growth?
2. In contrast to other European nations, how was England favored by the early achievement of a unified nation, religious tolerance, and a parliamentary form of government?
3. What was the objective of mercantilism? How was this goal supported by the ideas of bullionism, self-sufficiency, and colonialism?
4. Mercantilist policy relied upon what methods of direct government action? What methods of indirect action, or influence on individuals?
5. What conditions and experiences in the North American colonies shaped the individualistic attitudes of the people? The habits of self-government?
6. How did the economic interests of the northern colonies clash with the mercantilist policies of England? What mercantilist policies did the colonial legislatures themselves attempt to adopt? Why did the northern colonies depend upon trading outside of the British Empire?
7. What problems plagued the new Nation? Because of these problems, what major powers were granted by the Constitution to the central government?

8. In addition, what three main sets of policies were adopted by the first administration that further dealt with the initial problems? What mercantilist policies were not adopted?
9. What criticisms of mercantilism were made by the writers advocating a laissez-faire policy? Why did they argue that government need not direct production?
10. Why was bullionism criticized as self-defeating? How were tariffs thought to hurt the whole Nation?

Chapter 4 INDUSTRIAL REVOLUTION

The United States was born in the midst of three revolutionary changes that marked the beginning of the modern or industrial era of mankind. These often have been referred to as the Commercial Revolution, the Political Revolution, and the Industrial Revolution. All three, of course, came about gradually over several centuries; but it is interesting that the climax of all three major changes can be dated around 1776. That was the year of the signing of the Declaration of Independence and also the year when Adam Smith wrote *The Wealth of Nations.* The major changes in industrial technology that started the modern age also have been identified by historians as occurring in England in the last half of the 18th century.

The political, economic, and technical aspects of modern society are so intermingled in popular thinking and experience that it is important to be able to distinguish them separately. A market economy developed prior to democratic government, and to some extent it has been possible for authoritarian governments to use and encourage market forms of economic organization. Industrial technology was developed in a market economy, but it also has been possible for some nations to use this technology in centrally controlled command types of economies. The mixture of these three aspects of modern society, therefore, has varied among nations and over time. Some people have questioned whether the advanced stages of industrial technology can be completely compatible with a market economy, but others have questioned whether a command type of organization can be compatible with democracy. Certainly modern problems require study and clear thinking about how these three aspects are interrelated and what the effects may be of different variations.

The term Industrial Revolution commonly has been used to refer to (*a*) the historical period in England (*b*) when modern industrial methods were introduced and (*c*) rapid economic growth first started. While the term is convenient and continues to be useful, it initially conveyed a misleading impression. It erroneously suggests that most changes to modern technology came about suddenly in one short historical period. Actually a long sequence of discoveries and improvements preceded that period, and some of the discoveries in that period were not widely adopted until much later. It also erroneously suggests that the improvements in methods were limited to manufacturing. Actually, the improvements in agriculture, transportation, and other fields that preceded and accompanied the manufacturing improvements, made them possible, and may have had greater immediate effects on output. Rapid growth did start, but it may have started somewhat ahead of the inventions in manufacturing. The term, therefore, should be placed in a broader historical setting and understood as referring to a number of related developments in different economic fields. (See 4–1.)

4–1. Historical Setting of the Industrial Revolution

	Major Fields of Change				
Century	*Resources*	*Transportation*	*Manufacturing*	*Trade*	*Markets*
15th		Navigation improved	Guilds, custom manufacturing, handcrafting	Rise of trade	Emergence of factor markets
				Exploration	Farm "surplus" traded in cities
16th	More wool raised			Spanish gold	Inflation
	Displaced farm labor	Shipbuilding	Cottage textile manufacturing	Increased trading	Growth of London
17th	Timber shortage	Coastal shipping	Diversity of industries	Colonies	Income rise
	Use of coal		Use of water wheels, power transmission equipment		New products consumed
18th	Improved farming Released farm labor	Canals Roads	Coke Textile machines, better iron, tools Steam engine	India cotton goods imported American cotton	More food Population rise More cities War demands
19th	Improved extraction methods	Steam railroad Steamships	Standard parts Steel	Free trade	American expansion

The historical interpretation of the effects of the Industrial Revolution also has undergone considerable change. The first historians to use the term looked back with horror on certain conditions of living during the period as they were described by contemporary reformers. This led them to adopt an oversimplified explanation of the causes of those conditions, for they attributed them to the new methods and organization of production. In spite of later research correcting this error, the initial impression has stuck. Paradoxically, Western literature and ideology has been infused with a mythology of shame about the changes that brought revolutionary improvement in material conditions of living for the bulk of the people.

THE PREPARATION

England was the first nation to undergo an industrial revolution. Yet in 1500 England had been a weak and relatively backward country. Even for the next two and a half centuries, France was regarded as the most advanced manufacturing nation. What advantages did England have that helped her prepare for this first leap into the modern industrial age?

England's Advantages

Undoubtedly England was favored in its geography and natural resources. As an island nation, its fishing and shipping industries were developed early. Coastal transportation was easily available and cheap. The main part of the country was relatively flat and afforded few barriers to travel. Agriculture was prosperous enough to permit production of a surplus. Around the major export crop, wool, an export surplus of manufactured woolen textiles also was developed. Finally, materials of special importance to the industrial age, coal and iron, were locally available. These conditions, of course, were not entirely unique. The Lowlands, northern France, and the German Rhineland had similar juxtaposition of transport, agriculture, coal and iron.

Political conditions also were favorable. The transition from feudalism was more advanced, national unity was achieved, and a long period of peace had been experienced. Civil liberties and a degree of religious tolerance also were favorable to individual initiative and enterprise. Skilled workers had come as refugees from France. Some of the exclusion of minority groups from the church and government offices may have helped to divert talent into industrial lines. The high state of development of education, universities, and scientific societies provided a good environment for imaginative minds. Finally, the rise of parliamentary legislation and the influence of a large middle class undoubtedly encouraged the kind of legislation and economic policy which would be more favorable to market activities. Mercantilism never had been as restrictive as in France.

Most important, perhaps, was the advanced stage of commercial and industrial development England already had achieved by the middle of the 17th century. Its farming was highly commercialized. It had a large middle class. It had a large merchant fleet and an active world trade. It had well-developed financial institutions and large accumulations of capital. Besides its major industry in textiles, it had developed a wide diversity of manufacturing industries. If France still was the leader, England was a close second.

There were two features of England's industrial development which distinguished it from that of France. One was the larger size of factories in England, and the other was the concentration of production on low-cost, mass-consumption goods. Many of the new industries introduced in England early in the 16th century—paper mills, blast furnaces, sugar refining, and brass making—required heavy equipment and large numbers of workers. These industries required large accumulations of capital and management skill in handling large ventures. Experience in handling these industries helped to prepare for the new industrial modes of production. Furthermore, while France long had excelled at artisan skills in producing luxury goods, England produced cheaper goods consumed by the middle classes and the higher income workers and farmers. Being produced and sold in greater volume these goods were easily adapted to use of the new industrial methods soon to be introduced. With the rise in population, income, and trade throughout Europe, the demand for these products was expanding more rapidly than the demand for skilled craft products.

The more rapid expansion of manufacturing production in England than in France also appeared to be due to a more rapid improvement in methods. This could have been stimulated partly by the more rapid expansion of mass markets among the common people, because large markets permit more specialization and large size of production units. In some industries, the larger production units may result in lower average costs. Specialization also encourages a search for improved methods in performing one type of productive operation. In large part, however, the stimulus may have come from the problems of rising costs resulting from certain resource scarcities.

Stimulus of Problems

England, which was faced with an early depletion of forest resources not experienced by France, found its firewood and lumber prices rising rapidly in the 16th and 17th centuries. While the plentiful coal in England quickly replaced wood for home heating and industrial furnaces, there were some industries that could not avoid the rising costs of lumber. Between 1540 and 1640, when grain prices quadrupled and most manufactured goods prices about doubled, the price of firewood increased four to five times. While coal could be substituted for firewood in most industries, lumber prices affected the costs of factory buildings and much of the machinery. Metal was used only for certain critical parts of machinery—the axles, gears, cutting edges, or boilers. Stone and brick were used for the furnaces; but the rest of a mill's building and machinery would be made of wood.

Mining and metal industries also began to run into rising costs in the 17th century. While charcoal prices did not rise as rapidly as firewood, the smelter frequently exhausted his local forest supplies and had to move. Certainly charcoal was more costly than in France, and the technology of iron making at that time did not permit the use of coal in smelting the ore. Mines began to run into rapidly rising costs as shafts had to be sunk down into the ground. Coal, especially, encountered rising costs. Initially found in outcroppings on the surface, the consumption of coal for heating purposes was so rapid that seams had to be worked farther and farther down under the surface.

Rising labor costs also may have provided some stimulus for improving methods. Rising food prices may have exerted some pressure on wages, and the rapid expansion of industry frequently outran labor supplies. Compared to capital supplies, at least, there were frequent indications of labor scarcity in some industries prior to the mid-18th century. This may have added to the early incentives to find laborsaving methods and the use of more capital equipment in manufacturing.

In any event, the 16th and 17th centuries were periods of considerable scientific advances and improvements in technology. While some of the early improvements helped to stimulate rapid industrial expansion after the mid-16th century, there was an apparent slowing down of industrial progress after the mid-17th century that appeared to be related to resource limitations. Further rapid advance seemed to await the solution to certain problems, after which the further revolution in methods took place in the late 18th century.

Many of the early improvements had been made in mechanical

machinery. The textile industry benefited from the invention of Jurgen's spinning wheel in 1530, the stocking frame for knitting in 1589, and the ribbon loom in 1621. A great number of ideas also were developed for mechanically transmitting power—shafts, pulleys, chain drives, sprockets, gears, roller bearings, universal joints, and coil springs. These permitted greater use to be made of windmills and waterwheels, as well as horsepower. Many of the early mills relied upon falling water and the overshot waterwheel to drive bellows for blast furnaces and to raise and lower hammers. The problems of shaft mining gradually led to many engineering advances. Removal of water from mines was a great problem, and suction pumps could lift water only so far and had to be arranged in stairstep series. Force pumps required stronger pipes to hold the pressure. Hoisting buckets of ore was worked out with gear ratios so that a horse or waterwheel could gradually raise a great weight. Bellows and ventilating pipes were used to bring fresh air down into mines. Drills were used to explore for underground veins.

Metallurgy underwent a basic change with the introduction of a crude blast furnace for smelting at the beginning of the 16th century. A very great heat was needed to obtain molten iron. The furnace structure was as much as 30 feet high and 20 feet square, with walls 5 or 6 feet thick. Then a blast of air was applied to the fire by means of a large leather bellows usually driven by a large overshot waterwheel. The molten metal could be poured into small convenient-sized ingots. Reheated later, the ingots might be hammered into sheets or drawn into rods or wire, again with the use of power from large waterwheels. After the middle of the 17th century, the further expansion of the iron industry appeared to be stymied by the shortage and high price of charcoal. Coal could not be used directly in the smelting furnaces because it did not provide a hot enough fire and its sulfur gases made the metal too brittle. The limited number of available sources of waterpower near mines and minerals also provided another limitation to the expansion.

Agricultural Surplus

While certain barriers had slowed down the advance of manufacturing, improvements in agriculture seemed to be accelerating. Perhaps the earliest improvement in English farming simply was a result of the stimulus to produce for sale in the market. In addition to the stimulus to produce more wool, there was a rising demand for food by the growing city populations. Efforts were made especially to increase the acreage of agricultural lands. The high demand for wood and the cutting of the forests helped to clear more land. Grazing in the enclosures also permitted more production of meat. The increase in cod fishing and the importation of foods from the colonies and the Netherlands helped to provide more food for the rising city populations. Then, in the early 18th century, very rapid strides of improvement were made in agriculture which began to expand the productive capacity of the available farmers and lands.

New crops were the main initial source of this improvement. Before the middle of the 17th century, the Dutch were having great success in raising clover and turnips in the fields usually left idle. Clover improved the soil and later productivity of grain while turnips took different elements out of the soil than grain. Meanwhile, instead of the land being idle, the clover provided a good food for livestock, while the turnips provided food for humans and animals alike. The potato was introduced into Ireland in about 1600, but the Scottish and English peasants regarded it with suspicion. Originally it was cultivated as a rich man's food, but gradually it was adopted as the common man's food; white bread remained the preferred staple, however. The potato had the advantage not only of being exceptionally high in food value, but also of growing abundantly even on very small patches of marginal land.

Large landowners in England played a leading role in developing and introducing improved methods using these new crops. Shortly after 1700, Charles Townshend popularized various plans of crop rotation involving the alternation of turnips and clover with barley and wheat. While Italians in the 16th century had used a seed drill and small plows to cultivate vineyards, Jethro Tull developed horsedrawn machinery for plowing and planting seeds in rows. Then, in the latter half of the 18th century, Robert Blakewell introduced selective methods of livestock breeding; and Arthur Young wrote books and published a monthly magazine to spread the information on new methods.

One of the changes that helped to make these improved methods possible, of course, was the use of large fields for machine cultivation of crops and the enclosing of cattle grazing areas. In 1750, about two thirds of the land already was enclosed when a new series of enclosures was begun. This time resort to parliamentary acts and the courts provided a more formal procedure for the reorganization of land claims. Considerable attention was given by early historians to the parliamentary efforts to stop the enclosures during the 16th century and the legal steps to facilitate them during the late 18th century. The historians assumed that large masses of peasants were forced off the land to become a source of cheap labor for industry in the cities. This conclusion is valid for the 16th century. Recent population studies, however, show that in the 18th century, rural population was increasing rather than being reduced by enclosures. With a very high birthrate, the rural population was more than reproducing itself, and heavy migration to the cities was occurring. Up to 1750, most of the migration was to London; but after 1750, when the Industrial Revolution was under way, the rural migrants in the northern countries supplied much of the rapidly growing population of nearby industrial towns and cities.

A major effect of the agricultural improvements beginning early in the 17th century was the very rapid rise in population that then began in about 1740 and showed up as a continuous rapid rise thereafter. Early in the 18th century, farm output rose faster than did population, and it became obvious that with the extension of the improved methods and with a higher productivity, English agriculture had a capacity for supporting a much greater population. Thereafter, production of farms expanded rapidly with the rise of population and the shift to cities.

For a long time historians have debated the reasons for the sudden upturn in population trends in the middle of the 18th century. At first it was assumed to result from a decline in the death rate with improvements in medicine and sanitation. Such improvements, however, are not known to have occurred in the 18th century. Only in London, where death rates had been unusually high, partly due to the gin craze, was the rise in population prior to 1800 primarily due to lower death rates. In the rural counties, especially in northern England, the population surge was due primarily to a rise in birthrates. Presumably this involved earlier marriages. Marriage at younger ages might have resulted from the greater freedom of the peasant from the restraints of the feudal manor; also the improved economic conditions for food raising and employment made it easier to marry and support more children. Virtually everywhere in Europe population growth appeared to accompany the wider use of potatoes and the improvements in agriculture. In the late 17th and early 18th centuries, work opportunities appeared to improve, for complaints of labor scarcity were frequent and average wage rates were rising. Whatever the reasons, the rapid population increase beginning in the mid-18th century was important to the industrial expansion both for the increased labor supply provided and for the increased demand for industrial products.

THE TAKEOFF

The first nation's Industrial Revolution, therefore, came after a long period of preparation. Trade was well developed, national consumption levels were high, population was expanding, farm output was improving, a wide diversity of industries had been established, workers had developed handicraft skills, large mines and factories were in operation, and a great demand had been established for more products of industry. In terms of Rostow's analogy with an airplane takeoff into flight, the English economy had gathered momentum to a certain point and was ready for more rapid sustained growth.

Output Trends

The main reason for continuing to identify the late 18th century as the start of the Industrial Revolution is the upturn in rate of increase

4–2. British 18th-Century Growth

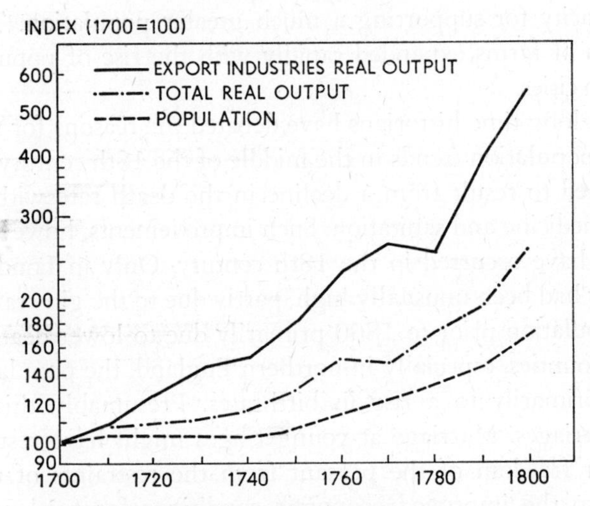

Note: The data plotted are decade averages.
Source: Phyllis Deane and W. A. Cole, *British Economic Growth, 1688–1959* (London: Cambridge University Press, 1962), p. 78, Table 19.

in output which occurred then and continued for over a century. The rate of increase in output was undoubtedly very rapid after 1790. Between 1790 and 1815, the Napoleonic Wars on the Continent undoubtedly provided a stimulus of demand for war materials and a period of rapid inflation. The American Revolutionary War, however, had interrupted an important colonial trade between 1775 and 1783. Except for this interruption, the start of the rapid increase in output might be dated near the middle of the century, when population began to rise rapidly.

Recent estimates of the total real output of Great Britain in the 18th century suggest that it rose very little up to 1740 but then more than doubled by 1800. These conclusions reflect separate estimates for all major segments of the economy. Over the century, agricultural output increased in value only by two fifths, or less than the population gain of more than 50 percent. Home industries, rents, and services probably gained about the same as population. Government and defense services were erratic, fluctuating widely with wars.

It was manufacture for export that provided consistently the most rapidly increasing segment of the total output of the national economy. The rate of increase in the output of export industries (involving both manufacturing and trading activities) was already rapid prior to 1740, but the ratio chart trend line becomes more steep between 1740 and 1770 and even more steep after 1780. Over the century manufacturing output as a whole more than quadrupled. (See 4–2.)

Three Clusters of Inventions

Simultaneously with the rapid rise of output in the 18th century, there was a quickening of technological improvements which made the expansion possible and gave it a cumulative impetus. Much of the Industrial Revolution has been identified with the rapid improvements in cotton textile manufacturing. Although cotton textile output was not large enough to influence total output trends much prior to 1780, by 1800 cotton textiles output had grown to about half of all English textiles and the new machinery had begun to be widely adopted. It was in the early 19th century that the English industrial expansion was strongly influenced by cotton textiles. However, the characteristic methods which have come to be identified with modern manufacturing were first applied extensively in textiles. It was the combination of three clusters of inventions that brought about this first application of modern manufacturing methods.

First, there were the inventions of machines to make standard consumer products on a large scale in the ***cotton textile*** industry. A series or cluster of inventions was involved. In 1733, John Kay invented the flying shuttle to speed up weaving. Weaving involved the interlacing of two parallel rows of threads while a third thread was passed back and forth between them at right angles, carried by a wooden shuttle. The shuttle had had to be thrown or pushed by hand, back and forth. The flying shuttle was knocked by a mallet or hammer released by a lever at the right moment. This so speeded up the work a weaver could do, that it soon became difficult to find enough spinners to keep up with the weaving. For spinning, John Wyatt and Lewis Paul invented, in 1738, a series of rollers which could give a loose strand of carded fiber a twist like that usually done with the fingers. Their spinning rollers did not work too well and frequently broke down; but in 1764, James Hargreaves invented an improved and practical version, the "spinning jenny," named for his wife. Instead of the one horizontal spindle on the home spinning wheel, he used several vertical spindles in a row so that a carriage moving back and forth could feed loose bands of cotton fiber from large spools while the spun fiber was wound on a bobbin. Together, the flying shuttle and spinning jenny were a great success. It soon became evident, however, that with the operations now mechanical, power could be applied and the number of units could be multiplied. In 1769, Richard Arkwright developed the water frame, that is, a spinning frame that could be driven by a waterwheel; and in 1779, Samuel Crompton invented the "mule," a cross between the roller and spindle method which produced stronger, finer threads. Then, in 1785, Edmund Cartwright invented a power-operated loom. These machines became widely adopted after 1790, and thereafter many improvements were made on the details of their operation.

With the sales of cotton textiles rapidly mounting, other improvements soon were added in the other stages of manufacture. Richard Arkwright made a carding machine in 1775 and then developed a crank and comb to turn out the carded fiber in a ribbon easily made into rovings. In 1785, chlorine was used to bleach cloth instead of just exposing it to the sun. In 1783, a cylindrical press was used for printing cloth. An especially important laborsaving invention for the separation of seed from fiber at the raw material stage was the cotton gin invented by an American, Eli Whitney, in 1794.

The second group of inventions was in ***metals and machine tools.*** The new textile machines were largely made of wood, but they required metal parts; and the power-driven machines required improved metals and accurate fittings. While the textile inventions produced a cheaper product for the consumers directly, the metal and machine tool industries helped bring about better machines in this industry and many others. In addition it affected directly those consumer products made of iron, such as nails, kitchenware, and firearms.

The major improvement in ironmaking came about with the development of coke. Long after coal was widely used as a fuel in many other industries, the iron industry still required the use of wood charcoal, which had become scarce and high priced in England. About 1709, Abraham Darby reduced coal to coke by burning off its gas and other impurities in an oven, much as wood is reduced to charcoal. In 1761, it was found that the coking fire could be made hotter by use of a blast of air from a piston air pump instead of a leather bellows. Coke quickly became important in England, although charcoal continued to be used for many decades in France and America where it was inexpensive.

Further improvements also were made in converting the pig iron into wrought iron, which is more malleable and less brittle. In 1784, Peter Onions and Henry Cort independently discovered "puddling," whereby pig iron was heated in a reverberatory furnace (out of direct contact with the fuel) and the molten mass was stirred (or puddled) to increase the burning-off of impurities. This reduced the amount of hammering needed to produce wrought iron.

Also, in the 1780's, the heavy labor of producing wrought iron was reduced by use of Watt's steam hammer and Henry Cort's rolling mill. Around 1750, Benjamin Huntsman improved the process of converting wrought iron into steel by heating it in a large crucible with a certain amount of ground glass in it.

Toward the end of the 18th century, better machine tools also were developed. In 1774, John Wilkinson made a drill for boring cannon. This led to the more general use of firearms with rifled bores, and it also led, just after 1800, to the making of accurate cylinders with horizontal and vertical boring machines. Henry Cort's rolling mill in 1783 also produced a low-cost boiler plate. In 1797, Henry Maudslay invented an all-metal lathe using a slide rest and accurate screw device. This facilitated accurate cutting and made possible such automatic devices as the screw-making machine. A nail-making machine was produced in 1790. John Wilkinson made the first iron bridge in 1779 and the first iron boat in 1787; he also made cast iron pipe.

The third key group of inventions was to provide the source of power to drive the machines—the ***steam engine*** and its improvements. The idea of steam was old. In the mid-16th century, Solomon de Caus showed that if a closed tank were filled with steam and then the tank cooled to condense the steam, it would produce a vacuum. Various efforts then were made to design a steam engine to pump water from mines. In 1708, Thomas Newcomen developed the first usable steam engine, although it was quite inefficient. It involved pushing a piston by steam pressure, then cooling the single chamber to condense the steam and pull the piston back with the vacuum. Alternate heating and cooling, however, was slow and inefficient in use of fuel. It could be used in coal mining because a cheap coal fuel was readily at hand. In 1765, James Watt, an instrument maker at the University of Glasgow, invented an improved two-chamber steam engine. A steam pressure chamber was kept hot, then by valves the vapor was let into the cooling chamber for condensing and creation of a vacuum. At first the piston was just pushed and pulled at either end; then, in 1782, a piston arm was attached to a rotating wheel and a rapid and efficient action was obtained. The improved engine was applied to textile machinery in the 1780's, but it did not immediately replace the waterwheels already in use. Its great advantage was in providing a new source of power not tied to falling water locations. It quickly was used for pumping water in mines, running air pumps for blast furnaces, operating great hammers, and as the propelling power for transportation. Robert Fulton's first steamboat was demonstrated in 1807 on the Hudson River, and in England, Robert Stephenson demonstrated the first railway steam engine in 1814.

The Modern Industrial Method

With these inventions and the rapid mechanization of the cotton textile industry, the Industrial era of man was launched. There has been some confusion, however, about just what the "revolution" was. It was a revolution in production methods, not in organization. There have been misleading references to this revolution in terms of the changeover from the put-out or cottage system of manufacture to a factory system. The factory system is supposed to involve the congregating of large numbers of supervised workers in one building. The factory, however, was not new in the 18th century. Even in ancient times large numbers of workers had worked under the same roof. In the 16th and 17th centuries, hundreds of workers might be employed in mines and various manufacturing industries requiring large heavy equipment—frequently called "mills" or "works." Even under the put-out system in textiles, some merchants were responsible for hiring hundreds of workers, and sometimes a considerable number worked on his looms in the same shop. The newly mechanized textile mills did bring many workers together in one "factory" in this particular industry; since textiles expanded rapidly to national prominence and utilized newly invented machines, there was a tendency for the public to notice the new factories at this time.

It is more appropriate to identify the industrial age introduced by the Industrial Revolution in terms of characteristics of the methods of modern industry. Therefore, we may define the ***modern industrial method*** of production as (*a*) the use of nonhuman power sources, (*b*) to drive machinery, (*c*) in the repetitive manufacture of large numbers of standard products, (*d*) by methods involving the division of labor in the production process. Cotton textiles, then, became the first major mass-produced consumer products industry. The invention of textile machines, improved metals and machine tools, and the steam engine combined to introduce this first modern industry.

Again, while labels may be useful, we need to keep in mind the gradual process by which this change came about. The three clusters of inventions were merely the climax of prior developments. Furthermore, the new improvements were not immediately and universally adopted. Steam power was widely adopted in cotton textiles only during the 1830's and 1840's. Machinery and power were much more slowly applied to woolen textiles. While a few large cotton textile firms had hundreds, even several thousand, employees, in the 1850's only about half of the textile workers were in cotton. The average woolen or worsted mill had about 45 workers. Furthermore, even in the mid-19th century, about half of the workers in woolen textiles worked outside of factories in cottages or small shops.

CONTRIBUTING CONDITIONS

The coincidence of several clusters of inventions and the rapid rise of total output in the last half of the 18th century in England does not necessarily tell the whole story. What comes before is not always the cause or the only cause of what follows. Some of the same types of conditions that brought about the earlier revolution in the 16th and 17th centuries again may have been present. In any event, it is important to learn from history what conditions influenced a trend, both favorably and unfavorably.

Markets and Transport

A large and expanding market demand was an underlying condition of great importance in the first nation's Industrial Revolution. England already was a nation with a large internal market and fairly prosperous population. After 1750, the rapid population increase brought a rising demand for clothing, household articles, and housing. But England also already had an active ocean trade with world markets. European and American population also was rapidly rising in the late 18th century; there was a very active demand for the mass-manufactured consumer goods of England. The total output estimates clearly show that exports were increasing more rapidly than any other segment of the economy. An important element in this rising export demand also was the shift in demand toward certain new products. There especially was a rapidly rising demand for the new and lighter cloths—not only cotton but also worsteds. Under initial restrictions on imports of calico, the British manufacturers had learned how to print cloth, had learned initially how to manufacture cottons in combination with linens, and had developed new machinery for mass production of cottons. The import restrictions on cotton were thrown off in 1774. In two and one-half decades, cotton production then rose to half of textile output and had become the largest single export product. At the same time there was a shift from woolens to worsteds. Due to the lightness, finer weave, and new patterns, worsteds became much the preferred fabric by European consumers.

The Napoleonic Wars also provided an important part of the demand stimulus. Shortly after the French Revolution in 1789, England joined other European countries in a war against France, in 1793. Austria and England did not sign the peace treaty in 1795 and continued the struggle against Napoleon. There was a brief peace between 1802 and 1805, then the wars resumed and continued until the final defeat of Napoleon at Waterloo in 1815. Thus, for over two decades, England was mobilized for war. Military service absorbed over 10 percent of the labor force. There were great demands for increased building of ships, dock facilities, and armaments. Since the British navy dominated the oceans, trade generally expanded; although France cut off some of the European ports. In addition to the stimulus of increased government purchases of manufactured goods, there was a general price inflation. Between 1790 and 1805, the general price level about doubled, while wage rates lagged behind. So, some manufacturers and merchants undoubtedly experienced inflation profits.

Improvements in transportation also played a major role in making mass production and sale to larger markets possible. At the end of the 18th century, England had about 46 percent of the Western world shipping tonnage, and the United States accounted for another one fourth. Its coastal harbors and rivers gave most parts of the country ready access to world markets. Furthermore, after 1760, a network of canals was built to extend the river navigation inland and interconnect them. James Brindley built the first major canal in 1761 to connect the Duke of Bridgewater's coal mines to Manchester; then he linked Liverpool with Manchester and built the Grank Trunk Canal linking the Midlands with North England. These and other canals, incidentally, were mostly built by joint-stock companies. Water transportation, of course, provides the cheapest form of movement of heavy bulk commodities, such as coal, iron, and bales of cotton. Iron rails also were used for horsedrawn railways in coal mines and between mines and the nearest waterways. The steam engine was not used until the 1830's.

Internal communications and distribution of lighter goods between cities and towns were improved by a period of rapid road building in the 1760's and 1770's. Two Scotsmen, Thomas Telford and John McAdam, developed the basic method of modern road building which eliminated the problems of deep mud and washouts that slowed down early wagon travel. This involved laying a base of rocks, covering them with smaller gravel, topping these with a smooth surface of clay or asphalt, and crowning the road top and digging gutters to provide drainage and prevent washouts. The main roads, or turnpikes, were built by private companies which were authorized by parliament to charge tolls in order to recoup their investment. Thus, considerable private capital was used to provide basic social facilities. Costs were greatly reduced and speed and safety increased in travel and the transport of goods. The reduced transport charges made goods less costly and easier to sell to more people, and the enlarged markets helped achieve the lower costs of larger and more specialized industry. Since early transportation costs often were a major part of the cost of final goods delivered to city markets, these transport improvements (and those to follow) may have been as important as the manufacturing inventions in making goods cheaper and expanding output.

Supply of Resources

The availability of productive resources was another condition important to England's Industrial Revolution. The invention of coke for use in making iron released England from one of its major natural resource limitations, the shortage of forests. At the same time it unlocked the technological door to using its great natural wealth of fuel resources in the form of coal. This permitted both a great expansion in ironmaking and the development of a new source of power in the steam engine, which required strong iron boilers and pistons. At the same time, another natural resource was unlocked with the improvement in agricultural methods. With the new products, methods of cultivation, and reorganized landholdings, it was possible to produce more food per acre and per farmer. Finally, the rapid expansion of the cotton textile industry was made possible by the access by ocean transport to expanding cotton supplies in America. While more cotton supplies might have been obtained from India, the costs might have risen rapidly if the American southern planters had not shifted rapidly to the new crop and opened up vast new lands in the interior Mississippi regions. Thus, whether by discovery or by invention, advantageous new and unlimited resource supplies became available that made possible rapid industrial expansion without steep cost increases.

The ***labor supply*** also increased rapidly. Part of this was due to the impact of improved agricultural methods on standards of living and population growth. Far from being pushed off the land by enclosures, the rural population was rapidly increasing in the 18th century in spite of rapid migration to the cities. The growing labor supply and its movement to the cities enabled industrial production to be rapidly expanded without running into the labor shortages that were complained of around 1700. The technology of the textile industry also permitted the use of more of the population in the work force, because the light nature of the work made it adapt well to labor by women and children. Of course, woolen textiles and the manufacture of clothing and many other handicraft products already employed a great number of family workers in the home, in small shops, or under the put-out system. But in contrast to coal mining or iron works where female and child labor was inefficient, the large textile mills could make use of these types of workers to expand output faster than the population growth. Again, as in the case of natural resources, industrial expansion could take place without straining the labor supply and running into steep increases in wage costs. Later, in the 1830's and 1840's, the rapid introduction of steam power in cotton textiles and extension of machinery into woolen textiles began to cause problems of technological unemployment. In the late 1840's, the Irish potato famine caused the influx of many more immigrants looking for work than could be quickly absorbed in industry. For a while, then, the labor supply was too plentiful.

Rapid expansion in the supply of the third productive factor, ***capital***—the accumulated resource—was especially vital to England's Industrial Revolution. While the new inventions enabled output to expand faster than labor supplies, capital, and raw materials might be expected to expand at least as fast as output. Expanding production requires expansion in "working capital," the funds that must be advanced to purchase materials and pay for labor services before the final goods are sold. A larger stock must be built up of raw materials inventories, goods in process, and final goods inventories being stored or shipped prior to sale. In addition, the new machine methods of production required more "fixed capital" in the form of buildings, machines, and tools. This meant an increased ratio of capital to labor and materials. Clearly, capital inputs had to increase faster than any other resources but not necessarily faster than output since technological changes could make new units of capital more productive.

England undoubtedly had a fairly high standard of well-being among the masses and a large and growing middle class with wealth. The Protestant ethics valued hard work, thrift, and the management of resources to accumulate more. Saving, however, usually was accompanied by investment in one's own property or business. In the 18th century, there was very little investment in stocks or bonds by many individuals, except in the case of the securities of the canal and turnpike companies and the bonds of the government. Falling interest rates for government long-term bonds did suggest that the available capital funds were becoming more plentiful; legal rates fell from over 8 percent in the early 17th century to about 3 percent in the mid-18th century.

The major source of business capital accumulation was profits. New manufacturing firms usually were started by one or two men already wealthy from other businesses. Then, the rapid growth of manufacturing firms depended upon their success in earning profits and reinvesting them in the business (instead of being withdrawn as consumable income by the owners). During a period of rapid price inflation, such as occurred during the Napoleonic Wars, some inflation profits rose from the rise in value of the inventories and goods in process before they were sold. Another source of inflation profits, at least for a temporary period during the Napoleonic Wars, was the lag in wage rates behind prices. With the major improvements in methods and machinery, however, the profits from reduced costs must have been large enough to account for most of the rapid accumulation of capital out of profits.

Enterprising Management

The story of the Industrial Revolution, however, would not be realistic without considering the role of the key individuals who decided and acted to bring it about—the new industrial managers. The leaders of the Industrial Revolution usually combined many roles in one person—an inventor, financier, organizer, supervisor, and salesman. The single proprietorship or partnership still was the chief form of business organization. So the owner (or owners) usually had to be the complete businessman or all-around manager. The most successful managers demonstrated outstanding characteristics that enabled them to see and take advantage of opportunities and to organize and expand great business firms. All of them were strongly motivated by a desire to make profits and accumulate wealth. They were especially alert to recognize new needs and opportunities, and they were willing to run great risks in investing their own capital and undertaking the responsibilities of making commitments and organizing the efforts of others in production. It is very appropriate, therefore, that they should be called by the French term ***entrepreneur;*** because daring and initiative are associated with this term.

It is important at this point to distinguish between the terms "invention" and "innovation," because there has been too much interpretation of the Industrial Revolution in terms of the former rather than the latter. To invent means to think up or imagine for the first time a new technical method, device, or process for doing something; but to innovate means to introduce something new into practical use. The new industrial leaders were not merely inventors, they were innovators. They were motivated to find and use new methods and products.

England at this time provided a very favorable intellectual environment for invention. The scientific age was relatively new and the philosophy of rationalism widely encouraged the idea that man could control and change his environment. Men were excited with the possibilities of discovering ideas of how to make material improvements in production. Since science was in its beginning stages, physicians and chemists were in close contact with businessmen, writers, and other educated persons. Even though knowledge was expanding rapidly, in those days the total stock of knowledge was small enough that an intelligent layman could be familiar with developments in a wide variety of fields. Many businessmen were on the list of the Fellows of the Royal Society, which was devoted to scientific studies and discussions. Historians also have noted that many of the new industrial leaders were members of minority religious sects—such as Quakers, Methodists, and Scottish Presbyterians. This has been widely interpreted as meaning they were nonconforming individualists. Probably more relevant than their dissenting views, however, was their education, for these religious minorities constituted the better educated section of the middle class. The Scottish system of primary education and the Scottish universities were the most advanced in the world at this time. Other dissenting groups also emphasized education and established academies in England. Actually, while the minorities were heavily represented, the inventors and innovating industrialists came from all religions, social classes, and parts of the country.

More important, probably, than technical knowledge was the keen sense of market opportunity possessed by English entrepreneurs. It should not be forgotten that cotton textiles and woolen worsteds were much in demand and there was a great opportunity for those who found ways to produce them cheaply. There also was keen competition with manufacturers in other countries in selling to European consumers. Much of the competition was on a quality basis—a lighter, stronger cloth with brighter dyes and more attractive patterns. The same was true of makers of rugs and china; not nearly as much expansion in sales resulted simply from a lower price as resulted from a new or better product at the same or lower price. The development of new products or designs often required close coordination of production with sales strategy; many merchants frequently made their success by going into business of manufacturing a product they saw was needed. Often it took a newcomer to the industry to see the opportunity of new machines and of reorganizing the various crafts and stages of production into a large integrated production unit. A sure sense of the size and demands of the market provided the confidence for more daring in organizing large-scale production.

EFFECTS AND CRITICISM

The industrial era ushered in during the late 18th century in England brought with it truly revolutionary changes in productive capabilities and living standards. Per capita output in England today is about 10 times as high as it was in the 17th century. Poor countries still at that 17th-century level today are anxious to achieve similar progress for themselves.

Surprisingly, the first experience with industrialization commonly is regarded with disapproval as a bad example of how to bring about the revolution. The traditional interpretation of historians, which is reflected in much of our literature, was that the initial progress was not shared by the workers. It long has been assumed that the workers suffered a worsening of their living conditions.

In the more lurid versions, a "story" was told of contented peasants being dispossessed of their lands, herded into slums devised to profit from their misery, driven at the treadmill pace of machinery by slave-master factory owners, and paid a bare subsistence wage. The dragon of the story was pictured as a brutal capitalist running rampant in a free market. The white knight who rescues the workers comes in the form of social reform legislation and interference by government in the market. More recent studies and new information have caused historians to revise this interpretation. While it long has been recognized that workers have been sharing in society's general progress and now have unparalleled living standards, there now appear to have been no initial "bad years" which were removed by social reform. The workers' share in progress appears to have been rather substantial from the beginning of the Industrial Revolution.

Rural migrants came from conditions that by today's standards were impoverished. They entered an urban-industrial environment in which life was about as brutal as it had been on the farm. Child and female labor was not an innovation of the Industrial Revolution. Women and children had been farm workers before they became industrial laborers.

The Industrial Revolution raised the productivity of workers in agriculture, mining, and manufacturing. And, contrary to the traditional interpretation, the benefits of higher productivity were shared by workers in general. There were of course cases in which workers failed to make the necessary adjustments required by a transition from rural to urban life. And other workers chose to migrate just as a depression was producing widespread unemployment in the cities. But for the great mass of workers the Industrial Revolution meant a rise in living standards. The contrary interpretation by earlier historians appears to have arisen out of the peculiar problems and political conditions in England during the first half of the 19th century, after the Industrial Revolution was well under way. These problems and conditions will be discussed in this section.

Rise in Living Standards

Recent estimates of population trends and total output of all segments of the economy provide a basis for measuring the rise in general living standards in 18th-century England. It seems clear that in spite of the remarkably rapid rise in population after the mid-century, agricultural output had kept pace until the Napoleonic Wars. Export industries had expanded much more rapidly and had brought about a faster rise in total output than in population. Output per person, therefore, rose about 60 percent during the 18th century. Fully half of this gain occurred in the last two decades of the century, which reflects the accelerating growth rate. The rate of growth continued to increase in the early 19th century, so that per capita income doubled between 1800 and 1850; it doubled again by 1900. (See 4–3.)

Now the faster rise in total output than in population does not necessarily mean that the products consumed by workers increased faster than their numbers. Yet in view of the rapid total output rise, it would be surprising if the workers did not experience some gain. The improvements in crops and rise in population suggest that the bulk of the farm workers had improved consumption standards. In northern England the migration of rural population switched from a movement toward London to a movement toward the new industrial cities after mid-century. This probably reflects an attraction of employment opportunities that the workers regarded as superior. Furthermore, the expanding textile industries provided work opportunities for women and children that added to total family income.

Some data are available that permit construction of indexes of changes in prices and in wage rates of employed workers. While there

4–3. British Real Per Capita Output, 1700–1830

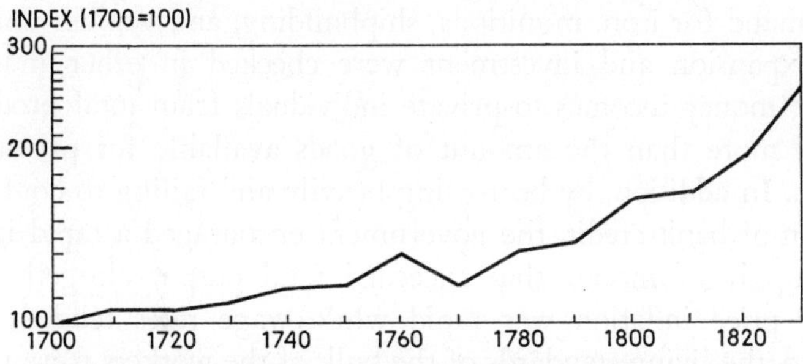

Source: Phyllis Deane and W. A. Cole, *British Economic Growth, 1688–1959* (London: Cambridge University Press, 1962), Tables 19 and 72, pp. 78, 282.

are serious limitations in the available figures, they indicate the nature of broad trends. Between 1700 and 1760, both prices and money wages were fairly stable, and there was no clear or substantial change in real wages, i.e., wages after accounting for price-level changes. Between 1760 and 1790, both prices and money wages rose, but important differences in trends occurred in different regions of the country. In London, wage rates apparently rose less than prices; early historians accepted this as evidence of the depressing effect on real wages of the Industrial Revolution. However, in the northern parishes where the new industrial cities were growing, wage rates rose faster than prices. It is only because the northern employment was not yet as large as the southern that the overall average real wages may have declined slightly. (See appendix to this chapter on "Real Income.")

During the Napoleonic Wars (1793–1815), temporary inflation conditions distorted the trends. It is clear that from 1790 to 1810, prices rose faster than wage rates—about doubling, while wage rates increased about three fourths. So real wages fell early in the war. In the later years of the war and afterwards, prices also fell faster than wage rates. So, in 1815 real wages had risen to their prewar level, and they continued to rise thereafter. While the price trend continued downward to 1850, wage rates stabilized after 1830. The rise in real wages was about 25 percent from 1800 to 1825, and about 40 percent from 1825 to 1850. For the next hundred years the rise in real wages continued to be rapid.

Problems from Other Sources

The Industrial Revolution obviously was not responsible for the Napoleonic Wars nor the problems that accompanied them. As in any war, much of the resources of the nation was diverted from private consumption and construction to national defense. While this created more demand for iron, munitions, shipbuilding, and woolen uniforms, output expansion and investment were checked in other industries. Thus, the money incomes to private individuals from total production increased more than the amount of goods available for private consumption. In addition, by borrowing heavily and failing to control the expansion of bank credit, the government encouraged a rapid increase in the supply of money that exceeded total output altogether. The resulting price inflation was rapid while wage rates tended to rise slowly; so, the living standards of the bulk of the workers were reduced while profit margins increased.

While population continued to increase and move to cities, building was restricted during the wartime. The import of timber from the Baltic was reduced, and the cost of other construction, as well as labor, increased. During the war interest rates also rose rapidly; and since a major part of rent consists of interest on the invested capital (as well as its amortization), house rents rose rapidly. Since the rural workers moving to cities earned low wages and could afford only very small rents, the dwellings had to be small and cheaply constructed. It was not a lack of government regulation of the private builders that made many of the row houses dark and drab; rather it was largely those local government regulations which determined the type of construction. The regulations were extensive and aimed to prevent fires rather than to provide comfort and sanitation. High taxes on windows and on bricks and tile also tended to discourage ample light and drainage.

The wealthy landlords were still in control of parliament in the early 19th century, and it was against their economic and political powers and policies that a worker protest movement developed. At the beginning of the wars, bad harvests added to monetary inflation, and the wheat price rose more than double by 1795. The Speenhamland system of poor relief enacted that year involved a form of food subsidies and poor relief. In the relative prosperity of 1798–99, the farmers and the workers attempted to maintain their real wages against price increases by various organized actions, sometimes involving local bread riots as well as worker strikes. Fears of the example of the French Revolution led government officials to repressive measures, including the Combination Acts of 1799 and 1800. Much class animosity was stirred up by the repeal of the income tax after the war.

The Corn Law of 1815 also attempted to preserve for the landowners their wartime rents and grain prices by forbidding the milling of imported grain whenever the price fell below a specified minimum. Nothing was done, on the other hand, to encourage more imports when harvests were bad and grain prices soared. During the postwar years, therefore, there was much complaint about the power of the wealthy landlords in parliament, and agitation for extension of the vote. It was only after the French July Revolution in 1830 that the Reform Bill of 1832 finally was passed. Generally, the merchants and manufacturers favored more liberal policies, politically and economically. The repeal of the Combination Acts in 1824 and the tariff reforms of the 1820's both were results of a trend toward laissez-faire policies.

The protests and riots of workers in the postwar period also reflected the unemployment of workers outside of the new textile factories, especially during periods of depression. Just as the guilds had protested against the movement of the wool industry to rural areas in the 16th century, and the woolen workers had violently protested the introduction of imported cotton goods in the early 18th century, the traditional handcraft workers in the textile industries protested their displacement by the new power-operated machines in factories during the first half of the 19th century. The protests against landlords and the riots about food prices were mixed with protests against machines. These protests usually became violent during depressions when unemployment was high. In the depressions of 1811 and 1816 the Luddites destroyed stocking frame machines in the Midlands. In 1817 and 1819, hungry and jobless workers marched and demanded reforms, but were met with repressive actions by a frightened government. Many handloom weavers also were active in the Chartist movement, with its uprisings in 1839, 1842, and 1848.

Unemployment conditions also were made worse by the immigration of Irish workers in the postwar period. Ireland had experienced the same rapid population increase as England but without England's expansion of industrial job opportunities. The potato initially had enabled a much larger rural population to exist on small patches of land in Ireland, but overpopulation already was causing considerable migration to England in the 1820's and 1830's. The Irish Potato Famine in 1841 and 1845–47 brought a much larger influx of immigrants. These immigrants began to compete for factory jobs with the women and children who had previously been employed. The existence of unemployed male workers provided a strong popular support for the factory reform legislation that restricted employment of women and children.

Reform Movement

It was in the midst of these postwar problems in England that a social reform movement took shape among middle-class intellectuals and reached a climax in the factory legislation of the 1840's. In addition to the economic problems, there were certain political and intellectual forces that helped to shape the movement.

The main political power struggle was between the wealthy agricultural landowners and the new middle class of merchants and manufacturers. The latter worked for less government restrictions and more free trade; and the Corn Laws were finally repealed in 1848. The landowners were hostile to new manufacturing industry and sought every means to discredit the new leaders of industry. The parliamentary commissions set up during the 1830's and 1840's to investigate conditions in the factories and new industrial cities frequently were dominated by Conservative party members, and their written record of hearings frequently reveals a very biased approach to investigation. It is from the written record of these commissions that historians and other writers later were to draw most of their conclusions about the effects of the Industrial Revolution.

Certain social attitudes also colored the views of middle-class reformers and intellectuals of the times. On the one hand, there was a strong Puritan attitude of disapproval toward new forms of consumption. Pleasure-seeking and the consumption of luxuries were regarded as sinful. Not only was there opposition to drinking of alcoholic beverages and the use of tobacco, but even tea drinking and the purchase of more colorful clothing were regarded as both wasteful and sinful. Accordingly, even the benefits of industrial employment in the form of increased income for consumption were regarded as an evil by some reformers, for this led to sinful consumption. On the other hand, there was a romantic philosophy about rural living and about the ideal conditions of "natural" human behavior before it was corrupted by social customs. Comfortable middle-class intellectuals living their lives in big cities, especially London, philosophized about the delights of carefree life in rural villages and the bountifulness of Nature before it was spoiled by mines, smokestacks, and slum dwellings. These were popular ideas when the leaders of London society were wealthy absentee landlords who occasionally visited their pleasant manor estates. Everything about lower class living conditions in the cities and in the factories looked especially horrible compared to this romantic rural ideal.

On top of this, methods of social study were still weak. There was an unrealistic crudeness about the observation and analysis of economic and social conditions by the early intellectual reformers and early historians. A few events and outstanding cases were quickly taken to represent general conditions. There was none of the sophistication about statistical averages, nor care in collecting complete information which has come to characterize modern social studies. Thus, the few large cotton textile factories were regarded as typical of British manufacturing at a time when the great bulk of the workers was still in small shops and cottage industries. Legislation to control working hours and conditions for women and children tended to single out the large cotton textile factories ignoring the prevalence of similar hours and conditions in the small plants, in the cottages, and in domestic service of all kinds.

Furthermore, the spotlight was thrown on conditions at one point in time, either with no consideration of prior conditions or with a presumption that prior conditions must have been better. Many of the current reformers in London had limited acquaintance with the conditions in the industrial northern cities and were shocked by rather brief visits or accepted lurid stories or testimony of others. In later times, historians and writers already accustomed to much improved living standards brought about by rapid industrial and social progress read descriptive accounts of early 19th-century conditions with great horror and shock. Only in recent times have studies of conditions in the 17th and 18th centuries in London put the housing and health conditions in the new industrial cities in a different perspective. Rapid urbanization itself was a problem that society has only gradually learned to cope with. It was not the factory that determined the social practices of urban life, although it did speed up urban growth.

In the long sweep of history, the remarkable thing about the reform movement was that it was the first such movement in history. It occurred first during the Industrial Revolution not because living conditions were extremely bad, but because there was rapid improvement. In those times, as in underdeveloped countries today, there were rising aspirations as to what living conditions could be like for the masses, and there was a great impatience to achieve new dreams immediately. The development of scientific knowledge spread the idea that the natural environment of man conformed to rational principles which could be discovered and used to improve human conditions. Together with the spread of belief in human dignity and rights, these ideas led to attempts to improve social conditions as well as natural conditions. The Industrial Revolution brought about rapid improvement of living conditions and gave rise to optimism that better conditions were possible for all men, not just the elite ruling classes.

The reform movement also was essentially a self-criticism by the new middle classes. In the long struggle against royalty and landowning nobility, the merchant frequently had been allied with the common people; and the ideas of individual liberty and democratic representation could hardly be reserved for the new middle classes. After a long struggle against mercantilist restrictions of government using the new ideas of laissez-faire as his weapons, the cotton manufacturer can hardly be blamed for feeling surprised and unfairly discriminated against by new government regulations singling out the large factory. Some factory owners undoubtedly spoke out expressing an ages-old attitude of indifference toward the welfare of the masses. The reformers, however, reflected the social conscience of the new middle class. Some of the large factory owners, such as Robert Owen and Sir Robert Peel, themselves were in the forefront of reform experiments and advocates of the factory legislation.

The reform movement was above all based upon the false premise that a redistribution of the annual flow of wealth either through regulatory legislation or more radical means would raise the lower classes out of their shocking misery. In fact, national income in Britain, the most materially advanced nation, was not large enough to have enabled bringing about this end. What England and other nations needed was a continuation of growth so that all might enjoy higher levels of living or so that redistribution policies would have some chance for success.

The Myth of Exploitation

The reform movement also reflected a crisis in the intellectual philosophy of the times. The popular intellectual philosophy involved a combination of romanticism—about human innocence and harmony in a natural primitive environment uncorrupted by social customs—and optimism—about human perfectibility and progress through reform.

Both romanticism and optimism received a jolt from the events and conditions at the end of the 18th century. The rapid rise in population through Europe during the last half of this century created overwhelming problems of overpopulation and urban crowding. The violence and chaos of the French Revolution and its Napoleonic aftermath created doubts about political democracy as a sure means to greater welfare.

One strand of rational thinking became more pessimistic or conservative about what could be accomplished by governmental reforms. Thomas Malthus reasoned that improved economic conditions would reduce death rates and encourage early marriage and high birthrates; so population was bound to outrun improvements in production and keep the masses at a subsistence level. David Ricardo could not see any inevitable harmony in the economic interests of different classes; because as population and capital expanded, land became more scarce, and rising rents stole the benefits of progress. So, at the very time that the laissez-faire ideas of Adam Smith were beginning to influence government policy, the economist began to express doubts. Economics became known as the "dismal science." It was argued that efforts of workers to improve their wages would only increase the population and reduce the accumulation of capital needed to employ them, thus lowering worker incomes to subsistence again.

Another strand of rational thinking became even more optimistic or utopian about the possibilities for improvement of human welfare through government reforms. Unrealistic optimism, however, requires some "devil theory" to explain away what holds back progress. The devil was identified by a German refugee, Karl Marx, as the "capitalist." After the French Revolution of February, 1848, which stirred a series of revolts in Germany, Italy, and smaller European countries, Marx and Friedrich Engels issued their *Communist Manifesto* urging the workers of the world to throw off their chains. It is ironic that this appeal should have been directed to the new industrial workers: the industrial changes were only beginning to come to Europe, and the middle classes there were finally overthrowing the autocratic powers of royalty backed by landowning nobility. It was further ironic that England, the most advanced European nation in living standards and political freedom at that time, should be used as their prime example of the oppression of workers. Drawing upon the writings of reformers, economists, and parliamentary commissions of the 1840's, Engels wrote on *The Condition of the Working Classes in England in 1844,* and Marx wrote *Das Kapital.*

There were other utopian and socialist writers, but Karl Marx turned the "story" of worker oppression in the Industrial Revolution into a theory of inevitable worker exploitation by capitalist factory owners for all times. While we cannot presume to give a complete explanation and critique of Marxian economics, we can briefly summarize his theory so that the reader can get at least a preliminary feel for the nature of Marx. In what follows note that Marx presents an appealing package of ideas which have a lustre for poor people in spite of the refutation of those ideas that history may have delivered. This thumbnail sketch of Marx's thought makes it easy to see why many underdeveloped nations are Marxian today.

Marx reasoned as follows: labor alone was productive; labor produced a surplus above its subsistence needs; the owner of capital tools had the power to expropriate this surplus as profits; reinvestment of profits in more machinery displaced the worker; competition among the "army" of unemployed workers bid down the wages to a subsistence level; capital accumulation made a few more and more wealthy; a struggle for survival among capitalists reduced their ranks to a few great monopolists; a need for expansion of markets led to imperialist seizure of colonies; and ultimately the masses of workers would revolt and establish a utopia on Earth involving no private property and no government. This oversimplified economic theory borrowed many existing ideas and wove them into a logical whole that had an appealing neatness to many minds. It seemed to explain everything, and it had a religious quality of enlisting converts to a social cause (revolt) that would inevitably end in utopia.

The theories of Marx, of course, had a number of logical flaws. One was in failing to see that consumer preferences determine the value of products, and not just the "cost" of production. Another was the failure to attribute to all productive resources—natural, human, and accumulated—their separate contributions to production. Still another was the failure to see the social benefits in the role of risk-taking enterprise and efficient management of resources in achieving greater production.

Perhaps his gravest logical error was in assuming that all invention and mechanization reduced the employment of labor. Now, while modern industry sometimes has used more capital-intensive methods—that is, requiring more capital per unit of output and not just larger sized machines and bigger factories—the savings in labor costs usually have been so great as to reduce total costs. The attraction of greater profits per capital investment leads to rapid expansion of total output and the hiring of more labor. Nevertheless, all inventions have not been simply laborsaving and capital-using; a great part of the technological advance in modern times has involved productivity gains for all resources. Much of invention has been capital-saving and material-saving, as well as laborsaving. In either case, reduction in total resource costs creates a technological surplus which can be reinvested to expand production without necessarily reducing labor or wages. It is the failure to see any other possibility of growth, except by accumulating profits at the expense of lower wages, that has led many people to accept the "labor exploitation" theory of capitalistic industrial growth.

The greatest disproof of Marxism, however, has been the historical contradiction of his predictions. Wages have not fallen. The poor have not gotten poorer. The wealthy have not gotten fewer. Capitalism has not broken down from its own growth and resulted in revolution in the countries where it has existed the longest and grown the most.

APPENDIX TO CHAPTER 4 ON REAL INCOME

"Real" is an innocent-looking little word that economists have a habit of inserting in their texts, but it has a special technical meaning. It is used because of the difficulties caused by changes in the general level of prices. A general increase in prices of most goods reduces the purchasing power of the dollars of income people receive. That is to say, price inflation reduces the value of money, and price deflation increases the value of money. Accordingly, if we wish to measure an increase in production and income over a period of history in which we know most prices have been rising, we must realize that the increased money income received will not be all "real" because rising prices will have diluted the purchasing power of the increase in income. By the term "real income," then, economists mean the ***quantity of purchasing power that would have been received if prices generally had not changed.*** The term is used to compare changes in income at the same prices.

To compare real incomes at two different periods, we first need a composite index of general prices for the two periods. Using the hypothetical illustration from the appendix to Chapter 3, let us suppose that it represents a composite price index not just of wheat and rum, but of all goods produced. Starting with an index of 100 in the base year, 1750, the composite price index rose to 117 in 1760. Let us suppose it also rose to 125 in 1770. Now, let us assume that we have data on the wages paid all employed workers in the colonies, and that we can say the average wage was $6 per week in 1750. Suppose the average increased by $0.75 in each of the two decades. What happened to labor's "real" income, or real wage? Did it increase at all? Did it increase by the same amount each decade?

To find out what happened to any series of money income figures (the amounts currently received in money terms), simply *divide by the indexes of composite prices* for the same years, and then multiply by 100 to move the decimal. In the illustration following, the money wages divided by the price index and multiplied by 100 equals the real wages. The real wages fell from 1750 to 1760, but increased from 1760 to 1770. This is because the decade-to-decade percentage increase was greater for prices in the first decade, but greater for wages in the second decade. In this example, the changes in the two periods were canceling, so real wages in 1770 ended at the same level as in 1750.

Year	*Money Wages* ÷	*Price Index* × 100=	*Real Wages*
1750	$6.00	100	$6.00
1760	6.75	117	5.71
1770	7.50	125	6.00

Interpretation of any real income series is complicated by the possibilities of error either in the income figures or in the price index. It should be kept in mind that either set of figures may have errors of ***inclusiveness*** and of ***weighting.*** Some of the early estimates of changes in real wages during the Industrial Revolution were based on existing data on wage rates of construction workers in London and on the prices paid by certain institutions for selected foods. Obviously this did not measure wages received by all types of workers, nor did it measure the prices of all goods consumed by workers. The wage series, incidentally, is not an income series. It could tell only what the rate of pay was for one worker working full time. It would not tell how regularly the worker worked nor how much other members of the family worked. The weighting of a price index also would assume that the types and proportions of goods consumed were constant.

The early historians' interpretations of the effects of the Industrial Revolution were based heavily upon poor data. Recent studies use much more comprehensive data. While some of the weaknesses of data and indexes still remain to throw some doubt on the accuracy of estimates of real wage trends, the preponderance of evidence shows that real income of the bulk of working people must have risen. Production rose faster than population; the bulk of the production was in goods consumed by the masses; the types and qualities of consumer goods improved; health improved (death rates fell); more family members worked as more women and children were employed; and the migration of rural population was predominantly toward the new industrial cities rather than toward London.

STUDY QUESTIONS

1. What was "The Industrial Revolution?" Why may the term be misleading?
2. What conditions in England prepared for the Industrial Revolution occurring there first? What advantages did England have? What problems provided a special stimulus? What agricultural improvements were under way?
3. As a result of the Industrial Revolution, in what periods of time and in what industries did production rise most rapidly? As an immediate cause, what clusters of inventions first introduced the modern industrial method of production, and how were they related?
4. How did improvements in transportation and expansion in markets contribute to the rapid rise in output? How did expansion in the three basic types of resources facilitate production expansion?
5. What kind of men brought about the Industrial Revolution? Compare the roles played by the inventor and by the entrepreneur.
6. What was the effect of the Industrial Revolution upon average incomes in England? What reason is there to believe that from the beginning workers shared in its benefits?
7. What other forces brought economic hardships during this period? What other political struggles and political reform movements occurred? What social attitudes colored interpretations of events at the time?
8. What was the difference between pessimistic and optimistic thinking about the future progress of man that followed the French Revolution and Napoleonic Wars? What has been the greatest disproof of Marxist theory of capitalist exploitation of workers?

PART II

Start of National Growth: 1783–1860

Chapter 5 EXPANDING TRADE

Political independence did not bring immediate economic independence for the United States, nor could economic independence have brought immediate progress in living standards. The American economy remained predominantly agricultural and closely tied to the European market. The chief commercial crops still had to be sold abroad, and most manufactured goods still had to be imported. Not only was the existing high level of per capita income dependent upon specialized production for trade, but also the prospects for raising per capita income in the next half century were closely tied to the fortunes of trade. There would not have been any advantage in seeking to make the United States immediately self-sufficient.

Not only was the American economy not ready to become a modern industrialized economy at the end of the Revolutionary War, 1783; at least half a century was to pass before it became ready for rapid industrialization. The new nation started with a relatively high income consumer market, an active commercial class, and political institutions favorable to business enterprise. Ample resources for manufacturing were readily available on the eastern edge of the North American continent, and vast resources awaited discovery inland. Yet natural resources were not enough. They had to be combined with an adequate supply of labor and capital, and new knowledge on how to combine them was needed. The Industrial Revolution in England already was revealing an advanced technology, and England's example was showing the way to national power and high living standards. However, the United States did not yet have the economic organization and management needed to launch its own Industrial Revolution.

The early development of the American economy involved a long period of extensive growth that led up to a brief period of rapidly accelerating per capita growth just prior to the Civil War. This chapter and the next two chapters deal with the period of history between the

Revolution and the Civil War, 1783 to 1860. While the rapid rise of modern industry is associated with the rapid growth beginning just prior to the Civil War, the establishment of industry came about slowly at first. The extra expansion and prosperity of the Nation depended largely upon major developments in trade, agriculture, and transportation, and each of these developments contributed to the later rapid acceleration in national growth.

While all developments were interrelated, separate chapters will be needed to give adequate attention to the sequence of events in different parts of the economy. This chapter begins by presenting overall trends of the whole economy during the entire period. Then, the influence of foreign trade on national growth will be considered during the early and later years of this period.

OVERALL TRENDS

Rapid economic expansion was the dominant characteristic of nearly everything about the American economy in the first half of the 19th century. There was a rapid rise in all of the resource inputs—additions were made to the territory and natural resources, population continued to double every generation, and wealth in the form of capital goods of all sorts accumulated at a rapid pace. It is no wonder, then, that a rapid rise also occurred in estimated national income. What we shall be interested in determining is when and how growth got under way. Estimates for certain data for the total economy give us both perspective and clues as to how the economic organization of the economy developed to bring about this growth.

Westward Movement

The peace treaty with England established the claim of the United States to all of the western territory between the Appalachian Mountains and the Mississippi River from the Great Lakes to Florida. With this initial doubling of land area, successive additions to territory were to triple that area again by the middle of the 19th century. This wide band of territory stretching across a continent from coast to coast was to provide a rich potential in natural resources. But natural resources do not contribute to production until people gain access to them and bring them into use. The frontier line (or westernmost boundary of settled areas), therefore, provides a better indication of the expanded use of land in national production. In 1800, the frontier line hardly extended beyond the western slopes of the Appalachian Mountains except in the central areas of Kentucky and Tennessee. By 1860, it extended beyond the Mississippi, and isolated settled areas had developed on the West Coast.

The pattern of the initial spread of western settlement was shaped by both geographic and human barriers. In the beginning, hostility by Indians was encouraged by the British in the Great Lakes area and by the Spanish in the regions near Florida. Early pioneers, therefore, moved over the Appalachian Mountains into the central regions. Some moved through the Cumberland Gap to settle along the Ohio River near Louisville and along the Cumberland River at Nashville. Others moved across near the Maryland-Pennsylvania border and settled in the Pittsburgh area. These early pioneers depended upon river transportation down the Mississippi River to New Orleans in order to get their products out to world markets. For a few years the Spanish attempted to restrict the use of this port. Then, in 1803, shortly after the French had acquired certain Spanish colonies, the United States was able to negotiate a purchase of Louisiana; and with this purchase came a vast territory stretching to the north and west of the Mississippi. The War of 1812 finally removed the Indian hostilities in the Great Lakes region. Shortly thereafter military action also forced Spain to concede the Florida territories.

With these barriers removed, rapid settlement occurred in both the Gulf states and in the Great Lakes states. The first surge of rapid settlement occurred immediately after the War of 1812, between 1815 and 1819. Another rapid surge of settlement occurred early in the 1830's. With the opening up of the Erie Canal in 1825 and with high wheat prices in the East, large numbers of settlers rushed to open up a vast grain farming area near the Great Lakes. At the same time, high cotton prices caused rapid expansion of the cotton plantations in the Gulf states.

The final phase of territorial additions began with the pushing of a few pioneering settlers into foreign or disputed territories in the West. Some Americans, who had opened up cotton farms and cattle ranches in Texas, fought for their freedom from Mexico in 1836 and sought admission as a state in 1845. The northern boundary of American-claimed Oregon territory was settled by treaty with the British in 1846. In the same year a war was waged with Mexico because of disputes over the southern border and our desire for territories in the Southwest. The peace settlement in 1848 gave California to the United States just before gold was discovered there. By 1860, however, only a few isolated settled areas existed in the Far West. The frontier line of the main settled regions was still on the edge of the plains just west of the Mississippi River. (See 5–1.)

Throughout this westward movement, government policy on land sales, as well as the relative abundance of land, made it increasingly easy for small farmers to acquire ownership of land. Some of the last vestiges of large feudal landholdings was ended by seizure of lands of loyalists during the Revolution. Then, when the original states gave up their conflicting claims to western lands, the federal government assumed ownership of new territories and established a uniform policy for sale of lands to individuals. The Land Ordinance of 1785 had required

5–1. Expanding Land Area

surveying of land in the Northwest Territory into rectangular townships of 36 sections of 1 square mile each. As we have noted, a minimum of 640 acres—one section—had to be purchased at an auction price of not less than $1 an acre. The Land Act of 1796 extended this system to all new territories, with the minimum price raised to $2 and with a year's time allowed for payment.

Since it was difficult for small farmers to raise this much money, political pressures gradually reduced the initial cash requirement. In 1800, minimum acreage was reduced to 320 acres, and half of the payment was to be in cash and the remainder in four years. Since the farmers frequently failed to make later payments, in 1820 full initial payment was required, but the minimums were reduced to 80 acres at

$1.25 each acre. In 1832 the minimum size was cut to 40 acres; so a farmer could buy a farm with as little as $50 in cash.

Part of the pressure for easier purchase was due to the widespread practice of early pioneer settling on land before it had been surveyed. While illegal, it was hard to prevent. The Pre-emption Act of 1841 finally gave squatters first right to purchase a quarter section of land they had occupied. The Graduation Act of 1854 also provided for gradual lowering of the price of any land that long remained unsold. During the 1850's political agitation increased for making land free for small farmers.

Finally, the Homestead Act of 1862 provided 160 acres for a nominal fee to any adult citizen who would live on it and cultivate it for five years. Or, he might purchase it immediately at $1.25 an acre. Title to such lands, of course, frequently was purchased later by speculators or large farmers.

Population and Production

In spite of the rapid extension of territory, population grew even faster. And considering the fact that most of the territory was far in the west and included much uninhabitable space, the history of America's westward movement was also a history of increasing population density. In spite of vast additions to territory, the United States increased its density of population per square mile from 4.5 in 1790 to 10.6 in 1860.

Until 1860, the westward movement consisted mostly of the increased settlement of the central Mississippi basin region of the continent. The proportion of the population living west of the Atlantic coastal states rose from 4.2 percent in 1790 to 50.4 percent in 1860. Very few people, however, were beyond the frontier line just west of the Mississippi. Furthermore, in spite of the westward movement to settle vast new farming regions, the percentage of the population living in cities increased in every decade except one (1810–20). American economic development from the beginning has been as much characterized by the "great urban movement" as by the "great westward movement." (See 5–2.)

Given plentiful natural resources, American economic expansion and growth depended upon the increase in human and accumulated resources. Economic expansion, of course, could take place solely through a westward movement which added more and more small farms with the same ratios of labor and capital per acre as on the previous farms. More intense settlement, however, meant an increase in

5–2. Population Settlement Trends

Year	Land Area (million square miles)	Population (millions)	Density Persons per square mile	Percent of Population in: Non-Atlantic States	Urban Areas
1790	0.86	3.93	4.5	4.3%	5.1%
1800	0.86	5.31	6.1	8.7	6.1
1810	1.68	7.24	4.3	16.3	7.3
1820	1.75	9.64	5.6	24.4	7.2
1830	1.75	12.87	7.4	29.9	8.7
1840	1.75	17.07	9.8	38.7	10.8
1850	2.94	23.19	7.9	43.9	15.2
1860	2.97	31.44	10.6	50.4	19.7

Source: U.S. Department of Commerce, *Historical Statistics of the United States* (Washington, D.C.: U.S. Government Printing Office, 1960).

the ratios of labor and capital per acre. Higher density and urbanization also reflected a development process by which greater specialization and division of labor would occur. The result was economic growth—what we described earlier as a rise in production per worker (productivity) and a rise in income per person (living standards).

Production, therefore, soon increased faster than population. It is not surprising in an expanding economy to see that virtually every record or measure of economic activity of any sort is rising. The important thing to note is the products that increase faster than population. With population in the United States increasing about one third every decade, production needed to grow at least this fast just to provide for more people at the same average consumption levels.

Unfortunately, data on many kinds of production were not very fully recorded during the first few decades of the 19th century; and the composite price indexes available for valuing and adding together total production are very crude. However, national income estimates for the decennial census years have been made by R. F. Martin for as far back as 1800. When adjusted for average changes in prices, these reflect real income, income of constant purchasing power, and thus are an approximate measure of total production. These estimates of total real income, then, may be compared to the trend of increase in total population. (See 5–3.)

Apparently, total real income did not begin to rise faster than American population until after the first quarter of the 19th century. At least this is all we can be very sure of; reliable and fairly complete data do not start until about 1840. Martin has estimated that real income grew more slowly than population prior to 1830 so that the ratio of real income per capita fell. Other scholars, however, recently have disputed the implication that per capita incomes ended up lower in 1840 than 1800. As we shall see in the next section, there is reason to believe that Martin did exaggerate the decline in per capita income in the first two decades. So, although we lack any authoritative figures, we may think of Martin's estimates for 1800 and 1810 as needing revision to levels somewhat below that of 1840. (See 5–4.)

American per capita income, then, began to rise rapidly in the second quarter of the 19th century, almost half a century after our

5–3. Expanding Population and Income

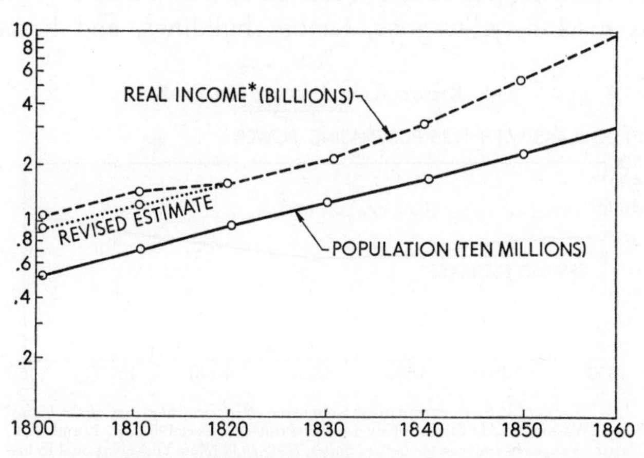

* In dollars of 1926 purchasing power.

Source: U.S. Department of Commerce, *Historical Statistics of the United States* (Washington, D.C.: U.S. Government Printing Office, 1960), p. 7; and R. F. Martin, *National Income in the United States, 1799–1938* (New York: National Industrial Conference Board, 1939), pp. 6–7.

Note: Income is for the year preceding each decennial census.

Nation began. It has continued to rise rapidly for over a century since then. There apparently was little change in per capita income prior to 1830. While no data are available prior to 1800, we suspect that there was a slight rise in per capita incomes during the period of early trade prosperity (1790–1810), as well as a slight decline afterwards. In any event, population and production evidently were expanding throughout these early decades, even though growth, a rise in per capita income, had not yet started.

Capital, Methods, and Industrial Organization

Of first importance in explaining the early 19th-century rise in income per capita is the rapid rise in capital. Mere expansion, of course, would require more of all types of productive resources, but increased production per worker usually involves some improvement in the ratio of resources used with labor. From the beginning of the American colonies, land was abundant while both labor and capital were scarce. As we have noted, rising productivity involved a faster increase in labor than land; for more intensive settlement has permitted more complex organization of labor. We now note that capital increased even faster than labor; so, workers benefited from an accumulation of more resources to help them in production.

For data on capital we have only estimates of the total value of "tangible, reproducible wealth" in this country for two early years, 1805 and 1850. These figures reflect the stock of man-made economic assets —such as machinery, wagons, factory buildings, and homes. They

5–4. Rising Real Income per Person

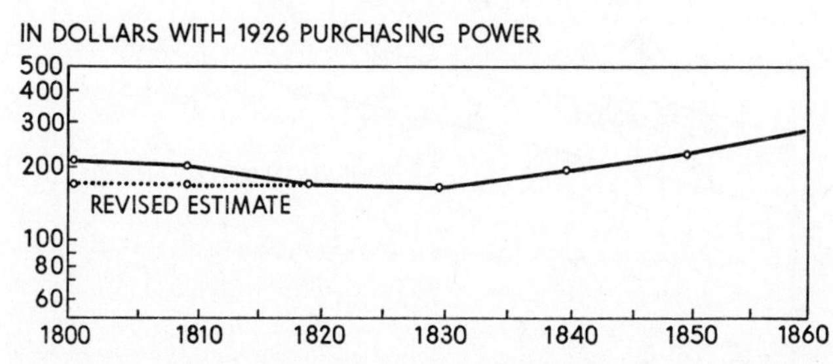

Source: U.S. Department of Commerce, *Historical Statistics of the United States* (Washington, D.C.: U.S. Government Printing Office, 1960), p. 7; and R. F. Martin, *National Income in the United States, 1799–1938* (New York: National Industrial Conference Board, 1939), pp. 6–7.

exclude land values, intangible ownership claims (such as debts and patents), military equipment and facilities, and semidurable or perishable civilian goods inventories. Adjusting for price changes, they may be expressed in real values, as though purchased in the same year. These estimates show tenfold increase between 1805 and 1850. Population increased only four times in the same period.

On a per capita basis, real wealth almost ***tripled*** according to these estimates, rising from $166 in 1805 to $441 in 1850. In comparison, even after some downward revision of Martin's early years estimates, real income per capita rose only about ***one third*** in the same period. Thus, the very rapid increase in capital undoubtedly was a powerful aid in raising production per person in the United States; and, if we assume that this accumulation gradually gathered momentum, it would help to explain the rise in income per person sometime after 1830. (See 5–5.)

Another important source of explanation for the rise in incomes per capita would be any general improvement in the technology or methods of production. This would permit the same resources to produce more of the same types of goods. It is difficult to show an overall measure of improved methods, but inventions and innovations of many kinds undoubtedly played an important role in raising the productivity of American resources during the first half of the 19th century. Furthermore, there is reason to believe that both the number of improvements and the extent of their application accelerated during the second quarter of the century. Examples of this will be cited in later chapters.

Still another source of explanation of rising per capita income, however, comes from various evidences of the changing organization of production in the economy as a whole. Not only are methods of making

5–5. Rise in Income and Wealth per Person

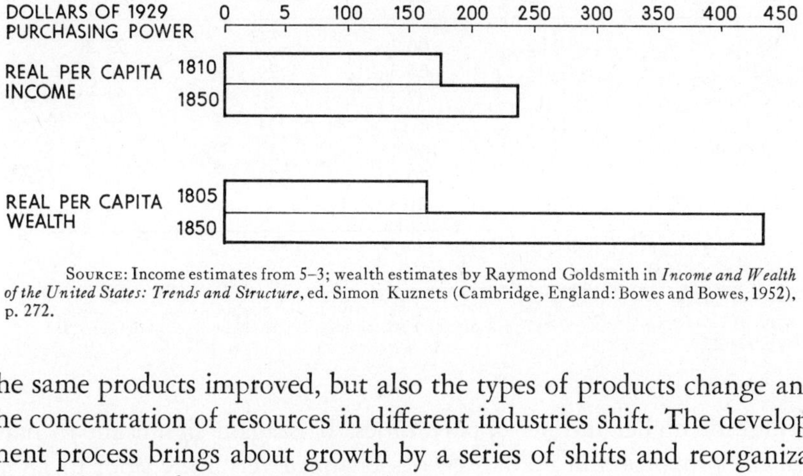

DOLLARS OF 1929 PURCHASING POWER 0 5 100 150 200 250 300 350 400 450

REAL PER CAPITA INCOME 1810 1850

REAL PER CAPITA WEALTH 1805 1850

Source: Income estimates from 5–3; wealth estimates by Raymond Goldsmith in *Income and Wealth of the United States: Trends and Structure*, ed. Simon Kuznets (Cambridge, England: Bowes and Bowes, 1952), p. 272.

the same products improved, but also the types of products change and the concentration of resources in different industries shift. The development process brings about growth by a series of shifts and reorganization in the use of a nation's total resources.

Certain changes in the data on population alone give clues as to how income per capita was raised. One is the rise in proportion of workers in the total population from 29 percent in 1800 to 33 percent in 1860. This occurred due to both an increase in the proportion of adults (aged 10 or over) in the population and an increase in the proportion of the adults (especially women) gainfully occupied. With more of the people working, income per head was likely to be higher. It is interesting to note that while these proportions did not change between 1800 and 1810, they rose in the following four decades.

Another noteworthy change was the rising proportion of white population from 81.1 percent to 85.7 percent. With slave importation curtailed to smuggling, the Negro population declined in importance.

Because the Negro slaves were mostly illiterate, unskilled, and occupied in farm labor, they can be assumed to have been among the least productive workers; so, their relative decline may reflect a rising average productivity of the total work force.

Still a third change was the rising proportion of all gainful workers who were doing nonfarm work, which was 27.2 percent in 1800 and 41.1 percent in 1860. There are two important implications of this change which have characterized economic development throughout history: (1) productivity of farm workers has to rise in order for more labor to be devoted to other forms of production, and (2) nonfarm work usually is more productive and attracts workers out of farming

5–6. TRENDS FAVORING RISING INCOME PER PERSON

	Percent of Population			*Percent Workers*
Year	*White*	*Adult**	*Workers†*	*Nonfarm*
1800	81.1	66.1	29	27.2
1810	81.0	66.3	29	28.2
1820	81.6	67.3	30	28.2
1830	81.9	67.1	31	29.5
1840	83.2	68.1	32	31.5
1850	84.4	70.9	33	36.3
1860	85.7	71.3	33	41.1

* Persons 10 years or older.
† Gainfully occupied persons.
SOURCE: U.S. Department of Commerce, *Historical Statistics of the United States* (Washington, D.C.: U.S. Government Printing Office, 1960); and early estimates by Simon Kuznets (ed.), *Income and Wealth of the United States: Trends and Structure* (Cambridge, England: Bowes and Bowes, 1952), pp. 224–25.

because of higher income opportunities. It is again significant to note that the proportion in nonfarm work changed very little prior to 1830 but rose rapidly thereafter. (See 5–6.)

Other data also provide clues as to the trends in per capita income. The early phases of pioneer farming undoubtedly resulted in low family income and living standards; consequently much of the early westward movement was not likely to help raise national incomes per capita. Estimates of per capita income by state for 1840, in fact, show lower averages in the western regions; and the increased percentage of the population in the non-Atlantic states would tend to lower the national average. This would help to explain the decline in per capita incomes prior to 1830. After that date, the rapidly rising proportion of population in cities and the rapidly rising proportion of workers in nonfarming would tend to raise per capita incomes. Furthermore, while pioneer farms were distant from markets so that high transport costs offset the use of more fertile lands, later improvements in transportation rapidly reduced costs and raised the productivity of western farms. Increasing surpluses of cotton and wheat were sold for export. Rapid improvements in farm machinery also raised crop production in the later decades. Finally, the rapid rise in manufacturing began to have substantial effects on national production in the later decades of the pre-Civil War period.

Thus we have many indications both of improved methods and of shifts in types of production that would lead to higher productivity and incomes in the 1830's, 1840's, and 1850's. With this brief survey of trends and of clues to their causes, we can turn now to examine the events in more detail in separate industries and regions. The rest of this chapter deals with foreign trade.

EARLY TRADE FLUCTUATIONS, 1783–1815

Immediately after the Revolutionary War, the new nation was very dependent upon foreign trade and thus much affected by world trade policies and wars. The foreign sector provided both problems and opportunities of economic development. Trade prosperity was to provide the high incomes and capital needed to grow, and market limitations and trade interruptions were to provide the stimulus to develop domestic industries.

Colonial Production and Trade Patterns

The foundation on which the new nation built its economy was the production and trade system that had evolved over the Colonial period. Although the bulk of the colonial population was engaged in high-subsistence general farming, a market sector did grow and prosper during colonial times. The nature of the market economy varied in the three colonial regions according to the dictates of those regions' respective natural resource endowments.

The New England colonies specialized in naval stores, shipping, shipbuilding, fishing, and raising livestock. New England's exports from these industries went to England in exchange for manufactured consumer and capital goods. The middle colonies specialized in grain production, chiefly wheat, which was also exchanged in England for manufactured products. The South's plantation economy produced staples—rice, indigo, and tobacco—and naval stores which gave southern colonists access to British manufactured products.

Superimposed upon these bilateral (two-way) trade relations were the triangular trade patterns we discussed earlier. Their chief importance came from the fact that multilateral trade relations gave the colonists the opportunity to buy a wider variety of foreign-made products and made possible the importation of slaves to work the southern plantations.

In addition to their trade with the rest of the world, a pattern of coastal trade among the Colonies emerged. Free trade among the Colonies enabled each geographical region to further intensify its specialization and trade off its surpluses for the surplus production of the other regions.

Extensive and intensive colonial growth brought colonial per capita income to at least the British level by the Revolutionary War—a remarkable record! That record is in part attributable to the colonies' rich natural resources. However, perhaps quantitatively far more important is the fact that the Colonies were able to specialize in outputs in which they enjoyed a comparative advantage from a production-cost standpoint. In turn, the fact that until the eve of the Revolution mercantilist laws favored them or, in most cases, fettered them only slightly, permitted this specialization pattern to develop.

Trade Restrictions

Immediately upon winning their freedom, the American states found themselves dependent upon the former mother country, England, for imports of manufactured goods. France did not capture the market as might have been expected. The former colonists were familiar with British goods and merchants, and English manufacturing industries at this time were more efficient in producing for mass consumer markets. An immediate wave of buying to meet a backlog of demands pushed prices very high. Most of the imports, however, were financed by credit, and a heavy debt burden quickly piled up. Currency drained out of the country to England to pay debts and finance new imports. With this rapid reduction in the supply of money, prices fell drastically.

The depression period of the early 1780's, however, arose not from excessive imports but from a slump in exports. As a new nation outside of the British Empire, the United States found itself facing important restrictions on the size of its export markets. In the South, farm production initially was down because of severe wartime devastation and the capture and removal of slaves. Then, British import duties on tobacco restricted British consumption and lowered the price to American farmers. France also at this time turned over to one agency a monopoly of all purchases of tobacco, which tended to depress prices received by American importers. Rice exports also were affected by British import duties; but indigo and naval stores suffered a decline because they no longer were encouraged by British bounties.

In the North, British duties also struck a blow to the whaling industry, which was reduced to one third its size. Fur exports became monopolized by Canada; and crude iron no longer was free of British duties. American-built ships no longer could be accepted into British registry; so New England shipbuilding activity slumped to a small fraction of its prewar levels. British restrictions on American trade with British colonies in the West Indies also limited exports of codfish, salted meats, corn, wheat, and flour. Opening up French colonies on the Caribbean islands helped offset some of this decline, but the French also excluded wheat and flour.

Exclusion from British registry also restricted the freight earnings of American shipowners who previously carried much British cargo. The carrying of British cargo from the West Indies to England was eliminated; and even France excluded American ships from handling its colonial sugar exports. No longer protected by the British flag, American ships lost protection from piracy off the Barbary Coast in the Mediterranean Sea.

As we pointed out earlier, some of the American states, especially in the North, attempted to retaliate by restricting British imports from the American domestic market. Tariffs were placed on imported luxuries and whiskey mostly in order to provide government revenues; but tariffs also were used to favor American shipowners and manufacturers. Extra duties were charged on goods carried by British ships, and tariffs were raised on goods which American manufacturers were producing. The larger American manufacturers of some goods soon found that local consumption in their own states did not provide a large enough market. Sales in other states and in the South were hampered by high transportation costs overland and by the competition of low-priced English imports. The lack of uniformity in tariffs among the states made federal tariffs necessary, and this contributed to the support in northern states for adoption of the Constitution in 1789.

Neutrality Prosperity

In the 30 years after 1790, three favorable lines of economic development took place that revived the economy and helped to prepare the way for later growth. The Napoleonic Wars brought an immediate temporary boom to the northern states in the shipping and shipbuilding industries. Southern agriculture was more permanently revived by a shift to a new export crop, cotton, that became increasingly important as time went by. Although subsequent interruptions in the wartime trade brought depressions in the North, they gave a stimulus to new manufacturing industries that were to become important later on.

The wars between France and England began in 1793 and lasted until 1815. Since nations at war tend to purchase more supplies from other nations in order to supply their armies, build up their industries, and make up for losses, the United States enjoyed a rising world demand for its exports, both from the North and the South. Exports of American goods, therefore, doubled by 1795. While this level was not maintained in the next few years, it was achieved again after 1800.

American-owned ships, of course, benefited from carrying an increased volume of exports; but the greater part of the shipping boom was in reexports. This term refers to foreign-produced goods brought to American ports and reloaded into American ships for export again to the warring European nations. The ships of a neutral nation were not subject to attack by the warring nations; so both sides relied upon neutral ships to help bring supplies from their West Indies colonies into their own ports. The volume of foreign-made goods carried soon became much larger than the expanded volume of American made goods. Total exports, therefore, more than doubled by 1795; and by 1805 total exports were more than five times larger than in 1792. (See 5–7.)

The result in terms of income, of course, was considerable prosperity for the Americans due to the European wars. Production and prices of farm products rose. Demand for new ships rose among American merchants as well as foreign merchants; and the annual tonnage of new ships built after 1800 was five or six times larger than it had been in the good years prior to the Revolutionary War.

Most important undoubtedly was the income earned from shipping. Net freight earnings rose about four times from 1792 to 1806. These earnings were quite large compared to the total value of exports —about one third as large. Why? Because they were earned on carrying imports as well as exports. Also, freight charges in early times were high in relation to the value of goods carried. According to Martin's estimates, income from all forms of transportation and communication around 1800 was about one fourth of total national income. Foreign shipping undoubtedly was an important part of all transport incomes; so the boom in net freight earnings was quite important to total national incomes. These freight earnings provided wages to large numbers of seamen from the New England area as well as large profits to shipowning merchants.

At the same time that the North was prospering from a boom in neutral shipping, southern agriculture began to be revived by a shift to a new major export crop. Georgia and South Carolina especially were suffering from the decline in indigo production and low prices for rice. Virginia also suffered from low tobacco prices between 1791 and 1796. So, a new crop was badly needed. Cotton, at first, did not seem very

5–7. Neutrality Trade Boom

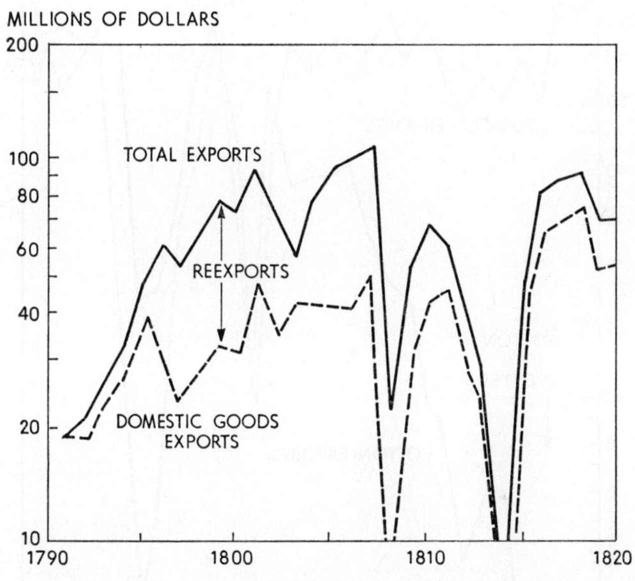

Source: U.S. Department of Commerce, *Historical Statistics of the United States* (Washington, D.C.: U.S. Government Printing Office, 1960), p. 538.

promising because of the large amount of tedious hand labor required to remove the seeds from the lint of the short-staple variety. It took one person a whole day to clean one pound of cotton. In 1793, Eli Whitney's invention of the cotton ginning machine removed this bottleneck to the production of cotton. It enabled one worker to clean 50 pounds a day. The cost of American cotton was drastically reduced at the same time that demand for cotton was rising by leaps and bounds in England's textile industry, due to the new methods of the Industrial Revolution.

Cotton quickly rose to be the major export crop of the South. From just a few thousand bales in 1793, production rose tenfold by

1800 and doubled again in the next decade. The national export value of cotton in 1811 was more than 50 percent larger than for tobacco. About three fourths of the cotton production was concentrated in Georgia and South Carolina, and another 19 percent was centered in

5–8. Tobacco and Cotton Exports

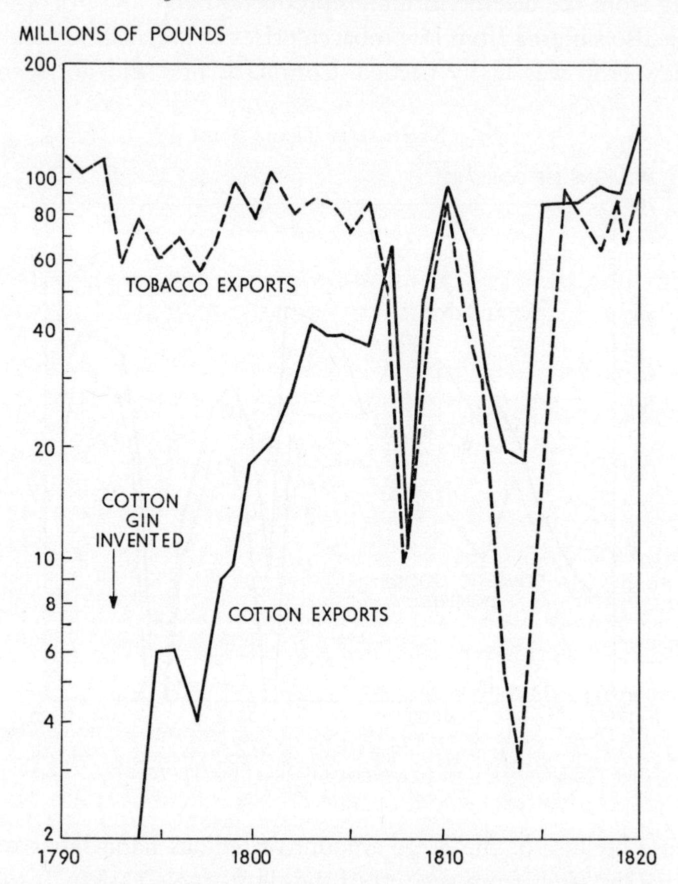

Source: U.S. Department of Commerce, *Historical Statistics of the United States* (Washington, D.C.: U.S. Government Printing Office, 1960), p. 547.

North Carolina and Virginia. The rest already was being produced in middle Tennessee and the lower Mississippi Valley before the War of 1812. (See 5–8.)

The new export crop also proved to be very profitable to farmers. Around 1800, cotton could be produced at a profit if the price was 12 cents a pound. Prices during the early years were very much higher, reaching a peak of 44 cents a pound in 1800 and averaging 15 to 19 cents during the next decade. Many small farmers moved up into a prospering middle class. Production, however, relied heavily upon unskilled slave labor; and the prices of slaves soon tripled. Only the most successful farmers and those with the best lands could afford to expand into large plantations.

The neutrality prosperity in the North, however, was short-lived. There was a trade slump during 1803 when England and France were briefly at peace. Not long after the war was resumed, both sides began to deny neutral ships access to enemy ports, and many American ships were seized by both sides. President Jefferson attempted to retaliate through the Embargo Act (passed in December of 1807) which forbade our own ships to trade with Europe. This hurt our own trade so much in 1808 that it was repealed early in 1809. Conflict with England over our neutral rights, as well as trouble on our western borders, led finally to a declaration of war against England in June of 1812.

Although the wartime interruption of trade caused a general depression, it provided a further stimulus to efforts to start new manufacturing firms in the United States. Cut off from English textile goods and faced with a large surplus of cotton, American merchants seized the opportunity to invest their capital in cotton spinning mills. In 1807, there were 15 mills already in operation using copies of the English Arkwright machines. By 1815, the number of American mills had grown to 213. In other industries less-dramatic but significant new ventures were launched. The preceding period of prosperity had increased consumer incomes and enlarged local markets. Plentiful capital also was available for starting new ventures because of the accumulated profits in the hands of merchants at a time when trading ventures were less promising. While these beginnings in manufacturing were not quantitatively important in the national economy at first, within a few decades the industries started were to provide a major source of national economic growth, and the experience gained in this brief period was invaluable.

LATER TRADE TRENDS, 1815–60

After the war with England ended in December of 1814, a trade boom got under way that lasted until the slump of 1819. The boom involved an increase in both exports and imports, but the imports were much larger. A pent-up wartime demand for English manufactured goods was matched by a drive by English merchants to dispose of surplus goods, restore their markets, and utilize the rapidly expanding capacity of the rising English manufacturing industries.

The import boom also was fed by loans and investments that expanded production capacity of export crops in the South and West. With the initial high prices for cotton and wheat after the war, profits were high in farming. There was a rush to settle new farmlands in the Mississippi and Ohio valleys. New farms needed capital for tools and for an initial stake of consumer goods; and credit was forthcoming from English merchants, American merchants in the Northeast, and the numerous new banks in the West. The purchase of goods by the new farmers at first exceeded their sale of products for export. Eventually as supply expanded a fall in prices brought a halt to this farm prosperity and expansion in debt.

During the initial boom, however, the Northeast did not participate in the prosperity. Shipbuilding declined, and American ships again faced restrictions in trading with England and its colonies. More drastically affected were the new manufacturing industries that now faced stiff competition from lower prices and often better quality English imports. Transportation improvements had produced lower freight rates both internally and between the United States and its trading partners. The initial impact of lower freight rates was to intensify the British comparative advantage in manufacturing and thus bankrupt many of the American manufacturing firms that had gotten a "false start" in the period of interrupted trade. Many cotton spinning mills closed, while the surviving mills tended to adopt the power loom and thus to adopt the more efficient integrated spinning and weaving operations common in England. Other industries also felt the competition of English manufactured imports in domestic markets without compensating enlargement of foreign markets. Only after the American market had grown significantly larger than its 1815 size did American manufacturing join in the general expansion of the economy.

Tariff Issue

The political demand for higher tariffs on imported manufactured goods arose as a policy issue that was to be prominent for many decades. Opinion was divided, of course, because people had different economic interests and were affected differently. Northeastern manufacturers and workers favored protection of their industries and jobs, although some of the merchants were more interested in handling expanded imports. Southern cotton and tobacco farmers were opposed to tariffs, which did not help their incomes and only raised the prices they paid on manufactured goods. Western opinion, however, was at first on the side of higher tariffs. Many small manufacturers and craftsmen serving relatively isolated local markets in the West were under pressure from lower-priced manufactured goods being transported into their areas. Northern and western farmers were selling grain and meat products primarily in American cities; so they had an interest in any tariff measures which would increase incomes of city workers. The western clamor for cheaper land and for federal aid in building roads and canals also added political support to tariff proposals, because land sales

5–9. Average Tariff Duties

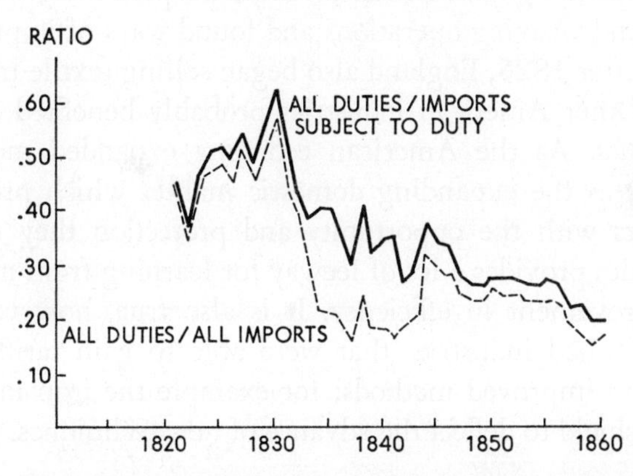

Source: U.S. Department of Commerce, *Historical Statistics of the United States* (Washington, D.C.: U.S. Government Printing Office, 1960), p. 539.

and tariffs were the two main alternative sources of federal revenues and thus the means of financing any spending programs.

A series of tariff laws successively raised duties on imports to quite high levels by the early 1830's and then progressively lowered them to low levels before the Civil War. The tariff rates passed in 1816 were about double the prewar levels. The depression in 1819 stimulated the political pressures for protection so that rates were again raised in 1824 and to a peak in 1828. The South, however, objected strenuously and got the rates lowered progressively beginning in 1833. An increase in 1842 was quickly reversed in 1846, and further reductions again were made in 1857. Political embarrassment over surplus government revenues aided in getting the latter two reductions. While the duties applied to particular types of goods varied widely, the effects of these rate changes are reflected in a rough measure of the average rates—the ratio of duties collected to the value of imported goods subject to duty. This ratio was between 0.45 and 0.50 in the 1820's, reached a peak of 0.62 in 1830, and fell to 0.16 in 1860. A rapid increase in the proportion of goods imported free of duty in the mid-1830's lowered the effective average rates even more rapidly during that decade. (See 5–9.)

The influence of the tariffs on manufacturing industries was mostly confined to the early years when new industries were getting started. High duties and falling prices after the War of 1812 tended to close out the cheapest coarse-quality cotton textile goods from England. American manufacturers were able to produce such goods for a growing domestic market while learning the skill and efficiency needed to produce higher quality goods. American mills adopted integrated methods of spinning and weaving operations and found ways of improving their machinery. After 1825, England also began selling textile machinery to Americans. Other American industries probably benefited similarly in the early years. As the American economy expanded more rapidly, however, it was the expanding domestic market which provided new manufacturers with the opportunity and protection they needed; for expanding sales provides a lot of leeway for learning from mistakes and gradual improvement in efficiency. It is also true, however, that the already established industries that were able to gain tariff protection failed to adopt improved methods; for example the iron industry used its tariff as a shield to deflect the advance of new techniques.

Expanding Exports and Imports

After the postwar boom and recession, trade data reflect the accelerating expansion of the American economy. From 1820 to 1830 the value of exports and imports remained at about the same level. In the late 1830's, trade activity was about 50 percent higher, and by 1860 it more than doubled. (See 5–10.)

The rate of expansion, however, may have been more steady than the value figures indicate, because prices continued their postwar declines until about the mid-1840's. If adjustment is made for the declining prices of exports, their real value (or physical volume) appears to have increased at a steady rate between the War of 1812 and the Civil War.

The rapid expansion in production and export of cotton played a major role in this rising trend of total exports. Already in 1815, cotton was about one third of the value of total exports. This share was boosted by more than half after the mid-1830's, when another great western land boom occurred. Exports of wheat and many other goods expanded also, but no other major export expanded as rapidly as cotton during the middle decades of 1820 to 1840. During this period, the American expansion was dominated by the production of this surplus farm product for export.

A division of trade statistics into three different categories of goods —materials, foods, and manufacturers—provides some indication of the changes that occurred during this long period of expansion. In exports, materials rose in relative importance, mostly due to the rise of cotton. Tobacco and lumber exports declined in relative shares. Foods declined in overall importance, with a decline in the export shares of wheat and flour, rice, and fish. Meat products increased in importance,

5–10. Value of Exports and Imports, 1815–60

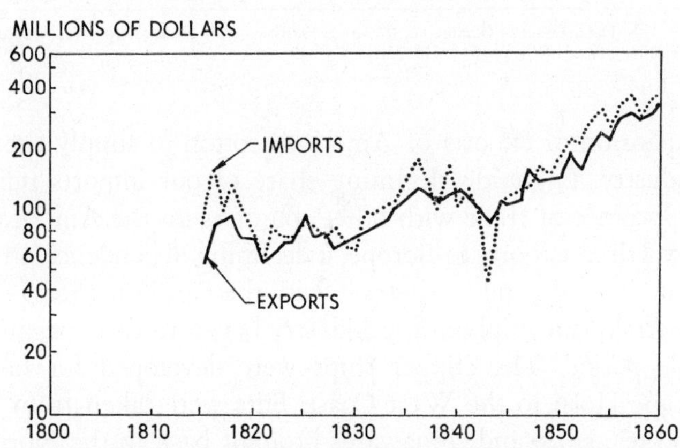

Source: U.S. Department of Commerce, *Historical Statistics of the United States* (Washington, D.C.: U.S. Government Printing Office, 1960), pp. 538 and 563 (based on revised estimates by Douglas C. North).

although they remained a small share of the total. Manufactures declined initially, but after 1840 they began to increase in percentage of total value of exports. In imports, there was little change in the importance of food products. These consisted primarily of imports of sugar, coffee and tea. Materials—such as hides, iron, and chemicals—initially rose in importance while manufactures—especially textiles—declined; but after 1840 these shares remained about the same. (See 5–11.)

A similar division of trade statistics by country of origin and destination also shows a change in America's relations with other trading nations. England remained the largest country in our total trade; but our imports from England declined in relative importance to our total imports while exports to England increased in relative importance. The increase in share of exports to England was largely due to the

5–11. CHANGES IN COMPOSITION OF U.S. TRADE

	Exports			*Imports*		
	1820	*1840*	*1860*	*1820*	*1840*	*1860*
Distribution by Type of Goods:						
Materials	61	68	69	5	12	11
Food	23	18	16	30	31	30
Manufactures	16	14	15	65	57	59
Distribution by Country:						
England	35	44	50	44	33	39
European	31	30	24	20	29	22
Americas	27	24	21	28	24	29
Other	7	2	5	8	14	10

SOURCE: U.S. Department of Commerce, *Historical Statistics of the United States* (Washington, D.C.: U.S. Government Printing Office, 1960), pp. 545, 551–53.

steady expansion of exports of American cotton to supply the English textile industry. England's declining share of our imports reflects the rising importance of trade with other countries on the American continent, a growth in exports to Europe, a declining dependence on English manufactured goods, and rising trade with the Far East. (See 5–11.)

The American shipbuilding industry began to thrive again during this whole period. The clipper ships were developed for fast travel around Cape Horn to the West Coast. Furs were taken from there to China, and tea, silks, and chinawares brought back to the Northeast.

The major seaport cities also prospered from foreign trade. Even though manufacturing industries were depressed immediately after the War of 1812, shipping, warehousing, transporting, and financing activities prospered. These were concentrated mainly in a few main port cities—especially Boston, Baltimore, Philadelphia, and New York. American laws restricting coastal shipping between American ships tended to encourage foreign ships to unload at one centrally located port, from which goods could be reshipped to several other ports. This gave American shippers and merchants an advantage in the South; and northeastern merchants did much of the lending, wholesale merchandising, and cotton brokerage business in the southern plantation areas.

New York developed certain advantages for shipping that soon enabled it to overtake Philadelphia as the largest American city. A regular public auction helped in obtaining quick disposal of cargoes not destined for particular merchants. Because of New York's central location it also was the logical terminal for the first regularly scheduled passenger and mail ships—or "packets"—which began between England and the United States in 1818. The opening of the Erie Canal later was to accelerate New York's growth as the terminal for the main overland route from the Great Lakes states to the East Coast.

After 1840, there are indications that internal developments rather than foreign trade were becoming increasingly important in American expansion. The importance of cotton in total exports remained about the same. Martin's estimates of national income indicate that agriculture's relative importance declined while that of manufacturing, trade, and services increased. Another crude indication, perhaps, is that the tonnage of shipping in domestic trade—coastal, rivers, and lakes—quickly surpassed the tonnage of American ships in foreign

5–12. Foreign and Domestic Trade Shipping Tonnage

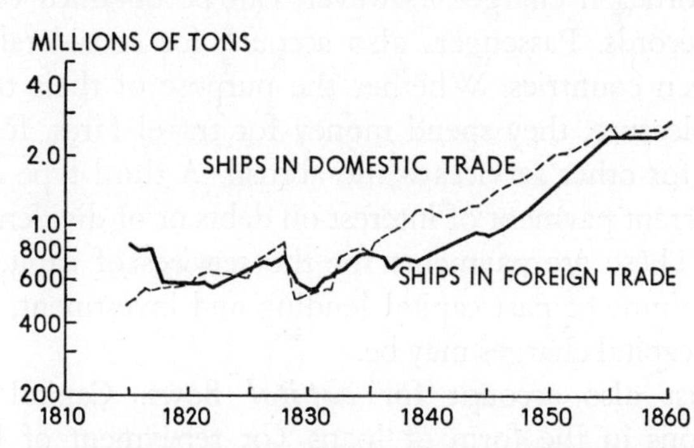

Source: U.S. Department of Commerce, *Historical Statistics of the United States* (Washington, D.C.: U.S. Government Printing Office, 1960), p. 445.

trade after the mid-1830's. After the mid-1840's, foreign shipping began to catch up again, but the rise of railroad transportation also was taking much of the domestic cargo carrying away from inland shipping. (See 5–12.)

Paying for Imports

Throughout the pre-Civil War period, the value of imports tended to exceed the value of merchandise exports in most years. This is what traditionally has been called an "unfavorable balance of trade." Unless some other way could be found to pay for the excess of purchases over sales, shipments of specie—gold and silver—would have to be made to pay for the difference. During the early post-Revolutionary years in the 1780's, some drain in specie from the United States did take place. But until the California gold discovery of 1848, little specie flowed out of the United States and considerable amounts flowed in. How is this to be explained?

To explain the total balance of payments between nations, a broader set of accounts is needed than we would need to compute the ***trade*** balance (exports less imports of goods) or the ***specie*** balance (outflow less inflow of money metals). We need to account for international service transactions which with the trade balance make up the ***current*** payments balance. These payments are called the ***invisible items,*** because they represent payments for services rather than for physical goods.

The freight charges on carrying goods, as well as various port fees, are not shown on the usual records for value of goods shipped (such as the records of tariff duties collected on values of goods imported). These transportation charges, however, can be obtained or estimated from other records. Passengers also account for considerable flow of money between countries. Whether the purpose of their travel is for business or pleasure, they spend money for travel fares, for food and lodging, and for other services while abroad. A third type of invisible item is the current payment of interest on debts or of dividends on prior investments. These are payments for the services of capital; and the greater the volume of past capital lending and investment, the greater these current capital charges may be.

We must also account for ***capital*** flows. Capital may flow between nations in the form of loans (or repayment of loans) and investments (or withdrawal of investments). It may be helpful to think of capital movements as transactions in paper claims to assets which are similar to the transactions in physical goods. When a New York state bond (or a merchant's I O U) is "exported" to London in exchange for an English investor's (or lender's) money, we can say that the capital transaction is positive and involves an inflow of funds. The transaction is negative when Americans invest or lend abroad (or pay back loans). In cases when merchants extend loans, physical goods usually are exchanged directly for paper claims (I O U) without any immediate money exchange. Capital also may flow between countries, however, as one-way transfers of funds without anything else being exchanged. Some transfers are between governments, as when the United States paid for the Louisiana Territory. Some transfers are by or between individuals, as when immigrants bring funds with them or send back money to their relatives. (See 5–13.)

For each of these four types of accounts, the positive (inflowing) payments may exceed or fall short of the negative (outflowing) pay-

5–13. U.S. BALANCE-OF-PAYMENTS ACCOUNTS, 1860
(Dollar amounts in millions)

Accounts	*Receipts*	*Payments*	*Balance*
Trade: goods sold and purchased	$ 335	$ 367	$ −33
Invisibles: payments for services	42	67	−25
(transportation charges)	(35)	(17)	(18)
(travel and other expenditures)	(2)	(20)	(−18)
(returns on past investments)	(5)	(30)	(−25)
Specie: gold and silver shipped	66	9	57
Capital*:			1
(transfers of funds)	—	—	(8)
(changes in debts and investments)*	—	—	(− 7)

* Estimate (for balance only) is derived as a residual; and the sign is opposite to the net balance on other payment totals (trade, current, specie).

SOURCE: U.S. Department of Commerce, *Historical Statistics of the United States* (Washington, D.C.: U.S. Government Printing Office, 1960), pp. 538 and 563–65.

ments. The account then may be said to have a positive or negative net balance. It often is convenient to analyze just the net balances rather than the total transactions.

People do not need to make all of their payments across the seas. In New York City an importer who may need English pounds can trade his dollars with an exporter who already has received English pounds and wants them converted to dollars. At the same time, in London, the corresponding exporters and importers there may be trading their dollars. Actually, by making payments with bank checks, the money transfers can be cleared through the banks. As long as all payments balance out, money actually need not be shipped between countries.

When the transactions are not in equilibrium, there tends to be some movement of gold or silver between countries to complete the balance of payments. Except for errors in records, therefore, the net balance for all four accounts will be zero.

By examining just the positive and negative net balances of each of the four main types of accounts, we can gain a useful perspective on certain international aspects of national development. In addition to noticing the size and type of exports and imports in relation to total national production, we can examine (with the aid of the balance accounts) how differences in trade were paid for and the extent to which outside capital aided national growth. We may ignore the varying pattern of short fluctuations in the different net balances from year to year; but the very large fluctuations in a few years are important indications of business conditions—the booms and depressions. Also, each of the four types of accounts may tend to have a persistent tendency or trend toward the positive or the negative side. (See 5–14 and 5–15.)

5–14. U.S. Balances of Trade and Invisible Items, 1815–1860

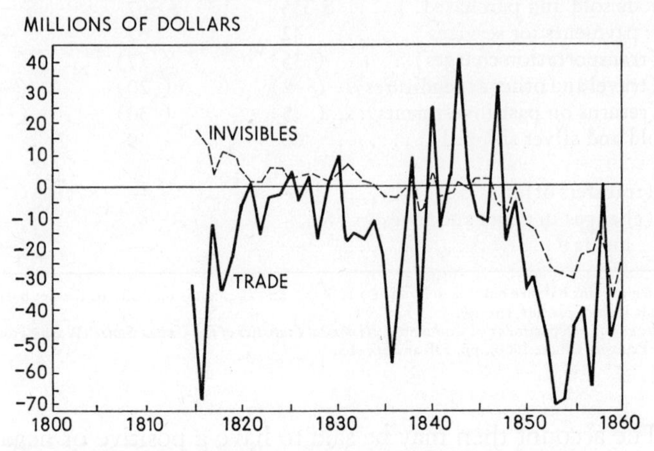

Source: U.S. Department of Commerce, *Historical Statistics of the United States* (Washington, D.C.: U.S. Government Printing Office, 1960), pp. 538, 563, and 565.

5–15. U.S. Balances of Specie and Capital Payments

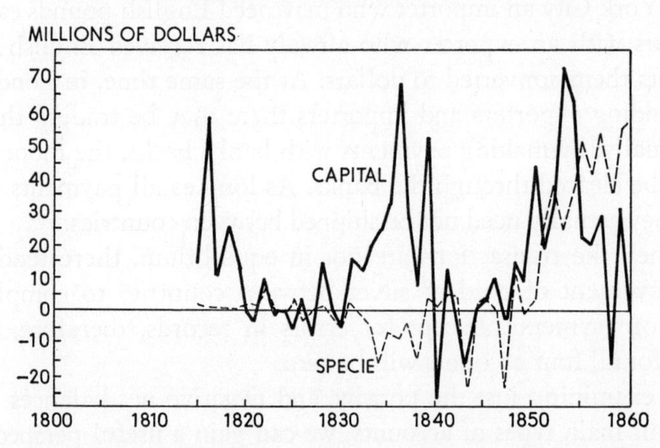

Source: U.S. Department of Commerce, *Historical Statistics of the United States* (Washington, D.C.: U.S. Government Printing Office, 1960), pp. 538, 563, and 565.

The ***trade*** balance usually was negative, meaning that imports usually exceeded exports. The excess of payments to other countries for imports reached large negative amounts in three different periods. The first was in 1816 and 1818 when a flood of English-manufactured goods was imported to meet pent-up postwar demands and to help provide supplies to the new settlers in the Gulf states and Great Lakes states. A second period of large excess imports took place in 1836 and 1839 when another western land rush occurred. The third period of large excess in imports came about during the mid-1850's as a result of a further boom in western land settlement together with the rapid building of railroads.

The ***invisible items*** balance usually was positive and thus helped to offset some of the negative trade balance. Immediately after the War of 1812 freight earnings (on carrying imported goods as well as exported goods) were high, although not quite as high as during the peak of the previous neutrality period. While freight earnings remained substantial, the net balance of charges on freight carried in American ships compared to freight carried in other nations' ships gradually declined in the following decades. The balance of travel expenditures also tended to fall during the 1840's and 1850's as Americans began to travel more abroad. Most important, the current payments of interest on debts and dividends on investments gradually became larger as the total of foreign lending and investment in America accumulated. The net balance of all current payments, therefore, gradually fell, and during the 1850's the balance became more and more negative.

The balance of ***specie*** movements usually was not very large; so they did not help much in offsetting the large negative amounts of trade balances during the first two boom periods. Until the 1830's the balance usually was slightly positive, representing a small outflow of money metals to help pay for excess imports. During the 1830's and 1840's, however, the balance usually was negative, meaning that money metals were being shipped in. Only in the 1850's did outward specie movements in large volume provide a major positive balance to offset the large negative trade balances. This was because gold itself became a major export commodity after the California gold discoveries in 1848.

Positive ***capital*** balances usually were required to offset fully the excess of imports. A transfer of funds brought by the increasing number of immigrants was an important part of the growing positive balances in the 1850's; but during all three boom periods especially large capital inflows occurred. In part, this represented Americans going into debt to finance an excess of imports and in part it reflected British investments helping America to expand. During the 1816–18 period, British merchants undoubtedly extended more credit to help finance the large inflow of British goods. During the later boom periods of the 1830's and 1850's, much credit was extended by British merchants as well as by American banks. Yet in these decades there also were substantial investment inflows of foreign capital funds to help build American canals and railroads. Most of the investments involved purchases of bonds of state governments and of railroad companies.

A persistence of positive capital balances during most years indicates a cumulative buildup of foreign-held American debt and investments. During the early decades of the century, the debt accumulated during boom periods tended to be paid off in later years. During the 1830's and 1850's, however, the investment flows during the boom periods of canal and railroad construction were not offset by later outflows (although some debt repayment reduced the cumulative for-

5–16. Foreign-Held Debt and Investments in the United States

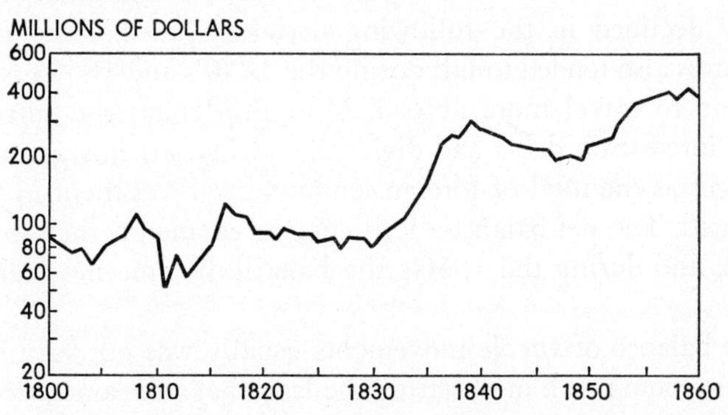

Source: U.S. Department of Commerce, *Historical Statistics of the United States* (Washington, D.C.: U.S. Government Printing Office, 1960), p. 566.

eign-holdings during the 1840's). The accumulated net balances of the capital account, therefore, tend to reflect the extent of permanent foreign capital investment which aided American growth. The absolute rise in the 1850's was almost as great as in the 1830's, but the percentage rise was much greater in the 1830's. Compared to the size of total production and private investment in the economy, therefore, outside investment problably was most important during the canal-building period. (See 5–16.)

STUDY QUESTIONS

1. Between 1790 and 1860, which of the Nation's resources increased faster, natural or human? In spite of the westward movement of population, what evidence was there of intensive development?

2. Over the period 1783–1860, when did production clearly increase faster than population? What indication is there that productivity was raised by increased capital per worker? What other clues are there to the sources of higher productivity?
3. In the first decade of independence, why did this Nation have depressed economic conditions? Why did we experience prosperity during the Napoleonic Wars? Besides the European war, what restored prosperity to southern agriculture? How did the trade interruptions of the Embargo and the War of 1812 both hurt and help northern economic development?
4. Why did the tariff become a political issue after the War of 1812? Why did people in the different regions disagree on this issue? When were the tariff rates the highest and most likely to have been an influence on new American textile industries?
5. Between 1815 and 1860, what was the most important American export? How did the laws restricting coastal trade to American ships favor the main port cities in the Northeast?
6. In terms of mercantilism, why was an excess of imports over exports called an "unfavorable balance of trade?" How was the balance supposed to be paid for? Did America pay for much of its excess imports in gold prior to the gold discoveries in 1848? What other types of payments between people in different countries must be taken into account in the complete "balance of payments?"
7. What types of payments offset the very large negative trade balances in each of three periods: in 1815–20? in 1834–39? in 1850–60? Would you call the negative trade balances "unfavorable" to American economic development?

Chapter 6 AGRICULTURAL SURPLUS

For two and a half decades after the War of 1812, agriculture was the most expansive force in the national economy. In the Northeast, shipping activity was resumed at a lower level than during the neutrality period, and it never regained its relative importance in national income. Manufacturing industries also went through a period of setback due to the postwar flood of imported English manufactured goods, and not until the 1840's was manufacturing production large and growing rapidly enough to be a major influence on national economic growth. Between 1815 and 1840, then, agriculture held the center of the stage. This was a period of rapid westward movement of population and general expansion in farming. Production of surplus farm products for export, especially cotton, rose more rapidly than total production.

The regional production patterns of the nation also were firmly established between 1815 and 1840. The regional differences had begun in the Colonial period. Although New England's small farms produced little for export, the larger farms of the Middle Atlantic exported grain and meat products while southern plantations exported tobacco, rice, and indigo. By 1815, cotton had become the major southern crop. The westward expansion after 1815 then took this regional pattern of farm specialization with it. Cotton production spread across the Gulf States. Tobacco production spread from Virginia and Maryland into Kentucky. Grain and meat production moved into Western New York and Pennsylvania and on across the Great Lakes states to Missouri and Iowa. Inland transportation links were to tie this northern tier of states to the industrial and port cities of New England and the Middle Atlantic. The Northeast thus became even more specialized as the commercial and industrial region. While the Great Lakes states developed a basis for industrial growth later on, the South did not, and the reasons for this difference in development will be explored in this chapter.

Reduced transportation costs and expanding external markets played a major role in the development of each region. This also is a subject to be examined in this chapter, but the initial point to be kept in mind is that without sale to distant markets, the western farms would have produced only a subsistence income level. The pioneers, in fact, were largely self-sufficient, not only producing food for themselves but also making their own clothing, furniture, and tools. Regardless of how fertile the soil, the early isolated rural communities may have eaten well, but their total production and incomes were low. Limited local markets permitted little specialization in farm and nonfarm production. Even later, as a region obtained access to large external markets and began to specialize in high-income export crops, some of the farmers remained at a low-income, subsistence level because they remained in relatively isolated regions, such as in the Appalachian Mountains, or because they had a small acreage and poor soil, such as the more hilly and forested lands. The story of development of a farming region, then, is to be told in terms of the rising specialized production of major products for sale in markets, especially for export out of the region. Transportation to markets provides a vital thread to that story.

SOUTHERN COTTON FARMING

Supplying World Markets

Peace came to both North America and Europe in 1815, and with peace came the opening up of world markets to the cotton textile industry. The Industrial Revolution had given English manufacturers a head start in selling the new and cheaper cotton goods, but in the United States and elsewhere, new textile machinery was being put into operation. As one of the main cotton-producing areas of the world, the South was to benefit from high prices and rapidly expanding demand.

Cotton was the dominant and dynamic element in the southern economy, although there were other major crops. While tobacco production was shifting westward because of exhausted fertility of long-worked lands near the coast, the volume of tobacco exports did not expand for another two decades. While both rice and sugar were profitable export crops raised on large plantations, their production was restricted by the limited areas of easily flooded lowlands in South Carolina and southern Louisiana. Large acreage, of course, was devoted to grain and livestock, although not for export. While a large share of national production of corn and swine was in the South, the region did not supply all of its own needs. Most of the slave labor was concentrated on producing export crops that would return a cash income.

The South's rate of increase in cotton production was very rapid. Output continued to double every decade until 1840, after which the trend began to slow down. This was about twice as fast as the rise in real national income, which took over two decades to double after 1820, and increased about two thirds each decade after 1840. (See 6–1.)

6–1. U.S. Cotton Production

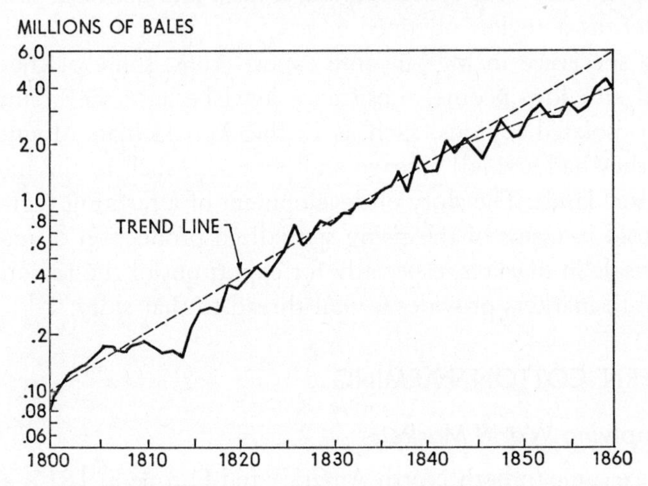

Source: U.S. Department of Commerce, *Historical Statistics of the United States* (Washington, D.C.: U.S. Government Printing Office, 1960), p. 302.

This dynamic sector of production was important not only in providing the major source of southern incomes; it also provided the major national export. As such it greatly facilitated the payment for imports of manufactured goods from England. The value of cotton exports quickly rose from one third to over one half of the value of all domestic exports (excluding the reexports). Usually about three fourths of the cotton production was exported, and American textile manufacturers in the Northeast purchased the rest. After 1840, the slowdown in output increases was accompanied by some lessening of the share of production exported and in cotton's relative importance in total exports. It was in the early decades, therefore, that cotton's importance was rising and its influence most dynamic (See 6–2.)

The increase in cotton production after 1815 occurred mostly in the New South, the territories to the west and southwest of the Appalachian Mountains, due to certain advantages in natural resources. While the climate was suitable for cotton in the whole southern half of the Nation, superior fertile soils were available in certain parts of the new Gulf states—especially in the "black belt" curving across central Alabama and in the lower Mississippi River Valley. By 1860 cotton production was still important in Georgia, but its output was exceeded by Mississippi, Alabama, and Louisiana, which together accounted for over half the total. Even the newest producing states of Texas and Arkansas ranked ahead of South Carolina.

6–2. Importance of Cotton Exports

	Cotton Exports as a Percent of	
Period	*Cotton Production*	*All Domestic Exports*
1815–19	64%	38%
1820–24	71	44
1825–29	70	58
1830–34	76	52
1835–39	71	65
1840–44	77	55
1845–49	74	45
1850–54	69	54
1855–59	67	51

Source: U.S. Department of Commerce, *Historical Statistics of the United States* (Washington, D.C.: U.S. Government Printing Office, 1960), pp. 302, 538, 547.

The New South, especially the Gulf states, had another natural advantage admirably suited to an export crop—easy access to ocean transportation. The Mississippi River provided a well-established transportation artery to a major port city, New Orleans. Other major rivers in Mississippi and Alabama provided barge transportation directly to the Gulf. The first settlers located along the rivers, and most other fertile lands were but a short wagon haul from the nearest barge landing. The ending of hostilities with England and the expulsion of Indians from western Florida opened up this rich-soil territory to ocean trade without the necessity of large capital expenditures to overcome land transportation barriers.

From the beginning of this period the New South's transportation advantage was a persistent influence. And as the cost of ocean shipping declined the region's transportation advantage was gradually enhanced.

Freight rates on cotton shipped to England from New Orleans in the late 1850's were about half their 1820 level. While commodity prices generally were also declining, some of the rate reduction was due to increased competition and greater efficiency in shipping. The design of sailing ships improved and larger cargoes were carried. New ships were increased in size from about 300 tons to over 1,500 tons.

In addition to access to markets through improved transportation, the growth of banking and credit facilities enable the "Cotton Kingdom" to grow. Plantation banks, financed in part by selling securities to British investors, provided credit facilities for the development of new lands and the internal slave trade. Also, the Second Bank of the United States became an important purchaser of cotton bills and for a brief period (1837–41) after it had become the U.S. Bank of Pennsylvania, it financed the shipment of cotton. Unfortunately the bank's foray into cotton speculation set in motion the process that led to its bankruptcy in 1841.

Surges in Expansion

The expansion in production capacity of cotton farming, however, was quite uneven. Sales of public lands in the Gulf states fluctuated widely. During most years the volume of sales was below $1 million, but in two brief periods, 1817–19 and 1834–36, very much higher volumes of land sales were made by the government. Land speculators undoubtedly accounted for much of these initial purchases from the public land offices; so not all of these lands were immediately put into full production. Nevertheless, the westward movement of population was not a steady even flow every year. During certain periods a land rush greatly expanded the number of farms and the production capacity for cotton.

Corresponding peaks of cotton prices suggest that market forces provided an uneven influence on the expansion of cotton farm capacity. While the long-term trend of prices was downward until the mid-1840's, peaks in cotton prices were reached in 1816 and 1835 at about the same time as the peaks in land sales. High cotton prices, of course, meant high profits on investments in cotton farmlands. So the rush to expand farmlands came especially during periods when high prices seemed to promise high rewards. In years of low prices, investments in new farmlands were correspondingly discouraged. (See 6–3.)

The fact that actual cotton production and consumption expanded more steadily than cotton prices, with less wide fluctuations, reflects a more complicated set of interactions between demand and supply conditions. Economic theory suggests an explanation in terms of demand and supply curves. At any one time in world markets, the quantities demanded and the quantities supplied may be quite inelastic, "sticky," in response to price changes. This means that price changes may fluctuate more widely than the quantities produced and consumed.

Over a period of time, the consumption demand for cotton may expand in steady but small amounts. The response of production supply, however, may be irregular and in large amounts. This is because of supply's relation to capacity and the time lags in expanding capacity. As long as existing farms have idle capacity, they can expand output

6–3. Cotton Prices and Land Sales in Five Southern States

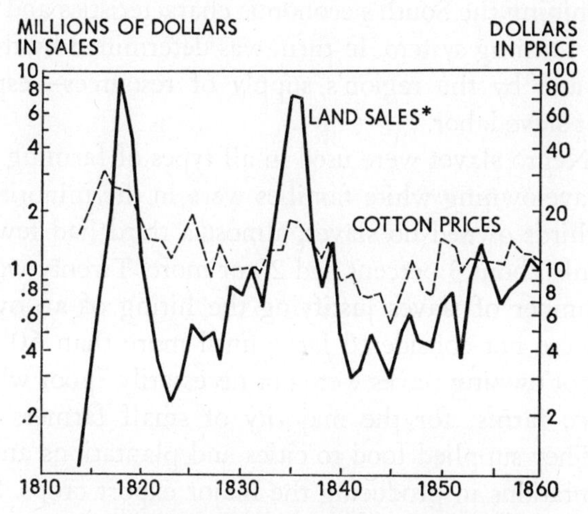

* Arkansas, Alabama, Florida, Louisiana, and Mississippi.
Source: U.S. Department of Commerce, *Historical Statistics of the United States* (Washington, D.C.: U.S. Government Printing Office, 1960), p. 124; and Arthur Cole, "Cyclical and Seasonal Variations in the Sale of Public Lands, 1816–1860," *Review of Economics and Statistics*, January, 1927, p. 52.

steadily and with about the same cost. As production approaches capacity, however, it becomes more difficult and costly to expand production. Production does not increase as fast as demand, and the price rises rapidly. Then the high price attracts new investment to expand capacity by opening up new farms or enlarging the cleared lands of existing farms.

Prices may remain high for several years because it takes time to expand capacity and to get the new lands into production. Finally, production begins rising rapidly, reflecting the new supply capacity. Since the supply expands faster than the demand, prices fall. As a result, capacity increases in a steplike fashion causing fluctuations in prices, while the price fluctuations cause the irregular capacity increases.

At the end of this chapter is an appendix which describes this process graphically. We suggest that the student finish the chapter, read the appendix, then return to this section for review. For purposes of the discussion that follows, the important thing to remember is that surges in the expansion of cotton capacity result from the normal operation of the market—from complex interactions between the growth of demand, the conditions of supply and capacity, and consequent fluctuations in prices.

The Plantation System

The way in which cotton production was organized played a large role in determining the South's economic characteristics and later development. The farming system, in turn, was determined by the nature of the product and by the region's supply of resources—especially the availability of slave labor.

While Negro slaves were used in all types of farming throughout the South, slave-owning white families were in the minority. In 1860, almost two thirds owned no slaves, almost a third had fewer than 20 slaves, and only about 3 percent had 20 or more. Twenty was about the minimum number of slaves justifying the hiring of an overseer, and plantations were not considered large until more than 50 slaves were used. Those not owning slaves were not necessarily "poor whites" living on subsistence farms; for the majority of small farmers were fairly prosperous. They supplied food to cities and plantations and competed with the plantations in producing the major export crops. Slave labor, nevertheless, produced a major portion of the region's exports; and because its competition had an effect on supply and prices, slave labor had a pervading influence on the labor income of free farmers.

The plantation system was carried over from the colonial period, in fact, it is still in use in various parts of the world. As a system, generally it involves the closely supervised employment of large numbers of unskilled workers with relatively low output per labor hour.

The amounts of land or capital used per worker may be moderate or very low, but the total amount used in the plantation as a whole is large. The workers are not only unskilled, they usually are destitute and have poor income alternatives. Whether they receive a wage, credit for merchandise, or food and other necessities supplied by the plantation, they ususally are dependent on the plantation for their current sustenance. The plantation, in turn, must have enough capital resources to meet labor and other expenses between crop sales. Thus, some current capital is invested in labor and supplies, while fixed capital is invested in land and equipment. Plantations may use free workers; but in colonial times free workers were unavailable and indentured servants or slaves had to be used; so some fixed capital had to be invested in labor.

Other than for slaves, the fixed capital requirements in cotton were somewhere between that for tobacco on the one hand and for rice and sugar on the other hand. Tobacco required almost no equipment and very little land, for one worker could tend only 2 or 3 acres of tobacco, and considerable close supervision and management skill was required. Sugar plantations required much investment in land improvements (to construct and maintain dikes and ditches). Cotton production required moderate acreage of land per worker and hardly any equipment. Since the work was simple and easily supervised, large acreages and many slaves could be managed in one farm unit.

The competitive advantage in large plantations, accordingly, was greatest for sugar and rice and least for tobacco. The first two were produced predominantly in large plantations, while tobacco soon became mostly a product of small farmers. In cotton, small and large farmers competed on somewhat more equal terms.

The large cotton plantation, however, did have certain advantages. The better farm managers tended to earn more profits, which could be reinvested in more slaves and land. Larger plantations tended to buy up the more fertile lands. Larger plantations also gained economies from greater division of labor, having more equipment, obtaining loans at lower interest, and making more favorable marketing arrangements.

Initially, high prices resulted in very favorable profits for both large and small farmers. The rush to settle the new lands in the Gulf states was by both large and small farmers. Small farmers hoped to get a start and grow larger by acquiring more land and more slaves. Some large tobacco farmers transferred into cotton; and even northeastern investors joined ventures in cotton plantations. On the frontiers of the South, some of the pioneer land was cleared by large planters with many slaves. Fortunes also were made in early land speculations and in the purchase and sale of lands as prices fluctuated. So large landholdings were obtained in various ways.

As the supply expanded and prices fell, however, widespread high profits disappeared and the basic condition of low-labor productivity held down small farmer incomes. Cotton was a labor-intensive crop; so, in competition with slave labor on plantations, the small farmer received a low income from his work. The slaves continued to be provided only a subsistence income in the form of crude clothing and food. Because of the large numbers of small farmers and slaves, average incomes were held down, and only a small percentage of wealthy plantation owners received high incomes.

The higher incomes were earned as a return from the larger amounts of capital invested in the plantations. On the average, taking into account the wide range in qualities of land and the variations in prices, a minimum-sized plantation with an overseer might require an investment of about $30,000. Almost two thirds of this might be the purchase price of the slaves and the rest the cost of land and equipment. Very large single plantations involved capital investments of several hundreds of thousands of dollars, and very wealthy men might own several large plantations.

The average profits in cotton farming as a whole varied with

6–4. ESTIMATED RATES OF RETURN ON CAPITAL INVESTMENT PER MALE SLAVE IN COTTON PLANTATIONS, 1830–60

			Rate of Return at Farm Cotton Prices of		
Land Quality	*Cotton Yield in Bales per Slave*	*Capital per Slave**	*7 Cents per Pound*	*8 Cents per Pound*	*9 Cents per Pound*
Poor	3	$1,250–1,300	2.2%	3.9%	5.4%
Typical	3.75	1,350–1,400	4.5	5.2	6.5
Better	4.50	1,600	5.0	7.0	8.0
Best	7	1,700	10.0	12.0	13.0

* Present value of total plantation capital outlays for 30-year life expectancy of slave.

SOURCE: Alfred H. Conrad and John R. Meyer, "Economics of Slavery in the Antebellum South," *Journal of Political Economy*, April, 1958, p. 107.

fluctuating prices, but they continued to be at least as good as on other investments in the national economy. Some historians have doubted this because the price of slaves rose—from $600 in 1802 to $1,800 in 1860 for a male field hand—while cotton prices had a long-term downward trend. Apparently, however, the productivity of labor used in cotton production rose as more production was concentrated in the most fertile lands of the Gulf States and as average farm size grew larger. Conrad and Meyer have estimated that the capital investment in the purchase of a male slave plus the land and equipment needed usually resulted in a net return to the owner of between 4.5 to 8 percent. (See 6–4.)

Dependence on Other Regions

Because cotton profits maintained their position relative to alternative sources of profit, southern resources continued to be concentrated in cotton production. Not only did cotton appear to be the most profitable use of most of the farmlands, but also there was little investment in nonfarm industries. Because of its concentration on cotton the South depended on other regions for supplying some of its needs.

The Great Lakes states and the border states found a considerable market for food supplies among the plantations near the Gulf. Productivity in raising corn and hogs was about twice as high on farms in the Ohio Valley as on plantations in the lower Mississippi Valley, and transportation down the Ohio and Mississippi rivers was cheap. When cotton prices were high or moderate, plantation owners found it profitable to concentrate even more of their slave labor on cotton production. Only when cotton prices were depressed did they try to make their plantations more self-sufficient. Small farms throughout the South, of course, also raised corn and hogs as well as cotton and supplied much of the plantation food needs locally.

The older farm states of the South Atlantic, as well as the border states, provided part of the supply of new slaves to the New South. After 1808, importation of slaves from abroad was reduced to smuggling, and the Negro slave population continued to expand solely through natural increase. The location of the slave labor, however, had to shift to the New South where cotton output was rapidly expanding. From 1800 to 1860, Negro population increased very slowly in the border states and South Atlantic region, while it increased very rapidly in the Gulf states and their near neighbors.

The bulk of the slaves that moved were brought to the New South by their masters who also migrated to the new farming areas. About two fifths, however, were sold in order to make the transfer. In some cases, the former masters were not consciously breeding slaves for the purpose of sale, but they found a need to dispose of an excess supply or to reduce their own operations. Certainly many southerners looked upon slave trading with distaste. Nevertheless, the effect was the same regardless of the intent. The Old South provided a breeding area for the expanding slave needs of the New South.

The production of slaves was an important intermediate product needed to carry out the whole process of cotton production. Furthermore, the production of slaves also was profitable and helped many small farmers and debt-ridden plantation owners in the areas of poorer soil to continue operating. Conrad and Meyer also have estimated that the rate of return was a little higher on the purchase of a female slave (who might raise 5 to 10 children), even though her work in the field was less productive than that of male slaves.

The Northeast supplied transportation, marketing, and financing services for the cotton planters as well as competing with English merchants and manufacturers in supplying consumer goods and machinery. Ships carrying cotton continued to be predominantly from the Northeast. The key businessman in handling cotton exports, however, was the broker (or "factor") at the main port cities, both in the South and in New York and Liverpool. He arranged for transporation to the port, weighing, storage, insurance, ocean shipment, and final sale; and for these services he charged a small commission. Usually the broker also was the planter's chief agent in arranging for loans and purchases of merchandise in New York or London.

Although the regions complemented each other in a mutually advantageous pattern during the period, the South's development might have taken quite a different course had it not depended so heavily upon staple crop specialization. Had the South been forced into other kinds of agriculture and more nonfarm pursuits it might have built a better foundation for the industrialization that it is struggling to complete today.

NORTH CENTRAL FARMING

Supplying Other Regions

Farming in the North Central region was influenced not so much by world markets as by expanding demand and limited supply in other regions of the nation. Food products did not bulk large in total exports, nor did food exports constitute a large part of total production. National population was expanding rapidly, and an increasing share of the people lived in cities and depended on purchases to supplement their own food production. East of the Appalachian Mountains, food production was limited by the declining fertility of worn-out soils on existing farms and by the increasing scarcity of unoccupied lands suitable for farming.

The northern lands west of the Appalachian Mountains had great natural resource advantages for grain and livestock production. Wheat production per acre was higher in western New York and Ohio than in most of the Northeast. Corn production per acre was higher in the Ohio Valley than in the New South. High yields on hay and other grains, together with the ample grazing space on uncultivated lands, made livestock raising advantageous.

The expansion of farm production occurred in surges in the North as well as in the South, and high market prices again provided some of the stimulus. Prices of wheat, for example, were very high at about the same time that peak sales in northern lands took place. Price changes, however, do not correspond fully to the surges in land sales in the late 1820's and the 1840's. (See 6–5.)

The major obstacle to farm production in the North Central region was the high cost of transporting surplus farm crops to distant markets in other regions. The high fertility of a farmer's soil and a high price in the market did not assure him a high cash income. High transportation costs might absorb a major part (sometimes as much as half) of the sale price of his products when delivered to a market. For this reason, transportation conditions were an especially important in-

6–5. Wheat Prices and Land Sales in Seven Northern States

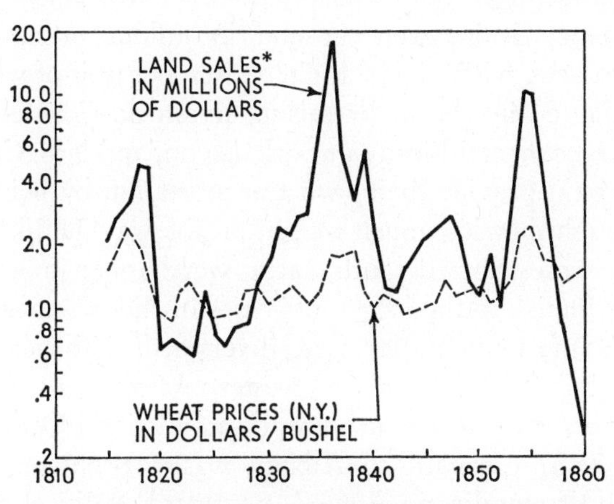

* Illinois, Indiana, Iowa, Michigan, Missouri, Ohio, and Wisconsin.

Source: U.S. Department of Commerce, *Historical Statistics of the United States* (Washington, D.C.: U.S. Government Printing Office, 1960), p. 124; and Arthur Cole, "Cyclical and Seasonal Variations in the Sale of Public Lands, 1816–1860," *Review of Economics and Statistics*, January, 1927, p. 52.

fluence upon expansion of farming in the North Central region. Major improvements in the interregional transportation links around 1825 and 1850, therefore, divide into three phases the history of northern farming before the Civil War.

In the first phase, prior to 1825, western farming was river-bound and oriented to southern markets. The earliest pioneers had settled along the Ohio River and its tributaries. The easiest mode of transporting farm products to markets was to build a raft or flatboat and float downstream via the Mississippi River to New Orleans. The ending of the War of 1812 relieved the settlers of harrassment by Indians near the Great Lakes and removed the ocean blockade of New Orleans. For several years prices for all farm products were high, and the expansion of southern plantations in the Gulf states provided a good market for northern food produts.

The trip downstream, nevertheless, was costly because it was long. Someone had to go with the goods and travel back again, being away several months. In 1815, the introduction of steamboats on the Mississippi and Ohio rivers speeded up the return trip for passengers and enabled the import of some manufactured goods. Yet most of the farm goods continued to be floated downstream.

High transportation cost had an important influence on the type of products moving out of the region. Usually, they were processed locally into semimanufactured food products in order to reduce their weight before shipment. Grains were ground into flour or converted into alcoholic beverages, which had a higher value per unit of weight. Grain also was converted into meat by raising livestock. Cornfed hogs were slaughtered and converted into salt pork, bacon, and lard. Cattle, on the other hand, could provide their own transportation by being driven to market, although they lost much weight on the way. Unlike most other products that were shipped south, cattle were driven mostly eastward across the mountains to the large port cities of the Northeast.

Farms in the Ohio Valley were diversified, with heavy emphasis on corn and hogs. Some farms in western New York and northern Ohio, however, specialized in wheat production. Overland transportation of flour eastward to Albany was a problem, as was the transportation of manufactured goods westward. Political agitation for public improvements in transportation in this area was important in bringing about a major change in interregional transportation.

Road and Canal Improvements

The transportation improvements that were to revolutionize North Central farming in its second phase began slowly and experimentally. Large investments were required, and the profit opportunities first had to be demonstrated. England, in the midst of its earlier Industrial Revolution, showed the way in road building and canal building by private stock companies.

Private toll road building in the United States was stimulated by the success of the Philadelphia and Lancaster Turnpike, built in 1789. During the next four decades more than 400 companies had constructed several thousands of miles of hard-surfaced highways in New England, New York, and Pennsylvania. Only the shorter, heavily traveled roads near or between large cities, however, were profitable. Stagecoach passengers, but little freight, moved over long distances. After the mid-

1830's, short plank roads were built for short farm-to-market travel because they cost less than the macadam-topped highways.

Government involvement in road building was limited almost entirely to the state and local levels, and even that was limited. When Ohio was admitted as a state in 1803, it was stipulated that part of the revenues from public land sales was to be used for state and federal road construction. After much controversy over implementing this stipulation, federal construction was authorized in 1811 for the National Pike (or Cumberland Road). It was completed from Cumberland, Maryland, to Wheeling, West Virginia, in 1818. Not until 1833 was it extended to Columbus, Ohio; it did not reach Vandalia, Illinois, until the mid-1850's. Other proposals to build a system of federal roads and canals were defeated largely because of sectional rivalries. New York and Pennsylvania were jealously vying for western routes connected to their own port cities; the New England states had built their own road systems; and the South, relying on ocean transport, preferred to mininize the need for federal tariff revenues.

Road building was not to prove revolutionary in any event, because it was costly to move bulky farm products by wagon. On a trail a horse could carry about three 60-pound bushels of wheat. Over a road a team might pull a wagon load of 25 bushels. On a canal barge, a horse could pull 50 times as much weight as it could on a wagon; so it is not surprising that average freight rates in 1850 have been estimated at around 15 cents a ton-mile by wagon and 1 cent a ton-mile on water. After deducting the costs of an average wagon haul of 80 miles, a Minnesota farmer might receive three fourths or less of the price of his wheat delivered at the nearest port. The longer the haul, the less the farmer received. An effective argument in favor of the proposed Erie Canal, which was begun in 1817, was that it would lower by one-fourth to one-half the transportation cost from Western New York to market. This could double the recipts of some farmers if prices held.

In 1825, completion of the Erie Canal from the Hudson River at Albany to Lake Erie at Buffalo marked the beginning of a canal-building fever and a new era in transportation. Very short canals connecting to ports had been built much earlier—even prior to 1800, in Maine and South Carolina. The Erie Canal was the first major undertaking, some 364 miles in length; and it was immediately apparent that it would be a financial success. Very fertile wheat lands lay between Rochester and Buffalo; so a heavy movement of wheat over nearly the full length was assured from the start. The more important use of the canal lay in the future, for it was apparent immediately that the Appalachian Mountain barrier had been overcome for east-west travel and that it now was possible to connect two large systems of water transportation, the Great Lakes and the Atlantic Ocean, via the Hudson River. Hitherto the Niagara Falls and the rapids on the St. Lawrence River had blocked navigation exit from the Great Lakes.

A burst of canal-building actvity followed in the late 1820's and early 1830's. Four western canals aimed to link the Great Lakes with the Ohio and Mississippi River system. Some of these were successful to a degree and helped to reverse the flow of farm products from a

6–6. Canals Linking Rivers and Lakes

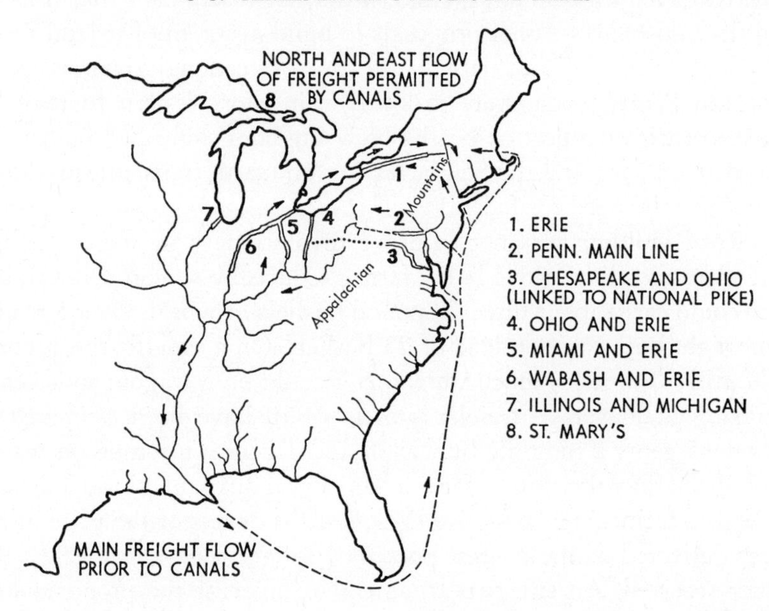

southward to an eastward direction after the mid-1830's. They also increased the traffic on the Erie Canal. Two other major canals aimed to compete with the Erie Canal by crossing the Appalachian Mountains. One was completed from Philadelphia to Pittsburgh and involved an ingenious combination of canals and rails (with the barges lifted onto rail cars to be pulled over the mountains). Another was completed only as far as Cumberland along the Potomac River from Washington. Neither of these was financially successful. Compared to the Erie Canal, they were more costly to build, they had less local traffic, and they provided little advantage of connection with an inland lake and river system (the eastward movement on the Ohio being an upstream one). (See 6–6.)

Other useful canals were built near the eastern port cities, but the canal-building fever was quickly over. The lack of early success, the depression after 1837, and the competition of railroads beginning in the 1840's all combined to cause financial losses and discourage further building. One exception was the building of St. Mary's Canal in the 1850's to open up navigation to Lake Superior and the iron ore mines in the Upper Peninsula of Michigan.

Specialized wheat farming received the greatest impetus from the new canal transportation. The location of most wheat farming also moved away from the Ohio River to the north and west, into more open country and prairies. The big increases in public land sales, during the 1834–37 boom, were in Michigan, Indiana, and Illinois. In spite of the depression following that boom, Illinois continued to have active land sales during the 1840's, when sales also began to be substantial in Iowa and Wisconsin. Farmers in all of these states could more readily make use of transportation of the products to eastern markets via the Great Lakes and the Erie Canal.

The Commercial Family Farm

The opening up of the prairies also was dependent upon development of farm machinery. Introduction of farm machinery, in turn, was encouraged by the shortage of labor and the land-extensive farming system that developed in the North. Since this type of farming developed around the family as the social unit, it may be referred to as the family farm. Since production became increasingly specialized for market sale rather than consumption and began to accumulate and use more capital, the label "commercial" may be used to distinguish it from the pioneer or "subsistence" farm.

In the 19th century, the greatest source of difference between farming in Europe and in America was the shortage of labor here. This was repeatedly observed by travelers visiting this country, and it helps to account for the higher farm wages here. Economic analysis, of course, leads us to expect that where one factor of production, land, is plentiful and the product is in demand, the other factors, labor and capital, will be more highly rewarded. The high rewards, then, will attract more of these factors in order to expand production.

The first source of farm labor supply was the farm family itself. A high birthrate produced many children, and they were put to work at an early age in the diversified work of a farm (gardening, milking, herding, churning, fruit picking) and finally the heavier work (haying, plowing, fence making, and so forth). As children grew to maturity they might be hired out to other farmers. Some left home to work as hired workers in new farm areas. The object of most was to own a farm, but many remained hired laborers. The next step might be to rent a farm as a tenant and share the crop with the landowner. Or, a small stake might be used to move west and buy public land to start a farm.

A second source of labor supply was the immigrant. Many had been farm tenants or farm laborers, and their object was farm ownership. Competition for such workers, however, was provided by city work and construction projects that could provide high wages and long steady periods of employment. Many of the immigrants came with enough funds to start their own farm, and it was not easy to find or hold farm workers.

From the earliest times it was characteristic of most American farmers to hold more land than could be worked immediately and to devote much labor initially to building up capital improvements. Before the prairies were reached, a farmer had to clear his land. He first cleared a small patch for a garden and corn to feed his family and a few livestock; then he tried to clear more and plant wheat to sell for cash. From then on he cleared, fenced, and expanded his operations. His methods might be crude and destructive of the fertility of the soil, but he had little incentive to improve as long as he had more land to expand onto.

Like the southern planter, the northern farmer frequently was heavily in debt trying to get started and to expand as fast as possible. The farmer borrowed to buy land, to buy livestock and tools, to build a house and barn, and to expand his operations. As long as prices held up, those loans were an investment in building up future production capacity and could be paid back out of expanded output. When the farmer speculated in more land than he could work or counted too heavily on very high prices, he took great risks of losing everything in mortgage foreclosures. The region, however, was fertile and provided profitable opportunties, the farmers were ambitious and optimistic, and owners of capital also were ready to loan at prevailing high interest rates. So the surges of land settlement brought streams of capital south and west as well as flows of labor.

Mechanization

The scarcity of labor was aggravated by the peak labor requirements in harvesting grains, especially wheat. The wheat had to be cut and shocked quickly within a few days after it was mature or the grain would fall off. Both the labor of plowing and harvesting were heavy. So many efforts were made to invent tools to make the work easier and faster. The farmer himself could make many tools out of wood, and the local blacksmith could forge and hammer out almost any part or fitting the farmer wished.

North Central and northeastern farmers became a font of technological improvement in reaction to competition from newer, more fertile western lands. As higher yield lands were cleared eastern farmers could leave farming, diversify into less competitive crops, or reduce costs and raise yields by developing better methods and better equipment. The latter alternative, of course, worked to the advantage of all farming and, ultimately, the consumer through resulting produtivity increases.

The first important improvement in farm tools was the making of a better plow. As early as 1797, Charles Newbold had patented a one-piece cast iron plow; but it was expensive and heavy. Between 1814 and 1819, Jethro Wood brought together a number of existing improvements to perfect a plow with three replaceable iron parts. It was simpler, lighter, and less expensive. The parts could be manufactured in factories in large numbers. In 1837, John Deere developed the first successful steel plow. The steel plow was especially important in facilitating prairie farming, since the sticky soil would push off the smooth polished surface more easily.

In the 1830's and 1840's, other inventions also faciliated wheat farming on large acreages with little labor. In 1833 and 1834, Obed Hussey and Cyrus McCormick patented reapers, which could be pulled by a horse and could cut many times as much wheat as a man swinging a sickle or a cradle. In the late 1830's, John and Hiram Pitts combined thresher and winnowing mechanical devices to a horse-powered treadle. Later portable steam engines were introduced to run the threshers. Because the machines were expensive, contract threshers moved through the wheat areas to do this for the farmers for a fee. Many other devices also were developed to save labor and use horse power—the mower, hay rake, the tedder, the horse fork (to hoist hay to the loft), the grain drill, and the corn planter.

By 1851, at the World's Fair in London, American farm machinery proved to be superior to that of any other nation. Factories in the East and in the North Central states were mass producing this equipment, and it was beginning to be used widely. This machinery increased the output per farm worker and enabled the family farm to be much larger in acreage. It also increased the capital needs of the farm, and had to be purchased rather than being accumulated by labor on the farm.

During this period the South made little use of the new farm tools.

This is in spite of the fact that many southerners were among those who took out patents on improvements. Apparently little laborsaving equipment was believed to be needed because of the low cost of slave labor. Work done elsewhere with horse-drawn equipment continued to be done with the hoe and the shovel plow. Only on the very large plantations was new steam-powered machinery introduced for processing the product after harvest.

The Prairies and the Railroads

In the 1850's, the third phase of North Central farming got into full swing with the help of new machinery and improved transportation. The specialized wheat farm on the prairies was the basis of the boom in land sales in the early 1850's. The large land sales were in Illinois, Wisconsin, Iowa, and Missouri. The steel plow, the horse-drawn reaper, and the thresher were enabling the family farm to handle a large acreage of prairie land. With large capital investments, the farmer concentrated on the wheat crop, and less-diversified production of other crop or livestock products was practiced. One exception was that some feed lots developed in the wheat region for fattening up cattle for market; Chicago developed as both a wheat-processing and meat-packing center.

The railroads also played an important role in the rapid development of the prairie, beginning in the 1850's. Rail lines were rapidly extended across the prairies in Illinois, Wisconsin, Iowa, and Missouri. This brought many areas remote from river transportation closer to the markets. Illinois counties which were distant from the river and previously sparsely settled had the most rapid population increases between 1850 and 1860.

Railroads also provided a new and better interregional link with the Northeast. Rail transportation was faster, less disrupted by weather, and permitted fewer transfers of cargo en route. While some railroad construction had occurred in the mid-1830's, it probably was delayed by the canal boom and then the depression in the late 1830's. During the 1840's, construction was mostly in the East, linking the coastal areas from north to south. But at the beginning of the 1850's, several mail lines were extended across the mountains in New York and in Pennsylvania, while a line was completed across Michigan to link Chicago and Detroit.

During the 1850's, there was a flurry of railroad construction that raised the total national railroad mileage from 9,000 to 30,000 miles. In the North Central states a network of lines was established connecting all of the cities and fanning out over the prairies. Rail lines could be laid hastily and cheaply across the flatlands, and the wheat crop promised to provide much freight traffic. In the South, railroad lines were fewer and usually connected the more isolated uplands areas with a South Atlantic port. Rail connections were made with the North only at Cairo, Lexington, and at Richmond. The river and ocean water routes apparently made rail lines along the previous traffic routes seem less needed. (See 6–7.)

During the 1850's also, the flow of immigrants (which had begun

6–7. Main Railroads, 1850 and 1860

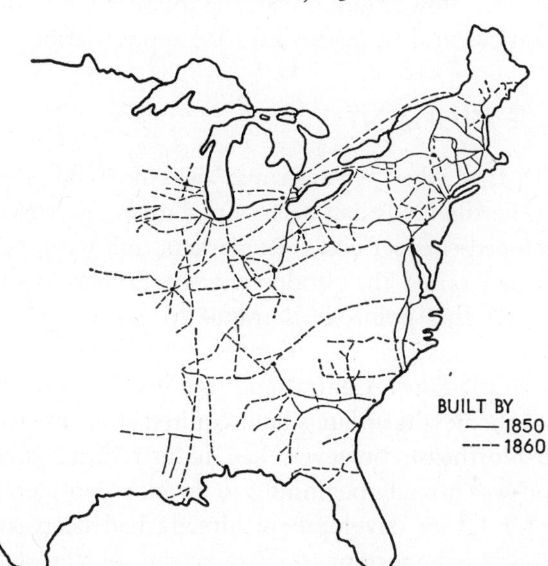

to rise rapidly in the 1840's) reached a peak. The Irish potato famine of the late 1840's brought many destitute Irish to the main port cities. But northern Europeans, the Germans and Scandinavians, began to flock to the prairie farmlands. Railroad developers helped to promote farm settlement along their lines. Land companies helped provide credit and settle whole communities.

The 1850's also was a period of awakening interest in improvement of farm methods and in education; and the competitive pressures brought to bear by the opening of new lands in the West contributed importantly to this awakening. Along with the efforts to find laborsaving machinery, there had been a slowly increasing interest in improved fertilization and crop rotation, in selective breeding, and in new species.

Decline in soil fertility and disease had hurt the wheat crops in the East, as well as cotton in the Old South. Farm magazines had been expanding in circulation and urging improved methods. Agricultural societies had flourished with the increased prevalence of the county fairs. State and federal governments also had taken more interest in providing information and technical aids to farmers. Beginning in 1830, 18 states had established geological bureaus and had made surveyes of soils as well as of rocks and minerals. Common problems of disease were studied. The patent office had established an agricultural bureau. Professors at leading universities were giving lectures on science in agriculture; and Michigan, Pennsylvania, Iowa, and Maryland pioneered in the 1850's in establishing agricultural colleges with state appropriations.

REGIONAL DEVELOPMENT

By 1860, then, the "farmer's age" was flourishing in the North Central states. Fertile lands had been settled upon, improved transportation had developed cheaper access to markets, and improved machinery and methods had raised the productivity of farmers on large-acreage family farms. At this point, it is useful to pause for a look at the interregional relations that had been established by the type of farm specialization in the South Central and the North Central regions. The competition of the new farmlands had required adjustments in the older regions. The Northeast, however, had industrialized, and the North Central region was already beginning to develop considerable industry. The pattern for future development already had been set before the Civil War, and it is important to examine the sources of this regional pattern of early development.

Income Differences

Estimates of per capita incomes by state in 1840 show that the highest income averages were mostly in the northern, highly urbanized regions. However, Louisiana and Mississippi also had very high average incomes, a considerable testimony to the profitability of large plantations in especially fertile areas. Also New Orleans was a thriving port city. The older farming states were somewhat lower in per capita incomes, both in the North and the South. The lowest income states were mostly pioneer or subsistence farm areas, usually somewhat remote from markets and thus having high transportation costs and, consequently, little specialization. The lowest income estimate in 1840, for example, was for Iowa, followed by Indiana, Michigan, Tennessee, Illinois, and Ohio. All of the cotton states fared somewhat better (See 6–8.)

Between 1840 and 1860, the average income per capita for the Nation rose rapidly, but all regions did not enjoy the same rate of increase. The Northeast had the most rapid gains, and its income per capita rose even higher relative to the national average. The North Central region had about the average gain, and its income remained about the same percentage below the national average. Gains in its older settled states were offset by the lagging of income in its more western pioneer farming area. All parts of the South, however, had slower than national gains in per capita income. The South Atlantic had sunk to

6–8. Total Income Per Capita by State, 1840*
(Current Dollars)

New England		East North Central		South Atlantic	
Maine	57	Ohio	48	Virginia	54
New Hampshire	64	Indiana	41	North Carolina	51
Vermont	65	Illinois	47	South Carolina	56
Massachusetts	107	Michigan	44	Georgia	57
Rhode Island	118	Wisconsin	80	Florida	69
Connecticut	91				
		West North Central		East South Central	
Middle Atlantic		Iowa	38	Kentucky	52
New York	80	Missouri	53	Tennessee	47
New Jersey	83			Alabama	53
Pennsylvania	75			Mississippi	84
Delaware	68				
Maryland	63			West South Central	
				Arkansas	68
				Louisiana	113

* Income originating in commodity production and distribution.

Source: Richard A. Easterlin, "Interregional Differences in Per Capita Income, Population, and Total Income, 1840–1950," Conference on Research in Income and Wealth, *Trends in the American Economy in the Nineteenth Century*, Vol. 24 (Princeton, N.J.: Princeton University Press, 1960), pp. 97–98.

become the lowest income region, and the East South Central fell below the East North Central. (See 6–9.)

Prior to the Civil War, therefore, the South had become established as the low-income major region. Among smaller regions, the more isolated farming areas—in northern New England, the Appalachian Mountains, and the western fringes of the North Central region—also had low incomes. The higher income states and regions were more urbanized and usually more industrialized.

For the most part, this pattern of regional income differences was maintained in the later history of the Nation. The East North Central, however, was an exception. It continued to gain in relative income level. Even before the Civil War it was becoming more urbanized and getting manufacturing industries. The South was lagging behind the

6–9. Regional Shares of Personal Income per Capita, 1840 and 1860

	Percent of U.S. Average	
	1840	*1860*
United States	100.0	100.0
Northeast	135	139
New England	132	143
Middle Atlantic	136	137
North Central	68	68
East North Central	67	69
West North Central	75	66
South	76	72
South Atlantic	70	65
East South Central	73	68
West South Central	144	115

Source: Richard A. Easterlin, "Regional Income Trends, 1840–1950," *American Economic History*, ed. Seymour E. Harris (New York: McGraw-Hill Book Company, 1961), p. 528.

Nation in income gains before the Civil War, and that war only caused a further setback by destroying much of its capital—especially its accumulated wealth in slaves.

Adjustment to Change

Underlying these statistics on regional income levels and their shifts was a changing set of economic opportunities and differing ways in which a region adjusted to them. In the early years of the Nation, the Northeast benefited from its foreign trade prosperity. While limited in agricultural surpluses, it had long had a timber-based shipbuilding industry, a fishing industry, seafaring people, and major port cities with good harbors. Then, when cut off from trade during wartime, its business leaders turned increasingly to manufacturing. Waterfalls provided power, large cities provided markets, and a labor supply came readily from immigrants and the farms, where opportunities were poor.

The rapid development of the central regions had an accelerating impact on the development of the Northeast. Supplying credit and merchandise to the new regions helped build up northeastern financial and trade businesses; and the domestic market for manufacturers was expanded. For the farmers in the Northeast, however, the canal and railroad improvements brought a flood of cheaper grain and meat products to compete with local supplies. Disease crippled some of the wheat production in the older areas. Fortunately, nearby city markets for food products were expanding. So the northeastern farmers began to diversify and produce more dairy products, fruits, and vegetables. Methods were improved and more capital was invested per farm. Many of the smaller farmers with poorer land, however, were hard pressed. Some moved west and others sought work in the cities. Young women from farm families in New England were especially an important source of labor supply to the textile industry.

The South Atlantic region had initially found its great opportunity in raising cotton for export. Then, as the more fertile lands of the Gulf states were developed and cotton prices continued to fall, the breeding of slaves for the newer regions became a supplementary export industry for the older region. The older southern regions also began to diversify their products somewhat and to try to improve farming methods. They did not benefit, however, from expanding markets in large nearby cities. Their farm population was not able to move to nonfarm work in nearby cities.

The amount of manufacturing and the enterprise of local businessmen in the Old South was quite limited. We do not have any confident answers as to why this was so, but historians usually have pointed to the dominant culture of a class society based on slave labor. The attitude of the country gentleman was to look down on physical labor and to devote much time to leisure activities. We should not overlook, however, the economic influences of a single-industry economy and of a product that did not favor other local activities; these influences are discussed in the following section.

The East South Central and West South Central regions were to suffer the same slowdown in their growth as soon as the initial expansion boom was exhausted. It is not that the regions lacked initial opportunities or resources. The profits in cotton and sugar were large. Capital flowed into the region, and every farmer tried to make the most of his opportunity to expand and accumulate wealth as rapidly as possible. After 1840, however, prices remained low and the growth of cotton production was at a slower pace. The northern freight traffic through New Orleans as a port also began to slacken in its growth as the canals and railroads shifted most of the freight increase eastward.

The East North Central region, in contrast, began to pick up momentum in its economic development and resulting growth in per capita incomes. The economy of this region initially was based upon shipments to other regions of processed grain and meat products. Improved transportation greatly enhanced the farmers' incomes. The opening of the prairies provided a new source of specialized production and export income. In addition, major cities grew up around food-processing industries, and the manufacture of farm machinery and other diverse goods began to appear. The region was developing the basis for a highly diversified, urbanized economy.

Development Influences

A number of contrasts between the South as a whole and the North Central region provide some insights into the economic conditions that influence cumulative growth. Basically, the differences seem to derive from the characteristics of the products initially specialized in and the type of transportation that was available. The social influences also were important, but they too were related to the type of production organization used for the main export crops.

First, the southern crops required intensive-labor cultivation on a small acreage. The available slave labor was plentiful, destitute, unskilled, and required supervision because of lack of incentive for personal advancement. Accordingly, there was little to be gained from building up capital improvements on the farm and using laborsaving machinery. The productivity and income per worker was low.

Second, the income distribution was very unequal in the South, where slaves were numerous, where many poor white farmers were subsistence farmers or competed with slave labor in producing export crops, and where wealth was based on ownership of land and slaves.

Third, a lack of support for public education was partly a consequence of the low and unequal incomes. The higher income planters gave their children private education and sent them away to finish their education. There was little incentive for them to support higher taxes to provide public education, and the poorer whites could ill-afford to support it alone. The North, however, continued a tradition of Protestant emphasis upon the virtues of education; and, in a more uniformly prosperous population and diversified economy, publicly supported education was more widely accepted and generally beneficial. Education, of course, then affected the quality and skills of the work force and tended to provide a source of native business leadership from families of rather humble origin.

Fourth, there was a limited consumer market and few cities with active trade and service industries in the South. The planters could travel to the Northeast or England occasionally, and they could order merchandise through their cotton brokers. The slaves and poor whites required very limited goods and services from city merchants. This lack of a large local market would be an important barrier to the starting of new manufacturing industries. In the North, the cities were numerous and did a thriving business selling diverse goods to prosperous farmers. The sale of farm machinery to northern farmers also was important to the development of metal industries in the Great Lakes area.

Fifth, southern agriculture did little to stimulate activity in related industries within the region. Most of the nonhuman inputs were produced more efficiently elsewhere. Once produced, the southern crops did not require much local processing. Sugar was an exception, but the heavy machinery required usually was provided by the very large planters themselves. Cotton required only simple crude machines on the larger plantations for ginning and baling. And cotton was spun, woven, and sewed at lower cost in the North. In contrast in the North, high transportation costs and the nature of the products made a wide variety of food-processing industries necessary. Cities, such as Cincinnati and Chicago, developed as ports and processing centers. The workers in these industries then required trade and service industries, too.

Finally, the easy access to ocean transportation by most of the South made the importation of manufactured goods very inexpensive. The freight rates on imports also tended to be low because the bulky nature of the export crops left most of the returning vessels almost empty, and competition was keen for some freight on the backhaul.

This meant that from the early stages of development of the region, any potential local manufacturer faced the prospect of low-competitive prices from established and efficient large manufacturers in the Northeast or England. There would be little differential in prices between the South and the Northeastern ports. In addition, any potential manufacturer also had a very small and limited regional market, because of the low incomes and few cities in the South. In the North, even after transportation was improved, the overland freight rates still provided substantial price differentials between midwestern cities and eastern cities. In addition, the market was large and growing rapidly in prosperous farm regions and in their trade center cities.

Consequently, we see in the negative example of the South and the positive example of the North some of the same influences that helped start the Nation on its path of cumulative development and rapid growth—a leading export industry that requires services from other diversified industries, urbanization and a growing local market, and energetic local business leaders. The culture and education of the South may have played a role in influencing the quality of leadership in that region; but these were not unrelated to the technical production characteristics of its chief export product, and these characteristics also resulted in a deficiency of demand for services of other industries. While specialization is important to high productivity and income initially, a diversity of industries helps to provide new sources of expansion when an older industry slows down. Furthermore, as the next chapter will show, increased size and number of industries in an area provide many economies of scale internally (in machinery) and externally (in the common use of specialized services).

APPENDIX TO CHAPTER 6 ON DEMAND AND SUPPLY CURVES

Economic theory uses demand and supply curves as a logical tool for mentally picturing the results of the interactions between buyers and sellers in a market for a particular good. Like an X-ray picture, the curves do not describe the full body of details of what happens, but only a skeleton outline of the relations of price and quantity sold. The pictures are static, "snapshots" showing relationships at one instant in time. By redrawing the curves to reflect the introduction of controlled, successive changes in conditions, the economist achieves something like a moving picture in analyzing the results implied by those successive changes.

The material that follows may be somewhat difficult to comprehend upon first reading if the student has not had some introduction to economic theory elsewhere. Further, we do not expect the student to master this analysis on the basis of these few paragraphs. What we are attempting to demonstrate is that economists have developed analytical tools that permit organizing, interpreting, and explaining the seeming chaos of price and quantity movements in real world markets. We will be gratified if the student is able to gain an appreciation for the power of these analytical tools in explaining historical occurrences. More specifically, we hope that the student can follow with greater insight the explanation of the relationship between cotton prices and expansion of capacity presented under the heading "Surges in Expansion."

Let us approach this by plotting theoretical data for demand and supply on a graph just as the economist would do in working with an actual historical problem. (See 6–10.) Note that we show prices on the vertical axis and quantity per time period on the horizontal axis.

Demand curves are illustrations of schedules that pair quantities that purchasers would buy with various alternative prices assuming that other factors are constant. For example, in 6–10, at 15 cents per unit buyers would purchase 0.6 units (say, millions of bales) per year. This

6–10. Theoretical Demand and Supply Curves

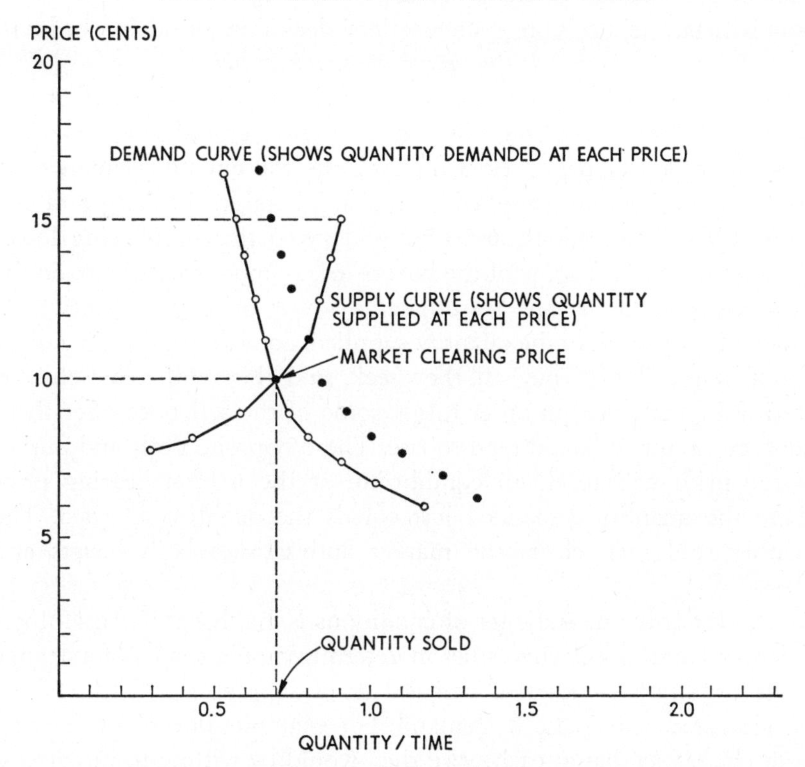

you can determine from the graph by locating 15 cents on the vertical axis, moving at a right angle from that point until you reach the demand curve; then move down parallel to the vertical axis until you strike the quantity axis at 0.6 units. If the price were lower, let us say 10 cents, then a greater quantity, 0.7 units, would be purchased. The less expensive is a given product, other conditions held constant, the more of that product are people willing to purchase. Thus the demand curve which is drawn by linking the various price-quantity points slopes downward to the right. (For now ignore the solid dots to the right of the demand curve.)

Correspondingly, supply curves are illustrations of schedules that pair quantities that sellers would be willing to bring to market with different prices. The higher the price, the greater the willingness of producers to supply the product. Thus the supply curve we get by linking our price-quantity points slopes upward to the right.

At the price of 10 cents we have a unique price-quantity combination. Only at that point in our price-quantity geometric space does the quantity demanded, 0.7 units, equal the quantity supplied. Only at 10 cents will buyers' decisions match sellers' decisions. In other words, 10 cents in our illustration is the ***market-clearing price.***

Let us see why 10 cents is the only price at which the market will clear. This can be understood by considering buyer and seller reactions to higher or lower prices. At a higher price the quantity demanded is less than the quantity supplied. Some suppliers are in danger of not selling all of their goods, and they will avoid this by offering lower prices in order to get some of the buyers to buy more from them. So the price would tend to fall. Starting at a lower price the quantity demanded is greater than the quantity supplied. Some buyers are in danger of not being able to buy all they seek, and they will avoid this by offering higher prices in order to get some of the sellers to offer them more. So the price would tend to rise. These opposite pulls and pushes on the price will reach an equilibrium at the market-clearing price where the quantity demanded just equals the quantity supplied. The quantity sold then clears the market and satisfies both buyers and sellers.

So far only one static set of conditions is involved. The usefulness of demand and supply curves lies in determining the results of a change in the conditions—either of demand or of supply or of both. Let us consider first an increase in demand. For example, buyers' preferences could change so that at each price they would be willing to purchase a greater quantity. The solid dots plotted to the right of our original demand curve illustrate this. This would shift the entire demand curve upward and to the right as you can see by linking the new points together.

Now a new market-clearing price-quantity combination would come about. Because buyers are willing to pay more per unit sellers are able to bear higher unit costs in bringing a larger quantity to market with the result that price would rise to 11 cents and quantity sold would advance to 0.8 units. You can picture similar results on the assumption that the demand curve remains constant, but that a cost-reducing innovation causes the supply curve to shift to the right. As you might guess, the market-clearing price would fall while the quantity sold would increase.

At this juncture let us add a realistic element to our analysis by turning to 6–11, which illustrates the cotton market in the antebellum years. The dots in 6–11 show the actual price and production data for the years 1827 to 1836, when prices reached a peak. The curves are hypothetical but are drawn so as to approximately fit the observed data.

6–11. Hypothetical Shifts in Cotton Demand and Supply

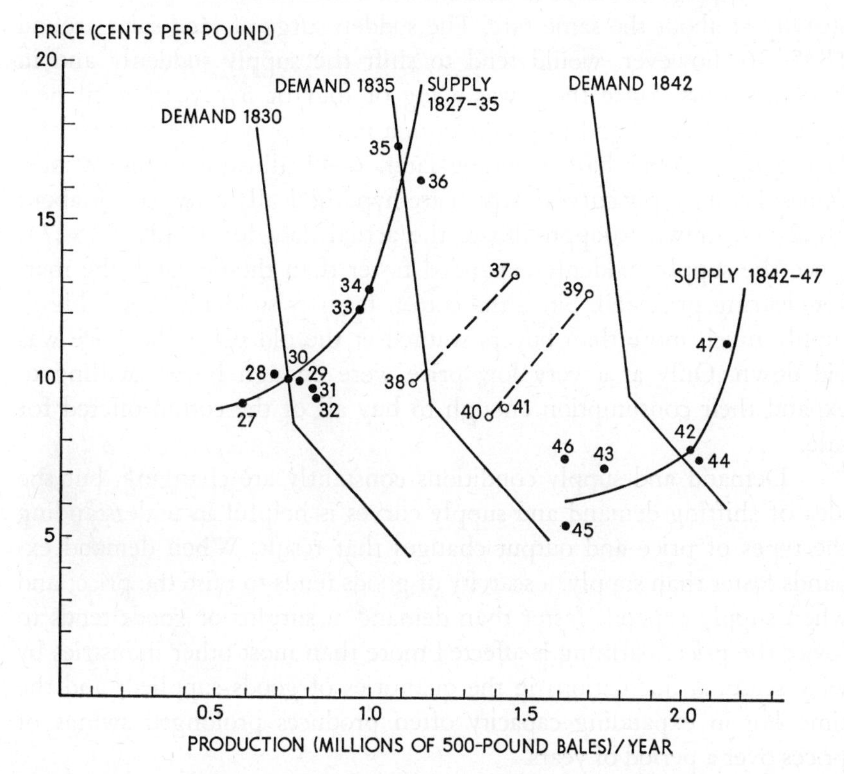

They suggest the relations that might explain the data but do not provide any proof that our illustration actually accounts for the observed price-quantity changes.

We can imagine that in 1830 the demand and supply curves looked somewhat as pictured. In that year almost 8 million bales were exchanged at 10 cents per pound or $50 per 500-pound bale. By 1835 demand had increased, for reasons that we have already discussed, and produced a new demand curve as noted in 6–11.

With the basic conditions of supply assumed to be unchanged, the market clearing price rose to about 17 cents per pound and output increased to over 1 million bales. Existing cotton farms were limited in their capacity and thus could only expand output at higher unit costs—less productive acreage had to be employed, products that were usually grown for plantation consumption had to be purchased at higher prices, and more field hands had to be bought in a rising market. Consequently, a higher price was necessary to draw forth more output.

Further shifts now may be introduced for both the demand curve and the supply curve. We assume that demand continued to expand steadily at about the same rate. The sudden surge of land sales around 1835–36, however, would tend to shift the supply suddenly and in large amounts. Since there was a lag of four or five years until new lands were cleared and in production, a new supply curve emerged far to the right about half a decade later. 6–11 illustrates this by new demand and supply curves (which are hypothetically assumed for about 1842 and drawn to approximate the actual data for 1842 to 1847). Since the supply suddenly expanded faster than the demand, the market-clearing price fell. Since the cotton farmers suddenly were able to supply much more than buyers wanted at the old price, the price was bid down. Only at a very low price were enough buyers willing to expand their consumption enough to buy all of the cotton offered for sale.

Demand and supply conditions constantly are changing, but the idea of shifting demand and supply curves is helpful in understanding the types of price and output changes that result. When demand expands faster than supply, a scarcity of goods tends to raise the price; and when supply expands faster than demand, a surplus of goods tends to lower the price. Farming is affected more than most other industries by wide seasonal fluctuations in the quantities of goods supplied; and the time lag in expanding capacity often produces prolonged swings of prices over a period of years.

STUDY QUESTIONS

1. From 1815 to 1840, what was the major expanding sector of the American economy? Why was much of national growth dependent upon one major export product?
2. Why did expansion of cotton farming occur in surges? How did supply shifts, in turn, affect cotton prices?
3. The plantation system of farming tends to develop under what types of conditions as to crop requirements and resource supplies? How does this explain the predominance of large plantations for sugar and rice, small farms for tobacco, and a mixture of large and small cotton farms? Why was cotton farming profitable for large farmers but a low-income occupation for small farmers? How did the rapid expansion of cotton production in the Gulf states affect the South Atlantic region?
4. In the North Central region what was the major initial barrier to rapid development of farming? Why was early development of this region oriented to the South? What besides price caused the major surges in land settlement in the North Central?

5. Why were roads not a major factor in the early economic development of the Nation? Why was the Erie Canal a major influence on the development of the North Central region? Why weren't other canals as successful?
6. Why was the northern farm based on small single-family units? How did the family farm and the requirements of crops influence the development of farm machinery? What developments in both farm machinery and in transportation brought another surge in farming expansion in the North Central during the 1850's?
7. How was farming in the Northeast affected by the development of the North Central region? How was other economic activity in the Northeast stimulated by the development, first, of southern farming, and later, of North Central farming?
8. Why was per capita income in 1840 highest in Rhode Island, Massachusetts, and Louisiana? Lowest in most East North Central states? Why did per capita income between 1840 and 1860 rise fastest in the Northeast and slowest in the South?
9. How did the characteristics of the major export crop eventually become a retarding factor in the economic development of the South prior to the Civil War?

Chapter 7 RISE OF MANUFACTURING

In the 1840's, the United States entered its initial period of rapid economic growth. As already indicated, the rise in per capita income between 1840 and 1860 was phenomenal; even England did not have such a rapid start in the Industrial Revolution. As a producer of agricultural surpluses, America had built up a flourishing export trade in cotton, and the wheat from its central plains was beginning to be an important export item. However, the most dynamic part of its national growth was due to the rise of manufacturing in the Northeast.

Manufacturing expansion may be regarded as being on the "intensive frontier" of American development, while agricultural expansion was mostly on the "extensive frontier." The rise in farm output was mostly a result of settling new farmlands. Extensive expansion of output meant more of the same type of production—not only more farms but also more trading towns, more processing of farm products, and more transportation of crops to markets. The increasing percentage of urban population, however, reflected something different—a more intensive concentration of production. As the economy expanded, the organization of all types of production became more complex, and greater specialization and division of labor resulted in higher output per worker. Farming, of course, participated in this rising productivity, but the greatest overall gain was from the rising importance of nonfarm production. In part, this was because America was able to provide for itself more of the high-valued manufactured goods. It also reflected an increasing shift of production from the home to the factory and the tremendous gains from introduction of modern industrial methods as this Nation began to participate in and contribute to the ongoing Industrial Revolution.

America's start in manufacturing, however, was not something deliberately chosen and suddenly launched for purposes of national self-sufficiency or of higher consumer incomes. Early efforts to foster American manufacturing industries were not very successful. Conditions, at first, did not seem favorable. Manufacturing industries grew slowly over several decades from a diversity of small beginnings. However, before the War of 1812, many inventions and a few successful manufacturing starts had been made.

When European strife and the War of 1812 led to curtailed imports between 1807 and 1815, the United States got a "false start" as a manufacturing nation. Although many of the new firms failed after imports once again freely entered our ports, the educational experience of our first large-scale venture into manufacturing was invaluable. Not until the 1820's did the first major industry, cotton textiles, become firmly established in domestic markets. Then, rather suddenly in the 1840's and 1850's, a great variety of industries began to flourish, and by 1860, the United States was among the leading industrial nations.

America's experience, therefore, raises two questions. Why was the start of manufacturing delayed and slow to get under way? And why did it grow so rapidly once it got under way? Answers to these questions are not to be found simply in a description of the historical events. Nor do the availability of natural resources and the timing of particular inventions provide satisfactory answers either. Consideration also must be given to the market environment and other resources required by modern industry. The various parts of an economy need to be viewed as interrelated and changing over time. In short, the answers must be sought in terms of evolving conditions and a developmental process. While detailed knowledge of the process of America's economic development is limited, a better understanding and perspective on the main events can be obtained by attempting to consider them in these terms.

EARLY BEGINNINGS

Types and Trends of Industry

In 1790, the United States was an agricultural nation that exchanged surplus farm products for specialized manufactured products from England. The American farmer, however, was quite self-sufficient and produced for himself most of the things he consumed. He not only raised his food and built his own house, but also he and his family made most of their own clothing, shoes, furniture, and other household items. This "home manufacture" continued for a while to provide an important part of consumer goods, but in the next half century the rise in production and sale in markets gradually removed this type of production from the home. The displacement of household manufactures by factory-produced imported and domestic manufactures followed closely the development of roads, canals, and railroads. As improved transportation routes penetrated the hinterland, home manufacturing steadily declined in all but the least accessible regions.

In the towns and cities skilled craftsmen supplemented the production in the home by providing things the farmer could not make for himself. The merchants and other city dwellers also relied upon craftsmen to make things for them. The better quality of goods from specialized craftsmen also was preferred by all who could afford to pay for it. Thus, the early cities and later western towns had their blacksmiths, cobblers, hatters, tailors, weavers, coopers, and other types of craftsmen. As his trade grew, the craftsman would expand his production by hiring apprentices and journeymen to work in his "shop."

In addition, some larger scale production was carried out in "mills." Grist mills were needed to grind wheat and corn, and sawmills provided lumber. Also, there were ironworks, breweries, tanneries, and brickyards. These required a number of workers and considerable capital equipment.

While statistics on production in the early decades were scattered and inadequate, the production of the shops and mills falls into the category of manufacturing industry. The rapid expansion of this industry in the first half of the 19th century was partly a matter of increased specialization and production for market—that is, a decline in home production. The major change, however, was the rapid expansion of production in "factories," using power-operated machinery to replace hand manufacture. This resulted in an improved quality of products at so much lower costs that time spent on home manufacture no longer seemed worthwhile to the family.

The trend of production in manufacturing industries undoubtedly was rising somewhat faster than national output for a number of decades, but it was not until after 1840 that manufacturing production was large enough and rising rapidly enough to provide an important stimulus to national growth. The available data, of course, are extremely inadequate prior to 1840, but the number of workers was small and could not have changed much faster than population throughout the early decades. In estimating national income, Martin indicates a rise in the share of income arising from manufacturing from about 5 percent in 1800 to around 7½ percent in 1820. Census data suggest that about 7½ percent of all workers were in manufacturing industries in 1820. By 1860, manufacturing's share of workers had risen to 12 percent. While Martin's estimate of manufacturing's share of income (in current prices) rose only a similar amount, recent estimates of commodity production suggest a much faster growth of physical production in manufacturing after 1840. Reduced prices in manufacturing would diminish the gain in dollar value of manufactured output, but even then the value of manufacturing output probably grew faster than employment. Both measures, however, show that manufacturing was increasing faster than national totals and thus was rising in relative size in the national economy. (See 7–1.)

7–1. Rising Importance of Manufacturing

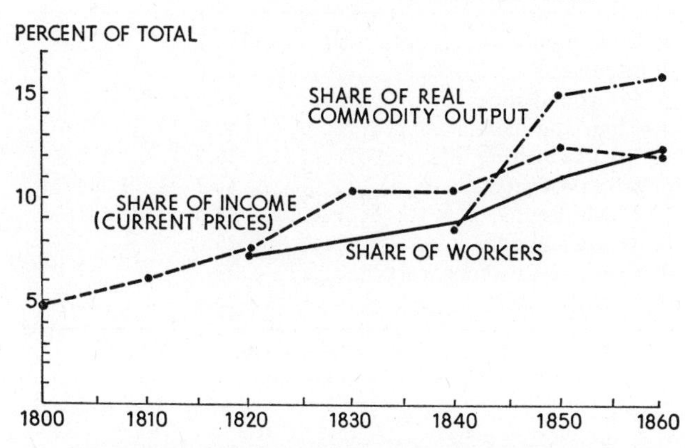

Note: Commodity output is treated here as half of GNP.

Source: R. F. Martin, *National Income in the United States, 1799–1938* (National Industrial Conference Board, 1939); and R. E. Gallman, "Commodity Output, 1839–1899," *Trends in the American Economy in the Nineteenth Century*, Conference on Research in Income and Wealth (Princeton, N.J.: Princeton University Press, 1960).

The types of industries that were important in this rise of manufacturing are suggested by the census of 1860. (Only in 1850 and 1860 were the census data fairly detailed and comparable to later data.) Lumber and flour mills were important from the beginning, and they were still the second and fourth ranking manufacturing industries in 1860. The first ranking industry, however, was cotton goods, and woolen goods placed eighth. These textile industries were virtually nonexistent in America in 1790; and they constituted the first leading "growth industry." Boots and shoes and men's clothing, the third and fifth ranking industries, had begun by 1860 to move from the large shop to the factory; but their relative importance also reflects the extent to which people no longer made their own clothing at home. Iron products and machinery were the sixth and seventh ranking industries. Altogether, this list suggests that the rapid rise of manufacturing industries is to be explained in terms of the development and use of power-operated machinery to produce textiles, clothing, and shoes in factories rather than in the home. This was characteristic of the Industrial Revolution in England, which was well under way by 1790. That revolution did not get into full swing in America until about half a century later. (See 7–2.)

7–2. TEN LEADING MANUFACTURING INDUSTRIES, 1860

Industry	*Value Added (Millions)*	*Employees (Thousands)*
1. Cotton goods	$54.7	115.0
2. Lumber	53.6	75.6
3. Boots and shoes	49.2	123.0
4. Flour and meal	40.1	27.7
5. Men's clothing	36.7	114.8
6. Iron products	35.7	49.0
7. Machinery	32.6	41.2
8. Woolen goods	25.0	40.6
9. Carriages, wagons, carts	23.7	37.1
10. Leather	22.8	22.7

SOURCE: *Eighth Census of the United States, Manufactures* (1860).

Textiles' Early Lead

It was in cotton textile manufacture that the Industrial Revolution got its start in England, but the Revolutionary War cut this country off from immediate access to the technological know-how of the new inventions. In England, the single spinning wheel quickly was replaced by the invention in 1764 of the multiple spindle "spinning jenny." Without much delay, in 1775 at the start of the Revolutionary War, the new spinning jenny was used in a factory established by a new joint-stock company in Philadelphia. Already, however, the English textiles were leaping rapidly ahead with the application of waterpower to run Richard Arkwright's water-frame machines (invented in 1769) with the improvement in quality made possible by Samuel Crompton's "mule" (invented in 1779). After the war, in the 1780's, the cheaper imported English cotton goods began to flood the American market, and several unsuccessful efforts were made to start American spinning factories. English laws, however, barred the export of textile machinery, inventions, or even skilled workers. In 1786, one set of brass models of the Arkwright machines was confiscated by the British government before shipment, although another set of models and descriptions did come into the possession of the state of Massachusetts. Machines were built from these models in Massachusetts, Connecticut, and Rhode Island, but difficulties were experienced in getting them to operate satisfactorily. Moses Brown, a Providence merchant engaged in making rough cotton goods for sale to southern plantations, bought a set of the machines and tried to run them with waterpower.

The first successful American spinning machinery was built for the firm of Almy and Brown by an English immigrant, Samuel Slater, who brought the technical know-how with him. Slater had spent six and a half years as an apprentice in the Strutt and Arkwright mill in England, where he had been allowed to experiment and make improvements in the machinery. Slater had memorized the key dimensions of the machines as well as being familiar with all of the parts. Knowing of the opportunities for similar factories in America, he dressed as a farm laborer and secretly boarded a ship for New York, where he was put in touch with Moses Brown. After demonstrating the success of his first machines in December of 1790, Slater became a partner with Almy and Brown and built a small factory in Pawtucket, Rhode Island. In the next few years Slater and others who learned from him built Arkwright machines for several other factories in New England; so, by 1807 there were 15 spinning mills operating.

Between 1807 and 1815, the embargo and the War of 1812 cut off the import of British textiles and gave a great stimulus to the construction of spinning factories in America. In 1810, the Secretary of the Treasury reported 87 mills built or under construction. By 1815, 213 mills were reported to be operating. With the return of peace, however, cheaper British goods again flooded domestic markets and many of the American mills were forced to close. While American manufacturers were learning to build the waterpowered spinning mills, England had gone on to build power-operated looms, based on the Cartwright invention in 1784. American spinning mills only made yarn and then "put out" their yarn to workers in their own homes. These "cottage" workers wove the yarn into cloth on handlooms and returned the cloth to the mill for marketing. This handwoven cloth, however, could not compete with the cheaper English cotton cloth made on power looms.

Fortunately, another breakthrough in acquiring the British technology had been made by an American manufacturer just before the end of the war. In 1810 and 1811 while traveling abroad, Francis Cabot Lowell, a member of a wealthy Massachusetts family, became interested in the cotton mills of Manchester and the possibility of introducing power weaving in America. After asking many questions and taking careful notes, Lowell returned to Boston where he persuaded several other wealthy families to join in the financing of an integrated spinning and weaving mill at Waltham. Making use of his mathematical training, Lowell made some intricate calculations on the key dimensions necessary to make the machines work and then developed some improvements of his own. The Waltham mill of the new Boston Manufacturing Company was operating very successfully in 1814; and to meet the postwar competition of British cotton goods, other American manufacturers quickly adopted the Waltham plan of combining spinning and weaving powered machinery in the same factory.

7–3. COTTON GOODS MANUFACTURED

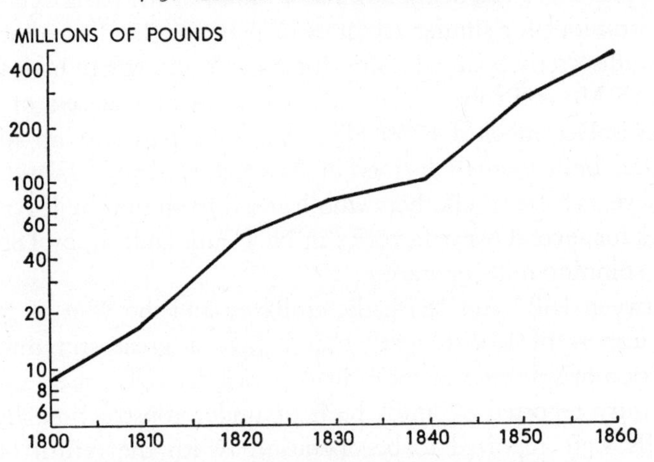

SOURCE: *Eighth Census of the United States, Manufactures* (1860), p. xv.

With the combined help of the new power looms and the Tariff Act of 1816, the cotton textile industry was fairly securely established in 1820. With further improvements in their own machinery, and with further tariffs, the output of the industry continued to expand. Production at first was concentrated primarily in the cheaper goods and coarser weaves of cloth where the tariffs were most effective and the acquired skill and quality of manufacture was least critical. In the 1820's, the combination of imports and domestic factories virtually eliminated handloom production of cotton cloth for market or home use. Then, in the 1830's, with these gains already achieved and tariffs declining, the growth of the industry slowed down. Finally, after 1840, rapid growth again returned with a general rise in demand and further improvements in waterpower and textile machinery. (See 7–3.)

The Diversity of Innovations

It is important to note that while the textile industry was leading the way as the first major mass-production industry, inventions were preparing for the beginnings of mass production in many other industries at the same time. Most of the discoveries were made quite independently, but so many were stimulated by developments in other industries or assisted developments elsewhere that it is difficult to disentangle them and discuss their history separately. The contributions of a few leading men may be cited as examples.

As early as 1787, a major existing industry, flour milling, benefited from a major invention by Oliver Evans. Considering the problem of labor shortages, as well as the backbreaking work of carrying grain sacks up stairways to the top of a mill, Evans developed a system of machinery that automatically performed the sequence of heavy labor and handling operations necessary to move the grain through the mill and emerge as barrels of flour. Power from the waterwheel was geared to a whole series of devices. A shoveling device, endless belts running over rollers, and buckets on a vertical lift conveyor did the initial work of handling the grain. Then the grain was allowed to fall between cracking and grinding stones, to be separated from bran, and to be packed into barrels by a series of chutes, valves, and rakes. Only two men were needed to operate the mill. While his system was adopted slowly and piecemeal at first, the advantages of continuous processing became so obvious that variations of automatic machinery were used nearly everywhere after 1815.

Numerous other ways were being found in other industries to use machines to perform repetitive tasks as well as in heavy work. In the 1770's, a device was introduced to head a dozen nails at once, and in the 1790's a machine cut and headed nails. In the 1790's, also, woodworking machines were cutting the teeth and forming the curved parts of cards and combs for the textile industry; and a lathe machine was used for turning wood to cut round and oval handles.

Eli Whitney, the inventor of the cotton gin, is credited with the first successful use of the idea of making standard parts in the manufacture of small arms. Having observed minting machines stamping out standard copper coins and wood-turning lathes, he decided to manufacture muskets by using a full line of guided tools. In 1798, he obtained a sizable contract from the U.S. Army for 4,000 muskets. Because of the time required to set up and perfect his machinery, he had only 500 ready for delivery a year later; but he put on a demonstration before President John Adams that gained him more time and further contracts.

He showed that by disassembling a number of guns, scrambling the parts, and reassembling them he still had guns of the same quality. Standard parts thus had advantages for repair and replacement of products in use, as well as for economy in manufacture.

Simeon North also produced arms about the same time using even greater specialization of workers on narrow phases of the manufacturing process. The government armories at Springfield, Massachusetts, and Harpers Ferry, Virginia, also deserve special mention in connection with the beginnings and development of interchangeable parts. Later, refinements in these methods enabled Samuel Colt to develop and mass-produce his revolving barrel pistol during the Mexican War.

Clockmakers were the first to adopt the idea of making standard parts in their industry. In 1807, Eli Terry built a larger mill fully using Whitney's methods of punching out and cutting standard wheels and cogs. Clocks previously selling for $25 were now sold for $5. Many of these parts at first were made of wood, but the introduction of metal parts further lowered costs and improved quality. This development, in turn, was aided by the development of light metals industries. The patriot, Paul Revere, had introduced large-scale copper rolling in order to sheath the bottom of the navy's ship, "Constitution," as well as the dome of the Massachusetts State House. In 1802, the brass industry began to develop in Waterbury, Connecticut. While the heavy metal industries were more advanced in England, America took an early lead in mass-producing light metal products and light machinery used in mass-production factories.

Development of specialized machine-making businesses was stimulated by and contributed to all of these developments. Oliver Evans and Eli Whitney were heavily engaged in making their own machinery. When Samuel Slater built his first textile mill, he had the help of an ironmaster named David Wilkinson. After helping Slater build several mills, Wilkinson opened up his own machine-building shop at Pawtucket in 1810, the same year Alfred Jenks started his machine shop near Philadelphia. These American machine builders independently discovered, or introduced from England and improved upon, the basic machine tools—the slide lathe, milling machine, and gear cutters.

By 1840, machine tools were produced for commercial markets as machine toolmakers grew in number and gradually displaced many of the machine shops that were merely departments within textile, armament, and other types of plants. As these shops grew in number the number of inventions, improvements, and innovations they accounted for mushroomed. Some examples are the Blanchard shaper, the milling machine, the turret lathe, improved grinders, and precision measuring devices such as the verier caliper, the micrometer, and Johannsen blocks.

Enterprise and Invention

These examples suggest the wide diversity of inventions that prepared the way for rapid expansion of manufacturing industries after 1840. The possibilities of mass production of consumer products had been demonstrated by British textiles. While American businessmen borrowed British know-how, they were quick also to adapt and improve

7–4. PATENTS ISSUED

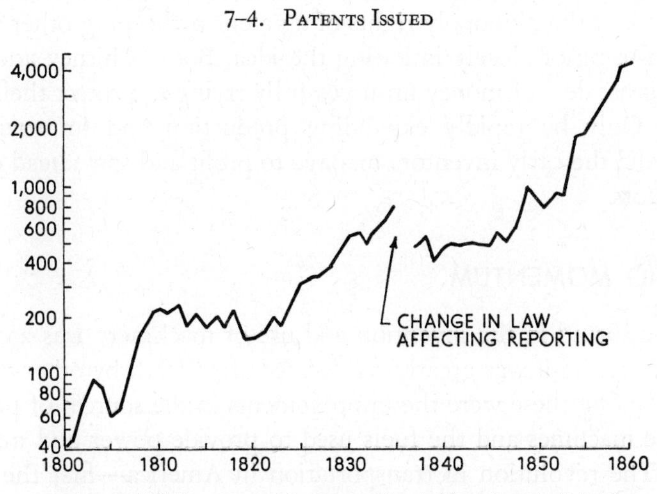

SOURCE: U.S. Department of Commerce, *Historical Statistics of the United States* (Washington, D.C.: U.S. Government Printing Office, 1960), p. 608.

upon these methods by their own inventions. Scarcity of labor in this country led to emphasis upon laborsaving machinery doing repetitive tasks. The idea of standard parts enabled complex products to be produced with specialized machinery and workers. Improvements in light metals and machine tools aided in the construction of the needed machinery in this country.

Some idea of the rise in inventive activity is suggested by records of patents issued by the national government. Patents at first were issued under loose standards and without checking for duplications, so after a change in the laws in the mid-1830's the figures are a little more reliable. Nevertheless, the total record suggests three periods of rapid rise in inventions—1807–14, 1825–35, and 1850–60. Each of these was a period of rising business activity; so, it might be argued that inventions were forthcoming when business opportunities were good. (See 7–4.)

Most of the early inventors, in fact, were businessmen, became businessmen, or were backed by businessmen. Slater was financed by Brown and became a partner in several textile firms. Oliver and Whitney established their own manufacturing industries. Lowell was a man of wealth who acquired the necessary technology and started a manufacturing firm with the aid of a group of wealthy merchants.

The history of invention, furthermore, is full of stories of long neglect or business failure. A number of people, for example, experimented with the steamboat and the steam railroad before successful models were developed and businesses established. Seldom was it possible to exploit the monopoly rights of a patent by keeping other producers from using or closely imitating the idea. Both Whitney and Evans spent a great deal of money unsuccessfully trying to protect their initial patents. Only by rapidly expanding production and improving the product did the early inventors manage to profit and stay ahead of their competitors.

GAINING MOMENTUM

The spread in the invention and use of machinery was a cumulative process, and it was greatly accelerated after 1840 by other developments. Among these were the improvements in the sources of power to drive the machines and the fuels used to provide power and make the metals. The revolution in transportation in America—first the steamboats and canals and then the railroads—magnified many times the effect of income and population growth in providing a rapidly expanding mass market, the essential environment for rapid conversion to mass-production methods. Finally, the resources required for expanding industry—the labor and the capital—became available fast enough to meet the demand.

Production Methods and Market Size

We have already developed the idea that specialization among firms and division of labor within firms raises productivity. Specialists, you will recall, produce more efficiently because they become more proficient, waste less time, and can utilize laborsaving, mass-production machinery. However, the capital goods used in mass production are "lumpy" in the sense that each unit built is very large (using the minimum level of daily output when fully manned as a measure of size). And each unit is very costly.

What this means is that modern industrial production requires a mass market so as to spread the cost of massive capital investment over as many units of output as possible. Otherwise unit costs of production would be prohibitively high by other than labor-intensive production methods. Imagine how high automobile manufacturing costs would be if today's market were only, say, 1 million units rather than 9 million units per year. With today's plant and equipment annual production could then be produced in about 40 days leaving auto plants idle for the balance of the year and producing, compared with actual costs, a nine-fold increase in annual capital costs per unit. In lesser dimensions exactly this situation threatened the potential American manufacturer in the early 19th century.

As we can see from the above, rapid manufacturing growth in the United States could not be initiated by inventions, innovations, and enterprising spirit alone. The period was the dawn of mass production; as long as the American market was small and scattered it was cheaper to import manufactured goods from nations such as England that had large, concentrated markets and thus could use modern production techniques.

On the other hand, once income and population growth had increased the market and transportation improvements had welded it together, the manufacturing sector was poised for a takeoff. That takeoff appears to have begun in about 1840. By that time natural population increases, augmented somewhat by immigration, and the rise in total income attributable to extensive growth of output had carried many manufacturing industries over the cost threshold that made domestic production possible. And with the greater momentum in manufacturing growth came an accelerated increase in per capita income increases. Thus we have here an example of the principle we cited in Chapter 1: namely that economic expansion—extensive growth—can aid economic or intensive growth.

Steam Engines, Iron and Coal

From earliest colonial times, the power to drive the machinery of mills and the bellows of furnaces was readily available from water-wheels on the numerous streams leading down out of the Appalachian Mountains. The early textile factories were located at some of the same river sites of the older mills. As these sites became crowded and more power was needed, large dams were built to provide a greater fall, use more of the water, and provide more regular flow throughout the year. The great concentration of textile industries at Lowell, Manchester, and Lawrence in Massachusetts was due to the development of waterworks on the Merrimac River in the 1820's. Attempts also were made to improve the efficiency of the waterwheel, and this led to additional experiments with the water turbine. Practical water turbines were first introduced for use by textile mills in New England in 1843. American improvements in the turbine in the next few years made important contributions to their technology and were widely adopted in the 1850's.

Because of the availability and cheapness of waterpower, steam engines were not rapidly applied to manufacturing. While low-pressure steam engines already were being used, in 1804 Oliver Evans obtained a patent for a high-pressure steam engine, which he developed to drive his flour mill machinery. By the War of 1812, about a dozen of Evans' engines were in use, but the spread of use in manufacturing was slow. The cost of the steam engine itself was high, and fuel and maintenance costs added to operating expenses. As late as 1840, steam power near eastern Pennsylvania coal sites was four times as expensive per horsepower as waterpower at Lowell. Steam engines were used principally at sites where waterpower was not readily available and in connection with driving bellows for furnace industries where the heat could be used to generate the steam.

The rapid development of steam engines was due largely to their use in transportation. Steam engines were quickly demanded to operate steamboats on the western rivers and lakes. Engine-building firms existed in Philadelphia and New York in 1803, and others quickly were started in Pittsburgh, Cincinnati, and other Ohio River cities. After 1830, the development of steam-powered ocean vessels and steam locomotives for railroads rapidly expanded the demand for steam engine makers in the East. With the Evans high-pressure engine and the improvements in steam economy and control invented by George H. Corliss, American-built locomotives soon were among the best in the world and much in demand as exports in the 1850's. Then, seeking to enlarge their domestic markets, American firms introduced small, standardized steam motors with interchangeable parts for use not only in small factories but also with farm machinery, as pumps, and in small shops. By 1860, these small engines were sold by catalog.

Improvements in ironmaking were required by the high-pressure boiler of the steam engine, and these improvements in turn helped to rapidly reduce the cost of the steam engine and permit its wide use. In 1815, ironmaking technology in America still was about the same as it had been for the previous century. Fairly large furnaces were required to smelt iron ores into pig iron, and waterwheels were used to drive the air bellows. Large forges also might use waterpower to drive drop hammers in making bar iron. The small-town blacksmith also operated small forges and hammered bar iron into shaped parts for farmers and local shops. Foundries usually reheated iron and poured it into molds for cast-iron pots, stove parts, and fancy ironwork. Forges also hammered out sheets and frequently were connected with slitting mills that made the rods for nails.

In 1817, puddling and rolling techniques, already used for three decades in England, were introduced. The rolling mills substituted for the hammering to make wrought iron. This greatly reduced labor costs and produced a more uniform sheet iron for making steam boilers. The puddling process heated the metal without direct contact with the fuel, and this was important in permitting the use of coal instead of charcoal. In 1833, patents were obtained and commercial use begun of the hot-blast method of smelting iron ore. This improved the puddling method by introducing a blast of hot air that already had been preheated by the otherwise wasted heat escaping from the furnace.

The technology of steelmaking was not substantially changed until the invention of the Bessemer furnace in 1851. This process forced a blast of cold air through the molten iron to decarbonize it. Yet this method was not used for a significant volume of production until after 1860.

The use of coal as the fuel in ironmaking was limited at first to anthracite (hard) coal. Bituminous (soft) coal did not stand transportation as well and was not as available in suitable quality in the East. Experiments were made prior to 1840 using coke made from bituminous coal in smelting iron, but this method was slowly adopted in America, except west of the Appalachians where anthracite was not readily available. The quality of iron made from wood charcoal was regarded as superior for such products as nails, hardware, and agricultural tools. Anthracite fuel, however, produced satisfactory iron for large-scale rolling of sheet iron and rails; so the use of anthracite coal in ironmaking became important in supplying the railroad industry.

The use of coal instead of wood charcoal as a fuel had important effects upon the location of the iron industry. Prior to 1830, iron industries were widespread because of the availability in every state of small quantities of iron and the universal availability of forests to make charcoal for fuel. In many places, however, local supplies of iron and of charcoal had begun to be depleted. A good quality iron in considerable quantities was available in the Lake Champlain area and anthracite coal was available near water transportation in eastern Pennsylvania. The iron industry prior to 1860, therefore, began to concentrate in New York, New Jersey, and eastern Pennsylvania. In the 1850's the opening of St. Mary's Canal gave access by water transportation to a large supply of high-quality iron on the shores of Lake Superior; and iron industries began to develop at Detroit, Buffalo, and Cleveland. The supply of this Great Lakes iron ore and the large bituminous coalfields of eastern Pennsylvania were destined after 1860 to attract a concentration of the steel industry in the Pittsburgh area.

The impact of these developments on overall manufacturing expansion is suggested by production trends of iron and coal. Pig iron production was set back by British imports after 1815 and in the depression of 1820, but data for the later census years show a steady and rapid rate of increase. Bituminous coal output began to rise faster after 1815 and increased faster than iron until 1855. Anthracite coal had a phenomenal expansion after it began to be used in ironmaking in the 1830's, and after 1840 it achieved about the same importance and matched the growth rate of bituminous coal. (See 7–5.)

Rapid Railroad Expansion

Transportation improvements had revolutionary effects on manufacturing as well as on farming. Even before the 1840's, steamboats, roads, and canals were lowering the costs of raw materials, widening markets and causing a concentration and larger scale of manufacturing. The rapid railroad expansion after 1840 intensified these effects as well as adding to the demand for products of certain industries.

Reduced transportation costs rapidly lowered the cost of raw materials for factories and permitted the concentration of production. Between 1815 and 1860, freight rates on coastwise and downstream water shipments fell about 75 percent, while upstream rates fell over 90 percent. The Erie Canal reduced freight rates from Buffalo to New York over 95 percent. In the mid-1820's, wagon freight rates were about 15 cents per ton-mile, and the early railroad rates were about half of this; but by 1860 all-rail shipments of wheat from Chicago to New York cost about 1.2 cents per ton-mile. The northern branch of the Erie Canal brought high-grade iron ore from Lake Champlain to the New York City area, and canals also brought anthracite coal from eastern Pennsylvania to the same area. Water transport also gave Philadelphia easy access to the same resources combination. This permitted the concentration of large-sized iron rolling mills in the Philadelphia and New York area. Railroads permitted even greater volumes of bulk

7–5. Railroad, Iron, and Coal Trends

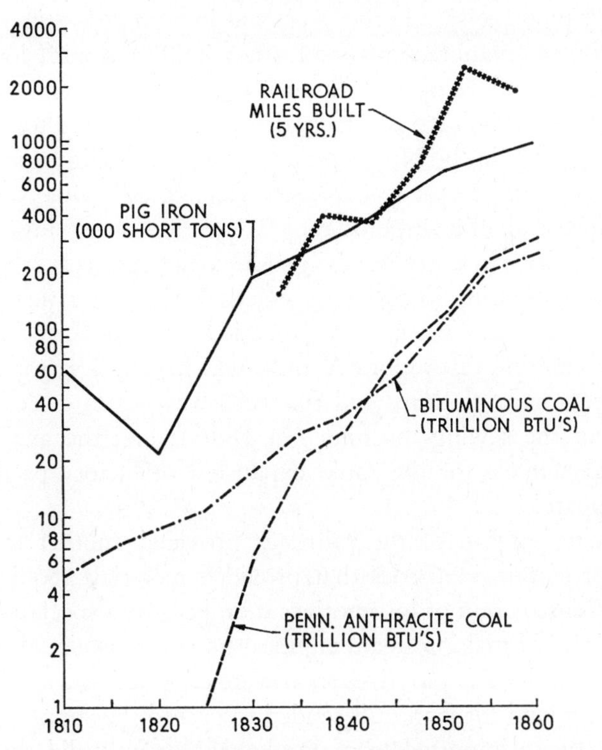

Source: U.S. Department of Commerce, *Historical Statistics of the United States* (Washington, D.C.: U.S. Government Printing Office, 1960).

shipments and a greater flexibility as to factory sites. After 1860, the steel industry grew not only in the East but also in the Pittsburgh area. A combination of water and rail transport permitted a combination of Lake Superior iron ore and western Pennsylvania coal at Pittsburgh.

Lower transportation costs also widened the markets for manufacturing firms. Western farmers not only could deliver wheat inexpensively to New York, but New York manufacturers could deliver machinery and consumer goods inexpensively to Chicago. The Erie Canal eliminated the necessity of shipping manufactured goods via New Orleans to the Great Lakes area. This, at first, was of greatest advantage to producers in the New York area. Railroads soon provided equal access to the West by manufacturers in Boston, Philadelphia, and Baltimore. Industries with large potential economies from mass production then began to expand rapidly in the Northeast. On the other hand, manufacturing of the same items on a small scale was discouraged elsewhere because of the competition of low-priced goods that could be shipped in. Manufacturing expansion in the West was in food-processing industries, farm machinery manufactures, and other industries with local advantages or ability to develop on a large scale.

A number of industries, which already were tending to concentrate in particular areas in the Northeast and were benefiting from mass-production economies, began to expand rapidly after 1840. Northeastern textile industries had a surge of rapid expansion in serving large markets, and the clock industry was helped in achieving mass production by the ease of distributing its products widely. The preservation of food in tin cans and glass jars was rapidly expanded after 1840, and during the 1850's the canning of evaporated milk was begun. The mass distribution of ready-made clothing and footwear was begun even before the invention of the sewing machine (in 1846); and the availability of mass markets made for the rapid expansion of factory production of wearing apparel.

Rapid expansion of the railroads provided another stimulus to demand for certain industries that provided materials required by the railroads. Construction of locomotives soon became a specialized branch of the business of making steam engines; however, as already indicated, improved American locomotives soon were exported as a surplus export item. The demand for iron rails tended to exceed the supply, and many of the rails were imported from England. Not only did the miles of railroad construction rise much faster than iron production (see again 7–5), but the early demand of railroads for rails exceeded the capacity of American rolling mills. Meeting this demand of railroads helped develop the larger scale heavy metals industries in the United States, which previously were more advanced in England.

Prior to 1860, coal was not yet demanded as fuel for the steam locomotives, but the demand was great for cordwood and ties. Timber cutting and sawmills underwent a great expansion after the 1830's. Due to depletion of forests in more settled areas, this industry became concentrated first in Maine and later in Michigan and Wisconsin. The need for railroad ties provided part of the surge in timber demands, as well as the need for urban housing and rural housing on the open plains. The construction of the railroads also provided a demand for labor, and helped bring many immigrants to settle the plains. Also, the railroad terminals and repair shops helped to create larger urban centers. So, the railroad's own needs added to the urbanizing trends in the economy and the rising demand for manufactured goods.

Organization of Production

Mass production was made possible by the technological innovations in machinery and engines and by the improved transportation that enlarged the markets. To exploit these technical and market possibilities, however, required changes in the organization of production in manufacturing. Larger quantities of capital had to be invested in machinery, production became more specialized in a few standard products, more operations were closely coordinated in a single building or a single management, larger numbers of workers were employed and closely supervised, and particular industries became concentrated in one or several strategic locations.

The mechanization of manufacturing required large amounts of capital. On the one hand, many of the new pieces of machinery were quite large. The blast furnace was larger than ever, the iron rolling mills required huge rollers, and larger ladles and cranes were required for large foundry castings. On the other hand, a greater number of machines were required to perform separate operations. Evans' continuous process flour mill required moving belts and many devices for the successive operations. The making of standard parts required many specialized machines performing different cutting and forming tasks. The textile mill operated many spindles along with each power loom. Furthermore, large buildings were required to house this machinery, and large sums of money were required to provide the large volume of raw materials that had to be on hand in inventories and in the process of being changed into products.

The making of standard products in large volume also led to greater specialization by the typical manufacturing business. As the machines became more specialized and the capital requirements grew, the full resources of a business were absorbed in making one product or one type of product. The making of iron rails became separated from rolling sheet iron, and the making of locomotives became a specialized type of steam engine manufacture. Machine shops that started as departments of textile mills soon became separate businesses specialized in making and repairing machines for many textile mills. A textile mill might concentrate on a particular type and quality of cloth.

At the same time, greater coordination of production operations was required. In part, this was due to a need for assuring the quality of materials and accuracy of parts to meet the requirements of a later process or final assembly. It was also to assure adequate and timely supply in order to maintain a high volume and steady flow of production. New types of mass production frequently had more special requirements than previous production and other industries. A major change introduced by Lowell's textile mill at Waltham, therefore, was the integration of spinning and weaving operations in the same building. The making of guns and clocks required close coordination of many types and stages of production. In making new engines and machines, initially the manufacturer might have to produce certain parts or metals himself. For example, in making iron rails, Abram S. Hewitt looked for a better iron ore and purchased the Andover mine.

Coordination of marketing and production was made important by mass production. In 1803, Eli Terry might make a few clocks and then load them into a wagon and drive to another town in order to sell them. But as machines provided mass production and improved transportation provided larger markets, the manufacturer could sell large volumes of goods to large merchants who would undertake to distribute them to distant cities. In some industries the mass distribution came first. Large merchants anxious to sell large quantities of shoes in many distant cities would urge shoemakers to produce more. Craftsmen in shops near the large port cities were closer to the merchants who were seeking to make large purchases. Certain towns, in fact, frequently got a leading start in mass production of particular products and became famous for the quality and low cost of these products. On the other hand, handicraft manufacturing all but disappeared from the Nation's hamlets.

The geographic concentration of the production of certain products in particular towns or cities resulted both from economies of large-scale production within the business firm and from economies of large-scale production in the same area by many firms—often referred to as "external" economies or as "neighborhood" or "agglomeration" effects. Market centers always tended to form as a convenience to many buyers and sellers in contacting each other with a minimum expenditure of time and effort and with a maximum range of choice. Production by many small producers, therefore, frequently tends to be attracted to some market center. The congregation of many similar producers, moreover, tends to create a demand for specialized suppliers of materials, parts, or machinery, who may produce more cheaply by concentrating on specialized operations needed by this industry. Also, new and expanding businesses find it easier to obtain skilled workers in the same area where other similar businesses are already operating. Thus, producers in such a center may find they have lower costs of marketing, of purchasing materials, and of hiring labor than more isolated produecrs in other areas. When these external economies are combined with large-scale machine methods of production, one center of production may begin to supply a large share of the national consumption of a particular product. Thus, manufacturing in the Northeast began to be concentrated in a few main cities for textiles, clocks, hats, shoes, rolled iron, and locomotives.

The employment of numerous workers had long been the characteristic of a mine, mill or large shop; so, the growth of large specialized manufacturers in some industries merely increased the scale of employment. However, the mechanization of repetitive operations and the coordination of the making of standard parts and of performing successive operations introduced the factory system of production. This system involves the hiring of large numbers of workers, the assigning of workers to narrowly defined tasks, and training and close supervision of the workers in performing these tasks, the pacing of the work by a machine and according to a uniform time schedule, and the coordination of all workers by a manager.

The dull routine of production-line tasks had some of the negative effects that Adam Smith anticipated when he observed production through the division of labor in a pin-making factory—discontent and frustration came both to skilled workers whose jobs were eliminated by the factory system and to the new factory workers who as human beings were required to work with the precision, constancy, and repetition of a mindless machine.

In some industries—the early spinning mills, the gun factories, and the clock factories—the factory system directly supplanted production in the home or in the shop. In other industries, however—such as weaving, shoemaking, and apparel—another system was used before new machinery caused production to be centralized in factories. This was the put-out or cottage system.

The cottage system usually was organized by merchants who wanted to obtain goods for sale in a large and expanding market in far-flung areas. As long as the method of production involved hand labor by individuals working alone, he needed only to contract with a large number of individuals to produce what he wanted. If craft skills were required, of course, he would contract with a number of shops. But if home-manufacture skills and little machinery were involved, the work could be done by workers and their families at home. Besides providing the demand, the merchant usually had to provide the materials and sometimes the tools. The cottage system sometimes involved the use of rural workers in farm families, as a means of using idle time to supplement family income—as, for example, in the making of straw and palm-leaf hats in New England. In other industries, such as shoemaking and apparel, workers in towns or cities were engaged in this work as their sole means of income. Not until the sewing machine was introduced did the factory system begin (during the 1850's) to dominate production of shoes and wearing apparel.

Labor Supply

The revolution in industrial production methods had a paradoxical relation to labor supply. On the one hand, mechanization is laborsaving; thus, machine production is encouraged by a shortage of labor supply and high labor costs. On the other hand, the economies of mass production are so great that its products tend to supplant those produced by hand methods everywhere. However, because technological changes reduced costs and, therefore, prices, total production and quantity sold increased. Consequently in the aggregate, total demand for labor remained constant although the composition of that demand shifted away from handicrafting to machine operation.

Specialized factories employing the new techniques were required to serve a large and expanding demand. In order to concentrate large-scale production in one place and to expand production rapidly without incurring rising cost barriers, a factory had to be able to obtain a large and increasing supply of workers where the factory was located. Accordingly, the geographical distribution of manufacturing labor demand also changed.

America continued to have a scarcity of labor compared to the older settled areas of England and Europe, and wage rates tended to be higher in this country than elsewhere. Also, because of the availability of new farmlands and the opportunities for starting new shops, employers had to pay higher wages to hold their employees. This labor scarcity and high cost, together with competition from low-priced British imports and a rapidly expanding demand, gave manufacturers a great incentive to invent and apply laborsaving machinery. The machine permitted a limited labor supply to produce a large output and high wages to accompany low prices.

The development and rapid expansion of concentrated factory production, however, was made possible in the Northeast by the rapid expansion of labor supply available to the new factories. The first source of this labor supply to the early textile mills was in the rural areas of New England. A second source was the foreign immigrants arriving in the great port cities.

New England farm areas provided a surplus labor supply in the late 1820's and 1830's because of the competition of cheaper wheat products from the Great Lakes region. New England farms never had been very productive and the Erie Canal brought a much lower price for grain and meat products in the East. Besides seeking to diversify their farm production, the farmers began to seek nonfarm work to supplement their incomes, or moved into the growing cities. Many New England farm families were able to supplement their incomes by various forms of cottage work—at first weaving and then making straw hats. Since the first textile mills were located in small towns near waterfalls, workers were initially drawn from local farm families. As the textile factories expanded, farm workers had to be recruited from a larger rural area and moved to the towns.

Two labor systems were used in the textile mills. In southern New England, the family system involved hiring men, women, and children from the same families. Women and children could do much of the light work in threading, watching and operating the machines, while the men repaired the machines and did the heavier work. In northern New England, as in the first Waltham mill, the dormitory system was used. Young women from farm families were recruited to live in dormitories and work in the factories. Many of the young men were away as apprentice seamen, so this employment was attractive to the young women as a temporary career and a way to supplement the family's income. They worked long hours in the factories, not too much unlike the long hours of farm work or of dawn-to-dusk work in home manufacturing or cottage work. In spite of long hours, the young women often received schooling or engaged in self-improvement activities under the encouragement of paternalistic Puritan factory owners. By the 1840's, however, labor conditions began to change and the dormitory system later was abandoned.

A large inflow of foreign immigrants in the 1840's and 1850's furnished much of the labor supply for rapid manufacturing expansion in the Northeast during the 1840's and 1850's. These workers crowded into port cities and larger towns. A large supply of unskilled men began to supplant the women and children in textile mills. The textile mills would have had difficulty in continuing their rapid expansion without this additional labor supply. In large cities, whether in their tenement quarters or in large factory rooms, the immigrants were employed in large numbers to expand production of shoes and ready-made apparel.

Migration of Europeans to America, a process which had been taking place during two centuries of colonial growth, began to take on a new characteristic during the 1840's: the furnishing of an urban labor supply. The expansion into new farming areas west of the Appalachian Mountains continued to attract farm settlers from England and Germany. However, in the 1840's, famines in Ireland and the revolutions of 1848 began to cause larger numbers of migrants to come to America in a relatively destitute financial condition. They arrived in port cities seeking immediate work as unksilled laborers. The total numbers of immigrants to the United States (for which we have records only since 1820), therefore, rose rapidly with the westward expansion in the late 1820's and 1830's, but were especially high in the 1840's and 1850's.

7–6. NUMBER OF IMMIGRANTS

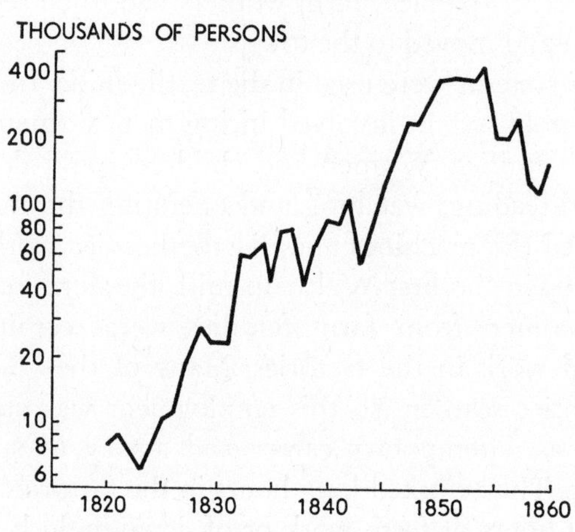

SOURCE: U.S. Department of Commerce, *Historical Statistics of the United States* (Washington, D.C.: U.S. Government Printing Office, 1960), p. 57.

Immigrants accounted for 3.9 percent of the total population increase of the Nation during the 1820's, 12.7 percent in the 1830's, 23.3 percent in the 1840's, and 34.0 percent in the 1850's (although there was some decline in the late 1850's). (See 7–6.)

The result of the rapid expansion of labor supply while manufacturing was rapidly growing was that wage rates (although relatively high in the United States) rose very little. It is very difficult, of course, to estimate meaningful wage averages during the early years. Apparently real wages in farming rose in most decades. In nonfarming there was little change prior to 1830, a higher level in the 1840's, and a slight decline in the late 1850's.

As in England during the same period, however, there was considerable labor discontent. In a land with opportunities for settling new lands, starting businesses, and achieving higher incomes there was a spirit of optimism and high hope. Frequently the urban worker, however, felt disappointed and frustrated. The new mass-production methods, based on division of labor and mechanization, tended to eliminate the craft shop as a small business and to break down the skills and lower the status of the high-paid skilled worker. The factory organization regimented the worker, and the large numbers of employees tended to depersonalize the relations between worker and employer. Urban growth and crowding of new immigrants into big cities fostered slums. The cheaper machine methods and a large immigrant labor supply intensified competition for jobs and put a downward pressure on wages. With fluctuations in business conditions, workers dependent solely upon urban employment suffered the hardships and uncertainties of prolonged periods of unemployment. Accordingly, early efforts were made to form trade unions and strike for better wages and working conditions. These efforts met with more success in skilled trades and during periods of prosperity; but on the whole the success was limited and short lived prior to the Civil War.

Capital Supply and Business Organization

Rapid manufacturing expansion and the new mass-production methods required large amounts of capital and new forms of business organization. Since nearly all of the capital was accumulated within the United States, a considerable share of the national production each year had to be saved, or withheld from current consumption. These funds also had to be invested in activities that promised to expand future production, but activities for which there was limited information, considerable uncertainty, and grave risk of losses.

The men who became manufacturers in the early period were either merchants who saw new market opportunities or small shop craftsmen who themselves invented new methods. For the former group, the initial capital was supplied out of funds earned in other business activities. The New England traders who had accumulated wealth in the re-export trade, the fur trade, and the China trade faced restrictions on their foreign activities during the Embargo and the War of 1812. Many of them also found profit opportunities in world trade less attractive after 1815. They had developed business management abilities, however, and had accumulated wealth needed to finance new ventures in other industries; so, they turned to manufacturing as a new opportunity. In the South, some men of wealth also turned to manufacturing, but the opportunities in cotton plantations continued to look most promising. They were not forced to look for new fields, and the plantation culture may have discouraged energetic management activities.

In addition to the help received from the transfer of wealth out of other industries, manufacturing was helped in gaining momentum by the opportunities for large profits which could be reinvested to expand the business. The innovator in a field might double his capital in a few years. Later businesses might not be as profitable; but even after an industry had many similar firms, profits of 10 to 20 percent were fairly common. On the other hand, it must not be forgotten that risks were great, and many firms went broke. After the rapid construction of textile mills between 1807 and 1815, for example, many had to close down with the return of British competition.

Most manufacturing businesses before the Civil War were owned by individuals or by partners. Evans, Whitney, and other inventors and craftsmen built up sizable fortunes in their lifetimes. Slater, who came to this country penniless, left over two thirds of $1 million in assets when he died about four decades later. Lowell started his first mill, however, by getting several other wealthy merchant families to join with him. This group of families continued to join in building up several other mills and invested jointly in other industries. They became known as the Boston Associates and long were prominent in manufacturing and financial leadership in Massachusetts.

Prior to 1860, the corporation was not widely adopted as the legal form of business in manufacturing. The chartering of corporations by specific acts of legislatures had traditionally been used to establish monopolies in which the state and the public had a special interest. It was used mostly for banks, public utilities, and transportation. However, some beginning steps were made toward wide use of corporations when Masachusetts passed a statute in 1830 giving corporate shareholders limited liability for the debts of a corporation if it went broke; and in 1837, Connecticut passed a sweeping act permitting anyone to apply for incorporation. Other states soon followed these precedents. For a long time, however, there was public suspicion of incorporation.

Outside capital also was not readily forthcoming for manufacturing in the form of loans. Banks made very short-term loans. With little incorporation, there was little sale of bonds by manufacturing firms, and little use was made of mortgages. Most long-term loans were made by wealthy individuals—sometimes one of the partners. Sometimes large merchant-distributors of the manufactured product advanced loans to the manufacturer, usually in times of stress and at high rates.

More frequently, the manufacturer found he had to advance loans to merchants because of the widespread practice of selling by shipment on consignment with payment made later. It was not easy, therefore, to raise capital outside of the manufacturing firm. The rapid expansion of manufacturing production out of the plowing back of profits, therefore, is all the more remarkable.

Some of the financial institutions, which later became important means of assembling the savings of individuals and making them available for investment in manufacturing, did have their beginnings prior to the Civil War. Insurance companies were started prior to 1800; by 1860, fire and marine insurance companies had nearly $3 billion of insurance in force, and life insurance in force amounted to $160 million. The latter provided a partial source of savings, but perhaps more important were the savings and loan associations, mostly in the Northeast, whose deposits reached over $150 million. Government bonds, mostly issued by states, provided a more important form of saving and capital formation initially. They also helped to accustom the public to purchasing securities and helped develop a private market for handling them. Prior to the 1830's, some states had run lotteries to raise money, and some of the same brokers who sold lottery tickets later dealt in bonds. Banks also did much buying and selling of bonds. Some large "investment banks" became specialized in handling initial flotation of bonds, especially selling them in other regions and countries. Stock exchanges had developed in Philadelphia, New York, and Boston prior to 1820; and much of the early transactions was in government securities. Banks, turnpike companies, and railroads provided most of the private securities that were widely purchased. Since manufacturing businesses usually were not incorporated, and even then their securities might be held by few people, they did not benefit much from the new financial institutions prior to 1860.

ROLE OF GOVERNMENT

In the remainder of this chapter brief consideration is given to the role of government in the economic development and accelerating economic growth of the country. This review is complicated by the variations in actions among governments at the state and local level as well as at the national level. It is necessary, also, to analyze the effects of general patterns of government actions without regard to the varying and often conflicting purposes behind specific events.

As an individualistic, frontier-minded people, Americans feared strong central government and tended to minimize government activities. But Americans were pragmatic in seeking whatever government actions appeared useful for immediate purposes. Economic theories of laissez-faire policy were not widely advocated prior to 1860. And as opportunities for transportation improvements and manufacturing growth appeared, a mixture of familiar mercantilist methods were frequently applied. In fact, government marched west with the pioneers, subsidizing their explorations and, later, transportation improvements, aiding them in their combat with hostile Indians, and favoring them with increasingly liberal land policies by which the public domain passed into private hands.

Whether it intends to or not, a government by its action and inaction influences the economy in two ways. On the one hand, it influences the environment within which private organizations and individuals make their decisions. On the other hand, it directly participates in decisions on how resources are used to affect production. The following sections, then, deal first with matters that appear least related intentionally to economic development and end with those more deliberately intended to direct and participate in economic decisions.

Government Finance

The minimum role assigned to government is reflected in the small size of expenditures by all levels of government. Federal expenditures rose gradually with the national income but remained between 1 and 2 percent of national income prior to 1860. State and local expenditures combined probably were less than this until the 1850's, but less is known about these expenditures in all areas. In 1819, for example, government expenditures on a per capita basis may be compared as follows: $2.29 federal; $0.47 for New York state; and $2.18 for the city of Providence. By 1860, the federal and state amounts remained about the same, while the city figures were more than tripled. Local expenditures, of course, varied widely and were much lower in rural areas.

Taxes, accordingly, were light. The main source of revenue for the federal government was the tariff on imports, and a secondary source was the sale of western lands. Many states initially had no trouble meeting their earlier small needs with miscellaneous revenues (such as land sales, lotteries, licenses, bank taxes, and interest on federal bonds); but after the 1830's, most states had to raise greater revenues mostly from property taxes—the mainstay of local governments.

The unstable source of federal revenues resulted in variations in the budget balance. National fiscal policy was formed primarily with the object of rapidly paying off war debts in order to establish and protect the federal government's reputation as a borrower. During the War of 1812, this enabled the government to increase its borrowing to meet sudden increases in expenditures in the face of a slowness of Congress to increase taxes. Increased tariff rates and import volume accelerated the repayment of debt during prosperous peacetime years. By 1835, the United States was one of the few modern nations to have completely paid off all debts. (See 7–7.)

During the 1820's and 1830's, the states were doing the opposite.

7–7. Federal Government Debt

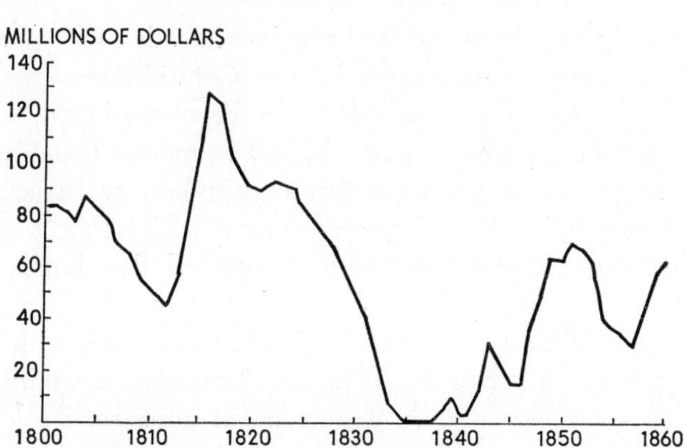

Source: U.S. Department of Commerce, *Historical Statistics of the United States* (Washington, D.C.: U.S. Government Printing Office, 1960), p. 721.

Starting with virtually no debts, the states rushed to build canals, turnpikes, and railroads, and to establish banks with money raised by selling state bonds. The state debts reached $66.5 million in 1835 and zoomed to $174 million by 1838—adding $108 million in just three years! This may be compared to the peak federal debt of $124 million in 1816. The optimistic assumption that revenues from the publicly built projects would pay for themselves was proven false in the depression after 1838, and the states found themselves unprepared to suddenly raise taxes to meet their debt obligations. Nine states defaulted on some part of their payments when they fell due, and three states and one territory actually repudiated bonds totaling over $13 million. This established a bad reputation for state bonds in the minds of private investors for many decades afterwards.

While government debt was regarded as a necessary evil in terms of government's own affairs, the effects on the private economy had beneficial aspects. As already noted, the sale of government bonds helped to establish the public habit of buying securities, the business of brokers, and the operation of stock exchanges. A large inflow of foreign capital in the American economy during the 1830's took place in the form of purchase of state bonds by private investors in London and elsewhere. Government bond ownership also provided a means of holding wealth in readily transferable form. As such it was used as a near-money. It was used by both individuals and governments to purchase bank stocks and thus become part of the capital reserves upon which the banks justified the issue of their own notes, a form of paper money.

The power to coin money and regulate its value was given exclusively to the federal government by the Constitution. The evils of inflation in the Revolutionary War had been attributed largely to irresponsible issue of paper money by governments. Paradoxically, it was regarded as more sound for government to borrow (issue promises to pay with interest) than to issue paper money (issue promises to pay without interest). It was not widely recognized that bonds held by banks and used to support issue of more bank notes could produce an equal or greater inflationary expansion in the money supply. It seems to have been assumed that bankers, as private businessmen, would be more responsible and conservative in issuing paper notes than a legislature would be; and, of course, the requirement that interest be paid must have had some braking effect on the total promises that were issued. Federal policy, therefore, was not consistently directed toward nor effective in controlling the supply and thus the value of money. One consequence was that the federal government did not provide an adequate supply of coins and paper bills to facilitate the Nation's production and exchange activities. Coin mintage long was inadequate to provide enough small coins. Rural areas and the western regions continually were short of any kind of money. Barter was widely resorted to in rural areas. Many kinds of institutions—railroads, insurance companies, and cities—issued various kinds of notes or promises to pay that had some circulation as a kind of money. State-chartered private banks, therefore, filled a real need by issuing notes; and the expansion of state banks, while at times inflationary, helped to expand the supply of money and credit to meet the needs of an expanding economy.

Before examining the control of bank credit, the effect on the economy of variations in government finance should be noted. In the early 1800's, little attention was given to the disturbances that government might cause in the private economy resulting from the way the

Treasury handled its own monetary affairs. Rapid repayment of government debt had a deflationary effect when it removed government securities from banks. A budget surplus accumulated in the Treasury also removed money from private circulation. During the 1820's and 1830's, the federal surplus varied between a fourth to almost half of budget revenues. Quite unintentionally, however, the peacetime surpluses and deficits may have had some stabilizing influence on the private economy; for during periods of prosperity and rising prices, tariff revenues automatically tended to rise and remove some money from circulation. During depressions the opposite occurred.

The disposition of government funds also could have disturbing effects. When held by the Treasury, accumulation of surplus removed money from circulation. When deposited in private banks, it enabled those banks to increase their note issue. With its own debt paid off, the federal government contributed to the boom-and-bust in 1836–37 by an act that distributed the federal surplus to the states. This not only encouraged their public works spending, but it precipitated a financial crisis by transferring large amounts of cash reserves from eastern banks to western banks. The eastern banks suddenly had to restrict their loans for this purpose, and this helped to check private investment in 1837. At about the same time the federal government had become worried about excessive issue of bank notes and required payment in specie on sales of public land. This also required western banks to draw upon their reserves in eastern banks to obtain enough specie to finance these payments.

In short, government was far from neutral in its effect on the economy merely in running its own fiscal affairs. Treasury policy had matured by mid-century and the passage of the Independent Treasury Act. That act was designed to put the Treasury on a cash basis and thus to make the Treasury independent of the private financial market. But, in quite a different spirit from that in which the Independent Treasury Act was passed, Treasury policy turned toward a conscious effort to stabilize the private money market by purchasing government bonds in times when bank reserves were low and retaining surplus tax revenues when they were high. Our secretaries had learned something of the importance of the Treasury's transactions from a half-century of influencing the money market.

Regulating Bank Credit

Closely related to the government role in issuing and regulating the value of money is its control of bank credit. Like money, loans are important in facilitating exchange and production. Many short-term transactions, as well as much seasonal production, rely upon loans to facilitate purchases and expenses prior to final sale of finished products. Because the use of capital and the risk of loss by individuals are involved in each loan, the extension of credit is like other private business activities and requires able management. A bank is partly a specialized credit institution and thus earns a profit on its loaned-out capital like any other business. But it also has a "public" nature in being entrusted with depository funds, in facilitating transfers of other people's money, and in issuing promises to pay in the form of deposits and notes.

In order to ensure the financial environment needed to encourage private production activities in the economy, government may need to regulate banking with three objectives in mind. First, an ample supply of loan funds at low interest needs to be encouraged to facilitate expansion of private production. Second, the people need to be protected against loss of money entrusted to banks due to failure or bankruptcy of banks. And third, excessive expansion or contraction of the money supply needs to be avoided in the collective behavior of all banks.

In regard to the last two objectives, it is the close relation of bank loans to money supply and their joint relation to inflations and depressions that are a public problem requiring government regulation. Rapid price inflation involves a loss of purchasing power by the money people hold. This may involve hardships and inequities for those receiving pensions or other fixed incomes and those holding savings deposits. It also may discourage accumulation and efficient investment of funds. In depressions, rapid price declines usually are accompanied by reduction in output, unemployment, and losses from sales of goods and assets at low prices.

Before discussing bank operations, therefore, a brief review is needed of the historical record of instability in prices and money supply prior to 1860. The greatest inflations always have occurred during war periods, and the War of 1812 was no exception. Two other rapid price rises occurred, in the mid-1830's and the mid-1850's. Following each sudden inflation came a period of sharp price declines. During these price declines production decreased, investment halted or slackened, and many people suffered from unemployment and losses of income and capital. (See 7–8.)

Now it must be recognized that some variations in economic activity are unavoidable. When people rush to take advantage of new inventions or resource opportunities they may start a rapid pace of investment that cannot be maintained continuously. Also, the extent of new opportunities may not be predictable, and investors may be overoptimistic and overinvest. This may be followed by a period of losses, contraction, and some waiting for opportunities to catch up before the pace of investment is continued. Total production is much affected by such variations in the rate of investment. It should not be forgotten, however, that the instability of business fluctuations (often referred to as business cycles) usually has been associated with rapid economic growth. Higher production levels are achieved even though the upward path is irregular and suffers some severe setbacks. Prior to 1860, the three main depressions were influenced by such worldwide events as wars, bad harvests, the Irish famine, gold discoveries, and the sudden

7–8. Average Wholesale Prices

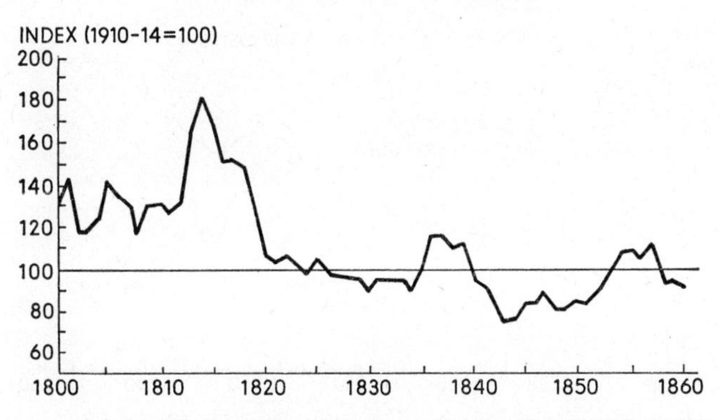

Source: U.S. Department of Commerce, *Historical Statistics of the United States* (Washington, D.C.: U.S. Government Printing Office, 1960), p. 115.

surge of canal building and railroad building. Because world markets were interrelated by trade, migration, and foreign investments, other nations experienced business fluctuations at about the same times as did America.

Nevertheless, the instability of money supply and bank credit in the United States undoubtedly magnified these price and output fluctuations. A measure of the total money supply must include not only the currency (coins and notes) issued by the federal government, but also the bank notes and deposits in banks. All three tended to expand faster than national output during the three historic boom periods and contract faster during the ensuing depressions. (See 7–9.)

The way a private bank operates to create additional money supply can be illustrated in terms of the balance sheet of a hypothetical state-chartered bank in about 1836. Suppose the bank was started by a group of merchants who, in exchange for $40,000 worth of stock certificates of ownership, paid in $40,000 worth of assets—$6,000 in U.S. currency; $7,000 in other bank notes; $13,000 in U.S. bonds; a $13,000 note secured by a mortgage on the bank president's mining property; and a city lot and store building estimated to be worth $1,000 (to be used as the bank building). Now, suppose that their first large depositor, on their grand opening day, is the mayor, who deposits a check for $10,000 drawn on a New York City bank. The owners decide to mail the check to the New York bank and ask that a deposit in the name of their bank be set up in the New York bank, in order to facilitate their transacting any check clearance business in New York,

7–9. Money Supply, 1800–60

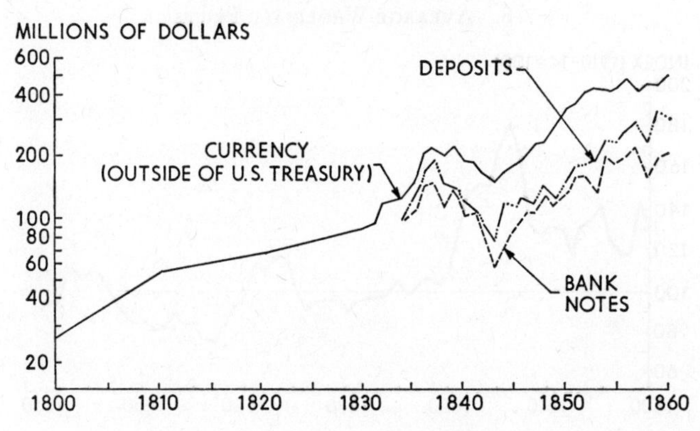

Source: U.S. Department of Commerce, *Historical Statistics of the United States* (Washington, D.C.: U.S. Government Printing Office, 1960), pp. 624–25 and 647.

and to establish their credit there. Now, the bank has $50,000 in assets (on the left side of the balance sheet) and the same amount in liabilities, composed of a $10,000 depositor's claim and $40,000 in ownership claims. The owners cannot make any profit unless they acquire more earning assets (more, that is, than the securities, mortgage, and the New York deposit, on which they already may receive some interest). They advertise that they are willing to lend, and a stream of local merchants and farmers come in to borrow money. The town is prosperous and all of these loans are likely to be paid back out of crops and store receipts. So, in the first week loans totaling $50,000 have been made for periods varying from 30 days to 6 months. The interest on the loans, when repaid, will produce a profit for the bank. (See 7–10.)

But what did the borrowers receive? The bank decided to print up its own I O U's, or bank notes, for half of the loans, and simply set up deposit accounts on its books for borrowers of the other half. When the borrowers spent money, some of it would go to Baltimore and other distant cities and some of it might circulate from hand to hand locally. But it would not all come back at once with claims to be exchanged for currency. Likewise, checks would be written on the deposits, some locally and some to distant persons. Some of the distant claims could be paid by transfers from the New York bank account and some would return to the bank claiming payment in currency or other bank notes. At the same time, many of the local people who received notes or checks would deposit them in the bank; so some of the drawdown of deposits would be offset by new deposits.

There are several points to note in this illustration. It was in the

7–10. Balance Sheet of a State-Chartered Bank
(Illustration)

Assets		*Liabilities*	
Reserves:		Obligations:	
Currency	$ 6,000	Deposits	$ 35,000
Other bank notes	7,000	Notes in circulation	25,000
Deposits in banks	10,000		
Earning assets:			
Securities	13,000		
Short-term loans	50,000		
Mortgages	13,000		
Fixed assets:		Owners' capital:	
Land, building, furniture	1,000	Stock and surplus	40,000
Total	$100,000	Total	$100,000

process of making loans that the bank issued new notes and deposit accounts that it did not have before. Since people accept and use these as money, the bank has "created" an additional supply of money in the act of expanding credit. The obligations of the bank now exceed the cash reserves that the bank has on hand, but there is no difficulty as long as all depositors and noteholders do not present their claims at once. In any event, the bank has enough valuable assets to meet all claims, if it has enough time to get its loans paid back or sell some of its assets. It holds only a small part of its assets as cash reserves to meet sudden claims.

Now, with this balance sheet in mind, we can consider the two main ways that the state banks got into trouble. The first way was to overexpand loans and leave cash reserves too slim. During the boom of 1836, everyone was optimistic and wanted to expand production by borrowing capital. The banks also were optimistic and tended to expand their loans as well as their deposits and notes too much. Cash reserves became too small relative to the claims and relative to total assets. When a fall in prices shook confidence in people's ability to pay back their loans, banks began to restrict their lending. This meant that money flowed less easily and people tried harder to get hold of cash. To get more cash, perhaps to pay back loans, more goods had to be sold immediately even at low prices. With more sellers than buyers, prices began to fall more rapidly. Banks then began to call in loans and depositors began to draw out more cash. Other banks in need of currency presented the bank's notes sooner for repayment. Thus, there was a cumulative panic. Some banks which had allowed cash reserves to get very slim suddenly found they could not pay all claims upon demand and had to close their doors. The closing of some banks scared depositors everywhere so that they might rush to their own banks to get their deposits out in cash. A "run on the bank" usually was a disaster because few banks could pay off all deposits and notes immediately. If they tried to cash in their securities with prices low, they took a loss on their former value.

The other way banks got into trouble was to keep part of their cash reserves deposited with big city banks. This was convenient for small banks and gave them some interest; but the big city banks treated these deposits like any others and expanded their loans on the basis of the currency the depositors had left with them. Each spring, the country banks tended to be short of cash and withdrew most of their city deposits. This caused the city banks to contract their lending in the spring. For this reason some of the panics, such as the one in 1857, occurred in the spring, when the big city banks were hard pressed to meet all of their cash needs. At the same time, the U.S. Treasury was accumulating a surplus in its own vaults; so the pressure for cash was doubly severe.

In earlier decades the federal government had made some efforts to control the excesses of bank credit fluctuation. The first Bank of the United States, started in 1791 with its stock partly owned by the government, was able to curb some excesses of private bank note issue by presenting promptly all notes that fell into its hands to that bank for immediate repayment in currency. It also was able to help a bank faced with a "run" by depositing some of its currency with that bank. But the charter of the first bank was allowed to expire in 1811. The second Bank of the United States, established in 1816, operated similarly; but it, too, was allowed to expire in 1836.

There also were some experiments in various states with ways to control banking. The Suffolk Bank of Boston developed a private system of policing the overissue of notes by small banks, for it regularly collected all country bank notes and delivered them back to those banks for repayment in currency. In 1829, New York state enacted a safety fund system which required payments into a pooled cash reserve and regular inspection of each bank's operations. While previously banks had been chartered by special legislative acts, New York in 1838 passed a Free Banking Act which allowed anyone to charter a bank provided a sufficient reserve deposit of securities was placed with a public agency. In 1842, Louisiana required its banks to keep a cash reserve equal to one third of note and deposit liabilities. The state regulations, however, were not uniform in all states, and many proved inadequate in the crash of 1857, partly because of the practice of placing reserves on deposit in large city banks.

Thus, it was largely through inaction or insufficient control that the government role in stabilizing bank credit and business fluctuations was poorly performed prior to the Civil War. But it has taken many more decades for governments and the public to learn the lessons of bank regulation.

Regulating Business

Because of the widespread political belief that the central government should exercise only limited powers, the federal government did little to encourage or regulate private business activities. The most important government action, of course, was the tariff. Although initially devised merely to raise revenues, it was raised in 1816 and in the next decade as a means of protecting and encouraging the development of American textile and iron industries. The patent laws also were designed to encourage the development and commercial use of inventions in industry. In the field of foreign commerce, legislation was passed restricting intercoastal commerce to American ships, and higher ship registration fees were required of foreign ships in American ports. American ships were required to hire a minimum percentage of American seamen; and laws protected conditions for seamen and for immigrants. In the realm of interstate commerce, federal inspection was required on the safety of steamboat boilers. Laws regulated trade with the Indians and prohibited sale of alcoholic beverages to them.

Americans, however, had little hesitancy about regulating business, and many colonial practices were carried over by state and local governments. Pennsylvania continued to inspect the quality of food products exported. Cities continued to inspect quality of bread, and in the 1850's milk also came under inspection. City price regulation applied to bread, produce markets, hackney rates, wagon transport rates, ice, gas, and water. Regulation of rates and of operations were included in the charters of canal and railroad companies. Since many of these activities had the characteristics of local monopolies, it commonly was assumed to be necessary to apply restrictions as well as to confer a privilege of licensed operation.

Much of the emphasis in the early decades, however, was upon conferring and granting rewards to encourage private business to undertake some kind of production that was regarded as serving the public interest in development. The federal government spent money on navigation aids and river and harbor improvements in order to assist shipping. In George Washington's first term, a duty was placed upon salt to finance a bounty paid to operators of cod fishing boats, and this subsidy remained until after the Civil War. The small arms industry was encouraged by granting contracts with liberal interest-free advances to the new arms manufacturers, such as Eli Whitney. For a few years subsidies were granted to American companies experimenting with ocean steamships.

Much of state government legislation was to grant special privileges in the charters of companies which were encouraged to provide new services. Bounties were given to shipbuilders in southern ports and to farmers for raising silk in New England. Many states provided tax exemptions for new manufacturing firms. Industrial fairs sometimes offered prizes for high quality or innovations in products.

No doctrinaire policies of laissez-faire seemed to stand in the way of governments regulating or giving privileges and subsidies to private business whenever there was a public demand for it.

Public Enterprise and Mixed Investment

From the earliest times, there was an assumption that certain large-scale activities, which broadly benefited most of the public but could be performed by a single firm, should be state enterprises rather than private monopolies. The federal government began its postal service initially as a revenue-earning division of the Treasury. Other federally operated projects included the lighthouse service, the mint, armories, Indian trading posts, and hospitals for seamen. The first telegraph line from Baltimore to Washington was built with federal funds and then turned over to the post office to operate. The longest and most expensive of turnpikes was the National Road, although Congress turned down other road-building projects.

It was at the state level that public enterprises were more prevalent. At the local government level road building was regarded as a public function, although the alternative of chartering private monopoly companies to build toll roads frequently was used. When it came to building canals, however, the size of the projects seemed far beyond what any private company of those times could handle. Whereas the capital investment in building a turnpike might be a few hundred dollars, a canal of any considerable length seldom cost less than $1 million. The Erie cost about six times this, and later branches and enlargements cost several times as much again. The state of Pennsylvania spent over $60,000 million on its canals.

In those times no private company had ever collected together such large pools of capital. A way was needed to draw upon the small savings of a large number of people, and New York demonstrated that the sale of state bonds could be used for this purpose. The major trans-Appalachian and western canals were entirely state enterprises, but many of the private canals also were heavily dependent upon public investment funds or subsidies. State and local governments made large purchases of the stocks and bonds of chartered canal companies. In some cases other loans were made to the companies. Even the primarily private canal ventures on the East Coast received special lottery and banking privileges.

The federal government at first refused any support for the Erie Canal, but this policy was not followed consistently. Large purchases of stock were made in the Dismal Swamp, the Chesapeake and Ohio, and the Chesapeake and Delaware canal companies. Indiana and Ohio were aided and encouraged by large federal land grants.

In the 1840's and 1850's, when the wave of railroad construction got under way, the emphasis had shifted almost entirely to private companies, but heavy government investments and subsidies were extended to the railroad industry, continuing the tradition of government encouragement of particular types of economic activity. Some railroads had been started in the 1830's, but the popularity of canals probably hindered their rapid development. There was some initial opposition from local interests and businesses with a stake in the canals because of a fear of competition for funds and traffic. Then, the failure of many canals to make a profit created somewhat of a bad reputation for state enterprises; and the railroad companies began to use laissez-faire arguments to stave off potential competition from public enterprises.

While the cost of all canals may have been almost $200 million, the cost of railroads prior to 1860 was something over $1 billion. Many of the railroad companies, however, were small and had relatively short lines. This facilitated the starting of such companies with relatively small stock investments. Local business leaders anxious to obtain the advantages of railroad transportation for their communities invested heavily themselves, but they also enlisted the support of municipalities to make investments, loans, and grants. States also were drawn into heavy investments in railroads. Of all the state bonds issued by 1838, about two thirds as much of the amount invested in canals already had been invested in railroads, and during the late 1840's and 1850's, state debts again increased to finance railroads. It has been estimated that in the South over half of the capital for railroads was provided by state and local governments, and even higher proportions were recorded for some northern states; so, perhaps half is a reasonable rough estimate nationally for the share of government in railroad capital costs prior to 1860. The state charters also gave the private companies many privileges to encourage them—monopoly of routes, power of eminent domain, exemption from taxes, and lottery and banking privileges.

Congress generally resisted the public clamor for financial aid to the railroads. However, many early railroad surveys were made by federal engineers at government expense. Tariff duties on iron also were reduced especially to help the railroads. Finally, in 1850, political representatives from southern and western states combined forces to get an act passed to give federal land grants to the states of Illinois, Mississippi, and Alabama in order to support a north-south railroad from Chicago to Mobile. This set a precedent for similar grants in the 1850's and after the Civil War. Two-hundred-foot right-of-ways and alternate even sections of land, 6 miles deep, were granted to the railroad companies. These subsidies gave them the immediate revenues or ability to borrow that enabled them to finance construction. When completed in 1857, the Illinois Central Railroad had cost over $23 million, of which stockholders contributed about one sixth, and sale of bonds secured by mortgages on federal lands raised most of the rest.

These public enterprises, investments and subsidies in the field of transportation played a major role in the rapid improvements in transportation early in American history. As we have seen in earlier chapters, the transportation improvements played an important role in reducing production costs, permitting regional specialization, and creating national markets to support mass production in industry. Without government assistance, large capital accumulations from private individual savings might not have been possible for several decades. State credit helped to bring in considerable foreign capital from private investors.

The public interest in encouraging the rapid construction of transportation was obvious. The benefits were widespread to a whole community or region and far exceeded the revenues that could be obtained by the operating agency from tolls on passengers and freight. Land values in the area would rise, many businesses would experience lower costs and greater sales, and personal incomes would rise. Transportation, moreover, has peculiar characteristics that arise from its high capital costs. The fixed capital costs are very large compared to the relatively low operating costs. Once built, the facilities need to be used heavily to justify the cost, but heavy use requires a large number of customers and perhaps relatively low rates. Not only are the facilities durable, but this spreading of fixed costs over a large volume at low rates requires many years for capital investment to be recovered from revenues. The total size of investment also must be very large because the fixed equipment cannot be built in small pieces to allow the business to grow by gradual expansion. A railroad or canal must extend all the way between two places, not just part of the way.

Accordingly, in a newly developing region with a small immediate volume of traffic, it might not be profitable for a private company to incur the large and heavy capital costs and wait a long time for enough traffic to build up revenues large enough to justify the investment. The government for the region, however, can take account of the broader social benefits that appear as lower costs for all industries and/or lower prices for consumers. It may determine that these outweigh investment costs and undertake or subsidize certain capital projects. It also can draw upon present and future taxes to share those costs.

For these reasons, as we pointed out in Chapter 1, economists today refer to the investment costs of transporation and public utility facilities (for gas, electricity, water, sewerage, and roads) as "social overhead capital." There is a public interest in insuring that such investments are made early so that a multitude of other private investments in a region will be worthwhile. Only the government may be able to take account of the indirect benefits that will result in deciding whether to incur these costs. Thus, the government plays an important role in supporting economic development investments as well as in providing the proper environment of laws and monetary stability.

In American history prior to 1860, then, governments played a limited but important role in achieving rapid economic growth. Without any consistent or well-defined conscious policies, the federal, state, and local governments applied a mixture of actions to encourage, support, or regulate private enterprises. By hindsight, a mixture of shortcomings and successes may be attributed to government action and inaction; but in 1860, there were no clear-cut ideas widely held about the distinct roles of private and public agencies in economic affairs.

STUDY QUESTIONS

1. England's Industrial Revolution began in about the 1760's; so why didn't ours begin about the same time? What were the early barriers to the development of an American textile industry, and how were they overcome? What kind of man played a major role in this development?
2. What other types of manufacturing existed at the start of our Nation? What conditions stimulated the development of machinery, and what major types of inventions were discovered that were to become increasingly important?
3. While waterpower was readily available for manufacturing, why was the steam engine important to the early rise of manufacturing? How was this related to ironmaking improvements and to the use of coal? Why were the railroads important to the pre-Civil War growth of manufacturing?
4. How did the new inventions and mass-production methods affect the organization of manufacturing production? What impact did exclusive growth of the U.S. market have upon manufacturing growth? Why did production of certain types tend to concentrate in particular cities or regions? Why did larger markets tend to stimulate more use of the "cottage" system of production at first?
5. How did the scarcity of labor encourage the mechanization of manufacturing industry? At the same time, why did a more plentiful labor supply attract textile mills to New England farm regions and apparel and shoe industries to northeastern port cities?
6. What type of men became manufacturers during manufacturing's early development? What form of business organization remained most common prior to the Civil War? Where did the initial capital come from that started new manufacturing firms? What were the chief sources of capital for expansion?
7. In spite of the minimum functions assigned to the federal government and the effort to handle its own affairs on a "sound finance" basis, its taxes, debt repayment, and handling of Treasury funds had disturbing effects on the private economy. Explain.
8. How do banks increase money supply by making loans? Why do bank loans tend to expand when prices are rising and contract when prices are falling? Why do some banks run out of cash when prices fall? How does the fear that this may happen cause a "panic" which helps make it actually happen? How did the state governments attempt to regulate banks? What weaknesses remained?

9. In what ways did state governments regulate or grant special privileges to private business? Did the federal government attempt any regulation or grant any special privileges or protection to private business?
10. Why was canal building primarily a state government enterprise? Did the federal government lend any support to canal building? Why was railroad building left to private enterprise? How did states and local governments provide most of the railroad financing? How did the federal government aid railroads prior to the Civil War? On what basis might public investment be justified in transportation improvements?

PART III

Sustained Rapid Growth: 1860–1920

Chapter 8 THE INDUSTRIALIZATION PROCESS

England introduced the Industrial Revolution to the world at the end of the 18th century. In the middle of the next century America led the race of other nations to industrialize. By 1860, the United States already was the second ranking industrial nation, producing about one fifth of world output. In technology, Americans had attracted attention with their superior farm machinery and locomotives at London's Crystal Palace Exhibition in 1851. Again in 1867 at the Paris Exposition, Americans won prizes for their pianos, firearms, sewing machines, and machine tools.

The rate of American expansion and rise in productivity after the Civil War was phenomenal; and manufacturing continued to provide the main impetus to this rapid increase. Between 1860 and 1913, the share of world manufacturing production in the United States rose from 23 to 36 percent. The share in England fell from 32 to 14 percent, and in France it fell from 10 to 6 percent. A rising share went to Germany (13 to 16 percent), the rest of Europe (9 to 11 percent), and the rest of the world (13 to 17 percent). By 1913, America's manufacturing output alone was equal to the combination of its three nearest rivals![1]

Paradoxically, this period usually is regarded as a dark chapter in American history. The achievement is taken for granted, and the business leaders who helped bring it about are cited with shame as "robber barons." In the perspective of a long sweep of history, this critical attitude becomes understandable as a consequence of the great changes that were transforming the methods and organization of production in the national economy. This also was a period when new problems were shifting the economic role of government and requiring new methods of public administration. The following two chapters will consider

[1] League of Nations, *Industrialization and Foreign Trade* (Geneva, 1945), p. 13.

these growing pains of the rapidly industrializing economy. This chapter will consider the record of rapid growth and the ways in which that growth was achieved. The pace of growth was not even and automatic; so, attention will be given to the major innovations and waves of investment that accompanied the surges of most rapid growth.

POST-CIVIL WAR TRENDS

Production Achievement

As we noted in Part II, American manufacturing capacity began to grow rapidly around 1840. Then of course the Civil War took its heavy toll through war damage and by diverting our efforts in favor of arms production and retardation of investment in growth-inducing undertakings. The postwar period saw us resume the expansion and growth begun in the 1840's.

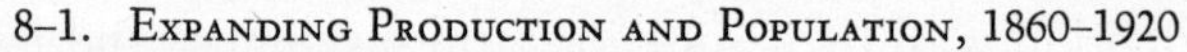
8–1. Expanding Production and Population, 1860–1920

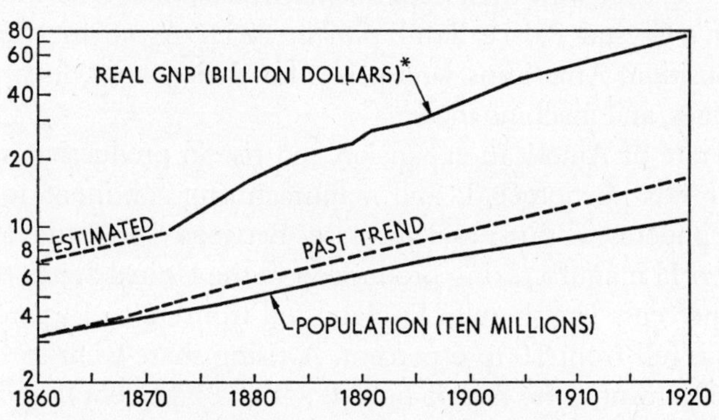

* Five-year averages, in 1929 prices.
Source: U.S. Department of Commerce, *Historical Statistics of the United States* (Washington, D.C.: U.S. Government Printing Office, 1960), pp. 7, 139; Kuznets' concept prior to 1890.

During the first six decades of the 19th century, America increased its population six times and raised its real income at least nine times. This resulted in a rise of income per capita of one half (or more). In the next six decades, population was to grow less than four times, while total production would increase 10 times. The result was an increase in production per person of about three times. (See 8–1 and 8–2.)

This was an unparalleled record of rapid and long-sustained increase in a nation's total production, and it was achieved in spite of a gradual slowing down of the rate of population increase. From 1830 to 1879, population had an annual average rate of increase of 2.7 percent

8–2. Rising Production per Person, 1860–1920

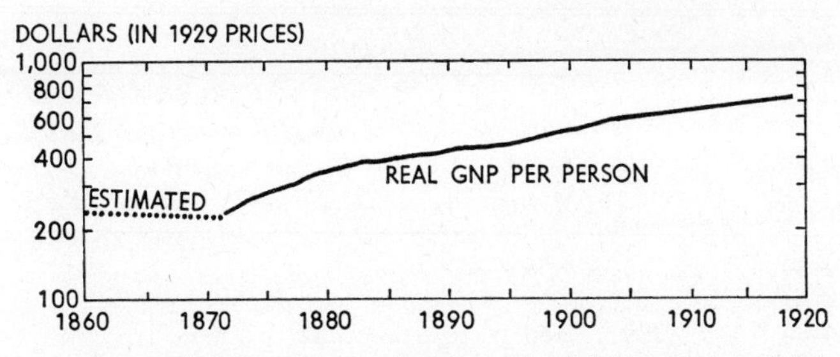

Source: U.S. Department of Commerce, *Historical Statistics of the United States* (Washington, D.C.: U.S. Government Printing Office, 1960), p. 139; Kuznets' concept prior to 1890.

which fell to 1.9 percent from 1879 to 1919. During the same two periods real gross national product averaged annual increases of 4.3 percent and 3.7 percent. Real GNP per capita, therefore, actually increased faster in the later period, rising from a rate of 1.55 percent per year to 1.76 percent.[2]

The rate of expansion and growth, however, did not occur at the same steady pace. The most rapid rates of economic growth occurred just prior to and immediately following the Civil War. The Civil War apparently interrupted or slowed down the rate of growth of total production, including both North and South. Shortly after the war, total production fully recovered and underwent the most rapid rate of increase in American history. From the year 1869 to the year 1879, the real gross national product is estimated to have doubled. The exact estimates for single years that long ago, of course, are not regarded as very reliable, but they may be averaged for longer periods. Nevertheless, alternative estimates, whether for census years or five-year averages, tend to confirm the conclusion that the 1870's was the decade with the fastest rate of increase in production in our national history. The next fastest increase was in the decade just before the Civil War. Another 10-year period of rapid increase came around the turn of the century, especially between 1897 and 1907. (See 8–3.)

During the century of rapid growth prior to World War I, therefore, there were three main surges of especially rapid growth. The first was in the 1840's and 1850's, a period of rapid railroad construction as well as manufacturing expansion. The second was between 1867 and 1882, another period of rapid railroad construction and of rapid devel-

[2] See Testimony of Raymond W. Goldsmith, U.S. Joint Economic Committee, *Employment, Growth, and Price Levels: Hearings*, Part 2, A59 (Washington, D.C.: U.S. Government Printing Office, 1959), p. 271.

8–3. DECADE RATES OF INCREASE IN PRODUCTION

Overlapping Decades	Alternative Estimates (Percent Changes)		
	National Income (Martin)	Commodity Output (Gallman)	Gross National Product (5 Years Average) (Kuznets)
1829–39	58		
1834–44			
1839–49	66	52	
1844–54		69	
1849–59	69	62	
1854–64			
1859–69	−4	23	
1864–74			
1869–79	75	62	77*
1874–84		70	85
1879–89	54	63	49
1884–94		41	37
1889–99	44	36	47
1894–04			59
1899–09	41		48
1904–14			33
1909–19	31		29

* Less than a decade.

SOURCE: U.S. Department of Commerce, *Historical Statistics of the United States* (Washington, D.C.: U.S. Government Printing Office, 1960); R. F. Martin, *National Income in the United States, 1799–1938* (New York: National Industrial Conference Board, 1939); and Robert E. Gallman, "Commodity Output, 1839–1899," Conference on Research in Income and Wealth, *Trends in the American Economy in the Nineteenth Century* (Princeton, N.J.: Princeton University Press, 1960), p. 16.

opment of the steel industry. The third was around the turn of the century when the electric utility and street railway industries were rapidly built up. The later sections of this chapter will describe the major industrial changes that accompanied the surges of growth after the Civil War.

Paradoxically, the decade of most rapid growth in our history also experienced the second longest depression. Each of the three decades after the Civil War, in fact, had its major depression—1873–78, 1882–85, and 1892–94. Speeches and writings during these decades of rapid growth, therefore, were filled with critical comments about unfavorable business conditions and distress among farmers and workers. How do we reconcile this evidence of business depressions with our data on trends of rapid growth?

A long-term decline in average prices throughout the economy was a major condition hiding some of the real growth and causing considerable distress. Inflation during the Civil War had doubled the index of wholesale prices, and not all of this inflation had been eliminated in the postwar price decline by 1870. During the 1870's, wholesale prices fell by one third, and finally reached the prewar level by 1879. In the following decade and a half, a further decline of almost one third occurred. Only after 1896 did prices generally begin to rise, and after 1910 prices exceeded the pre-Civil War level. After 1896, therefore, both prices and output were rising, and business depressions seemed shorter and milder. Before 1896 the falling trend of prices

8–4. WHOLESALE PRICES, 1860–1920

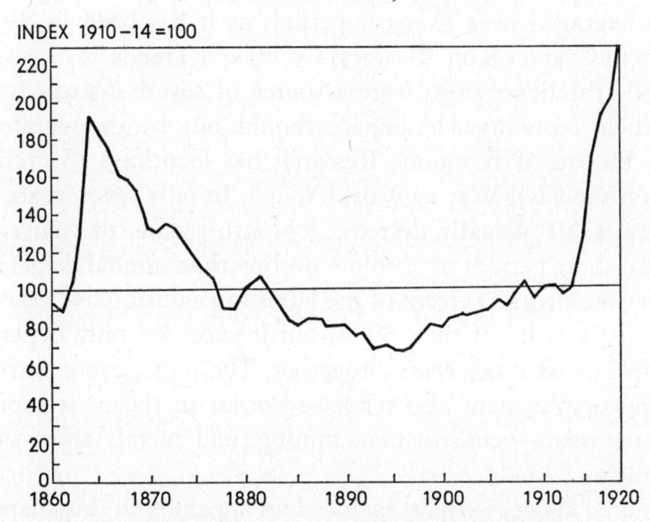

SOURCE: U.S. Department of Commerce, *Historical Statistics of the United States* (Washington, D.C.: U.S. Government Printing Office, 1960), pp. 115–16.

made money incomes increase more slowly than physical production and intensified the sudden price declines in business depressions. Businessmen, who purchased goods at one price and had to sell after prices had fallen, took a loss on their inventories. Farmers, who had borrowed to buy land and machinery when prices were high, had difficulty paying off their mortgages as prices of their products fell. Wage rates failed to increase or were reduced. In the midst of rapidly rising trends of production, therefore, there was much discontent with economic conditions. There is no clear evidence that either the early price deflation or the later price inflation helped or hindered the long-term trend of economic growth. (See 8–4.)

Short-term fluctuations in output and prices also tended to obscure the long-term trends. In a rapidly expanding economy, people are prone to take for granted the periods of increasing output as normal and to be deeply concerned about years of disappointing increase or actual decrease. Periods of rapid expansion in output and rapid rise in prices most often were followed by severe setbacks such as had occurred in 1837 and 1857 and occurred again in 1873 and 1893. These frequently started as financial crises and were referred to as "panics." Later the frequency of the setbacks in output and prices became widely recognized, and the term "business cycle" came to be applied to their repeated recurrence. Since the fluctuations usually took only three to five years from peak to peak, the longer term trends are more apparent when output is averaged over five-year periods as it has been in 8–1. (See Appendix to Chapter 8 on "Business Cycles and Trends.")

While the depressions were a source of severe distress for many people, their economywide impact should not be exaggerated. The National Bureau of Economic Research has identified 13 cyclical declines from the Civil War to World War I. In only seven years did the annual real GNP actually decrease. (Monthly data, of course, would show more short periods of absolute decline than annual data.) Unemployment exceeded 10 percent of the labor force during five years of the 1870's and six years of the 1890's, but it exceeded only 6 percent in perhaps five or six other years altogether. The most severe decreases in output and employment also tended to occur in the most rapidly expanding industries—construction, mining, and metals and machinery manufacturing.

As noted above, we have included an appendix in this chapter that introduces business cycles and their relationship to long-term trends. That discussion provides the basis for a fuller appreciation of the preceding several paragraphs. In addition it offers helpful background information for understanding the changing structure of the economy discussed in this and the last section of the text.

End of the Frontier

To account for the remarkably rapid trend of increase in national output, we first turn to broad measures of the resource inputs. To be sure, all of the inputs—land, labor and capital—were expanding. Yet there are three aspects of their growth which deserve special attention. First, the rate of increase slowed down for all three of the inputs. Second, the average rate of expansion in land was the slowest, while the rate of expansion in capital was the fastest. Third, while the rate of growth of output also slowed down somewhat, it continued to rise faster than any of the inputs; and the growth in real GNP per capita became even faster. This suggests the important role played by improvements in methods and organization.

Natural resources are difficult to measure as an input factor. In a sense, the natural resources were all there to begin with and remained as a fixed quantity. The continental territory of the 48 states had been acquired by the Nation prior to 1860. The history of development after the Civil War was one of settling the virgin territories and raising the average density of population, from 10.6 persons per square mile in 1860 to 35.6 in 1920, as total population more than tripled. However, the utilization of natural resources did continue to undergo an upward trend as more farmlands were placed under cultivation and more mineral deposits were discovered and subjected to mining operations. Better transportation and changes in landholding patterns increased our access to a fixed quantity of natural resources.

In just three decades after the Civil War, total farmlands in the Nation doubled. This means that as much new land was settled in these three decades as had been settled in almost three centuries of prior history. This rate of settlement, however, merely kept pace with the population growth, which about doubled in the same period. After 1900, the increase in farm acreage almost came to a halt. Large tracts of remote and otherwise uneconomic unoccupied public lands remained, but the frontier line of settlement had disappeared. No longer could the American people move westward to settle vast new territories. Further land use was a matter of filling in the gaps of less-desirable or less-accessible lands that still were idle. Because of this slowdown, the total farm acreage in 1920 reached only about two and one-third times its 1860 level, while population reached three and two-thirds times its 1860 level. (See 8–5.)

The discovery and use of timber and mineral resources also underwent a rapid burst of increase followed by a slowdown after the turn of the century. The centers of lumber production moved westward and also south, with the older areas becoming cut over and exhausted of the best tree stands. While lumber production is not a good measure of the resource availability, the decline after 1910 did coincide with reduced cutting operations in the older forest areas of the East and North. Likewise, the number of mining workers rose very rapidly before 1890 but increased very little after 1910. While productivity increases slowed down employment more, the increase in production of all minerals also slowed down—doubling from 1900 to 1920 after having tripled in the previous two decades. The continued rapid growth was mostly due to

8–5. Slowing Down of Natural Resource Use Expansion

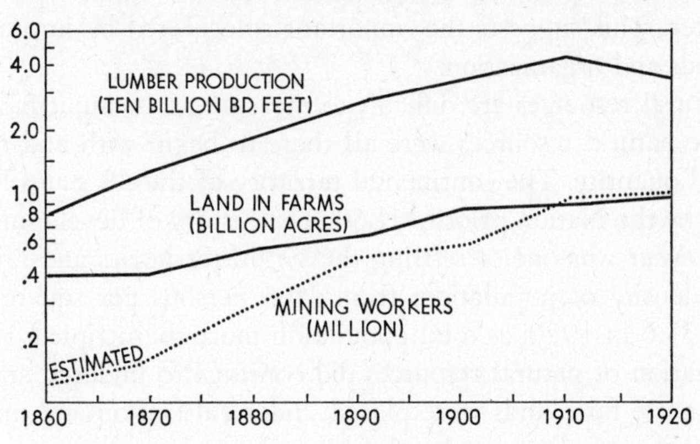

Source: U.S. Department of Commerce, *Historical Statistics of the United States* (Washington, D.C.: U.S. Government Printing Office, 1960), pp. 278, 312, 349.

the increased importance of mineral fuels; for bituminous coal output again tripled between 1900 and 1920 while petroleum output increased six times. The growth of metal mining slowed down the most.

Labor inputs maintained the most steady rate of increase. As already indicated, population more than tripled between 1860 and 1920, but the labor force grew even faster, almost quadrupling during the same period. This is largely accounted for by the increase in median age of the population from 19.4 years in 1860 to 25.3 years in 1920. The number of children below 10 years of age fell from 14 to 11 percent of the population. This reflected some decline in birthrates as the population became more urbanized, but chiefly it was due to the large inflow of immigrants, who were mostly young adults. In the early 1870's the peak number of immigrants arriving yearly in this country exceeded 400,000 as it had in the early 1850's. Even greater numbers arrived during the 1880's and early 1890's. A slump occurred with each depression, because jobs were hard to get and relatives were less able to help new arrivals. After 1900, the numbers again rose and reached peaks of over 1 million in 1905–07, 1910, and 1913–14. Since some people also left the country, the net gain was less. Elizabeth Gilboy and Edgar Hoover have estimated that during the 1880's and 1900's net immigration accounted for about one third of the population increase (measured in the preceding decade) and during the other decades about one fifth.[3] (See 8–6.)

[3] Seymour E. Harris (ed.), *American Economic History* (New York: McGraw-Hill Book Co., 1961), pp. 266–67.

The measure of labor input, however, is a little more complicated than just the number of workers. The number of hours worked and the degree of skill also are important. In 1860, the usual working day for nonfarm workers was over 10 hours, and the workweek was six days. This meant working for over 60 hours a week. By 1920, the average weekly hours for nonfarm workers had fallen to about 50 hours. Taking into account the number of days of idleness during the year and including farm and government workers, the average workweek for the total labor force was a little less to begin with, and it declined only about 9 percent between 1869 and 1919. Total man-hours of labor input, therefore, increased somewhat slower than the labor force. Dur-

8–6. Immigrants Arriving in the United States, 1860–1920

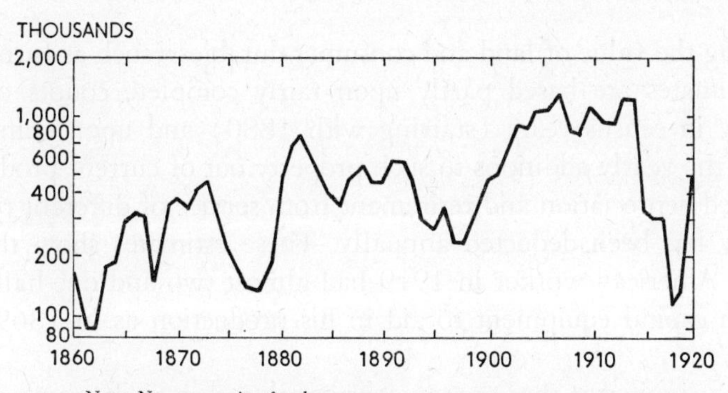

Note: Not accounting for departures.
Source: U.S. Department of Commerce, *Historical Statistics of the United States* (Washington, D.C.: U.S. Government Printing Office, 1960), pp. 56–57.

ing this period, there also was a shift toward a greater proportion of workers in the higher skilled jobs. This was mostly due to an increased proportion of workers in nonfarm jobs, which had a higher value of output per worker than in farming; and also the more skilled jobs in the faster growing industries tended to have a greater influence on the average. Using the average annual earnings in different industries as an indication of skill levels, it has been estimated that the real value of total labor inputs increased somewhat faster than the number of workers, even after allowing for the reduction in average hours worked. (See 8–7.)

The input of capital increased almost as fast as output. While no figures are available for 1860, estimated real capital stock rose from $27 billion in 1869 to $227 billion in 1919 (both in 1929 prices). These estimates are for the value of reproducible tangible property including buildings, machinery, inventories, and money metals, but

8–7. Measures of Change in Labor Input, 1869–1919

INDEX (1869=100): 0 100 200 300 400
POPULATION
LABOR FORCE
AVERAGE WEEKLY HOURS
MANHOURS
LABOR INPUT

Note: Not accounting for departures.
Sources: U.S. Department of Commerce, *Historical Statistics of the United States* (Washington, D.C.: U.S. Government Printing Office, 1960), p. 7; and John W. Kendrick, *Productivity Trends in the United States* (Princeton, N.J.: Princeton University Press, 1961), Tables A VII, A IX, A XI, and A XIII.

excluding the value of land and consumer durables (such as furniture). The estimates are based partly upon fairly complete counts of such property in census years (starting with 1880) and upon cumulative data on the yearly additions to such property out of current production. Estimated depreciation and retirement from service of different types of property has been deducted annually. These estimates show that the average American worker in 1919 had almost two and one-half times as much capital equipment to aid in his production as in 1869. (See 8–8.)

It is significant that energy consumption rose at the same pace as capital stock prior to 1900 and then rose even faster in the following

8–8. Expanded Use of Capital and Energy

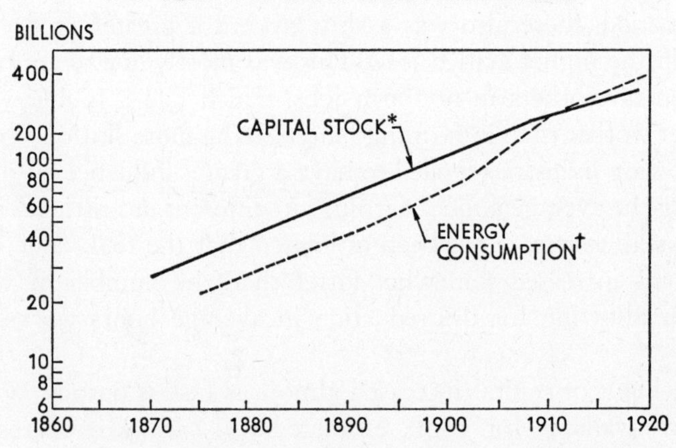

* In dollars of 1929 purchasing power.
† Horsepower-hours, for work; starting with 1870–80 decade average.
Sources: Simon Kuznets, *Capital in the American Economy* (Princeton, N.J.: Princeton University Press, 1961), Table 3; and J. F. Dewhurst, *America's Needs and Resources: A New Survey* (New York: The Twentieth Century Fund, 1955), Table L.

two decades. We have seen that the revolution in modern industrial methods involved the application of nonhuman energy to run machinery in making standard products. So the rapid pace of industrialization in America was marked by the use of more machinery and more fuel for power. After the turn of the century the widespread adoption of electricity and the gasoline motor rapidly expanded the use of various forms of energy, both for production and for direct consumption purposes. The American worker was given tremendous amounts of power at the control of his fingertips to both lighten his work and vastly increase his productivity.

Productivity and Rewards

The increase in output at a faster rate than the increase in inputs suggests that something more happened than mere expansion. Improvements in methods and organization of production must have taken place. An increase in productivity commonly is used as a measure of the results of such improvement. The term productivity refers to the ratio of the amount of production achieved in relation to the amount of resources used. Frequently, the term is used merely to refer to labor productivity, or the ratio of output to the labor input alone. This does not mean that labor alone was responsible for the output. It merely is a short-cut measure using the most readily available data. It also satisfies our interest in the potential consumption implied by a greater increase in product than in workers.

In studies of productivity, economists frequently have resorted to a division of inputs into only two categories, labor and capital. Capital, in this sense, refers to the amount of property or wealth devoted to production, including the value of land or natural resources as well as the accumulated stock of reproducible property. Estimates of capital in this special sense have been made starting with 1889. They show that in the three decades prior to 1920, capital input in the private sector of the American economy increased at an average yearly rate of 3.4 percent. Labor input, taking account of changes in hours and in skills, increased a yearly 2.2 percent. The combined inputs of labor and capital (each weighted by their share of national income), therefore, increased at an in-between rate of 2.6 percent per year. Total output, however, rose 3.9 percent. With output rising faster than total inputs, the total factor productivity ratio increased 1.3 percent annually. (See 8–9.)

Two things should be clear from these comparisons. An increasing amount of capital was being used per worker in order to attain the rising output per worker. And output was increasing faster than either the labor input or the capital input. Improvements in methods and organization, therefore, were enabling the combined inputs to produce more output. It also should be noted that the new methods usually required investment in more capital in the form of new types of machinery. While labor accounted for more than three quarters of the total cost of production, capital was contributing more to the increase in productivity.

Historically, the assumption frequently has been made that modern industrial progress was achieved at the expense of workers. The myth has been spread that not only did property owners expropriate the

8–9. Productivity Trends, Pre-World War I

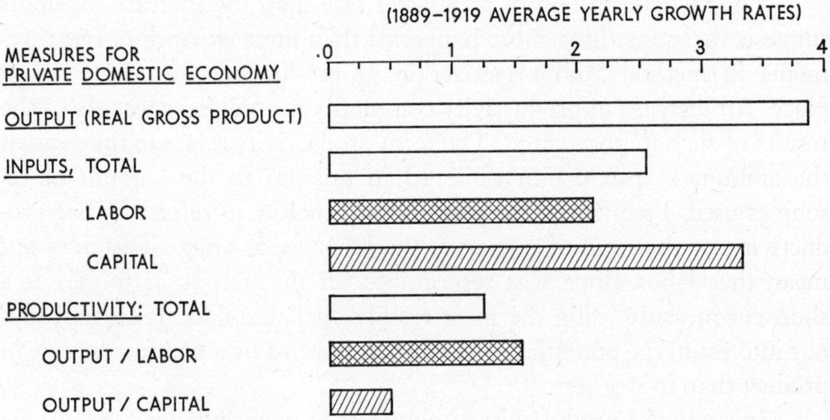

(1889–1919 AVERAGE YEARLY GROWTH RATES)

MEASURES FOR PRIVATE DOMESTIC ECONOMY .0 1 2 3 4

OUTPUT (REAL GROSS PRODUCT)

INPUTS, TOTAL

LABOR

CAPITAL

PRODUCTIVITY: TOTAL

OUTPUT / LABOR

OUTPUT / CAPITAL

Source: John W. Kendrick, *Productivity Trends in the United States* (Princeton, N.J.: Princeton University Press, 1961), Tables I and A XXII.

gains in productivity for themselves, but also the profits were obtained partly by reducing the real wage incomes of workers.

The productivity studies mentioned above have provided some basis for contradicting these charges. While an increasing proportion of capital was used in production from 1889 to 1919, it has been estimated that the average unit price of capital increased much more slowly than did the unit price of labor. The real income going to capital owners, therefore, is estimated to have increased less rapidly than the real income going to labor.

Other types of studies have tended to lead to a similar conclusion. Data on wage and salary payments have shown them to be rising in relation to national income, although this is thought to be mostly due to the increasing proportion of people who have become hired workers rather than working for themselves on a farm or a small business—the proprietors or self-employed. Proprietors' income, of course, involves both labor and capital rewards and there is no clear way to separate them. Economists have concluded that the share of total income going to labor has tended to remain about the same, although there is much doubt concerning the exact trends. With a rising proportion of capital being used and with about the same total share of income going to capital, the rate of reward for capital must have been falling. This is confirmed partially by data showing falling average interest rates on bonds between 1860 and 1920.

Studies also have been directed at estimating the average wage rates and annual earnings of workers. The general declines in prices

8–10. Worker Gains in Real Earnings, 1860–1920

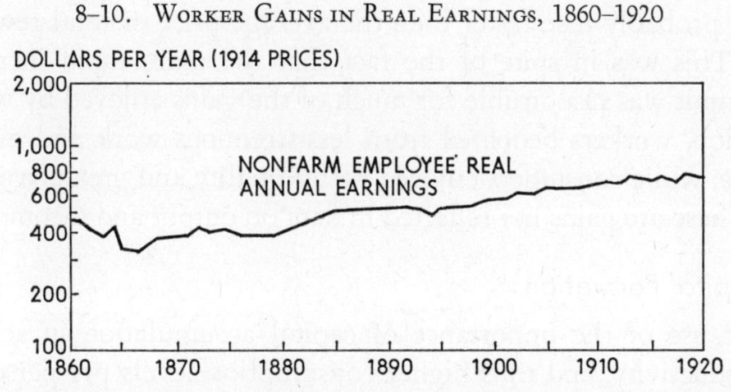

Source: Stanley Lebergott, *Manpower in Economic Growth* (New York: McGraw Hill Book Company, 1964), Tables A17, A19.

were accompanied at times by general declines in wages, and for a while it was thought that real wages may have had a long-term decline prior to 1914. Recent studies, however, have provided more comprehensive wage and price data that show a pronounced upward trend in real wages from the Civil War to World War I. (See 8–10.)

This does not mean that all individuals shared equally in the gains in real income. Undoubtedly this was a period when a few families became enormously wealthy, and the contrast (or spread) between the incomes of the poor cotton sharecropper and the very rich must have increased. But is there evidence of substantially greater inequality of income distribution during this period? Unfortunately, there are no adequate data on individual incomes prior to the start of the federal income tax in 1914. After that the shares of total income going to the top 1 percent and top 5 percent of families remained fairly constant for two decades and then declined somewhat. Income tax data from the

Civil War and immediately following years are inconclusive but suggest little difference in the top group's share in 1869 and in 1920.[4] The process of industrialization and urbanization undoubtedly increased the relative size of the middle classes. The proportion of workers also increased in nonfarm jobs and in the more skilled industries. Thus, the distribution of incomes may have shifted in favor of the middle and upper middle incomes and away from the very lowest income groups. This does not necessarily mean that any group was worse off in absolute terms.

The conclusion must be drawn, therefore, that the benefits from America's period of most rapid economic growth and early industrialization were shared by workers generally and thus were widespread throughout the economy. The price of labor and labor's total income rose and probably rose faster than the average price or total rewards to capital. This was in spite of the fact that the more rapid increase in capital input was responsible for much of the gains enjoyed by workers. In addition, workers benefited from less-strenuous work and more leisure time, while consumers enjoyed better quality and greater variety of goods. These are gains not reflected in data on output and incomes.

Capital Formation

Because of the importance of capital accumulation in achieving high productivity, and thus higher consumption levels per person, it is important to consider where the increased capital came from. How was it accumulated? Data on gross national product provide some general information on this. They also provide additional evidence confirming the widespread benefits to consumers from the rising trend in output.

The gross national product represents the total value of all goods and services produced in a year. Not all of the products, however, go to consumers and are used up in current consumption each year. Some of the products are in the form of capital goods—buildings, machinery, inventories. Some of the current production is needed to replace capital goods that wear out or lose their value from obsolescence each year. This is referred to as an allowance for "capital consumption," and it is required merely to maintain the value of the total capital stock existing at the beginning of the year. Some of the new capital goods also go to expanding the total stock of existing capital. It is this net addition to capital stock that is important to expanding the gross national product

[4] Simon Kuznets, *Income and Wealth of the United States* (Cambridge, England: Bowes & Bowes, 1952), Table 29 and footnote on p. 144 (citing work of Rufus S. Tucker).

in the future. This net addition is called the "net capital formation," and the total of nonconsumed goods—capital consumption plus net capital formation—is called the gross capital formation.

In the years 1917–21, the annual gross capital formation still was about one fourth of the gross national product, as it had been in 1869–73. Capital consumption, however, required an increasing share of GNP. This probably reflects the increased importance of durable goods in the capital stock (and less importance of inventories), a shorter useful life of capital goods because of rapid obsolescence with

8–11. Changing Components of GNP

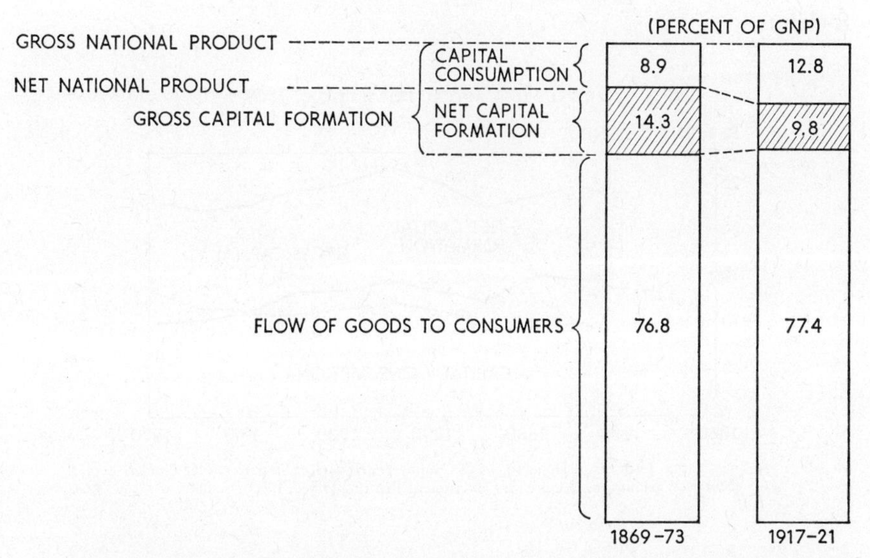

Source: U.S. Department of Commerce, *Historical Statistics of the United States* (Washington, D.C.: U.S. Government Printing Office, 1960), p. 144.

technological change, and some slowing down in the rate of growth of GNP itself. In any event, net capital formation absorbed a declining share of GNP. The GNP was slowing down partly because a smaller share of the total output was being reinvested to expand capital stock and thus raise future output. (See 8–11.)

Business firms were the chief users of capital goods, taking initially almost three quarters of the total, while households initially took over a fifth. Governments initially absorbed a small share, but their share rapidly increased, especially for local governments. On the other hand, personal savings provided almost two thirds of total savings (including farmers and unincorporated businesses with individuals), and corporations provided over a fourth. The transfer of savings to enable capital users to purchase more capital goods was arranged mostly through financial intermediaries—banks, savings and loan associations, and insurance companies—which received individual savings and made loans and investments in businesses.

These long-run trends fluctuated somewhat with the rate of increase in gross national product. When output growth was slowest, during the depressions following 1873 and 1893, the flow of capital goods required the highest share of output (in the five-year periods 1874–79 and 1894–99). The subsequent rapid growth of output reduced the percentage share of output in the form of capital goods. (See 8–12.)

8–12. Trends in Capital Formation, 1869–1919

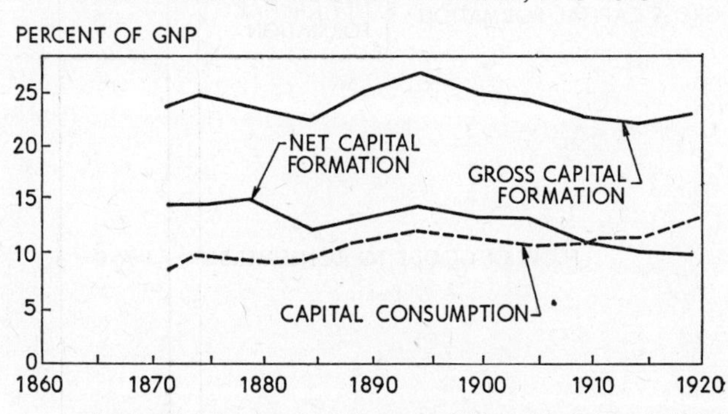

Source: U.S. Department of Commerce, *Historical Statistics of the United States* (Washington, D.C.: U.S. Government Printing Office, 1960), p. 144.

Note that as total output expanded, consumer goods were expanded in about the same proportion (as shown in 8–11). This means that the gains of increased output were proportionately shared by consumers. They did not have to tighten their belts and sacrifice in the present in order to build up capital for expanding output in the future. In fact, after deducting allowance for capital consumption, the net capital formation rate, which approximates the saving rate out of total incomes, fell to about 10 percent of GNP while gross capital formation (gross saving) remained at about 23 percent of GNP.

In other words, about the same ratio of total output was consigned to replacing worn-out capital and providing new capital in the two time segments presented in 8–11. As our capital stock grew, the absolute amount of capital "consumed" in the production process grew also. To replace ever increasing amounts of worn-out capital we chose to reduce our new capital formation as a percent of GNP rather than reduce consumption as a portion of total output.

In his productivity studies for the private domestic economy (involving slightly different proportions than above), John Kendrick pointed out that between 1889 and 1898 about 83.6 percent of the GNP was used to maintain the existing capital goods, to maintain consumption standards of the initial population, and to meet national security needs. About 6.7 percent of the GNP was required to provide the additional capital goods and consumption goods for the increase in population. This left a margin of 9.7 percent for economic progress. About 1.2 percent was used to raise average consumption levels per person, and 8.5 percent went to expand capital and thus help raise future output. By 1909–19, the maintenance and national security requirements took 88.4 percent, and after allowing for population growth the margin for economic progress was down to 5.6 percent. After using 1.3 percent to raise consumption levels, only 4.3 percent went to expand capital.[5]

During the early periods of our most rapid national expansion in output, then, a substantial part of current output was saved and reinvested to expand capital. An increasing stock of capital per worker was important to raising productivity. The workers and consumers generally tended to increase their incomes and standards of consumption. The proportion of income saved and reinvested gradually declined and with this there was gradual slowing down in the rate of increase in total output. Because population growth slowed down more, the rate of growth in income per person was maintained.

EXPANDING TRANSPORTATION AND MANUFACTURING

In the two decades prior to the Civil War, national economic growth had begun to accelerate largely because of the rapid expansion of manufacturing. This trend had started slowly with the early establishment of one major mass-production industry, cotton textiles. At the same time a diversity of innovations had laid the basis for a spread of mass-production methods to other industries. Then in the 1840's, the rapid construction of railroads gave an added impetus to the metals and heavy machinery industries. At the same time, it provided cheaper transportation to tie together the regions, expand agricultural production, and provide mass markets for the newly mechanized industries.

[5] John W. Kendrick, *Productivity Trends in the United States* (Princeton, N.J.: Princeton University Press, 1961), p. 100.

The Civil War provided an interlude of somewhat slower growth. While there might be expected to be a rise in demand for guns and clothing for the armies, some of the wartime demands diverted materials from civilian uses. Pig iron production remained almost the same from 1860 to 1865, and the mileage of new railroads constructed increased only 15 percent. Textile manufacturing shifted from cotton to wool. A few types of production—such as coal and farm machinery—rose as fast or faster; and some military suppliers and speculators got rich. Wartime inflation, which doubled wholesale prices, made the dollar value of sales much larger. Estimates of real commodity output, however, show a very low rate of increase during the decade of the 1860's—perhaps about the same as the rate of population increase. The South especially suffered much destruction and loss of property in the war, and for every southern state, estimates of real personal income in 1880 show a level little better than in 1840. Immediately after the war, the rapid pace of national expansion was resumed, manufacturing and railroad construction again spurted ahead, and even in the South both farm and factory production soon recovered and grew.

Completing a Railroad Network

The building of a complete national railroad network was a major stimulating force in the economy in the two decades immediately after the Civil War. The prewar rate of increase in railroad mileage, which had tripled during the 1840's and again in the 1850's, was not quite reached; but track mileage doubled in the first 8 postwar years and doubled again in the next 14 years. After this, construction slowed down, with little more than 50 percent added in the next three decades combined. (See 8–13.)

The most dramatic part of this railroad construction was the spanning of the western plains and mountains to reach the Pacific Coast. After having authorized engineering surveys of several routes in 1853, Congress passed the Pacific Railway Act of 1862, authorizing the Union Pacific and Central Pacific railroads to build toward each other from Omaha and Sacramento. The linkup was made in 1869 just west of Ogden, Utah. Not until 1883 was another link provided by the Northern Pacific, but by 1893 the Great Northern and Southern Pacific added two other routes.

The largest concentration of new track was laid in the Great Plains states. Chicago became the primary focus of a network of railroads, called the Granger roads that fanned out westward over the plains and interlaced vast new farming areas. From Chicago eastward,

8–13. Railroad Mileage and Traffic, 1860–1920

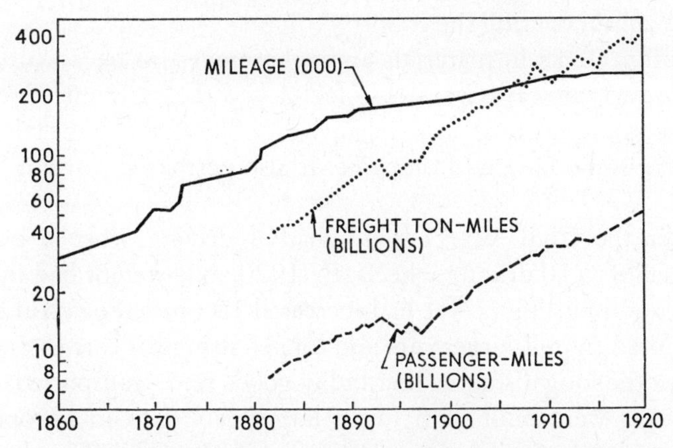

Source: U.S. Department of Commerce, *Historical Statistics of the United States* (Washington, D.C.: U.S. Government Printing Office, 1960), pp. 427–29.

five major systems were built up during the 1860's and 1870's: the Grand Trunk, the Pennsylvania, the New York Central, the Baltimore and Ohio, and the Erie. These railroads (called the trunkline roads) filled in gaps, built feeder lines, and provided multiple connections between major cities. A number of smaller railroad companies (the coal roads) specialized in connecting the Appalachian coal mines with the East Coast or the Ohio Valley. Construction lagged about a decade in the South, but by 1900 the national railroad network was virtually completed in every region and state.

Along with the increased mileage came rapid improvements in methods that helped to lower costs and improve service. In the first decade of building, the improved interconnection of rail lines itself brought a big improvement, and bridges crossed many rivers for the first time. This greatly reduced the labor cost of unloading and reloading freight at points of transfer between types of transportation. The same problem, however, had to be overcome in moving freight over different companies' lines and equipment. This required a prolonged effort to achieve uniformity. In 1871, 23 different track widths, or gauges, were in use. By 1880, four fifths of the mileage had been reduced to one standard gauge, and in 1886 the southern lines finally converted to standard gauge, too. With standardization of cars, and especially their coupling devices, freight could move over different lines in the same car without reloading. Special freight handling companies organized fast freight service over several companies' roads. Standard bills of lading and standard classifications of products were developed;

and, in order to standardize time schedules, agreement was reached on four time zones covering the country.

Improvements in materials and equipment also began to increase speed and carrying capacity. A big factor was the early introduction of steel rails, and the rails also began to be longer and heavier. This permitted a smoother and faster ride. It also permitted carrying heavier engines.

After the Civil War engines had 4 driving wheels, but soon engines had 8 to 10 driving wheels. By 1920, axle weight had increased 3½ times and pulling power had increased 10 times. Powerful engines were required to pull larger cars and longer strings of cars in one train. Because of the long distances that bulky goods were transported, American railroads were built with much larger cars than in Europe. Coal cars, for example, carried about 10 tons after the Civil War, but up to 100 tons by 1920. Safety devices became increasingly important with the faster speeds; so, in 1887 the automatic coupler and air brake both were introduced, and later came the electric block signal system.

These technological innovations including managerial improvements all contributed to lowering freight rates. Larger cars, more cars per train pulled by more powerful engines, more trains per time period, and more mileage all reduced unit costs which the forces of competition translated into lower prices.

Increased traffic, as well as improvements in methods and equipment, helped to lower costs and rates. When a rail line first was built, there was seldom enough traffic to fully use the capacity of the line. As traffic grew, more trains and longer trains could be run over the same rails and use the same terminals. Later, double tracks could be laid on the same roadbed, and improved equipment carried more traffic faster on the same mileage. The costs of building the lines initially were financed by bonded debt, which had to be paid off with interest by annual payments. As traffic and efficiency increased, these fixed costs could be divided over more units of sales and thus result in lower costs per unit. During the 1870's, the rate of increase in freight and passenger traffic little more than kept pace with the rapid construction of new rail mileage. But during the following decades traffic continued a rapid growth while new construction slowed down. (Refer again to 8–13.)

Historians have estimated that land transportation costs were cut in half between 1860 and 1900. A discussion of rates will be postponed to a later chapter, but this was a period of generally declining rates. It is difficult to separate the influence on rates of declining prices in the economy as a whole, and this was a period of rapid technological advance in many other industries. Yet, freight revenues per ton-mile fell at least as fast as general wholesale prices prior to the mid-1890's and continued (along with passenger revenues) to fall thereafter when wholesale prices rose. There is no way to measure the value of the improved quality of service also performed.

The stimulating effects on the national economy resulting from this railroad expansion were partly due to services rendered and partly due to opportunities created for other businesses. The new network of transportation opened up vast new farming regions and tapped mineral resources in previously inaccessible locations. Lowered costs and faster delivery created large national markets for the mass producers of consumer goods. These benefits were reflected in the rising land values near the rail lines. Opportunities for investments in new farms, mines, and factories were created; new towns sprang up along the rail routes; and major cities grew at key rail intersections and terminals.

Another type of effect was the development of the national capability for mobilizing resources for construction. The success in building the railroads prepared the economy for other building tasks. Labor and capital resources were drawn from many domestic sources and new supplies were drawn from abroad. Labor construction gangs included many immigrants who later bought farms and settled in the West. To finance the construction, private savings had to be mobilized on a large scale. Governments at all levels initially helped with land grants and loans. The funds, however, actually came from the purchase of both private and public securities by many individual investors both here and abroad. Sale of these railroad and government securities helped to develop stock markets which later helped finance other industries. Railroads alone absorbed about one eighth of the gross capital formation in the Nation during the decades of the 1870's and 1880's.

Still another major effect of the railroads was the direct stimulus to other industries provided by purchases of equipment and materials. The railroads had to purchase large quantities of steel rails and wooden ties to build their rail lines. Then they had to order engines and various types of cars. Finally, large quantities of coal were used to run the trains. To the degree that large orders from the railroads allowed these industries to realize economies of large-scale production, the railroads lowered the costs and prices of supplier industries and thereby benefited the entire economy.

The traditional interpretation of the railroads' impact upon American growth is highly impressionistic in attributing revolutionary effects to railroad development. Such interpretations imply that in the absence of the railroads, extensive and per capita growth would have been stalemated. In fact we had a transportation system prior to the railroads. That system not only reached the greatest part of our agricultural land, but in addition freight rates over that system were falling owing to improvements in efficiency. Further, the industries that supplied the railroads existed before and would have grown in the absence of the railroads, although they would not have achieved scale economies as early as they did in the presence of railroad building.

Recent quantitative studies of the impact of railroad development debunk the various assertions of revolutionary gains. But they do assign a very significant, albeit not overwhelming, role to railroads in our national growth. For example, one of those studies shows that the superiority of railroad transportation compared with water and other land conveyance added about 5 percent to the gross national product in 1890.[6] Additional gains were doubtless realized from induced scale economies, but the range of industries affected was narrow and thus the effect would be modest. For example, let us assume that in 1889 the productivity of all manufacturing was 10 percent greater than it would have been in the absence of railroad purchases, ***a very generous assumption.*** Given that manufacturing accounted for 19 percent of national income, scale economies attributable to railroads would have been only 1.9 percent of national income.

Giving the railroads a generous margin for errors in estimation, GNP was perhaps 10 percent greater in 1890 than it would have been in the absence of railroads. Instead of increasing by about 90 percent from 1860 to 1890, GNP per capita would have increased by 70 percent—this presents quite a contrast with assertions that growth was almost wholly dependent upon the railroads in this period. Also it is worth noting that over shorter time periods the stimulus to the total economy provided by waves of railroad activity would be quantitatively more important than over a three- or four-decade span.

Other transportation and communication industries should be mentioned at this point. Because of greater speed and more direct routes and year-round operation, railroads greatly reduced transportation on the rivers and canals. Only the traffic on the Great Lakes increased, largely because of the iron ore carried from Lake Superior in large lake boats. On the oceans, American shipping also declined as iron hulls and steam engines took over from wooden sailing ships. American construction and labor costs were high compared to those of European shipbuilders.

[6] Robert W. Fogel, *Railroads in American Economic Growth* (Baltimore: The Johns Hopkins Press, 1964).

Foreign ships carried nearly all of American foreign trade, but American shipping increased in the protected coastal trade.

Improved communications, however, developed parallel to improved rail transportation. The first transcontinental telegraph line, in fact, was completed a decade earlier, in 1861. This meant that messages previously requiring weeks to deliver could be communicated in hours or even in minutes.

A successful transatlantic cable was laid in 1866. The basic patents on the telephone were filed in 1876, and during the 1880's telephone lines were strung across the country and covered cities with a maze of poles and wires. Experiments in radio were begun in the 1890's, but by World War I, the main use still was in shipping.

Developing Metal and Fuel Industries

Along with rapid expansion of the internal transportation network came rapid improvement and cost reduction in basic metals and power sources that were essential to mechanized mass production. Iron and machinery industries had developed with the leading industries, textiles and railroads, prior to the Civil War. After the war, expansion of railroads and rapid mechanization of other manufacturing industries required an accelerated growth of metals and machinery, because construction of machinery was a first step in expanding other industries. Increased use of power-driven machinery also accelerated the demand for fuels.

Ironmaking underwent a rapid cost reduction through the introduction of coke as a fuel and the building of larger blast furnaces. Cokemaking was developed especially in southwestern Pennsylvania where large quantities of soft coal were readily available at little cost. A large supply of iron also was available in this region because of cheap water transportation up the Ohio River from Missouri mines and down the Great Lakes from mines in upper Michigan and Wisconsin. The blast furnace also was made more efficient by being built on a larger scale with higher blast pressures and temperatures. The weekly tonnage of furnace output was raised from 300 tons to 600 tons in the decade after the Civil War; and the capacity of furnaces was raised another six times in the next two decades. Thus both concentrated sources of fuel and mineral supply and the great size of furnaces began to concentrate iron production more heavily in a few industrial areas.

At the same time, the "steel age" was being introduced by the Bessemer converter furnace. While invented in the 1850's, the first commercial production of Bessemer steel in this country came after the

Civil War. Bessemer steel was not as hard as tool steel, but it was much harder and stronger than wrought iron. Although more costly at first, it was preferred and heavily demanded immediately for steel rails. Later improvements were worked out in the process of achieving large-volume production, and as its cost fell it substituted for wrought iron in a wider variety of uses. Production of all steel expanded 10 times during the decade of the 1870's alone, and by the mid-1880's virtually all rails were made from steel. Meanwhile another type of furnace, the open-

8–14. Output Of Iron, Steel, and Rails

Source: U.S. Department of Commerce, *Historical Statistics of the United States* (Washington, D.C.: U.S. Government Printing Office, 1960), pp. 365–66, 417–18.

hearth furnace, had been improved and was rapidly being introduced. This furnace had the advantage of being able to utilize scrap metal along with some types of iron that could not be used in the Bessemer converter; and it also permitted greater control over the type and quality of steel produced. So by 1908 steel production from the open-hearth furnaces exceeded that from Bessemer converters; and total steel output by that time had again increased more than tenfold. (See 8–14.)

Along with the steel furnaces, large rolling mills were required to produce rails. The same techniques and facilities permitted the production of structural steel for construction of bridges; and in the 1890's steel was used to build skyscrapers. In the 1880's a naval expansion program called for armor plate and sheet steel for ship hulls. Rolled steel plates also were used in boilers, and various types and sizes of pipe were required for transporting oil and gas and for hydraulic mining and irrigation in the West. Steel began to replace iron in wire, nails, and many other uses.

New types of heavy machinery industry also were developed which greatly benefited from the lowered costs and improved qualities of iron and steel. Production of farm machinery and locomotives continued to expand. Railroad cars increasingly were made of steel. In addition, other types of machinery makers began to specialize in meeting the needs of certain industries—in the making of dredging and excavating equipment, conveying and elevating machinery, mining and well-drilling equipment, and refining equipment. Machine toolmaking was a specialized field that benefited from development of high-speed cutting tools of steel.

The steam engine was used more and more in factories, and by 1870 it surpassed falling water as a direct source of power. Boilers were improved and made safer with the use of banks of tubes instead of one large water cylinder; and fuel economy was raised with mechanical stokers, forced draft, and superheaters. The engines were improved with new types of valves and gears, as both larger engines and small compact types were developed. In the development of better engines as well as other machinery, the improved qualities of metal and improved methods of cutting and shaping metals were key factors in achieving better performance.

With these expansions in metals and engines, there had to be another acceleration in the output of a prior stage of production—the mining of metallic ores and fuels. Rapid development of American industry was greatly aided by the early discovery of large bodies of high-grade ores in convenient geographic locations and often near the surface. The discovery of ores was aided in the 1850's by systematic geological surveys by state governments and universities in the East, and in the 1860's the federal government undertook much of this work in the West. For ores found at the surface, open-pit mining techniques were rapidly developed, using huge shovels and other earth-moving equipment operated by steam engines. For shaft mines, however, the steam engine was limited to operating hoists, pumps, and ventilating equipment. At the end of the Civil War, underground mining still was a hand pick-and-shovel operation. During the 1870's the piping of compressed air to drills and the use of blasting powder were major developments. Further mechanization awaited the development of the electric motor. Above the surface, new equipment had to be invented to crush rock and separate ores, and new processes had to be developed to utilize low-grade ores. Like the steelmaking operations, some of the mining operations involved very large-scale capital investments.

Iron mining was expanded in three main locations after the Civil War: northern Michigan and Wisconsin, southeastern Missouri, and northeastern Alabama. Technology, however, favored the first of these; for the mines near St. Louis played out in the late 1880's, and the Alabama ores were of a type that was unusable in the Bessemer process of steelmaking. On the other hand, in the late 1880's the Mesabi ore field was found near the surface in northern Minnesota, and after some experimentation, ways were found to handle this softer ore mined with open-pit techniques.

Some shifts in location also occurred in other metals. Copper first was developed in northern Michigan, but in the 1870's and 1880's large mines also were opened in Montana and Arizona. Southwestern Missouri also had the early zinc and lead mines, but later production was developed in Nevada, Utah, Colorado, and Idaho.

The use of coal as the major fuel in ironmaking and in steam engines rapidly made this the major mining industry. Technological considerations long had delayed the use of bituminous or soft coal in ironmaking. Development of the anthracite or hard coal in a few sites in eastern Pennsylvania had helped the early development of iron industries in that region. After the Civil War, however, the conversion of soft coal to coke permitted its large-scale use as the major fuel in ironmaking. Due to the ample soft coalfields in southwest Pennsylvania and the concentration of coke making at Connellsville, Pittsburgh early became the major ironmaking center of the Nation. Because of the larger bulk of coal required, it was cheaper to transport the iron to this area, via the water routes of the Ohio River from St. Louis and the Great Lakes from northern Michigan. During the 1880's natural gas in the western Pennsylvania area also was used in steelmaking, but coal also became used to manufacture gas.

Petroleum also was first discovered in Pennsylvania before the Civil War, where it was close to convenient transportation and markets. The supply of whale oil was limited, and the demands for lamp oils and machine oils were rapidly rising. Kerosene at first was the main product, although by the 1890's fuel oil was increasingly used in steam engines, especially in western states. In 1893, Ohio forged ahead as the major well-producing state, to be succeeded in 1903 by California. Up until World War I, a simple distillation process was used, until the rising demand for gasoline brought a shift to a thermal conversion process (called "cracking").

Mass-Producing Consumer Goods

With these improvements in both transportation and in machinery, the means of mass production and mass selling were made possible for a whole range of consumer products. In a nation with a rapidly expanding population and rising per capita income, the opportunities would seem to be unlimited for starting and expanding new businesses. The history of consumer goods industries, however, shows that the path for individual businesses was precarious. The process of mechanization usually led to a smaller number of firms of larger size. New products and qualities frequently meant a shift of consumption patterns away from older products. Many industries that became localized and flourishing in one area experienced a shift in market or producing centers to other regions.

These trends can be illustrated in textiles, which was the oldest mass-producing industry and still in 1919 the largest employer (as a major industry group). In cotton goods, mechanical advances continued to be introduced, with the ring frame increasing the speed of spinning and the automatic loom tripling the number of machines one worker could tend. The result was that between 1870 and 1890, the number of cotton factories declined by 50 percent while employment increased by 64 percent. Spindle machinery increased 100 percent and raw materials processed increased 200 percent. So, the size of factories was increasing. Much of the increase in production, however, occurred in the South, as the regional pattern of location in the industry began to shift. In woolen textiles, the major change was a shift in types of fabrics. Between 1869 and 1909, the value of output of woolens declined by one fourth, while it increased fourteenfold for woolen worsteds. Worsted factories also tended to be larger. Even so, woolen textiles lost first place in value of output to cotton goods; and new branches of the industry—knit goods and silk goods—gained on the rest.

Neither the apparel nor the shoe industry went very far in the trend toward large factories. In clothing the sewing machine already had been introduced in the 1850's. Subsequently many specialized machines were developed—buttonhole making and sewing, cloth cutting, and steam pressing—and power was applied to run the machines. But the equipment remained small; piecework could be contracted out to small shops, often in slum tenement buildings, and style variation and specialties tended to preserve the small producer. Because of rapid style changes, women's wear concentrated in New York, but men's garments were made in most of the major cities. Specialized sewing machines for shoes were not introduced until the 1860's, and power soon was applied to create factory operations. By 1895, it is said that the labor cost of making a pair of shoes had been reduced to one ninth what it was in 1865. Still, the sewing could be done in relatively small shops with the material buying, cutting, and final selling done by a larger firm. Also, the patent rights on the machines were used to set up a machine-leasing system; so one firm built the machines and sup-

8–15. Size of Manufacturing Industry Groups, 1904 and 1919

	Value Added (Millions)		*Wage Earners (Thousands)*	
	1904	*1919*	*1904*	*1919*
1. Iron and steel and their products	$1,009	$ 4,588	868	1,586
2. Textiles and their products	908	3,834	1,163	1,611
3. Lumber and its remanufacture	702	1,710	734	839
4. Paper and printing	550	1,706	351	510
5. Food and kindred products	539	2,327	354	684
6. Miscellaneous	491	3,313	408	1,227
7. Chemicals and allied products	442	1,863	227	442
8. Liquors and beverages	361	381	68	55
9. Stone, clay and glass products	268	677	285	299
10. Metals and metal products (other than steel)	263	850	199	339
11. Leather and leather products	244	896	264	349
12. Tobacco manufactures	205	529	159	157
13. Railroad repair shops	167	807	248	516
14. Vehicles for land transport	143	1,561	137	496
Totals	$6,294	$25,042	5,468	9,096

Source: U.S. Department of Commerce, *Statistical Abstract of the United States* (Washington, D.C.: U.S. Government Printing Office, 1909 and 1921).

plied them to the many small operators. The location of this industry, however, did undergo a shift from the region around Boston, where foreign hides had been imported, to St. Louis, Milwaukee, and Chicago, where domestic hides from the meat-packing industry were available.

The development of meat-packing industries, in fact, helped to maintain the food products industry group among the first ranking industry groups. (See 8–15.) The railroads again had an important influence by developing cattle raising and wheat growing on the Plains and concentrating the rail terminals in a few big cities such as Minneapolis, St. Louis, and Chicago. The development of refrigerated rail cars also helped to concentrate meat slaughtering in a few big firms at cattle yard markets in these terminal cities. And because refrigeration and canning provided new ways to preserve beef, there was a shift of consumption away from pork toward beef. The development of canning techniques also created additional demands for tin can and glass jar industries. Very large flour mills were concentrated in Minneapolis, although mills continued in many other cities. Brewing and distilling industries, based on grain products, also were widely disbursed but a few grain centers like Milwaukee and St. Louis became notable for their concentrations.

Somewhat similar trends occurred in another major industry group, lumber and its products. Lumber mills began to mechanize and become larger with the use of band saws and gang saws and the mechanical handling of materials. The lumber industry also shifted its regional concentration. Production reached a peak in the Great Lakes states by 1890 and began to rapidly build up in the South. Furniture making also began moving toward the Great Lakes region from New England and New York.

Without further surveying of the great variety of industries that developed, it should be noted that many individual products became quite localized in production and identified with a particular town. For example, early historical concentration of production has identified hat making with Danbury, gloves with Gloversville, knit goods with the Mohawk Valley, clocks with Bristol, buttons with Waterbury, guns with Hartford, sewing machines with Bridgeport, cameras with Rochester, and cigarettes with Durham. Historical accident or the enterprise of a local firm explained initial production in these towns, but sometimes advantages of locating other firms near the same suppliers, skilled labor supply, and market headquarters tended to attract a concentration of similar firms. (These are sometimes referred to as "agglomeration advantages.") Nevertheless, initial concentration did not protect areas from decline in sales if new resource discoveries or innovations shifted the advantage to other producing areas or if consumer tastes and markets shifted elsewhere.

IMPACT OF MAJOR INNOVATIONS

After the burst of rapid growth following the Civil War, it might have been reasonable to expect a noticeable slowdown in the rate of industrial expansion. After all, the construction and equipping of a national railroad network was completed, the resources of the continent had been made accessible, the metal industries had been established, and mechanization of most industries was well under way. At the very least, it would take successive starts of new growth in many industries even to maintain the initial burst of growth, for in each industry the rate of increase tended to slow down as the new mechanization was achieved.

The remarkable rate of American economic growth, however, continued at almost the same tempo, and a further surge of rapid growth has been noted around the turn of the century. Some economists have attributed this to a new wave of major innovations that created new investment opportunities. Once the potentialities of machines, steam and steel had been pretty well exploited, there came a whole set of new investment opportunities related to new inventions in electric power and internal combustion engines during the two decades prior to World War I.

Electric Power

The Industrial Revolution introduced the use of massive sources of power to substitute for human and animal muscle power in doing work. The machinery merely extended the use of levers, wheels, and gears to convert this energy in handling tools. In the United States, the ready availability near the eastern coast of waterpower initially, and large coalbeds later, therefore, was vital to industrial development. Introduction of electricity generation and transmission did not provide a new basic power source; but it provided a very flexible means of transmitting that power over distances and subdividing it into small units of convenient usefulness. The sites of falling waterpower that could be harnessed practically for industry were few and often poorly located for transportation of materials. The steam engine was not a cheaper source of power, but it enlarged the power supply and provided greater mobility of factory location. Still, the steam engine tended to be large and heavy, and the transmission of power within a factory from either source involved complicated systems of shafts, gears, and pulleys which were expensive and not flexibly controlled. What electricity now made possible was a combination of power transmission by wire and power application by use of small electric motors. This has permitted great flexibility in the location of the factory and in the internal arrangement of machinery. It has permitted control of the speed and timing of operations; and it has permitted machinery to be made responsive to the finger touch or to be controlled automatically.

The innovations came first in the transmission of electricity for nonpower uses. Invention of the telegraph before the Civil War and of the telephone in 1876 applied electricity transmission to communication uses. In the 1870's, electric lighting also was developed. Arc lights were used in Wanamaker's department store in Philadelphia in 1878 and also at the Paris Exhibition that same year. In 1880, Edison's incandescent light bulb provided a means of using very low current for lighting. The idea of ladder circuits indicated the feasibility of providing current to a large system which could be turned on and off for particular local uses. With financial backing, Edison designed and built in 1882 a central power generating plant and wire delivery system for providing stores electric lighting in New York City. In the late 1880's, many cities quickly developed electric companies and adopted plans of street lighting. Transportation uses quickly followed. In 1887, an electric trolley street railway was operated in Richmond, Virginia. Already horse-drawn, steam-engine-propelled, and cable-pulled streetcars had been used for city public transportation; and New York City even had elevated tracks. Beginning in 1890, 7,082 miles of street railway track were operated, and only 1,262 of it used electricity. By 1902, 21,902 miles of electrically operated street railway existed and only 676 miles of other systems remained. And by 1918, mileage reached its peak of 44,949. Nearly every city quickly built a streetcar system within the city, and by 1900, Boston and New York City had subway systems. In addition, electric railways were extended outside the city to provide frequent and fast transportation to suburban towns and even to connect nearby cities. By 1914, it was possible to travel from Portland, Maine, to New York City and from there to Chicago by a combination of electric interurban trains and electric street railways.

The big need immediately apparent was for a more efficient and constant speed steam engine. In England the design of the water turbine was copied in developing a steam turbine in 1884, but it was not until 1896 that Westinghouse bought the rights and began large-scale production. At about the same time, in 1895, the first large use of falling water to produce electricity was begun with the installation of water turbines and electric generators at Niagara Falls.

It should be noted that the rapid expansion of electric utility companies and electric railways in the 1890's and 1900's required a large volume of capital investment. Just as the construction of railroads was tapering off, these new industries came along to provide another major spurt of capital formation. Between 1900 and 1910, the combined investments in street railways, electric light and power, and telephones about equaled that in railroads; and all "regulated" industries (including railroads) absorbed about one fifth of the gross capital formation in the Nation at that time.

Factories had hardly begun to use electric motors to operate machinery in 1900, but by 1920 over half of all power applied in factories was by electric motors. Most of the electricity was generated initially by the factory's own steam engines; however by 1920, over two thirds of

8–16. Horsepower of Prime Movers

MILLIONS
RAILROADS
FACTORIES
MINES
CENTRAL ELECTRIC STATIONS
AUTOMOTIVE
1860 1870 1880 1890 1900 1910 1920

Source: U.S. Department of Commerce, *Historical Statistics of the United States* (Washington, D.C.: U.S. Government Printing Office, 1960), p. 506.

the electricity was purchased from the central stations of electric utility companies. Shortly thereafter utilities surpassed factories in primary power production of all kinds. (See 8–16.)

The development of large sources of electricity also made possible the use of electrolytic processes and electric furnaces. The introduction of the Solvay process in the 1890's and the electrolytic process in the 1900's were responsible for development of a large-scale chemical industry in the United States prior to World War I. An electrolytic process also was used in refining both copper and aluminum. Some iron ore was smelted with electric furnaces, but this method was used mostly for refining high-grade steels.

Internal Combustion Engine

During the 1880's and 1890's, over 12 million bicycles were built in America, and many mechanics tinkered with ways to produce self-propelled vehicles for the highway. The internal combustion engine, using gasoline as fuel, first was used to operate a motor vehicle in Europe in 1885, and not until 1893 were any built in America. Both steam engine and electric motor vehicles had been built first and introduced earlier for commercial sale. Furthermore, interest was not limited to the passenger vehicle; for buses, trucks, and motor-driven farm implements were developed at the same time. The gasoline engine soon gained favor, however, because of its efficiency and high power with compact size. As early as 1903, Orville and Wilbur Wright used a gasoline engine to run the first flying machine. Four- and six-cylinder engines quickly demonstrated the possibilities of smoother and more powerful engines; and the self-starter and many other innovations quickly appeared.

One of the remarkable things about the automobile industry was its rapidly skyrocketing production volume. In 1899, the U.S. Census reported production of 3,700 motor vehicles, only part of which used gasoline engines. In 1908, the year the Model-T Ford was introduced and General Motors was formed, the industry produced 65,000 gasoline motor vehicles. The next year this doubled, and it doubled every two years thereafter to reach 1,746,000 in 1917. Output slackened in the war, but another doubling occurred by 1923, after which output leveled off. But by 1929, motor vehicles had become the first ranking manufacturing industry in value of product.

Another aspect of this industry was that it quickly became an industry of large mass-production firms. Ransom Olds began producing 600 cars in 1901 and raised this to 5,000 in 1904, thus demonstrating early that quantity production of a standard product was possible. Ford led the way in further demonstrating the possibilities of mass-production methods, especially the moving assembly line, and of developing mass markets with a low price. General Motors initially reflected a strategy of growth by merger of a number of companies. About four fifths of the auto producers had gone out of the business by the mid-1920's.

From the beginning, however, auto making was largely an assembly operation. So the industry is made up of a few large producers and many small-parts makers, specialty suppliers, and toolmakers. Some major industries also have grown up as virtually specialty suppliers—rubber tires and flat glass, especially. The chemical industry received a great stimulus from auto demands for paints, lacquers, and plastics. Furthermore, the auto industry became a major purchaser of steel aluminum, and many other materials. Petroleum refining expanded into a major industry to supply the users of motor vehicles.

The effect of the auto industry on the economy, however, has been most revolutionary by indirectly changing the way of life of consumers. The rapid rise in use of automobiles led to a demand for massive highway construction, which got under way after World War I. The freedom of movement afforded to the auto owner led to a decentralizing movement of city dwellers to the suburbs and to the small family residence, which stimulated a construction boom. So, while the electric railways and electric elevators helped to build up the central city, the "auto age" has tended to spread out city dwellers over a wider territory.

APPENDIX TO CHAPTER 8 ON BUSINESS CYCLES AND TRENDS

In Chapter 8 we referred to this appendix as providing a basis for understanding the deviations from our long-term growth trend, known as "business cycles." It is presented at this point because in the post-Civil War period fluctuations in economic activity became more severe and prompted various governmental actions which we shall discuss, especially currency and banking reform. In Chapter 12 we will dwell on business cycles in the context of an actual historical event, the Great Depression.

In markets where individuals and firms are free to make choices, there is a great deal of variability in the measures of economic activity over short periods of time. Daily quotations of stock market prices jump up and down erratically. Clearings of bank checks may vary widely from week to week. Monthly new housing starts will vary seasonally but no one year's season is exactly like another. The longer the period of time considered, the more these variations will offset each other and average out to a smoother trend line. But different types of economic activity do not necessarily offset each other. A great number of economic measures move together in their expansion and contraction phases, which extend beyond the purely seasonal changes within a year. The observed frequency of recurrence of these short swings in general economic activity led to their being called business cycles.

A theoretical business cycle and the economy's basic trend look as pictured below. For observation we can interrupt the cycle as GNP has climbed above its long term trend and is expanding very rapidly under what are often called "boom" conditions.

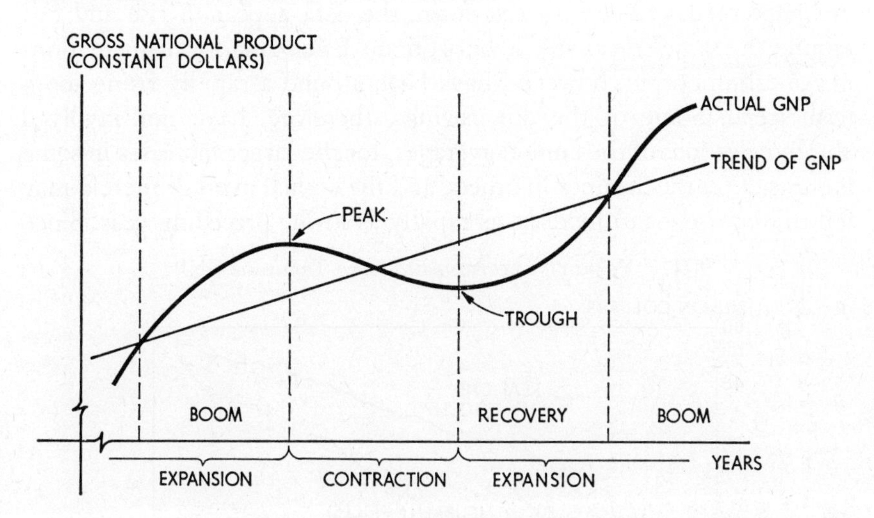

At some point the forces producing expansion play out and the cycle reaches its "peak" and thereafter the economy enters a "contraction" phase called a "recession" or "depression." When the "trough" of contraction is reached the economy is ready to turn around and enter an "expansion" phase. The early stages of expansion, known as "recovery" blossom into a full-fledged boom as GNP crosses its trend line. The boom continues until the contraction phase of the next cycle gets underway.

Studies of business cycles, however, have not found them to be as regular in duration or severity as pictured above. In spite of much advance in economic knowledge and the statistical arts of forecasting, they still are not very predictable. Only the severity of the swings seems to be subject to control and moderation by deliberate government monetary and fiscal policies. Studies of business cycles during more than a century, however, have shown that they average about four years in length from peak to peak, with about a year and a half of contraction and about two and a half years of expansion. Yet they have varied from as short as two and one-half years to as long as eight and one-fourth years. Because of their short and irregular length, they usually are measured on a monthly basis rather than annually. Thus, it is possible for an absolute decline between the middle of one year to the middle of another, as between July, 1890, and May, 1891, to fail to result in a decline in the yearly average between the two years.

Charts of business cycles sometimes are shown in measures of deviations from a long-term trend line—in fact we present such a chart in Chapter 12 (12–1). In this form, the data appear to rise and fall around the same constant (or horizontal) level. Historical fluctuations in American output, however, have been around a rapidly rising long-term trend. Some of the downswings, therefore, have not involved absolute declines of the annual averages; for the larger increases in some months offset the declines in others, and the annual average merely may fail to increase, or to increase as rapidly as in the preceding year. Since

8–17. Yearly Variations in Rising Trend of GNP

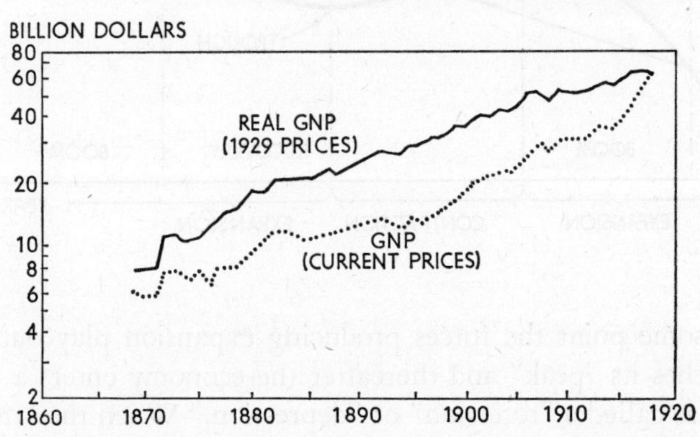

Source: Simon Kuznets, *Capital in the American Economy* (Princeton, N.J.: Princeton University Press, 1961), Tables R22 and R23, using moving averages in R25 and R26 to obtain implied annual estimates prior to 1889. See also charts in U.S. Joint Economic Committee, *Employment, Growth and Price Levels: Hearings*, Part 2 (Washington, D.C.: U.S. Government Printing Office, 1959), pp. 232 and 441.

prices tend to fall in the downswing, and usually fall more than output, the annual dollar value of output in current prices appears to fall more frequently and more severely than does real output. (See 8–17.)

Business cycles are not measured solely in terms of real output, for price declines are a major focus of the interest in cycles. Many different types of measures of economic activity also tend to rise and fall at the same time. Even without an accurate measure of total output in the early years of our history, therefore, it has been possible to identify the peak and trough turning points of past business cycles by the concensus of turning points among a large number of different series of data.

The term "trend" refers to some sort of continuing change in the same direction over a long period of time. It may be continuous at a fairly steady rate, such as the population increase in America prior to 1860 (on a ratio scale), or the rate may be gradually speeding up or slowing down, as did the population after 1860. The trend also may reflect some average rate of change over a long period in which yearly changes may increase or decrease. This sort of average change also may be a straight line or some gradual curve. When the average rates of change for successive long periods are sharply different, or even in opposite directions (as in the case of wholesale prices before and after 1896), they are not regarded as being a part of the same trend.

In the study of economic growth, attention is given to long-term trends and to changes in trends. We have noticed that around 1840 a distinctly faster trend of increase in total output began in this country. Around 1900 there also appeared to be some slowing down in this rapid rate of increase. The average rates of change for some decades also were noticeably faster or slower than others. Some economists have suggested that these variations in trends take a repetitive pattern as long cycles.

The study of trends and changes in trends requires some sort of averaging methods. One method is to compare changes from peak to peak (or trough to trough) of the business cycle. This is similar to comparing monthly data with data for the same month in the previous year in order to avoid the influence of purely seasonal changes. Another method is to average periods long enough to offset short fluctuations. Annual averages thus average out the seasonal changes. Business cycles, however, are not as regular in duration as seasons. Because most business cycles last for less than five years, five-year averages provide one simple way of smoothing out the cyclical fluctuations in data in order to observe the trends and long-term swings. Five-year averages of real GNP between the Civil War and World War I, for example, show two periods of especially rapid "surges" in expansion. Referring back to the annual data, and using the cyclical turning points, these can be pinpointed between 1867 and 1882, and between 1897 and 1907.

The causes of business cycles and of long swings in trends are not fully understood. Some of the recurring aspects of business cycles are related to adjustments in business inventories. As production expands, inventories also must be expanded to handle the larger sales; so, for a time output must expand faster than sales. Once inventories are large enough, output may slow down. This slowdown may cause some investors to be more pessimistic; for the future is quite uncertain, and slight changes may give an early warning of trouble. A slowdown in investment spending, then, may cause a sharp decline in output and in prices. When inventories get low and producers realize that expansion will continue, output may increase more rapidly again. Some of the longer swings and the more severe depressions are related to changes in population growth, changes in construction, and changes in investment in new plants and machinery. To some extent, the slowdowns are an inevitable consequence of prior periods of rapid expansion. A new invention may set off a wave of production increase to take advantage of the new opportunity or the demand for a new product. At some point the opportunity for rapid expansion along the same line diminishes, and this source of output expansion slows down. For example, when streetcars were introduced, there was a period of rapid construction until most large cities had built the main lines they most needed; and then the rate of building new streetcar lines had to slow down. Both business cycles and the long swings also are affected by noneconomic events, such as bad weather affecting harvests and wars which destroy property and redirect production. The economic organization of society and government economic policies also may affect the business cycles and long swings. Economists study fluctuations in the hope that a better understanding will lead to policies speeding adjustments to unpredictable changes and moderating the magnitudes of disturbance.

STUDY QUESTIONS

1. What evidence could be cited for calling the period from 1860 to 1920 one of unparalleled economic progress? Indicate the periods and reasons for the two main surges of growth. Why was there also much economic distress and political protest in the period?
2. How did the "end of the frontier" slow down American economic expansion? Which of the three major inputs rose the slowest? The fastest? What effect did the change in relative proportions of the inputs have?
3. Why was labor productivity increasing? What evidence is there that the American people widely shared in the benefits of economic progress? Explain how a declining share of output could be used for expanding capital goods while about the same share was used for consumer goods.
4. Why were land transportation costs cut in half from 1860 to 1900? How did the railroads affect the economic growth of the Nation?
5. What major improvements and expansions in mining and metal manufacturing industries occurred soon after the Civil War? Indicate how this affected the major consumer-goods industries. How did the ranking of major manufacturing industries in 1904 differ from 1860? (See 7–2 and 8–15.) From 1919?
6. What new sources of power conversion became important after 1890? Since these did not use really new basic sources of energy, what new advantages did they have? Why did they have an important effect on national economic growth trends?

Chapter 9 TRANSFORMATION OF THE ECONOMY

In a few decades after the Civil War, the United States had become the largest manufacturing nation in the world. Besides expanding over a continent and more than tripling its population, the Nation had managed to triple its production per person. This was a remarkable record of economic growth, and it did not come about merely by getting bigger and doing the same things in the same manner. It was a result of economic development—a cumulative process of change in production methods and organization. The result was a complete ***transformation*** of the whole economy.

The American economy was basically different in 1920 from what it had been in 1860. The distribution of workers among industries and occupations had shifted drastically, reducing the proportions in farming while increasing those in manufacturing and other nonfarm activities. The concentration of manufacturing industries had stretched westward toward Chicago in a long belt, while most of the South and West developed as vast raw material-producing regions. Meanwhile, more and more of the total population lived in cities. Finally production also had become concentrated in larger production units, and specialized financial and management organizations supported and directed these units.

The sweeping nature of these transformations of the whole organization of national production became more and more apparent in the decades after 1920; yet the changes were under way from the beginning of the industrializing process. The main elements and the bulk of the change had occurred by 1920, but (as we shall see in the following chapter) public attitudes and policies had not yet fully adjusted to them. An examination of basic changes in the organization of the economy prior to 1920, therefore, is important to an understanding of the history of that period and of the whole process of American economic development.

STRUCTURE OF INDUSTRIES

The Nation got its start as an agricultural economy producing a surplus for export and depending upon imports for most of its manufactured goods. During the middle of the 19th century, however, the rapid rise of manufacturing production completely altered this. The value added in manufacturing production began to exceed the value of agricultural commodities in the mid-1880's; and after 1920 the number of workers occupied in manufacturing also exceeded that of agriculture.

9–1. Industrial Distribution of Gainful Workers

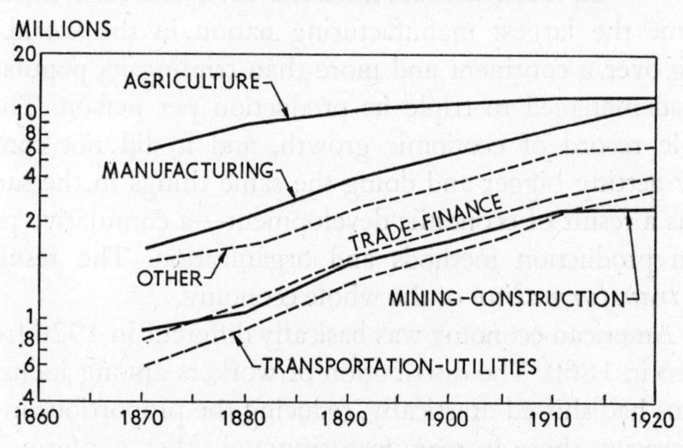

Note: Solid lines for commodity production and broken lines for services.
Source: U.S. Department of Commerce, *Historical Statistics of the United States* (Washington, D.C.: U.S. Government Printing Office, 1960), p. 74.

The number of workers in other nonfarm activities also expanded somewhat parallel to the rise in manufacturing. (See 9–1.)

Agricultural Progress

If it were not for the more rapid expansion of other parts of the economy, the rise in agricultural output itself would have been regarded as quite rapid prior to 1900. Farm output expanded faster than population. Food was produced in surplus and continued to be an important part of exports. This rise in farm output was due to both an expansion in farm acreage and an improvement in productivity. Over the whole period, 1860 to 1920, gross farm output rose about three and three-quarter times while population rose about three and one-half times. The rate of increase by decade, however, was not steady; most of the rapid gains came in the early years after the Civil War. The war itself drastically curtailed cotton production until the early 1870's. Both cotton and corn output then had a rapid and steady increase until the 1890's when the trend slowed down. Wheat production had been maintained during the Civil War despite the military drain on farm manpower. Then, when the railroad expansion came a very rapid increase in wheat acreage and output followed. The increase in the last four years of the 1860's alone made the decade show the same rate of increase as the 1850's, and this decade rate of growth was matched by the 1870's. The slowdown in this very rapid output trend in wheat began in the 1880's, a little earlier than for other major cash crops. Altogether, total crop production was twice as large in 1880 as in 1860. The same was true for livestock production, but both increased only 50 percent by 1900 and about 25 percent by 1920.

A large part of the increase in farm output was a result of increased farm acreage in the process of settling the West. Yet much was due to rising productivity and improved yields resulting from both mechanization and improved methods. Grain production especially benefited from mechanization.

While 70 percent of the wheat in the North Central states already was cut by the reaper in 1860, continuous improvements were made in the reaper and its use was extended. The Marsh brothers' harvester was introduced during the war but began to be widely adopted late in the 1870's. In 1878 the Appleby twine binder was invented, and it enabled one man to cut and bind 8 acres of wheat a day—a task previously requiring three men using a harvester or eight men using a hand cradle. The chilled iron plow was introduced widely in the 1870's, and the disk harrow in the 1890's. In this last decade mechanization also was extended to corn production with the wide adoption of the corn binder. The overall trend of mechanization is shown by estimates of the rate of real investment in machinery and implements prior to 1900 (as reflected in manufacturing output of such equipment). The expanded use of farm work animals also shows the early substitution of power for human energy. (See 9–2.)

The gains in mechanization were mostly laborsaving, not increases in yield per acre. The wheat yield, for example, averaged only 13.9 bushels to the acre in 1900 compared to about 15 in 1840, while man-hours required to produce a bushel had fallen from 233 to 108. Corn yield likewise was 25.9 bushels per acre in 1900 compared to 25 in 1840, while man-hours per bushel had fallen from 276 to 147. Cotton, on the other hand, did not benefit from mechanization; yet, partly because of the continued movement to more fertile new lands in

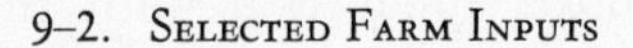

9–2. Selected Farm Inputs

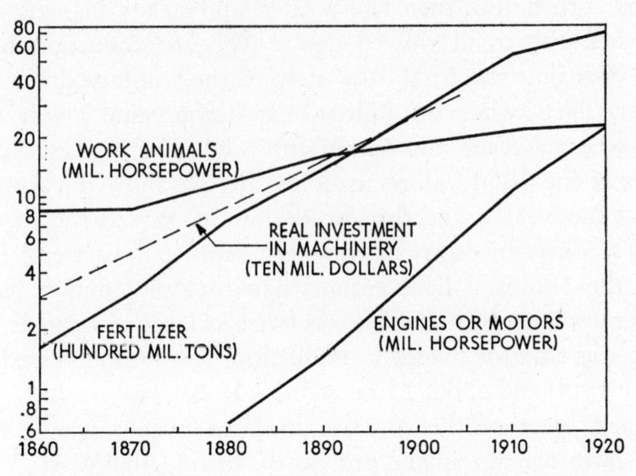

Source: U.S. Department of Commerce, *Historical Statistics of the United States* (Washington, D.C.: U.S. Government Printing Office, 1960), pp. 284–85, 506. Machinery real investment estimates by decades (in 1910–14 prices) from Marvin W. Towne and Wayne D. Rasmussen in Conference on Research in Income and Wealth, *Trends in the American Economy in the Nineteenth Century* (Princeton, N.J.: Princeton University Press, 1960), p. 276.

the Southwest and partly because of increased use of fertilizer, the yield rose from 147 pounds of lint per acre in 1840 to 191 in 1900. With less than a fifth reduction in man-hours per acre, the man-hour requirements per bale fell over one third—from 439 to 280. Increasing use of fertilizer also helped raise the productivity of diversified farming in the older eastern areas as well as in the South.

John W. Kendrick's estimates of output per unit of combined inputs show about the same increase in farming as in manufacturing from 1869 to 1899—about a 50 percent increase in productivity. In terms of labor inputs only, agricultural productivity gained faster in the 1870's, but in the 1890's manufacturing's faster gains more than offset this to achieve greater overall laborsavings by 1899. In the two decades following 1900 farming showed no gain in productivity, while the gains continued in manufacturing and elsewhere in the economy.

The gains in farm productivity, however, brought about a problem that was not common in most other industries—a problem of surplus production owing to a slow rise in demand. It is a characteristic of human consumption that the demand for increased food becomes less urgent as higher income levels are reached. Economists refer to this characteristic as low "income elasticity" of demand—percentage increases in food purchases are characteristically less than percentage increases in income. Studies of how city workers spend their incomes, for example, show that in the same year the higher income workers spend a smaller percentage of their family budgets on food. Also, over time, even the lowest income worker families spent less proportionately for food as their average incomes have risen historically. In the mid-1870's, the average city worker spent about 58 percent of his income on food, while by 1919 only about 41 percent was spent on food. (See 9–3.)

Throughout history and in all nations, economic development has involved a declining share of agriculture in total productive activity. The basic necessities of life have had to be provided first, and as man's productive capacity in farming has increased, his ability to devote time to other activities has increased. This shift in concentration of production activity has depended, first, on the rise in productivity in farming

9–3. Percentage of City Worker Budget Spent on Food

	Low Income	*Average Income*	*High Income*
1874–75	64%	58%	51%
1901	51	43	37
1917–19	46	41	37

Source: U.S. Department of Commerce, *Historical Statistics of the United States* (Washington, D.C.: U.S. Government Printing Office, 1960), p. 181.

itself and, second, on the slower rise in demand for food products than for other products as incomes have risen. Basically, it may be said that the ***development role of agriculture*** is to minimize the use of labor in providing essential food and materials so that labor and other resources can be "released" for other types of productive activities. At first, a surplus of farm products may be traded for specialized products of other nations. Later, a nation may develop its own specialized types of nonfarm production with the labor and other resources released and transferred out of farming.

In the United States during the three decades after the Civil War, the faster rise in farm output than population created a domestic surplus of food. Per capita consumption of food already was high in the United States and did not increase much thereafter. Fortunately, until the early 1880's when European tariffs rose exports of wheat and livestock increased very rapidly to absorb most of the domestic surplus. Yet, part of this draining off of the surplus was made possible only by the rapid declines in American prices. Later it became increasingly difficult to sustain a rapidly rising output. Further increases in productivity with little more output demanded necessarily meant less need for labor in agricultural production. Gradually, an increasing share of the national work force had entered nonfarm activities. Agriculture's proportion of all gainfully employed workers fell from 55 percent in 1860 to 37 percent in 1900, and to 27 percent in 1920. By 1920, in fact, the total number of farm workers had begun to decrease.

Strains of Farm Adjustment

This release of labor from farming did not come about without some strains of "pushes" as well as "pulls." Throughout American history the faster rise of jobs in cities has pulled or attracted workers out of rural areas, and the rapid rise of manufacturing industries during this period helped to accelerate this process. However, overproduction and declining prices in farming also tended to push or force some people out of farming in a more unpleasant way. During the early years of expanding wheat farming in the North Central states, for example, farmers in the East were facing the competition of lower-priced western wheat. Many were compelled to leave farming and find jobs in cities, and others survived by improving methods and finding other products to produce for local markets in nearby cities—especially fresh fruits, vegetables, and dairy products. Late in the 19th century, many western farm areas faced similar problems. Falling prices forced them either to become larger, more efficient, and more mechanized or else to sell out and seek employment in nonfarm activities.

It was not merely a surplus of farm products that was forcing a decline in farm prices. As the last chapter pointed out, a severe decline in all wholesale prices occurred in the economy as a whole from the peak of the Civil War inflation to the depths of the depression in the mid-1890's. The most severe part of this decline occurred early in the postwar expansion and the long depression of the 1870's. There was a temporary recovery in the early 1880's, and then a further decline to the mid-1890's.

It is important to note that farm prices generally did not fare any worse than wholesale prices of all staple products, except for short periods such as from 1868 to 1872, 1881 to 1885, and 1893 to 1896. The ratio of farm prices to other wholesale prices, in fact, tended to be at a higher level in the 1880's and 1890's than in the 1860's and 1870's. In addition, farmers benefited from improvements in farm machinery, reduced transportation costs, and improved consumer products at lower prices; and these gains were not reflected in price measures alone.

Eventually after the mid-1890's, the farmer's price picture reversed. Wholesale prices generally rose and farm prices rose even faster. With farm output lagging behind population growth and farm productivity gains slowing down, farmers began to experience a rising demand for their services, as their output became relatively scarce. Conditions began to be so favorable to farming that the pre-World War I years were looked back to in later decades as the "golden years" of farming. (See 9–4.)

Immediately after the Civil War, the financial position of the individual farmer made him especially vulnerable to the drastic and continued price declines. To begin with, the American farmer always has been optimistic and speculative. The westward movement was filled with people with high hopes and expectations of owning their own

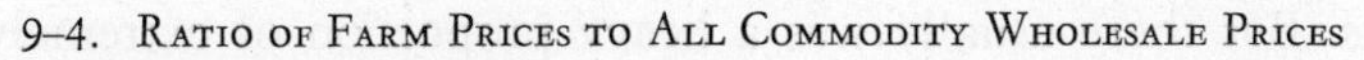
9–4. Ratio of Farm Prices to All Commodity Wholesale Prices

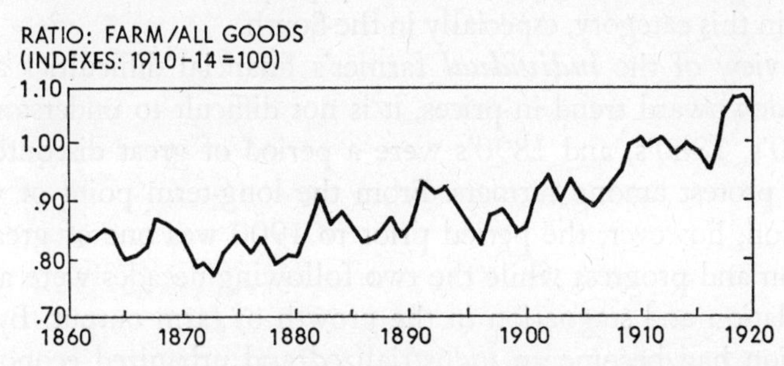

Source: U.S. Department of Commerce, *Historical Statistics of the United States* (Washington, D.C.: U.S. Government Printing Office, 1960), pp. 116–17.

farms and accumulating modest wealth. Considerably more initial capital was required than most settlers possessed in order to buy land, stock it with animals and equipment, and supply family consumption needs for the first year or two. As we have noted, it was customary to borrow heavily to get a start. A large proportion of western wheat farms were mortgaged. Farming seldom was easy, and the risks of bad weather were great. Adverse weather took its greatest toll when a poor harvest at home coincided with falling world grain prices brought about by bumper crops on other continents. In addition to the catastrophes of nature that ruined many farmers, the declines in prices from good harvests and overproduction brought less income than expected.

On top of all this, the general secular and cyclical price declines in the national economy wreaked special havoc with those farmers who were heavily in debt. Those who bought farms and machinery during the Civil War were saddled with especially high prices frozen into debt while their crops sold at successively lower prices. Those who settled later during boom times in new areas where land prices were speculatively high soon faced further declines in product prices. Loan money usually was scarce in rural areas, and partly because of the high risks in farming, interest rates tended to be high. The technical requirement for success and survival—that of mechanizing and operating a larger sized farm in order to produce at lower unit costs—only added to the financing and debt problems. These financing problems were reflected in the rising statistics on size of farm, capital investment per farm, volume of farm mortgages, and proportion of tenant farmers. While the earlier extent of renting is not known, about 25 percent of the farmers were tenants in 1880 and 40 percent in 1920. For many, of course, tenancy was a step upwards on a ladder—from farm laborer, to tenant, to mortgagee, to full owner—that was more common among younger farmers. But there usually was a heavy proportion of extremely poor farmers in this category, especially in the South.

In view of the ***individual*** farmer's financial difficulties and the general downward trend in prices, it is not difficult to understand why the 1870's, 1880's, and 1890's were a period of great discontent and political protest among farmers. From the long-term point of view of the Nation, however, the period prior to 1900 was one of great farm expansion and progress while the two following decades were a period of retardation and stagnation in the growth of farm output. By 1920, the Nation had become an industrialized and urbanized economy, although the adjustment away from a farming economy was not yet complete.

Emergence of Mass Distribution

With the revolutionary reductions in the costs of producing commodities, it is not surprising that other activities would be left with a larger share of the workers. Commodity distribution is estimated to have used 6 percent of the labor force in 1870 and 10 percent in 1920. All other services (including government) also increased in share from 18 to 28 percent. Part of this was due to a slower rise in productivity in trade and services, although measurement of the "product" is more tricky for services than for physical commodities. With increased specialization and decline in rural living, people also were buying more goods from stores and requiring more services. With higher incomes, essential commodities became relatively less important and more services were desired. Also improvements in quality and variety of intermediate services were embodied in various physical goods prior to sale.

Technological changes also were bringing about great changes in the ways of distributing goods. Mass production required large and steady outlets for the mass distribution of goods. The national railroad network provided manufacturers ready access to a large national market of customers. The bewildering variety of goods available to consumers, however, led to intense competition among fewer and larger producers of similar standardized products. At the same time the consumer's greater shopping mobility and greater discretion in choosing how to spend a higher per capita income led to more intense competition in quality, variety, convenience, and service, as well as in price. Modern technology, therefore, was transforming the emphasis of business from production to selling. The economy was becoming consumer oriented.

Part of the organizational change in distribution has been the reduced number and role of "middlemen" between the manufacturer and the retailer. For farm goods, the opposite occurred, of course. The specialization of farm areas in producing for national and international markets led to specialized middlemen connected with storing, transporting, and exchanging commodities in central auction markets. The increased processing, packaging, refrigeration, and precooking of foods also placed a new group of manufacturers between the farmer and the consumer. It is easy to understand why the farmer would blame "the greed of middlemen" and the increased spread between farmer and consumer prices of food as the cause of the farmer's misery.

For distributing manufactured goods, there were two levels of middlemen in 1860. In the northeastern manufacturing centers and port cities, large commission merchants advanced credit to manufacturers and undertook to handle the distribution of factory output to wholesalers in major cities throughout the Nation. ***Wholesalers*** in turn distributed to retail stores in a local region. In doing this, they performed for retailers the traditional roles of the import trader—the advantageous purchase of a variety of goods from far-flung sources, the handling of bulk shipments, the storage and prompt delivery of goods locally, and the advance of credit to the retailer. The prominence of the wholesaler probably reached its peak in 1880. Changes in technology, however, already were under way that began to eliminate the need for these middlemen, and both the manufacturer and the retailer began to seek to deal directly with each other.

Immediately after the Civil War, manufacturers began to handle more of their own distribution as the cost-reducing advantages of mass production made larger and steadier sales volume more and more necessary. Competition from other large producers for a larger share of the market also became more intense. Credit became less critical as profits were reinvested in their own business by successful manufacturers, and as specialized financing institutions developed. With their capacity to produce increasing faster than their sales, manufacturers became impatient with the passive order-taking practices of wholesalers and hired their own regional agents and traveling salesmen to promote sales through direct contact with retailers. In the case of large durable goods or where single-line specialty stores existed (such as for sewing machines and shoes), some manufacturers found it advantageous even to develop their own direct sales agents and retail stores.

Methods of selling manufactured products also were drastically changing. Products no longer were simple familiar objects whose quality could be judged by inspection or touch. Farm machinery, the sewing machine, and other durable goods involved technical features and new uses that had to be explained. Quality and durability of new materials might become evident only after long use. Foods no longer could just be pinched to test for ripeness. An increasing variety of foods and other products could be pre-weighed, counted, and handled more conveniently in packages that prevented visual inspection. Increased processing, refrigeration, and precooking of foods also required quality control and sanitary packaging. As in the case of drugs, these products required consumer trust in the reputation of the manufacturer. Nationwide distribution of some products also presented to the consumer a bewildering variety of choices. The manufacturer's reputation for quality, special guarantees, and recognizable brand names, therefore, all became important factors in consumer selection of goods.

Under these conditions ***advertising*** began to assume a new character, and advertising expenditures soared rapidly in the 1890's. While customer satisfaction and repeat sales were essential, the initial buildup of a large volume of national sales depended heavily upon getting consumer recognition and initial selection of the product. Increasingly the consumer was flooded with choices among suppliers of the same type of product, new products were rapidly being introduced, and the consumer was exploring new ways to spend his rising income. The manufacturer, therefore, began to compete for a greater share of the national market by advertising its brand name and product advantages in newspapers, in magazines, on outdoor billboards, and on the radio. It no longer was enough simply to announce the manufacturer's location, products, and terms. It became necessary to educate the consumer about the product and its uses and to persuade him that the product's quality and satisfactions would be superior to other products. In some cases where different manufacturers actually had virtually identical and uniform products, of course, the advertising served mostly to stabilize consumer purchase habits and concentrate sales on a few widely known brands. The initial advertiser gained an increased share of the market, but there was little advantage to each when all manufacturers advertised. Yet for other products, such as for cigarettes prior to World War I, advertising helped to introduce new products more rapidly and even to increase consumption for the whole industry.

During the same period ***retailing*** also was rapidly changing. For a while after the Civil War the country general store continued to have a place in the rural West and South. It handled all types of goods and frequently served as a social meeting place. It often accepted local food products for resale or as payment for debts. In the South the post-Civil War lien laws formalized the storekeeper's claim on crops as security for credit, and it became the chief consumer credit institution for the poor southern sharecropper. The retailer, in turn, relied heavily upon wholesalers for credit. The chief retail innovation in the rural areas was the introduction of the ***mail-order*** business. While some specialty mail-order firms existed in 1860, the first large general mail-order firm was established by Aaron Montgomery Ward in 1872. Low prices were made possible by large bulk purchases made directly from manufacturers, by skipping the middleman and the retailer, and by use of the low-cost delivery services of the federal postal system. Catalogs provided a much wider range of choices than was available in the rural country store.

In the cities, the general store had given way by 1860 to numerous speciality stores—groceries, dry goods, shoes, hardware, and so forth. The introduction of the soda fountain in the apothecary's shop (or drug store) was one example of a continuing adaptation of each store to consumer needs and habits. One major retail change that developed from this specialization trend was the ***chain store.*** In the late 1870's, the Atlantic & Pacific Tea Company had been converted from a small chain of tea shops to a major chain of "economy" grocery stores. Again the low cost was achieved by buying in large quantities directly from food processors and skipping the middleman. In addition, a cash-and-carry policy cut out the costs of consumer credit. Similar principles were applied at about the same time to F. W. Woolworth's 5 and 10 cent variety stores.

The large city ***department store*** represented a different trend in retailing—a trend away from specialization. The emphasis was upon offering a full range of shopping opportunities at one location convenient to concentrated transportation facilities in the downtown center. By expanding to a large enough size, each department could compete with specialty stores in the variety of choices offered. Large-quantity purchases could be made directly from manufacturers to eliminate the costs of middlemen. The department store also could extend credit in one account to a consumer to cover a whole range of types of purchases. Catering especially to women, the department store attempted to gain favor through offering deliveries, refunds upon return of unsatisfactory goods, and other special customer services.

The changes in distribution, therefore, involved contradictory trends affecting distribution costs. On the one hand, in nearly every type of store the distribution margin tended to rise—that is, as the price of

9–5. DISTRIBUTION SPREAD BY TYPE OF STORE

	1869	*1899*	*1919*
		(Percent of Retail Price)	
Grocery, independent	27.3%	28.3%	29.7%
chain	—	19.0	20.7
Shoes, independent	27.3	33.5	37.6
chain	—	33.5	32.0
Dry goods	31.5	36.7	44.9
department	—	29.4	35.6
Furniture, independent	37.3	39.0	46.4
chain	—	44.0	44.0
Drugs	39.8	46.7	51.1
Jewelry	46.9	46.5	51.7
All groups	32.7	35.4	36.5

SOURCE: Harold Barger, *Distribution's Place in the American Economy since 1869* (Princeton, N.J.: Princeton University Press, 1955), p. 92. Selected from Table 26.

goods tended to fall, the costs of wholesale and retail distribution tended to rise as a percentage of the final retail price. At the same time, new types of large retailing organizations tended to have lower margins. The overall trend of the distributive margin, therefore, rose moderately. Throughout this period and later, however, a diversity of methods of distributing continued. The independent store did not tend to disappear, and the low-margin, cut-rate store did not attract all the customers away from the full line, multiservices store (See 9–5.)

FOREIGN TRADE

During the last half of the 19th century, the foreign trade of the United States also underwent a drastic shift in emphasis as it continued to expand. The expansion itself was rapid. Value of exports tripled from 1860 to 1880 and tripled again by 1915. By 1920 it had more than doubled again, although much of this was due to an inflation in prices. The most rapid expansion again was in the decade and a half after the Civil War and another surge occurred around 1900. Yet the foreign-trade expansion was less rapid than the expansion in domestic production. As a percentage of gross national product, imports fell from 7.9 percent in 1869–73 to 4.4 percent in 1907–11. It was the shift in the composition of trade which was most important. There was a shift in the balance of trade, in the types of goods, and in the countries dealt with.

Shift to an Export Surplus

Throughout its early economic growth the American economy had been heavily dependent upon its imports. In nearly every year, imports of goods exceeded exports of goods. The difference had been made up by performing shipping services for other nations and attracting foreign capital investments. These trends continued during the further railroad boom and settling of the Far West in the decade after the Civil War. After the mid-1870's, however, the balance of trade permanently shifted the other way. In nearly every year exports were larger in value than imports. America simultaneously became one of the major exporting nations of the world when it became the leading industrial nation (See 9–6.)

The heavy shift toward manufacturing emphasis in the American economy also was reflected in the types of goods most important to its

9–6. U.S. Exports and Imports, 1860–1920

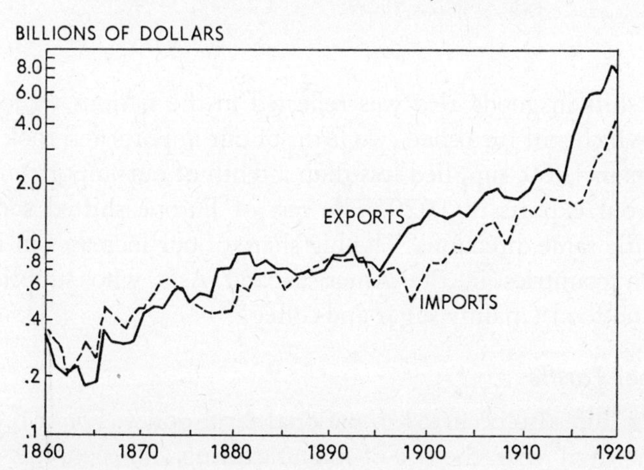

Source: U.S. Department of Commerce, *Historical Statistics of the United States* (Washington, D.C.: U.S. Government Printing Office, 1960), pp. 537–38, 562–63 (excluding specie).

foreign trade. Between 1860 and 1880, exports of crude materials, which were mostly cotton, had given away the position of prominence to foodstuffs, mostly wheat and flour. Then, manufactures, which long had been about 15 percent of the value of all exports during the pre-Civil War period and still were in 1880, began to rise rapidly in the late 1890's and were over half in 1920. Imports shifted just as drastically. Manufactures fell from just under half of imports to about a third. Crude materials rose from about a fifth to about a third, as rubber, copper, tin, and various other materials were imported to meet the needs of expanding industry. (See 9–7.)

9–7. Composition of Trade, 1880–1920

	Exports			*Imports*		
	1880	*1900*	*1920*	*1880*	*1900*	*1920*
Distribution by type of goods:						
Materials	29.5%	24.8%	23.3%	21.3%	33.2%	33.8%
Food	55.7	39.8	25.2	32.6	27.2	34.4
Manufactures	14.8	35.4	51.5	46.1	39.6	31.8
	100.0	100.0	100.0	100.0	100.0	100.0
Distribution by foreign areas:						
England	54.3%	38.3%	22.2%	31.6%	18.8%	9.8%
Europe	31.7	36.6	32.1	24.0	33.1	13.5
Americas	11.1	16.3	31.0	31.7	26.4	45.9
Other	2.9	9.1	14.7	12.7	21.7	30.8
	100.0	100.0	100.0	100.0	100.0	100.0

Source: U.S. Department of Commerce, *Historical Statistics of the United States* (Washington, D.C.: U.S. Government Printing Office, 1960), pp. 544–45, 550–53.

The shift in goods also was reflected in the nations traded with. England, which still furnished two fifths of our imports and took half of our exports in 1860, supplied less than a tenth of our imports and took a fifth of our exports in 1920. The rest of Europe shifted somewhat slower in the same directions. The big share of our increases in imports came from countries in the Americas and Asia who supplied raw material and food (mainly sugar and coffee).

Higher Tariffs

A big shift also occurred in national tariff policy. For two decades prior to the Civil War, the rise of manufacturing and economic growth had occurred under a low tariff policy, with average duties on all imports well below 20 percent. The Republicans came to power in

1861 committed to raising duties to protect American manufacturers, and the absence of southern congressmen enabled the tariff to be raised before Lincoln took office. On the excuse of raising war revenues, protective duties were then raised further until the average duties on all imports reached 47 percent in 1867. A 10 percent reduction in tariff rates in 1870 was reversed again in 1875; but some goods removed from the duty list were not affected, so the duties as a percentage of all imports remained considerably lower. The Democrats campaigned against the tariff and in the second Cleveland administration managed

9–8. Average Tariff Duties, 1860–1920

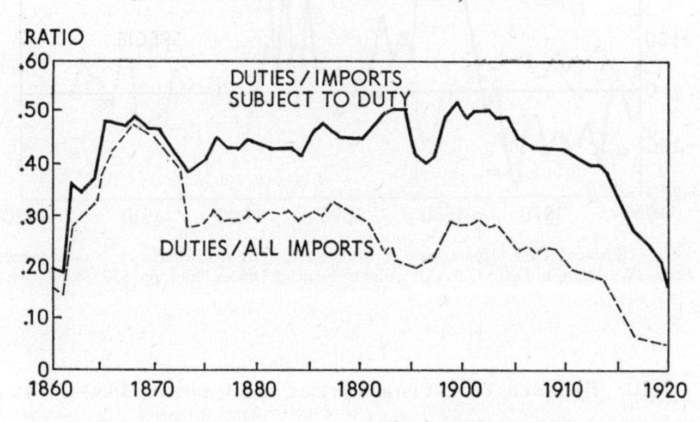

Source: U.S. Department of Commerce, *Historical Statistics of the United States* (Washington, D.C.: U.S. Government Printing Office, 1960), p. 539.

again to lower the rates temporarily in the mid-1890's. The increasing importance of imports of materials with low duties or none caused most of the decline in average duties collected on imports after 1900. (See 9–8.)

Balance of Payments

The composition of the balance of payments also changed to accommodate the shifts in trade emphasis. While the net balance of shipments of gold and silver fluctuated only moderately and played little role in the balance of payments, the negative balance of invisible items became progressively larger. In part this reflected the rising interest and dividend payments on the growing stock of foreign capital which had been invested in this country. In part it reflected the shipping charges for freight increasingly carried on foreign ships, the remittances by immigrants to their relatives, and the increasing travel abroad by Americans. (See 9–9 and 9–10.)

Reversals in the flow of capital movements was the major source

9–9. Balances of Trade and Specie, 1860–1914

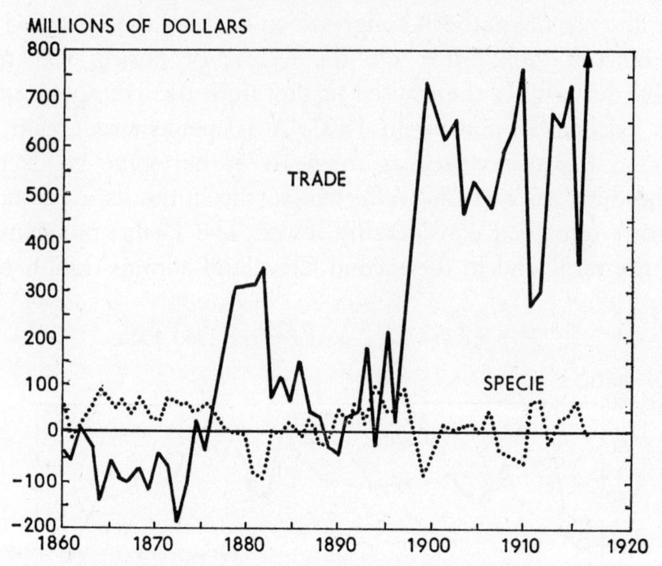

Source: U.S. Department of Commerce, *Historical Statistics of the United States* (Washington, D.C.: U.S. Government Printing Office, 1960), pp. 537–38, 563–64.

9–10. Balances of Invisible Items and Capital, 1860–1914

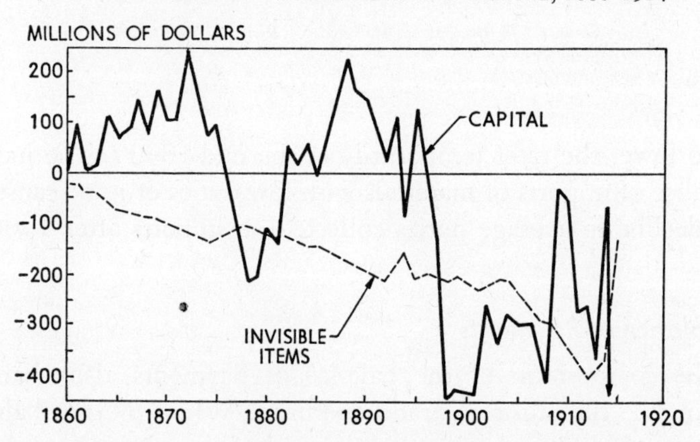

Source: U.S. Department of Commerce, *Historical Statistics of the United States* (Washington, D.C.: U.S. Government Printing Office, 1960), pp. 537–38, 563–64.

of offsets to the wide swings in balance of trade. In the early years when imports exceeded exports and between 1882 and 1895, when trade was nearly balanced, foreign capital continued to flow into this country. This helped to finance construction of the railroads first and later the electric utility industry. But when manufacturing exports boomed and the trade balance soared after 1895, it was a large outward flow of American capital that helped to finance the excess of exports. In this, the United States was acting much as England had earlier: the rising trade with South America and Asia involved some extension of credits with the sale of manufactured goods and some investment in foreign mines, plantations, and transportation facilities. Even before World War I, the United States was on the way to leaving its status as a debtor nation and becoming a creditor nation. The war speeded this process. (Since the whole scale of payments balances was magnified several times by the war, discussion and representation in charts of this experience is postponed to Part IV.)

LOCATION OF PRODUCTION

Our discussion shows that the American economy was quite different in 1920 than it was in 1860. The economy had been transformed from a predominantly agricultural to a predominantly manufacturing industrial structure. At the same time the population was expanding and settling a continent. The transformation, therefore, did not occur uniformly across the country. Economic activity had a geographic pattern that took shape early; then it was elaborated and changed gradually. The 1920 pattern is largely the one that persists today.

Regional Specialization

Economic development is largely a process of increasing specialization and more complex organization of exchanges between more numerous and distantly located people. This permits greater productivity to be achieved, partly because the greatest advantage is taken of particular resources in different regions and partly because of economies of scale from specialization. Each region of the country thus takes on a special economic character based on its main specialized activities. Distance serves as a separation between regions, much like the political boundaries between nations. So the main specialized products are like "exports," being produced largely for sale in other regions. The regional development of the economy, therefore, can best be understood in terms of the main "export" industries and their stimulus to other activities serving the local residents—often called the "residentiary" industries.

The early American economy was agricultural and developed around port cities and major rivers along the Atlantic Coast. Major differences in climate and resources led to different types of production in North and South. The early westward movement continued to be based upon agricultural specialization. Vast fertile areas were settled in the midcontinent basin of the Mississippi River system. Two important conditions influenced this process. First, the new lands were capable of producing more products at a lower cost than older areas near the eastern Coast or in Europe. Second, the invention and construction of improved means of transportation greatly reduced the cost of gaining access to these resources; and, in turn, the resource producers gained access to large markets. The early rise of manufacturing in New England and the Middle Atlantic states also benefited from the same two conditions of ***resource advantages*** and ***transport access to markets.*** Waterpower, iron, coal, and timber were readily available, as were ample labor supplies and capital. The port cities had had access to the South Atlantic and Gulf states, as well as to world markets; then, the canals and later the railroads opened up the farm-consumer markets of the North Central states.

Three other conditions helped the Northeast gain a cumulative advantage in manufacturing. First, there were ***economies of scale*** to be realized in larger-sized factories. These economies of scale were inherent in the technology of mass-production methods in textiles, watches, shoes, steel rails, and so forth. Second, there were ***proximity advantages*** (or "external economies") resulting from the clustering of industries in the same city or region. The concentration of industry helped each firm obtain supplies, labor, special machinery, capital, and marketing services more cheaply; and it enabled other firms to specialize in serving the needs of certain industries.

Third, there were ***large local market demands*** in the large cities and the industrial region itself. This meant that a major share of the output of manufacturers could be sold in nearby areas with little transportation. It also meant that firms serving local residents—the residentiary industries—could expand and specialize. For all three of these reasons, the areas that already had manufacturing and specialized urban services were favored to expand and develop more of the same. Cities that started in manufacturing by historical accident—as a port or river crossing, perhaps—had some advantage in continuing to grow (although this alone did not prevent stagnation and relative decline if all other advantages disappeared).

The Heartland and Hinterlands

The "industrial heartland" of the American economy, therefore, was already well established in 1860. The main development in the next six decades was extension westward as an urban-industrial belt reaching to Chicago. The technology of the steel industry played a large role in this shift of industry westward. Cheap water transportation of iron ore on the Great Lakes brought iron supplies into close contact with the coalfields of western Pennsylvania. As noted, since coal was more bulky and consumed in greater amounts, the early steel industry concentrated in the Pittsburgh area near the coke-making center at Connellsville. Later as improvements in steel furnaces economized on fuel consumption, newer steel mills were located on the shores of the Great Lakes at Cleveland, Gary, and Chicago.

Other conditions influencing this industrial belt were related to the type of agricultural specialization in the region. Wheat farming in the Great Lakes prairies led to the early construction of an east-west railroad network and the concentration of meat-packing, flour milling, and farm machinery industries in this region. This helped to create cities and a diversity of manufacturing. With a national rail network permitting distribution to the rest of the Nation, this region continued to attract most of the new manufacturing factories that were built. For example, the auto industry, a heavy steel user, concentrated in Detroit, and its location in turn influenced the location of rubber and glass industries.

While manufacturing did have some tendency to spread out with the growth of the national economy, the proportion of manufacturing employment in the manufacturing belt (East North Central, Middle Atlantic, and New England states—except Maine, New Hampshire, and Vermont) already was 72 percent in 1870 and fell only to 66 percent by 1920. (See 9–11.)

9–11. Regional Specialization of Production, 1900

The rest of the country continued to specialize primarily in agricultural production and other raw material "extraction" from Nature —mining, forestry, and fishing. East of the Rocky Mountains a semicircle of raw material "hinterlands" bordered the industrial heartlands, while isolated valleys and cities in the Far West were like distant colonies.

West of the Mississippi highly specialized farming and a few mining and lumber centers developed. Wheat production moved westward across the plains, crowding cattle ranges into the more arid or mountainous lands. Corn production was found to be more advantageous in the prairies nearer the Great Lakes, as was dairy farming. Accordingly, hog production and cattle feeding concentrated in this region near the meat-packing centers. Irrigated farming flourished in the valleys of California and the Southwest fed by mountain streams. At other scattered points, mining and lumber production were concentrated, and several major port cities arose on the Pacific Coast.

The South also continued to concentrate in agricultural activity, with cotton and tobacco still the major crops. Pre-Civil War levels of cotton production were not achieved until the early 1870's and part of this reflected the continued westward shift into new cotton lands in Texas, and later the irrigated areas of the Southwest and California. Loss of slaves hampered prodution until the sharecropping system of tenancy was established to redeploy the workers who had been transformed from "capital" to "labor" by emancipation. Since this system was heavily financed by seasonal short-term credits extended by merchants, such emphasis was placed upon cash crops that corn and cattle production were neglected, and the region was not self-sufficient in food.

Beginning in the 1880's, the South began to expand its manufacturing activities, based partly on its raw material resources and partly on its large surplus of low-income workers. Textile factories, with the latest improvements in machinery, began to be built in the southern Piedmont area (the eastern slopes of the Appalachian Mountains between Virginia and Georgia) at a faster rate than nationally. Between 1880 and 1900, cotton spindles increased eight times in the South, and by 1912 southern textiles were using more than half of the cotton consumed by the industry. A little later, furniture industries began to flourish in the same area, partly due to the rapid expansion of lumber production. By 1890, the older forests in the Great Lakes region were nearing exhaustion and production was shifted primarily to the South and the Pacific Northwest. A great boom in southern lumber production occurred between 1890 and 1910.

Mineral production also began to flourish in certain areas. Coal production expanded with extension of railroads into West Virginia and Kentucky. Iron production in the South accounted for about one fourth of the national output in 1890 in spite of the unsuitability of the southern ores for Bessemer furnaces. With the increased use of the open hearth, the steel industry in Alabama began to flourish after 1900. After 1900, the Texas and Louisiana area had a boom in both chemical and petroleum industries. Large underground sulfur beds overlying salt domes were discovered; these were important in making various chemicals, insecticides, explosives, rubber, paper, and many other products. Rich oil and gas fields discovered in eastern Texas in 1901 soon skyrocketed this state into surpassing California as the leading petroleum producer.

Regional Growth and Development

In the westward march of the American people, each region has gone through successive stages of being a frontier outpost, a specialized raw-material producer, and a more diversified and urbanized economy. This process of early rapid expansion and later slowdown as some degree of maturity was reached is reflected in the census data on population trends by region. The three eastern regions—New England, Middle Atlantic, and South Atlantic—had population trends between 1860 and 1920 more like the national trends of later decades. If these trends are taken as an indicator of "maturity," the East North Central already had completed its period of rapid rise and reached maturity by 1870 and the East South Central by 1880. The West North Central reached its maturity level in 1890 and then began to recede somewhat from the national rate of population increase. The West South Central reached its maturity in about 1920. Only the Mountain and Pacific regions still were being settled and rapidly expanding by the end of this period. (See 9–12.)

The rate of population expansion alone, however, is not a reliable guide to economic growth and development. It has been pointed out that the pioneer subsistence farming areas were those of lowest per capita income in 1840. Once good transportation access has been opened up to a region, however, resource advantages may create profitable opportunities that attract capital and labor resources. Wage rates and producer incomes tend to be very high in boomtowns and rapidly expanding regions.

Estimates of per capita incomes by region reflect both the high-income opportunities in developing new regions in the far West and the

9–12. Regional Population Trends, 1860–1920

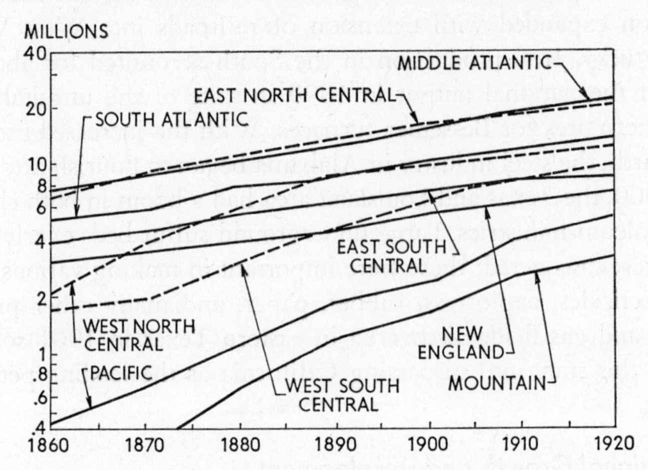

Source: U.S. Department of Commerce, *Historical Statistics of the United States* (Washington, D.C.: U.S. Government Printing Office, 1960), pp. 12–13.

relatively low incomes in purely farm areas. The highest relative incomes were first in the Pacific and Mountain regions and secondly in the urban-industrial areas. The heavily farming regions of the Plains and the South had the lowest incomes. (See 9–13.)

It should be noted that the spread between the highest and lowest

9–13. Personal Income Per Capita by Region, 1880, 1900, 1920

Regions	Percent of U.S. Average		
	1880	*1900*	*1920*
Northeast			
New England	141	134	124
Middle Atlantic	141	139	134
North Central			
East North Central	102	106	108
West North Central	90	97	87
South			
South Atlantic	45	45	59
East South Central	51	49	52
West South Central	60	61	72
West			
Mountain	168	139	100
Pacific	204	163	135

Source: Richard A. Easterlin, "Regional Income Trends, 1840–1950," in Seymour E. Harris, *American Economic History* (New York: McGraw-Hill Book Co., 1961), p. 528.

incomes was much wider in 1880—from 204 to 45 percent of the national average—than it had been in 1860—from 144 to 67 percent. This reflects partly the new income opportunities in the Far West and also the post-Civil War depression of the economic status of the South. The South already was lagging behind national development prior to 1860; but the war greatly worsened its relative position.

It also should be noted, however, that the spread in income levels began to lessen thereafter—a trend that has continued in recent decades. This partly reflects the growth and maturity of successive regions. Relatively high incomes are experienced in rapidly expanding industries and areas. Later the expansion rate slows down as the basic resource opportunities are more fully exploited. Each region tended to catch up in its development of residentiary and service industries appropriate to the level of incomes generated by the specialized "export" production of the region.

The widening and then narrowing of the spread of regional incomes also reflected the simultaneous influence of forces of ***change*** and ***adjustment.*** Areas with relatively high incomes and rapid expansion trends may be viewed as benefiting from changes in technology and demand. A discovery of resources, an invention, an improvement in transportation, or a favorble shift in market demands created favorable economic opportunities. It then took a period of time for these opportunities to be fully exploited. Other areas, conversely, suffered exhaustion of resources, new competition from other areas, or some reduction in consumer demand for their products. In American history, many local areas experienced such relative declines in major industries—eastern wheat farming, New England shipbuilding, lumber in New England and the Great Lakes, New England textiles and shoes, southern cotton, and western wheat.

In cases of both rapid expansion and relative decline, some adjustment of economic resources was necessary. Labor and capital resources were needed in newly expanding areas, and high-income opportunities provided an incentive for these resources to move to where they were most demanded and in shortest supply. At the same time, where an imbalance of resources developed in some region, mobility of resources between regions also helped equalize conditions. Thus, in the post-Civil War period, the South found itself short of capital and with a surplus of labor. Gradually a flow of northern capital investments into the South helped to develop its industry and resources. At the same time, out-migration of population from the South—both westward and northward —helped to minimize the surplus of labor. Farm areas throughout the

Nation have been forced to make most of their adjustment in terms of labor migration as long as the growth of demand for agricultural products was slowing down and the opportunities for investment were limited.

Rise of Cities

The rise of cities has been the demographic counterpart of the increased share of the labor force in manufacturing and in trade, service, finance, and government activities. From the beginning of the Nation, the rate of expansion in total population has been exceeded by the rate of expansion in urban population. This has been referred to previously as the intensive dimension of development, as contrasted with the extension of settlement over more space. The main thing to note during the period 1860 to 1920 is that urban population finally exceeded rural population at the end of World War I. (See 9–14.)

9–14. Growth of Cities, 1860–1920

	1860	*1870*	*1880*	*1890*	*1900*	*1910*	*1920*
Population (millions):							
Rural	25.2	28.7	36.0	40.8	45.8	50.0	51.6
Urban	2.6	9.9	14.1	22.1	30.2	42.0	54.2
Number of Cities*							
Under 10,000 population	299	495	716	994	1297	1665	1970
10,000–100,000	84	154	203	326	402	547	684
Over 100,000	9	14	20	28	38	50	68

* Places with population of 2,500 or more.

Source: U.S. Department of Commerce, *Historical Statistics of the United States* (Washington, D.C.: U.S. Government Printing Office, 1960), p. 14.

The American economy finally was an urban economy as well as an industrial one. The building of American cities had provided employment for a large share of the work force in construction as well as in lumber—the predominant building material. Shortly after the railroad-building boom, a heavy flow of capital investment had been absorbed in building public utility facilities, not only for industry but also for city residents. Electricity generation was demanded for lighting streets and houses, and telephones were installed in homes. Structural steel and elevators made the skyscrapers possible, and an electric street railway system was necessary to carry people to concentrated places of work, factories and office buildings. Water and sewer systems were required by a concentrated population. The automobile created an early demand for paved streets and later for paved highways between cities.

It is important to note that urbanization was widespread throughout the country. Each region developed its own trade and financial centers. The number of medium-sized cities of 10,000 to 100,000 population increased somewhat faster between 1860 and 1920—increasing eight times compared to about seven and a half times for larger cities and six and a half times for smaller ones. The fastest growth in both number of cities and urban population occurred during the 1880's, and the number of cities of over 1 million in population rose from one to three at this time. The basic changes in utilities, buildings, and transportation, however, occurred in the next two decades to create the modern appearance and characteristics of urban life.

ORGANIZATION OF PRODUCTION

A transformation of the American economy also occurred in the ways that production was organized, financed, and managed. A shift occurred not only from agriculture to manufacturing and from rural to urban living but also from individual or small group activities to large social organizations of coordinated productive activity. Mass production and national networks of transportation and distribution were accompanied by large-scale business organizations and new methods of finance and management.

Big Plants, Giant Businesses

Even before 1860, the railroads and a few manufacturing firms were experiencing the problems of directing large numbers of workers. The Pepperell textile mills averaged about 800 workers during the 1850's, and the New York & Erie Railroad by the mid-1850's hired more than 4,000. These, however, were exceptions. Most manufacturing still hired small groups of workers.

By 1920, plants the size of the Pepperell mills had become quite common. There were 10,000 manufacturing establishments with more than $1 million in annual sales and averaging 500 workers. Prior to 1900, census statistics available are heavily weighted by very small "hand and neighborhood industries," but even these statistics show a rise in average workers per manufacturing plant, rising about one third from 1870 to 1890. From 1900 to 1920—without the hand industries in the data—another 50 percent increased occurred. In view of the laborsaving and productivity increases achieved, this understates the increase in size. Real capital invested per plant doubled from 1880 to 1900 and had doubled again by 1920. The plants with over $1 million in sales accounted for two thirds of manufacturing output. (See 9–15.)

In railroads the increase in size came earlier and was more related to technical operating needs. The large trunk-line systems in the Northeast were formed by linking up smaller lines and adding feeder routes. By the late 1880's, the Pennsylvania Railroad hired close to 50,000 employees. These workers were spread over hundreds of miles and were engaged in a wide variety of activities—construction, maintenance, repair, freight handling, warehousing, train operation, and selling services.

In manufacturing, however, the biggest part of the expansion in size of firms, when it came, was not so much in the size of the plant

9–15. Average Size of Manufacturing Plants

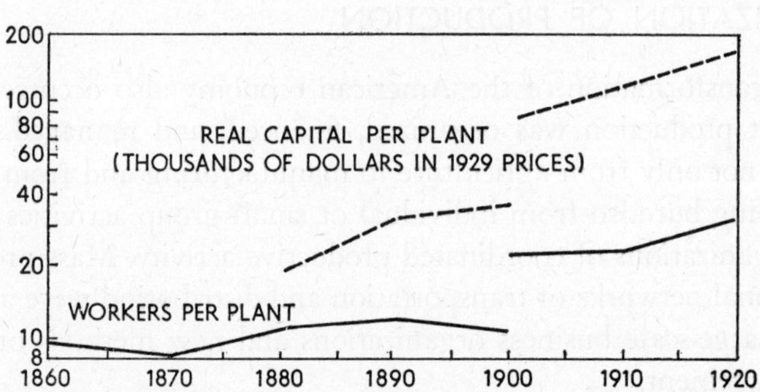

Source: U.S. Department of Commerce, *Historical Statistics of the United States* (Washington, D.C.: U.S. Government Printing Office, 1960), pp. 409–10.

Note: Wage earners; and fixed plus working capital. Prior to 1900 averages are held low by inclusion of numerous small "hand and neighborhood industries."

production unit as in the number of plants directed by one firm. As individual firms expanded their plants to put new technologies to work they were forced to invade each others markets to gain sufficient volume. This "overcapacity" problem was solved through "horizontal combinations" in which competing firms merged and, thus, created multiplant operations.

The big change came around 1900 when the first big merger movement took place. John Moody reported that in 1904 the 318 important manufacturing trusts had 5,288 plants, or an average of 17 each. United States Steel alone controlled 785 plants. Consolidations of firms also were common among public utilities and railroads.

In most cases a large part of this increase in size of business firms was neither required nor justified in terms of the technological economies to be achieved from large-scale mass production. Rather, in part it arose as a consequence of mass marketing. There were advantages to be gained from capturing the allegiance of a large share of the Nation's consumers through advertising and brand identification. One firm could distribute more than it needed to produce in one plant. It also arose from the losses resulting from severe price competition that tended to force manufacturers to seek protection in various forms of monopoly.

Concentration and Modified Competition

Prior to 1900, American industry experienced falling prices and severe price competition. Outright "price wars" tended to result from two conditions: high fixed costs and a small number of sellers. When a firm had made very heavy investments in machinery and buildings, it found that the variable costs for labor, materials, and power were a small part of the total costs it needed to recover in the price of its products. If demand fell or its competitors cut their prices, the firm had an incentive to cut its price in order to maintain a large volume of sales. Its fixed costs of depreciation and interest on capital would continue even if it closed down. As long as the price was greater than its relatively low operating costs, the firm was better off continuing to operate even at a low price. When there was a large number of firms, none could control the price; and the price might fall in response to general oversupply, as it does in competitive farm markets. When there were only a few firms, however, they were in greater rivalry for a larger share of the market. If one sought an advantage by setting a lower price, the others might react by cutting their prices even lower. In competing to have the lowest price, all sellers would suffer more loss than necessary.

The railroads were the first to demonstrate the folly of price wars. A very large part of their costs was fixed, and between major cities a few major companies were in intense rivalry. When one railroad appeared to be gaining too much of the traffic another might cut its rates. Matching cuts might drastically lower rates for several months at a time, and all railroads would suffer losses before rates finally were restored to normal again.

Many manufacturing firms also had made large capital investments in order to achieve the operating economies of mass production. The salaries of managers, skilled workers, and a distribution organization also continued regardless of volume of production; so, there was a strong incentive to keep up the volume of output by lowering prices when necessary. New technology and rapid construction of new plants tended to produce an oversupply. New and more efficient producers were entering markets and gradually forcing smaller and older producers out of business. As long as prices did not fall as low as operating costs, however, the inefficient firms hung on for a long time.

The bitterness of price competition was aggravated by other sources of price declines. Farmers were not the only producers with high debts affected by the falling general wholesale price levels of the Nation from 1865 to 1895. And the manufacturing overcapacity was felt most keenly during the depressions beginning in 1873 and 1893.

Attempts were made, therefore, to resort to various forms of monopoly as a protection against severe price competition. One of the oldest forms, of course, was for one firm to gain control by price cutting its rivals out of business, seizing control of a raw material supply or getting some exclusive arrangements with distributors. Another traditional effort was to reach a "gentlemen's agreement" on maintaining prices, or perhaps to divide up the volume of sales by some sort of "pooling" arrangement. Yet, businessmen, desperate to increase sales during a depression or seeing an unusual profit opportunity, could not be counted on to be "gentlemen" and abide by their agreements. All forms of collusion tended to be temporary and to break down eventually.

The solution usually arrived at was to combine the rivals into the same organization in some way. The "trust" was introduced during the 1880's as such a device. Various firms turned over their voting stock to a small group of trustees in exchange for trust certificates which gave rights to common dividends but no voting rights. The company leaders acting as trustees, therefore, could control the actions of all firms and distribute the common revenues. When both state and federal legislation outlawed this type of trust, the "holding company" became a substitute device. A newly formed corporation, frequently from 1889 on under the very permissive laws of New Jersey, simply purchased controlling shares of the stock of various operating companies. Prices and other general policies of the operating companies thus were decided by the holding company board, while operating decisions might be left up to the operating company officers.

The big merger movement that occurred between 1895 and 1904 involved both holding companies and also the outright combination of operating companies into one larger company. The latter usually involved buying out the assets of a smaller company or the exchange of each stockholder's stock in older companies with issues of stock in a new company.

The big merger movement, which was stimulated by a prosperity boom and a permissive court interpretation of the Sherman Antitrust Act, slowed down drastically after 1904. The economies of scale and the monopoly advantages may have been overestimated by industrial leaders. As it happened, inefficient plants were often acquired on which losses had to be absorbed and large rival combinations kept any one group from dominating in most industries. By 1920, not more than a third of all manufacturing output was in industry classifications in which even the top four firms controlled over half of the output.

In industries with a few large firms, however, a new or modified kind of competition was ushered in. Price wars were avoided by keeping announced prices the same for long periods of time. (This price rigidity has come to be referred to as "administered pricing.") Instead, rivalry for market control was expressed through expenditures on advertising, sales promotion, and product improvement. The rivalry for markets extended across wider territories and even internationally; and competition for the consumer's spending extended to rivalry between different industries producing materials or products with similar uses—such as competition among steel, aluminum, lumber and concrete as building materials. At the individual consumer's level, there may not have been much loss of buyer's choice as the usual seller's rivalry among a few local or regional manufacturers was shifted to a sellers' rivalry among a few national manufacturers competing in all local markets. As the total economy expanded, the big new firms tended to lose somewhat their dominant position in each market. At the end of our study period, mergers were most common in the emerging new product industries, such as in the auto industry.

Ownership, Control, and Financing

Manufacturing was slower to adopt the corporate form of business organization than the railroads. For one thing, the canals and railroads had been chartered by individual legislative act as franchised monopolies vested with a public interest. For another, they required huge sums of capital from the start, and many small investors were solicited for funds in the midst of considerable publicity. Manufacturing firms usually were built from small beginnings, with an inventor or resourceful businessman seizing a profitable opportunity and then plowing back his profits to expand. Bank loans and merchant credit were the most important outside sources of funds at first.

In the rapid industrial expansion from 1850 to 1873, many of the successful individual manufacturers were swept upwards to great wealth with the surge of general national expansion. As individual proprietors, partnerships, or family businesses, they had managed to finance most of their own expansion. In the depression of the 1870's, however, continued needs for capital to expand and mechanize in the face of stiff competition and falling prices caused many firms to incorporate and take in other wealthy shareholders. In most cases, however, the early manufacturing corporations long remained closely held by a few owners, and their stocks were not offered for public sale. In the late 1880's, only one large manufacturing company's stock was listed on the New York Stock Exchange. It was in the merger movement of the late 1890's that many major manufacturing corporations began to list their stocks for public sale. Soon such manufacturing corporations had many thousands of stock owners, but very few had a large share of the ownership.

At this point the separation of ownership and control became important in manufacturing, as it had been in railroads. Even in closely held corporations, not all investors could follow all affairs of the business and left it up to the largest owner or the officers to run the business. Thousands of small stockholders had even less chance of an effective voice in management. The board of directors, accordingly, became largely self-perpetuating and dominated by the officers who might hold only a small share of the stocks.

The investment banker also began to play a key role as one of the directors on many boards of railroads and manufacturing firms. This began first in the railroads when many went bankrupt in the depressions of the 1870's and 1890's. While some large individual officials and wealthy investors created scandals out of their manipulations of the stock market, the investment banker tended to be a stabilizing influence protecting the interests of investors. An investment banker generally was a stockbroker who undertook to buy and then resell large issues of bonds or stocks of railroads or industrial firms. Both wealthy investors and financial institutions relied on their advice about the soundness of the management of the firms. So, when bankruptcy occurred, before more funds could be loaned or invested, investment bankers were called in to assure that the firm was properly reorganized. To make sure the reorganized firm would continue to be well managed the investment banker was placed on the board of directors.

With the creation of giant corporations, it took very large capital resources to be able to handle the sale of new issues of stocks and bonds; so a loose alliance or "syndicate" of investment bankers usually was formed. Investment bankers also tended to hold stock and directorships in large commercial banks and insurance companies, which had large funds to lend or to invest. So they acted as the go-between for both large institutional investors and large industrial firms. Yet, these widespread financial interrelations tended to be pragmatic alliances that depended for their continuance upon trust, successful service, and mutual advantage for all parties. So the "power" of investment bankers was quite restricted.

Professional Management

With the disappearance around 1900 of the so-called "industrial capitalists" who had built major manufacturing firms in the mid-century period of growth, and with the rise of so-called "financial capitalists" interested mostly in sound finance, it fell to a new group, the "professional managers" to run the business. These generally were men with middle-class family backgrounds and better-than-average educations who had risen to officer rank with long experience in the business or who had been specialized advisers to firms. Even the great industrialists of earlier days had not done all of the managing alone. There had been a team of leading managers, including several of the chief stockholders and an increasing group of department heads and staff advisers.

By trial and error, and beginning primarily in the railroads, the modern practices of management had evolved. Better methods of accounting and better flows of routine information were the first needs in the far-flung railroad operations. Accounting consultants and a separate controller's staff usually were introduced as an early step. Then, departmental responsibilities were delegated for different phases of the operation—construction, operations, maintenance, selling, etc. As the railroads were consolidated into large systems, and as the manufacturing firms were combined in mergers, decentralized authority had to be placed in regional divisions and subsidiary officers. The central office management group and its staff then acted more in a policy setting and supervisory role.

One consequence of the large scale of corporations and the new basis of competition was the development of specialized research laboratories. Taking their lesson from universities, technical schools, and government research on agriculture, the major companies began to realize the importance of systematic search for improved methods, materials, and products. Because of their large corporate size, expensive laboratories cost only a small fraction of current sales. Also, with increasingly diversified operations, some of the firms, in chemicals and drugs especially, could make use of unexpected findings in a wide variety of fields. In 1920–21, a National Research Council survey identified 525 industrial research laboratories as being in operation.

Another development in methods was referred to as "scientific management." Around the turn of the century systematic study was being applied by Frederick W. Taylor and others to the detailed operations of the factory—to piece rates, to the use of cutting tools, to the hand motions of workers, to factory organization, and to cost records.

One notable change in manufacturing methods and a further development of mass production was the perfection of the ***continuous assembly line.*** This was primarily an innovation in management methods rather than in technology. All of the technical elements were at hand—the standardized products, interchangeable parts, precision tools, scientific work study methods, and even the continuous belts. Workers had been specialized to do the same operation on all units of product, and the moving belt was used to move the units slowly past a line of workers who completed their operations in turn until the assembled and finished product emerged at the end of the line. The final assembly line itself was a marvel to behold of layout design, but behind it also lay a wonder of organization and planning to achieve on schedule the purchase, fabrication, and movement of materials to the assembly line. At the selling end, too, a flow of mass distribution and sales had to be maintained.

Employee Relations

The transformation of production organization, however, also changed the nature of work for the individual laborer. In the first place, very few persons still worked for themselves. America had become a nation of "employees" in the last half of the 19th century. Not only was there a diminishing proportion of workers who were farmers, but also there was a decline in the proportion of self-employed shopkeepers and craftsmen. This is reflected in the faster rise of nonfarm employees than of the labor force (which includes the self-employed) during the 20th century, the years for which these data are available. (See 9–16.)

Organizational changes also transformed the nature of the relations between worker and employer. No longer was work performed individually or in small informal groups. Meaningful communications, let alone personal contacts, were lost between the top management and the lowest worker as the numbers of people and the layers of supervision were multiplied in the giant business organization. The possibilities for misunderstandings and human grievances were multiplied. Furthermore, the morale and cooperativeness of workers were lowered by the depersonalized condition of modern technology. The factory subjected

9–16. Rise of Employee Status and Union Membership

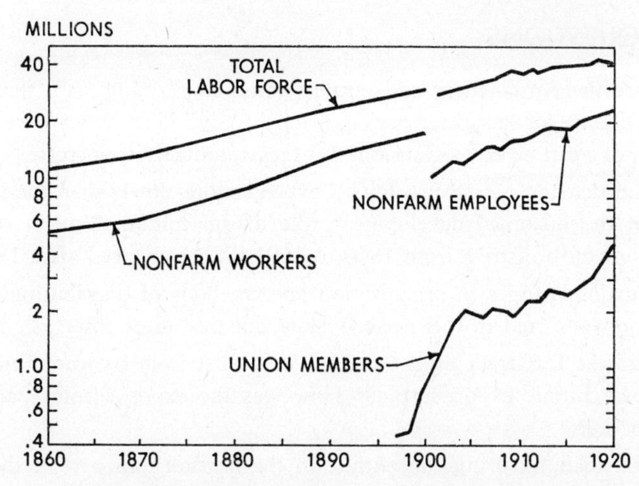

Source: U.S. Department of Commerce, *Historical Statistics of the United States* (Washington, D.C.: U.S. Government Printing Office, 1960), p. 97; and Stanley Lebergott, *Manpower in Economic Growth* (New York: McGraw-Hill Book Co., 1964), pp. 510–13.

the worker to the discipline of the clock and the machine, the process was too vast for the worker to see the consequences of his efforts, and the repetitiveness of his tasks produced boredom and human frustrations.

If these human frustrations were not enough, the worker also had economic incentives to organize to serve his own interests. In this, the American worker was just as pragmatic as businessmen, farmers, and other producers in seeking group organization to solve his economic problems. Generally it was the most skilled and highest paid workers who succeeded in organizing first. In times of rising demand for scarce workers, they had the best opportunity to bargain for higher wage rates. In times of depression and in the face of floods of unskilled immigrant workers, they tried to protect their jobs and privileged positions of skill by restricting the entry and training of new workers and the hiring of nonmembers.

No attempt is made here to recount the history of unionism, but it is important to note that the transformation of the American economy included a sudden rise of worker organization around 1900 at the same time that business mergers were occurring. While the railroad brotherhoods and building craft unions led in the rise of union membership, during World War I industrial unions also began to gain considerable strength. Still, in 1920, only about 12 percent of the labor force and 22 percent of nonfarm employees were union members.

STUDY QUESTIONS

1. Compare the employment and output trends in farming with those in the total economy for successive periods after the Civil War. What were the main sources of farm output expansion? Of farm productivity increase?
2. Why did demand for farm products expand more slowly than total income? Explain the historical development role of agriculture. Explain the major sources of farm distress from 1860 to 1895. What changed after 1895?
3. What major changes in organization and methods of distributing goods to consumers occurred in this period? How did this affect costs?
4. Why did the U.S. trade after the Civil War shift from a chronic import-surplus to a chronic export-surplus? How was the export-surplus paid for by other nations?
5. Why did manufacturing concentrate in the northeastern part of the United States initially? Why did the industrial belt later shift toward Chicago but not spread out to other regions?
6. Why were per capita income averages highest in the West and the Northeast? Why was the trend of per capita income by regions converging (the highs and lows moving closer to the middle)?
7. Why did an increased share of urban population accompany economic development? Why was urban expansion more widespread than manufacturing?
8. Why did the average size of business firms rise? In railroads and manufacturing, explain how both a high proportion of fixed costs and a small number of competing firms might lead to price wars. In what ways did business firms attempt to solve this problem?
9. How did the growing size of business firms affect their ownership and control? Their management? Their employee relations?

Chapter 10 ENLARGED ROLE OF GOVERNMENT

The great changes that were transforming the American economy could not help affecting government and changing its role as well. Government policies and organization that had served for a small agricultural nation were not adequate for a large nation with a modern industrial complex.

The changes in both cases came about gradually, but the government adjustments tended to lag somewhat behind economic conditions. Just as the market economy was not invented suddenly in earlier centuries, so also in the 19th century the structure of modern industrial organization was not introduced suddenly as though it were a new machine. The economic changes came about piecemeal and irregularly over a number of decades. Nor did changes in government policy and organization come about smoothly and painlessly. Adjustments were made by a trial and error learning process. Learning was slow, and errors often were repeated. Public understanding lagged far behind the changes in economic conditions. In spite of our wealth of experience and economic sophistication, today some of the problems of modern industry and urban living are not fully understood or adjusted to.

Three major trends appeared to be enlarging the role of government during the six decades from 1860 to 1920. First, there was an increased use of federal powers to influence economic affairs. While the Nation had been formed as a union of states in the midst of popular suspicion of central government powers, increasing popular demands were made for government action at the federal level. Greater government responsibility especially was demanded for the proper functioning of the national economy. Second, the emphasis of government economic policy shifted from development to regulation. While the early task of government was seen as that of stimulating and aiding private business to undertake the building of social overhead capital and the expanding of basic industries, later the task of government came to be regarded as that of restraining and regulating private business. Third, administrative machinery expanded at all levels of government. In part, this was a consequence of the growing size of the nation and of the burdens of financing and administering a federal government charged with military defense. At the state and local levels, however, there also were rapidly rising demands for public services due to the new complexities of industrial and urban society.

Throughout this period of rapid change, a great tumult of political controversy and protest arose over government policy, and the then current attitudes and opinions have tended to confuse later historical interpretation of the general economic conditions and trends of the period. Considerable enlightenment may result, however, from reversing this process and using our improved information on economic conditions to better understand the political controversies. The preceding chapters have described the trends and basic transformation of the economy, and the changes in government policy and organization to be described in this chapter may be regarded as early efforts of the Nation to cope with these new economic conditions. Since the basic economic changes were poorly understood and their causes often misinterpreted, the political leaders and writers of the times often were misled into oversimplified explanations and wild charges of blame.

CHANGING SOCIAL PHILOSOPHY

The furor over economic policies took place in a controversial intellectual context. On one side the laissez-faire teachings of Adam Smith and later British and American economists received considerable support and amplification from a school of thought labeled by intellectual historians as "Social Darwinism." This philosophy was first articulated in detail by Herbert Spencer, the British philosopher who coined the term "survival of the fittest."

Essentially Social Darwinism, which came into vogue shortly after the Civil War, involved a wholesale transfer of Darwin's theory of natural selection to the realm of social philosophy including economics. Human perfection in both a biological and social sense was held to be inevitable through the operation of natural evolutionary processes. The good life would emerge naturally via technological improvements, and the actions of individuals in trying to maximize their respective self-interest would promote social welfare.

In this doctrine the state had only a minimal role to play in the affairs of man. Governmental attempts to steer society in the direction of improvement were misguided—if they were effective in any way it would be for ill, resulting in maladjustment of nature's carefully engineered machine for progress. For example, laws designed to increase the income of the poor would only trip off a Malthusian mechanism by which higher birth and survival rates would flood the labor market, depress wages, and defeat the intent of the law.

Society existed for the benefit of its component individuals and had no identity or consciousness apart from that of its individual members. Consequently the state per se could have no goals, another basis for restricting government activity. It is only fair to Spencer to add that the popular conception of Social Darwinism represented a gross oversimplification of Spencer's philosophy which was not nearly so optimistic in its predictions for mankind.

Andrew Carnegie, certainly one of the fittest among the survivors, summarized this oversimplified, popular view of Spencer and used it to rationalize income inequality and business concentration. Carnegie asserted in his "*Gospel of Wealth*" that

> the price which society pays for the law of competition . . . is . . . great; but the advantages of this law are . . . greater still. . . . But, whether the law be benign or not, we must say of it: . . . It is here; we cannot evade it; no substitutes for it have been found; and while the law may be sometimes hard for the individual, it is best for the race, because it insures the survival of the fittest in every department. We accept and welcome, therefore, as conditions to which we must accommodate ourselves, great inequality of environment, the concentration of business, industrial and commercial, in the hands of a few, and the law of competition between these, as being not only beneficial, but essential for the future progress of the race.

In opposition to the Social Darwinists were those who advocated extensive social reform. While accepting the evolutionary nature of society in principle, this school did not equate evolution and progress. Rather they felt that individual actions left unfettered could produce deterioration of man's condition. Accordingly they advocated an active role for the state in guiding the forces of change in society along a path that would produce widespread participation in the benefits of economic progress.

This vein of intellectual development can be thought of as starting with the philosopher-economist John Stuart Mill. Near the end of his career he broke intellectually with his fellow classical-liberal economists whose tradition had been founded by Adam Smith. Mill did so by declaring that the laws of production may be "natural" but that the distribution of income was a decision for society to make through conscious deliberation.

From Mill's time on, the social reform movement atomized into a vast collection of advocates of state control of widely different beliefs and generally sharing only one principle, a lack of faith in laissez-faire economics. At one extreme were the Marxists with their advocacy of violent overthrow of bourgeois society. At the other pole were those who felt that the state could modify man-made social institutions in a way that would force the economy to operate as the Social Darwinists insisted it would operate automatically if freed from the perverse influence of government.

Paradoxically the formation of the various social reform movements emanated from the scientific approach to society that fostered Social Darwinism. The growth of those disparate minorities was encouraged by the economic changes that had made the material aspects of life more rewarding but more complex and subject to sharp variations and risk. The actual changes in government policy that came about were less dramatic than one would suppose. The various dissident minorities agitated loud and long about both real and imagined grievances suffered at the hands of an impersonal market mechanism or powerful interest groups. Out of this political tug-of-war came the Greenback movement, Populism, Progressivism, the Muckrakers, and perhaps a half-dozen minor isms each concerned with a narrow range of reforms. Eventually minority opinion became majority opinion, and with traditional American pragmatism in defining government's role, social welfare and regulatory legislation were enacted.

Now that we have reviewed the intellectual background of government's changing role over the five decades after the Civil War, let us consider the political climate of the times. This can perhaps best be done by noting the political alignment of major economic interest groups. At the start of the Civil War, the Republican party had come into power, and it dominated the federal government most of the time during the next five decades. Since industrial and financial leaders were strongly allied with this party, there was a shift away from the agricultural viewpoint which had dominated during the first half of the century. Because the following decades constituted a period in which great changes occurred in the size of businesses and in the conditions of farming, much of the minority political protest was from farmers, workers, and small businessmen vying with "big business."

The socialist ideas of Marx and others, while never widely and rigidly held in America, were used to suggest that farmers and workers were oppressed by an inherently greedy class of giant capitalists. Government regulations and reforms, therefore, were sought as ways to restrain the exploiter and help the oppressed.

The laissez-faire of Social Darwinism, while frequently ignored in practice, was used to suggest the superiority of an economy run by private business entirely free of interference and regulation by government. Neither of these extremes of oversimplified ideology, however, was very useful in understanding the major changes taking place in the economy and the changing adaptations of actual government policy.

CONTROL OF MONEY AND BANKING

Increasing demands for the exercise of central government powers occurred in several fields of government activity. One of the first fields in which the shift of powers from states to the federal government took place, however, was in money and banking.

This was a field in which there might have been the least question about the constitutional basis for the powers and a field in which the federal government earlier had taken steps and then withdrawn. The first Bank of the United States had been chartered in 1791, but the recharter of the second Bank of the United States was effectively vetoed by President Jackson in 1832. This also was a field in which the major consideration in enlarging government's interference in the private economy was most dominated by its own needs to handle the government's internal fiscal affairs. Yet, oddly enough, our steps to regulate banks and the money supply were hesitant. The Independent Treasury Act (1846) is a classic illustration of this hesitancy. Although the act became the legal basis for Treasury intervention in the private money market, it was the intent of Congress to maintain the Treasury aloof from the private money market, unrealistic as that goal may have been.

Civil War Financing

The Civil War created great money problems for the federal government which continued to plague it for the rest of the century. At the start of the war, tariff duties provided nearly the only source of revenues, and a continuous deficit had been experienced since the recession of 1857. From $35 million in 1861, military expenditures alone jumped to $431 million in 1862, and by the end of the war had reached the awesome peak of $1.15 billion.

The government started out somewhat cautiously and unrealistically, expecting to raise taxes only moderately and pay for the war by borrowing. Initial efforts to sell bonds to the public, however, were not very successful and attempts to borrow specie from the banks drained them of reserves. The early reverses of the war caused a loss of public confidence, and people began to hoard gold. At the end of 1861, the banks had to suspend payment of specie on their notes and checks. Early in 1862, the government was forced to issue noninterest-bearing Treasury notes, that also were not redeemable in specie. These notes, popularly called "greenbacks," were made legal tender for all private and public debts except payment of customs duties and interest on U.S. bonds and notes. This was the first real paper money issued by the United States, and it was not until 1869 that the Supreme Court settled the issue of its constitutionality.

While an omnibus revenue bill had been passed in mid-1861, it was not vigorously administered until the next year, when a more thoroughgoing tax bill added to the types and rates of taxes. It took time, however, to organize a staff of tax collectors; and the policy of relying upon every conceivable type of tax rather than upon high rates made administration more cumbersome. By the end of the war, half of the revenues were collected from excise taxes, the largest sources being the taxes on manufactures and on whiskey and tobacco. The rest of the revenue came primarily from higher tariffs and from a new federal tax on personal incomes. While revenues were slow in rising, they did reach almost one fourth of total expenditures by the end of the war. Altogether, the tax burden was rather regressive—that is, it took a larger proportion of the incomes of the lower income families.

While introduced as a temporary and limited expedient, the issue of greenbacks was extended to $450 million by 1863, which amounted to almost half of the currency in circulation at the time. On the private market a premium was demanded for gold, which in 1865 required more than $2 in greenbacks in exchange for $1 in gold. Small silver coins also disappeared from circulation, and for a while postage stamps had to be used in place of coins until fractional paper notes were issued. Prices generally also rose rapidly because of shortages of goods as well as an increase in money supply. The Treasury, refusing to recognize its own part in the inflation, tended to blame private speculators for bidding up gold prices and state banks for excessive note issue.

Since the greenbacks initially were convertible to bonds (a provision removed in 1863) and since depreciation of greenbacks made the interest payment in gold very attractive, the market for bonds began to brighten late in 1862. Having failed to sell its own bonds very well, the Treasury contracted with a private banker, Jay Cooke, to act as general agent in selling bonds for a commission of ½ of 1 percent. By hiring a large crew of agents and by extensively advertising throughout the country, Jay Cooke was extraordinarily successful in quickly selling the bonds. He also repeated this feat later in the war; and his success is credited with introducing much of the public to the practice of buying bonds as a form of personal saving and investment. Most of the bonds, however, were purchased in financial centers and held by banks.

It was largely to help the Treasury in its financing problems that the National Banking Act was passed in 1863. This act gave national charters to groups of individuals forming banks; and, it required them to purchase national bonds, place them on deposit with the Treasury and receive national bank notes in their place. The objective was to help the Treasury sell its bonds as well as to introduce more uniformity in bank notes. The number of new banks, however, was disappointingly small until 1865, when a 10 percent tax was placed on notes issued by state banks. This quickly eliminated the issue of state bank notes and brought the conversion of many state banks to national charters.

Debt Retirement and Hard Money

After the Civil War, the Republican party leaders were anxious to return to "sound finance." It was regarded as prudent and moral to pay off the debt, reduce taxes, and restore the former value of the dollar in exchange for gold.

Federal expenditures were cut to one third of the war peak by 1867, but hopes of cutting them nearer the prewar levels were not realizable partly because of the heavy interest burdens. The occupation costs in the South and continued skirmishes with the Indians in the West slowed the decline in military costs, but by 1873 defense expenditures were leveled off at about double the prewar level. Pensions were more than 10 times higher at the end of the war, and this doubled by 1873. Costs of tax collection, other administrative expenditures, and public works outlays also were much higher than prewar. Nevertheless, total federal expenditures in 1873 were only about 4 percent of the gross national product, and rapid growth of the economy was reducing this percentage.

Taxes were rapidly cut or eliminated, but revenues fell somewhat less rapidly because expanding production and imports yielded more revenues than anticipated. Most taxes on business and manufacturing were eliminated, but excise taxes on liquor and tobacco were continued at substantial levels, as were the tariffs. The income tax was reduced in 1867 and eliminated in 1872. Long afterwards, the controversy generated by this form of tax resulted in an 1880 Supreme Court decision that it was unconstitutional.

Since expenditures fell faster than receipts, a surplus resulted; and the Treasury used this to pay off debts and reduce the supply of paper money. The short-term debt was paid off first and every effort was made to refund the debt with new issues for longer terms and lower interest. A brief effort also was made to repurchase and retire greenbacks; but political protest quickly caused this to be stopped after less than a third of the outstanding supply was withdrawn. (See 10–1.)

10–1. Federal Finances, 1860–1920

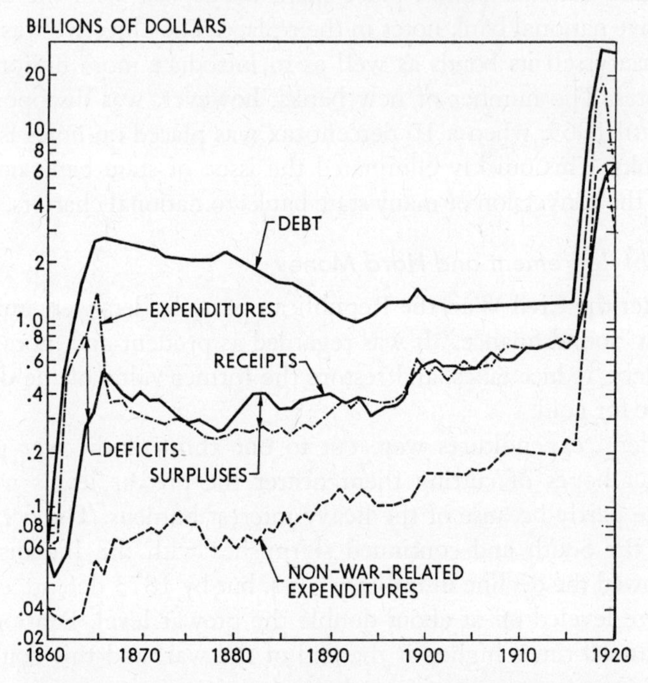

Note: Interest on debt and veterans' pensions and benefits are treated as war-related.

Source: U.S. Department of Commerce, *Historical Statistics of the United States* (Washington, D.C.: U.S. Government Printing Office, 1960), pp. 711, 718.

The continued postwar decline in prices aroused much political controversy over the financial policies of the Republicans. After the panic of 1873 a prolonged depression intensified the popular demand, especially among farmers, for an easy money policy. Since price inflation had accompanied the flood of paper money in the war, there was a demand for more greenbacks in order to raise prices. A National Greenback party even ran a candidate for president in 1876, although it did not poll a significant share of the total vote. Business recovery helped to stay these political pressures, and the favorable balance of trade beginning in 1876 helped bring an inflow of gold. The Treasury also was able to acquire an adequate gold reserve by sale of bonds at more favorable interest rates than in most European countries. So, in 1879 greenback values finally reached a parity with gold, and the Treasury resumed the redemption of greenbacks with specie upon demand. This brought the Nation back to a metallic currency standard after having an irredeemable paper currency for 17 years.

The political protests against declining price levels then shifted to a demand for increased issue of money in the form of silver coins (or silver-backed certificates). During the 1870's, great new silver mines in the Rocky Mountains began to pour out large quantities of silver, while the world demand was not expanding. In fact, most nations already were on a gold standard and some were switching from silver to gold. This caused a fall in the price of silver; so, the popular demand to expand money supply was combined with an appeal to aid the western mining industry by Treasury purchases of silver at prices well above the market. A compromise was reached in 1878, when the Bland-Allison Act obligated the Treasury to purchase between $2 and $4 million worth of silver a month at above-market prices to issue in coins or to support the issue of silver certificates. Later, the Sherman Silver Purchase Act of 1890 further required the Treasury to purchase silver and issue treasury notes redeemable in either silver or gold. Shortly afterwards, however, the Panic of 1893 led to a run on the Treasury to exchange treasury notes and greenbacks for gold, and in the midst of world de-

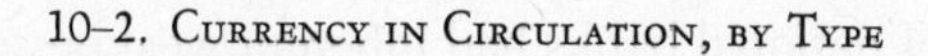
10–2. Currency in Circulation, by Type

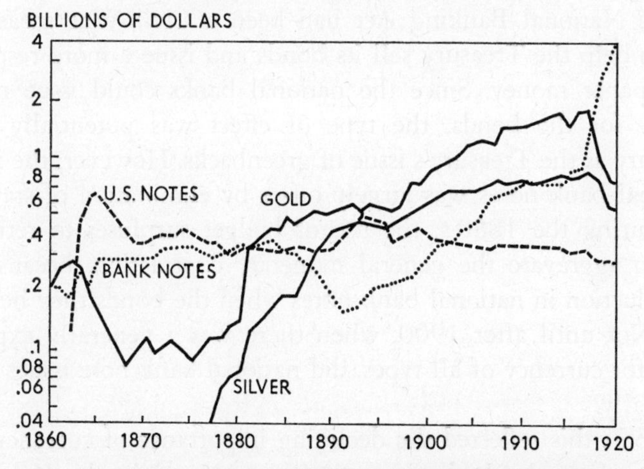

Note: Bank notes include state bank notes prior to 1879 and Federal Reserve notes and Federal Reserve Bank notes after 1915. Minor coin are included in silver. Fractional currency, Treasury notes of 1890, and other U.S. currency are included in U.S. notes.

Source: U.S. Department of Commerce, *Historical Statistics of the United States* (Washington, D.C.: U.S. Government Printing Office, 1960), pp. 648–49.

pression there was a gold outflow from the Nation. So, the silver act had to be repealed. Then, in the presidential election of 1896, William Jennings Bryan proposed a silver money standard as his major campaign issue. His decisive defeat seemed to settle the issue politically.

A change in economic conditions in the mid-1890's also helped to bring a decisive end to the political controversy over the form of national currency. During the 1890's, new discoveries of gold were made in Africa, Australia, and Alaska. An improved, cyanide process of extraction also increased output. World gold production rose from 5.7 million ounces in 1890 to 13.9 million ounces in 1898. A favorable balance of trade also brought an inflow of gold to the United States. Between 1896 and 1898, it is estimated that the Nation's gold stock increased 40 percent. With the rapid business recovery in the late 1890's, the general price level also began to rise. So the economic basis of the political controversy had been removed when the Gold Standard Act of 1900 finally defined the value of the dollar solely in terms of gold. (See 10–2.)

Bank Regulation

Unfortunately, this did not settle all questions of money supply, for banks were increasingly responsible for a large part of the money supply. During the next decade public discontent with the inflexibility of the banking system during business fluctuations was to result in further banking reform legislation. For a long time it had been evident that the system of national banks had inherent weaknesses.

The National Banking Act had been a Civil War measure designed to help the Treasury sell its bonds and issue a more respectable type of paper money. Since the national banks could issue notes in exchange for the bonds, the type of effect was potentially just as inflationary as the Treasury's issue of greenbacks. However, the increase in national bank notes was largely offset by elimination of state bank notes. During the 1880's, the use of budget surpluses to retire debt tended to aggravate the general monetary contraction, because there was a reduction in national bank notes when the bonds they held were retired. Not until after 1900, when there was a generally expanding demand for currency of all types, did national bank note issues expand substantially.

In part this reflected the declining importance of currency in the total money supply. In business transactions and in the larger cities increasing use was made of checks and bills of exchange instead of transferring large amounts of currency. It was mostly in rural areas that currency still was relied on heavily for transactions. By 1870, in fact, demand deposits in banks exceeded the total currency in circulation in the Nation; and thereafter, deposits continued to grow more rapidly than currency.

As a means to create a more uniform type of banknote issue, the national bank system was successful. The 10 percent tax succeeded in driving state bank notes out of existence. For a while the number of state banks had dwindled; but it soon became apparent that banks did not need to issue notes to make loans. The setting up of a bank deposit for a borrower was just as effective as issuing him notes. Since most of the state regulations on types of loans that could be made and on reserves required were less restrictive than the national regulations,

10–3. GROWTH OF NATIONAL AND STATE BANKS

Year	Number of Banks		Assets (Millions of Dollars)	
	National	State	National	State
1860	...	1,562	...	1,000
1870	1,612	325	1,566	215
1880	2,076	1,279	2,036	1,364
1890	3,484	4,717	3,062	3,296
1900	3,731	9,322	4,944	6,444
1910	7,138	18,013	9,892	13,030
1920	8,024	22,885	23,267	29,827

SOURCE: U.S. Department of Commerce, *Historical Statistics of the United States* (Washington, D.C.: U.S. Government Printing Office, 1960), pp. 626, 628.

state charters again became popular. By 1890 both the number and assets of state banks exceeded that of national banks. (See 10–3.)

While the restrictions were greater on national banks, it soon was apparent that the system was not much help in preventing recurrent bank crises. Numerous national banks failed during each of the depressions. While there was national inspection and supervision, there was no central control over the system. The major weakness was that the law itself had allowed and encouraged a pyramiding of bank reserves without allowing any flexibility in the supply of money in times of emergency. Country banks were required to keep 15 percent of their deposits on reserve, but three fifths of this reserve could be held as deposit in a city bank. City banks had to keep 25 percent reserves, but they could keep half of them on deposit in New York City banks. Only banks in New York City and other reserve cities had to keep their 25 percent reserve as currency in their own vaults.

Since the practice then was to pay interest on reserve deposits, banks tended to make full use of the opportunity to keep part of their reserves in city banks and in New York. This was safe if only a few banks had sudden need for currency, for they could withdraw their reserves individually without causing a problem. But in times of money shortage if all banks tried to call back their reserves from city banks and from New York, the banks holding those reserves might find it impossible to provide enough currency suddenly. This is because they did not hold these deposits in currency but put them out to loan commercially. Thus any increase in demand for currency in the Nation as a whole was likely to cause a crisis in New York banking and financial circles. This experience was repeated regularly in the panics of 1873, 1884, 1893, and 1907. After the Panic of 1907, there was a political demand for banking reform. New York had become an international banking center, and even international bankers were impatient with the weakness of the Nation's banking system. In 1908, the Aldrich-Vreeland Act provided as a temporary measure that groups of banks could form associations that could borrow from the Treasury in an emergency. Meanwhile a national Monetary Commission was appointed to study the banking system and make recommendations. The results of the Commission studies began to be publicized in 1911, and the debates over various alternative legislative proposals began, culminating in the signing of the Federal Reserve Act in December of 1913.

The Federal Reserve Act did not create a strong central bank, such as many European nations have, but it did correct some of the weaknesses of the previous national bank system. Twelve reserve banks were created in districts, with national banks as members participating in the election of boards of directors. A central Board of Governors of the Federal Reserve System was appointed by the President and given supervisory powers. One function of the Reserve banks was to liquidate the old national bank notes and issue new Federal Reserve notes. This new issue was to be limited by a 40 percent gold reserve requirement of the Reserve banks themselves. Member banks were required to keep specified reserve percentages on deposit in the Reserve banks. The Reserve banks were to act as a clearing system for checks drawn on member banks; and the member banks were able to borrow from the Reserve banks.

The flexibility to create more money supply was inherent in the power of Reserve banks to issue their own notes to purchase government bonds and short-term commercial loan notes in the open market. Restraint on excessive issue of bank credit in boom times also was possible by raising the interest rates on their loans to member banks, and setting higher reserve requirements. There was little opportunity to test these powers prior to World War I; but in that war one other function of the system immediately came into use—the power to act as a fiscal agent for the Treasury.

World War I Financing

Even prior to America's entry into World War I, the war had a disturbing effect on the American economy. Initially the outbreak of aggression had caused a panic sale of securities, and the sales by many foreign investors caused an outflow of gold and strain on the money supply. Since the Federal Reserve System was not yet in operation, the Treasury used the powers of the Aldrich-Vreeland Act to lend emergency currency to banks, and more of the Treasury's own cash was deposited with banks. Still, some business depression and unemployment in the economy as a whole resulted.

In 1915, business conditions were reversed by a rapid rise in exports, as European nations placed heavy orders in America for war munitions and supplies. In three years, exports increased sixfold, and the real gross national product increased 20 percent. Since imports did not rise as much, the net export balance tripled, and the total balance in these three years was almost as large as the total of all previous export balances in American history. To settle this balance, foreign nations liquidated about half of their American securities, and about $2.7 billion in foreign government bonds was sold to Americans. Shipping services and gold flows each brought in another billion. These gold imports were the largest in history, and the American gold stock was the largest any nation had held. The gold imports greatly expanded bank reserves and enabled credit to expand to handle the increased business activity. Bank deposits (adjusted for interbank holdings) increased 30 percent; and the new Federal Reserve System encouraged credit expansion by lowering rediscount rates.

In mid-1916, federal military expenditures began to increase. In this preparedness period, tax rates were increased; and the 1913 constitutional amendment and law restoring the federal income tax helped provide more revenues. The Treasury also was authorized to begin emergency short-term borrowing.

With the declaration of war in April of 1917, expenditures shot up much faster than revenues. Expenditures tripled in 1917 and rose ninefold by 1919. After an emergency tax increase in March of 1917, Congress was slow in debating and raising tax rates, which it did in

October of 1917, and again in February of 1919. Many persons regarded the rates as confiscatory, for the basic tax on personal income reached 12 percent while the maximum surtax was 65 percent. Corporation taxes also were 12 percent and excess profits taxes were 65 percent. Excise taxes were increased much less, and no increase was made in tariffs. In this war, therefore, the tax burden was progressive, falling proportionately more on higher income families. Revenues, however, fell from 60 percent of expenditures in 1917 to 26 percent in 1919. On the whole, about 30 percent of the war costs were paid by taxes.

The remaining 70 percent had to be raised by borrowing. While this might have been noninflationary if all the borrowing had removed funds from the people, about one fifth of the money was borrowed directly from banks. The Treasury also urged people to borrow while buying bonds on the installment plan. The Federal Reserve System, through its own policy and through legislative amendments, greatly expanded the money supply to enable banks and individuals to borrow to buy the bonds and to finance increased private spending. Between 1916 and 1919, deposits of member banks doubled, while deposits of nonmember banks actually declined slightly. The Federal Reserve deposits and notes also expanded. So, while the government did not appear to be printing money to finance the war in an obviously inflationary manner, the same effect was achieved through using the Federal Reserve System to rapidly expand bank deposit money.

Money Supply and Prices

Thus, in the two wars at the beginning and end of this period, the government in handling its own finances had a strong disturbing effect on the economy in the form of rapid price inflation. Being unprepared and unwilling to finance the sudden large military expenditures through taxes, the Treasury had to resort to printing money or borrowing from banks in a way that expanded its note issue or deposits.

Furthermore, in attempting to put its own house in order after the Civil War, the government also disturbed price levels in the private economy but in the opposite direction. This resulted from policies that contracted or retarded the growth of the stock of money available in the economy while production was expanding rapidly. Late in the 1870's, there was an effort to withdraw greenbacks. Bond retirement resulted in some contraction of national bank notes in the 1880's. (Refer again to 10–2.) Most generally, however, it can be said that the major weakness in government policy was what it failed to do. It failed to expand currency fast enough to meet the needs of an expanding economy, and it failed to prevent contraction of bank deposits during depressions. If it had not been for the trend toward more rapid expansion of bank deposits during the three decades after the Civil War, even greater downward pressure might have been placed on the price trends. Even the rapid deposit expansion was due more to the state chartered banks than to the national banks. (See 10–4.)

The quantity theory of money provides a way to analyze how a grand variety of forces transmitted through the money stock influence the general price level. Let us start from the simple definition that a price is the ratio of the amount of money exchanged for a quantity of

10–4. Currency, Deposits and Money Stock

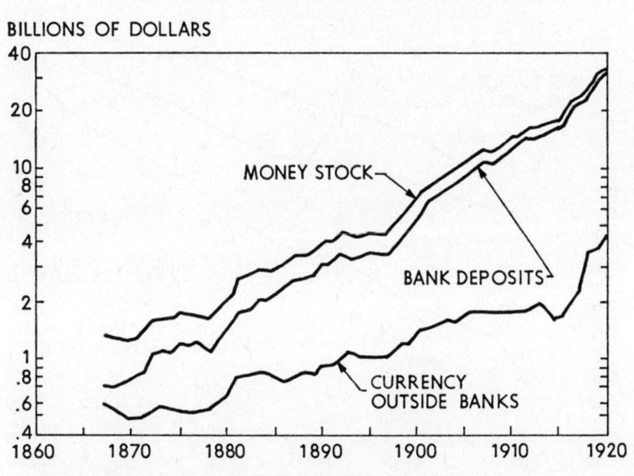

Note: Includes time and demand deposits.
Source: U.S. Department of Commerce, *Historical Statistics of the United States* (Washington, D.C.: U.S. Government Printing Office, 1960), pp. 646–47.

goods divided by that quantity of goods. Then for the total economy the theory states that the price level depends upon the money stock (M) times its velocity of circulation (V) divided by production or real income (Y), as shown by the measure net national product. This is shown symbolically by the equation:

$$P = \frac{MV}{Y}.$$

If the velocity (or rate at which the money stock changes hands in producing the annual income) is fairly stable, then faster (or slower) changes in the money stock than in production are likely to result in increases (or decreases) in the general price level. Many other things, of course, affect the velocity, especially in short periods of time; so it should not be assumed that prices are influenced only by money stock. Yet, the availability of money has been important historically in influencing wartime price inflations, depression price declines, and long-term secular price trends. (Refer to 8–4 in Chapter 8 for wholesale prices.)

Again we stress that there is not a simple mechanical relationship between the quantity of money and the price level. Rather a host of economic forces influence the quantity of money which in turn influences spending and thereby affects price levels. The precise nature of

10–5. National Production, Money Stock and Prices

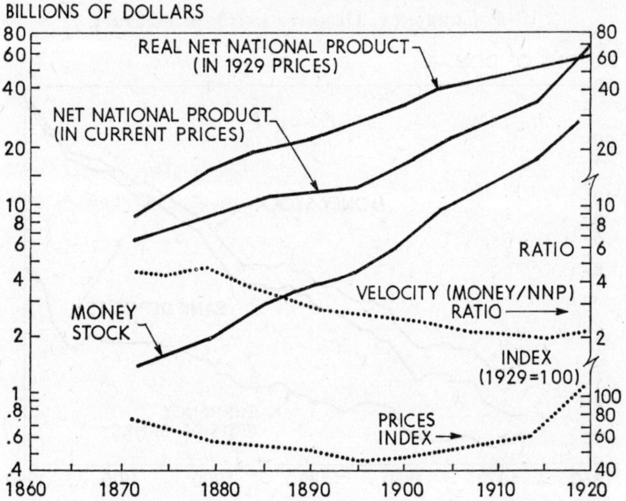

Note: The implicit price index for adjusting real net national product is used, and it is shown in five-year averages on a ratio scale; so it looks different from the wholesale price indexes previously shown.

Source: U.S. Department of Commerce, *Historical Statistics of the United States* (Washington, D.C.: U.S. Government Printing Office, 1960), pp. 139, 144, 646–47

these interrelations is still hotly debated by economists, especially as far as short-run problems are concerned. We, however, are interested in longer time periods over which money stock and price-level changes are useful sources of insight.

We can use 10–5 to trace the relationship of these variables over our study period. The national output rose very rapidly immediately after the Civil War, and the money stock rose with it from 1868 to 1872. Yet from 1872 to 1879, when resumption of specie payment finally was achieved, the money stock stayed almost constant. This was a period of depression and precipitous price declines, which continued the rate of immediate postwar price declines. During the decade of the

1880's, the money stock rose about as fast as the national production, but velocity fell steeply. This was a period of rapid growth of bank deposits (some for saving purposes), and this form of money evidently changed hands less rapidly. Consequently, prices continued a downward trend. Between 1892 and 1896, during another depression and period of price declines, the money stock again stopped expanding. After 1896 and virtually until World War I, the money stock rose much faster than national production and more than offset the continued downward trend of velocity. The long-term price trend, in turn, was rising during this period. During World War I, an even more rapid rise in the money stock was again accompanied by a rapid inflation in prices.

It is not necessary for the money stock to have been the sole influence on prices for this analysis to be relevant. The point is that the money stock was one of the major influences on price levels, and the federal government had the constitutional powers and responsibility to control the money supply. At times it exercised its powers in such a way as to account for a large part of the wide fluctuations in price levels—especially in wartime and during the post–Civil War effort to get back on the gold standard. At other times, it permitted price fluctuations to occur from other causes without adequate efforts to offset them—as in the depressions and during the long-term decline that continued in the 1880's. If it had not been for the expansion in state bank deposits, the lack of a federal effort to provide an expanding money supply for an expanding economy might have brought even worse price declines. And if it had not been for the fortunate rise in world gold production, there might not have been an upward trend in prices after the mid-1890's.

It should be noted that monetary disturbances can wreak havoc throughout the private economy. Rapid price inflation can cause a wasteful diversion of capital funds into hoarding of gold and speculation in land and inventories instead of into new productive investments. Inflation hurts people who depend upon relatively fixed money incomes—whether in the form of salaries, rents, interest, or pensions. Falling price trends, on the other hand, hurt people who have borrowed money, invested in productive equipment, and are holding inventories. Farmers, small businessmen and manufacturers all were hurt by falling prices in the three decades after the Civil War. The bankruptcies were intensified in railroads, where fixed capital costs from large initial investments were important.

In the midst of monetary disturbances, it is the private market and individual businessmen that tend to get blamed for the difficulties everyone is experiencing. Then, the assumption too easily is made that some type of government interference with the private market is needed to "reform" the private economy. The extent to which government policy itself is at fault may be overlooked. This was often the case over the period 1860–1920.

SUBSIDIES AND REGULATION

Other fields in which the federal government exercised an increasing influence over economic affairs were closely related to its constitutional powers and traditional functions. Setting tariffs and sale of western lands always had been federal government functions. Federal government subsidies for railroad construction in the form of land grants already had begun in the 1850's.

Shortly after the Civil War, however, the emphasis in government policy began to shift. Formerly the emphasis was upon encouraging private business to undertake the risky investments needed to build the country. When the expansion across the continent was nearing completion, and as industries and cities began experiencing new problems of large size and complexity, government policy began to emphasize regulation of business. The aim was to restrain and guide the methods of a few in order to protect the many. That is, the emphasis shifted from stimulating the private economy to regulating the way it worked. The type of government interference was changing.

Development Subsidies

It was primarily through the exercise of its powers to set tariffs and sell public lands that the federal government initially tried to stimulate, support, and protect the productive activities of individuals in developing the country. That is to say, it was not through spending public funds but through the granting of special privileges and protections that the government encouraged the rapid exploitation of the natural resources of the continent.

Controversies over the tariff dominated post–Civil War politics almost as much as the money issue. The Republican party had come into power in 1861 dedicated to a high-tariff policy, and the Democratic party tried to lower tariffs during the Cleveland and Wilson administrations. Since the Republican party was more identified with business leaders, the high-tariff policy frequently has been cited as serving the class interests of manufacturers and demonstrating the domination of government by big business. This is a gross oversimplification that ignores the diversity of interests among business groups, the support of tariffs by some farm and worker interests, and the importance attached to tariffs as a source of revenue.

The railroads favored low rates on steel, the steel companies wanted low rates on iron and coal, the woolen manufacturers sought low rates on wool, exporters of machinery favored low-tariff reciprocity, and merchants usually favored free trade. On the other hand, farm groups wanted higher rates on wool and sugar. Workers in manufacturing industries generally feared the competition of foreign imports because of the lower wages in most European countries; and during depressions the competition of imports threatened employment as well as wage rates. Further, pressures for tariff legislation fluctuated with the business cycle. It was during the depressions of the 1870's and 1890's that rates were raised, and during prosperous periods there were efforts to lower the rates.

Throughout the post–Civil War decades, the main justification offered for the high tariff was the need of the federal government for revenues to pay off its debts and support higher expenditures. Nevertheless, the high-tariff policy of the federal government must be regarded as a form of privilege and protection for certain producing groups.

Government policy on the sale of public lands was a compromise between the desire for revenues and the desire to help farmers. During the Civil War, the latter motive became dominant. During 1862, several measures were passed that were designed to aid farmers. The Homestead Act removed the price on public lands (except for a nominal filing fee) for the small farmer. At the same time, the Pacific Railway Act was designed to encourage the building of railroads to open up new farmlands in the West, as well as to provide a connection with the West Coast.

Also in 1862, the Morrill Land Grant College Act was passed, and the Department of Agriculture was established. These measures aimed to raise farm productivity and incomes by encouraging research and the dissemination of new knowledge. While the Morrill Act involved only grants of federal lands, in 1887 appropriations began to be made for grants-in-aid to states in support of research at agricultural experiment stations. In 1906, a federal program was undertaken to stop the spread of the boll weevil on southern cotton farms. In 1908, Congress doubled the support to agricultural colleges; and in 1914, the Smith-Lever Act provided federal funds to support an agricultural extension service. The expenditures of the Department of Agriculture were $3.6 million in 1900, reached $22.2 million in 1914, and rose to $66.6 million in 1920.

In the disposal of public lands to business interests, there was a similar policy of stimulating rapid development but with a little more concern for government revenues. Beginning in the late 1840's, Congress had sold mineral lands at higher prices than those for agricultural lands. Legislation after the Civil War set similar prices for mineral lands in the West with the hope of bringing in additional revenues to reduce the national debt. Congress, however, frequently passed special measures exempting particular areas. Also, the administration of the land offices was lax until the end of the 1880's. Just as pioneer farmers had practiced squatting on public lands, many of the early timber cutters did not always bother to acquire the lands they cut. The early cattlemen also grazed their cattle on public lands. The lax enforcement of the Homestead Act then enabled large holdings of timber, mining, and grazing lands to be assembled by paying small farmers to "settle" the land and then buying their claims. Nevertheless, most of the timber and mining lands were purchased under the laws established for this purpose.

Late in the 19th century, some public leaders began to express concern over the dwindling of public lands and the need to conserve natural resources. Eastern leaders were aware of soil depletion in farming, exhaustion of mines, and cut-over forest lands; and they advocated the setting aside of reserves of public lands in the West. Western merchants frequently opposed this as tending to slow down the economic development of their areas. Congress authorized the setting aside of public lands as national forests and the creation of national parks. In 1902, the Reclamation Act provided for the proceeds from the sale of public lands to be used in a fund for construction of dams and irrigation of farmlands in the dry regions of the West. Thus, in its land policy generally, the federal government shifted from a give-away policy designed to stimulate rapid development to a more restrictive conservation policy; and public funds began to be used to improve the methods of utilizing natural resources.

Brief mention also may be made here of the rising expenditures of the federal government on rivers and harbors. While the traffic on canals and rivers had been greatly reduced by the competition of the railroads, there were continual pressures on the federal government to subsidize improvements in waterways, partly as a measure to force lower competitive rates on the railroads and partly to aid communities on the rivers and coast. Expenditures on rivers and harbors increased during the depressions of the 1870's and 1890's. By 1914, annual expenditures on rivers and harbors were $48 million, larger than for any yearly construction expenditure on the Panama Canal.

Financing the Railroads

The major development effort of the federal government was in the form of land grants to aid the construction of western railroads. Railroads also were the first major industry to become a focus of public regulation. Much of the history of government and business relations, then, can be recorded in terms of what happened to railroads. The preceding comments on government policy in regard to tariff protection and agricultural land grants, provide a useful background perspective on initial public attitudes toward aiding private business.

In 1862, when Congress decided to encourage the building of a railroad link to the West Coast, federal aid commonly was believed to be necessary to bring this about. Previous canals and railroads had demonstrated that there could be public benefits broadly diffused to a whole region; but it took a long time to build up traffic to begin recovering the costs of construction. Customarily, railroad construction had been financed with combinations of grants and loans by local and state governments. In the 1850's, the Illinois Central had been built with the aid of a federal land grant to three states, who in turn gave land grants to the railroads. Construction in the West, however, posed a problem. Vast territories had to be crossed where there were no settlements and no states or local governments able to give aid. There also was considerable uncertainty about the costs of construction through two mountain ranges. The size of the capital funds required also would be large, and the federal government, already incurring a large wartime debt, was not anxious to undertake all of the financing.

The making of large land grants to the railroads, therefore, seemed like a reasonable solution; for the railroads could sell their own bonds to private investors secured by the mortgages on this land. Eventual sale of the land, as land prices rose along the railroad line, would be expected to provide funds to pay off the bonds. Still, the original promoters of the Union Pacific hesitated to get under way with construction; so, the 1862 act was modified in 1864 to increase the land allotments. Under the law both the Union Pacific and the Central Pacific were to receive a 400-foot right-of-way, 10 alternate sections of land on each side of the tracks (or 12,800 acres per mile of track), and government loans ranging from $16,000 to $48,000 per mile, depending on the difficulty of construction. The government loans were secured by second mortgages on the land, and the railroads pledged toward bond retirement 5 percent of their net revenues and one half of any revenues on movement of troops or government freight.

During the next seven years, federal land grants also were extended to other western railroads. Over the whole period, 1850 to 1871, 175 million acres had been granted by Congress, although 35 million were forfeited and returned when part of the construction contracts were not fulfilled. It has been estimated that one fourth of the land in Minnesota and Washington was in railroad grants and from one fifth to one eighth in other western states. In addition, some states added about 48 million acres in land grants of their own. Only six of the railroads received government loans, but the toal amounted to over $64 million. Virtually all of the loans were repaid in full with 6 percent interest by 1899.

Obviously these land grants were on a huge scale and represented very sizable subsidies to privately owned railroad companies. Historians have disagreed about the proper valuation of the land grants and whether they were justified in terms of the real costs of building the railroads. The government, of course, did not have to put up the money, and there is little doubt that the cost to the government was recouped eventually. Public land during this period was selling for less than $1 an acre. Since the railroads sold their land over many decades and captured much of the rewards of rising land values, they received an estimated $3.42 an acre from sales. Thus, the value of the federal land grants has been estimated anywhere between $131 million and $448 million. Yet the rate savings to the government for its own freight and troops carried by land-grant railroads alone has been estimated at well over $500 million.

A public outcry later arose over certain scandals that were revealed in the financing and construction of the railroads. A congressional investigating committee in 1873 reported that the actual construction costs of the Union Pacific were no greater than the government loan and the amount of first mortgage bonds issued by the company; yet the construction firm, the Credit Mobilier, had received much more. About 48 percent of the construction costs were its profit. This construction firm turned out to be owned by a group of the railroad's directors and officers; so, they had overpaid themselves for the construction at the expense of stock owners and bondholders in the railroad.

This type of maneuver by inside promoters was not unusual, and it was one of the ways by which railroad companies became overcapitalized—or their stock became "watered"—a condition in which the value of the property is worth much less then the face value of the bonds and stocks issued. Sometimes new stocks were issued as "dividends" to create the impression of profits and expansion. In the late 1860's and early 1870's, a few unscrupulous men—such as Jim Fisk, Jay Gould, and Dan Drew—milked their firms dry of funds and manipulated stocks to make a fortune in the stock markets. Usually these maneuvers were not clearly illegal, but in a few cases, there were outright frauds, such as when the president of one railroad issued unauthorized stock for sale and then left the country with the funds. However, we should note that "overpricing" of railroad stocks and bonds reflected the high risks born by the construction companies since they often agreed to take payment in securities of the railroad which they might not be able to dispose of except at considerable discount.

The popular concern over these scandals was not so much over the excessiveness of federal subsidies as over the financial losses that were widely experienced. In addition to the federal help to western railroads, local aid had continued to be poured into eastern roads. The southern states also went heavily into debt on behalf of southern railroads. Furthermore, bonds and stocks of railroads had been widely purchased by many thousands of small businessmen and farmers. As the railroads lost money or went bankrupt, many people suffered losses on their investments. Likewise, the farmers' complaints about high freight rates were aggravated by a belief that "insiders" had overloaded the capital costs and were making fortunes at rate payers' expense. It was during the depression of the 1870's that public disillusionment with railroad financing set in and also when agitation for state regulation began.

Railroad Rate Discrimination

It was at this point in American history that we first faced semi-monopoly business conditions on a national scale, thus the public was slow in understanding the nature of the problem. In theory, a single-producing firm in a particular market tends to restrict its output and sell at somewhat higher rates than a similar competitive firm would. On a state and local level, therefore, it long had been recognized that any unavoidable monopoly required public regulation of prices. Even in Colonial times, some grain mills were regulated; and in the early years of the Nation, state incorporation of a bank, canal company, or railroad was assumed to involve the granting of a monopoly privilege which then was hedged with restrictions, such as rate limits. Later, however, the popular desire to promote railroad development left out considerations of rate regulation. The public gains from any railroad service were expected to be large while the prospects for railroad profits looked limited.

Conditions in railroading were confusing. Along the routes through rural areas and small towns a railroad might provide the only transportation service and thus be a monopoly; but between the larger cities there were several parallel lines and a web of indirect routes operated by competing railroad companies. Both sets of conditions tended to produce varying freight rates that discriminated among types of products, size of customers, and localities. It was this inequality in rates that caused the most protest. What the public did not understand was that it was not immoral skulduggery but something inevitable in the ***economic conditions of this type of industry which caused both price discrimination and rate wars.***

The basic difficulty was the high proportion of fixed costs to total costs in railroads. Most of the cost was in building the tracks and terminal facilities to begin with, a cost which had to be paid for in terms of fixed annual payments of interest and amortization on borrowed money. The costs of maintaining the rails and operating the trains also were relatively fixed; they did not change much with carrying more passengers or freight. Therefore, the more traffic that was carried, the more units that fixed costs could be divided by in figuring costs per unit of traffic; thus, higher volume meant lower rates. Conversely, if the demand for services was limited, the average costs would be high, for the fixed costs could not be reduced to fit the demand. In fact, any manager would have to recognize that the ***additional*** costs for handling any particular unit of traffic (the costs that vary solely with output) might be very low; and if any revenues in excess of these added costs could be earned by adding traffic even at very low rates, it would contribute that much more toward paying at least part of the fixed costs.

Now, it is a characteristic of monopoly pricing that a firm will charge different prices for the same product or service if its customers can be kept separate and if they have different demands. Even today, "natural" monopolies—such as local gas and electric companies—are permitted by public utility commissions to charge lower rates to some types of customers so long as it seems necessary to cover total costs and earn only a normal profit. It was inevitable, therefore, for railroads to charge ***discriminatory rates*** for different ***types of goods*** and different ***classes of customers*** along their exclusively monopolized routes.

The locations of larger shippers, moreover, usually gave them special bargaining power with the railroads. In larger cities, where the shipper had a choice of railroads and routes, he could bargain to give all of his business to the company which gave him the lowest rate. Sometimes, even though the large shipper was served only by one railroad, competition in national markets might force him out of business if his railroad did not give him rates similar to those of his competitors on other lines; and if a railroad did not recognize this in time, it might lose the revenues entirely of a firm on its line that was forced out of business. One way or another, therefore, the ***large shippers*** tended to have the bargaining power to force railroads to give them ***special rates.*** In order to keep other railroads from knowing and to avoid dissatisfaction with other customers, the special rates often were secret, sometimes in the form of special discounts or rebates. Naturally, there was much public protest when news leaked out about the low rates or rebates obtained by large firms, such as Standard Oil. Yet it should be noted that the railroads were trapped into this and suffered as well as other shippers.

One form in which special rates frequently showed up was in the difference in long-haul and short-haul rates. Sometimes the long-haul locations had more competitive rate situations than the short-haul locations. Another source of rate differences by distance, however, arose simply from a cost difference. Unlike passengers who simply ride the train and get off, freight must be loaded and unloaded on both ends; and these handling costs are an important part of the total transportation costs. Also, once a train had been assembled and sent on its way, the additional cost of traveling some extra distance, speaking comparatively, is not very great. So the cost per ton of a short haul tends to be larger than for along haul. In other words, transportation costs do not rise in proportion to the distance traveled. Similarly, there is some cost saving in handling large bulk shipments and full boxcar loads; so there is some cost justification for offering somewhat lower rates to large shippers.

Railroad Rate Wars

From the point of view of the farmer or small businessman, rate discrimination simply looked like the railroads were exercising their monopoly powers in charging the little fellow whatever high rates they wished. Because of their location in low-density areas farmers especially had to ship from the high-cost, noncompetitive shipping points. To the railroads, however, their competitive position seemed very precarious. They could not earn enough from the limited traffic from small towns and rural regions to cover the high costs of running a regional rail network. Yet between the larger cities there was keen competition for the remaining available traffic. Unfortunately the railroads in many cases overbuilt in trying to round out their access to major commercial centers and distributing points and in seeking to keep up with the services offered by their rivals or in some cases in seeking to drive them out.

Here again the high fixed costs (as well as the limited number of rivals) plagued the railroads, for there was the constant temptation to undercut the rates of rival railroads between the major cities in order to gain a larger share of the traffic. Even at very low rates, the added revenues still might exceed the additional variable costs of adding a few more boxcars to the train. The danger was that the same temptation faced the rival railroad, and both rivals had the capability of drastically lowering rates. Yet whenever they engaged in a rate-cutting war, both tended to lose revenues without any substantial increase in overall traffic. Thus, rate-cutting was mutual suicide or "throat-cutting." It was this peculiarly unstable kind of competition (between a very few firms with high fixed costs) that has tended to give competition a bad name among businessmen. It is important to note, however, that "cut-throat competition" does not reflect highly competitive conditions, but semimonopolistic conditions.

Beginning in the 1850's, the railroads experienced their first rate wars, but the 1870's brought their most severe struggles. The depression reduced traffic and they found themselves overbuilt. A climax was reached in 1876–77, when freight rates from the East Coast to Chicago fell temporarily to one fifth their previous level. Passenger fares were cut almost in half. The rate wars, of course, were aggravated by the generally falling price conditions permitted by the government, as well as by the depression in traffic.

It might have been expected that the farmers would be happy about the temporary rate cuts. Farmers and other long-distance shippers, however, were angry when they found rates had fallen after they had shipped; for they had missed a saving by not waiting a little while. This put shippers into the position of having to speculate on what would happen to transport rates. The merchant especially was angry if his competitors shipped at a different time at lower rates and could undersell him in the destination markets.

The rate wars usually affected only the routes between major cities; so the farmer might hear about low rates elsewhere that he could not get locally. Furthermore, the rate wars only "proved" to the farmers what they already had suspected—the railroads could charge much lower rates at will. When the rates rose again, they seemed unnecessarily high. Thus, rate instability as well as discrimination stirred up protests.

Decline in Average Rates

During the depression of the 1870's, there was a widespread belief, therefore, that railroad rates were unjustifiably high. This view was frequently expressed at the local level, and nationally a congressional committee in 1874 argued this case. In wartime, increased taxes and higher prices had forced railroads to raise their rates. After the war, taxes were reduced and all prices were falling; but it was charged that railroad rates had not fallen as much as agricultural prices. The multi-

10–6. Railroad Freight Unit-Revenues

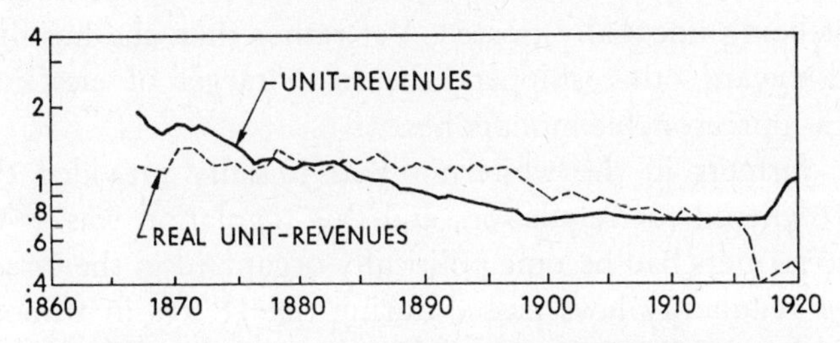

Source: U.S. Department of Commerce, *Historical Statistics of the United States* (Washington, D.C.: U.S. Government Printing Office, 1960), pp. 115–17, 428–31. Data prior to 1881 from *Report of the Industrial Commission* (Washington, D.C.: U.S. Government Printing Office, 1902), Vol. XIX, p. 280.

tude of different rates between particular places, however, made this difficult to determine one way or the other.

Actually, there appears to be little basis for the common belief that railroad rates generally were too high or too slow in falling. Average rates for all American railroads can be estimated by comparing total revenues with the total freight tonnage carried and the miles it was transported. These estimates clearly show that average revenues per ton-mile were falling during most of the period from 1867 to 1879 and were falling as fast as general wholesale prices. In the last chapter it was noted that farm prices fell no faster than all wholesale prices in this period. Furthermore, the average railroad revenues per ton-mile continued to fall at about the same rate as wholesale prices, dropping from 1.92 cents in 1867 to 0.73 cents in 1900. Thereafter, rail rates rose less rapidly than wholesale prices. Accordingly, the "real" rates (in dollars of constant purchasing power to the customers) were approximately constant until 1900 and declining thereafter. (See 10–6.)

Furthermore, the profit record of railroads does not show that they were prospering from exhorbitant rates. During depressions there were many bankruptcies and reorganizations. Yields on railroad bonds before World War I were little more than half their level immediately after the Civil War. While common stock yields for railroads in 1871–73 tended to be higher than for industrial and utility companies, during most years thereafter, the stock yields tended to be lower for railroads.

Regulation of Railroads

It was under these peculiar economic conditions in the railroad industry—semimonopoly, high fixed costs, discriminatory pricing, and cutthroat price wars among a few firms—that the first movement toward regulation of business was introduced at the national government level. The chief source of discontent was price discrimination—a feeling of being unequally treated. Yet rather than the hostility being expressed toward other shippers, the main target of attack was the railroads as unreasonable monopolies.

The farmers in the western plains initially provided the main source of demand for regulation, and this regulation was at the state level. The farmers had become politically organized in the Grange, and a series of regulatory laws passed during the 1870's in Illinois, Iowa, Wisconsin, and Minnesota are referred to as the "Granger Laws." Earlier regulation, of course, had been practiced in New England, and many of the initial railroad charters had incorporated rate limits; but the rapidly falling prices and rates in the post-Civil War period made these limitations ineffective.

State railway commissions were established to set rates and determine services and safety practices. Rate-setting, however, was a complicated matter; and if flat rates were arbitrarily set for all railroads regardless of differing conditions, one road might prosper while another went bankrupt. The attitudes of state legislatures in the western farm states tended to be unsympathetic toward railroads controlled by eastern investors. The railroad companies fought back by using funds to bribe or politically support legislators and to challenge legislation in the courts. In 1886, the Supreme Court severely limited state regulation by a ruling in the *Wabash* case that an Illinois law prohibiting short-haul-long-haul discrimination was an encroachment on the federal powers of regulating interstate commerce.

The passage of the Interstate Commerce Act of 1887 appeared to be precipitated by the Court's limitation of state regulatory powers. There also was some opinion at the time that state regulation was not fully effective against large railroad networks operating across numerous states. The railroads were the first giant corporations, and there was some public alarm at the potential powers of big business. Nevertheless, the impetus of the movement for federal regulation came not solely from the farmers protesting high rates. Rather, it also came from urban merchant groups and from the railroads themselves, both concerned with competitive rate-cutting. Congress actually had been debating regulatory legislation for several years, and both houses had approved different versions prior to the Supreme Court decision in 1886.

Eastern merchants and oil producers especially played a leading role in demanding federal regulation of railroads because they feared that rate-cutting by rival railroad trunk lines was hurting their interests, and the trunk lines were beyond the control of any one state. In 1881, the New York Central had initiated a particularly severe eastern rate war, claiming that lower rates to Baltimore and Philadelphia had diverted to those cities much of the east-west traffic and import-export business that would have gone to New York City. Independent oil producers claimed that Standard Oil had favored the Erie and victimized the Pennsylvania and other railroads.

Most of the railroads actually favored federal regulation, although their disagreements over particular measures in different bills frequently gave the appearance of opposition. This railroad viewpoint might seem surprising because of their opposition to state regulation; but the fear of more severe regulation at the state level was one source of their desire for federal action. Also the Great Railway Strike of 1877 had thoroughly frightened the railroad companies. The National Guard and federal troops had been used to maintain order. It was not unusual for businessmen of those times to look to government intervention to serve business interests, and regulation appeared to be an excuse to continue such intervention.

The main motivation of the railroads in seeking federal regulation, however, was a desire to prevent disastrous rate-cutting among themselves. Their own efforts at voluntary self-controls through rate agreements and "pools" (which involved allocating traffic among lines at agreed-upon rates) had utterly failed. Repeatedly the railroad companies had tried to make agreements and form associations to maintain rates. Always these agreements had broken down because independent railroads refused to join or some ambitious or hard-pressed line violated the agreements. While the newspapers and critics of the railroads viewed the pools with alarm as evidence of the great monopoly powers of railroads, the railroad leaders were discouraged with their inability to make the pools lasting or effective. It is not surprising, therefore, that a railroad lawyer wrote one of the proposed bills and that most railroad men testifying in congressional hearings favored some sort of federal legislation. What the railroads opposed was any provision outlawing pooling.

The legislative compromise in the Interstate Commerce Act resulted in a vaguely worded law to be administered at the discretion of a commission. With the appointment of commissioners identified with railroad interests, the result was largely a regulative failure from the shippers' point of view. Exceptions were allowed for certain forms of pooling. Shippers had to take the initiative of complaining and had the burden of proof. The Commission made it clear that it was chiefly concerned with unreasonably low rates that hurt investors and might impair service.

During the late 1890's, the Supreme Court made a series of decisions that limited the discretion of the Commission and denied it the power to regulate rates. Pooling also was declared a violation of monopoly laws. This returned the railroads to a chaotic condition of competitive instability. Between 1898 and 1903, the railroads participated, along with other businesses, in the merger movement. This may be interpreted as another attempt to escape the dangers of rate-cutting. But the railroad consolidations were not complete enough to include all competitors in a region, and the large networks still were plagued with small independents who would cut rates.

During the next few years a series of laws were passed that strengthened the powers of the Interstate Commerce Commission. Ironically, these laws provided the protection against competitive rate-cutting that the railroads desired, but they were interpreted by the public and by later historians as restrictions imposed on railroads against their will.[1] The Elkins Act, 1903, which was drafted and supported by railroad men outlawed rebating. Since rebating was defined as a deviation from published rates, and since nothing prevented railroads from publishing higher rates, the law obviously restricted secret rate-cutting. In 1906, the Hepburn Act required railroads to publish their rates, gave the Commission power to set and enforce maximum rates, and put the

[1] The traditional interpretation by historians resulted from a concentration on views of farmers, shippers, and politicians as revealed in newspapers, hearings and legislative debates. What the railroad leaders were saying and writing in their trade journals, however, has been skillfully analyzed by Gabriel Kolko in *Railroads and Regulation, 1877–1916* (Princeton, N.J.: Princeton University Press, 1965), which was awarded the Transportation History Prize by the Mississippi Valley Historical Association.

burden of proof on the railroads in appealing to the courts against the Commission's decisions. In 1910, the Mann-Elkins Act gave the Commission power to suspend a railroad's new rate until it had been investigated, and the Commission's power was restored to determine exceptions to the prohibition against higher rates for short hauls. While these powers could be used against the railroads, the policy of the Commission continued to be favorable to the railroads; and in 1914 a general rate increase was granted the railroads on the principle of allowing a fair return on investment. In 1913 and 1914, the Supreme Court also supported the supremacy of federal regulations over state regulations. Throughout this history, it was mostly the continued controversy over particular alternative proposals and the public statements of politicians that gave the appearance of federal regulation being forced upon an unwilling industry.

Antitrust Movement

Federal legislation regulating the railroads set the precedent and prepared public opinion for regulation of business monopolies generally. As in the case of the railroads, there was a background of state action. By 1890, 14 states had prohibitions of monopoly and restraint of trade in their constitutions, and 13 had specific laws on the subject. In the presidential campaign of 1888, both parties advocated federal antitrust legislation; but when legislation was introduced it was passed without hearings and little debate or amendments.

The initial regulatory effort was feeble. The Sherman Act was simple and vague. It outlawed "every contract, combination in the form of trust, or otherwise, or conspiracy in restraint of trade" and prescribed light fines or punishment for persons violating the law. Enforcement efforts also were limited. There were five cases filed in court during Harrison's administration, seven started under Cleveland, and five begun under McKinley.

The initial interpretation of the Supreme Court probably was a strong stimulus to the merger movement among businesses, which was opposite to the intention of the law. In 1895, the Court ruled in the *E. C. Knight* case that a merger of several companies into the American Sugar Refining Company, increasing its control from 65 to 98 percent of the Nation's production, did not constitute a violation of the law. Since the Court consistently held in other cases in the late 1890's that agreements between two or more businesses affecting prices or markets were illegal, the obvious message was that agreements were illegal but merger was not. Not until the *Northern Securities* case in

1904 did the Court declare that a merger that could destroy competiton was illegal. A very great number of business mergers, therefore, occurred between 1895 and 1904 as a direct result of the encouragement given by a combination of federal law and court interpretation.

The public reacted with alarm to the merger movement. The *Northern Securities* case was begun in 1902, and in 1903 Congress passed the Expediting Act giving preference in the courts to railroad and antitrust cases. A Department of Commerce and Labor was created with a subsidiary Bureau of Corporations which, as a purely research agency, began investigations of the Standard Oil and American Tobacco companies. President Theodore Roosevelt in the 1904 campaign promised vigorous antitrust prosecution, and 42 cases were begun in his administration. Fifty-two cases were started under Taft and 95 under Wilson. Although Wilson's prosecution score was higher than his predecessors' he had less faith in "trust busting" of "bad" business combinations than Taft or Roosevelt. Rather, he looked upon restoration of competitive markets through strict enforcement of trade regulations by the Federal Trade Commission as a resolution to problems arising from great industrial concentration.

Supreme Court decisions in 1911 then ordered the dissolution of both the Standard Oil Company and the American Tobacco Company. The Court, however, based its action on a "rule of reason" whereby combinations might be lawful as long as the restraint on competition was not unreasonable. The Court considered significant the evidence that the past history of these firms showed an intent to monopolize and that they had used predatory practices to this end—namely, the use of discriminatory rebates and price wars to drive rivals out of business.

Two decisions at the end of World War I further limited the application of the law against big business. In the *United Machinery Company* case the mergers were not declared illegal because the former companies had not been direct competitors. In the *United States Steel Corporation* case it was found that the company did not possess the power of complete monopoly and did not evidence the predatory practices that would indicate an intent to monopolize. "The law does not make mere size an offense," the Court said, "or the existence of unexerted power an offense."

In 1914, Congress had passed the Clayton Act and the Federal Trade Commission Act. The Clayton Act forbade price discrimination, exclusive selling and tie-in contracts, and price-cutting where it was intended to destroy a weaker competitor—although these provisions were difficult to enforce. The act excluded union and farm organizations from being considered monopolies. The Federal Trade Commission was created to enforce the Clayton Act, using the Interstate Commerce Commission as its model. It was given powers to investigate, to hold hearings, to issue "cease and desist" orders, and to initiate appeals to federal courts for enforcement.

On balance, the antitrust legislation was not severe nor very effective. The Sherman Act was vague, and the Clayton Act added provisions difficult to interpret and enforce. The Court vacillated between allowing, not allowing, and allowing mergers as monopolies. Its "rule of reason" and "mere size" principles seemed to recognize the status quo for any consolidation that had not been achieved by specifically disapproved practices.

Clearly the American public had become alarmed by the growth of big businesses. The principle of government intervention at the federal level to regulate business also had been established. There was no clear definition, however, of just what a monopoly was and exactly what business practices might be illegal; and so far, there was little willingness by political leaders to prosecute the antitrust laws vigorously. The high point of business mergers and industry concentration probably was reached in 1904. Thereafter, the extent of monopoly remained about the same or decreased. The antitrust laws may have had some dissuading value, but the growth of the economy and the vigor of competition by other growing firms also restrained the power of individual firms in most industries.

PUBLIC ADMINISTRATION AND SERVICES

The government also began to play a larger role in the economy in another way. Running its own affairs became increasingly complex and expensive, and the size of government operations gained a larger share of total economic activity. This was partly because government was called upon to perform more public services as well as to regulate private activities more.

Rising Government Expenditures

As we have seen, government expenditures tended to rise largely because of military expenditures, which remained higher after each war. Yet in comparison to the growing national output, the 19th-century expenditures of government were quite small and usually declining during peacetime. In 1860, total government expenditures at all levels may be estimated as around 6 percent of the gross national product. In 1870, they were nearly 15 percent, but the faster growth in national output reduced this to about 8 percent by 1890. After this, government expenditures about kept pace with the expansion in production. Then, by 1920, after the wartime demobilization, government expenditures had risen to about 11 percent of gross national product.

Except for the war-related expenditures, neither the largest amount nor the greatest increases in expenditures were at the federal level. In 1860 and in 1913, before each major war, the largest expendi-

10–7. Per Capita Government Expenditures

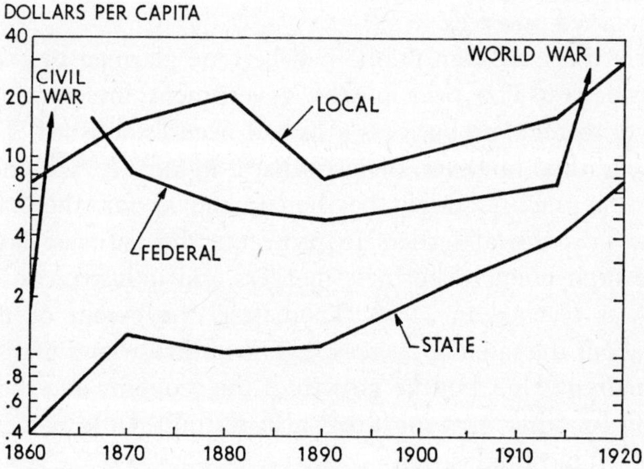

Source: Paul Studenski and Herman E. Krooss, *Financial History of the United States* (New York: McGraw-Hill Book Co., 1963), Table 1, p. 7.

tures were at the local levels of government. On a per capita basis, local governments were spending about $7.27 per person in 1860 compared to only $2.26 per person by the federal government and $0.43 by the state governments. In 1913, the corresponding amounts were $15.02, $7.01, and $3.89. The federal expenditures skyrocketed during wartime. In peacetime, local government expenditures rose especially rapidly right after the Civil War and again around the turn of the century. Over the whole period, it was the state government expenditures that rose the most rapidly compared to the others. (See 10–7.)

State governments had contributed materially to the military costs of the Civil War, and after the war they also provided large sums for veterans' bonuses and pensions. In the South, there were heavy reconstruction costs. Aid to railroads and construction of highways were important expenditures in the immediate postwar years. Heavy debts were incurred for all of these purposes.

The cities also engaged in an intensified rate of spending between 1866 and 1873. Rapid urban growth required enlargement of waterworks and sewer systems. There was a widespread move to pave city streets, first with bricks and after 1870 with asphalt. Bridges were built and gas pipes were laid. There also was a great surge in the construction of public buildings. Police and fire stations had to be added, and imposing city halls and courthouses were built. Museums, zoos, and parks were created. A great expansion in public education required the construction of schools and colleges. Cities also lent their credit freely to railroads; and New York City started construction of an elevated steam railway.

With the depression in the 1870's, both states and cities experienced a drop in revenues and sharply curtailed their spending. Both were hard pressed to keep up payments on their debts, and some states and some cities defaulted on their debt payments.

In the late 1880's and the late 1890's, there were further booms in city construction expenditures. Along with further extensions of waterworks, sewers, and streets, there was a surge of public utility construction to provide gas pipes and electric street lights. An electric street railway system was rapidly built in most major cities, and suburban lines were extended beyond the city limits. By the time of World War I, there was a rising demand for paved highways to accommodate the rising use of automobiles. State governments increased expenditures on highways, education, and public welfare, and both federal and state governments provided aid to lower levels of government for these purposes. (See 10–8.)

These rising expenditures not only increased government employment and activities, they required rising revenues. The collection of taxes, as well as government spending, affected the expenditures of private individuals and businesses. In 1902, the federal government still relied heavily upon customs and excise taxes (which may be considered as types of sales taxes), and its chief revenues were from land sales and postal charges. The reintroduction of corporate and individual income taxes just before World War I shifted the burden of taxes toward the higher income groups. State governments had the most diversified sources of taxes, and by 1922 they had increased their use of sales taxes and introduced income taxes also. The local governments continued to rely heavily upon property taxes. The revenues from various local utility services were the other main source of increased revenue. Because of the

10–8. Government Expenditures by Function
(Dollar Amounts in Millions)

	Federal		*State*		*Local*	
	1902	*1922*	*1902*	*1922*	*1902*	*1922*
Totals	$572	$3,763	$188	$1,397	$959	$4,567
Defense, foreign, veterans	306	1,300	...	80	...	...
Interest	29	988	10	45	58	337
Intergovernment	7	118	52	312	...	...
General	34	126	23	69	118	244
Postal and utility services	126	553	...	...	131	548
Transportation	22	308	4	303	171	991
Education	3	8	17	164	238	1,541
Police, fire, correction	...	14	14	68	90	344
Health, hospitals, welfare	7	103	42	163	55	214
Resources, parks, recreation	8	79	9	61	29	85
Other	30	156	17	78	69	242
Insurance trust	...	9	...	54	...	21

Source: U.S. Department of Commerce, *Historical Statistics of the United States* (Washington, D.C.: U.S. Government Printing Office, 1960), pp. 725–30.

limitations that states usually placed on the types of taxes that could be levied by local governments, a heavy transfer of funds from state to local governments was used to supplement local revenues. The federal government also began to provide more aid to state governments for highway, education and welfare programs. (See 10–9.)

10–9. Government Revenues by Source
(Dollar Amounts in Millions)

	Federal		*State*		*Local*	
	1902	*1922*	*1902*	*1922*	*1902*	*1922*
Totals	$653	$4,261	$192	$1,360	$914	$4,148
Intergovernment	...	...	9	126	56	321
Taxes:						
Property	...	...	82	348	624	2,973
Sales	487	1,152	28	134	...	20
Income	...	1,939	...	101	...	...
Other	26	281	46	364	80	76
Charges and other revenues	140	850	27	181	154	742
Insurance trust	...	40	...	106	...	16

Source: U.S. Department of Commerce, *Historical Statistics of the United States* (Washington, D.C.: U.S. Government Printing Office, 1960), pp. 724, 727–28, 729.

Problems of Administration

This increasing scale of expenditures and services created internal problems of administration in government, just as it was causing problems in business and the economy as a whole. Previously, American politics had been encouraged by the simplicity and small scale of government to use a patronage system of filling government jobs. It was assumed that anyone could run for office and that any of his supporters could perform the duties required in government jobs. As the size and complexity of government agencies increased, the incompetencies and corruption that accompanied this system were less tolerable.

Even before the Civil War, the rise in expenditures in large cities had created administrative problems and gave opportunities for politicians to divert funds to their own uses. Cities acquired more taxing and borrowing powers from legislatures, and reforms were attempted to give mayors more centralized administrative control. Council members, however, continued to meddle in administration and divide responsibility. In New York City the council came to be called "The Forty Thieves." In many states civic leaders attempted to reform the conditions by having the state legislature intervene more in municipal affairs, setting up numerous state-appointed state commissions. But this only perpetuated the problem of "invisible government," whereby independent authorities were responsible to no one.

Boss Tweed's political machine long ruled New York City for its own profit. In 1869–71, it reached the zenith of its power when it controlled both the city and the New York state legislature. An investigating committee estimated that a private business could have run the city government for one tenth the cost, and half of the city's debt was said to represent politicians' plunder. In Philadelphia, another political group was entrenched in a city-owned gas company run by trustees appointed by the city council. It employed 15 percent more workers than necessary and neglected repairs and maintenance until service broke down. With the depression of the 1870's and the default of many cities on their debts, a number of states adopted legislation or amendments limiting the borrowing and spending powers of cities.

Various reform movements, therefore, were started to curb the corruption and wasteful spending in local government. Reform charters were adopted for New York City in 1873, Boston in 1885, and Baltimore in 1898. Reformation centralized administrative power in the mayor, gave budget making and fiscal powers to a small financial board, and made the school board independent.

In spite of previous bad experiences with corruption and mismanagement in government, municipal ownership of some public utility services became more prevalent. In 1900, virtually all sewer systems were publicly owned, but only about half of the city waterworks were. The gas works and the street railways were almost completely private enterprises, but the electric light companies, which started later, were affected by the trend to municipal ownership and were about 15 percent publicly owned. Part of the reason for the popularity for government ownership of these "natural" monopolies was to be found in the disappointing experience with regulatory commissions. They had to deal with complicated and detailed matters. Emphasis upon reports, publicity and complaint procedures did little good if the public was not actively interested. The men appointed to the commissions tended to be from the ranks of those being regulated or were susceptible to their influence. Reform movements tended, therefore, to be passing public fads. Neither public ownership nor public regulation provided an easy solution to the problem of social control in situations where only one agency was needed to provide a service.

In the 1880's, a reform movement also had begun in the federal government. After the Civil War, Congress had wielded much power over the executive offices; and the legislators had been able to maintain their political organizations in their own states by appointing many workers to jobs in customhouses, post offices and various bureaus. Special legislation was passed to provide pensions as well as special business privileges. Scandals were revealed affecting officials in Grant's administration as well as members of Congress. So demands began to grow for reforms in the federal government and the appointment of government workers on a merit basis. In 1883, Congress passed the Pendleton Act setting up a Civil Service Commission and providing for competitive examinations in certain classified jobs.

President Cleveland tried to improve further the federal administration. The Navy and Interior Departments were reorganized. Greater independence from congressional interference was asserted by the President in making appointments. Studies of the Treasury resulted in some improvements in fiscal procedures. But for many years the division of appropriating responsibilities among many committees of Congress prevented any unified budget decisions. President Roosevelt also made efforts to have the organization and methods of the federal government studied and improved; but no centralized budget-making procedures or powers were developed.

The federal government tried to copy business organization in operating some agencies that sold services, but there was little uniformity in the way they were organized or administratively supervised. The postal service was operated as a separate entity, and only its operating deficits or surpluses were counted in the budget. The Panama Canal, the Alaska Railroad, the Reclamation Service, and the Inland Waterways were operated as subsidiaries of major departments; but their expenses were listed as a part of the department appropriations, while their receipts were shown as miscellaneous receipts of the Treasury.

War Mobilization

World War I threw a tremendous burden of administration on the federal government for which it was greatly unprepared. The rapid establishment of a selective service system enabled large numbers of men to be drafted, but there were delays in training and equipping them for the mechanized nature of modern war. If it were not for the Allies' provision of transportation, American troops might not have gotten to the battlefields before the war was over. When they got there, they fought with French and British cannon. American production of ships and arms was just beginning to reach its peak when the Armistice was declared.

World War I was the first war in American history for which the entire economy needed to be organized, for over 20 percent of the national production needed to be shifted to wartime needs. A War Industries Board was organized purely by administrative directives from the President, and it was served mostly by volunteer workers from industry who received only the nominal pay of one dollar to indicate their official status. These so-called "dollar-a-year men" operated in industry sections to allocate scarce materials, set priorities, and fix prices. A Food Administration was set up to persuade the public to reduce consumption of scarce foods and to stimulate production. For the latter purpose it established the U.S. Grain Corporation to serve as a centralized purchasing agent on all purchases of grain for the government, the Allies, and the Red Cross. The Sugar Equalization Board similarly purchased all the U.S. and Cuban sugar crops and sold them to refineries. The U.S. Fuel Administration was established to encourage production, conserve supplies and distribution, and fix prices of fuel—especially of coal. A Railroad War Board of railway executives was established to facilitate shipments to the East Coast; but because of a jam of boxcars in eastern freight yards, the President had to order an emergency seizure of the railroads to put them under direct government operation. The efficiency of this operation is a matter of dispute, but the railroads were compensated for their loss of normal profits during the government's period of operation. A Shipping Board was established to build merchant ships, and an Emergency Fleet Corporation was set up as a subsidiary to operate the ships. A War Labor Board was established by administrative order with no legal authority, but it relied on persuasion and public opinion to settle worker disputes with management. For the emergency period, the union representatives on that board won for unions the right of workers to join unions and not be discharged for union activity.

All in all, this first great war mobilization effort was a mixed success, but it set many precedents and stirred up much re-thinking of government administration. The National Defense Act of 1920 authorized peacetime planning for industrial mobilization; and later an Army-Navy Munitions Board and an Army Industrial College were formed to study procedures and train personnel for future war mobilization needs. Reform of government fiscal procedures also was stimulated in the passage of the Budget and Accounting Act of 1921, which established both the Bureau of the Budget and the independent General Accounting Office. The rapid establishment of large new federal agencies and independent corporations to undertake emergency tasks was to influence public proposals for government action in the emergency of a major depression during the 1930's.

STUDY QUESTIONS

1. In American history why have major price inflations occurred only in wars? Compare the government financing of the Civil War and World War I.
2. After the Civil War what was the "sound finance" policy and what effect did it have on the economy? What types of currency expanded in 1875–85, 1895–1904, and 1916–20? Over the whole period, 1870–1914, what part of the money stock expanded the fastest? What control did the federal government exercise over the money stock?
3. What was the purpose of the National Banking Act, and how did it work? What was the purpose of the Federal Reserve Act, and what did it provide?
4. Using the quantity theory of money, explain the changes in the wholesale price index from 1870–80, 1880–95, 1895–1915, and 1915–20.
5. How did the federal government use two major sources of revenue partly for its own purposes and partly as a stimulus to development? Why were land grants to railroads thought to be necessary? Why were they later criticized?
6. What happened to the trend of average real prices of railroad service in 1870–1900 and 1900–20? What was the basic source of criticism of railroad

rates? What were the main sources of discriminatory rates in railroads? Why did railroads engage in rate wars? Why did rate-cutting not please shippers?

7. Why did government regulation start in railroading? Why did the railroad companies favor a shift to federal regulation? Why was antitrust legislation initially stimulating to mergers and later not very effective?
8. What were the main sources of increased per capita government spending? How was increasing size of organization a problem for government as well as for business? Why was the mobilization of the economy for World War I only a "mixed" success?

PART IV

Adjusting to Growth, 1920 To Current Times

Chapter 11 THE CHANGING BASIS OF GROWTH

By the end of World War I the United States had achieved not only world leadership in production and per capita income but also a new type of economy. Historians have found it useful to apply the term "Commercial Revolution" to the transformation of a feudal traditional economy into a market economy. The term "Industrial Revolution" has been applied to the transformation of production methods through the use of machinery and power to mass-produce standardized goods. Perhaps someday it will be useful to refer to recent decades as the period of the "Scientific Revolution"; the chief characteristic of the modern economy and the basis for its continued growth is the extent to which the systematic effort to discover and disseminate new knowledge is changing not only productive activity but also consumption and social patterns.

Technology's transformation of society has produced a sweeping disruption of previous patterns, and such broad social change is seldom smooth and easy; it requires sweeping adjustments that affect workers, farmers, urban dwellers, governments, and the business community. Thus the rapid growth of the American economy is not entirely a success story. The record is full of problems as well as achievements. The changes that brought growth have introduced strains in social relations as well. New conditions have required new forms of organization, and attitudes have been slow to adjust to new conditions.

As we all recognize, the periodic wars and continual international hostility among nations that have characterized modern history have introduced stress and the need for readjustments in our economy. But even without the influence of international competition for political power, the technological changes that have given our growth a new basis would have produced significant adjustment problems. What is more, the arrival of the Scientific Revolution in only that part of the world which we call developed has constituted a basis for international tensions.

The story of recent economic development, therefore, is a story of continuing rapid change with attendant problems of incomplete adjustment. This chapter begins with a survey of trends and is followed with an analysis of the nature of technological change and concludes by discussing the shifts in industrial structure that have occurred since the end of World War I. Later chapters take up the problems of national instability, group and individual insecurity, the problem of increased size of business organization, and world rivalries—all as consequences of rapid economic growth.

TRENDS SINCE WORLD WAR I

Rate of Growth

By the time of World War I, the United States had become the greatest industrial nation in the world. But could it continue its rapid pace of growth?

This question might have been suggested by the experience of other nations. The first industrial nation, Great Britain, already had slowed down in its growth late in the 19th century. In 1913, the newer industrial nations, Germany and Japan, were growing at a faster rate than the United States. The United States, in fact, also had had its fastest growth in its early industrialization and railroad building periods just before and after the Civil War.

During the booming 1920's there were few who doubted that America's capacity for continued rapid progress was unlimited. Then the Great Depression of the 1930's struck. Unemployment was more severe and prolonged than ever before. Recovery was slow so that it was virtually a decade of depression. The blow to American optimism was shattering.

The question then was raised publicly: Has long-term growth leveled off? Must a mature economy stagnate? Three main conditions seemed to provide a basis for a gloomy outlook.

The first basis for fear of stagnation was the slowdown in the rate of population increase. The United States along with other European industrial nations had experienced a decline in birthrates while the death rate had leveled off after its earlier decline. Therefore, the natural increase in population (the births minus the deaths) was slowing down in modern societies. Immigration into this country also had been drastically curtailed by laws passed in 1921 and 1924, which set limited quotas on new entrants by country of origin. Whereas immigration had provided almost half of the population increase in the first decade of this century, it accounted for only one fourth in the 1920's and less than one tenth thereafter. While total population increased 21 percent in the first decade, it increased 15 percent in the next two and only 7 percent in the 1930's (although it recovered to 19 percent in the 1950's). Over the long sweep of American history, the rate of increase in population has slowed down gradually. In 50-year intervals, national population was four and one third times larger in 1860 than in 1810, three times larger in 1910 than in 1860, and two times larger in 1960 than in 1910.

The second basis for fear of stagnation was the limitation of natural resources. The continental territory of the United States had been established by 1853, and the westward movement to settle this territory initially had been completed around the turn of the century. In a sense, the natural resources were fixed, and only more intensive utilization was possible. Between 1870 and 1900 land in farms doubled, but by 1956 a peak of farm acreage (about one-third larger) had been reached. Also very little virgin timberland outside of national forests remained. The reserves of minerals in the ground still were being explored, but much of what was discovered was found at greater depths or in lower grade concentrations. For each of the extractive industries—agriculture, timber, and minerals—output increased slower than total national output. By 1940, the United States had become a net importer in all three major extractive industries.

The third basis for the fear of stagnation was uncertainty about the continued pace of technological change. Previous periods of most rapid economic growth had been associated with major technological breakthroughs that had led to rapid investment in new industries. Early in the previous century, the cotton gin and farm machinery had laid the basis for rapid expansion of farm exports. Also, innovations in machinery, metals and steam power had started the industrialization process. In the middle of the century, heavy investment in railroads had stimulated investment. Around the turn of the century, heavy investments in electric power and street railways had occurred. The auto industry obviously was a major stimulator of investment and growth just before and after World War I; but the growth of this industry, too, could be expected to slow down after a few decades of rapid investment. Studies of many industries have revealed a common pattern of rapid initial expansion followed by a slowing down to the all-industry average rate or less. In the midst of the depression of the 1930's, therefore, no major new industries appeared to be providing the new stimulus to expansion —or so people thought. In each generation, the major technological changes causing rapid expansion have been clearer in retrospect, while the source of future expansion remained uncertain.

Yet, these fears have not been confirmed by the historical record of the postdepression decades. National economic growth has continued to be rapid in spite of the long interruption of the Great Depression. To be sure, some slowdown did occur in the trend of total output along with the slowdown in population increase. As shown in Chapter 8, real gross national product had annual average rates of increase of 4.3 percent and

11–1. Continued Expansion of Production and Population

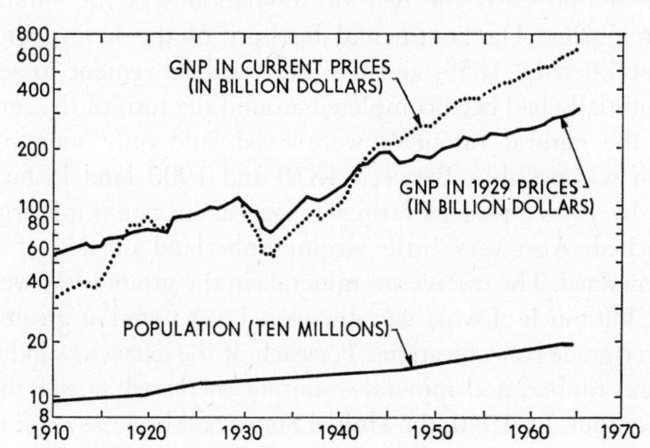

Source: U.S. Department of Commerce, *Historical Statistics of the United States* (Washington, D.C.: U.S. Government Printing Office, 1960), pp. 7, 139; data after 1954 from *Economic Report of the President, 1966* (Washington, D.C.: U.S. Government Printing Office, 1966).

3.7 percent during the two 40-year periods of 1839–79 and 1879–1919. During 1919–59, it was about 3.0 percent. Yet, the output slowdown was not as great as the population slowdown; so, the growth rate of output per person was maintained. The annual average rate of increase in GNP per person had been 1.55 percent in 1839–79, and 1.76 percent in 1879–1919, and during 1919–59 it was 1.64. (See 11–1 and 11–2.)

Real fluctuations around this trend were magnified by price changes. Inflationary price increases in World War I suddenly raised the level of national output in dollar values. There was little postwar setback to prices, and during the 1920's the long-term trend continued. The Great Depression of the 1930's, however, brought a severe decline in price levels generally as well as a reduction in real output. Another

11–2. Rising Trend of Production per Person

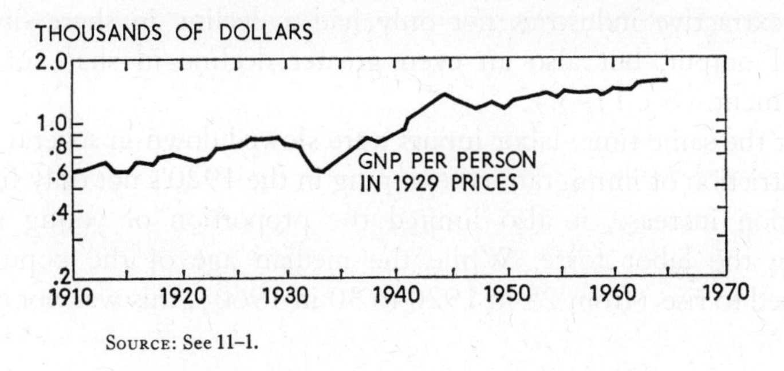

Source: See 11–1.

period of rapid inflation along with rising output occurred during World War II. Then, the continued inflation after the war disguised a setback in real output which was not fully overcome until the Korean War. The continued rapid growth of output with stable prices from 1955 to 1965, however, reestablished the pattern of the long-term trend.

Sources of Gains

What explains this record of continued rapid intensive growth in spite of a slowdown in the rate of expansion? This question cannot be answered in exactly the same manner as for previous periods because the end of the frontier limited the rate of expansion of natural resource inputs. Scarcity of natural resources might be expected to raise the cost of output in terms of more required labor and capital inputs. A rising output per worker still might be maintained if capital inputs were increased much faster. Yet, during the depression, many people feared that it was mechanization that was putting workers out of jobs. Fortunately, the historical record did not bear out the fears of either resource scarcity or labor displacement. While the proportions of factor inputs did shift, output gains continued to be rapid in the face of a slowdown in all inputs.

While resource inputs slowed down the most, there is little indication that scarcity was a seriously limiting factor. Instead of the costs of labor and capital rising, extractive industries generally (agricultural, timber, and mineral products) had faster reductions in labor and capital requirements per unit of product (or productivity gains) than did all other industries. Also, as income and consumption levels rose, people did not consume more raw materials per person. Instead, they demanded an increase in processing of commodities (both farm and industrial) and more distribution services as well as other services. As a result, extractive industries not only had a decline in share of total national output, but also an even greater decline in share of total employment. (See 11–3.)

At the same time, labor inputs were slowed down in several ways. The restriction of immigration beginning in the 1920's not only limited population increase, it also limited the proportion of young adults entering the labor force. While the median age of the population continued to rise (from 25 in 1920 to 30 in 1960), this was not due to

11–3. RESOURCE TRENDS, 1920–54

	1920	*1954*
Prices relative to all wholesale prices (Index, 1947–49 = 100):		
All extractive industries	83	90
Agriculture	78	82
Timber products	62	104
Minerals	105	107
Output as percent of GNP (1954 prices):		
All extractive industries	21	12
Agriculture	14	8
Timber products	2	0.69
Minerals	4.9	3.3
Employment as percent of total employment:		
All extractive industries	28.5	11.8
Agriculture	25.2	10.1
Timber products	0.4	0.3*
Minerals	2.7	1.2

* Data for 1950.

SOURCE: J. L. Fisher and E. Boorstein, *Study of Employment, Growth and Price Levels,* Joint Economic Committee, 86th Cong., 1st sess., Study Paper No. 13 (Washington, D.C.: U.S. Government Printing Office, 1959), p. 43.

a decrease in the proportion of children, but to an increase in the proportion of persons over 65. The total labor force, therefore, increased slightly less than did population after 1920, and no longer were gains in output per capita aided by a greater proportion of the population being in the labor force. At the same time, average hours worked continued to fall so that total man-hours did not increase as much as the labor force. (The resulting increase in leisure time, of course, was one of the intangible benefits of progress that is not recorded in the measure of increased output.) Offsetting these trends retarding the increase in labor input was the continued shift in the distribution of workers toward the more productive industries and skills. This increased effectiveness of man-hours is reflected in the labor input measure by means of weighting man-hours by the average annual earnings in each industry. The resulting measure of total labor inputs shows a somewhat larger increase than man-hours but still less than the increase in population; so, labor input did not contribute to the gains in output per capita in this period. (See 11–4.)

Input in capital also slowed down. Gross capital formation actually continued at about the same proportion of gross national product—about 20.2 percent in the 1946–55 decade compared to 20.6 percent in the 1909–18 decade. Because the capital stock grew larger, capital consumption absorbed a larger proportion of gross national product—15.1 percent compared to the earlier 10.7 percent. As a result, net capital

11–4. Measures of Changes in Labor Input, 1919–57

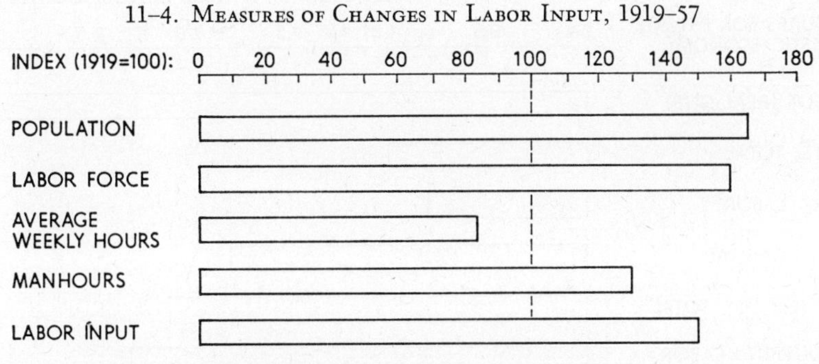

Source: John W. Kendrick, *Productivity Trends in the United States* (Princeton, N.J.: Princeton University Press, 1961), Tables AVII, A IX, A XI, A XIII.

formation slowed down—from 9.9 percent to 5.1 percent of gross national product. During the depression and war decades it had been even smaller; so the increase in capital stock over the whole period was greatly retarded. Continued military defense expenditures in the 1950's, in fact, still reduced the margin for economic progress shown by Kendrick's estimates. While he had estimated a margin (after provision for consumption, capital maintenance, and population increase) of 5.6 percent in the 1909–18 decade, the margin was only 1.9 percent in 1954–59. Allowing the same 1.2 percent for increasing consumption per person, only 0.7 percent was left for expanding capital per person.[1]

Still, capital inputs continued to grow faster than labor inputs. Between 1919 and 1957, capital stock in the private domestic economy almost doubled, while labor input increased little more than a third.

[1] John W. Kendrick, *Productivity Trends in the United States* (Princeton, N.J.: Princeton University Press, 1961), p. 100.

The result was a continued rise in the ratio of capital per worker. This meant that workers had more and more assistance in their labors—more machinery, buildings, and inventories to work with. (Continued rise in fuel and power per worker aslo reduced the muscle power needed.) The higher ratio of capital to labor again helped to raise the productivity of workers and thus contributed to the continued rise in output per capita.

Only a small part of the growth, however, can be explained by the increased capital per worker alone. Several economists independently have estimated that only 10 to 15 percent of the growth in output per

11–5. PRODUCTIVITY TRENDS, POST-WORLD WAR I

1919–1957 AVERAGE ANNUAL RATES (PERCENT)
MEASURES FOR PRIVATE DOMESTIC ECONOMY:
0 0.5 1.0 1.5 2.0 2.5 3.0
OUTPUT (REAL GNP)
INPUTS, TOTAL
LABOR
CAPITAL
PRODUCTIVITY, TOTAL
OUTPUT / LABOR
OUTPUT / CAPITAL

SOURCE: John W. Kendrick, *Productivity Trends in the United States* (Princeton, N.J.: Princeton University Press, 1961), Table A XXII.

capita could have resulted from the faster rise in capital if no change in initial technology had taken place. This leaves a large unexplained residual, which usually has been attributed to technological change.

The most outstanding fact about the continued rate of rapid growth in recent decades has been the upturn in the rate of productivity increase. The annual rate of increase in the ratio of output to total factor inputs was 1.2 percent during the 1889–1919 period, but during 1919–57 it was 2.1 percent. A similar rise occurred in the productivity ratios for each factor separately because output increased faster than any major input. The annual rates of increase in the two periods rose from 1.6 percent to 2.3 percent for output per unit of labor and from 0.5 percent to 1.3 percent for output per unit of capital. (See 11–5.)

Technological change, or improvement in methods, is implied by this greater increase in output than in any of the inputs—materials, labor or capital. While technological improvement was not new to the modern period, the dependence of nearly all of the growth on technological change was new and significant. In spite of the slowdown in all inputs, rapid growth was maintained by a more rapid rise in productivity. This alone is good reason for suspecting that the modern period is a new age of technological advance.

Before jumping to the conclusion that investment in capital no longer was important to continued growth, however, three qualifications about the measures used may be noted. First, most of the improvements in methods had to be embodied in new machinery through investment before output could be expanded. New labor skills also had to be acquired. The improvements also involved new types of materials and products. Second, the quantitative measures of inputs and outputs do not take adequate account of these qualitative changes in both the factors and the products. And third, the improvements in methods were achieved largely with the aid of new forms of capital investment that were not recorded in the measures of tangible property. Both investments in research and investments in education of workers may be considered as creating intangible forms of capital. The basic idea of investment or capital formation is that current nonconsumption uses of resources raise future production capabilities. This is true of expenditures to develop a new process or product and to educate workers as well as of expenditures to build a machine. Yet customary accounting practice does not record expenditures on research and education as additions to the stock of capital assets in a business or in a nation. So hidden forms of capital investment may be involved in modern technological advances.

Shares of Rewards

In view of the continued importance of capital and the heightened importance of technological change in maintaining economic growth, how were the rewards of progress distributed? This question needs to be reexamined for each historical period because of the traditional fears that progress may be achieved at the expense of workers; that property incomes will take a larger share of the pie, and that incomes will be distributed more unequally.

In spite of the faster rise in capital inputs, the labor share of national income payments increased after 1920. Wage and salary compensation averaged around 60 percent of the national income during the 1920's and rose to 70 percent in 1957. In part, of course, this was due to the decline in self-employment and in the number of proprietors of unincorporated small businesses (mostly in farming). Incomes of proprietors and the self-employed fell from 17 to 12 percent of national income. Incomes in the form of rent, interest and corporate profit, however, also declined from 23 percent to 18 percent. In order to make his productivity estimates, John Kendrick subdivided the income of the self-employed group into labor and capital shares on the assumption that the same rate of income on their own labor was earned as the average rate paid to hired labor in the same industry. Accordingly, he estimated that labor's total share of income rose from 72 percent in 1919 to 81 percent in 1957 while capital's share fell from 28 percent to 19 percent. Regardless of the accuracy of this method of estimation, it is clear that labor's share rose and capital's share fell.

Since labor inputs increased more slowly than capital inputs, it is logically implied that the real earnings per man-hour must have risen more than did the income per unit of capital. Yet, since output increased much more than the combined inputs, it is possible that the real earnings per unit rose for both labor and capital. John Kendrick, in fact, has estimated that the real income per unit of capital rose at an annual rate of only 0.3 percent. He interprets this as due to a slight increase in the prices and quality of capital goods for he saw little change in the rate of return on investment. Real earnings per unit of labor, on the other hand, were estimated to have increased at an annual rate of 2.7 percent. This is faster than the increase in labor productivity of 2.3 percent per year. The conclusion Kendrick reached is that labor absorbed nearly all of the increase in total productivity.[2]

This conclusion is confirmed by other attempts to estimate labor productivity and real average hourly earnings, both for manufacturing alone and for the whole nonfarm sector of the private economy. Real hourly earnings indexes usually start lower and rise higher than the indexes of output per man-hour over long periods of time. (See 11–6.)

Again this does not mean that all individuals shared equally in the gains in real income. Some individuals received very large salaries which are included in the labor earnings; and relatively few people were owners of a large share of the wealth—which provides rent, interest, and profit incomes. It is only since the start of the federal income tax in 1914 that statistics are available on individual incomes, and in the early decades only the upper income groups reported incomes for tax purposes.

In regard to the very wealthy group, the top 5 percent of all

[2] *Ibid.*, chap. V.

11–6. Nonfarm Labor Productivity and Earnings

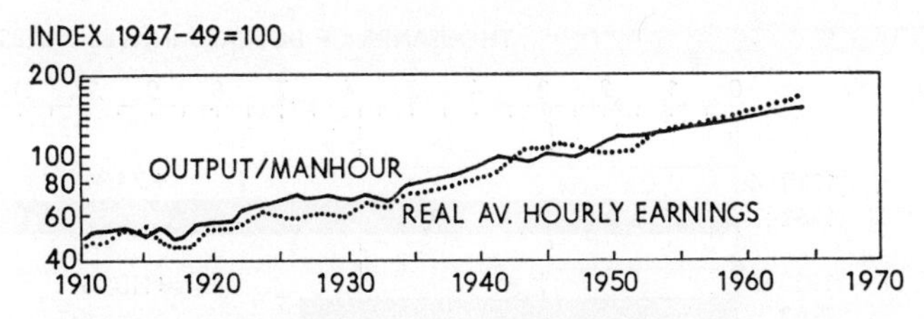

Source: Joint Economic Committee, *Productivity, Prices, and Income: Materials Prepared by Staff*, 85th Cong., 1st sess. (Washington, D.C.: U.S. Government Printing Office, 1957), Table 49; extended by U.S. Department of Commerce *Statistical Abstract of the United States, 1965* (Washington, D.C.: U.S. Government Printing Office, 1966), Table 317.

income receivers, the record shows that they received a declining share of total incomes after taxes. This top 5 percent of families received around 25 percent of incomes in 1917 and in the late 1920's but less than 20 percent in the early 1960's. Most of the decline occurred during World War II when income tax rates were raised; but some long-term declines also came about during the 1930's and the 1950's. The lowest 20 percent of income receivers, on the other hand, do not show as definite a trend. Their share was about 4 percent during the 1930's and rose to 5 percent during World War II. But during the late 1950's and early 1960's this gain was partly lost (when their share declined to 4.6 percent). (See 11–7.)

A more detailed picture of the long-term change in income distribution can be gained by comparing incomes in 1935–36 and 1962 for each fifth of the families ranked by incomes after taxes. Two main facts should be noted from this comparison. First, as the Nation progressed and the average real incomes of all families rose 98 percent, all

11–7. Trends in Shares of Income Received by Highest and Lowest Income Families

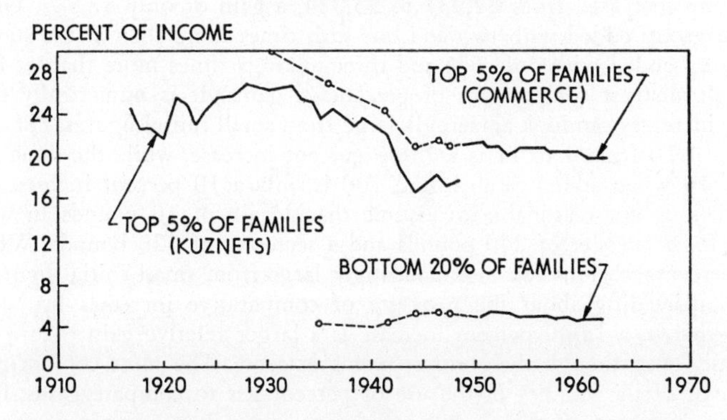

Source: U.S. Department of Commerce, *Historical Statistics of the United States* (Washington, D.C.: U.S. Government Printing Office, 1960), pp. 166–7 (Kuznets' data 1917–47; Commerce data 1950 on, with earlier comparable estimates).

11–8. Average Real Income by Income Groups, 1935–36 and 1962

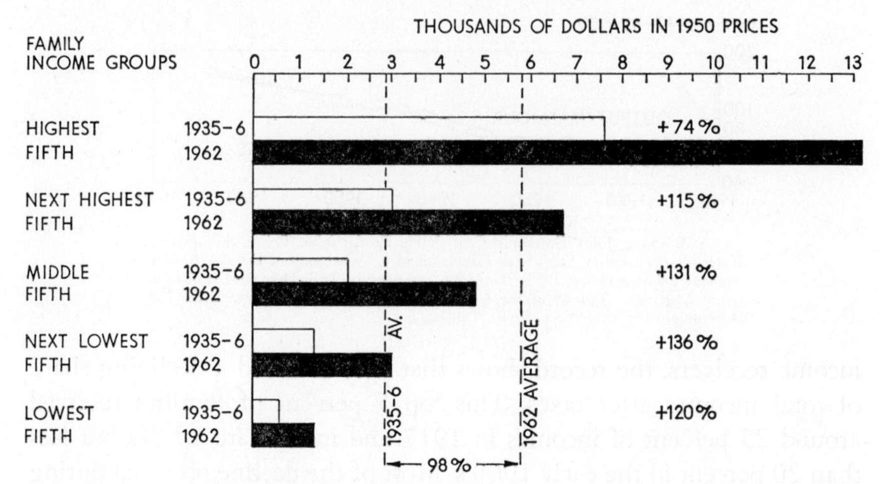

Source: U.S. Department of Commerce, *Statistical Abstract of the United States, 1965* (Washington, D.C.: U.S. Government Printing Office, 1966), p. 340.

groups of income receivers shared in the gains absolutely. Second, it was the lower three fifths of the families that made the greatest percentage gains. The only group increasing slower than the national average was the top income group and the next highest income group had the next lowest percentage gains.[3] (See 11–8.)

These comparisons of relative gains in income by groups are seen even more clearly in terms of shares of total income. The highest

[3] As a statistical footnote, it may be noted that there is much confusion over the appropriate measures to use when comparing income gains among high- and low-income receivers. This is because the ***absolute gains*** are larger for those who start at a higher level. The top group, for example, started with an average income of $7,591 and increased their average to $13,236, a gain of $5,645, while the bottom group increased from $2,937 to $5,824, a gain of only $2,887. Of course, the bottom group ended with two and one-fifth times more than at the start, while the top group ended with only one and three-quarters times more than at first. Yet many people distrust comparisons of percentage gains. It is numerically true that percentage increases can look amazingly large from small initial figures. For example, an increase of 10 from 1 to 11 is a 1,000 percent increase, while the same absolute increase of 10 when added to an initial 100 is only a 10 percent increase. On the other hand, it is not reasonable to assume that a gain of 10 pounds in weight is equivalent for a wrestler of 240 pounds and a secretary of 120 pounds. While it is true that percentage gains can look amazingly large from small initial figures, there is nothing misleading about the ***ranking*** of comparative increases by percentage measures—that is, a 1,000 percent increase is a larger relative gain than a 10 percent increase, even though the contrast seems extreme. The most convincing argument in favor of the validity of the use of percentages to compare gains, however, can be made in terms of ***shares.*** Whenever one group has a larger percentage increase than the total for all groups, it necessarily must have increased its share (or percent of total).

11–9. Percent Shares of Income by Income Groups, 1935–36 and 1962

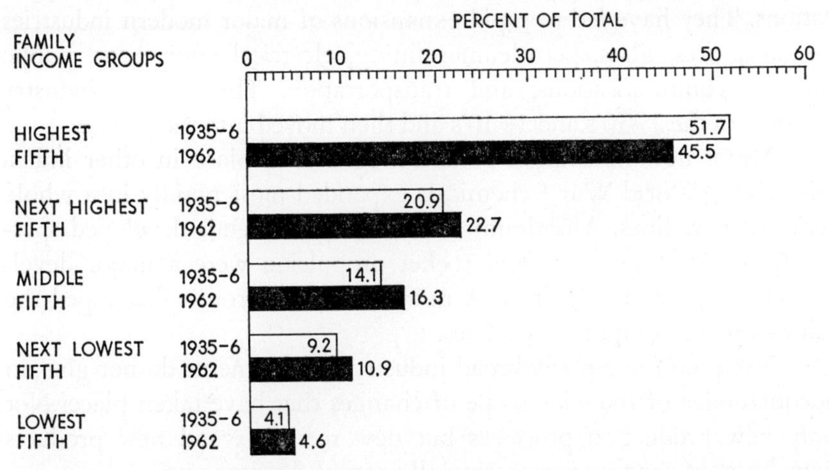

Source: Department of Commerce, *Statistical Abstract of the United States, 1965* (Washington, D.C.: U.S. Government Printing Office, 1966), p. 340.

income group alone decreased its share of national income, and it alone had a smaller percentage increase in real income than the national percentage increase. All other income groups not only shared in the absolute gains in real income during the Nation's progress but also they increased their shares of national income. This is indeed a noteworthy record of progress. (See 11–9.)

RAPID TECHNOLOGICAL CHANGE

The overall record of increased productivity, which maintained the high pace of growth in spite of a slowdown in all inputs, has suggested the importance of technological change in the modern period. A more detailed examination of industries and products reveals two important characteristics of this modern technological change. First, the changes have been widespread throughout the economy. In contrast, previous surges in American growth were spurred by a few major innovations backed up by a host of lesser inventions and innovations. Second, the source of technological change has been related increasingly to scientific knowledge. We seem to have discovered a process of bringing about change more continuously through organized research and widespread education.

Diversity of Innovations

Much of the recent progress is a continuation and broadening of the major innovations that began before World War I. Electrical and automotive energy both have continued to find more widespread applications. They have led to rapid expansions of major modern industries —autos, tires, glass, petroleum refining, electrical equipment, public utilities, communications, and transportation. The aircraft industry boomed in the 1930's and 1940's and then moved into the jet age.

Major new innovation breakthroughs took place in other industries. After World War I chemicals expanded most rapidly in a whole series of new lines. Aluminum and other light metals developed spectacularly. Atomic energy and rocket propulsion were a major development after World War II. A new field of electronics developed the television and computer industries.

Yet even these many broad industry developments do not give an adequate idea of the wide scope of changes that have taken place. Not only new production processes but new materials and new products have brought changes permeating all parts of the economy.

New materials have made a whole range of new products possible and also have done much to eliminate the danger of scarcity in natural resources. Beginning with rayon in the 1930's a whole new group of synthetic fibers have been developed, and they reduced cost and introduced new qualities in clothing. Synthetic rubber was developed during World War II; and a wide variety of new plastic materials has been found. Lumber and brick in the building industry have faced new competition from aluminum, lightweight steel, plywood, and molded composites. A vast selection of paper, plastic and metal containers have revolutionized packaging and merchandising of products. New fertilizers and insecticides have helped to raise agricultural output. Antibiotics, antihistamines, various vaccines, and countless other new types of medicines have reduced the toll of major illnesses.

Radically new types of products not only have created vast new industries but have altered consumer styles of living. Television, automatic record players, tape recorders, transistorized pocket radios, home movie cameras, quick-developing film, and electronic musical instruments have created new patterns of home entertainment. Plastic motor boats, ski lifts, aqualungs, trailer coaches, and automatic bowling pin setters have made possible new forms of outdoor living and active recreation. Reading materials and written communications have been facilitated with new processes in typesetting, offset printing, and photo or magnetic copying. The drudgery of housework has been reduced with vacuum cleaners, automatic washers and dryers, and dishwashers. The new stoves, refrigerators and home freezers, in conjunction with all sorts of precooked and frozen foods, have made for great convenience and variety in home cooking. Electric blankets, shavers and hair dryers, as well as air conditioning and thermostatic heating controls have made for greater personal comfort and convenience in the home.

Many of these new materials and products involve qualitative changes that are not easy to measure in the record of output and productivity progress. Yet many of them have involved drastic savings in costs of materials and use of capital equipment as well as in labor. In addition, a wide variety of innovations has been made in the methods or processes of production.

Previously, the Industrial Revolution had evolved gradually from the initial discovery of machinery producing standard products to the standardization of parts and to the assembly line. In the modern period, further innovations were introduced to remove more completely human handling of materials, to make the machines more automatic, and even to mechanize the controls and routine decisions.

The forklift truck was added to the conveyor belt and overhead crane; and with it came the palletized storing and transporting of boxes and bulky objects. Metal and plastic tanks, pneumatic tubes, long-distance pipelines, and rotary pumps are used to move all sorts of liquids and crushed solids. Continuous process plants were developed early in petroleum refining and various chemical industries, and with these came various measurement and control instruments. Increasingly the routine decisions were made automatic by establishing a feedback from the measurement devices to the control switches. An early shift to automatic continuous operations also was made in bottling, canning, and packaging machinery; and recently, the possibilities for computerized instructions to machine tools has introduced automation to previously skilled or small job-lot operations. Even old industries, like steelmaking, have been rejuvenated by new techniques and processes, such as high-pressure oxygen furnaces and continuous pouring and rolling.

As production labor was reduced and organizations became larger, the paper work and clerical tasks mounted until they, too, could be automated. Tape recording and copying devices have reduced secretarial operations. Electric adding and calculating machines, accounting machines, and punched cards made great strides in recording and handling figures; but these are being supplanted rapidly by sensitized inks, magnetic tapes and electronic computers.

Even selling labors are being reduced while convenience to the customer is enhanced. Self-service and the check-out counter are being used more widely in stores. Automatic vending machines provide convenience items when and where the customer chooses. Coin machines collect fares and tolls. Dry cleaning, car washing, and various other labor services are being mechanically provided on a self-service basis.

One field of innovation deserves special mention because it illustrates the widespread effects of technological change. That field is agriculture. After the adoption of farm machinery in the middle of the last century, little change occurred in farming methods until the introduction of the tractor. This caused a rapid reduction in the use of draft horses during the 1920's, which in turn released more acres from merely supplying feed to horses. The real changes in labor productivity and in yields per acre, however, came after the mid-1930's. The development and introduction of new fertilizers, seeds, and insecticides began to bring rapid gains in output per unit of input. Newly irrigated lands in the Southwest brought higher yields in some crops. Cotton picking machines have been widely introduced in the South since World War II. Improved farm management and the breeding and feeding of animals also had widespread effects.

Role of Science and Education

Innovation always has played an important role in economic growth, and its source has been in the intangible conditions of a society rather than in physical quantities. Historically, innovation has depended upon both a favorable social environment and the qualities of individuals. The environment must provide opportunity and freedom as well as the motivations of rewards and competition. The individuals have had to have the capabilities that come from experience and education as well as traits of imagination, ingenuity, daring, and vigor.

Innovation is a broader term than invention, which may be regarded as just one stage in the innovating process. To innovate means to introduce or bring into practice something new and improved. The process of innovation may be divided into several stages, although there may be no clear dividing lines between them. First, there is a background of knowledge—knowledge about a problem and the need or opportunity to solve it, and knowledge about available materials and methods that might be pertinent to a solution. Second, there is the invention of a new way of combining knowledge that potentially may solve the problem. The initial idea may be very crude or it may merely point the way. Third, there is the working out or development of the practical application of the new idea. Adaptations and improvements may be needed to make it economical or adaptable to mass production. Fourth, there is the introduction and wide dissemination of the use of the idea through mass production and mass distribution.

What has distinguished innovation in modern times is the extent to which it has been intertwined with scientific knowledge and the role of large organizations. The uncertainty of innovation and the individual qualities of imagination and daring remain just as important, but the individual approaches new ideas with a greater background of knowledge and requires more organization to put them into effect.

Innovations in modern times increasingly are the result of the combined efforts of many people, frequently (but not always) as a team within one large business organization. New ideas on materials, processes and products are being based on a greater background of knowledge. This knowledge has accumulated not only from trial and error experience but also from scientific theories and deliberate experiments. More organized research is being used deliberately to uncover new ideas. Then, after new ideas are found, the many specialized skills of the production and marketing specialists are applied to develop a practical application and put it into widespread use.

Beginning with the chemical and drug industries around World War I, large corporations increasingly have established research laboratories and experimental teams to improve their processes and bring out new products. The success of some research leaders, such as Du Pont and Bell Laboratories, as well as the government-sponsored research during World War II, has led to more widespread private industrial expenditures on research and development (commonly called "R. & D."). It is estimated that such expenditures amounted to less than 1 percent of the gross national product in the 1920's, but have risen above 2 percent in the 1960's. They may reach 3 percent by 1970. Private industry performs about two thirds of all research, while government laboratories and universities split the rest. About two thirds of all the funds, however, come from government, which contracts with both industry and universities for most of its research. (See 11–10.)

As already indicated, these R. & D. expenditures may be regarded as a form of investment, a use of resources currently in order to expand future productive capabilities. During the 1950's, a close correlation was observed between the percentage of sales devoted to research in various industries and the rates of return on net worth in subsequent years. Also, there seemed to be considerable substitution between expenditures for capital equipment and expenditures for research. Over several decades, the proportion of gross national product spent on capital equipment has declined while the proportion on R. & D. has increased; yet their combined proportion has remained about the same. Since R. & D. has reached about a fourth of all private investment, the

11–10. Industrial Research and Development Expenditures

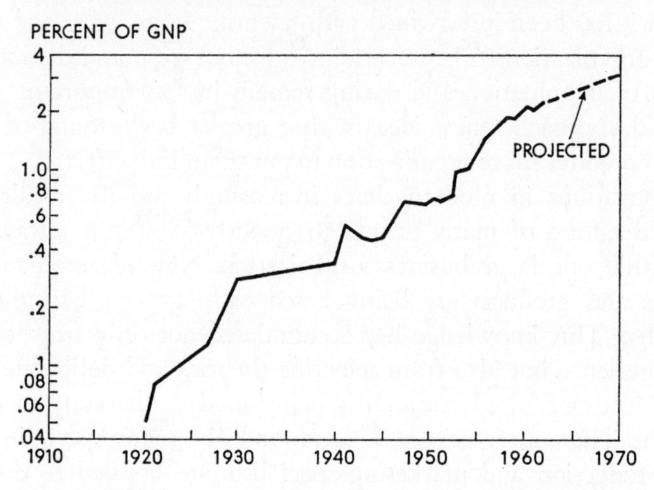

Source: Yale Brozen, "Trends in Industrial Research and Development," *Journal of Business*, July, 1960, Table 2, U.S. Department of Commerce, *Statistical Abstract of the United States, 1965* (Washington, D.C.: U.S. Government Printing Office, 1966), p. 548.

rising trend of such expenditures may soon level off at a more constant percentage of gross national product.[4]

Some qualifications must be noted, however, lest assumptions be made that are unrealistically optimistic about the future outlook for invention through organized research. It is not true that organized research groups completely dominate the field of inventions. Studies of patents and of recent major inventions show that individual inventors still supply a large share of the new discoveries. Small companies and sources outside of an industry often provide the major breakthroughs. It also is not true that organized research can be planned with a reasonable certainty about the results. Discoveries still are largely accidental; and the applications of research results may occur unexpectedly in other fields than those for which they were intended.[5]

There is no doubt that modern technology is placing an increased emphasis on an increased store of scientific knowledge, and the individuals who participate in this process must acquire this knowledge through education. In addition, the men who develop the practical products and the improved processes require professional knowledge and skills in science and engineering. Those who manage mass produc-

[4] Yale Brozen, "The Future of Industrial Research," *Journal of Business*, October, 1961, Tables 3 and 4.

[5] Richard E. Nelson, "The Economics of Invention: A Survey of the Literature," *Journal of Business*, April, 1959.

tion and marketing also must have professional training and technical skills in engineering and business administration.

The emphasis in the modern age of science is upon brain power, not brawn. Not only is a higher level of education and training required to innovate and raise productivity, it also is needed to carry out current production. Machinery and materials handling equipment now do the muscle work, and the routine decisions are made by control instruments. Increasingly, the worker is limited to making the more complex decisions, to planning, and to repairing the machines.

This shift to a higher type of labor skills can be seen in the distribution of the labor force by occupation. Between 1920 and 1960, the total labor force expanded about 50 percent. The number of farmers and farm laborers declined absolutely, as did the number of manual laborers outside of farming. The number of operatives also began to decrease during the last decade. Over the four decades, however, managers, clerical workers, and service workers tripled, while professional and technical workers quadrupled! (See 11–11.)

Our economy has been able to meet the requirements of modern technology for a better quality of workers because of the rising supply of better educated workers. As incomes have risen, Americans have been able to give more financial support to public school systems, and a greater proportion of the youth has completed high school and gone to

11–11. Distribution of Occupations, 1920 and 1960

	1920	*1960*
White-collar workers		
Professional and technical	2,283	7,475
Managers and proprietors	2,803	7,067
Clerical	3,385	9,783
Sales	2,058	4,401
Manual and service workers		
Craftsmen and foremen	5,482	8,560
Operatives	6,587	11,983
Laborers	4,905	3,665
Private household workers	1,411	2,216
Other service workers	1,901	6,133
Farm workers		
Farmers and farm managers	6,442	2,780
Farm laborers and foremen	4,948	2,615
Total	42,206	66,681

Source: U.S. Department of Commerce, *Historical Statistics of the United States* (Washington, D.C.: U.S. Government Printing Office, 1960), p. 74; and U.S. Department of Commerce, *Statistical Abstract of the United States, 1965* (Washington, D.C.: U.S. Government Printing Office, 1966), p. 228.

11–12. The Rising Level of Education by Age Groups

Age Groups in 1960	*Median Years' Schooling*
25–29	12.3
30–34	12.2
35–39	12.1
40–44	11.8
45–49	10.6
50–54	9.7
55–59	8.8
60–64	8.6

Source: U.S. Department of Commerce, *Historical Statistics of the United States, Continued to 1962* (Washington, D.C.: U.S. Government Printing Office, 1965), p. 32.

11–13. Relation of Education Level to Income.

Years of Education Completed	*Average 1963 Income, Males*
Less than 8	$ 3,641
8	4,921
9 to 11	5,592
12	6,693
13 to 15	7,839
12 or more	10,062

Source: U.S. Department of Commerce, *Statistical Abstract of the United States, 1965* (Washington, D.C.: U.S. Government Printing Office, 1966), p. 117.

college. Gradually the work force has gained a higher average level of education. This can be seen in the average number of years of schooling that each age group in the population had in 1960.

Those who were in their early sixties, having started working around 1920, had a median of school years completed of only 8.6. Those in their late twenties had a median of 12.3 years. The other age groups rank successively between these two. (See 11–12.)

The idea that education is a form of investment—an investment in an improved quality of human resources—is relatively new. It is clear, however, that education is costly—not only in tuition and expenses but also in wages that are foregone while devoting time to studies rather than to working. Yet the high initial cost is justified on the basis of the improvement that results in future productivity and earning power. During 1963, for example, it is estimated that men with 12 or more years of education averaged an income almost three times as large as those with less than eight years of education. On the basis of such information, some economists have estimated that the rate of return on investment in education is about comparable with the rate of return on investment in physical capital goods. (See 11–13.)

SHIFTS IN INDUSTRY STRUCTURE

While technological changes were widespread throughout the economy, they were not uniform. As a result, there were widely differing rates of change in productivity among industries. Likewise, as consumer incomes rose and as technology presented new types of products to choose among, output did not increase at the same rate among industries. These changes in output and productivity brought considerable shifts in the distribution of employment among industries.

Among the major sectors of the economy, two of the extractive industries had the slowest increases in output. Yet this was not due to any lack of progressiveness in these industries. On the contrary, the annual rate of increase in productivity for mining exceeded the national rate during 1919–29 and 1929–38. For agriculture, it exceeded the national rate during 1937–48 and 1948–53. Since 1953, agriculture has continued to have productivity gains exceeding those of manufacturing or other nonfarm sectors combined. As already noted, a virtual revolution in farming technology has occurred since 1938. Yet, as a result of the slow expansion in sales and the rapid expansion in productivity, the labor requirements in both mining and agriculture fell absolutely. Transportation was the only other sector to experience a reduction in employment.

The fastest increases in output were in the communications and public utilities sector and the manufacturing sector. Manufacturing had an annual rate of increase in productivity exceeding the national average during the first decade, 1919–29. Communications and public utilities had a faster than average rate during the first three decades, with some acceleration in its gains to 1948. Since World War II, however, the productivity gain in these sectors has been about average. (See 11–14.)

Within manufacturing, the industry groups that had the slowest gains in output were based on extractive industries and traditional labor skills. These were leather, lumber, textiles, tobacco, food, and apparel

11–14. Output and Employment Changes, by Sector

Broad Sectors, Private Economy	1953 Indexes (1919 = 100)	
	Output	Employment
Agriculture	138	67
Mining	200	76
Construction	307	256
Manufacturing	399	165
Wholesale-retail trade	294	222
Transportation	278	89
Communications and utilities	734	223
Finance, insurance, real estate	227	259
Service		180

Source: John W. Kendrick, *Productivity Trends in the United States* (Princeton, N.J.: Princeton University Press, 1961), Tables A IV, A VII.

products. Productivity gains also were relatively slow in most of these industries. Where output grew slower than productivity—in lumber, leather, and textiles—there was an absolute decline in employment.

The fastest gains in output were in chemicals, electrical machinery, transportation equipment, petroleum products, paper, and instruments. These were the industries in which technological changes combined to bring about new materials, new processes and new products. These also tended to be research-oriented industries. During 1963, for example, the largest industry expenditures on R. & D. were as follows: aircraft, $4,835 million; electrical equipment, $2,483 million; chemicals, $1,253 million; autos and other transportation equipment, $1,103 million; machinery, $977 million; instruments, $497 million; and petroleum products, $315 million. The productivity gains in most of these industries also were so high that the differences in employment gains among industries were not as startling. Employment grew more than twice the all-manufacturing rate only in electrical machinery. Paper, chemicals, fabricated metals, and machinery expanded employment at about twice the all-manufacturing rate. (See 11–15.)

Between 1953 and 1965, the above trends were roughly similar; so, the present structure of income and employment may be examined in contrast to that of 1919. Within manufacturing, transportation equipment and ordnance is the largest industry group in terms of income and employment. By number of workers, food, machinery, and electrical equipment are the next ranking industry groups. Manufacturing as a whole, however, employs about one fourth of the total labor force, and produces one third of the income. (See 11–16.)

11–15. Changes in Output and Employment, Manufacturing Industries

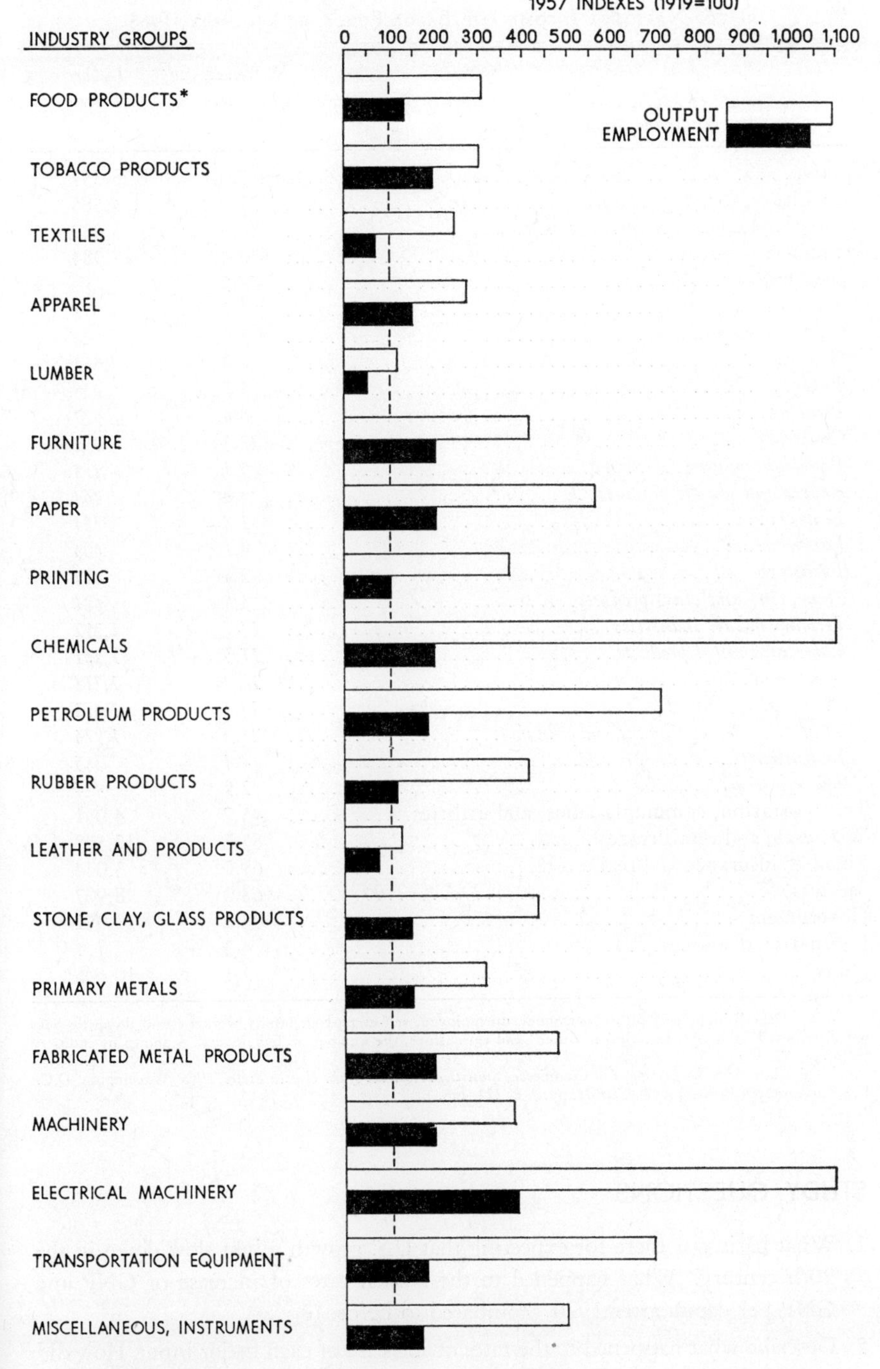

* Excludes beverages.

Source: John W. Kendrick, *Productivity Trends in the United States* (Princeton, N.J.: Princeton University Press, 1961), App. Tables A IV, A VII.

11–16. NATIONAL INCOME AND LABOR FORCE, BY INDUSTRY, 1965

Industry Sectors or Groups	*National Income (Billions)*	*Labor Force (000)*
Totals	$559.0	78,357
Agriculture, forestry, fisheries	21.0	4,585
Mining and construction	34.8	3,839
Manufacturing	170.4	17,984
Food products	*14.5*	*1,737*
Tobacco manufactures	*1.2*	*84*
Textile mill products	*5.9*	*920*
Apparel	*6.6*	*1,351*
Paper	*5.7*	*638*
Printing	*8.6*	*977*
Chemicals	*12.3*	*902*
Petroleum refining	*5.1*	*178*
Rubber and plastic products	*4.0*	*464*
Leather	*1.8*	*354*
Lumber	*4.1*	*606*
Furniture	*2.8*	*429*
Stone, clay and glass products	*5.8*	*621*
Primary metals industries	*14.7*	*1,292*
Fabricated metal products	*11.3*	*1,261*
Machinery	*18.4*	*1,714*
Electrical equipment	*14.2*	*1,672*
Transportation equipment and ordnance	*26.0*	*1,976*
Instruments	*4.4*	*385*
Miscellaneous	*2.9*	*424*
Transportation, communications, and utilities	45.7	4,031
Wholesale and retail trade	83.6	12,588
Finance, insurance and real estate	61.0	3,044
Services	63.0	8,907
Government	75.2	10,051
International sources	4.3	...
Other*	...	10,606*

* "Other" includes military personnel, unemployed, self-employed, family workers, and domestic help not distributed by sector. Except for "other" and agriculture, the number of "employees" is shown by industry sector.

SOURCE: U.S. Department of Commerce, ***Statistical Abstract of the United States**, 1966* (Washington, D.C.: U.S. Government Printing Office, 1967), pp. 218, 222, 236.

STUDY QUESTIONS

1. What basis was there for expecting that U.S. growth might slow down in the 20th century? What happened to the annual rates of increase of GNP and GNP per capita after 1920 (compared to before)?
2. Describe what happened to the rates of increase of each major input. How did each factor contribute to raising output per capita before and after 1920? What became the major source of growth?

3. Under modern capitalism what has happened to the labor share of income? To wage changes compared to productivity changes? To rates of return per unit of labor compared to capital? What has happened to the long-term trends in the shares of income of the top income families? To the equality of income distribution of all income groups as a whole? What evidence can be cited for the latter?
4. Why is technological change considered to be more diverse and widespread in the economy after 1920 than before?
5. How has research been related to modern growth? To invention and to innovation? To capital investment? How has education been related to modern growth?
6. Among major sectors of the economy, which grew the slowest in employment and which the fastest? Why? Among manufacturing industry groups, which grew the slowest in employment and which the fastest? Why?

Chapter 12 GROWTH AND INSTABILITY

The Great Contraction of 1929–33 served as a dramatic reminder that economic life is often highly unstable. In an economy in which growth and change are central themes, variations in total economic activity are part of the fabric of economic life. The pattern that 12–1 shows is typical of the ups and downs of economic life in a market-oriented growth economy.

In the underdeveloped economy, growth is measured over centuries rather than decades. Very few major innovations, the prime generators of growth, come along to produce massive shifts in total spending patterns. But the rapidly growing economy is quite different in this respect. When new inventions create new products, better methods of production, or improve access to productive resources, people rush into the affected fields to expand production. When the initial surge of expansion plays out because supply catches up with demand, investment opportunities all but disappear. Because new inventions do not occur continuously, predictably, or controllably over time, new fields of expansion are not always at hand to replace those that are petering out. As a consequence, the developing economy often responds to its growth stimuli in a staccato fashion. Periods of very rapid expansion, booms, are followed by periods of slowdown or contraction, recessions or depressions. What is more, the growth economy's problems are intensified by the same things that devastate other economies—wars, crop failures, and natural disasters.

The relationship of growth and instability does not stop with the destabilizing impact of innovations. The cumulative gains of growth tend to make economies more vulnerable to various shocks. Growth is associated with—indeed, speeded by—the expansion of the market sector. And, the higher income levels that growth produces mean that capital goods and durable consumer goods—items which are easily postponed—take up a larger portion of the national budget.

12–1. American Business Activity Since 1790, Plotted as Deviations from Trend

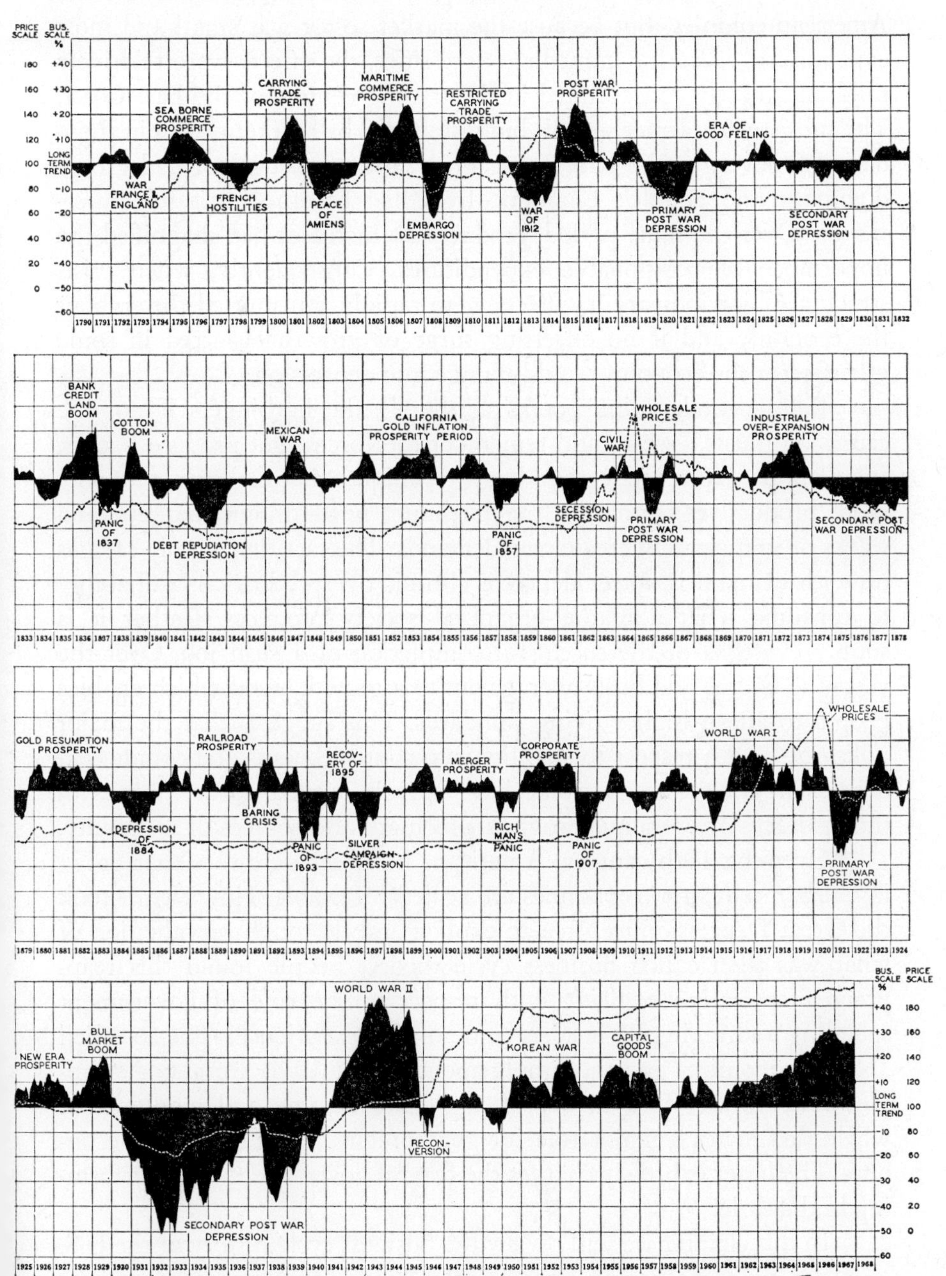

Source: The Cleveland Trust Company, by permission.

In the late 18th-century economy, British depressions spread to the American colonies. But because the market sector was small and most expenditures were for immediate necessities, the effects were relatively mild and mostly concentrated in the trading centers of the East Coast. The subsistence farmer was all but untouched by market events in those days. However, by the late 19th century, the market sector had grown dominant and people's economic lives had become intricately interwoven. Over the same period, productivity increases had magnified the importance of postponable expenditures. Consequently, when crisis struck a major industry its effects were rapidly transmitted throughout the economy and if no offsetting surge of growth occurred in some other sector the economy would plunge into depression.

Before condemning booms as merely the harbingers if not the causes of "busts," we should remember the forces that produce booms. Innovations—new products and new techniques that make the economy more productive—jumps in the birthrate, new foreign markets, and waves of immigration create new demands. The fact that supply catches up with demand is not evidence of chronic overproduction or inability to consume what a market-organized society produces. Rather it is simply evidence of the successful completion of a rush job. Over the years the booms and busts average out to a growth trend which enables people to attain higher living standards. This suggests that the major policy task with respect to stability is to control booms and countervail depression forces, not, as some have naïvely argued, to do away with those sources of economic progress which are also sources of instability.

Over the 19th century, Americans had become aware that growing, urban industrial economies are at heart unstable. However, it took the Great Depression to force an explicit and thorough reevaluation of what was then called business cycle theory; people found this reappraisal especially agonizing with respect to the role of government spending and taxing. What has come of this experience? The so-called "New Economics" and the Employment Act of 1946 are major examples. The former is a theory of aggregate income and employment which designates a major role for government in stabilizing the economy. The latter expressly charges the federal government with performing in that role.

In this chapter we will review the business cycle history of the U.S. economy over the period since World War I. Our attention will be focused upon the business cycles themselves, the economic theory that developed as students groped to better understand economic fluctuations, and the governmental institutions and policies that were developed over this 50-year span. At this point it would be useful for the reader to review the Appendix to Chapter 1 on "National Accounts" and the appendix to Chapter 8 which discusses business cycles in general.

THE CYCLICAL RECORD

Prosperity Decade

The 1920's were generally prosperous years. Employment, income, production, and worker productivity all advanced with a minimum of interruption for business cycle declines. We had fought "a war to end all wars" and had entered, in the opinion of many, a period of "normalcy" in which growth and prosperity were considered the normal course of events.

At the end of World War I, the economy quickly returned to a peacetime status but with a continuation of war prosperity. Government expenditures remained high; in 1919 spending was $13 billion higher than taxes, while building construction, automobile manufacturing, and increased exports filled the gaps left by reduced armament expenditures. In general, after a few hesitant months in 1918, the United States experienced boom conditions until the depression of 1921.

The postwar depression set records both for the rapidity of the 1921 contraction and for 1922's abrupt reversal of economic activity and rapid climb back to prosperity. Exports were cut almost in half from 1920 to 1921 as Europeans who had increased their own production bought less from us, especially from American farmers. Further, discontinued government loans abroad and curtailed domestic government expenditure pushed the Treasury into a surplus position so that it was reducing rather than adding to purchasing power in the economy. However, by 1922, changes in private domestic spending turned the economy around again and economic growth was resumed.

The recovery of 1922 initiated a period of expansion which led many scholars and most laymen to conclude that a new era had dawned in which the economic ups and downs of the past would be replaced by a "permanent plain of prosperity." Purchases of new consumer durables such as refrigerators, radios, and mass-produced automobiles were made easier through innovations in consumer credit. The new consumer goods plus expanded sales of investment goods more than offset the fall in government expenditures and exports that had precipitated the 1921 contraction.

Signs of prosperity seemed to be at every corner. By 1929, industrial production had reached an unprecedented height after following an expansion course marked by only a few minor interruptions. Gross national product expressed in 1963 dollars rose from slightly over $100 billion per year in 1922 to over $125 billion per year in 1929, while real income per person rose from $938 to $1,041 over the same period.

However, to the worker, the executive, the shopkeeper, the industrialist, and the public servant, the most convincing evidence of prosperity was the stock market boom. By 1927, Dow Jones and Company had become a household term and the stock prices index that bore its name reached dizzying heights as people from all walks of life poured money into the market. The Dow Jones Industrial Average moved from a low of 153 in January of 1927 to 381 in September of 1929. In less than two years, speculation in the bull market had more than doubled the price of stocks. We know now with the insight that comes with hindsight that the bull market was covering up signs of trouble in the economy. When the stock market crashed in October of 1929, the problems of the economy were not only revealed, they were intensified.

Depression Decade

The stock market crash of October, 1929, heralded a depression which in fact was already upon the stage and was to become the most severe business depression in U.S. history. From August, 1929, to the low point of the cycle in March of 1933, the economy established new records for contraction. Real net national product, wholesale prices, and the money supply all declined by more than one third. Unemployment rose from 3.2 percent to 25 percent of the labor force. As can be seen in 12–2, by 1933 the economy had literally been set back more than a decade—in 1933 real gross national product was about 5 percent less than its 1922 level. By June, 1932, the Dow Jones average toppled from its lofty 1929 altitude of 381 to 41, barely more than 10 percent of its bull market peak.

Nor did the economy recovery rapidly. As 12–1 shows, the Great Depression is the longest on record. In fact it was so long that as we noted in Chapter 11, people questioned whether we have entered upon an era of stagnation. It was not until 1939 and the stimulus provided by the preparations for World War II that GNP surpassed its 1929 peak and not until 1943, well after Pearl Harbor, did unemployment fall below the 3.2 percent of 1929.

The data in 12–2 shows the huge cost of the Great Depression and the impetus to recovery provided by World War II. Note the dashed

12–2. Real Gross National Product by Expenditures

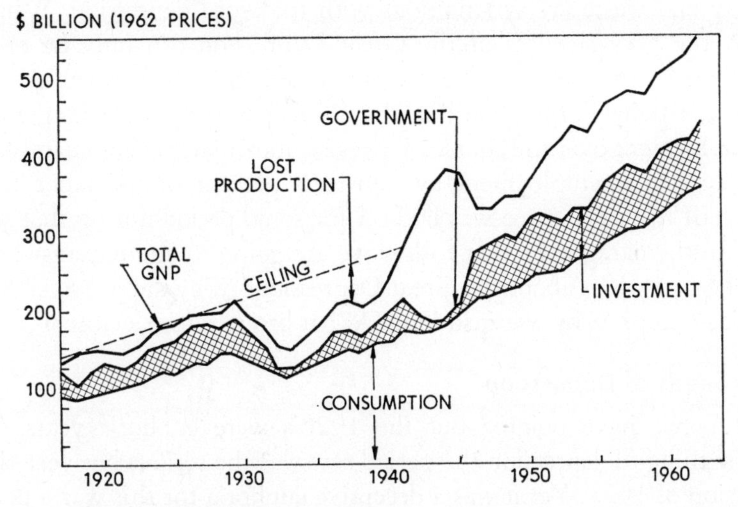

Source: U.S. Department of Commerce.

line that is extended from GNP's peak in 1929 to the GNP level achieved between 1940 and 1941. This line can be thought of as ceiling output under peacetime conditions. It is essentially a hypothetical extension of GNP at its long-term growth rate using 1929's record output as a starting point. As such it illustrates what we could have produced each year in the absence of any cyclical downturn. What we actually produced is, of course, shown by the line labeled "Total GNP." Now note that the dashed ceiling line is also extended back in time to the World War I period. Again we can note the contrast between actual GNP and maximum possible output.

Just a quick glance at 12–2, for the period from the late teens to the early 1940's shows the vast difference in economic performance before and after 1929. In the 1920's, the toll taken by depression was relatively modest in both pecentage and absolute terms. In sharp contrast the lost production of the 1930's was astronomical by either relative or absolute standards. One additional statistical observation may help in grasping the magnitude of the Great Depression: the production lost through idle capacity was about equal to our share of the cost of World War II, the greatest war in history.

The data cited above give some notion of the severity and persistence of the Great Depression. The figures also imply what a tragic period it was in American economic history. In the developed economy, figures on unemployment and income contraction tell about the same human story as famine statistics tell in the underdeveloped economy. Misery and waste are synonomous with the word depression. What is more, the pervasiveness of the Great Depression can only be appreciated when the viewer realizes that unemployment figures relate to a particular point in time and that the number of people who experience unemployment over the course of a year is much larger. For example, in 1933, when unemployment averaged 25 percent of the labor force, over half the work force was laid off for some period during that year.

In the paragraphs that follow we are going to attempt answers to four key questions about the Great Depression: Why did it strike? Why was it so deep? Why was it so long? What brought it to a close?

Seeds of Depression

As we have pointed out the 1920's were euphoric years. The closest thing to depression the period saw was the serious but very short recession of 1921. Yet it was a deceptive euphoria for this was a period in which the seeds of the 1929 "crash" were sown. Perhaps economists will never agree on a precise explanation for the Great Depression—the data for the period are just not good enough—but in a broad sense there is agreement as to the kinds of forces that were at work during the latter portion of the 1920's decade. To get some insight into the operation of these forces, let us summarize the interrelationship of the various expenditure sectors of the economy.

12–3 is a variation of the description of national accounts presented in the appendix to Chapter 1. The first thing to notice is that it reflects the fact that by definition the economy's total income is equal to total output. Second, notice that the bars summarize the relationship between income, spending, and production. The left-hand bar shows that income that is not allocated to consumption of domestic production is either saved, paid in taxes, or used to finance imports. The middle bar shows that the spending offsets to the nonconsumption allocations of income are domestic investment, government purchases, and foreign purchases. The right-hand bar shows the components of total production associated with the division of spending shown in the center bar.

The information summarized in 12–3, plus a general knowledge of the economy, are enough to permit some deductions about the operating relationships of income, spending, production, and employment. First, we can see that spending is the vital link that joins income and production—as long as total income is spent the entire GNP will be cleared from the market given that total income equals total output. Second, if the output level reflects production at full employment of

12–3. NATIONAL INCOME AND PRODUCT

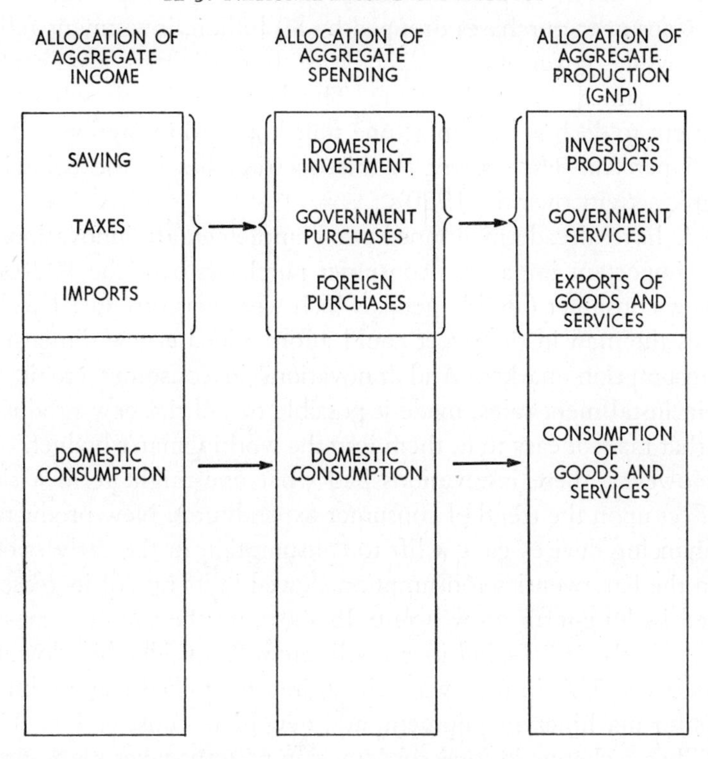

available human and material resources, full employment will be maintained as long as total income is spent. Third, it follows that to maintain full employment, if any combination of spending sectors reduces its purchases, some combination of the remaining sectors must compensate by expanding expenditures by a like amount. Otherwise total sales will decline, and, therefore, production and employment will be reduced, and a downturn will ensue.

Further, the initial contraction will breed additional contraction. As furloughed workers reduce their consumption expenditures, sales will fall further inducing more layoffs and further consumption expenditure reductions until a full-fledged depression is under way. This cumulative effect of an initial expenditure change is referred to by economists as a ***multiplier*** reaction: an initial change in investment spending sets off a chain reaction in which income, employment, and total spending change further. The cumulative total change in spending becomes some multiple of the initial change.

Between the boom year of 1929 and the depression year of 1930,

GNP fell by about 15 percent, a drop of $19 billion expressed in 1963 prices. Consumer purchases dropped by $9 billion, investment fell $13 billion, while government expenditure rose slightly, and net sales abroad remained about the same. The key question is what caused investment to decline by almost one fourth and consumption to fall by about 5 percent. The answer to this question lies in the behavior of economic activity over the 1920's.

We have already mentioned two complementary innovations that had an important impact on consumer purchases over the 1920's decade. New consumer durable goods which were mass-produced and sold at prices the man in the street could afford added a new dimension to the consumption market. And innovations in consumer credit, especially in installment sales, made it possible to sell the new products on terms that made it easy to fit them into the workingman's budget.

However, these innovations had what one might term a single-shot effect upon the trend of consumer expenditures. New products and new financing devices gave a lift to consumption in the early twenties, then in the late twenties consumption slowed in its rate of increase as it resumed its long-term growth rate. In short, on the average, consumption grew in the 1920's, but its growth rate was considerably slower late in the decade. This in turn was echoed in a magnified way by business outlays for machinery, equipment, and new plant construction.

When a change in total consumption patterns takes place, producers must retool, build new plants, and in general expand purchases of capital equipment. This, in turn, will lead to a sharp rise in investment spending in the total economy. But once the capital demands of the affected consumer goods industries are satisfied, investment spending will decline to levels appropriate to provide for replacement and long-term growth. Thus, for example, a 10 percent bulge in consumer spending could cause a 100 percent increase in investment, followed by an equally precipitous decline as consumption resumed its normal growth rate.

Economists call this process an ***accelerator*** reaction: changes in the rate at which consumption expenditure grows can induce absolute increases or decreases in investment spending. Thus, investment expenditure declined in 1929 because the rate at which consumer purchases grew slowed down in the late 1920's as the dramatic effect of introducing new products and financing methods waned.

Investment in residential construction also declined in the last part of the decade. By 1925, the postwar housing boom had reached its peak. Thereafter, new housing starts declined every year. After 1929, the other components of investment that had offset the housing decline gave way in the accelerator reaction we outlined above. The result was the drastic cutback in investment that most economists feel started the Great Depression.

There were complicating factors at work in the 1920's that at least fortified the tendency to collapse that was building in the economy. First, farm income never recovered from the postwar depression. Second, productivity grew much faster than wages with a consequent shift of income distribution toward upper income groups; although, because the total pie was growing, labor's income share grew in total terms. And, third, the stock market boom probably siphoned funds away from plant and equipment investment as firms which floated new issues put the proceeds of their security sales back into the market instead of purchasing production equipment and building new factories.

The Great Contraction

By September of 1929, the economy had turned around. The decline that followed is the most often cited example of the multiplier at work. By 1933, the gap between full employment and actual performance had widened to a point that total production was almost 40 percent less than potential GNP. The multiple contraction of the economy resulted in 75 percent of the work force producing only 62 percent of potential output—the inefficiency of depression pulled real per capita GNP down by 31 percent by 1933.

However, economists are coming to believe that a contraction as great as that described above is too monumental to assign solely to the multiplier. As it happened, financial and monetary events as well as government fiscal policy exacerbated the situation and thus turned a rather commonplace recession phase of a business cycle into the Great Contraction.

The most important financial and monetary forces, which reinforced the 1929 decline and explain why this depression was so deep, were:

1. The stock market crash of October, 1929, which occurred almost two months after the economy had turned down and was inevitable at some point given existing conditions in the market.
2. Three waves of bank failures which were attributable to a combination of poor loans and investments and restrictive monetary policy.
3. Britain's departure from the gold standard which promoted the expectation that the United States would follow suit and caused foreign holders of U.S. securities and bank accounts to cash them in for gold.

4. Restrictive monetary and fiscal policy, which intensified the ills of the business community.

Just why the market crashed when it did we do not know, but most generally, it is obvious that it had to collapse. Prices had been pumped up almost solely on the expectation that it did not matter at what price you bought because the bull market would pull your stock up and you could always sell at a profit. Stock prices grew to magnitudes which bore no realistic relationship to the factors which are usually crucial to a buyer's decisions—current and prospective dividends and profits, value of physical plant and equipment, and the quality of company management. The source of profit to the share buyer became the next owner of the stock rather than the company.

No market can persist by feeding on itself in this way. At some point a wave of "profit taking" (selling out to cash in accrued appreciation) will depress prices enough that a wave of scare selling will start a snowball effect. In 1929, securities buyers financed their purchases with loans for which their stock was collateral. When the market broke the banks wanted their cash back, so people had to sell.

The crash affected an already bad situation in a number of ways. Low stock prices meant that business firms now had to issue more shares to finance a given amount of additional plant and equipment which naturally discouraged investment. The crash also ended the willingness of banks to finance stock purchases on what amounts to a low down payment plan, so a source of funds to finance plant and equipment dried up. And we should not neglect the psychological impact of the crash—many business managers who were charged with investment decisions were traumatized by their personal losses in the market and retrenched in their business decisions. What is more, consumers from all walks of life had been "in the market"—if "Old Man Depression" hadn't gotten a man's job and so reduced his spending, the stock market took his savings and made him tighten his belt.

The crash came early in the Great Contraction but was probably not as important as the bank failures. The first came in October, 1930, the second in March of 1931, and the third came in the last quarter of 1932 and continued until Franklin Roosevelt declared a nationwide banking holiday on March 6, 1933. In each banking panic poor business conditions bred fright in depositors. They feared that their banks would soon become insolvent, so they all rushed to convert their deposits into currency. Because banks did not (and do not now) keep 100 percent currency reserves against deposits, they had to sell other assets, principally bonds, to get cash for depositors. The more depositors panicked and demanded currency, the more bonds and other assets were sold and the lower the prices of those securities fell. Soon many banks found that their securities were worth less in the market than the accounts they owed depositors. These banks failed and wiped out many depositors in the process. Further, many nonfinancial business firms and individuals were forced under as a part of the banks' death throes. In their fight for liquidity banks demanded payment of loans, and when business borrowers couldn't pay they were forced to declare bankruptcy.

Doubtless each of the banks that failed, and many that did not, had made loans in the late 1920's which were fundamentally unsound even for a boom. But today many economists believe that even if every loan had been sound by very conservative criteria most of the bank failures would have occurred anyway. Why? Primarily because a falling bond market was wiping out the assets of bank after bank in this period. Even a bank without a single commercial loan in default would have found it very difficult to pass an examiner's test in those dark days. And why was the bond market falling? It is too easy to say that in bad times the bond market falls—rather the Federal Reserve System simply failed to purchase bonds in amounts great enough to offset the forces that were pushing bond prices down. The system had the statutory power to do so, but not the will.

What effect did the bank failures have on the economy? We only have to review the comparable paragraph dealing with the stock market to answer this question. In addition to personal and business bankruptcies, widespread bank failures constrict the flow of credit and alarm both consumers and those who must make capital spending decisions.

When Britain left the gold standard in September, 1931, foreign holders of bank accounts and securities that were payable in dollars cashed in those assets for gold. The run on U.S. gold meant that the basis of the domestic monetary stock declined which, in turn, restricted the ability of banks to supply money and credit.

Each of the factors cited above operated to cut back spending and reinforce the multiplier through a variety of ways—in sum, they led to a contraction of the money supply, higher interest rates, reduced availability of credit, bankruptcies, and lack of confidence in the economic future. In turn, both investment and consumption were discouraged. While lack of confidence reduced the propensity to spend, high interest rates, credit shortages, and bankruptcies choked off some of that spending which would have taken place in spite of poor expectations. And, of course, the problem was compounded by the decline in the money stock because shrinkage of the money supply reduced the number of transactions that could take place each day.

Restrictive Policies

The United States was certainly subject to a paradoxical set of forces in 1929. In the midst of a recession, monetary policy makers produced a reduction rather than an increase in the supply of money and credit—a course of treatment about like prescribing hot baths for a patient in fever.

Just why our monetary policy was so restrictive is still a matter for debate that would justify an entire study in itself. However, students of the period now feel that monetary policy that would have braked the contraction was possible. The decision makers had adequate knowledge of the operation of the banking system and the relationship of monetary controls to the business cycle. The fact remains that in spite of their knowledge, those who made Federal Reserve policy preferred to open an economic vein and place the leach of monetary restriction upon it.

Fiscal policy was no better than monetary policy in this period. Herbert Hoover, who had taken over in the Presidency at nearly the peak of the boom was presented with a situation in which precedents were few. Further, many of his advisors, especially Secretary of the Treasury Mellon, were unyielding and doctrinaire in their approach to the situation—Hoover named them the "leave-it-alone liquidationists." Mr. Mellon saw only one alternative, to "liquidate:"

> Liquidate labor, liquidate stocks, liquidate the farmers, liquidate real estate. . . . It will purge the rottenness out of the system. . . . People will work harder, live a more moral life. Values will be adjusted, and enterprising people will pick up the wrecks from less competent people.

Hoover and some of his advisors were not so hidebound. Although much villified for his policies, the President did take a number of steps aimed at ending the contraction and speeding recovery.

At Hoover's urging, a number of antidepression policies were enacted. Tariffs were raised to reduce imports and favor American business in spite of protests from thousands of economists. The Reconstruction Finance Corporation was formed to make loans to crisis-racked railroads, financial institutions, and state governments. Other domestic counterrecession moves included additional public works projects, expansion of the federal employment service, a variety of alterations in the banking system, Federal Farm Board purchases of wheat and cotton to support their prices, and establishment of the Federal

Home Loan Bank to act as the Federal Reserve System of the home mortgage market. Internationally, immigration was restricted, a moratorium declared on war debt payments, and a world economic conference was organized to work for reciprocal tariff reduction.

Perhaps Hoover's principal tactic was to attempt to restore confidence in the economy so that the business community would feel secure in resuming precrash levels of activity. To that end he held a series of White House conferences, established various economic commissions, and with his Cabinet members made reassuring statements to the public. Above all the administration attempted to set a good example by balancing the federal budget. Thus, taxes were raised in 1932 and expenditures were reduced in a number of areas.

In sum, Hoover's attempts to cure the depression were a contradictory mixture of expansive and restrictive policies. Raising taxes cut private expenditures and fortified the contraction. The hike in tariffs invited reprisals that reduced our sales abroad. On the other hand, other policies were expansionary but too modest to accomplish their overall objective.

Such an assessment of Hoover's fiscal policies is clearly dictated given present-day knowledge of the economy. But, unlike the makers of monetary policy, authors of fiscal policy operated in a virtual knowledge vacuum in those days. Statistics were fragmentary—gross national product was a term known to only a few scholars who were designing a system of income accounts and at the time labor force data were so bad the level of unemployment was a matter for speculation and debate. Business cycle theory was about on a par with the quality of statistical information. Generally, it was felt that the economic laws governing the total economy made for a long-run trend of near full employment and that cyclical departures from this trend were self-correcting. Consequently, no set of rules of fiscal policy to stabilize the economy had been formulated or tested.

THE NEW DEAL

The third of our questions about the depression is why was it so protracted? It cannot be answered without examining the New Deal in some detail. The Great Depression so permeated the fabric of American life that the New Deal and the Great Depression are inextricable. Our economic woes became the focal point for both domestic and foreign policy. The energies of Roosevelt and his Cabinet were almost solely consumed by attempts to restore prosperity.

New Deal legislation was so extensive a reaction to the depression that it changed markedly the institutional framework of the American economy. These changes created a much modified environment for economic growth and, therefore, provide a second important reason for studying the economics of the New Deal.

Roosevelt's antidepression policies were logical deductions from his conception of the Great Depression. He interpreted the depression as a result of a collection of economic maladjustments that happened to come along at the same time. Consequently, he amassed a series of programs to deal with the causes and effects of the depression as he saw them. Formulation of policy was approached in a highly pragmatic manner. In one solution did not work another was tried. Advice came from all corners and was accepted. Often particular problems were treated by consecutive application of mutually exclusive formulas.

The Great Depression was not seen as a truly ***national*** phenomenon. As with Hoover's advisors, New Dealers failed to see that it resulted from the way in which a very large, high-income market system operates as a unit. Rather, legislation was enacted to offset what was regarded as failure of elements within the system—failures of state and local governments, failures of the business community, and failures of particular institutions such as the banking system. From this experience we learned that the federal government must have a national economic policy dealing with the economy as a whole, rather than relying upon distinct and, as it often happened, uncoordinated policies dealing with each of the separate segments of the total economy. As the economist would put it, we needed a ***macro***economic policy in addition to refurbishing our ***micro***economic policies. We shall discuss that policy and the theory underlying it in the section following this. At this point our task is to trace the attempts of Roosevelt and his advisors to deal with the depression as they diagnosed it.

Relief

Historians have found it convenient to classify New Deal economic policy under three headings—relief, recovery, and reform. Relief where the tragic effects of depression were concentrated. Recovery measures designed to restore income and employment. And reform to eliminate the social ills that to FDR and his advisors bred depression. Let us look at some major examples in each classification.

Work relief was established in May of 1933 with the Federal Emergency Relief Administration (FERA) which made grants to state and local governments for both direct relief payments and public work projects. A little later the Civil Works Administration (CWA) expanded the scope of FERA projects, then in 1935, the Works Progress Administration (WPA) was formed to employ directly a wide array of people from musicians to ditchdiggers in their respective occupations. At its peak the WPA, which lasted until 1942, employed as many as 3.3 million workers which was 6 percent of the labor force.

A second type of relief was furnished to the financial community. A bank holiday was declared by executive Order on March 6, 1933. The holiday, which was extended by Congress, lasted to mid-March. It was designed to end banking failures by giving federal and state banking authorities a chance to examine banks and license to reopen those which were sound. At the same time, FDR suspended gold redemption and shipments to foreigners in order to end hoarding and outward gold flows. When the sound banks reopened, the United States was off the gold standard and thus insulated from a principle source of monetary restriction.

There were, of course, many other relief measures—the "First Hundred Days" were punctuated with bills whose titles began with "emergency." Those discussed above are most significant in that they were the most sweeping. They also typified FDR's approach to the economy. We had an employment problem and a money problem and until the causes could be rooted out and dealt with, symptomatic measures had to be taken.

Recovery

To FDR recovery required a scatter-gun approach. Consequently, off the White House desk and through the Congress came PWA, AAA, TVA, and NRA. The Public Works Administration (PWA) was designed to stimulate recovery by employing the Nation's contractors to build dams, highways, and public buildings. The Agricultural Adjustment Administration (AAA) was formed to create scarcity and, thus, raise farm income and prices artificially by restricting acreage under cultivation. The Tennessee Valley Authority (TVA) established a federal corporation which was charged with development of the economy of that long-impoverished, highly rural watershed through construction of multiple purpose dams and opening the river and its tributaries for navigation.

The National Industrial Recovery Act (NIRA) was passed to make capitalism national by bringing together labor, capital, and the consumer in preparation of codes of "fair practice" which would set minimum prices and wages, regulate output, and set maximum hours of work. The idea was to achieve higher prices (then called "reflation"), spread work among more workers, and raise wages. If the vicissitudes for which the market was infamous had brought on the depression, the substitution of planning for the apparent chaos of the market seemed the thing to do.

A second approach to "reflation" came in our gold policy. In the period after the banking holiday, the price of gold was gradually raised to the current $35 per ounce. Roosevelt believed that raising the price at which the Treasury bought gold would cause other prices to rise and bring back prosperity. The gold purchase program was based on the following reasoning. Depression is essentially a problem of prices being too low; recovery, therefore, can be achieved through price inflation. Since the price of gold and commodity prices are positively correlated, it follows that prosperity can be restored by government purchases of gold at higher prices.

Prices did rise slightly after 1933, but the Federal Reserve System also had instituted an easy money policy at about the same time; so the data aren't convincing either way and by modern standards the theory is woefully inadequate. Perhaps the most telling criticism of New Deal gold policy was contemporary. John Maynard Keynes,[1] the famous British monetary economist, wrote the President that "the recent gyrations of the dollar have looked to me . . . like a gold standard on the booze." To Keynes the whole idea smacked of "trying to get fat by buying a larger belt," because price rises are an effect of expansion not a cause of recovery.

These were the most significant recovery measures employed by FDR. Taken together then exemplify the New Deal's analysis of the depression. Bad times emanated from a series of economic disorders in the Nation. Because there were so many simultaneously active sources of distress, the depression was "Great" and each of these sources required a specific remedy, hence the wide variety of recovery programs.

Reform

FDR was convinced early in the depression that reform was necessary if lasting recovery were to be achieved. He felt that the nation was on the road to "economic oligarchy" with a huge, perhaps overbuilt, industrial plant squeezing out the small businessman and displacing workers with laborsaving machinery. In times past the western frontier provided a safety valve, but in Roosevelt's view the frontier had been

[1] Keynes is pronounced to rhyme with rains, not teens.

pushed to the sea. Government, he felt, should provide the "maintenance of balance" as a compensation for the closing of the frontier.

Specifically government's tasks were to assure lifelong economic security for the individual; establish a monetary and financial system that would not permit the excesses of the precrash days; provide an environment in which labor could organize and bargain collectively; and conduct a program which would harness or atomize the power of the economic oligarchists.

The social security system, the Fair Labor Standards Act (maximum standard workweek), the minimum wage law, and unemployment compensation were aimed at providing economic security at a "living wage" and "decent hours" throughout the worker's years in the labor force, then a retirement income until death.

The monetary and financial reform legislation of the New Deal comprises a list too lengthy to enumerate here. However, we can get an idea of the reform philosophy of the New Deal by briefly surveying the general areas in which bills were passed. Legislation was enacted to provide a continuing government oversight of the stock market and investment banking through the Securities and Exchange Commission (SEC) and the Federal Reserve System. The latter was given the power to set the necessary "down payment" for stock purchases (called the "margin requirement"). One of the most vulnerable areas of the economy in the 1920's, public utility financing, was given a set of federal procedural and organizational ground rules.

Agricultural credit facilities were reorganized. Federal bank deposit insurance was instituted to avoid recurrence of the tragedies of 1929–33 in which bank failures wiped out many depositors. The Federal Housing Administration (FHA) was organized to insure lenders in home mortgage contracts, and the amortized mortgage was substituted for the 5- and 10-year "sudden death" mortgages whose terms had not only provided the crisis in hundreds of showboat melodramas but in thousands of real-life situations as well. The Federal Reserve Act was amended several times to centralize control of the system and shift the balance of that control away from the commercial banks and to the presidentially appointed Board of Governors. This shift was especially important with regard to the system's open-market purchases and sales of securities which control the volume of bank reserves in the country and, therefore, influence the quantity of money in the economy.

Reformation was extended to labor and capital. In Section 7-A of the National Industrial Recovery Act labor was given the right to organize and bargain collectively. After the NIRA was set aside as unconstitutional the Wagner Act—"Labor's Magna Charta"—was passed reestablishing that privilege and setting up the National Labor Relations Board (NLRB) to enforce the act's prohibitions against certain "unfair labor practices" on the part of management. The Norris-LaGuardia Act was a major factor in reducing violence in the union movement. It had been passed in the dog days of the Hoover administration, and, after 1937 when the Supreme Court held it constitutional, it was effective in eliminating the more flagrant antiorganization tactics of management.

The NIRA legislation suspended the antitrust laws and in effect gave business the right to form cartels to control prices and output industry by industry. But this awesome delegation of power was to be offset by multiparty industry policy making. Broad management policy was to be forged jointly by representatives of management, labor, and the consumer. In fact, labor and the consumer seldom got to the conference table, so Roosevelt's design to institutionalize a system of checks and balances never came to fruition.

Soon after the Supreme Court turned thumbs down on the NIRA, Thurmond Arnold, the Attorney General, launched an attack against the oligarchists whom FDR had renamed the "Economic Royalists" in the 1936 campaign. The "central planners" had failed in their attempts to influence policy in favor of a new NRA, and the "atomizers" had come to the fore. The idea was to splinter economic power so as to protect the system from its own force. A truly vigorous antitrust policy under the Sherman Act was begun in 1937 and was carried over, with occasional lapses, into subsequent administrations.

The foregoing makes clear that FDR's notion of reform did not mean radical social reorganization by which bankers and businessmen were to be replaced by civil servants. Rather, the decision makers of the private economy were to be boxed in by the law so that within its confines their individual profit-maximizing decisions would contribute to maximizing the national welfare as well. Reform to him meant "government acceptance of responsibility to save business, to save the American system of private enterprise and economic democracy."

What of the results of Roosevelt's experiments? Did they shorten or prolong the Great Depression?

The recovery and reform aspects of his programs get good and bad marks. The gold purchases were economic folly as Keynes pointed out. The Wagner Act and "trust busting" probably scared business as much as the earlier NIRA had encouraged it. Centralization of the Federal Reserve System probably enhanced the quality of monetary policy, or as some would say, lessened its ineptitude. The financial control acts definitely discouraged businessmen if their protests are criteria, but private securities sales did continue to rise even after these acts.

The public works projects, TVA and AAA, all increased aggregate spending. The NIRA's "reflation" strategy according to most students of the era met with little success—what recovery was achieved in the period before it was held unconstitutional has been attributed to other factors.

It appears that one way to summarize the New Deal is to say that its policies were a mixed bag of tricks whose contents appeared to offset each other. In other words, Roosevelt's policy, although more vigorous than that of Hoover's, was also contradictory. These observations give us one explanation for the protracted duration of the Great Depression—the net effect of federal antidepression policy under both presidents appears to have been at best neutral, the good offsetting the bad. However, before we settle for this judgment of Hoover or FDR, perhaps we should look at the entire depression period in fiscal and monetary policy terms. Then we can again pose the question of the depression's extreme length.

Recovery Policy Appraised

In discussing the factors that produced the 1929 contraction, we used 12–3 to depict the relationship between income, spending, production, and resource employment. In that discussion we pointed out that full resource employment can be maintained as long as total spending equals full employment output. We also noted that if any combination of spending sectors reduces its outlays some other combination must expand purchases by an equal amount if full employment is to be maintained.

Thus, if government spending minus taxes had been increased so as to offset the decline in business and consumer spending that took place during the Great Contraction, income, output, and employment would have been pumped up to ceiling levels again. In short, an expansive fiscal policy—some combination of lower taxes and greater government spending—could have filled the expenditure gap. In the period we are reviewing, this policy would have called for increasing federal budget deficits as a consequence of increased expenditures and decreased tax rates. Further, the "easier" had been monetary policy in that and similar situations, the lower would have been interest rates and accordingly the higher would have been private investment. In other words an easy money policy can reduce the size of the job assigned to fiscal policy.

Given the monetary policy of the period, just how big a fiscal policy task this was can be seen by comparing a few figures. We can trace the course of fiscal events between 1929 and 1930 by looking at Department of Commerce estimates of the main components of expenditure expressed in terms of 1958 purchasing power. As the figures cited below show, GNP fell by over $20 billion between 1929 and 1930. Assuming that all changes in consumption were induced by movements in income, this change in income was generated by the $13.1 billion decline in investment and net exports which was offset to only a modest degree, $2.3 billion, by a rise in government expenditure.

	Amount, 1929*	*Change,* 1929–30*	
Gross national product	203.6	−20.1	
Consumption	139.6	− 9.2	
Investment	40.4	−13.0	−10.8
Government	22.0	+ 2.3	
Exports less imports	1.5	− 0.1	

* In billions of 1958 dollars.

Fiscal policy would have had to raise nonconsumption spending by $10.8 billion to maintain income at its 1929 level—truly a Herculean task when you consider that total government spending in 1929 was only $22 billion. Some combination of increased government outlays plus increases in consumption and other outlays induced by tax reductions would have had to fill a spending gap equal to 50 percent of 1929's level of government spending.

The actual fiscal policy record was just the opposite of expansive. In 1929, government collected slightly more in taxes than it spent. Thereafter, as one student of the period's fiscal policy has shown, in every year but two over the entire 1930–39 period, all governments had a more restrictive effect on the economy than they had in 1929. Only in 1931 and 1936 did fiscal policy push the economy toward recovery.[2] Of course, taxes did decline and government spending did rise on the average from 1929–39, yet taxes fell as a response to falling income rather than rate reductions—in fact rates were raised—and spending fell by 8 percent from 1931 to 1933. The important point to note here is that the deficits incurred were chiefly the ***result*** of low income, producing low tax ***yields*** rather than rate cuts and massive spending increases.

We have already seen that monetary contraction was permitted to

[2] E. C. Brown, "Fiscal Policy in the 'Thirties': A Reappraisal," *American Economic Review,* Vol. XLVI, No. 6. (December, 1956), pp. 857–79.

intensify the business contraction of 1929–33. Thereafter, monetary policy was for the most part easier. However, many assign a significant role to the monetary restraint of 1936 in explaining the recession which a glance at 12–1 will show occurred in 1937. Thus when viewed from the standpoint of the spending relationships we have just reviewed, the Hoover and Roosevelt policies failed to effectively combat the Great Depression: tax policy was contractionary while spending was only mildly expansionary; monetary policy was perverse in the early phases and only modestly easy-to-perverse in later phases.

Any appraisal of the policies of either Hoover or Roosevelt must be made with reference to the fact that each of these men had to make decisions in a political context. Therefore, the area of applicable economic theory as they separately conceived of it was narrowed for each by what was politically acceptable in their respective views. Further, not only did their economic theory differ but their political environments were markedly unalike—Roosevelt had a mandate to experiment while Hoover was under pressure to retrench.

As we have seen, Hoover believed that a balanced budget was a prerequisite of recovery, especially in view of the clamor for fiscal prudence. It is almost inconceivable that the same public which pressed Mr. Hoover for balanced budgets, hard enough that Mr. Roosevelt felt he had to promise the same, would have permitted tax cuts and spending increases of sufficient magnitude to restore full employment.

Given the pressure for fiscal orthodoxy, it should come as no surprise that higher tax rates were legislated at all levels of government. The question is Why was there no grasp in the years of decline of the rather simple elements we are working with here? The answer probably is that what men knew, and knew correctly, blinded them to other knowledge. Deficits did cause, as Hoover and Roosevelt predicted, unrest and lack of confidence and thus adversely affected the economy. Further, household and business deficits in depression were folly, and it was this rule that the people and businessmen applied to their government as a criterion of performance. What is more, the accepted economic theory of the day backed up this view. Thus, both Presidents failed to see the following: if done on a sufficiently grand scale, taking less from the people in taxes than is paid out as spending and relief can stimulate business sufficiently to offset the adverse psychological effects of a deficit.

At this point we can again venture a judgment as to why the depression was so prolonged. As we have seen, during the 1920's the economy developed basic maladjustments which produced the 1929 downturn. Complicating factors, including restrictive monetary and fiscal policies, made the downturn more pronounced than it might have otherwise been. During the recovery phase of the cycle, after 1933, fiscal and monetary policies slowed the economy's expansion.

While the economy lingered at far less than full employment, making its plodding recovery, pessimism about the economic future reinforced the system's hesitancy. The birthrate dropped as marriages and children were postponed. Business and the financial community as well as many academicians began to accept the stagnation notion we sketched earlier in the text. For many this view was verified when the 1937 recession followed the relatively prosperous although not full-employment conditions of 1936. In 1938, the economy turned up again, but this recovery was also halting until defense and war spending changed the entire fabric of economic life.

In short, then, policy errors were to a very large degree responsible for the longevity of the Great Depression. Let us now address our fourth question, What restored prosperity?

WORLD WAR II "PROSPERITY"

Paradoxically war, the most wasteful of society's institutions, was responsible for lifting millions of Americans from privation and providing them employment and economic security. As the German military machine was rebuilt in the late 1930's, then displayed in Czechoslovakia in March of 1939, U.S. foreign policy shifted from one of isolation to international involvement. Government expenditure expanded accordingly—first, with our efforts to assist Britain, then through our own rearmament. In 1941, after Japan's December 7 attack on Pearl Harbor we began a massive reemployment and reallocation of resources into wartime outputs. War production became a force-draft effort to prepare for offensive warfare while stretching a desperately small stock of military supplies and equipment over months of retreat in the Far Eastern Theater.

Starting as we did from 15 percent unemployment, government purchases were able to more than triple from 1940 to 1942 while consumption, rather than declining, actually increased by 5 percent. As unemployment and underemployment declined in the face of military demand, a 60 percent increase in total industrial production made possible expansion in both the public and private economies.

However we soon bumped against the ceiling of our capacity as a revitalized civilian economy added its new demands to the growth in

12-4. U.S. DATA RELATED TO THE WARTIME ECONOMY

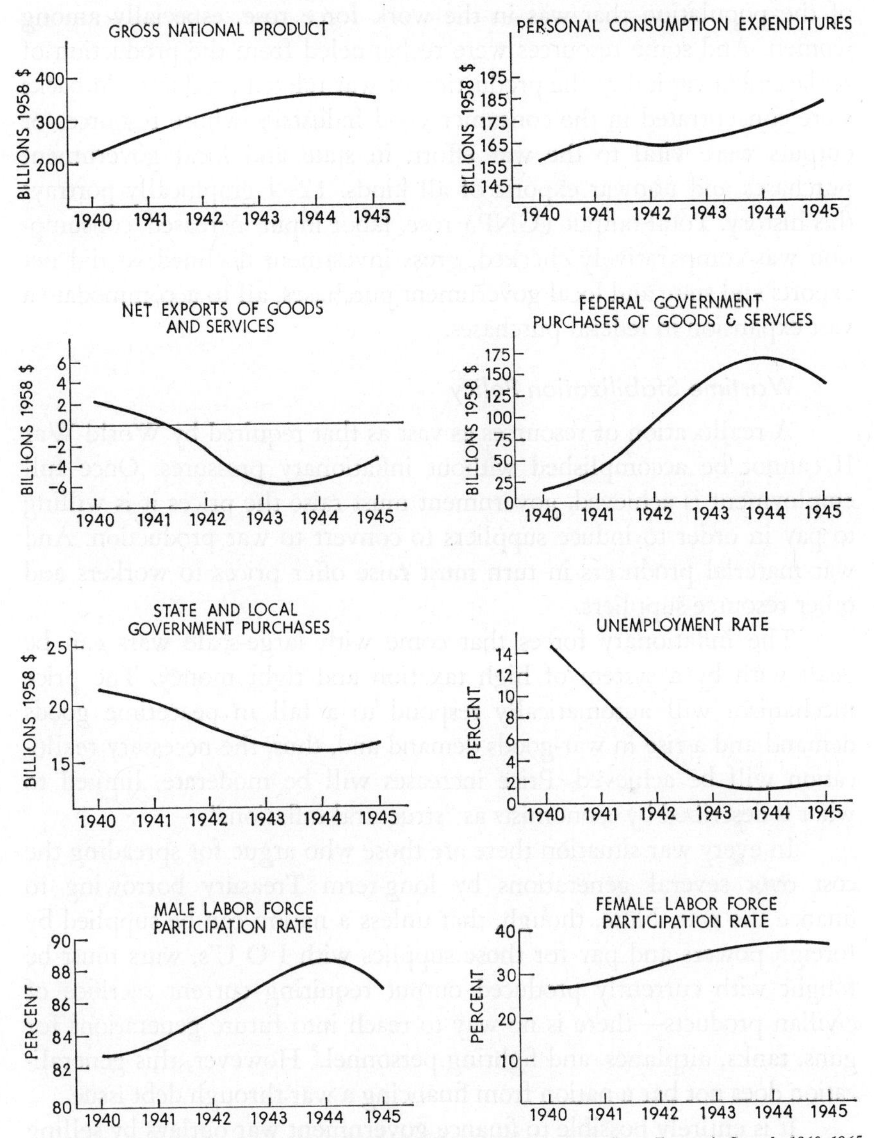

SOURCE: U.S. Department of Commerce, Bureau of the Census, *Long-Term Economic Growth, 1860–1965* (Washington, D.C.: U.S. Government Printing Office, 1966), Appendix 3.

government demand. Consequently from late 1942 until the end of hostilities in 1945, it was necessary to both expand our total capacity and to severely restrict the expansion of civilian production.

Capacity was stretched in a variety of ways. Working hours increased, especially in the direct production of war material. The portion of the population that was in the work force rose, especially among women. And some resources were rechanneled from the production of replacement capital to the production of war-related products. Cutbacks were concentrated in the consumer good industries whose resources or outputs were vital to the war effort, in state and local government purchases and nonwar exports of all kinds. 12–4 graphically portrays this history. Total output (GNP) rose, labor input increased, consumption was comparatively checked, gross investment declined, as did net exports and state and local government purchases, all to accommodate a vast expansion in federal purchases.

Wartime Stabilization Policy

A reallocation of resources as vast as that required by World War II cannot be accomplished without inflationary pressures. Once full employment is achieved, government must raise the prices it is willing to pay in order to induce suppliers to convert to war production. And war material producers in turn must raise offer prices to workers and other resource suppliers.

The inflationary forces that come with large-scale wars can be dealt with by a system of high taxation and tight money. The price mechanism will automatically respond to a fall in peacetime goods demand and a rise in war-goods demand and, thus, the necessary reallocation will be achieved. Price increases will be moderate, limited to what is described by economists as "structural inflation."

In every war situation there are those who argue for spreading the cost over several generations by long-term Treasury borrowing to finance the war. Note, though, that unless a nation can be supplied by foreign powers and pay for those supplies with I O U's, wars must be fought with currently produced output requiring current sacrifice of civilian products—there is no way to reach into future generations for guns, tanks, airplanes, and fighting personnel.[3] However, this generalization does not bar a nation from financing a war through debt issue.

It is entirely possible to finance government war outlays by selling bonds to the public and using the proceeds to buy war material and meet military payrolls. This means that in future generations taxpayers will bear the cost of debt service to bondholders. To restate the princi-

[3] The exceptions to this rule are capital replacement which may be abandoned thus leaving future generations with less capital and training of people that can leave future generations less productive. Neither hinges upon the way in which the war is financed.

ple, we cannot get around sacrificing current peace goods to supply a war effort by government borrowing, but government borrowing can be used to finance purchases of war goods.

Further, as our review of Civil War finance revealed, government can print money to finance a war. It need only print enough money to bid up prices in the war industries sufficiently to bring about the necessary reallocation of productive effort. With this statement of operating principles let us see how we did finance World War II.

12–5. Cash Income and Outgo of U.S. Treasury

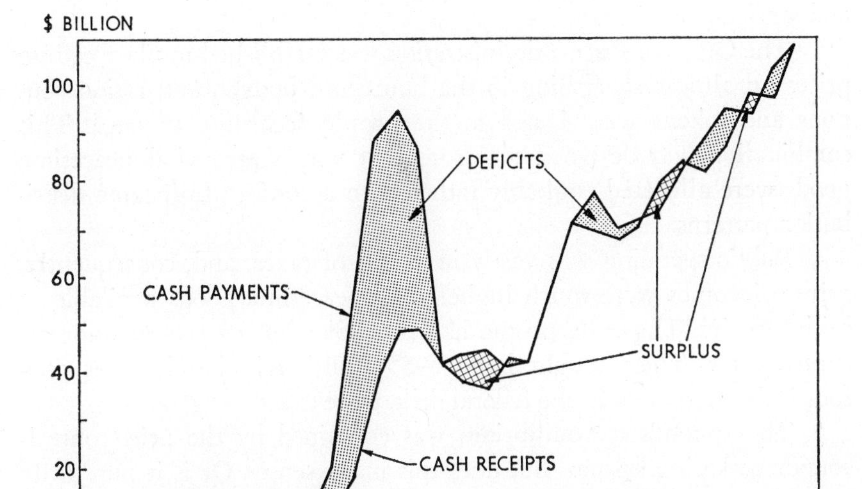

Source: U.S. Department of Commerce.

As it happened, we did not choose to finance our battles with Germany, Japan, and Italy on a current basis. Taxes were raised; but, as 12–5 shows, in addition to Treasury cash receipts rising very rapidly, the federal deficit grew tremendously during the war. And much of that deficit was in effect the result of printing the money; the federal government sold large bond issues to the Federal Reserve System which "created" new money to pay for the bonds.

At this point it is logical to ask why we chose to utilize all three financing alternatives open to us—taxes, borrowing, and money creation. No satisfactory answer can be given beyond saying that the public will demanded it. Some doubtless thought that the real costs could be spread over several generations through debt issues. Others preferred bonds to tax receipts. And, of course, taxes are unpopular per se.

Regardless of motivations we ended up with what John Kenneth Galbraith has named the "disequilibrium system."[4] Expenditures by government were sufficiently large compared with taxation that the total of private plus public spending would have far outstripped our ability to produce unless some brake was put on the private economy—instead of rationing private consumption by limiting purchasing power through taxation, we preferred to directly ration private sales of goods and services.

The Office of Price Administration was established to place ceiling prices on almost everything in the household budget, and ration coupons and tokens were issued to the people according to need. This combination was designed to assure that very scarce vital peacetime goods were allocated equitably rather than according to income distribution patterns.

Public spending was vastly in excess of taxes, and, consequently, private incomes were much higher than peacetime goods available at ceiling prices. Thus, the people had no choice but to save at unprecedented rates. They bought bonds—$54 billion in bonds, over one-fourth the increment in the federal debt, to be exact.

The system's disequilibrium was contained by the price-control-coupon-rationing system. But does this make sense? Or is it pure folly involving a rationing system which is more complex and less efficient than prices and taxes? Several telling points stand in favor of our rather pragmatic solution to war finance.

First, work incentives might have been damaged by taxation at higher rates with harsh results for the war effort. In some industries, people were asked to work 12-hour days, 7-day weeks, and some never took a vacation through the entire period. The question is, would they have been willing to put forth so much sustained effort if their gross pay had been split, say, 50–50 between tax receipts and cash? Under the disequilibrium system, people found their gross split between cash, tax receipts, and bonds. The bonds, many economists feel, represented future purchases and kept incentives intact.

Second, bonds were cashed and spent when civilian goods were again plentiful. Thus in periods of potentially weak demand after the

[4] J. K. Galbraith, "The Disequilibrium System," *American Economic Review*, Vol. 37 (June, 1947), pp. 287–302.

war, the disequilibrium system served to support stability in the postwar economy.

POSTWAR STABILITY

At this point, we might consider how well our economy has done in regard to business fluctuations since World War II. There have been five minor dips—in 1946, 1949, 1954, 1957, and late 1960. Since 1961 expansion has proceeded almost unabated. Throughout the period we have had a general tendency toward mild price inflation punctuated by accelerated price increases during the Korean and Vietnam military actions.

No other period in our history has had such a long span of growth with such mild fluctuations. However we should note that each cycle has ended with a higher unemployment rate than the previous cycle—or did so until the 1964 tax cut plus the war in Vietnam prolonged the last recovery and pushed the unemployment rate lower than it had been in 12 years.

Favorable Postwar Setting

A certain amount of groundwork should precede an evaluation of our post-World War II record. First, we should look at the basic economic setting into which we stepped at the close of the war. Second, we should trace the metamorphosis of business cycle theory as it evolved into a comprehensive theory of aggregate income and employment determination.

As the close of the war approached, many scholars and lay people fully expected a return to depression conditions. This expectation was rooted in the stagnation thesis that we discussed in the brief review of the past 50 years in Chapter 11. Stagnation you will recall was said to result from the general maturity of the economy, especially the decline in the birthrate, the closing of the frontier, and the changing nature of capital. All these factors reduced the productivity of new capital investment. Given the high incomes and therefore the high saving levels associated with maturity, the laissez-faire economy chronically tended to generate higher levels of saving than the low productivity of new capital could justify in the way of investment. Now the question to ask is: Did the postwar economy offer the same threat of stagnation that the 1930's seemed to pose?

After the war the economy instead of plunging into recession took up the task of doing over the Nation's plant and equipment for peacetime pursuits. The bulge in unemployment that came directly after the end of the fighting was partially checked in its economic effects by the unemployment compensation program inaugurated after 1936. And the short period of unemployment was attributable only to the time required to convert plants. Consumers had been starved for durables over the lean depression and shortage war years and had war bonds ready to finance automobiles, appliances, and house repairs. Consumer durables sales continued at high levels as the 1945 tax reductions took effect and led to increased consumption.

Prolonged high employment accelerated the birthrate and with it the investment in housing, facilitated to a large degree by the insured mortgages of the New Deal's Federal Housing Administration. A backlog of depression-spiked state and local government construction projects was put into action although the needs actually grew as the war babies suddenly descended upon the Nation's school systems. Spurred on by low-interest rates and easy money, state and local government deficits soon outweighed the combined deficits of the 1930's. And the AAA put a floor under farm incomes when European production shut out a large portion of U.S. farm exports.

Finally, the economy emerged from the war and the New Deal quite a changed system. With all its ills and privations, World War II was for many Americans an exhilerating experience which affected postwar thinking—in spite of stagnation talk, investors and consumers entered the years after 1945 with a free-wheeling optimism. The various Hoover and Roosevelt reforms added stability to the environment. Expansion was also enhanced by the continuing deficits of the state and local governments and by the progressive elements of the federal income tax.

Does this all say that the stagnation thesis was not valid, that events have disproved it? No! Rather, we must conclude that the proximate conditions that produce stagnation are no longer extant. The public sector is large, annual government borrowing is significant, and taxes do reduce the flow of savings, so private investment can fill the remaining gap. All the stagnation thesis ever stated was the tendency to chronic depression in the laissez-faire economy—what with growth of the public sector, we have never had a significant factual test of this thesis.

Change in Economic Thought

We have discussed the factual environment that constituted the postwar economy. We should now describe the economic thought that provides the basis for both our analysis and the policy tools that have been forged since 1945.

In 1936, John Maynard Keynes, whom we have already cited as a famous monetary economist, published his *General Theory of Employment, Interest and Money.* This book, whose contents are still hotly debated in academia and condemned in some lay circles, has already made as great a mark on economic life as Adam Smith's *Wealth of Nations.* Keynes presented to a stunned and mystified world an explanation for the longest depression in history.

Keynes's book is in excess of 300 pages and this is not the appropriate place to review it in detail. For our purposes Keynes' message can be summed up by three statements:

1. The mature, western market economy is basically unstable.
2. In the operation of the total economy, the movement of prices and the forces of supply and demand in individual markets do not collectively constitute an inherent tendency toward full resource employment without inflation—an economy could in fact stagnate at less than full employment.
3. In such an economy fiscal and monetary policy can be designed to achieve relatively full employment and price stability with only mild cyclical swings.

These three statements represent Keynes's contribution to what policy makers and the popular press refer to today as "The New Economics." Actually the New Economics is more than 30 years old and represents a synthesis in which the monetary theory of the 1920's was blended with extensions of Keynes's work to produce what economists call modern macroeconomic theory—especially in its monetary and fiscal policy applications. Yet people refer to the New Economics as the result of the Keynesian Revolution. To see why this evolution in thought is treated as a revolution it is necessary to review briefly the predecessor of modern macroeconomic theory.

In the early 1800's, Say's Law of Markets was articulated by several economists including J. B. Say, the theory's namesake. It can be briefly summarized as follows:

1. In the aggregate economy, supply creates its own demand because production of any one firm gives rise to income which is spent for other producers' output. (Recall the National Accounts relationships of income and production.)
2. Depression and inflation are momentary disturbances which are self-correcting—international gold movements plus the ability of prices to fluctuate in individual markets in order to equate supply and demand guarantee automatic restoration of prosperity and price stability.
3. Any governmental action to restore stability is at best redundant and at worst destabilizing.

Again we stress that the New Economics evolved over a long period. Thus one should not infer that the theory presented immediately above in its most abstract form was universally held without modification until 1936 when the Keynesian Revolution imposed itself. Rather the New Economics should be thought of as revolutionary in the sense that in one generation economists and policy makers reversed their position with respect to government's role in determining the level of total spending, output, and employment. That revolution was sparked by the depth and length of the Great Depression.

As the corpus of modern income and employment theory developed, the law followed, although somewhat reluctantly. Most significant of the legal developments is the Employment Act of 1946 which established the President's Council of Economic Advisors and announced this policy:

> The Congress hereby declares that it is the continuing policy and responsibility of the Federal Government to use all practicable means consistent with its needs and obligations and other essential considerations of national policy, with assistance and cooperation of industry, agriculture, labor and State and local governments, to coordinate and utilize all its plans, functions, and resources for the purposes of creating and maintaining, in a manner calculated to foster and promote free competitive enterprise and the general welfare, conditions under which there will be afforded useful employment opportunities, including self-employment, for those able, willing, and seeking to work and *to promote maximum employment, production, and purchasing power.* [Italics supplied]

To enable the federal government to carry out this mandate, two types of fiscal policy have been developed which with monetary policy give the public decision makers a formidable array of countercyclical weapons.

The Built-in Stabilizers

Stabilizing changes in federal tax collections and expenditures occur automatically when the economy starts to take a swing toward inflation or depression. These nondiscretionary fiscal policies which result directly from changes in the GNP are usually referred to as the ***built-in stabilizers.*** Ironically, although they are products of New Deal reforms they were proposed and enacted for their proximate results—equity or economic security for target groups. Since the 1930's lawmakers have come to recognize their aggregate stabilizing influence.

When GNP and employment fall, income tax receipts fall even faster than income (because of the tax's progressive structure) and government payments for unemployment compensation and relief, and often farm subsidies, automatically rise. Consequently, under current conditions, a fall in GNP of, say, 10 percent might result in a decrease in consumer disposable income of only 5 per cent. This in turn breaks the contraction of consumption and thus ***reduces the multiplier*** reaction we discussed earlier.

For example, a $10 billion initial decline in GNP would yield only a $5 billion decrease in disposable income; and, if consumers reduce their spending by 80 cents out of each dollar by which their incomes fall, the $10 billion decline of GNP will result in only a $4 billion decline in consumption. It is easy to see how much smaller the ***multiplier*** would be in such a case as contrasted with a similar situation in which there are no taxes or transfer payments such as unemployment compensation to drive a wedge between GNP and disposable income: in our example, if capital consumption allowances were, say, $1 billion, then the resulting decline in disposable income would be $9 billion and consumption would fall by $7.2 billion (0.8 × $9 billion). What is more, the stabilizers work in reverse—in this case, a rise of $10 billion in GNP would produce only a $4 billion increase in consumption, not a $7.2 billion rise.

Do the stabilizers do their job well? While they do not fully iron out the business cycle, several careful studies of their effects report that they have been significant in stabilizing the postwar economy. In fact we have learned that they may do their work too well in periods of postrecession expansion by checking recovery before full employment is reached, and thus some compensatory discretionary policies may be required.

Discretionary Fiscal Policy

Stabilizing policies which require an act of Congress or an Executive Order are classed as discretionary fiscal policies. We have already seen how tax cuts and/or expenditure increases operate to break recession and speed recovery. The principle you will recall is simply that the full-employment level of saving, taxes, and imports must be fully offset by private investment, exports, and government expenditure. Fiscal policy may bring this about by some combination of lower tax rates, higher expenditures for goods and services, or higher payment schedules for programs such as relief and unemployment compensation. Thus in recession, federal expansion and/or tax cuts should be the order of the day and the opposite during inflation.

Because federal stimulation can be obtained by spending more or by taxing less, there are disagreements about which is better. On the one hand, the question is one of what a nation needs most at the time—more government programs, more private products (tax cuts), or more of both. Only existing conditions and the public will can answer this question. On the other hand, the problem is one of strategy. Recent experience has suggested that public investment projects—such as the construction of dams and highways—take a long time to get under way; so they are not very flexible in the timing of expenditures. Theoretically, tax cuts could be voted quickly and take effect immediately; but Congress usually does not act quickly on tax measures. The latter point is especially true when tax cuts are necessary to compensate for the "overeffectiveness" of the built-in stabilizers during recovery.

A reversal of antirecession policy is all that is required to combat inflation—public and private spending must be reduced to full-employment levels. The problems of implementation are much the same as with antidepression policy. Public works are hard to stop midway to completion and tax increases are both slow to get through the Congress and politically unattractive.

How has our discretionary fiscal policy record been? On the inflation side, relatively good until recently. Recessions? If measured by intentions, performance has been bad; but if we consider the fortuitous tax cuts which were legislated for other reasons in the late 1940's and 1950's, the record is fairly good. The following paragraph summarizes Professor E. C. Brown's evaluation of discretionary action from World War II to 1960.[5]

Discretionary policy was mixed in its effects and underlying motivations and thus cannot be assigned much credit for the stability of the 15-year period. The tax cuts of 1945 were too early. In 1948, taxes were cut for "precisely the wrong reasons." In the 1949 recession, policy was mildly expansionary but fortuitously so since it was adopted for "other reasons." During the Korean War we moved decisively and effectively against inflation but in the recession that followed our withdrawal from Korea, policy was deflationary. In the 1955–57 inflation we did nothing to alter our fiscal posture. Finally the antirecession movements of 1957–58 were modest compared with the task. However, Brown asserts, "This is too harsh a judgment. There was less moving in the wrong direction and more understanding was acquired." However, the judgment stands that in the 1940's and the 1950's the actual fiscal posture of the federal government was more stabilizing

[5] E. C. Brown, "Federal Fiscal Policy in the Postwar Period," *Postwar Economic Trends in the United States* (New York: Harper & Row, 1960), pp. 185–86.

than we can assume it would have been in the absence of "wrong" and "other" reasons.

After 1960, policy improved markedly. The New Economics had "arrived." To boost the recovery from the 1960–61 recession, depreciation rules for tax purposes were relaxed and a tax credit based on new investment activity was enacted. Then, in February, 1964, corporate and individual taxes were cut. This action marked a watershed, the first tax cut undertaken ***explicitly*** to spur a recovery and head off another recession. In February, 1966, unemployment at 3.7 percent was lower than it had been since the July, 1953, peak of the 1953–58 cycle. This record is to a large degree accounted for by these tax cuts.

The logical question to address at this point is why wasn't our postwar fiscal policy record better? The answer seems to be that public, congressional, and executive attitudes persisted in the balanced budget orthodoxy of the 1920's. Even after a calamity like the Great Depression, the Employment Act of 1946 was passed as a much watered-down version of the original draft, and it had great difficulty getting passed. For many years high historical regard for laissez faire, as a corollary to individualism, and a penchant for drawing invalid analogies between household and public budgets overwhelmed the desire to make the economy more stable.

On the other hand, since the passage of the Employment Act of 1946, administrative and congressional leaders of both parties have shown a growing readiness to seek government action when a recession occurs. Why is this?

For one thing, people now realize that only the federal government can take responsibility for the behavior of the economic system as a whole. In an individualistic economy, what is nobody's business in particular must be everybody's business in general. For example, when everyone is trying to protect himself by getting hold of cash, only the government can step in and make sure that enough cash is available to restore public confidence. And, when state and local or private expenditure flows slow down, only the federal government can take the responsibility to keep everyone employed. This need not mean that the national government plans and directs private actions in the economy, but it may need to provide an environment of confidence and ample spending to encourage private activity.

Another factor is greater appreciation for the fact that idleness of men and plant capacity are both wasteful and a source of great individual suffering. The American people now appear determined not to have another depression like the one of the 1930's. World War II demonstrated that the government, if necessary, can put people to work and even draw into the labor force an abnormal proportion of the population.

Monetary Policy

The monetary weapons at the disposal of the Federal Reserve System have also been revolutionized since 1929. Hoover's and Roosevelt's monetary legislation vastly changed the nature of the financial sector. Prior to reform, the financial system was a destabilizing force, whereas today, given its new structure, it provides an excellent environment for countercyclical policy.

The tools of monetary policy are readily understood. As we said in Chapter 10, the Federal Reserve System was established to control the volume of money and credit in the system by changing the reserve requirements of member banks and altering the interest rate, called the "discount rate," at which it would loan reserves to member banks. Since 1913, the system's power to buy and sell securities in the open market has been significantly expanded and is now the most formidable countercyclical monetary tool.

In general, monetary policy stimulates a flagging economy by increasing the availability of reserves to the banking system and combats inflation by restricting reserves. Because commercial bank reserve accounts at the Federal Reserve are the basis for the money-creating activities of the banks, expansion or contraction of reserves produces like movements in the money supply.

If unemployment and deflation are the problems of the day, the System will lower discount rates and buy bonds in the open market. Member banks will now find it cheaper to borrow reserves. And banks in general will discover that the bonds in their portfolios can be sold at a profit since the System's purchases have pushed up their prices. Consequently banks will be more willing to increase their loans from the Federal Reserve and banks in general will sell bonds in the open market. These moves increase bank reserves and thus the ability of banks to make loans to customers. What is more, given their increased reserve position, banks now have incentive to make more loans even at lower interest rates; so they will lower interest charges and encourage heavier borrowing. The individuals and firms that borrow additional amounts increase their expenditures and the whole multiplier process goes into action. (If the system is dealing with an especially deep recession, it may also lower the reserve requirements of member banks which, of course, automatically raises the latter's ability to lend.)

Inflation is dealt with in reverse fashion—the discount rate will be raised and bonds will be sold at lower prices in the open market. Banks will be discouraged from borrowing reserves and will reduce their loan activity in favor of purchasing bonds which would be selling at bargain prices and, therefore, at higher yields than previously. Thus spending will contract and inflationary forces will diminish.

Let us review our monetary policy record. During the World War II period to 1951, the Federal Reserve was denied its most powerful weapon, open-market policy. It had agreed to sacrifice countercyclical goals in order to stabilize the bond market at very low rates of interest thus minimizing carrying charges on the war debt. Money was tightened on the average after 1951 with some easing with the 1953–54 recession. Since 1957, the System has permitted the monetary stock to grow but usually less rapidly than the economy as a whole; this amounts to a tight money policy. This policy came in the face of the secular rise in unemployment we mentioned earlier in this section.

Most economists will agree that on many occasions fiscal and monetary policy have been at odds, most often with fiscal moves being made to prod expansion accompanied by a monetary policy which brakes the economy. In an administrative sense, this can occur because the System now is organizationally centralized ***but*** very much independent of Presidential control. From a more fundamental standpoint the tug-of-war between fiscal and monetary policy arises because the goals of the Employment Act are mutually exclusive at close to full employment.

When an economy is in deep depression the goals of "maximum employment, production, and purchasing power" are compatible goals. Deficit government spending plus an easy money policy can promote higher employment and expanded output with no significant advance in prices. But when near full employment—say, 5 percent or less of the labor force unemployed—any advance in spending from any quarter will not only increase employment and production but will push prices upward as well. In short, there is a tradeoff relationship between price inflation and reduction of unemployment when the economy is near full employment.

No economist can dictate the right amount of employment and correspondingly the right degree of price inflation—that is, a value judgment. But economic policy makers cannot dodge the issue; they must make a choice. As it happens, bankers, who make monetary policy decisions, become more exercised over the unwholesome results of inflation than do congressmen and Presidents, and vice versa with respect to the ills associated with unemployment. Thus the chairman of the Federal Reserve System on the one hand and the President and the Congress' Joint Economic Committee on the other hand, often find themselves at loggerheads. They are both operating in the context of the New Economics yet advocating almost opposite policies. However, we should not despair that we are as vulnerable as in the 1920's because the policy makers cannot get together. Rather, it is only on this fuzzy borderline between inflation and unemployment that coordination suffers.

In sum, why has our postwar record been so stable? Certainly monetary and fiscal policy deserve a large part of the credit, even if the right things were often done for the wrong reasons. Second, the war changed the basic nature of the economy in favor of long-run exhilaration, pushing aside stagnation—nowhere have these basic changes been more pronounced than in the government sector where urbanization and population growth have placed great pressures. Thus a basically more stable economy has been given even more stability by improvements in contracyclical monetary and fiscal policy.

STUDY QUESTIONS

1. "Business cycles are 'normal' in a market economy in which technological changes are frequent". Explain this statement. Would you expect a subsistence income economy to be more or less stable than a mature western economy?
2. Why was the 1921 recession so short? Why were the 1920's so stable? Were the 1920's as healthy as their stability would imply?
3. What is the relationship between total spending on the one hand and GNP and employment on the other hand? If private investment were to decline would you expect GNP to fall by an equal amount? By more? By less? Explain your answers.
4. If consumer buying patterns were to change because new types of products came on the market, what would happen to private investment?
5. What were the proximate causes of the Great Depression? Why was it a "Great Contraction?" Why was the depression so long? What brought it to a close?
6. Evaluate Hoover's and Roosevelt's antidepression policy. Was fiscal policy as enlightened as it could have been in view of economic knowledge at the time? Monetary policy?
7. Why was conversion for the war effort relatively easy considering the magnitude of the task? We produced above capacity during the World War II. Explain this statement.

8. What is "The New Economics?" How does it relate to Keynesian economics? To monetary and fiscal policy?
9. Define discretionary fiscal policy and evaluate its postwar effects. What are the built-in stabilizers? How do they operate?
10. Full employment and price stability are compatible goals in depression but not when the economy is very near capacity. Explain this statement.

Chapter 13 CHANGING STRUCTURE: BUSINESS, AGRICULTURE, AND LABOR

We have noted several times that economic growth is associated with changes in the structure of the economy. Some of the changes are causes of growth whereas others are the result of higher incomes or the pace of growth. Some are costs, unfortunate side effects and dislocations, while others are the gains which make the pursuit of growth worthwhile. In this chapter we shall survey such developments in several sectors of the economy since 1920. Specifically we shall look at the implications of growth in the business, agriculture, and labor sectors of the economy. The household and government sectors are discussed in the following chapter.

Taken together the characteristics of these five sectors constitute the structure of the economy and the changes that are part of the growth process alter that structure. Throughout it is important to remember that the sectors are ***not*** mutually exclusive segments but are instead overlapping and interdependent categories. In sum, they constitute the medium through which the causes and effects of economic development are transmitted.

GIANT BUSINESS ENTERPRISE

By World War I, the United States had become the leading modern industrial economy and achieved a standard of living that was the envy of the world. Yet Americans remained very self-conscious and self-critical about their problems. They particularly were embarassed and uneasy about the extent to which giant business organizations had grown up with mass production and mass distribution.

There were three types of fears concerning bigness in business. Each of these fears concerned one of the useful functions of competition in a market economy.

First, there was the fear of loss of the ***regulating force*** of competition. The antitrust movement of the last century and the prewar reform movement continued to be a recurring political force. Competition is valued as a means of ensuring that business is efficient in serving consumers and does not have arbitrary powers to raise prices, restrict output, and profit through exploiting some exclusive position of market power. The giant corporation frequently was suspected of possessing and using monopoly powers.

Second, there was the fear of loss of ***incentives*** to improve. During the Great Depression, charges were made that giant businesses had rigidly administered prices that weakened the flexibility of the market economy and that the enterprising spirit was dying out in the bureaucracy of large-scale business organization. Competition also is valued as a means of motivating business leaders to make rapid adjustments and to strive to improve production and introduce new methods and products.

Third, there was a fear of loss of ***individualism and democracy.*** Competition is valued as a means of providing alternative opportunities to the individual and keeping power dispersed. After World War II, there was increasing concern over the plight of the "organization man" and the possible disappearance of small business. Individuals felt an increasing helplessness in a complex world in which issues seemed to be decided by the leaders of Big Business, Big Labor, and Big Government.

Big Firms in a Big Economy

The American economy has grown very large. Within this economy both the number of giant firms and the absolute size of these firms have increased. In 1901, the United States Steel Corporation became the first corporation with over $1 billion in assets. In 1962, 1,533 corporations had over $1 billion in assets, and 638 had over $2.5 billion—which is more comparable to $1 billion in 1901.

There undoubtedly is more concentration in production than in consumer incomes—for consumption takes place mostly in small family units. In 1962, the 638 largest corporations had 27.7 percent of all sales among a total of 1.3 million corporations. Corporations, in turn, accounted for roughly two thirds of all gross product among about 5 million business firms. This means that in recent times, close to 1⁄100 of 1 percent of the units provides a little less than 20 percent of business production. In family incomes, the top 5 percent receives about 20 percent of income.

Of what significance is this? It is difficult to determine. The prediction of Karl Marx, of course, was that capital ownership inevitably tends to concentrate a monopoly of economic power in fewer and fewer hands. This leads to a fear that the dispersion of economic power essential to a democracy will be lost. There is little evidence, however, that justifies the exaggerated claims of giant firm domination of the American economy today, and there is no trend toward greater monopoly in the economy.

Since the early 1930's, when the first studies of concentration were made, a sort of numbers game has been used to create the impression—or at least illustrate the potentialities—of concentrated power. Whenever there is a wide dispersion of sizes for any type of data, some small number will have some disproportionate share of the total. By selection of the number in the top group, an impressively large percentage share—say 50 percent—can be obtained. By eliminating banks, insurance companies, and other financial corporations—on the doubtful argument that they merely hold money and securities of the really productive corporations—the number of giants can be reduced. In 1962, 293 giants had 25.9 percent of the nonfinancial corporate sales. Eliminating the separate reporting subsidiaries of holding companies can further reduce the number of giants. In 1933, this adjusted the magic number of giants from 375 to 200. By speaking in terms of assets—rather than sales or employees—the share of the giants looks larger, because it is the capital-intensive technology of some modern industries that brought the giant firms into being. In 1962, the 293 giants had 44.5 per cent of the nonfinancial corporation assets. Previously, in 1933, the adjusted number of 200 giants had 55 percent of the nonfinancial corporation assets. By referring to specific sectors—those that are most concentrated and highly capital-intensive—even smaller numbers of firms and higher percentages can be obtained. In 1962, 118 of the giant corporations held 75 percent of the assets in all transportation and public utility corporations; and 141 giants held 48.6 percent of assets of all manufacturing corporations. By implication, these are the "key" sectors of a modern industrial economy, so a few firms in these key sectors are assumed to dominate the whole economy. By redirecting the focus, away from production to individual ownership, it can be pointed out that the key giant corporations are financially controlled by a relatively small number of giant corporations, wealthy families, or company officials.

It is on the basis of this type of study and the plentiful literature of the antitrust and reform movements early in this century that much of the rest of the world has gained its impression that the American economy is dominated by a few giant capitalists. When a group of leading Russian economists visited this country in 1960, for example, they seriously asked executives of large manufacturing corporations about their "orders" from Wall Street bankers. The Harrimans, Rockefellers, and Fords are regarded as behind-the-scenes rulers of our country.

The numbers game, of course, can be played in reverse. There are 5 million business decision makers, and 1.3 million corporations. There are a greater number of small businesses as the economy grows; and each year opportunities abound for new ones to start. By implication, the nongiants control 90 percent of business sales. The few giant corporations are not free to make any decisions they please, unless it could be shown (which it rarely can) that they have exclusive areas of decision making where they have secure monopoly positions.

The relevant number at which decision-making power becomes dangerously concentrated also is an important question that no one has been able to answer. Experience with pools and collusion, for example, suggests that business interests seldom are so harmonious or group discipline so strong that 20 or even 10 firms can act together for long. If the top 10 or 20 firms were spotlighted, the percentage shares of sales in the economy would not be so impressive. On the other hand, by selecting a high percentage, an initial impression is created without regard to whether the number of firms is 500, 200, or 100.

The word "control" also is highly ambiguous, both in terms of the consequences of percentage shares and the meaning of various types of linkages. How much power can be exercised over other firms when one firm has 10 or even 50 percent of the output of a product? While it may be conceded that a small percentage of stockholders may provide the leadership to a large corporation with tens of thousands of passive owners, to what extent can control be exercised contrary to the interests of the majority of stockholders? To what extent can company officers stay in their positions if their profit-making performance is poor? Are widespread security holdings evidence of far-flung controls for power purposes or of prudent diversification of investments?

The historical sources of business concentration, moreover, are technology and market size rather than ownership. Large corporations are a result of mass-production and mass-distribution technology; and concentration is greatest where capital-intensive methods are required. About the same technology and organization scale is adopted in all modern nations; but this involves a much greater degree of concentration in small nations. Most modern industrial nations have greater percentages of concentration of sales in large firms than does the United States. Even Russia has its giant production organizations in the same types of industries.

It should be noted that the greatest concentration is in sectors where it is technically unavoidable or socially desirable and where public regulation is exercised—that is, in transportation and public utilities and in finance. The transportation and public utility industries long have been recognized as having technical conditions requiring exclusive service facilities or as achieving economies with large single units; and historically these "natural monopolies" have been publicly regulated by special charter conditions or government supervisory commissions.

Financial institutions also have the social function of collecting large aggregations of savings to provide the capital for large-scale production units. Large financial institutions provide specialized analysts, diversify their investments, and handle large blocks of security issues needed by large corporations. Some public regulation also is exercised in securities markets and in banking.

Most important, there is no evidence of historical trends toward ever-increasing concentration in the modern economy. Little information is available on how much concentration existed in earlier times on a smaller and more local scale. The early manufacturer and banker frequently had a near-monopoly in his local community; and a small group of wealthy merchants were prominent in the early textile industry. Between the Civil War and World War I, however, when the basic industrialization of the economy occurred, it seems likely that national concentration of business increased. A great merger movement in business history took place around 1900 when large corporations were formed as horizontal integrations of many plants of the same type. Additional concentration probably occurred between 1920 and the mid-1930's, when major new industries took shape, many corporations integrated vertically (to control their own supply and marketing operations), and holding companies spread in public utility industries.

Since the 1930's, however, no clear trend has appeared. Expansion of the total economy has been rapid, and additional large firms have risen to share the position of previous leaders. While a new wave of mergers has occurred since World War II, it has been a new type of merger. Smaller firms have been acquired to diversify operations into different industries rather than to extend the market share or to integrate related operations within the same industry. Such mergers are called conglomerate mergers. For example, the *Annual Report of the*

Council of Economic Advisors in January, 1965 (page 132) stated that the 100 largest manufacturing firms had increased their share of all manufacturing assets and value-added from 1947 to 1962 but that "concentration within specific industries has shown no significant trend." (See 13–1.)

In addition to the lack of a distinct trend in concentration, the modern period has evidenced a rapid turnover in the identity of the top-ranking corporations by size. Of the 100 largest industrial firms in 1909 (omitting transportation, utility, and financial firms) only 50 still were among the 199 largest in 1919 and 31 in 1960. Of the 100 largest in 1935 only 65 still were among the 100 largest in 1960.[1] This

13–1. MERGERS IN MANUFACTURING AND MINING INDUSTRIES
(Five-Year Totals)

Period	Mergers	Period	Mergers	Period	Mergers
1895–99	1,649*	1920–24	2,235	1945–49	1,505
1900–04	1,363	1925–29	4,583*	1950–54	1,424
1905–09	440	1930–34	1,687	1955–59	3,365
1910–14	451	1935–39	577	1960–64	4,366
1915–19	625	1940–44	906		

* Note that the largest number for a single year was 1,245 in 1929, and the next largest was 1,208 in 1899.
SOURCE: U.S. Department of Commerce, *Historical Statistics of the United States* (Washington, D.C.: U.S. Government Printing Office, 1960), p. 572; U.S. Department of Commerce, *Statistical Abstract of the United States, 1965* (Washington, D.C.: U.S. Government Printing Office, 1966), p. 503.

is because the major technological changes of the modern period have shifted the relative importance of various industries—whole new industries (such as aircraft and electronics) have risen to prominence while others (such as coal, shipping, and leather) have stagnated. Some corporations (such as U.S. Steel and Standard Oil of New Jersey) have expanded and stayed in the 100 largest industrial firms but have been reduced to a smaller share of the output in their own industry group. Some corporations (such as S. S. Kresge, National Biscuit, and Wheeling Steel) have dropped out of the top 100, while others in their industry group (such as J. C. Penney, General Foods, and Kaiser Steel) have entered the top 100. So the dynamics of the modern economy has not assured the prominence of the same large firms.

The New Competition

Aside from the regulated utilities and financial industries, most attention has been focused on manufacturing as the next most concentrated sector. Yet the market power of a manufacturing corporation

[1] A. D. H. Kaplan, *Big Enterprise in a Competitive System* (Washington, D.C.: The Brookings Institution, 1964), p. 136.

depends more on its share of sales in specific subindustries or product markets than on its size ranking among all industrial giants. The studies of corporate concentration in the 1930's soon led to government-compiled statistics on the shares of assets, employment, and sales by the top firms in each subindustry.

In the motor vehicles and parts subindustry, for example, the four largest companies in 1954 had 70.7 percent of the assets, 69 percent of the employment, and 75 percent of the value of shipments. Some experiments with measures for the 1 largest, 4 largest, 8 largest, and 20

13–2. DISTRIBUTION OF CONCENTRATION IN MANUFACTURING INDUSTRIES, 1954

Industries in which the Share of Sales by the Four Largest Firms Was	*Number of Industries*	*Percent of Total Sales*
75 to 100%	40	7.8%
50 to 74	101	16.7
25 to 49	157	35.3
0 to 24	136	40.2
Total	434	100.0%

SOURCE: U.S. Senate Committee on the Judiciary, Subcommittee on Antitrust and Monopoly, *Concentration in American Industry*, 85th Cong., 1st sess. (Washington, D.C.: U.S. Government Printing Office, 1957), Table 17.

largest firms show that these measures vary little in their ranking of different subindustries. Any of the measures show that some industries —such as aluminum, tin cans, motor vehicles, and cigarettes—are highly concentrated while other industries—such as woolen and worsted goods, drugs, and medicines—are not.

These measures show that surprisingly few of the subindustry groups in manufacturing are very concentrated. Of 434 subindustries in 1954, only 40 had concentrations of sales of over 75 percent among the four largest firms. In only a third of all subindustries was concentration above 50 percent. Some subindustries, of course, are much larger than others. Still only 24.5 percent, or one fourth, of all manufacturing sales were in industries with concentrations of over 50 percent of the sales in the four largest firms. (See 13–2.)

These measures also show a long-term trend toward less concentration. A study compiling the same sort of concentration measures for manufacturing subindustries in 1901, showed that 32.9 percent, or one third, of value-added in all manufacturing came from industries with concentrations above 50 percent.[2] The comparable figure in 1947 was 24.0 percent, or ***one fourth.*** Since then there has been little change. According to the Council of Economic Advisors, the comparable figure for 1958 was 23 percent, in spite of the merger movement increasing the share of sales in the economy among larger firms.

While there is no evidence in these measures of any actual increase in concentration of power in markets generally, there has been a change in the awareness of the public about the presence of concentration. New ideas about competition began to appear in economic theory literature beginning in the 1930's. The simple idea of a dichotomy between monopoly and competition—which assumed an industry either was a monopoly (single seller) or it must be competitive—was replaced with more complex ideas. Monopoly power began to be considered as a matter of degree, and there was more than one dimension to consider in measuring that power. In theory, the conditions for pure competition were defined in rather severe terms so that pure competition became the unusual case rather than monopoly. Nearly all industries seemed to be only imperfectly competitve and had varying degrees of monopoly power.

Instead of the dichotomous approach to market structure, analysts have developed a more useful alternative. Today markets are considered to be characterized by different degrees of competition varying between the theoretical extremes of monopoly and what the economist calls pure competition. This represents theoretical recognition of the conditions of the modern economy. Contemporary theory takes into account the fact that there are many factors in addition to concentration which determine whether the useful functions of competition are performed.

One of the conditions to be taken into account was the extent to which advertising and product differentiation by each manufacturer created a special demand for its own output. It was found that sales could be expanded by product improvement and sales promotion as well as by cost reduction and price cuts. The preference of some customers for its product also gave a firm some discretion in charging a higher price than some of its competitors without losing much of its sales. In theory, this condition of product differentiation, when large numbers of firms were involved, was given the odd label of "monopolistic competition."

Another condition that affected the more concentrated industries

[2] G. Warren Nutter, *A Quantitative Study of the Extent of Enterprise Monopoly in the United States, 1899–1939* (Chicago: University of Chicago Press, 1951).

was the recognition by a few large firms that the demands for their product were mutually interdependent. One firm's demand depended on other firms' reactions. If one firm alone cut its price, it might gain a large increase in sales volume from customers who shifted from competitors' products. Yet, if other firms reacted by cutting their prices too, each of the firms might gain a very small increase in sales—reflecting the extent to which total customer sales would increase with a lowering of price. Whenever there were a small number of firms (or a high concentration among a few firms) each firm became very conscious of the potential reactions of its rivals. Business decisions, therefore, became much like a poker game—in fact, economic theory began to explore the "theory of games."

Unfortunately, economic theory still lacks adequate explanations and predictions for how a very few large firms in an industry will behave. There is an increased likelihood that they will attempt to make agreements about prices, just as the railroad pools once attempted to do. Or, each firm may begin to make pricing decisions very much like the whole industry would if it were organized as one big monopoly. Or, one firm may make such decisions and others may follow, believing them to be in their mutual interests. Since some of the theory for this condition evolved from considering one-firm and two-firm industries—the monopoly and duopoly cases—the label of "oligopoly" was applied to all cases of few-firm industries.

Still another condition requiring changes in the theory of market structure and performance was rapid technological change. This adds a dynamic dimension to competition; for now it may not matter so much how many firms there are, or who has the largest share of sales, as who first introduces a new or improved product. The modern consumer has demonstrated remarkable quickness in changing habits to take advantage of new product and service opportunities. Mass-production and mass-distribution techniques also are capable of putting a new product on the market and very quickly capturing a large share of consumer purchases in an industry. Consumer habits and trust in recognized brands then make it difficult for another firm to recapture the market without a superior product. The few large firms in an industry, therefore, cannot rest easy on their share of the market and a willingness to follow the leader in price setting. The new forms of nonprice competition—product improvement, advertising and promotion—potentially provide a very active form of competition.

Industry classifications also present a very crude idea of the markets within which a firm must compete. Some products are sold in rather local regions because of high transportation costs; and the competition from firms outside of the region is felt mostly in terms of number of sales at the fringes of the region. Some products whch are distributed nationwide by just a few firms, have to compete with other products that may be substituted by the customer to serve similar uses. Up until World War II, for example, aluminum was produced by a single monopoly firm; and it still is produced by only a few large firms. Yet aluminum firms now have to compete with producers of other metals and materials in many different markets. Aluminum competes with steel for auto parts and containers, with lumber for house siding, with copper for wire, and with plastics for many light household objects. Finally, nationally distributed products also have to compete with imported products domestically, and the large firms face worldwide competition for their exports.

John Kenneth Galbraith has suggested an additional way in which to view the structure of markets. In his *American Capitalism* he shows that checks on industrial concentration and economic power instead of just coming from "competitors" may emanate from customers as well. One illustration which he provides of his "theory of countervailing power" is Sears Roebuck and Company. Sears, according to Galbraith, can use its power as a very large customer to obtain tires from the highly concentrated tire producers at very considerable savings; these are then passed on to consumers in the form of lower prices. His general conclusion is that unless the economy is under severe inflationary pressure, when two industrial giants oppose each other as buyer and seller, the consumer comes away the victor. Of course if inflation is the order of the day, then incentives exist to encouage buyer and seller to make a compact which passes higher supply prices onto the consumer.

Galbraith's work which was first published shortly after World War II was enthusiastically received. Unfortunately, however, his more avid readers have assumed that countervailing power characterizes all highly concentrated markets and therefore "bigness" is no problem as long as inflationary pressures are held in check. Nevertheless, as we have noted, there are many ways in which the market power of giant firms in a concentrated industry are limited. New forms of competition can be highly effective.

Changing economic conditions have enriched our theories of market behavior. Instead of the two rather clear-cut and simple models, competition and monopoly, we have additional and more complicated analytical devices. Yet as the next few paragraphs illustrate, economic theory has not caught up completely with economic events. Economists would like to know a lot more about the operation of various markets.

Enterprise among Giants

During World War II, the giant corporations played an important role in helping to organize a production miracle. While a large government regulatory bureaucracy was set up, production could not have gotten under way as quickly as it did if large corporations had not taken over the management of mass-production orders of weapons and coordinated the activities of many small firms working on subcontracts for parts. This war record and the long postwar prosperity have helped to restore public confidence in business. In the 1950's, many business leaders and journalists took the initiative in defending corporations against the charge of excessive power. Some writers seemed to worship bigness uncritically. The giant firms, it was claimed, were more efficient because of the economies of large scale. Also, large firms were claimed to be more innovative, because they alone could afford large research laboratories.

That bigness is not a reliable indicator of lower costs, however, is suggested by the few studies that have been made of efficiency in large and small firms. Comparisons among firms of accounting costs and profits have suggested that medium-sized firms do as well or better than the very largest firms in most industries. The continued existence of many smaller firms in the same industries as the giants also attests to the limited difference in efficiency due solely to size. In some industries, the size of modern plants is very similar even though the size of firms varies widely. Larger plant size usually is associated with lower costs only up to some minimum optimum size, and larger plant sizes result in about the same production costs. The operation of multiple plants also has been estimated to provide very little savings in production costs. The efficiencies of large-firm size, therefore, must come primarily from large-scale marketing, large financial resources, and capable overall management.[3]

There is little reason to suppose that the particular size of giant firms was due solely to technological advantages. Firms have become

[3] See Temporary National Economic Committee, Monograph 13, 77th Cong., 1st sess. (Washington, D.C.: U.S. Government Printing Office, 1941); J. L. McConnell, "Corporate Earnings by Size of Firm," *Survey of Current Business,* May, 1945; Joe S. Bain, *Industrial Organization* (New York: John Wiley & Sons, Inc., 1959), pp. 346–52.

large from a variety of causes and motives. Some firms may have grown partly from desires to gain market power—through horizontal integration to gain a larger share of the market, vertical mergers to gain some independent control of strategic resources, and acquisition of patents to exclude potential new competitors. One study of a sample of 20 manufacturing subindustries showed that the four largest firms usually had a much larger share of market sales than would have been required if they each had one plant of the minimum optimum size estimated by engineers in the industry.[4]

Giant size also is not a reliable indicator of innovation. As already noted, the process of invention is uncertain and unpredictable. Most of the inventions still come from individuals, and often the major breakthroughs come from outside an industry. It is mostly in the development stage that a giant firm with a large research laboratory has an advantage. The giant firms also are in a better position to mass produce and mass distribute new products. There must be strong rivalry and competitive pressures on a firm, however, to ensure that it will try to bring quickly into wide use a new product or process that might involve some losses in its old products and plants.

Rapid changes in technology have brought some new firms into existence and enabled them to grow large rapidly. Two recent examples are the Xerox Corporation and Texas Instruments, Inc. In an economy with some giant firms, therefore, it still has been possible not only for some small firms to persist with costs little different from those of the giants but also for some small firms to innovate very successfully. The turnover in ranking of the 100 largest industrial firms likewise suggests that initial size is no protection against the need to be enterprising in a changing world.

On the other hand, some writers have bemoaned the decline of enterprising spirit that is assumed to result from the bureaucratic tendencies of large organizations. The era of the "entrepreneur" may be over in terms of the individual owner-manager who single-handedly built up a large firm. Even the close-knit family or the group of independent business associates no longer provides both the imaginative direction and able management for large industries.

Enterprise, and the entrepreneurial function, however, still survives in the giant corporation. It merely has taken a different form in the organization of management. The railroad and the multiplant manufacturing corporations required that management organization be split

[4] Bain, *ibid.*

into two levels. Separate, but similar, divisions had to have operating managers. The top executive, or even a team of top executives, continued to make policy and coordinate the operations of all divisions and plants. Within this coordinating group, functional specialities were developed to direct sales, production, and perhaps financial operations.

The modern trend of corporate expansion into diverse industries has created even another level or type of management—a level which specializes in the more enterprising aspects of management. As operations have become more diverse, coordinating responsibility has to be delegated to operating divisions that are essentially subsidiary companies, usually organized along industry lines. Each subsidiary unit has its executive or executive team that must coordinate many production units. The subsidiary unit has its own functional managers of sales and production. The top level of managers, or parent corporation board, primarily controls major financial decisions, the selection of top executives, and the planning of future strategies of product development and expansion. If there is a research laboratory, it may be attached to the parent corporation. It is primarily at the top of the management structure that the vision, the planning, the initiative and the risk-taking now must take place.

There are indications that giant corporations may be as sensitive to changing economic conditions and to stockholder interests as the owner-managers in former times—or more so. Top executives constantly study the profit performance of subsidiary corporations and divisional executives. Banks, large financial institutions, and individual investors also study carefully the performance of the large corporations. Whereas an owner-manager could stick to his opinions and to old methods regardless of current reverses or the criticisms of minority stockholders, the boards of giant corporations are sensitive to changing conditions and to the general opinion of investors about their success. Outside sources of financing and the price of securities can change; stockholder representatives on boards can change; and the top executives of giant corporations can be reshuffled.

Last, the question of bigness must be viewed in the context of the total economy's growth. While the average corporation has grown larger, the economy has also expanded. For example, today the steel industry is far more competitive than it was at the time of the United States Steel Corporation's birth when its formation set the pace in the great merger movement. Yet in absolute terms U.S. Steel is much larger, not smaller, than it was at the turn of the century. Domestic and foreign markets for steel have grown so much over this period that now several dozen giants compete in markets in which 20 years ago only several producers operated.

This example is not meant to suggest that the structure of the 20th-century industry is typified by the situation in which individual firm bigness is dwarfed by the total size of the market. Rather it is meant to suggest that the extensive and intensive growth of the national market, economic growth abroad, and continued reduction of trade barriers may importantly multiply the examples of this phenomenon.

The Quest for Social Control

While the worst fears of economywide domination or industry-by-industry monopoly do not appear to be justified in the modern economy, the American public continues to be concerned about the problem of exercising social control over giant firms. On the whole, the record of antitrust regulation has been favorable and improving; but as we have learned more the problem has appeared more complex and we are less satisfied.

The history of antitrust regulation has been uneven and gradually evolving, with the public reacting to major changes in conditions. As already noted, the merger movement around 1900 was partly encouraged by the Supreme Court's interpretation of the Sherman Act as prohibiting collusion but not merger. The merger wave set off a political reaction that led to greater enforcement efforts and new legislation before World War I. In the *United States Steel Corporation* case in 1920, the Court again applied the "rule of reason" and refused to see mere size as an offense in the absence of clear evidence of abuse of power. A new wave of mergers occurred during the late 1920's.

The unsettled world conditions after World War I and the depression of the 1930's brought a retrogressive political trend away from reliance on competitive markets. The raising of tariffs and the actions of trade associations were designed to prevent competitive pressures for price reductions. In the depression, the federal government was called upon to aid industry with loans—through the establishment of the Reconstruction Finance Corporation—and to protect industry against competitive price cutting—through the trade association codes approved by the National Industrial Recovery Administration (the NIRA). The Robinson-Patman Act in 1936 outlawed discriminatory or temporary price cutting intended to eliminate small competitors, but it was popularly referred to as an antichain store act. The next year the Miller-

Tydings amendment provided an exemption from the Sherman Act for contract agreements by retailers to charge no less than the manufacturer's list price in states with "fair trade" laws. Other legislative efforts in agriculture, bituminous coal, and crude oil, as well as the first minimum wage law were aimed to provide government protection to producer groups against competitive price reductions.

The depression, however, also brought a contradictory trend toward greater regulation of business. There were the Securities Exchange Act of 1934, the Communications Act of 1934, the Public Utility Holding Company Act of 1935, the Federal Power Act of 1935, the Motor Carrier Act of 1935, the Natural Gas Act of 1938, and the Civil Aeronautics Act of 1938. Thus, in the fields where natural monopoly was regarded as inevitable, public regulation was extended. Late in the 1930's, an effort also was made to step up the enforcement activity of the Department of Justice and the Federal Trade Commission, and Congress established the Temporary National Economic Committee to make a study of monopoly conditions.

While World War II interrupted these enforcement efforts, they were resumed and intensified in the postwar period. In 1945, the Alcoa decision ended the Court's narrow interpretation of the "rule of reason," and an effort was made under the Surplus Property Act to dispose of plants built by the government in wartime in such a way as to encourage competition. In 1950, the Celler amendment to the Clayton Act extended antimerger provisions to include the purchase of assets as well as stock. In the 1950's, the Supreme Court made several key interpretations—in the *United States Machinery* case in 1953, the *Du Pont Company* case in 1954, and the *Brown Shoe Company* case in 1962—that tended to limit the kind of merger permitted under the laws.

The evolution of interpretation by the Supreme Court has been away from reliance solely upon overt collusive or restrictive actions as evidence of monopoly practices. The trend has been toward recognition of the relative size of a firm within particular markets as creating a strong presumption that monopoly power exists. This concentration does not automatically convict a large firm, but it weakens somewhat the burden of proof of the prosecution that certain actions reflect abuse of market power.

Business spokesmen complain of the uncertainty forced upon normal business decisions by these court interpretations. Yet the basic difficulty lies in the inadequacies of our existing theories and knowledge about market power and how to control it. While some writers argue that the good performance of giant corporations should be the primary criterion of the legality of their size and practices, no one has proposed acceptable objective measures of performance by which the good monopolies can be distinguished from the bad.

The very sensitivity of business leaders to court interpretations is some evidence that the antitrust laws may have had some effect in deterring monopolistic practices. There is clearly less concentration in the American economy than among most industrial nations, where antitrust policy has been less pronounced. Also, the merger movement in the late 1950's and early 1960's has been in the direction of greater industry diversity rather than greater industry concentration—a trend that monopoly laws and court interpretations may have influenced.

The sensitivity of business leaders to public reactions against abuse of market power also has been evidenced in much talk about the need for greater "social responsibility" by giant corporations. Social responsibility, of course, is an admirable virtue on the part of any individual or group. Yet the very intensity of discussion of social responsibility by business writers has evidenced their awareness of possession of power incompletely controlled by external market forces. Without power to control, there is no issue of responsibility. Mutual moral "pep talks," however, are a poor substitute for external restraints—the public is furnished no guarantee that social responsibility will always be considered. The logic of interdependence in an oligopolistic industry provides powerful social pressures toward monopolistic behavior—as evidenced in 1961 by the criminal convictions for monopolistic collusion of highly placed executives in most of the leading electrical equipment manufacturing corporations of the country. Since nearly all major corporations have been involved in antitrust cases of one sort or another in recent decades, the pleading for social responsibility would not seem to provide a very promising solution to the problem of market power.

Recognition of the modern limitations on market power, on the other hand, has helped to popularize overoptimistic interpretations of the salutary effects of scale economies, technological innovation, interindustry competition, nonprice competition, social responsibility, and countervailing power. In fact there has been very little study which would lead to the conclusion that big business creates its own checks and balances.

Thus, the problem of maintaining highly active competition in industries with giant firms is only incompletely solved in modern America. Yet the alternatives to reliance primarily upon market competition to control private producers in the consumers' interests also have not been developed. So the public search continues for improved means of social control.

AGRICULTURAL ADJUSTMENT

A prerequisite of economic growth is an agricultural sector in which productivity is growing very rapidly—so rapidly that it outstrips food and fiber demands and thus releases men and capital to support the growth of other sectors of the economy. In American agriculture persistent increases in productivity in the face of relatively slow growth in demand have meant that many farmers have had to abandon farming.

We have spoken rather easily of "releasing labor" from agriculture. But this can be a very painful process. Similarly, the technological displacement of workers in particular skills and industries (which is discussed in the following section) can be painful. If the human side of this part of the growth process is ignored, it can cause trouble.

We also must consider the struggle of farmers to maintain or increase their relative share of the growing national income—the struggle to get a bigger slice of the "pie." When groups can organize privately to wield a monopoly power over the price for their services, they will do so. But when large numbers of people feel they are losing their relative economic position and are helpless to do anything about it privately, they will seek to organize politically to find a remedy. Both farmers and, as we will see, nonfarm workers have done this. Much of the hostile feeling of people in distress has been directed at private business organizations. Big business and monopoly frequently are blamed as the cause of their troubles, and the conclusion is drawn that monopoly tactics—that is, output restriction and price setting—must be used as a counterforce to protect themselves against "big business." This kind of popular reaction is perhaps one of the gravest dangers of business monopoly; for it can lead to a struggle between power blocs and a struggle to gain control over government.

This discussion of farm organization and the one that follows on labor organization do not aim to criticize the motives or right of any group to advance its own economic position. Rather, the purpose here is to consider whether the methods chosen help to bring about adjustments that come to grips with the causes of distress.

Talk abounds about "the farm problem" but in fact there is no single farm problem. Historically there have been two farm problems —one of chronic overproduction and another of rural poverty. The first, in turn, breaks into a wheat problem, a feed grain problem, a cotton problem, etc. Similarly the second aggregates the problems of the small tenant or sharecropper, the "hardscrabble" freeholder, and the itinerant picker.

Confusing as this array must seem, there are common denominators to each of these broad categories which permit us to analyze them meaningfully. Let us begin with overproduction.

Farm Overproduction

Overproduction arises from two sources: a slow growth in demand for food and fiber by consumers, and a very rapid rise in productivity. Between 1948 and 1960, farm output increased only 32 percent compared to an increase of 67 percent in all private industry; but farm output per man-hour (productivity) rose 78 percent compared to 62 percent in all private industry. In the same period, the demand for farm products rose even less rapidly than total output with the result that government acquired considerable stocks of surplus commodities. Now in the late 1960's, this latter trend has abated somewhat, but farm economists continue to feel that overproduction is still a basic tendency. Thus as a basic adjustment we must reduce the amount of resources—labor, capital, and land—that are devoted to farm production while continuing to increase the productivity of the remaining producers.

The symptoms of the problem, however, are declining prices—either absolute decreases or relative to other prices in the economy. Farmers who find it difficult to move out of farming would like to solve their problem simply by controlling the symptoms. Thus we have federal government programs to purchase surplus products in order to maintain prices and protect the incomes of farmers.

No one really thinks this is a solution because the price support program is not only expensive and costly to taxpayers, but also because the surplus stocks on hand tend to increase for many years at a time. Some notion of the cost of storage is implied by the size that the task can reach. For example, carry-over stocks in the fall of 1960 amounted to 130 percent of a year's requirements of wheat and other grain foods, 60 percent for cotton, and 60 percent for corn. Since 1960, carry-overs have declined but are still large for some products.

In blaming the price symptom, farmers early in the 1920's began to complain of the greater decline in prices of farm products than in the prices they paid for machinery, farm supplies, and consumption items. Later in the 1930's, it also was pointed out that while farm prices were more flexible than farm output, industrial output was more flexible than industrial prices. This they attributed to monopoly and the ability of big business to administer prices. While there is an element of truth in this argument, it is oversimplified because it does not take into consideration the differences in basic economic conditions affecting supply and demand in different industries.

13–3 shows the trend of farm output and prices over most of this century. Output has expanded fairly slowly and has been rather stable except for a moderate decline during the depression of the 1930's.

13–3. Farm Output and Prices

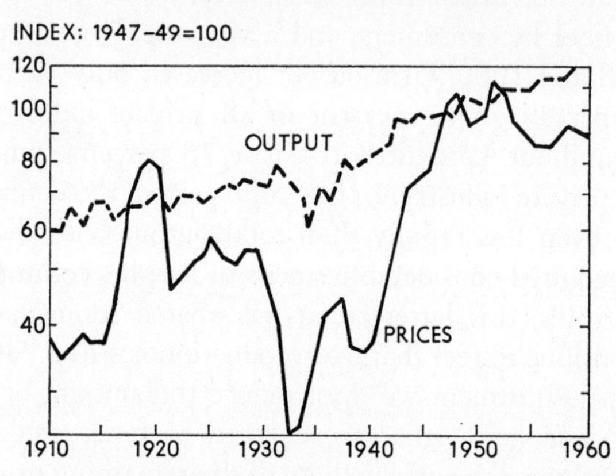

Source: U.S. Department of Commerce, *Historical Statistics of the United States* (Washington, D.C.: U.S. Government Printing Office, 1960), pp. 117 and 288.

Prices, on the other hand, have zoomed upward during war booms and postwar inflations and downward during depressions. Of concern recently is the continued decline of farm prices since the Korean War. Now, what are some of the long-run forces influencing these trends? Let us mention a few.

13–4 and 13–5 are hypothetical demand and supply curve situations similar to those of the appendix to Chapter 6. First, what happens when demand increases rapidly while supply conditions remain the same or only increase slightly? The diagram in 13–4 shifts the demand curve upward and to the right, from D_1 to D_2. At the initial price (P_1), D_2 suggests that almost 50 percent more output might be purchased; but the supply conditions indicated by S_1 show that producers can make only relatively modest increases in production and that they will do so only with the incentive of higher prices.

The "shortage" of supply relative to demand, therefore, is adjusted to both by the increased supply encouraged by a higher price and by the restriction in the quantities demanded as a rising price made the product more expensive and squeezed out some buyers. Even with a slight shift in supply conditions (due to technological improvements), the resulting price (P_2) is much larger than initially. This diagram reflects approximately what happened between 1940 and 1950 under the pressure of increased food demands for domestic consumers, the Armed Forces, and allied countries. Of course general price inflation exacerbated this tendency to higher prices.

13–4. Increase in Demand

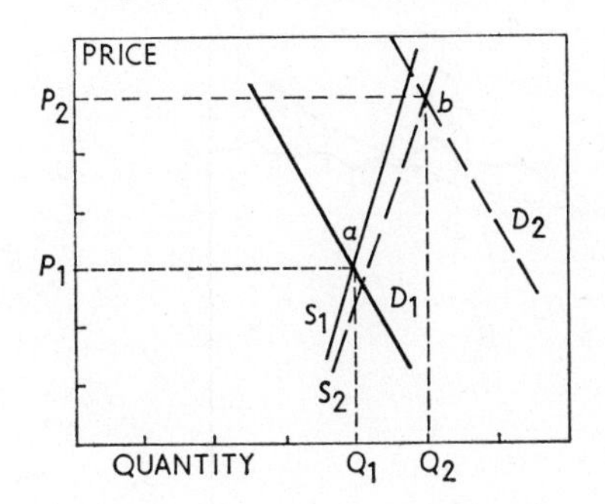

13–5. Increase in Supply

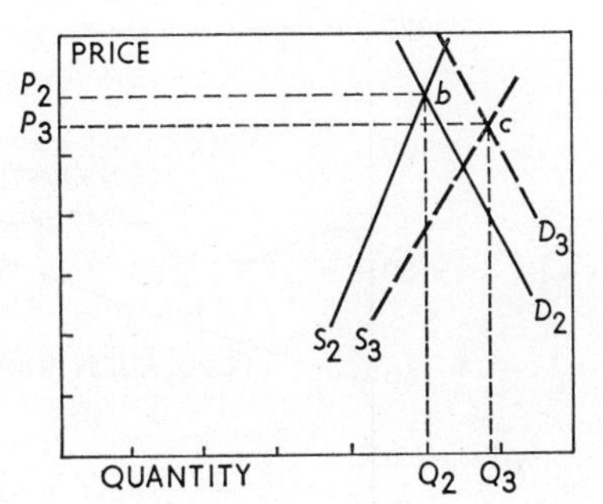

13–5 shows what happens when supply increases substantially while demand remains the same or increases only slightly. In the diagram the supply curve has shifted to the right (S_2 to S_3) to reflect substantial increases in productivity. That is, costs to produce the same quantity as initially are about one third less. Suppliers, therefore, would like to produce a much larger quantity at the initial price—perhaps 25 percent more. The demand of consumers, however, will absorb increased quantities only at lower prices. Even if demand gradually expands through extensive growth, say, to D_3, the quantity demanded may not increase enough to maintain the initial price. Thus, the result is an increase in quantity (Q_3), but a reduction in price (P_3). This diagram reflects approximately the conditions of change between 1950 and 1960 when productivity increased supply faster than demand. It teaches a very important lesson: technological change makes it possible to profitably produce greater quantities at a lower price because unit cost is lowered, but there is no guarantee that a price cut equal to the reduction in unit cost will stimulate demand enough to clear the increment in production.

Note that an increase in demand conditions (a shift in the demand curve) increases both the price and the quantity, while an increase in supply (a shift in the supply curve) ***increases*** output but ***lowers*** price. The opposite direction of shifts would reverse the effects. Thus, for example, in 13–4, a downward shift of demand from D_3 back to D_2 would reduce both quantity and price. Since supply conditions are rather inelastic (the curve is steep), price falls more than quantity of product. This reflects the kind of conditions that occurred during the Great Depression of the 1930's.

13–6. Demand Influences

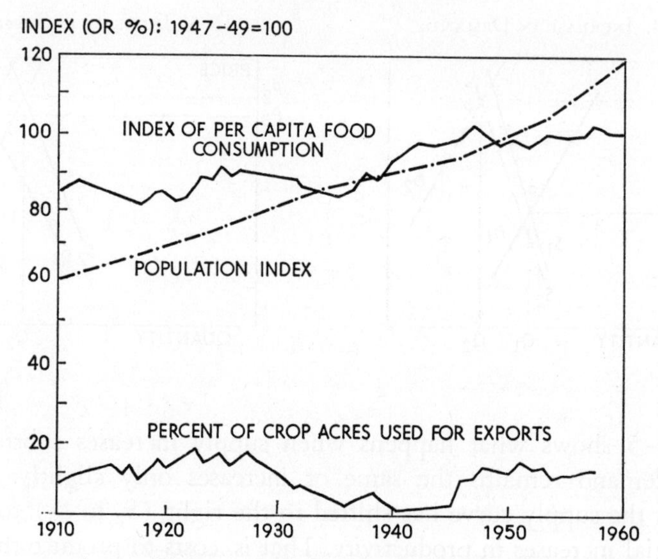

Source: U.S. Department of Commerce, *Historical Statistics of the United States* (Washington, D.C.: U.S. Government Printing Office, 1960), pp. 185, 281, and 7.

Now we can begin to explain price and output cycles if we can find major demand influences that rose or fell in particular decades. 13–6 shows that population rose fairly slowly and steadily (this growth rate has, you recall, corresponded closely to farm output). Per capita consumption did not change very much in the long run, but it did dip substantially during the depressed 1930's, and it rose most rapidly during the 1940's. At the same time, exports of farm products fell during the 1930's and recovered during the late 1940's. A good deal of the dip in the 1930's and the rapid expansion in the 1940's of both output and prices, therefore, is explainable in terms of demand conditions for food. The amount of land and the number of farms were fairly stable and were kept in production in good times and bad; so most of the demand fluctuation was reflected in price and income changes.

13–7 shows that while crop acreage was fairly stable, supply was increased by two major changes. The record of the 1920's was especially affected by the introduction of tractors and thus the decreased number of acres needed to grow feed for horses and mules. This trend continued to release acreage and increase food supply for several decades, but after 1950 the amount of change was very small. In the 1940's and 1950's, crop production per acre, or "yield," began to

13–7. Supply Influences

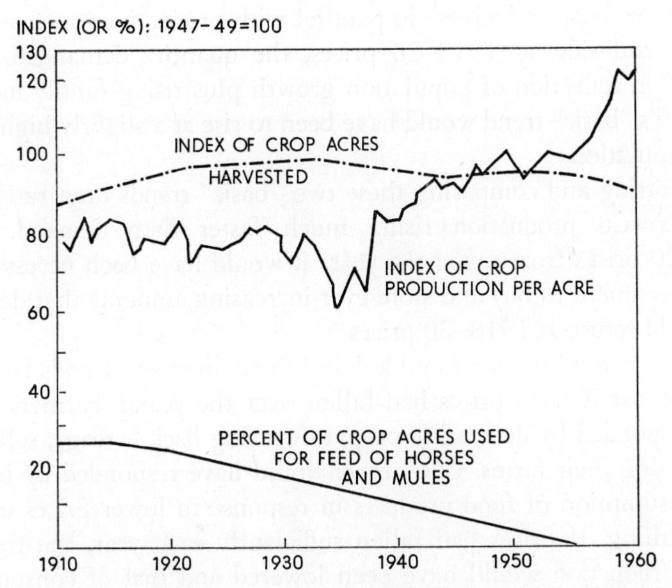

Source: U.S. Department of Commerce, *Historical Statistics of the United States* (Washington, D.C.: U.S. Government Printing Office, 1960), p. 281.

increase rapidly. This reflected the rapid increase in productivity mentioned earlier. Especially in the later part of the 1950's, this tended to shift the supply curve to the right and thus to reduce price while it raised output. Since consumer demand is not very responsive to price (low price elasticity), the price decreases might have been larger if it had not been for the gradual demand shift caused by rising population during the 1950's.

Our analysis so far has enabled us to explain the long cycles in agricultural prices, the protracted booms and busts. We must now turn our attention to a long-run trend that has been superimposed upon the forces we have just examined. Since 1920, agricultural productivity for all inputs taken together has increased very rapidly while the rate of population growth tended to decline. Per capita income in the economy continued to grow, of course, but food and fiber demand is not very responsive to growth in individual incomes.

In order to see the consequences of these developments, let us see what conditions would have been like if we could somehow go back and freeze farm prices at, say, their 1918–20 average levels. At 1918–20 prices, increases in productivity would have lowered costs each year and thus given producers incentive to increase production by expanding acreage and farming more intensively—the "basic" trend of output would have been to increase in parallel with productivity increases. On the demand side, at 1918–20 prices, the quantity demanded would increase in reflection of population growth plus rising family incomes. Demand's "basic" trend would have been to rise at a slightly higher rate than population.

Plotting and comparing these two "basic" trends on a ratio chart would reveal production rising much faster than demand. Were 1918–20 prices frozen over the years it would have been necessary for the government to buy and store ever-increasing amounts that demanders would refuse at 1918–20 prices.

How would the forces underlying these divergent trends be reconciled? What if farm prices had fallen over the years? Farmers would have responded by decreasing output—cutting back acreage, selling or abandoning their farms. Consumers would have responded by increasing consumption of food products in response to lower prices of food and clothing. If prices had fallen sufficiently each year, the trend of actual production would have been lowered and that of consumption raised so that the two would have been identical—the market would have cleared each year and no stocks would have had to be consigned to storage.

A relevant consideration at this point is to wonder what assures that the two trends would have matched up. The answer is perhaps most easily seen by assuming that such trends separate from time to time. If in such cases production starts to climb faster than demand, a cycle will start in which at first market prices will be driven down which both will encourage buying and drive some producers into bankruptcy, lowering supply. A new price will be established at which the market clears and which will assure remaining producers just enough profit to remain in production but not so much that people are encouraged to return to farming. On the other hand, if demand were to surge upward relative to output, prices would rise and new producers would come into the market until supply and demand trends were again equated.

Which curve would move the most? Our knowledge of consumer reaction to lower farm product prices tells us that the bulk of the adjustment task will fall to producers. Even a large percentage reduction in farm prices will produce only a minor increase in quantity demanded but will prove disastrous for farmers' profits. This in turn suggests that if in fact the two trends matched over the period we are talking about, a very large percentage of farm operators would have had to leave agriculture. The surviving producers would have operated profitably over the years, but many producers would have been forced out by heavy losses.

To state our conclusions again in different words, productivity increases make it possible for efficient farmers to operate profitably at lower prices and higher levels of output, to the benefit of consumers. But under typical demand conditions in agriculture, price reductions which are equal to unit cost reductions will not stimulate demand sufficiently for the market to absorb the increase in output. Therefore, some producers must leave the industry before supply will equal demand at a price that permits profitable operation.

However, in fact, the market has ***not*** operated in the manner described above. Government has had to stockpile farm products. And many unprofitable producers have hung on year after year because they do not have or do not recognize alternative opportunities. Thus we have an overproduction problem because prices have failed or not been free to do their job. Of course, the trends have moved toward each other—farm population ***fell*** by one third, 10 million, in the 1920–60 period, and lower relative prices certainly stimulated consumption—but the task has not been completed!

Low Income

The above analysis shows that it is not overproduction alone, but also the immobility of farm resources that prevents farm incomes from being maintained. Further, while farm incomes declined during the 1950's and have fluctuated in the 1960's, the most acute income problem is not the recent trend, but the long-term historical persistence of lower incomes in farming compared with other industries.

As 11–3 showed, agriculture has persisted in having a smaller share of GNP than of national employment. 13–8 shows that incomes are lower in farm residences than in urban or rural nonfarm residences in all parts of the country. There also are wide differences in farm incomes among regions. Farm incomes are highest in the West and Northeast and lowest in the Midwest and South, especially among Negro operators. In other words, the problem of low income in farming is especially acute in predominantly farming regions.

13–9 also shows that individual farms differ widely in income levels and size. Farms with over $10,000 in annual sales are substantial

13–8. Median Family Incomes, 1960

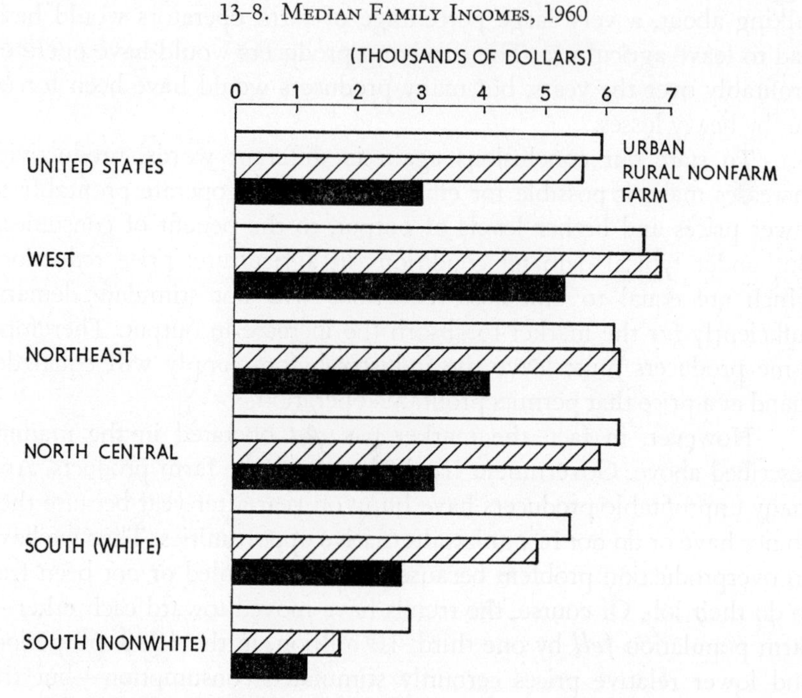

Source: Karl Fox, V. W. Ruttan, and L. W. Witt, *Farming, Farmers and Markets for Farm Goods*, Supplementary Paper No. 15 (New York: Committee for Economic Development, 1962), p. 80.

businesses and cannot be regarded as constituting a "low-income" problem in the Nation. They are not, however, in the big business category and like other small businesses, they face competition from other products, have a cost squeeze problem, and are constantly trying to adopt improved methods to lower their costs. The number of these larger farms is increasing, although most of the increase under the Commercial Farm heading is still in the "family farm" category rather than in large farming corporations.

The small and inefficient-size farm is the real income problem. The number of these farms is decreasing rapidly due to the pressures of falling prices and rising costs. The newer technology frequently requires more capital and the purchase of more adjoining land in order to take advantage of its cost-reduction benefits—options usually not open to the small farmer. Thus, small- and medium-size farmers are turning increasingly to off-farm work to supplement their farm incomes.

Frequently, a factory job will turn a small farmer into a sundown farmer with about the same farm output and income as before. Also, a working wife can supplement the budget and help add to savings that may go to improving and expanding farm output. Studies have demonstrated nationally that counties with the most urban and industrial employment also tend to have higher farm incomes and the reason

13–9. Number of Farms by Size and Class

	Number in Thousands		*Percent Change*
	1949	*1959*	
All farms	5,382	3,704	−31
Commercial farms:			
Sales $10,000 and over	484	794	+64
Sales $5,000 to $9,999	721	654	− 9
Sales $2,500 to $4,999	882	618	−30
Under $2,500	778	} 1,638	} −50
Part-time residential	1,670		
Subsistence (sales under $250)	247		

Source: U.S. *Census of Agriculture.*

appears to lie in the labor market. Competition for labor raises farm wages, and off-farm work supplements farm family incomes.

This brings us to the problem of migration of farm population. Most farm areas today are hoping that industrial development in rural areas will solve their problem. They hope that factories will move to them so they will not have to move away from their farms. Unfortunately, most farm areas probably will not solve all of their problem in this manner, because there are not enough new plants and new jobs free to move into rural areas. Also, the size of the labor adjustment needed in farming is very great. Between 1948 and 1960, the man-hours needed to produce farm output fell 46 percent.

At the same time, rural populations have higher birthrates and more young people entering the labor market. 13–10 shows that rural areas have a greater percentage of their population under the age of 14 and in the youth group of 14 to 19. The difference is a little less than in

1950 because of the growth of rural nonfarm population and the higher postwar birthrates in urban areas.

Most migration occurs between the ages of 20 and 25, rural areas have a smaller proportion of population in the remaining young adult group, ages 25 to 40. The older people, however, have greater difficulty moving. A farm owner in the 45 to 64 age group may prefer to live off his capital in order to maintain his home and present occupation rather than to sell out and make a new start in life.

13–10. Age Distribution of Population

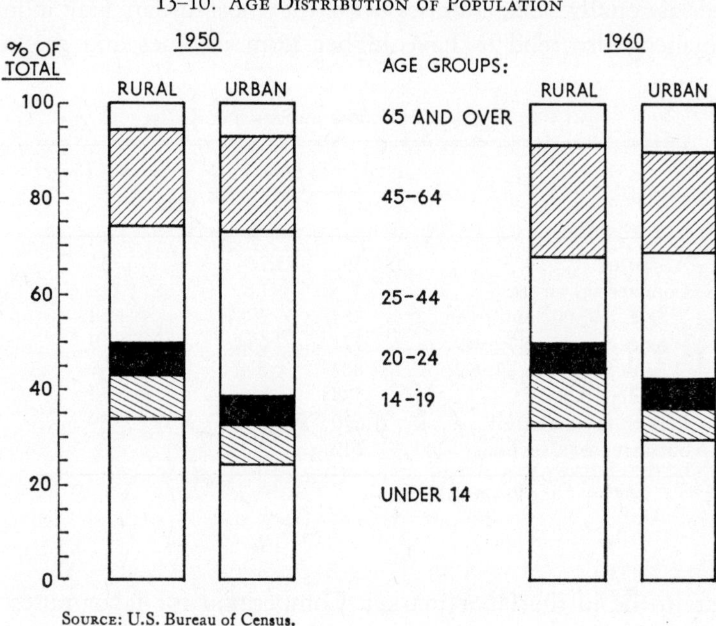

Source: U.S. Bureau of Census.

The farm labor adjustment problem is not only easier when industry moves into the rural area, it also is easier for labor to move when jobs are plentiful in urban areas. 13–11 shows that net migration of the farm population has been low in depression periods like the 1930's, 1954, and 1957–58, while it has been highest when industrial production was highest and expanding, such as during the decade of the 1940's and the expansion years of the 1950's.

It is also easier for young people to move and to find work when they have received a high level of education and training. Unfortunately, a low level of education and training is characteristic of low-income farming areas. Also, young people in rural areas which are out of touch with urban America need more counseling and public employment information services to help them determine what types of jobs are available and where. Currently, there is little assistance being offered to help people relocate in another community or state. Our employment offices are designed to help local employers find workers and to issue unemployment compensation—in no meaningful sense do we have ***national*** employment service.

13–11. ANNUAL AVERAGE NET MIGRATION FROM FARMS

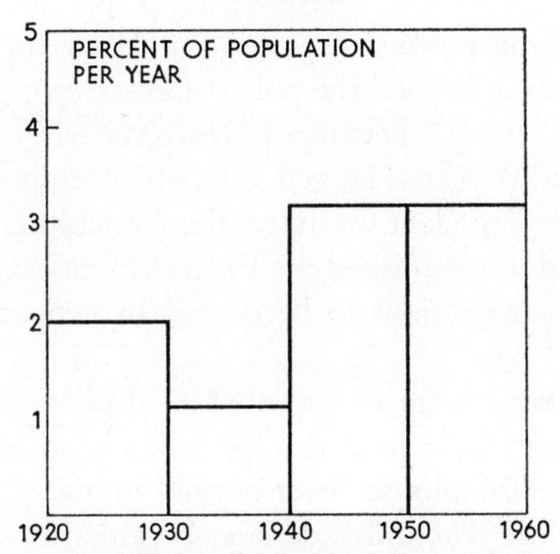

SOURCE: Research and Policy Committee of the Committee for Economic Development. *An Adaptive Program for Agriculture* (New York: Committee for Economic Development, 1962), p. 19.

A last note with respect to migration: even a massive migration of low-income farmers probably will not solve the oversupply problem that affects the incomes of the larger farm units. The very small units do not collectively account for enough production to dent the surplus problem. To have equilibrium in agriculture some of the medium-sized units will have to leave the market as well. And this is where the difficulty lies; how do you convince a man with a section of land and topsoil 3 feet deep that he is a submarginal farmer?

Farm Programs

We have discussed the economics of American agriculture with only passing reference to government programs intended to assist the farmer. Now it is appropriate to specifically analyze those programs with reference to the economic theory we have reviewed. Our survey of the history of farm legislation since 1920 will make several factors apparent—early debate over legislation showed a confusion over the basic causes of the farm problem, therefore the legislation that was actually enacted does not meet head-on either the overproduction or the low-income problem; and generally legislation has compromised the economics of the situation to meet political requirements.

In the peroid 1921–32, farm policy proposals largely ignored the long-run tendencies of agriculture and centered instead upon the cyclical sources of farm depression. Early in the decade, low prices were recognized as effects of the 1920–21 recession and the decline in exports resulting from postwar expansion of European agriculture. Yet since these causes were beyond the policy-makers' scope, proposals were made to maintain "parity" between prices received and prices paid by farmers. After the McNary-Haugen bill which embodied this notion was twice vetoed by President Coolidge, the Agricultural Marketing Act of 1929 was passed. It established the Federal Farm Board which was to found stabilizing corporations to be owned by cooperative marketing associations.

The corporations were to use a $500 million fund to purchase farm commodities in the market to support their prices. The basic idea was summed up by the phrase "ever-normal granary," coined in 1922 by Henry A. Wallace who a decade later became Roosevelt's Secretary of Agriculture. Prices were to be stabilized through purchases and storage of commodities when demand was weak and sales from stocks when demand was strong. The crash of prices in the recession phase of the Great Depression swamped all Farm Board efforts. Other stabilizing attempts of the period included tariff barriers and improved credit facilities.

From this review we can see that the implications of productivity increases were not apparent to policy makers. It just did not occur to them that a growing number of Americans would require fewer ***not*** more farmers each decade. Thus farm problems were attributed to business depressions and the weather, cyclical factors. People did not see that cost reductions would require a downward price trend and the exodus of farmers if chronic overproduction and low-farm incomes were to be avoided.

During the Great Depression, the parity price support concept was extended under the Agricultural Adjustment Act of 1933 and subsequent legislation. The goal was to maintain farm incomes by pegging the ratio of prices received to prices paid at the average that prevailed over 1910–14, the so-called "golden age of agriculture."

For some crops total acreage allotments, which were prorated among farmers, were designed to reduce production and thus enhance prices. Cooperating farmers were also paid a subsidy based on their output. Later in the New Deal, government loans were made to farmers on their crops by the Commodity Credit Corporation (CCC) at stated percentages of parity. Whenever market prices fell below loan values, farmers had the option of defaulting their loans and letting the CCC take title to and store their output. Starting with 1939, wheat, corn, cotton, and tobacco were stockpiled in large quantities. For crops that were not easily stored a system of marketing agreements was also established by the Secretary as a way of limiting output of other crops.

The farm programs of the 1930's also failed to deal with agriculture's basic problems. The marketing agreements, acreage restrictions, and marketing quotas did limit market supply and thus pushed up relative prices. But these plans were instituted by prorating production or acreage among producers according to acreage or past output records rather than the productivity of producers. To do otherwise would have been politically impossible. This meant that high-cost, inefficient farming units received allotments right along with the best farmers in the business. Furthur, pressure has always been applied to design the programs so that prices are high enough to make low efficiency units profitable. By contrast uninhibited market forces tend to push prices low enough to purge the least efficient producers, resulting in lower prices to consumers and profitable operating conditions for remaining operators.

The parity concept was also basically fallacious. It implies that prices paid by farmers reflect costs and thus a policy that maintains a constant ratio between prices paid by farmers and the prices at which they sell would guarantee them a constant real income. Here is where the fallacy lies: one of the parity notion's implied assumptions is that productivity increases will not come along to lower costs. Actually improved farming methods could more than offset higher prices paid by farmers. In fact agriculture's trend is for real unit costs to decline as compared with 1910–14 with the consequence that the parity price will contain an ever-increasing profit margin. Thus under the parity concept, some farmers have the incentive to stay in farming when under free market conditions they would leave the industry.

During World War II ceiling prices were placed on most nonperishable agricultural commodities. With the surge in demand, sales rose, prices hit the ceilings, and output was supplemented from government inventories. But after Europe again resumed production in the postwar period, surpluses again mounted. Legislative innovations were proposed and enacted such as the soil bank plan for long-term retirement of acreage. However, still no change in the broad framework of farm programs was made to acknowledge the root causes of agriculture's ills.

In spite of improved understanding of the problem, politicians feel they must continue to pledge the salvation of the family farm. Consequently, no concerted effort has been put forth to ease the movement of those high-cost, low-income, small acreage farmers who are 80 percent of all farmers and yet benefit little or not at all from current programs. Further, under current conditions producers of some crops have successfully campaigned against production limitations. They have gained a system of acreage restrictions that permit them to farm remaining acreage more intensively and thus undermine the entire program while benefiting from price supports.

Thus, the farm problem now facing the country is to find ways to speed up the flow of resources out of agriculture and at the same time to ease some of the hardships forced upon individuals and communities. Programs that merely try to control prices will bring only temporary relief, for prices themselves are the signals and incentives for bringing about adjustments in markets.

UNION BARGAINING

Union organization reflects the effort of another type of producer group to influence the price of its members' services and thereby increase their income share in the total output pie. But a union is more than an economic interest group. It is also a political organization composed of people trying to have some voice in determining the working conditions affecting their lives.

To a large extent, unions are "protest" organizations looking after the interests of individual workers in the giant, impersonal corporations of modern industry. Some writers have referred to collective bargaining as a form of "industrial democracy" in which the worker representatives participate in making rules regarding working conditions. The arbitration procedures for settling grievances have been referred to as a form of industrial jurisprudence, settling a worker's claims to job rights and protecting him from arbitrary exercise of supervisory authority. Many an employer has discovered that human attitudes and emotions cannot be ignored in running a business, that a smooth arbitration procedure and effective collective bargaining may avoid unnecessary strikes and slowdowns in productivity.

The Growth of the Union Movement

13–12 shows that the growth of the union movement has been uneven and recently has leveled off. After a burst of organizing and initial growth under the American Federation of Labor (AFL) at the beginning of the 20th century, unionization slowed down. Then World War I brought a peak of labor demands and cooperative union-management relations were encouraged by the common defense effort. After the war, unions lost ground until the mid-1930's when protective legislation gave unions a boost. World War II further spurred membership as the organized industries expanded. Frequently, new workers

13–12. Union Membership

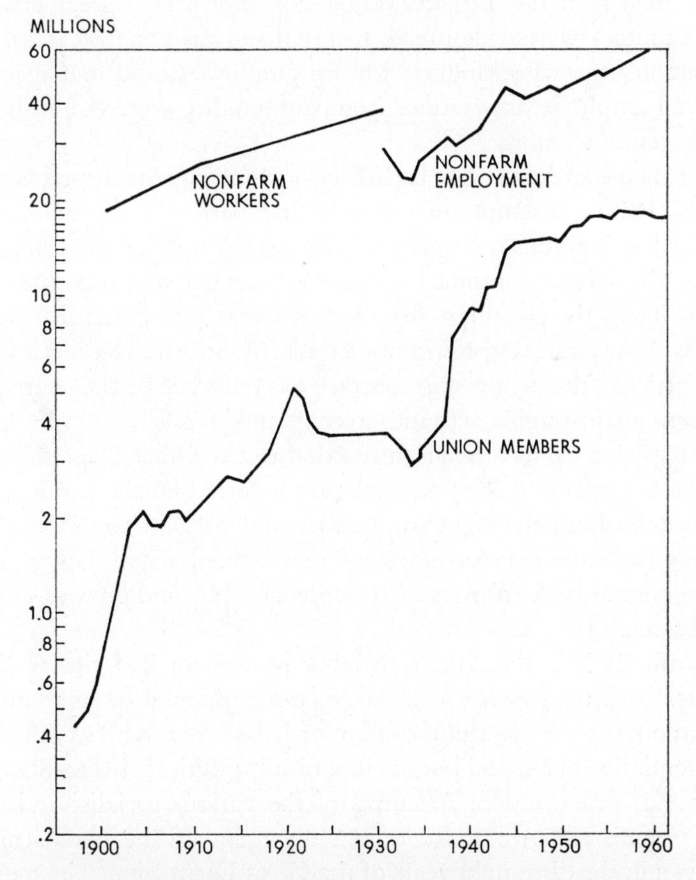

Source: U.S. Department of Commerce, *Historical Statistics of the United States* (Washington, D.C.: U.S. Government Printing Office, 1960), p. 98; and U.S. Department of Commerce, *Statistical Abstract of the United States, 1962* (Washington, D.C.: U.S. Government Printing Office, 1963).

were required to join the union which was bargaining with the company under "closed shop" agreements.

The growth in union organization that came in the 19th century and the first three decades of the 20th century occurred in a hostile political and legal environment. Social Darwinism and its economic corollary, laissez-faire, were interpreted to mean that organization of workers to influence wages, hours, or working conditions was morally and economically wrong. And the power of the state was invoked to give effect to this conviction.

Management employed a wide variety of devices to hinder unionization: "agitators" were discharged and blacklisted by employers; employers, in effect, went on strike by locking out workers; "scabs" were employed to replace striking workers, while private detective firms supplied men to harass pickets; yellow-dog contracts (agreements not to join a union) were widespread; paternalism was designed to kill the unionization urge with kindness toward employees; and management-dominated employee associations, company unions, were established to preclude genuine unions.

For their part, the courts backed up such management practices. In the early 1800's, attempts to organize and bargain collectively were interpreted as "criminal conspiracy." After overthrow of the conspiracy doctrine, the courts continued to rule against strikes, picketing, and boycotts. Then the Sherman Antitrust Act was interpreted to include unions as "conspiracies in restraint of trade." Until the Norris-La Guardia Act of 1932 the yellow-dog contract was enforced by the courts, and injunctions against union activities were granted freely.

Largely, as we have seen, in reaction to the Great Depression the Norris-La Guardia and Wagner acts gave a carte blanche to unions by legally establishing the right to organize and bargain collectively and outlawing the "unfair labor practices" enumerated above. Union membership bounced back from its early depression low and grew at unprecedented rates.

By the 1930's, the American labor movement had clearly established its character which was in large part implanted by its dominant organization, the American Federation of Labor. The AFL's philosophy was essentially bread-and-butter unionism, political neutrality, and craft-by-craft organization. Attempts of the various socialist and communist organizations to make unions an agent of the class struggle failed even in the distraught years of the Great Depression. The melting pot nature of America, the Nation's upward social mobility, and the identification of journeymen workers with their employers, themselves usually former journeymen, all militated against a feeling of class consciousness. Rather than exercise political control, laboring men reacted positively to a philosophy of organization that was economic. Labor wanted "more," as AFL President Samuel Gompers, an ex-"radical," put it, and was determined to get it by organizing each of the crafts.

This organizing philosophy has remained basically intact with one major exception. There had long been attempts to form organizations that included all workers regardless of craft that were employed in a particular industry such as steel production; but conditions were never right except for isolated instances, the most notable of which was the United Mine Workers. The labor legislation of the 1930's cleared the way for organization along industrial as well as craft lines. In 1936, the Congress of Industrial Organizations (CIO) was formed. The CIO's goal was to enlist all workers in a particular industry regardless of craft. The growth of the Steelworkers and the Auto Workers goes a long way in explaining the surge in union membership in the 1930's.

In the postwar period, however, union growth again slowed down and organization stopped growing in the latter part of the 1950's. Thus, starting in the mid-1930's, with 7 percent of the labor force and 11 percent of nonfarm employees, union membership had risen to 23 percent of the labor force and 32 percent of nonfarm employment. But there it stayed.

During the postwar period, two important labor acts were passed which regulated the activities of labor unions. The Taft-Hartley Act of 1947 established the following: "unfair labor practices" of unions—"featherbedding" is an example—to go along with the management practices outlawed by the Wagner Act; rules of conduct, especially financial, upon union management; certain collective bargaining agreements such as the closed shop that could not be made; and a procedure for avoiding strikes that might paralyze the Nation, e.g., a nationwide rail strike. The Landrum-Griffin Act of 1959 extended government regulation of union management. It was largely a response to the congress' labor-racketeering investigations of the late 1950's which spotlighted the alleged illegal conduct of the Teamsters Union leadership.

It appears that unions have about reached their saturation point. They have organized about all of the groups that are easy to organize and in which they have the greatest potentials for monopoly gains. The industries most highly organized tend to be the skilled crafts of the construction industry, the various transportation and utility industries, and the most highly capitalized and concentrated of the manufacturing industries. They are especially well organized in large plants and giant companies because they can mobilize worker protests where organizations are large and human relations most difficult. On the other hand, the atomized industries such as textiles and lumber in manufacturing and agriculture are the least organized. (See 13–13.)

In spite of much talk about "drives" to organize the South, the unions have had only limited success in this region. This is mostly because of the types of industries that are predominant in the region. When highly unionized industries open plants in the South, they tend to get organized; but the South has a higher proportion of its jobs in the less-unionized industries. Also, smaller plants, smaller cities, and the attitudes of workers (affected by job scarcity and individualism in a rural culture), tend to make union organization more difficult. As a

13–13. Extent of Union Bargaining in Manufacturing, 1958

Industry	*Workers in Plants Covered by Bargaining*		*Employment in Industry Group*	
	U.S.	*South*	*U.S.*	*South*
Highly Unionized:			21%	18%
Petroleum refining	90%	88%		
Primary metals	89	95		
Transportation equipment	87	86		
Ordnance	84	n.a.		
Rubber	81	n.a.		
Substantially unionized:			47	36
Stone-clay-glass	78	65		
Paper	76	79		
Electrical machinery	73	n.a.		
Fabricated metals	71	54		
Food products	68	41		
Machinery	68	63		
Chemicals	65	62		
Printing	65	61		
Moderately unionized:			17	16
Tobacco	63	72		
Apparel	60	30		
Miscellaneous	54	n.a.		
Instruments	52	35		
Furniture	50	28		
Lightly unionized:			15	30
Leather	49	32		
Lumber	44	27		
Textiles	30	14		
All manufacturing	67	46	100	100

Source: U.S. Department of Labor, *Monthly Labor Review*, 1962, p. 347.

result, in most types of industries, the South has a smaller proportion of its workers in plants covered by collective bargaining.

Unions also experience difficulty in trying to organize most sales, clerical, and professional employees; again, these fields are characterized by a large number of employers who often employ relatively small work forces. This is especially significant because these types of workers are becoming a larger part of the labor force. In short, there appear to be natural limits on the extent to which the labor force will be unionized.

The Bargaining Process

The primary purposes of collective bargaining are to further or protect the economic interests of members. The means of doing this first of all is to obtain a monopoly of the labor supply of a particular employer or in a particular trade. This involves organizing all of the workers, getting agreement from the employer to hire only union members or to require that workers once employed join the union, or pressuring nonunion workers to stay away. Secondly, it means having the power (and occasionally using it) to shut down a plant by striking. This is intended to hurt the profits of a company so that the company will be "persuaded" to seek an agreement, or contract, favorable to the union members.

Once established, unions attempt to influence the level of wages in three ways—by raising worker productivity, by restricting the number of workers who enter the market, and by striking collective bargaining agreements in which management is left free to decide how many workers will be hired but pledges itself to pay a prescribed minimum wage rate. The only important example of the first is provided by the garment workers who have cooperated in, often initiated, studies aimed at increasing productivity. The craft unions have long practised the second tactic as a way of putting teeth in their wage demands. And the last is the stock-in-trade of the industrial union which uses an all-or-nothing tactic, work or strike, as a bargaining lever.

Essentially, then, the bargaining process involves a lot of the tactics of a poker game and the use (or threat) of the strike weapon. Public policy essentially permits a certain kind of legalized monopoly and a certain kind of industrial warfare in order to let the parties to a dispute settle it among themselves. In practice, very few strikes occur. In no year since 1946 has as much as 1 percent of the man-hours of all industry been lost in strikes. However, there are a number of unsolved public problems. One involves the rights of a minority of workers who do not wish to join the union or pay dues. Another concerns the public interest in maintaining production in key public utility industries and in goverment bodies where workers are organized. Even in the nonutility industries, the public frequently gets hurt by a dispute. Still another problem is the extent to which wage bargains may cause inflation.

Wage Gains

The effects of wage bargains are difficult enough to determine, but even the wage increase itself is not always clearly due to the union's power. Under collective bargaining all wage changes will be made at specific times by mutual agreement between the company and the union. Some of the wage gains might have occurred anyway, especially in time of inflation or when the company is expanding and needs to recruit more workers. From the mid-1930's to the end of the Korean War, when the unions gained most of their strength and experience, there was an almost continuous rapid rise in prices and expansion of output in the country. Employers either wanted to give wage increases or put up little resistance. So-called "patterns" of wage increases and fringe benefits followed in one industry after another. This gave an impression of tremendous union power over wages in this country. Some economists, however, question how much of these increases was due to union power. A number of the nonorganized industries had faster wage increases during the 1940's; and study of World War I shows many examples of similar rapid wage increases at a time when unions weren't numerous enough to be a significant force.

13–14 shows that for over half a century, wages in manufacturing

13–14. Manufacturing Wages and Productivity

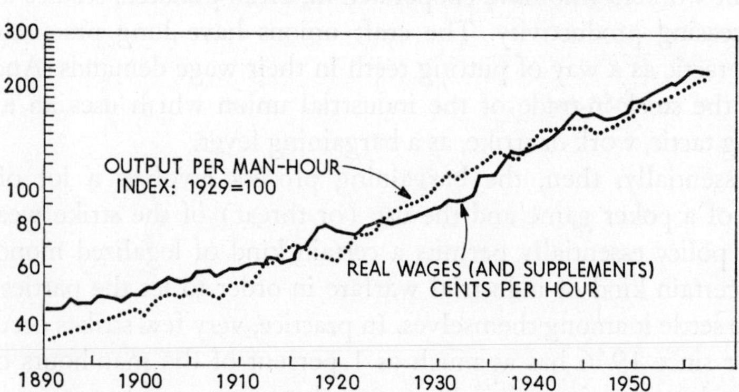

Source: Albert Rees, "Patterns of Wages, Prices and Productivity," The American Assembly, *Wages, Prices, Profits and Productivity* (New York: The Assembly, 1959), pp. 15, 27.

(after adjusting for price changes) have been keeping pace with the general rising trend in productivity. As indicated earlier, wages in manufacturing have risen as fast as output per man-hour and faster than output per unit of labor and capital inputs combined.

13–15 shows that the wage cost per unit in manufacturing has corresponded fairly closely to the wholesale price changes of finished goods. Compared to the base year, 1929, wage costs have risen a little more. This may be because material costs rose a little less rapidly and nonproduction workers may not have received wage increases as rapidly as production workers. Also the spread of skill differentials has narrowed with the general rise in educational levels.

13-15. Manufacturing Wage-Costs and Prices

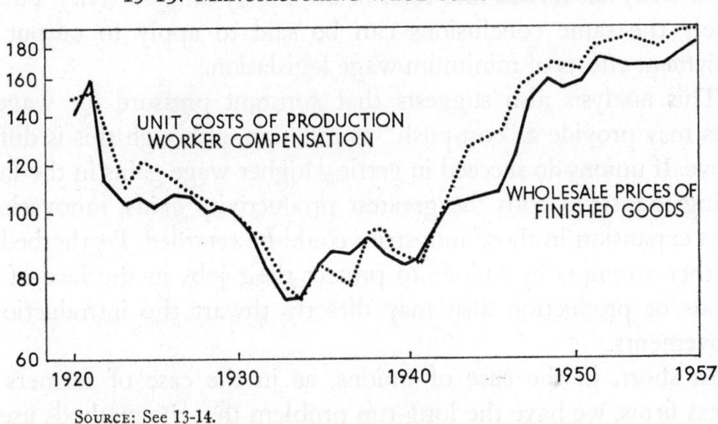

Source: See 13-14.

Economists have noted that labor's share of the national income has remained fairly stable during comparable periods in the business cycle. During depressions the profit share falls more, and during business booms profits rise more. With the decline in farmers, more people have become employees; so, total wages and salaries have increased somewhat in relation to national income.

If on a per-worker basis labor's percentage of the total output has not increased, it follows that union activity has not redistributed income over the years.[5] Further, if as we have seen, unit wage costs in manufacturing have not increased at the expense of profits, it follows that union wage gains resulted in either price hikes or dampened price reductions

[5] That union activity prevented a worsening of the worker's relative position is unlikely—in spite of recurrent depressions, this economy has historically been one of labor scarcity in which the drift of wages was upward well before unions had control over a significant portion of the labor force.

which in turn reduced production and employment or dampened increases in output and employment.

Thus we cannot escape the conclusion that unions, having failed to raise the share of the pie going to all workers, have increased the share going to union members. These policies have retarded the growth of organized industries and produced labor surpluses in unorganized industries such as farming, household services, retailing, and wholesaling. In short, very high wages may cause more people to seek certain jobs but mean fewer opportunities to obtain them. This conclusion seems paradoxical at first when one considers that union growth was often most rapid in the rapidly expanding industries. However, it is important to bear in mind the fact that this deduction only states that growth rates are ***retarded,*** not turned into rates of decline by union activity. Further, precisely the same conclusions can be said to apply to output and employment effects of minimum wage legislation.

This analysis also suggests that constant pressure for wage increases may provide a "cost-push" to inflation, although this is difficult to prove. If unions do succeed in getting higher wage gains in the fastest growing industries with the greatest productivity gains, innovation as well as expansion in those industries could be retarded. Featherbedding and other attempts by unions to protect their jobs in the face of new methods of production also may directly thwart the introduction of improvements.

In short, in the case of unions, as in the case of farmers and business firms, we have the long-run problem that the methods used by sellers to protect their own interests may hinder the adjustments that are necessary parts of the growth process and slow down the overall growth of the economy.

Labor's Progress

What can we say by way of summarizing labor's progress over the period since 1920? In spite of three wars, a continuing cold war, and a devastating depression, the American economy has achieved growth records and a level of living which only the science fiction of Jules Verne anticipated in the last century. The data show that from an income standpoint, labor has progressed in parallel with this growth. In nonincome terms, gains are even more impressive: hours of work have been reduced from an average of 47.4 per week in 1920 to 39.7 in 1960; physical working conditions have improved tremendously; and the average employee is now treated as a human being rather than a glorified beast of burden.

The workingman's lot today is at a vast remove from the wage slave days when a man could be prosecuted for quitting his job. The conditions which Marx and Engels described quite accurately are no longer typical simply because of the factor that both these men failed to comprehend—economic growth was carrying the ***entire*** economy to higher levels of material well-being. But while the average has moved up, the southern sharecropper, the unskilled urban laborer, the hard-scrabble farmer, and the Appalachian who toils at the face of a "scab" mine are not much better off than their counterparts of several generations back. We shall turn specifically to problems of poverty later.

What role did unions play in this history? From a wage standpoint we have seen that both union activity and minimum wage legislation have actually exacerbated the problems of the groups referred to above while improving the lot of the membership. Yet in a larger sense, the union movement through direct action and by influencing legislation may be responsible for most of the nonwage gains that labor has made since 1920—growth made them possible, unions may have directed them to labor in general.

STUDY QUESTIONS

1. If giant firms eventually dominate the economy, what dangers or disadvantages might this have? What evidence is cited that suggests considerable dominance now? Criticize this evidence.
2. Why is market power measured within industries rather than in terms of share of economy as a whole? What share of manufacturing output is sold where four firms have over half of the sales? What is the long-term trend in this measure?
3. How have ideas changed about monopoly and competition and the conditions affecting the degree of monopoly power a firm may have?
4. How do size of plant and size of firm relate to unit costs or efficiency? How does size of firm affect innovations? Where is the "entrepreneur" in the bureaucracy of giant firms?
5. Criticize the following statement: "Antitrust regulation has been tried historically and has failed." Criticize the idea of "social responsibility" as an alternative to competitive markets and antitrust regulation. Criticize the idea of "countervailing power" as an alternative to competitive markets and antitrust regulation.
6. Why do farm prices tend to be much more volatile than output changes in the absence of price stabilization programs. What impact on prices and output would you expect from a rise in farm productivity? An increase in

total population? A rise in per capita income? How has the historical record evolved in these respects?

7. Why must some farmers leave farming over the long run when productivity in farming is increasing? Why would price support programs tend to get more difficult to manage over time?
8. Distinguish between our "overproduction" and our "low-income" farm problems. What policies would tend to aid solutions to both? What solutions unique to each would be appropriate?
9. Why has unionization slowed down?
10. How have unions affected incomes for all workers? For union members?
11. What tactics do unions employ to raise wages?

Chapter 14 CHANGING STRUCTURE: INDIVIDUALS AND GOVERNMENT

INDIVIDUAL SECURITY AND OPPORTUNITY

Over most of the post-World War II period, public celebration of our "affluent society" served to sweep the notion of poverty under the rug—at least for 80 percent of the population. But beginning in the late 1950's, Americans began to ask themselves about the quality of life in the affluent society. Their investigation led them to the rediscovery of poverty—poverty in urban ghettos, in mountain hamlets, in depressed areas, in the rural South. Writers such as Michael Harrington spotlighted this sloppy housekeeping by pointing to the lump in the rug, by reminding the 80 percent of the 20 percent who live in *The Other America*—the "invisible poor" tucked out of sight in the "invisible land" well away from suburbia and well off the commuter's, the shopper's, or the vacationer's pathways.[1]

In the shock of rediscovery the celebrated man in the street overcompensated; he formed the impression that this country has a problem of "poverty" that is unusual among nations or is rapidly becoming worse. There is no evidence, however, that our lowest income groups actually are worse off than similar groups in any other country or than similar groups in previous decades. These days, the "poverty" problem almost always is discussed in terms of judgments about what is believed to be a "minimum standard" of living in some sense. What are called "minimum" standards however, are determined in terms of what is socially "desirable" or expected. As we will see, these desirable standards tend to be tied to "average" living standards and to rise with historical improvements in that average.

So far we have been concerned with the long sweep of economic growth not so much in terms of the size and power of the Nation as in

[1] Michael Harrington, *The Other America* (Baltimore: Penguin Books, Inc., 1962), pp. 9–12.

terms of the per capita income and welfare of the people. Clearly we have achieved the highest income standard of any people in the world. This growth in income has been dealt with necessarily in terms of averages for all the people; but we also have pointed out that wages of workers have kept up with national productivity gains and that the top income groups have recently been receiving a diminishing share of total income. Now we will turn to take a closer look at the lowest income group and also consider some of the hazards individuals may face in a market economy.

The Great Depression of the 1930's was a shock to public confidence in a free market system, and it caused a great deal of individual suffering. Reforms in institutions and changes in monetary and fiscal policies have gone a long way toward minimizing and offsetting slumps in production and income. A great deal of attention and some reforms have been focused on the hazards of individuals during both depressions and prosperity. In the most massive single piece of welfare legislation, the problems of old age and unemployment were dealt with by the Social Security Act of 1935. During the postwar period, more and more public attention also has been given to expanding social security coverage and improving medical care and education.

The process of economic growth produces threats to individual security and opportunity and, consequently, poverty for particular segments of the population; however, for others the growth process reinforces security and widens the range of economic opportunity and thereby produces affluence. And the fruits of growth include the ability to do something about problems of security and opportunity. Thus increased public concern does not reflect a worsening of conditions. It merely reflects our realization that we have achieved a ***greater ability*** to deal with these problems. We can do more so we have become more impatient and expect even greater achievements of ourselves.

Personal Income Distribution

We can perhaps best appreciate who are the poor and why they are poor if we have in mind what is implied by the term "personal income distribution." Personal income distribution simply refers to the division of aggregate personal income among consumer units (families and individual household heads). Underlying the personal distribution of income is "factor income distribution" which refers to the distribution of income to labor and owners of capital and land. From this we can see that personal income distribution depends upon the nature of the personal distribution of productive factors. Put another way, the more and better the labor, land, and capital controlled by a given household, the more affluent will be that household, and vice versa.

What besides the luck of the draw determines the quality of productive factors in a given household? Native abilities and the demand for those abilities, education and training, age, race, location, and market power all combine to determine the rates of pay that will be earned in each household.

14–1 shows that the distribution of income became slightly more

14–1. Percentage Distribution of Total Personal Income 1929, 1935–1936, 1944 and 1962

Quintile	*1929*	*1935–36*	*1944*	*1962*
Lowest fifth	12.5	4.1	4.9	4.6
Second fifth		9.2	10.9	10.9
Third fifth	13.8	14.1	16.2	16.3
Fourth fifth	19.3	20.9	22.2	22.7
Highest fifth	54.4	51.7	45.8	45.5
Total	100.0	100.0	100.0	100.0
Top twentieth	30.0	26.5	20.7	19.6

Source: U.S. Department of Commerce, *Survey of Current Business*, April, 1964.

equal over the period 1929 to 1935–36, then accelerated its tendency toward equality from 1935–36 to 1944, and since 1944 has changed only slightly. Further, it shows that the greatest part of the change in distribution from 1929 to 1964 came from the top 20's reduced share being directed to each of the four lower classes in such a way that the highest of the four got the largest gain in percentage points and so on. Thus, earnings have been redistributed toward the lower income groups but ***not*** radically so over the past four decades. From this we can conclude that distribution of factors of production has been similarly modified. Since we know that labor's share of the total pie has increased only very slightly we can reason that the ownership of other factors of production has been moderately redistributed in favor of the lower income classes.

However, it is important to note that the entire distribution structure moved upward in this period—real per capita disposable income has moved from $1,236 to $2,116 over the same period. In other words, had there been no downward redistribution the lot of Mr. Average Man in the lowest fifth of the population would still have improved markedly.

Concern about Poverty

The fact remains, though, that we as a nation are unhappy to note that the lowest 20 percent of consumer units receive less than 5 percent of total income. Why? First, poverty is expensive; the incidence of crime is concentrated among the poor, as are the special social services that are provided by government, and the low productivity of the poor exacts its toll in lost GNP. Second, as the absolute level of incomes has grown, our standards as to what constitutes poverty and what is equitable have grown too. Consequently, according to the guidelines of the President's Council of Economic Advisors, individuals who earn less than $1,500 per year and families that earn less than $3,000 per year are considered to live in poverty.[2] In 1963, there were 34.5 million people, 19 percent of the population, in these classifications. Comparable percentages for earlier years are 1958, 23 percent, and 1947, 32 percent.[3]

Why is it that society considers today's low incomes inadequate when they are in fact equal to yesterday's middle incomes and well above yesterday's poverty line? Why, in other words, have our standards escalated along with our incomes? We can only attempt a superficial explanation here.

By a generally accepted definition, poverty is the inability to purchase "necessities." We have traditionally had public and private agencies who dispersed assistance of one kind or another to those who met the agencies' respective definitions of poverty. The poverty criteria of these agencies have been drawn up by compiling budgets necessary to provide a family with at least a minimum level of subsistence. Over the years the dollar value of these budgets has been raised over and above adjustments for price changes as the responsible officials raised their conception of what constitutes an acceptable minimum. These officials, drawn from the American middle classes and subject to the same forces that shape the general public's attitudes, institutionalized changing standards of adequacy. However, it is noteworthy that in spite of expansion of the "subsistence" budgets they remain within a range that most

[2] There is much quibbling about where and how to draw the poverty line simply because such judgments are subjective in nature. The vital point is that a large segment of the American public, whether it is 10 percent as some hold or 30 percent as others say, live in circumstances that the balance of the population considers poor enough to warrant concern and effort.

[3] Herman P. Miller, "Facts about Poverty Revised," in *Poverty American Style,* ed. Herman P. Miller (Belmont, Calif.: Wadsworth Publishing Co., Inc., 1966), p. 117.

of us would consider subsistence, i.e., food, shelter, and clothing are defined in a minimal way, and medical services, entertainment, and reading material are sparsely represented. Our rising standards have not elevated our definition of necessities to include contemporary luxuries.

It appears that the greatest influence that economic growth has had upon the formulation of standards is through growth's impact upon the "workingman's" wage level and budget. 14–2 shows the historical

14–2. Subsistence Budgets and Low Wages

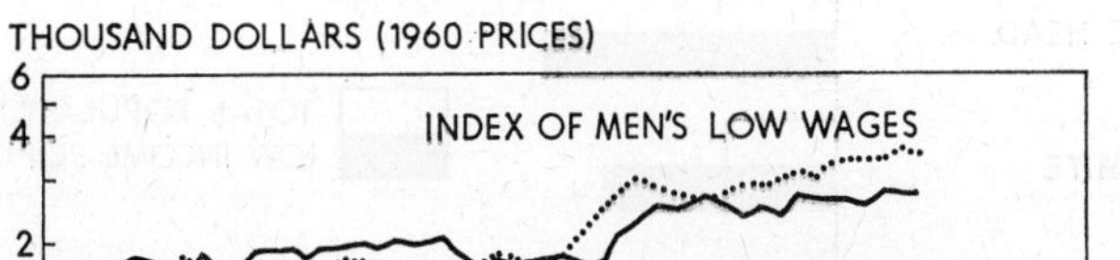

Source: Oscar Ornati, *Poverty Amid Affluence* (New York: The Twentieth Century Fund, 1966), App. 2, Table B.

movement of real wages earned by low-paid male workers and the real value of the minimum subsistence budgets which were defined in each of the years from 1910 through 1960. Two characteristics command attention. The wage index and the budget values have been very close in value over the period in spite of becoming inverted in their relative positions. And, secondly, the direction of movement of the two series has been very closely associated.

Who are the poor? If you are an elderly nonwhite female head of household, living in the rural South, in poor health, unemployed, and with less than eight years of education, the "probability" that you are ***not*** in poverty is in all likelihood less than 1 percent. The data in 14–3 summarize the characteristics of single individuals and of low-income families and their household heads. For this purpose, low income is defined for each family size in such a manner as to include only the lowest 19 percent of all consumer units. The percentage of low-income persons with a particular characteristic (in the shaded bar) is compared with the percentage of all persons in the total population with the same characteristic (in the light bar).

Lack of more than an eighth grade education is a handicap of two fifths of the population, but it is an especially common trait of the low-income family head—two thirds of whom are so limited. In addi-

14–3. CHARACTERISTICS OF LOW-INCOME FAMILIES, 1957

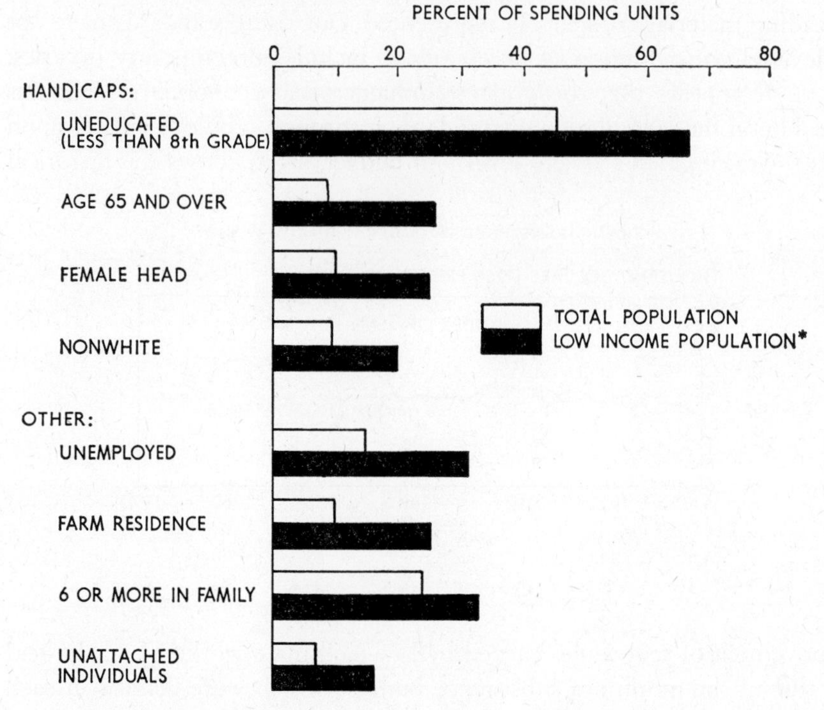

* See text for definition.
SOURCE: Robert J. Lampman, *The Low Income Population and Economic Growth*, U.S. Congress, Joint Economic Committee, 86th Cong. 1st sess. (Washington, D.C.: U.S. Government Printing Office, 1959).

tion, one fourth of the heads of low-income families are persons over 65 years of age, or are women, compared to 10 percent or less in the population. More of the low-income family heads also are nonwhite. Associated with age, sex, and race may be certain traits that limit productivity and income-earning power; but discrimination by employers also limits the opportunities of these groups. This is especially true of Negroes of both sexes and women. Traditionally certain jobs have been barred to Negroes and women quite apart from ability considerations. Usually these have been the higher paying jobs or the jobs that are stepping stones to higher positions. Thus families headed by Negroes and women tend to be low-income families in which characteristically health, education, and goals (goals not aspirations) are at lower levels than in higher income families. The result is that poverty is self-perpetuating along lines of race and sex.

In addition, low income also is associated with the unemployment of the family head. Also because of a surplus of rural workers and low incomes in farming, a large proportion of the people living on farms has low incomes. Note that although employment and rural residence are important poverty characteristics, many of those who reside in cities and people who work in low-skill, low-wage jobs everywhere fall in the poverty class as well. Finally large family size is associated with an income level that is low relative to the per capita needs, both for the very large family and for the isolated individual.

Now let us consider specifically the hazards of age and illness. One of the benefits of our rising income levels and advances in science is that people are healthier and live longer. This can be seen in 14–4 by the

14–4. Longevity and Households

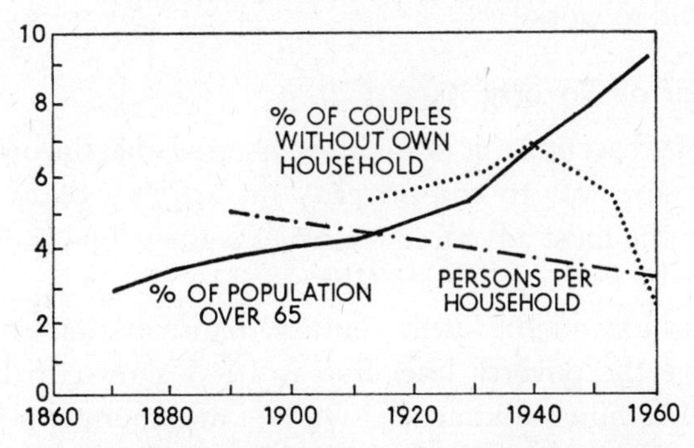

Source: U.S. Department of Commerce, *Historical Statistics of the United States* (Washington, D.C.: U.S. Government Printing Office, 1960), pp. 10, 15, and 16; and U.S. Department of Commerce *Statistical Abstract of the United States, 1960* (Washington, D.C.: U.S. Government Printing Office, 1961).

solid line indicating that an increasing percentage of the population is over 65 years old. This benefit, however, is not without its costs. The very old worker reaches a point where his capacity for work diminishes, and he may be discharged. Even before this time, older workers laid off for any other reason may find it difficult to find work again. Also, while medical science has brought better health, the costs of healing miracles may come very high. Treatment for major illnesses can run into thousands of dollars. Thus the average person who now lives longer may expect to incur increasing medical expenses in general and especially as he gets older.

At the same time that we are living longer, we also are abandoning some of the security of large family households, and we are losing some of the neighborliness of small rural communities. Fifty or a hundred years ago, when fewer people lived to an old age, they usually could count on the younger members of a family group to support them and care for them. On a farm, at least, there was still some work they could do that was useful to the family. Today, however, less and less productive activity (homemade articles and do-it-yourself services) occurs in the home. Also, as shown in 14–4, the average number of persons per household has long been declining—and not all of this is from having fewer children. Fewer relatives live with the family. Also, as shown in this chart, in the postwar years fewer married couples are without a household of their own. Our increasing concentration of population in large cities also tends to make social contacts more impersonal. Individuals, therefore, must rely more on themselves and less on family or neighbors for their protection when sick or when they become too old to work.

The War on Poverty

In the 19th century it was often asserted that income redistribution was the sure way to end poverty. In fact, as we have cited, total GNP in even the most advanced countries was too low over most of the century to make this mathematically possible. Growth we learned was the solution. Now in the 20th century, redistribution could raise all families above the poverty line. But as 14–5 shows, to bring the 40 percent of all families who are below the "minimum comfort level" to that level would require reducing the incomes of those above the minimum by one third of their above-minimum margin (note that the areas of the two shaded rectangles are equal). Such a massive shift is not politically feasible, so we have government programs by which we render service to the poor, a "war on poverty."

Leaving aside those whose infirmities bar them from the labor market, over the long run education and general economic growth are capable of pulling much of the poverty group up to higher income levels. However, poverty has an ethos of its own that, as we have seen, tends to perpetuate itself in particular families generation after generation. The corollary to this rule is that it is far more difficult for general growth and prosperity to enhance the economic position of the poor man than for the middle-income individual. This in turn suggests that although monetary and fiscal policy are the vanguard of the attack on poverty, supplementary programs are necessary—programs which deal with poverty's specific causes and symptoms (which are causes one poverty generation hence), programs which will aid the labor force to adjust to changing patterns of labor demand.

There is evidence to support this assertion. Sociologists have been studying poverty for the many years in which the problem was ignored in other quarters. Their findings have come as a shock to many who speak of a "culture of poverty" and attribute a unique set of aspirations to the poor. In fact, the great majority of the poor long for exactly those things that are the goals of the so-called middle class—home ownership, college for the kids, and a respected place in the community.[4]

14-5. Illustration of Income Redistribution

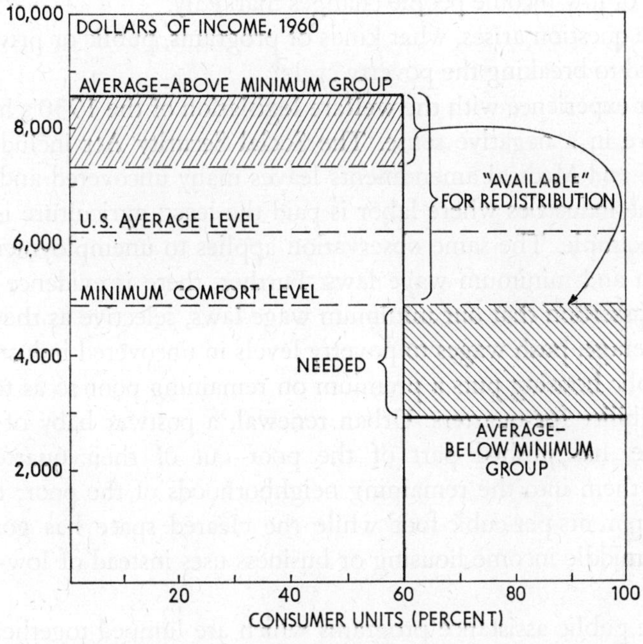

DOLLARS OF INCOME, 1960
AVERAGE-ABOVE MINIMUM GROUP
"AVAILABLE" FOR REDISTRIBUTION
U.S. AVERAGE LEVEL
MINIMUM COMFORT LEVEL
NEEDED
AVERAGE-BELOW MINIMUM GROUP
10,000
8,000
6,000
4,000
2,000
20
40
60
80
100
CONSUMER UNITS (PERCENT)

Source: Oscar Ornati, *Poverty Amid Affluence* (New York: the Twentieth Century Fund, 1966), Appendix 35; and U.S. Department of Commerce, *Statistical Abstract of the United States, 1965* (Washington, D.C.: U.S. Government Printing Office, 1966).

However, the poor recognize the futility of adopting these desires as goals. For the most part they feel walled in by the factors in their environment that are responsible for their low-income position—poor education, frail health, housing restrictions, employer discrimination with respect to age, race, and sex, etc. Thus they maximize their position behind the poverty wall in a life style that consists of setting and meeting goals that are different from their "middle-class aspirations"—

[4] See for example, Hylan Lewis, *Culture, Class, and Poverty* (Washington, D.C.: Cross-Tell, 1967).

and this involves behavior that often reinforces the tendency for poverty to infect successive generations. But, some say, if one bought very wisely, scrimped and saved, one could get along on $3000 per year even with six in the family. United States Department of Labor studies have, in fact, proved something like this, but to keep the regimen involved requires a bachelor of science degree in domestic science and the character of a Trappist monk. The frustrations of poverty produce an attitude which mortars the walls of poverty. However, if some force comes along to make it realistic to think of vaulting that wall, the actual behavior of low-income people changes markedly.

The question arises, what kinds of programs, public or private, are best suited to breaking the poverty cycle?

Our experience with the welfare legislation of the 1930's has been instructive in a negative sense. The Social Security Act including the Medicare and Medical amendments leaves many uncovered and especially in the industries where labor is paid the least; agriculture is an excellent example. The same observation applies to unemployment compensation and minimum wage laws. Further, there is evidence to support the assertion that our minimum wage laws, selective as they are in their coverage, push wages to poverty levels in uncovered industries.

Public housing puts a premium on remaining poor so as to maintain eligibility for quarters. Urban renewal, a postwar baby of 1930's parentage, has pushed part of the poor out of their quarters and crowded them into the remaining neighborhoods of the poor; this has driven up rents-per-cubic-foot while the cleared space has gone into high- or middle-income housing or business uses instead of low-income housing.

The public assistance programs which are lumped together under the popular label "the Welfare" and are typified by the Aid to Dependent Children program (ADC) were structured with the intention of preventing chiseling. But they have the side effects of becoming a cause of the conditions they were designed to treat symptomatically. Such programs as aid to the blind and disabled are exceptions to this observation. The school lunch program which subsidizes public school cafeterias and the surplus food distribution plans—both were designed as part of the farm program—get better grades. The former often constitutes the difference between a health-sustaining diet and malnutrition for some youngsters while the latter has prevented starvation for whole families. But the balance of the farm program amounts to welfare payments for the middle class, since most poor farmers benefit little or not at all from the support programs.

This all adds up to what one student has called the "paradox of the welfare state" and described by Harrington as "socialism for the rich and free enterprise for the poor."[5] What alternatives are there? Two lines of attack have been suggested: ***categorical assistance*** and ***income supplements.***

Categorical assistance involves programs to aid the poor who qualify in certain disability categories such as being blind, disabled, poorly educated, unemployed and without unemployment compensation, a dependent child, etc. Advocates of this approach suggest redesigning and adding to types of programs that came out of the New Deal. Causes and symptoms of poverty are to be identified and programs designed for those who are so afflicted ***but*** with adequate guarantees that incentives to become self-sufficient will be held intact or at best stimulated. Such programs are criticized because they combine some category criterion (e.g., having dependent children) with an income criterion in such a way that the grant falls by $1 each time income from other sources rises by $1; this constitutes a confiscatory tax and stifles incentives according to critics. Recent legislation, in fact, recognizes this problem by exempting a percentage of earned income in defining categorical eligibility.

Those who advocate the income supplements deny that a sufficient number of public and private programs can be designed to deal with all the causes of poverty that are open to change through social action. Rather, they advocate supplementing incomes sufficiently to bring low-income people up to a level that permits them to scale the wall and take for themselves the steps which assure economic security at "decent" income levels. And those who cannot participate in the labor force owing to disabilities would be similarly assured a decent standard of living. Incentives would be maintained by reducing income supplements by less than any increases in after-tax earned income so that it would always pay to raise one's earning power and income; this assertion is questioned by critics of this approach. In the current debate over how to end poverty the income supplement approach usually referred to is the ***negative income tax.*** It calls for a payment to all individuals and families that is subject to taxation so that taxpayers with sufficient incomes from other sources receive no supplement.

As we have noted, 14–5 illustrates the size of the income redistribution that would be required to bring the low-income group to a minimum comfort level. In turn the minimum comfort level would guarantee access to the educational, health, nutritional, and cultural levels that will sustain the average family at or above the minimum

[5] C. R. McConnell, *Economics* (3rd ed. 1; New York: McGraw-Hill Book Co., 1966), pp. 673–74; and Harrington, *op. cit.,* p. 157.

comfort level through its own efforts. Let us assume for sake of illustration that the tax legislation necessary to produce such a massive shift in incomes could be legislated. The relevant question then becomes will the jump in incomes be used to achieve these ends or will the life style of poverty prevent taking advantage of opportunities that become financially possible? Will "the cream" again rise to the top as opponents of income redistribution assert?

Again we have a case in which discussion has turned into polemics and advocates have polarized their positions. Yet review of the causes of poverty makes it apparent that a synthetic approach is called for. For example, consider the family in which the head of household fits the stereotype of the shiftless poor—lazy, drunken, sex-crazed, prolific, and illiterate. Income supplements would be wasted relative to the traditional goals of antipoverty legislation unless some sort of categorical assistance went with them to channel the funds into a permanent escape route from poverty for at least the children of the household.

Take as a second example, a middle-aged, Negro, female head of household with four children, who works as a "domestic." Obviously she cannot find the time, income supplement or not, to enter a training program in order to enhance her productivity. Yet a training program that pays a salary as if it were a job accomplishes this end. Of course compared to an income supplement the costs would be higher during the training period but they will terminate, whereas an income supplement would have to continue indefinitely.

The "War on Poverty" inaugurated by President Lyndon Johnson in 1964 is a mixture of these two approaches. Yet, as of this date, the programs are modest relative to the problems involved and constitute only a token recognition of the income-supplement approach. We can perhaps speculate as to the future of antipoverty legislation. Given our aspirations and impatience it is not unlikely that a basic system of income supplements will be enacted and complemented by a superstructure of specific programs which bolster productivity for particular categories of individuals. Such a system would enable those who are capable of raising their productivity to do so while those who cannot or will not could at least have sufficient income that the choices of the other members of the family will not be restricted to those that lie within the perimeter of the closed circle of poverty.

The budget outlays for any concentrated attack on poverty will be large. But if the programs they support do in fact reduce poverty to minimal levels they will be self-limiting and so will the ancillary costs associated with poverty such as crime. Further the higher productivity of those who are assisted will increase GNP. On the other hand, the self-regenerating nature of poverty promises to perpetuate the costs of poverty.

Our survey of the incidence of poverty and the special roles played by age and illness shows how particular characteristics of households make for low earning power of the individuals within them. Secondly, our survey suggests that there is a vicious cycle of poverty; low income means an environment in which the preconditions for another generation of poverty are present. Our earlier observation that poverty is self-regenerating along lines of race and sex can be extended to include almost all of the attributes of low-income households. Now it is appropriate to look at the various ways in which individual security and opportunity can be secured.

Assuring Individual Security

From the foregoing it is obvious that it has become increasingly important in an urban, industrial society for individuals to save, to accumulate financial reserves in order to protect themselves in times of need. Also, while their own times of illness are unpredictable, the proportion of people likely to be sick at one time can be predicted from social experience; so the risks of individuals can be spread by the insurance principle.

Fortunately, our rising incomes nationally also have been accompanied by a rise in real wealth per capita. The development of banks, savings and loan associations, insurance companies, and stock and bond brokers not only helped to finance the capital needs of industry, it also helped many individuals accumulate small holdings of assets in a diversified form. 14–6 shows how important these assets can be in relation to personal incomes for the nation as a whole. With all cash and savings more than offsetting debts (both consumer credits and mortgages), individual financial equity consists mostly of securities (stocks and bonds, both public and private) and the accumulated cash reserve values of insurance and pension funds. In addition, individuals own considerable tangible assets in the form of consumer durable goods (such as autos, furniture, and household equipment), homes, and land. In total, both financial and physical assets of individuals, clear of debt, amount to over four times the personal income in one year for the Nation as a whole.

While ownership of assets or wealth may be more unequally distributed than income, there is some tendency for it to be distributed in the favor of older persons and in favor of farmers and self-employed

14–6. Individual Income and Assets

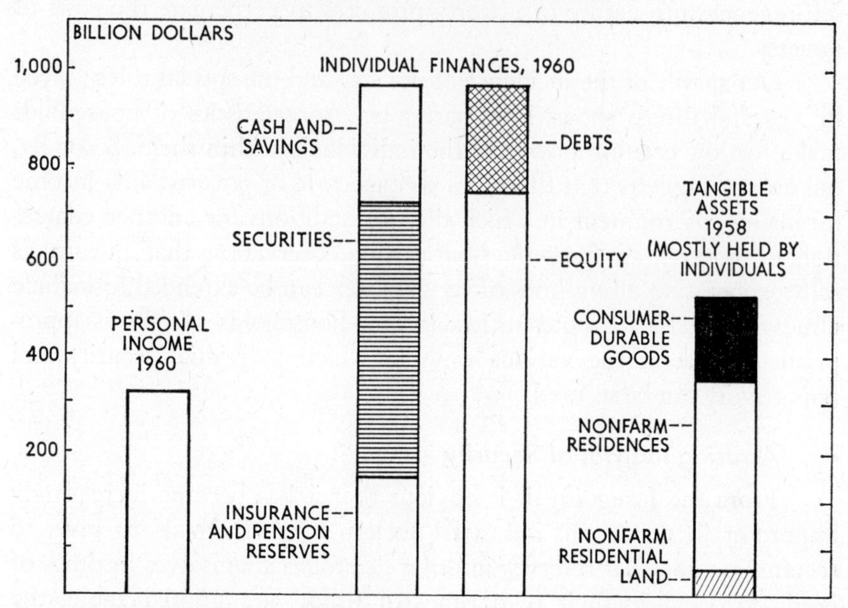

Source: U.S. Department of Commerce, *Statistical Abstract of the United States, 1962* (Washington, D.C.: U.S. Government Printing Office, 1963), pp. 328 and 338.

persons. For those who can remain employed not only does a person's income-earning power tend to rise with age (until a later age, in fact, for the higher income occupations), but also an older person has had more time to accumulate savings.

At the same time that rising incomes have enabled individuals to accumulate more wealth to protect themselves, rising incomes also have enabled our economy to have the luxury of devoting a larger share of resources toward public programs of insurance and forced savings. The biggest single change in our national income distribution pattern since the 1930's was, no doubt, the public pension program instituted under the Social Security Act. Since 1920, the largest increase in government expenditures, after the defense and interest items, has been for welfare, housing, and social insurance. 14–7 shows the relative importance of the expenditures within this group during 1960. Social Security pension payments are the largest item, and nearly all of this expenditure is by the federal government.

With the growth of the regular pension programs, little or no increase in public aid expenditures has been legislated in the last two decades. Since employees, as well as employers, are taxed to contribute

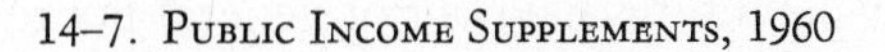

14–7. Public Income Supplements, 1960

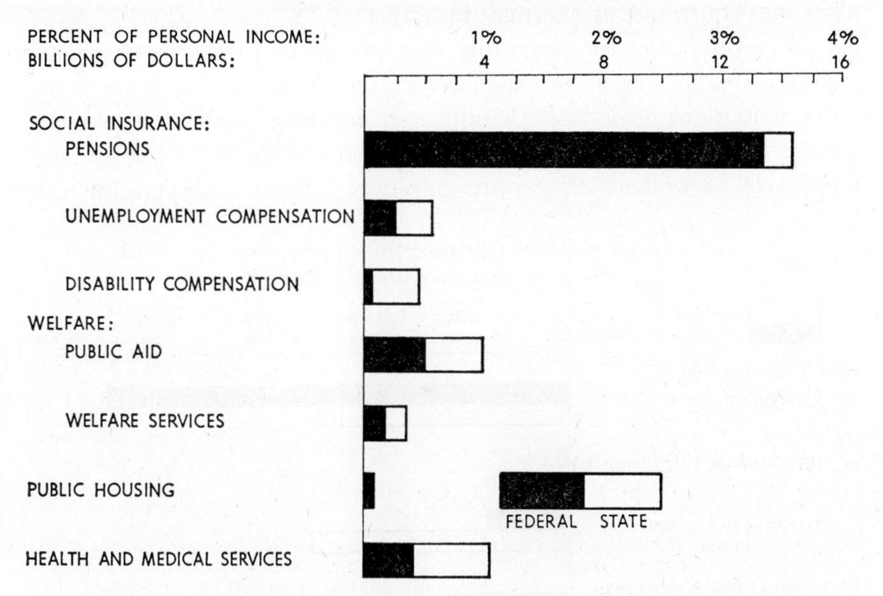

Source: U.S. Department of Commerce, *Statistical Abstract of the United States, 1962* (Washington, D.C.: U.S. Government Printing Office, 1963), p. 275.

to the buildup of a pension fund, the individual receiving a social security pension does not feel as though he is receiving charity. Actually, of course, the program was started by giving pensions to individuals who had not fully paid in advance for their benefits; and still today the program is not fully "funded"—that is, paid for in advance. Thus, as more people have started drawing their pensions, workers have had to pay higher taxes to cover part of the costs. Young workers in the next few decades, in fact, are going to be supporting both a larger proportion of old people and a larger proportion of children than perhaps any previous generations. But then, with rising productivity and income levels, this may not be too difficult a task.

Among the other items, disability compensation is paid for by employer taxes on truly an insurance principle; but unemployment is not properly an insurable risk, except during good times. During depressions many people draw compensation all at once, which is of course counter to the insurance principle. (Of course, this has the useful feature of providing an automatic countercyclical spending flow by government when private spending tends to slow down.) Public welfare services, public housing, and health and medical services tend to be general welfare expenditures paid out of general tax revenues. Individuals do not contribute as a form of insurance.

14–8 indicates the large role now played by private pension and insurance plans. Instead of expenditures, this chart deals with the regular contributions made by both employers and employees to support the various types of employee benefit plans—some of them for government employees as well as for private employees. Again, the pension pro-

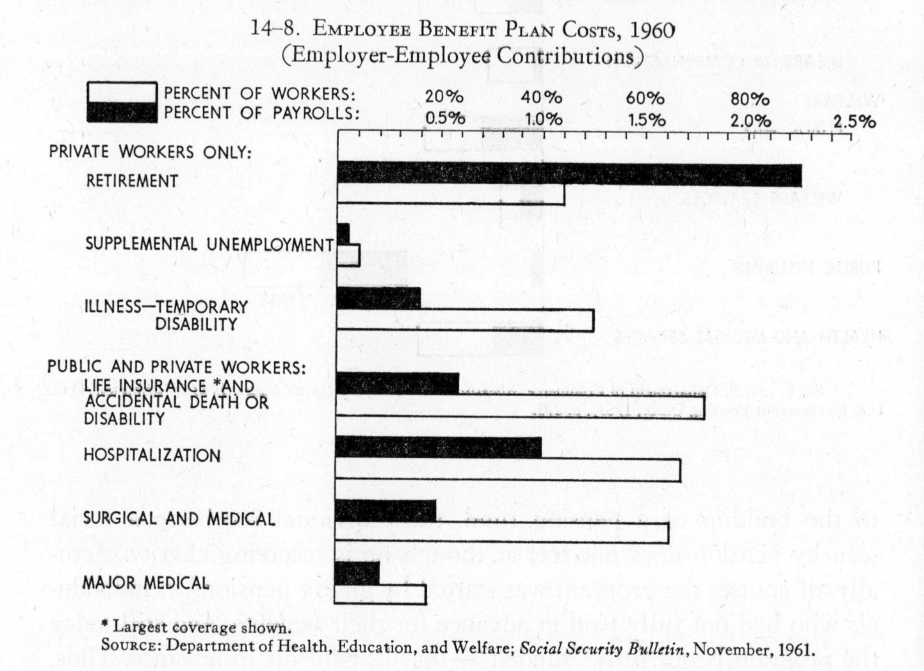

14–8. Employee Benefit Plan Costs, 1960
(Employer-Employee Contributions)

* Largest coverage shown.
Source: Department of Health, Education, and Welfare; *Social Security Bulletin*, November, 1961.

grams take the largest part of the payroll deductions. Life insurance and insurance against medical expenses account for most of the rest.

Now, whether the employer contributes all or only part of the cost, it really is the worker who pays; the payroll taxes are "labor costs" to the employer and increased "fringe benefits" tend to take the place of increased wage payments. This involves, of course, an element of "forced savings" which may make sense in terms of human psychology. As most insurance salesmen will agree, most people do not regularly make enough provisions for known future needs, let alone the unpredictable needs. By forcing everyone to make more provision for predictable social needs, there is less need for charity and welfare expenditures to take care of unfortunates who failed to take or never had the economic power to take adequate precautions.

Unemployment and Displacement

As we have said, unemployment associated with recessions and depressions is not simply an insurable risk of individuals. As 14–9 shows, almost one fourth of the labor force was unemployed in 1933. Unemployment of this magnitude is not predictable and thus not subject to the actuaries' calculations; it is a problem for monetary and fiscal policy. During the postwar years, we have succeeded in avoiding astronomically high unemployment levels. However, in recent years, there

14–9. Unemployment Rate-Yearly Average

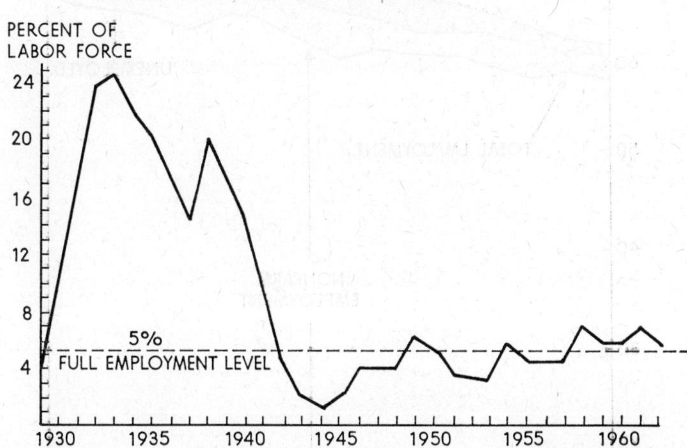

Source: U.S. Department of Commerce, *Historical Statistics of the United States* (Washington, D.C.: U.S. Government Printing Office, 1960), p. 73; and U.S. Department of Commerce, *Statistical Abstract of the United States, 1962* (Washington, D.C.: U.S. Government Printing Office, 1963), pp. 215 and 219.

has been increasing concern over gradually rising levels of unemployment, even during periods of prosperity. During the recoveries of 1953, 1956, and 1958, the unemployment rate was reduced successively less each time. This trend, which has been referred to as the "secular rise in unemployment," has been attributed to the changing structure of demand for labor and to an insufficiency in aggregate demand.

On the structural side, some studies have analyzed this unemployment in terms of the characteristics of unemployed persons; they have been found to have a higher percentage of the same characteristics as the low-income persons we discussed previously. Other studies have pointed to the persistently high unemployment levels in particular industries and communities. Textile towns, coal mining towns, and rural southern counties have been identified as "depressed areas."

There also has been some speculation that our efforts to "protect" workers also have tended to aggravate the unemployment problem. Seniority rules and pension rights on the job with a particular company make a worker less ready to change jobs or to seek work elsewhere

14–10. Labor Force and Employment

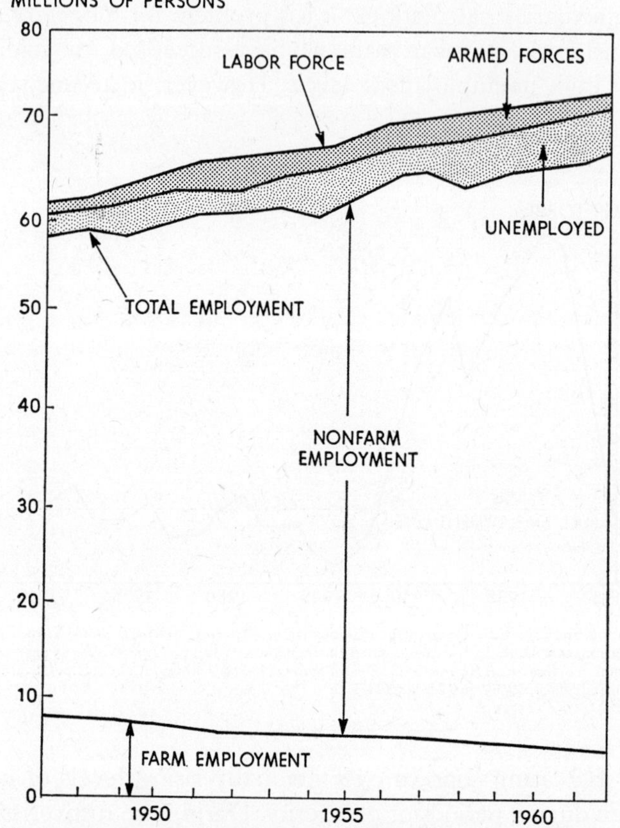

Source: U.S. Department of Commerce, *Historical Statistics of the United States* (Washington, D.C.: U.S. Government Printing Office, 1960), p. 73; and U.S. Department of Commerce, *Statistical Abstract of the United States, 1962* (Washington, D.C.: U.S. Government Printing Office, 1963), pp. 215 and 219.

when laid off. Present unemployment compensation rules may make workers less willing to accept lesser paying jobs; and for some seasonal or irregular workers, the unemployment compensation is an important part of their annual income that sustains them in a certain way of life. In short, our efforts to protect workers against the hardships of rapid change also may hinder or slow down the adjustments needed. Our whole experience with the unemployment compensation system is relatively new, and there is much that we do not yet fully understand about it.

On the aggregate demand side of the argument some public leaders believe that persistently high unemployment merely reflects our

14–11. Employment by Industry

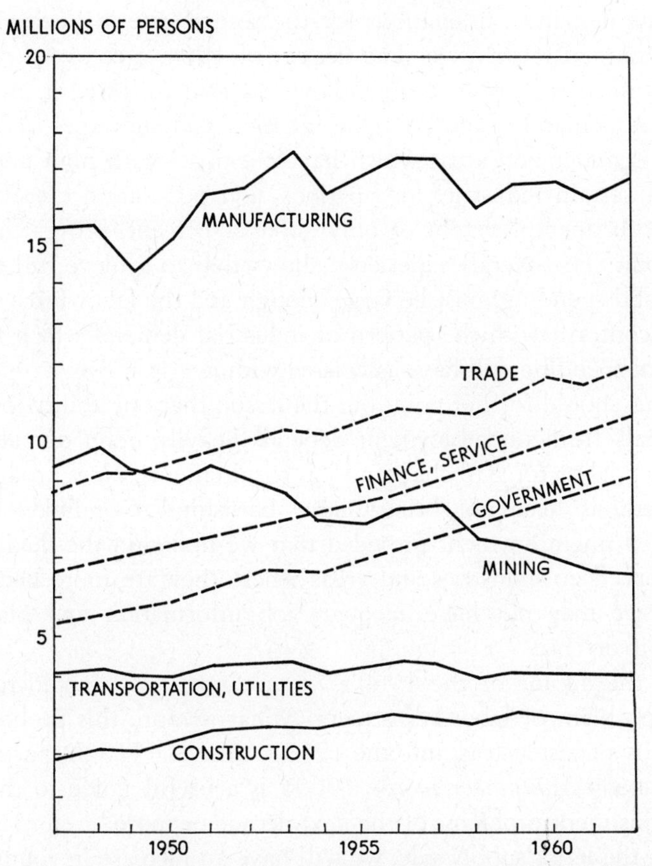

Source: U.S. Department of Commerce, *Historical Statistics of the United States* (Washington, D.C.: U.S. Government Printing Office, 1960), p. 73; and U.S. Department of Commerce, *Statistical Abstract of the United States, 1962* (Washington, D.C.: U.S. Government Printing Office, 1963), pp. 215 and 219.

"fiscal drag" and the problem of keeping national growth rates at high and stable levels. 14–10 shows that our labor force is constantly rising, and unless employment increases as much, we will have a widening gap of unemployment. With farm employment declining, nonfarm jobs must be increased to hire the new workers entering the labor force. 14–11 breaks down nonfarm employment by major industry groups. It shows that mining has been declining throughout the postwar period, while manufacturing employment has not exceeded its 1953 peak. On the other hand, trade, finance, services, and government are industries with rapidly rising employment. It is in these industries that the bulk of job increases from the expansion of aggregate demand will come.

The implication of our discussion so far is that the structural and aggregate demand explanations for the secular rise in unemployment are not mutually exclusive. The tax cut of 1964, a recovery year, and the continued reduction of unemployment that followed it proves the aggregate demand point. And the inflation and shortages of labor in certain high-demand areas which have coexisted with high unemployment in certain industries, occupations, and population classifications, along with unemployment of only about 4 percent, proves the structural point. The overall experience shows that to achieve full employment, total spending must be large enough and the labor force must be able to conform with the pattern of industrial demand which full-employment spending will have associated with it.

This should further point out the lesson that our ability to protect individuals from unemployment depends heavily upon our ability to adjust our labor force to changing job requirements. New products and new methods need not bring undue hardships to individuals from prolonged unemployment provided that we maintain the flexibility to shift workers to industries and areas where they are more needed. At present we may not have adequate job information and placement services to do this.

In the decade of the 1960's, we are faced with an increasingly serious problem of labor adjustment. What is more this problem will apparently persist at least into the 1970's. Thus the U.S. Department of Labor's study *Manpower in the 1960's* is a useful guide to the labor force adjustment problems of the next decade or more.

On the labor supply side, we will have an increase in young workers with few skills, although with more education. As 14–12 shows, the number of older workers over 45 will increase, in keeping with past trends toward rising population and longer lives. Also, more women are reentering the labor force in their middle years. We will have fewer workers in the most productive ages of 35 to 44 because of the low birthrates during the 1930's. Then we will have a rise in young workers 25 to 34, and a big increase in youth under 25, which reflects the high postwar birthrates between 1946 and 1955.

If we had trouble keeping all workers employed during the late 1950's, when young workers were more scarce, we will face increasing

14–12. Manpower Outlook in 1960 and 1970

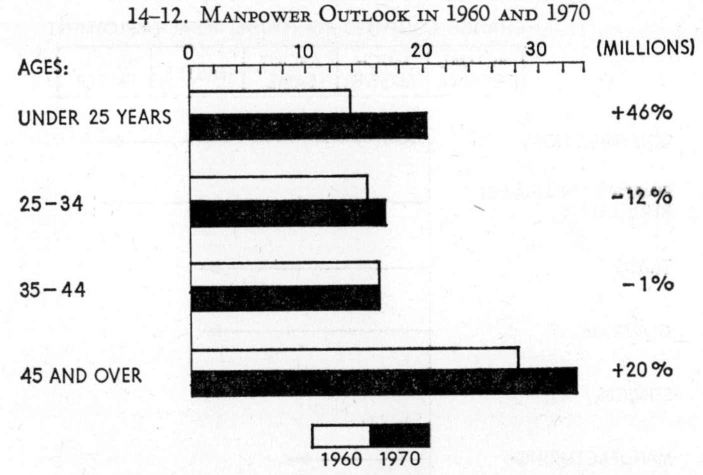

Source: U.S. Department of Labor, *Manpower in the 1960's* (Washington, D.C.: U.S. Government Printing Office, 1961).

difficulties in the 1970's with this new flood of young workers. To some extent, of course, these new young adults will help create their own demand by marrying, having babies, and creating a demand for new houses, appliances, furniture, and baby products.

On the side of demand for labor, we face further shifts in the types of jobs available, both by industry and by occupation, as is shown in 14–13 and 14–14. Construction may be expected to have a new spurt; but the bulk of growth in new jobs must continue to be in trade, services, finance, and government, if our tastes persist in their present pattern. Even more important, perhaps, is the fact that the largest projected occupational increase is for professional and technical workers. Unskilled jobs will remain about the same while farm jobs will continue to decrease.

14–15 shows the importance of education in the occupations that will grow the fastest. 14–16 indicates that those with less education are found more frequently among the unemployed; little education is correlated to some extent with the types of occupations which have the widest fluctuations in employment. Finally, 14–17 shows the relation frequently observed between education level and average annual income which again is correlated with occupation. The same type of relationship exists between income and vocational and on-the-job technical training of various sorts; this relationship will persist because there will be a need for many skilled and technical workers to complement professional and managerial workers.

14–13. EMPLOYMENT OUTLOOK IN 1960'S BY INDUSTRY

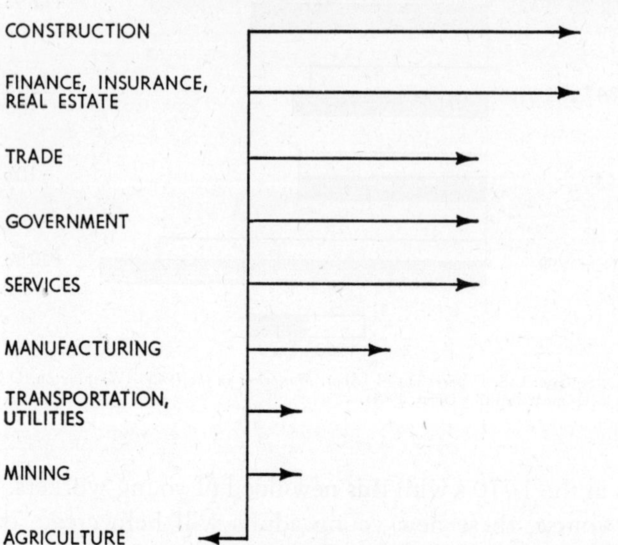

SOURCE: U.S. Department of Labor, *Manpower in the 1960's* (Washington, D.C.: U.S. Government Printing Office, 1961).

14–14. EMPLOYMENT OUTLOOK IN 1960'S BY OCCUPATION

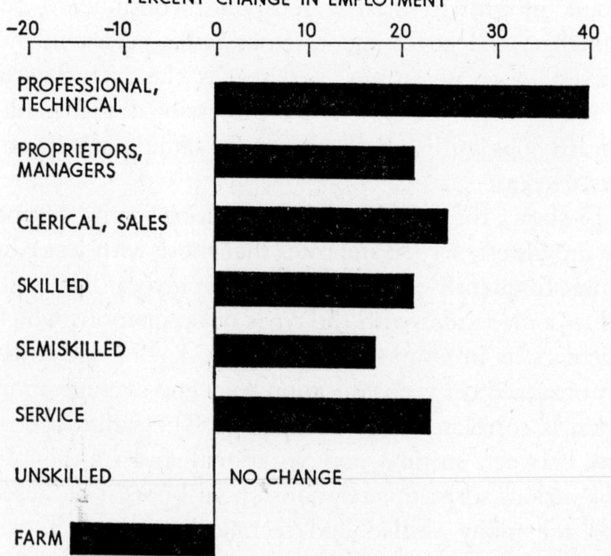

SOURCE: U.S. Department of Labor, *Manpower in the 1960's* (Washington, D.C.: U.S. Government Printing Office, 1961).

14–15. Education and Occupation

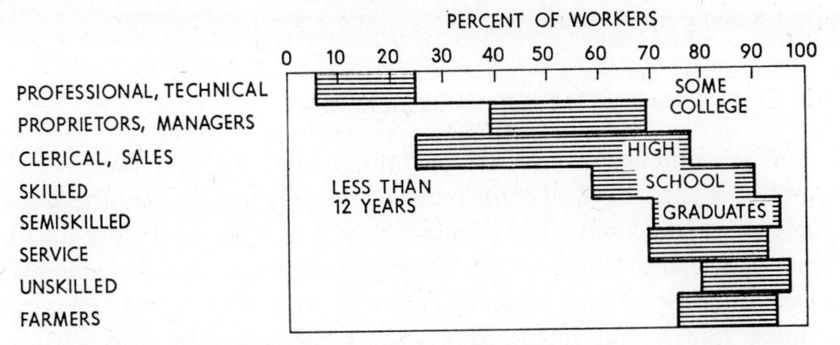

Source: U.S. Department of Labor, *Manpower in the 1960's* (Washington, D.C.: U.S. Government Printing Office, 1961).

14–16. Education and Unemployment, 1959

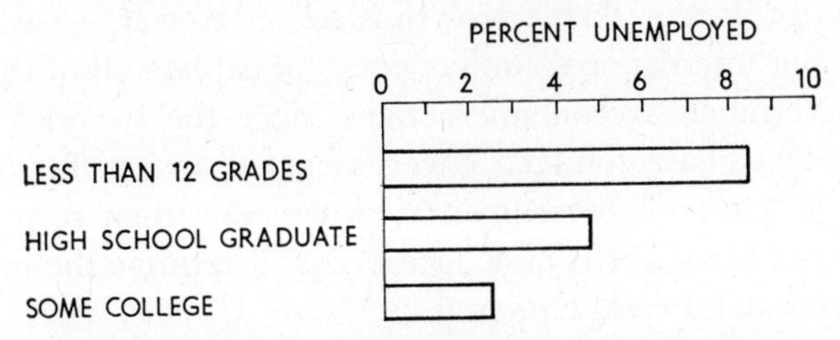

Source: U.S. Department of Labor, *Manpower in the 1960's* (Washington, D.C.: U.S. Government Printing Office, 1961).

14–17. Education and Income, Males, 1958

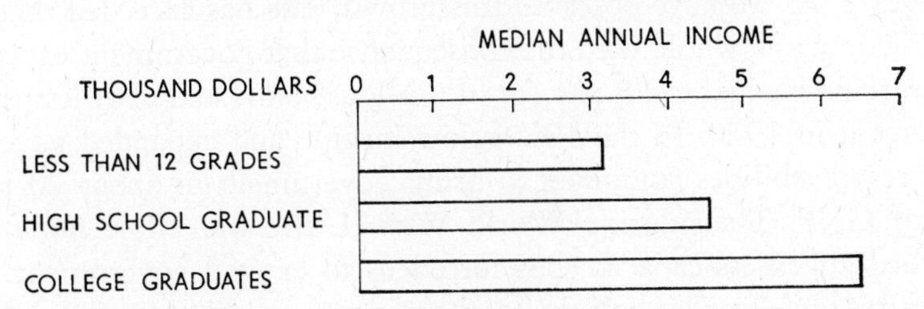

Source: U.S. Department of Labor, *Manpower in the 1960's* (Washington, D.C.: U.S. Government Printing Office, 1961).

The worker in the 1960's and 1970's, therefore, needs not only "protection" against excessive national unemployment rates; he needs to be flexible enough to adjust to new demands. To adjust he needs to prepare himself with adequate general education or specialized training. Our market economy will continue to provide opportunities for individuals to rise to higher income opportunities only if they prepare specifically for those opportunities.

THE CHANGING ROLE OF GOVERNMENT

War, depression, and the structural changes we have reviewed so far in this chapter have all contributed to the very rapid rise in the scope of government activity. The economy has grown fivefold since 1920. Population, real income, and per capita real income have all increased; so we would expect government to grow as well. More people carrying on more transactions require more government services. But what is especially important about our experience over the past five decades is the relative growth of government. While the economy grew by a factor of five and population by a factor of less than two, government at all three levels grew by a factor of eight.

Much of this remarkable growth is related to wars—past, present, and future. But international conflict does not explain all of the acceleration in government's economic activity since the twenties—general economic growth has promoted government expansion. Let us look at some of the details of government's growth and then reappraise the facts in light of some of the basic factors that determine the importance of government in the total economy.

The Growth of the Government Sector

A glance at 14–18 indicates the very rapid growth that has characterized both government expenditures and government revenues since the 1920's. As we have observed this growth rate has exceeded that of the economy as a whole with the consequence that government expenditures are now equal to 28 percent of GNP as contrasted with less than 10 percent in 1920. In the 1930's low income and expanded government responsibilities combined to bring government to about 20 percent of GNP. Then during World War II, the war effort not only absorbed all excess capacity, but forced us to expand government expenditures to just under half the total gross national product. Since then continued international involvement is the most important force which maintains the government sector at 25 to 30 percent of the aggregate economy.

In absolute terms the rapid growth of government expenditures is attributable to three main factors: (1) population increases, (2) rising prices, and (3) increased demand for defense and nondefense spending. 14–19 shows the per capita growth of government expenditures over

14–18. FINANCES OF FEDERAL, STATE, AND LOCAL GOVERNMENTS FOR SELECTED YEARS, 1922–65
(In Billions of Dollars)

Year	Total		Federal		State		Local	
	Revenues	Expenditures	Revenues	Expenditures	Revenues	Expenditures	Revenues	Expenditures
1922	9.3	9.3	4.3	3.8	1.4	1.4	4.1	4.6
1927	12.2	11.2	4.5	3.5	2.2	2.5	6.3	6.4
1932	10.3	12.4	2.6	4.3	2.5	2.8	6.2	6.4
1934	11.3	12.8	3.9	5.9	3.4	3.5	6.4	5.7
1938	17.5	17.7	7.2	8.4	5.3	4.6	7.3	6.9
1942	28.3	45.6	16.1	35.5	6.9	5.3	8.1	7.4
1946	61.5	79.7	46.4	66.5	8.6	7.7	9.6	9.1
1950	66.7	70.3	43.5	44.8	13.9	15.8	16.1	17.0
1954	108.3	111.3	75.8	77.7	18.8	18.6	22.4	23.8
1958	130.4	134.9	86.6	86.5	26.2	28.1	31.3	34.0
1962	168.0	176.2	106.4	113.4	37.6	36.4	43.1	45.3
1965	202.6	205.6	126.0	130.1	48.8	45.5	53.4	55.5

SOURCE: U.S. Department of Commerce, *Census of Governments* (Washington, D.C.: U.S. Government Printing Office, 1962); and *Governmental Finances, 1964–65* (Washington, D.C.: U.S. Government Printing Office, 1966).

14–19. PER CAPITA GOVERNMENTAL EXPENDITURES FOR SELECTED YEARS 1932–65

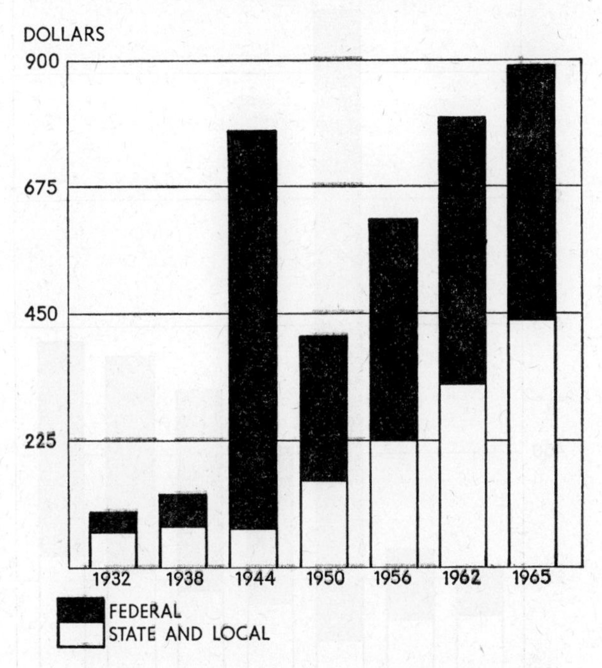

SOURCE: U.S. Department of Commerce, Bureau of the Census.

the period. The fact that the per capita trend is far less steep than the trend of aggregate expenditures is a reflection of the population explosion's impact on the government sector since World War II. Much of the growth of government is attributable to the population increase; so when we place the figures on a per capita basis, the rise in expenditures appears less imposing.

The prices which federal, state, and local governments have to pay have more than tripled since the early depression years. Consequently a large portion of the growth of government expenditures and receipts is a result of inflation.

In 14–20, the effects of price increase have been removed from the per capita data to show the trend of real expenditures per person.

14–20. Real Per Capita Federal, State, and Local Expenditures for Selected Years, 1932–65

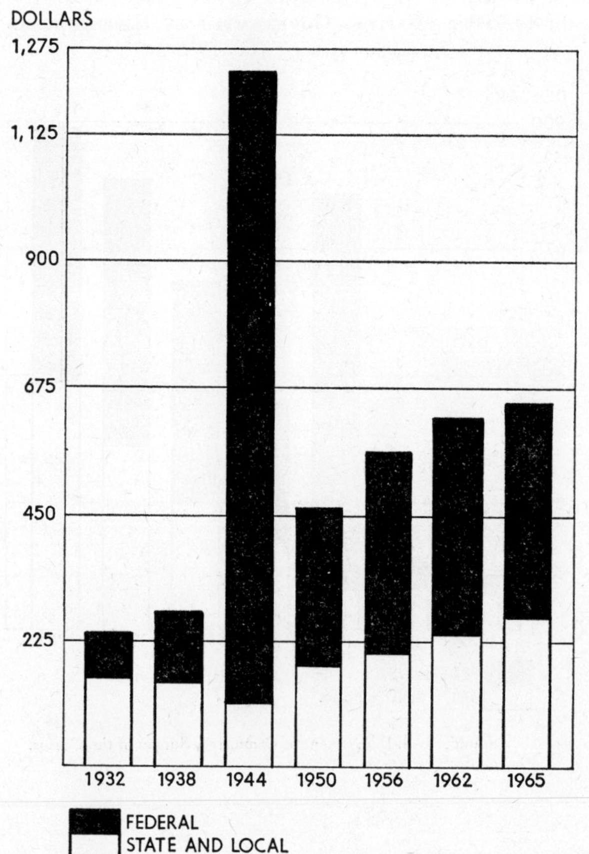

Source: U.S. Department of Commerce, Bureau of the Census.

This upward trend is in essence an index of the rising need per person for governmental services, especially defense. Note that per capita real expenditures reached a peak in 1944, the year of our most intensive war production, then declined until the upward trend was restored by the Korean War and expanded defense and nondefense requirements after the war.

This trend was reinforced by the state and local government sector which reflects the bulk of the rise in nondefense needs. During the war, state and local needs had to be deferred so that the combined expenditures of the two levels declined from well over half to less than 10 percent of the total government sector. Thus the state-local sector built up a backlog of needs. After the war this backlog was magnified by the rise in demand for state and local government services. Especially important in this regard was the postdepression baby boom which lowered the average age of the population and correspondingly raised the per capita requirements for schools and residential services. Much of the increase in state and local government operations has been concentrated among functions in which the federal government has traditionally or recently encouraged activity through grants-in-aid and consequently this federal expenditure item has become a larger and larger part of total general government expenditures. (See 14–21).

On the revenue side, the growth of government has been equally impressive. The growth of demand for services has not only required raising the real tax burden but has forced the national, state, and local governments to introduce countless innovations to their revenue systems.

At the federal level, World War II increased reliance upon individual and corporate income taxes, a reliance that continues. In the 1920's and early 1930's income taxes comprised 35 to 45 percent of the total general revenues of the federal government while taxes on sales including import duties hovered at around 25 percent of total collections. By 1944, individual income taxes were 44 percent of total revenues, corporate incomes taxes 30 percent, and the various sales taxes only 10 percent. More recently the figures have been as follows: individual income, 47 percent; corporate income, 25 percent; and sales, 17 percent.

The pattern of increases for state and local governments has also produced dramatic shifts within the revenue structure. Sales taxes rose during the depression and the war from less than 5 percent to more than 20 percent of general revenues, while property taxes declined from over 70 percent to a little more than 30 percent. Income taxes almost

14–21. PERCENTAGE DISTRIBUTION OF GENERAL EXPENDITURE BY FUNCTION FOR ALL GOVERNMENTS
(Selected Years, 1922–65)

	1922	1927	1934	1938	1944	1948	1957	1962	1965
All functions	100.0	100.0	100.0	100.0	100.0	100.0	100.0	100.0	100.0
National defense and international relations	9.9	5.8	4.6	6.4	79.3	32.1	41.7	35.7	32.1
Postal service	6.2	6.7	5.4	4.8	1.0	3.4	2.8	2.7	3.0
Education	19.3	21.2	16.6	16.3	2.6	15.4	13.8	15.3	17.7
Highways	14.6	17.2	15.1	13.2	1.1	6.1	7.2	7.0	7.1
Public welfare	1.4	1.5	8.1	7.6	1.1	4.3	3.2	3.5	3.7
Health and hospitals	4.0	4.1	4.4	4.2	0.8	3.9	3.8	4.1	4.4
Natural resources	1.6	1.9	10.3	12.8	2.5	4.4	6.9	8.2	6.3
Financial administration and general control	5.0	5.0	4.4	4.5	1.0	2.6	2.2	2.1	2.2
Interest on general debt	15.5	12.7	12.2	9.3	2.5	9.4	6.0	6.1	6.6
All other	22.5	23.9	18.9	21.0	8.1	18.3	12.4	15.2	15.9
Exhibit: Federal intergovernmental expenditure as percentage of total state and local general revenue	2.5	1.7	12.7	8.3	9.8	10.3	10.1	13.3	13.1

SOURCE: U.S. Department of Commerce, Bureau of the Census.

doubled in their importance during the war but are still less than 10 percent of total revenues. In particular states, though, they account for as much as 35 percent of state government revenues. Federal grants to the states and localities have grown faster than any revenue source so that currently they are about seven times more important in the budget than they were in the 1920's and account for almost 15 percent of revenues.

The separate patterns of change for state governments and local governments have been very similar; however, the resulting revenue structures are still quite diverse because property taxes were such a large part of local budgets at the beginning of the period compared with the states. In spite of new revenue sources, the property tax remains the dominant local levy in contrast to the states in which sales taxes have come from obscurity to assume a dominant role.

Taxes have not fully covered expenditures over the years; governmental indebtedness has increased at all levels of government. As we have noted, during the Great Depression sliding income and rising governmental responsibilities pushed the federal government into a deficit position. Then during World War II the "disequilibrium system," our option for financing the war, caused the debt to skyrocket. At the end of the war, the debt had reached almost $260 billion, about 130 percent of GNP and close to twice the value of private debt.

Since World War II, after dipping slightly, intermittent deficits have more than offset surpluses. The federal debt has grown slowly to over $320 billion in absolute terms. In the same period it has declined to about 45 percent of the value of GNP and less than one-third the value of private debt. This postwar rise in the debt can be attributed to two factors. First, built-in stabilizers pushed the federal budget toward a deficit in times of recession. Second, a latent sluggishness in private demand would have caused total spending to fall below the level required by full-employment without the prodding from a federal deficit. In general over this period, the federal government spurred aggregate demand by cutting private spending (through taxes) by less than it added to total spending through its outlays for goods, services, and transfer payments.

When converted to a per capita basis the growth in the federal debt turns out to be a very modest decline. But when adjusted for price level increases the decline is precipitous; at its 1946 peak the real value of the national debt amounted to almost $3,000 per person whereas in 1965 the figure was just under $1,500 per person.

From a debt standpoint, the state-local sector presents a marked contrast to the federal government. Rising need for long-term capital

14–22. Distribution of Real Per Capita General Nondefense Expenditures by Function for All Governments, 1922 and 1965

	1922		1965			
	Amount	*Percent*	*Amount*	*Percent*	*Percent Change*	*Change as Percent of Total Change*
Total	124.12	100.00	529.24	100.00	326.39	100.0
Health, education and welfare	38.39	30.93	231.72	43.77	503.59	47.73
Education	(26.64)	(21.46)	(139.00)	(26.26)	(421.77)	(27.73)
Housing and urban renewal	(.02)	(.01)	(10.32)	(1.95)	(*)	(2.54)
Public welfare	(1.99)	(1.60)	(30.14)	(5.69)	(*)	(6.95)
Highways and other transportation	24.86	20.03	70.77	13.37	184.67	11.33
Interest on the general debt	21.32	17.18	53.66	10.14	151.69	7.98
Postal service	8.60	6.93	24.69	4.67	187.09	3.97
General and financial administration	6.83	5.50	18.03	3.41	163.90	2.76
Public safety	5.63	4.54	19.24	3.64	241.74	3.36
Natural resources	2.17	1.75	51.59	9.75	(*)	12.20
Agricultural stabilization program	(...)	(...)	(27.24)	(5.15)	(...)	(6.72)
Other	16.32	13.15	59.54	11.25	264.83	10.67

*More than 1000%.
Note: All dollar amounts expressed in 1957–59 dollars of purchasing power.
Source: U.S. Department of Commerce, Bureau of the Census.

investment, principally in schools and roadways, has encouraged flotation of bond issues. The combined state and local debt has increased steadily at a significantly faster rate than the federal debt. Yet, like the federal debt, it has expanded much less rapidly than the debt of the private sector. In per capita terms, the state-local debt has expanded modestly, while after adjustment for prive level increase it is apparent that the real burden of the debt has actually declined since World War II.[6] Over a longer period (1922–65), for all levels of government the real interest burden of the debt has increased on a per capita basis. However, interest charges have declined as a percentage of total nondefense spending. (See 14–22.)

Why Has the Government Sector Grown?

In reviewing the chronology of government's expansion, we have pointed to three very general explanations for the growth of government expenditures and revenues. Now it seems appropriate to dismiss the effects of war and price increases as self-explanatory and approach the "why" of government growth by examining the catalog of reasons for government spending and control. Note that we are broadening the discussion beyond direct government spending to include the qualitative role government plays in influencing economic behavior and the pattern of spending in the private sector. Our discussion will reveal that the process of growth and the rising level of income associated with economic growth have caused the nondefense portion of the government sector to expand faster than population and income. (See 14–22.)

In the most general terms government economic activity is aimed at three kinds of goals: (1) to adjust the allocation of the economy's productive resources, (2) to alter the distribution of income among households, and (3) to stabilize the economy.

We have already seen how both automatic and discretionary fiscal and monetary policies have been employed to flatten out the business cycle. Since 1920, government's growth as a percentage of the economy has increased its ability to serve its stabilizing role. Further, our survey of fiscal policy performance revealed that especially since World War II the federal government has shown a growing sophistication in the matter of contracyclical policy. Over the same period, the state and local

[6] It is important to note that when the real burden of the debt is reduced by inflation, the taxpayer who must service the debt gains but the bondholder loses correspondingly.

expenditures have had a stabilizing side effect. The great relative and absolute growth of nonfederal expenditures has provided an offsetting force for any tendency toward secular stagnation.

As to income distribution policy, the growth of income taxes at all levels of government has tended to redistribute income ***after taxes*** slightly in favor of the lower income brackets. This tendency has been reinforced by expenditures for education, health, welfare, and other programs whose value to recipients tends to be a higher percentage of income the lower the recipient's position on the income distribution ladder. In fact, as we have discussed, our traditional approach to correcting inequality has been to give aid according to certain categories of need and to escalate that aid as the economy has grown. Thus, as 14–22 indicates, housing, urban renewal, and public welfare expenditures have grown very rapidly relative to total per capita nondefense expenditures.

Important as stabilization and distribution policies have made government's role, the public sector's economic influence has grown chiefly through its direct and indirect effects upon resource allocation. The term "economics" connotes the process by which a society divides its resources, its factors of production, among a limitless number of goods and services it finds desirable. In the American economy we depend most heavily upon the decisions of individuals made in market exchanges to guide the allocation of factors. This is because we feel that the operation of ***competitive*** markets generally tends to be compatible with one of our central economic goals—getting the most value out of our scarce productive factors. Often this proposition is put as follows: the ***competitive market solution*** is compatible with ***optimum resource allocation.***

What we shall now look at are often overlapping situations in which government through spending, taxing, or direct control influences resource allocation. As the discussion will make evident, government has been called upon to adjust the pattern of resource allocation either because the services required would not be provided at all by the private sector or would be privately provided but in insufficient amounts. Also, government has found it necessary to intervene in the private economy when regulation or other controls have been agitated for because the public has been dissatisfied with the operation of private markets.

Since 1920, the growth of the economy has meant that the economy is more urban, more highly industrialized, and more populous. These developments, as the following list demonstrates, have produced increasing government influence upon resource allocation. Note that we are not saying that this increase is good or bad—events have produced the growth of government and we shall review those events.

The productivity increases which have generated growth have raised education and training requirements, and the postdepression population explosion has increased the proportion of the population which is of school age. Although education could be, in fact is, produced and sold privately we choose to encourage education beyond levels that would result from a wholly private system. Thus we have traditionally required school attendance and publicly subsidized education at all levels. And we have elected to meet the increased demand for education by expanding public outlays. Per capita education expenditures increased in excess of 100 percent in the 1922–65 period and accounted for over one-fourth the growth in total nondefense expenditures. (See 14–22.)

Population growth in the cities has intensified the traditional problems of cities. What is worse the problems of the cities have taken on new dimensions. The flight to the suburbs which began in the 1920's has left the central cities of America without a leadership class and eroded the tax base. Negro migration from the rural South to the urban slums has copied past ethnic migration patterns except in one vital respect: deepseated prejudices and the Negro's visibility have all but blocked Negro assimilation. The American city has not proved a melting pot for black Americans. For Negroes the city has not proved to be the "frontier" that it was for Irish and European immigrants.

Thus the city has found itself with problems that grow faster than its population and a tax base that grows slower than its problems. The expenditure pattern which has emerged from the city's travails consists of rising per capita public safety outlays and very rapidly increasing welfare, housing, and urban renewal expenditures. (See 14–22.) In fact, most of the noneducation items such as sanitation, public health, and recreation included in the "Health, education and welfare" category of 14–22 have had growth rates that exceed the average for nondefense expenditures.

Governments have traditionally subsidized transportation for two reasons—good transportation facilities enhance economic growth and the high cost of collecting tolls prohibits private provision in most cases. Development of the automobile and the airplane as widely used transportation devices began in the 1920's. Accordingly, governments have been called upon to provide highways at unprecedented levels and in various ways subsidize the airlines. As compared with 1922 real per capita transportation expenditures had almost doubled by 1965. (See 14–22.)

Economic growth and especially industrial growth, is not without its costs. Most of these costs are borne directly by the private sector, e.g., households forego present consumption in order to save, making possible capital investment and, therefore, higher future consumption. But some of the costs of industrial expansion are very public in the sense that they do not fall upon producers of the products in question. Rather, they are shifted to the general public—such effects are termed neighborhood effects or spillover costs. Stream pollution is an example. When a paper mill is constructed which subsequently pollutes a river on which it is located, downstream communities which must install additional water treatment facilities are forced to bear part of the cost of increased paper output. Cases of this kind have multiplied as the Nation has become more crowded and industrial. So government has been called upon both to control the sources of some neighborhood effects and to spend to compensate for other such effects. The budget effects of this kind of government activity have influenced the overall growth of per capita expenditures by speeding the growth of the many government agencies whose outlays are summarized in 14–22.

The size and complexity that the private sector has achieved have added to the size and complexity of the public sector. In other words, growth of the industrial establishment has exacted tolls in addition to the spillover costs discussed above. On the one hand, the government must provide a legal environment which facilitates private market exchanges; as industrial and financial organizations have increased in complexity, the range of required government services has been extended. On the other hand, government has been called upon to protect or assist parties who are especially vulnerable to the costs of industrial transformation. In addition, government has had to act when competition gave way to collusion in concentrated markets or when competitive markets have produced results with which the public was not happy.

The Justice Department's antitrust activities, the various regulatory agencies, expenditures to assist small business, and the costs of the agricultural stabilization programs are all attributable to the industrialization process and the adjustments it requires. Tariffs constitute a system of negative incentives which change domestic resource allocation in favor of certain industries, and import quotas have about the same effects. Subsidies to the merchant marine are also designed to foster home industry. With the exception of agriculture, expenditures for these functions do not now and have not accounted for a very large part of the budget. Nevertheless, such expenditures have grown. But what is most significant, they affect the pattern of resource allocation well beyond their importance in the consolidated budget.

We have reviewed a rather lengthy list of factors which explain the 300 percent increase in real per capita government expenditures shown in 14–22. Yet the catalog is not complete without mentioning a complementary force that is directly attributable to economic growth. Growth has changed the pattern of final demand in favor of a larger relative role for government. Increased capacity makes production of a greater variety of final products possible. As an individual's income grows, he expands somewhat his consumption of food, clothing, and shelter, but the bulk of his increased purchasing power will be devoted to other items some of which will be new to his budget. By the same token, when national income grows, the public opts for both more private goods and more public goods. The reason for this is the complementary nature of the public and private sectors. In some ways, the two sectors are intimately complementary—automobiles require streets. In other respects, the connection is less direct, but nevertheless very important—the enjoyment of a nice house is increased by easy access to good public recreation facilities. So beyond those reasons we have cited above, government's role has grown faster than the national economy because the best allocation of our resources pointed in the direction of per capita government growth.

The Affluent Society

Whether the relative growth of government has been adequate, too great, or not great enough is now a more than decade-old debate. In the mid-1950's, critics of the social scene looked around at what they termed public poverty amid private affluence—an alleged situation of social imbalance. The spectacle of luxurious automobiles running on potholed roadways was accepted as evidence of general privation in the public sector. In the wake of the debate which ensued, the growth of the public sector's nondefense activities was accelerated.

What impact has this spurt in spending had? Whether social imbalance has been ended (if there was a deficit in the public column) or worsened (if the public sector was in fact too large at mid-century) no one can say with precision. The public will is difficult to interpret and equally hard to translate into legislation. And the statistical measures we have at hand are of little use because we do not have any reliable criteria that indicate what ratio of public to private activity is desired by the electorate.

We are left then with a dilemma in summarizing developments in the public sector since 1920. Growth of prices, population, international involvement, and the degree of urbanization and industrialization have generated increases in government expenditure. Collectively these forces have caused government to grow as a percentage of the economy. But whether government has grown enough to provide an optimum allocation of resources cannot be answered. Economic growth has been sufficient in its cumulative effects to allow a vast range of public-private combinations in resource allocation. But the social machinery does not exist to guarantee achieving what we would as a Nation consider the ***best*** combination.

STUDY QUESTIONS

1. Explain the relationship of *factor* income distribution to *personal* income distribution. How would economic growth affect each? How are they mutually related to growth?
2. What has happened to the distribution of income in recent decades? What has happened to the incomes of the poor over recent generations? To our "standards" of poverty?
3. Discuss the various public and private ways in which we assure individual security. In view of the theory presented in Chapter 12 discuss the assertion that recession unemployment is not an insurable risk. Is unemployment compensation, therefore, a poor policy?
4. Distinguish between categorical assistance and income supplements. Discuss the pros and cons of the two approaches. Why under categorical grant rules in force today, do we say that they constitute a confiscatory tax.
5. Discuss the growth of the government sector since World War I. Why has it grown as it has?
6. Distinguish between government's influence in directly allocating resources and its effects upon private resource allocation through regulation, incentive payments, etc.
7. Analyze this statement: "The per capita growth of government is the handiwork of crafty bureaucrats who have contrived ways to confiscate our incomes to further their empire-building schemes."
8. Analyze this statement: "We spend as much on liquor as we do on education in this country—surely this proves a social imbalance."

Chapter 15 INTERREGIONAL AND INTERNATIONAL ADJUSTMENTS

At this point we should review and expand upon the companion principles of specialization and exchange according to comparative advantage which were introduced in Chapter 2.

A process which is vital to economic growth is the ***division*** of the economy's work among ***specialists*** who in a relative sense excel at particular tasks. Specialization increases productivity. And the economy that is able to increase the degree to which it follows this maxim is able to increase its growth rate. But application of this principle is not as straightforward as it might seem at first blush. Complications arise because we find specialization ***among*** economies, ***within*** economies, and both ***among*** and ***within*** producing units within any economy.

Let us look first at this phenomenon as it occurs ***among*** economies. To use a trite but clear example, Brazil and the United States could each grow both coffee and soybeans. For the United States, coffee culture would be highly artificial requiring what amounts to giant hothouses. Thus we specialize in soybeans and through the market mechanism trade them for coffee beans. Why? The first response is to say "coffee growing would require too many men and materials per ton of coffee produced." That is a correct but partial answer. A more complete explanation is "compared with soybeans, coffee growing here would require so many men and materials that to produce each dollar's worth of coffee would force us to reduce soybean production by, say, two dollars."

In essence, the cost of any product is the alternative products the economy sacrifices to allocate resources to the product in question. So the best pattern of specialization and division of labor among national economic units requires that each trading nation minimize the value of products sacrificed in order to produce its actual array of outputs. We produce soybeans rather than coffee because our coffee production wouldn't be worth much per man-hour, whereas the Brazilians do the opposite because of the same cost considerations.

Do both Brazil and the United States benefit by this arrangement, Yes, of course! Both specialize at what they do best, produce a surplus, and trade off that surplus for what they do least well. For the United States, an acre of land will produce much more coffee by the indirect route of planting soybeans and trading the beans for coffee than by planting coffee directly. The reverse is, of course, true for Brazil.

The principle of specialization demonstrates why national economies produce surpluses and swap them off to each other in ***inter***national trade. The trading patterns that evolve are those dictated by the law of comparative advantage which we introduced in Chapter 2 and have just reviewed in our Brazil-United States example. Now let us turn to ***intra***national trade and see if these principles apply.

Within each national economy there is a wide variety of resources of greatly varying productivities. From this it follows that the production jobs the economy wishes to perform should be divided among its human and material resources so that overall productivity can be maximized. In short, the rule that productivity is increased by specialization applies to resources within an economy as well as among economies.

Specialization within national economies leads to regional differences within nations. Resource mixes vary from region to region, so quite naturally cost structures and, therefore, output mixes vary from region to region. Some examples may prove helpful at this point.

Cotton can be grown in both the Old South and the New South and so can tobacco. But cost considerations arising from differences in resource endowment make the midde or new South a cotton economy while tobacco dominates in the southern coastal states.

Clothing can be manufactured in both major metropolitan areas and remote rural areas. High-fashion clothing is made almost wholly in New York City, and the industry is one of the city's most important employers because a New York location offers certain vital inputs at very low cost—so low that high labor costs are overcome. On the other hand, inexpensive ready-to-wear clothing can be most efficiently manufactured in the remote hamlets of the southern agricultural states because labor costs are the most strategic input variable to that industry. Consequently, mass-produced garments are a specialty of the low-wage South.

In an engineering sense, both sawmilling and aerospace instruments can be produced at either rural or urban locations. But cost considerations dictate that sawmilling be performed very near the forests, whereas the precision instrument industry is found in the cities that have large universities. This pattern of specialization has emerged from the same cost consideration: trees and highly trained technical pesonnel are both very expensive to move.

Once again it should be easy to see how the notion of specialization applies in the third way we mentioned above—among and within producing units within an economy. Firms and plants specialize in particular products according to their comparative advantages. Within firms employees specialize according to the employer's assessment of comparative skill advantages.

Now let us see what kinds of general observations the above discussion leads us to.

First, nations and regions within nations are more productive when they specialize rather than when they attempt to produce the entire array of products desired. The same principle applies to production ***among*** and ***within*** business firms. The other side of this coin is that specialization and division of labor require larger markets than a highly diverse economy in order to spread high plant and equipment costs over a large sales volume.

Second, this requires a trade pattern ***among*** and ***within*** nations in which each nation and region trades the surplus it produces in its specialty for the specialty surplus of other nations and regions. In other words the export-base products of nations and regions are traded against each other.

Third, international and interregional trade requires a universal means of payment. Within the United States, dollars are just such a means and internationally gold and certain national currencies serve as a means of international payment.

Fourth, the productivity of the export base depends on the quality of productive resources and the world demand for the product mix of the export base. The higher the productivity of the export base, the greater will be the power to import and thus the more prosperous will be the economy, whether it be a city, a state, a region, or a nation.

Fifth, changes in the structure of world demand and technological innovations are capable of increasing or decreasing the productivity of the export base. Consequently the prosperity and growth rate of an economy will often depend upon the nature of such changes.

When we apply this fifth principle to the relationship between a national economy and its regions, we find that when the nature of a nations' export base changes the productivity of the export bases of each of its regions will change also. Consequently when a nation's export base mix changes, within that nation a reallocation of resources and a change in distribution of income among regions will take place.

Sixth, the larger is an economy, the more diversified it can be and the less dependent will it need be upon imports to satisfy its demands. Thus a state such as Arkansas devotes almost half of its resources to several agricultural mainstays, garment manufacture, and timber products, and exports about half of its total production, while the United States spreads its resources among a vastly wider variety of industries and exports less than 10 percent of its production.

Consequently the larger is an economy, the less will its growth rate and prosperity depend upon other economies. A corollary to this principle is that the larger is an economy, the greater is the number of variables that are susceptible to manipulation by public policy and the less is the degree to which a nation's economic fate is determined outside the economy and out of policy makers' reach.

Seventh, as we shall see, the conclusion we reached immediately above does not apply to problems relating to international payments. In the United States, gold flows overseas have become the tail that wags the dog in the sense that our adjustments to international payments difficulties have an impact upon all sectors of the economy.

With these observations regarding specialization and a nation's degree of prosperity and economic growth rate, we can look first at the varying development of regions within the U.S. economy and then at the relationship of the U.S. economy to the world economy. Finally we shall add a postscript designed as a capstone for our study.

REGIONAL DEVELOPMENT OF THE U.S. ECONOMY

The topic "Regional Development" returns us to consideration of another broad aspect of the national economy: its geographic structure. We have mentioned regional development prior to the Civil War and during our rapid growth up to World War I. In this chapter we will consider some of the changes in the modern period, especially in the recent decade of the 1950's.

We will be interested in more than just how regional specialization contributed to national productivity and growth. We also want to turn particular attention to the adjustments that regions have had to make as a result of changes in the national economy. In a sense, then, this topic concerns one more of the problems of our high-income growth economy. It is a problem that gained increasing public attention during the 1950's. Then in 1961 a new federal agency was created to deal with problems of "depressed areas." As we are constantly reminded, mass migration of low-income, low-skill workers to urban slums has produced a situation of socioeconomic peril. And the historical rural-urban struggle has taken on new intensity as legislative reapportionment has been required among and within states.

Let us start by considering the factors behind the regional speciali-

15–1. STATE PER CAPITA INCOMES, 1960
(Percent of U.S. Average)*

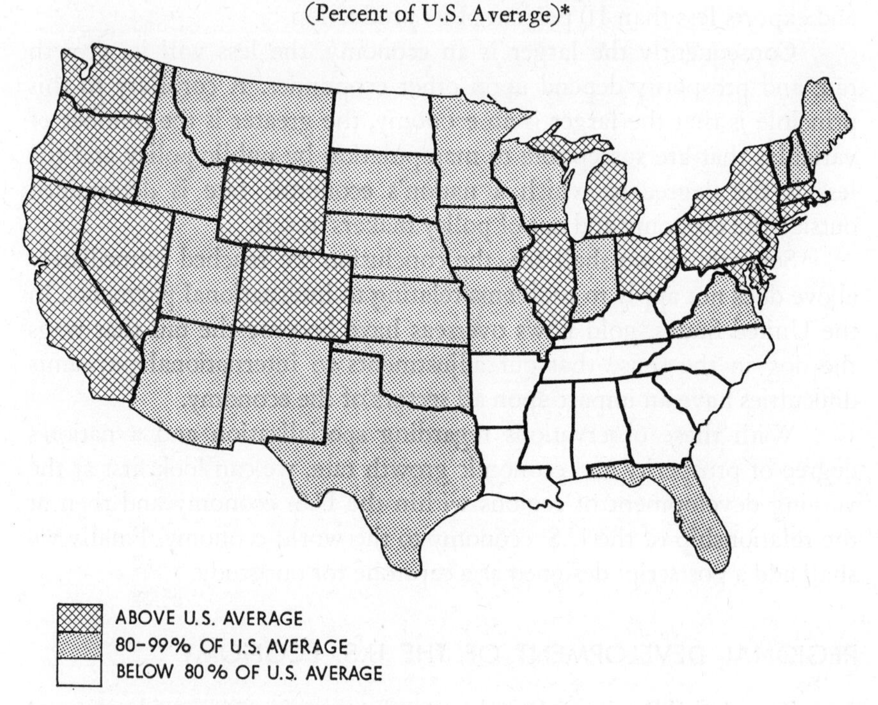

* U.S. average per capita personal income: $2,223.

SOURCE: U.S. Department of Commerce, *Statistical Abstract of the United States, 1962* (Washington, D.C.: U.S. Government Printing Office, 1963), p. 322.

zation of our national economy. It will help, to begin with, if we look at a map that is most representative of the regional structure of the economy. (See 15–1.) Since we are concerned with the resulting levels of individual welfare more than with size of total output, it is appropriate to make per capita income our basic measure of regional differences. 15–1 shows per capita income levels by state in 1960 expressed as a percentage of the national average, which in 1960 was $2,223.

Above average income levels generally are found in the northeastern industrial states and in the far western states. Below average income levels (except for North Dakota) are concentrated in the Southeast. 6–9, 9–13, and 15–2 show that this difference in regional incomes had developed by 1840 and has been characteristic ever since. These charts also show, however, that regional income differences have been narrowing; all regions are gradually becoming more alike in levels of income.

Now, how did we get that way? The answer lies in the pattern of regional specialization as we pointed out in the introduction to this chapter. 15–3 notes some of the basic influences on regional specialization and, therefore, productivity. In order to bring our discussion into historical focus, let us review the development of regional specialization we presented in several earlier chapters then consider the operation of the factors presented in 15–3 since 1920.

15–2. PER CAPITA INCOMES BY REGIONS

	Percent of U.S. Average	
	1940	*1960*
Northeast	131	116
New England	127	111
Middle Atlantic	132	117
North Central	102	103
East North Central	112	107
West North Central	81	93
South	66	79
South Atlantic	77	84
East South Central	49	66
West South Central	64	81
West	115	113
Mountain	87	94
Pacific	132	118

SOURCE: U.S. Department of Commerce, *Statistical Abstract of the United States, 1962* (Washington, D.C.: U.S. Government Printing Office, 1963), p. 319.

15–3. INFLUENCES ON REGIONAL SPECIALIZATION AND PRODUCTIVITY

1. Competitive resource advantages
2. Access costs (transportation)
3. Plant and market size
4. Relative prices of items in output mix
5. Proximity advantages
6. Local market demands

At least until the 1880's agriculture was our principal source of export income and the economic base of most American communities. Externally, changes in world food and fiber demand and, internally, changes in agricultural technology and transportation determined the relative prosperity of the various regions. The colonies developed around ports and rivers. Then with the rising importance of cotton and better inland transportation the East, West, and South developed the interdependent pattern of specialization that we reviewed earlier.

After farm productivity had increased sufficiently to release significant numbers of workers to manufacturing, regional income patterns changed in response to changes in regional specialization. Manufactured exports gained supremacy over agriculture. The manufacturing heartland developed and stretched westward to the Middle West. At the same time the balance of the Nation became a raw-materials (especially minerals) and agricultural hinterland for the Northeast and Great Lakes regions which had become the heartland of our export base. As 6–9, 9–13, and 15–2 show, income patterns followed the redeployment of the export base.

The heartland-hinterland relationship continued in this pattern until around 1920 by which time the movement of manufacturing into the hinterland had begun to blur the distinction between the two types of areas. With this change came the narrowing of regional income differences that we referred to above. Labor-intensive industries continued their movement South, while the West, especially California, and certain key cities in the Southwest were the recipients of capital-intensive, high-wage industries.

The South continued to specialize in cotton and more recently soybeans. Around the turn of the century, it also had a boom in lumber production which continued until the building slump of the 1930's, when its virgin forests also began to be depleted and competition was faced from western lumber areas. The Southwest benefited from a boom in oil, while the Gulf area benefited from both petroleum and chemical industry growth.

As the Nation continued to grow, certain nonresource influences continued to favor manufacturing expansion in the manufacturing belt and in large cities in particular. These were indicated as the last two points in 15–3. First, there was the advantage of proximity to other industry—both in the same type of production and in other fields. The economist refers to this advantage as an "external economy of scale." That is, the growing size of all industry in an area makes possible the specialization of certain types of supplier and service industries and minimizes certain marketing costs. An apparel manufacturer, for example, finds that a large city with many apparel plants has a large supply of experienced workers, nearby suppliers of machinery and cloth, and nearby centers of finance and marketing organizations. He can show his wares at annual shows and personally contact both customers and suppliers.

City planners also have referred to this same characteristic of industry to gather together in certain regions and in major cities as the tendency toward "agglomeration." It is a factor that has made our large cities larger. Improvements in city transportation—street cars, then buses and commuter trains—as well as technological improvements in construction of tall buildings made possible the concentration of more and more manufacturing, commercial, and financial businesses in close proximity to one another in our major cities, now called metropolitan areas.

A second influence on the growth of major cities was the last item shown in 15–3 —the growth of local markets. As more industrial firms located near each other in cities, more jobs in other industries were required to serve not only those industries themselves but also the worker population of the area. City planners have described this multiplication of local serving jobs by using a base industry-service industry scheme of analysis. In line with the analysis at the beginning of this chapter, they point out that the basic industries of a community exist largely to serve a regional or national market—that is, they "export" their goods and services from the local community. Manufacturing is a very important example. The locale-serving, or residentiary, industries, however, exist because of the size of the local work force or population. They expand or contract with that local work force—especially the portion that is employed in export industries—but are not primarily responsible for causing the expansion or contraction. Thus, community leaders are aware that the development of new manufacturing jobs is critical to the growth of their community. Of course, recreation, financial, and other industry specialization in particular communities also may be an export-base industry as well as a manufacturing firm.

In any event, the growth of residentiary industry was a further factor in the growth of major city centers early in our history. It also has become important in the development of cities in the hinterland regions more recently.

Influences on Regional Change

The basic structure of regional specialization in the Nation was established before the Civil War. By 1900, the economy had reached a peak in regional specialization. Let us now turn to consider some of the influences that produced different kinds and different rates of change in the various regions. 15–4 lists some of these influences.

11–13 and 11–14 show how technological change caused different rates of growth in different industries. Changes in consumer preferences will have, of course, a similar impact on the structure of total demand. We have also stressed the importance of different rates of growth in demand as incomes rose—that is, differing income elasticities of demand. It should be easy to understand, therefore, that regional specialization in different products exposed regions to different rates of growth because of what was happening to their major industries. For example, the competition of aluminum has cut into the production of steel, and thus affected the steel making cities. Western lumber expanded at the expense of southern lumber; and southern textiles and apparel expanded at the expense of New England textiles and apparel.

15–4. INFLUENCES ON REGIONAL CHANGE

1. Technological change
2. Income elasticity of demand
3. Changes in consumer preferences and, thus, structure of demand
4. Sunk costs
5. Changes in amenities
6. Growth of local markets

Farming and many consumer goods industries have experienced less rise in demand for their output than have other industries.

Changes between 1950 and 1960 in the major nonfarm industries using an employment measure are shown in 15–5. Mining and transportation, communications, and utility groups experienced decreases in employment, while manufacturing increased less than the average rate for all nonfarm industry. The highest rates of increase were in finance, real estate and insurance; services and miscellaneous; and government (primarily state and local government, incidentally).

Within manufacturing, also, different rates of change have occurred in different industries; and these changes also have affected regions differently. Between 1950 and 1960, decreases in employment occurred in tobacco, textiles, leather, lumber, and miscellaneous—which are low-wage industries—and also in petroleum refining and primary metals. Employment also decreased in auto vehicles and parts

15–5. Nonfarm Employment in the United States, 1950 and 1960

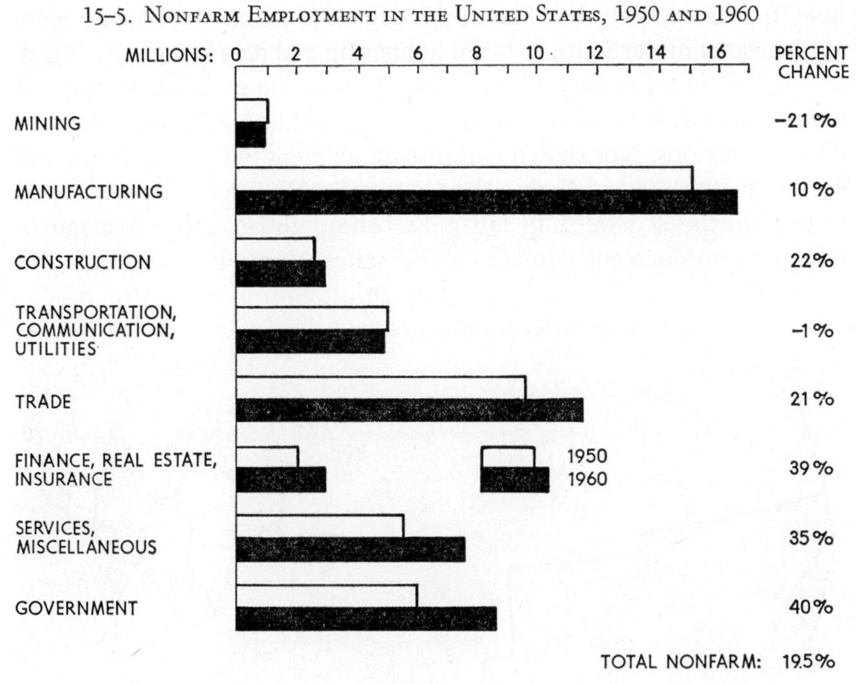

Source: U.S. Department of Commerce, *Statistical Abstract of the United States, 1962* (Washington, D.C.: U.S. Government Printing Office, 1963), pp. 219 and 223.

as well as in railroad equipment, although the transportation equipment group increased due to increases in aircraft (and missiles) and in boats. Otherwise, the increases continued to be led by chemicals, electrical machinery, and instruments; and growth continued in ordnance, machinery, fabricated metals, and paper and printing.

Different regions tended to fare well or poorly depending on which industries were concentrated there. Nevertheless, the biggest differences between regions arose out of different rates of growth within industry groups (although some of the group averages in the data merely result from different product concentrations).

New Regional Patterns

During the 1950's, there arose considerable public discussion and concern over certain "depressed areas," which experienced slow growth or declines in total employment while high unemployment rates held or even rose during periods of national prosperity. Notable among the urban "depressed areas" were New England textile towns, coal mining areas, railroad equipment or repair centers, and automobile or household machinery centers. The rural depressed areas, of course, were concentrated in the South in farm, lumbering and textile areas.

15–6 gives a very rough idea of how these different rates of industry and demand changes affected the total nonfarm employment in different regions. Not shown is farm employment, which of course was declining nearly everywhere. The chart shows that the industrial areas in the Northeast tended to lag most behind the national average in nonfarm employment growth, while states along the southern and

15–6. State Nonfarm Employment Changes, 1950–60

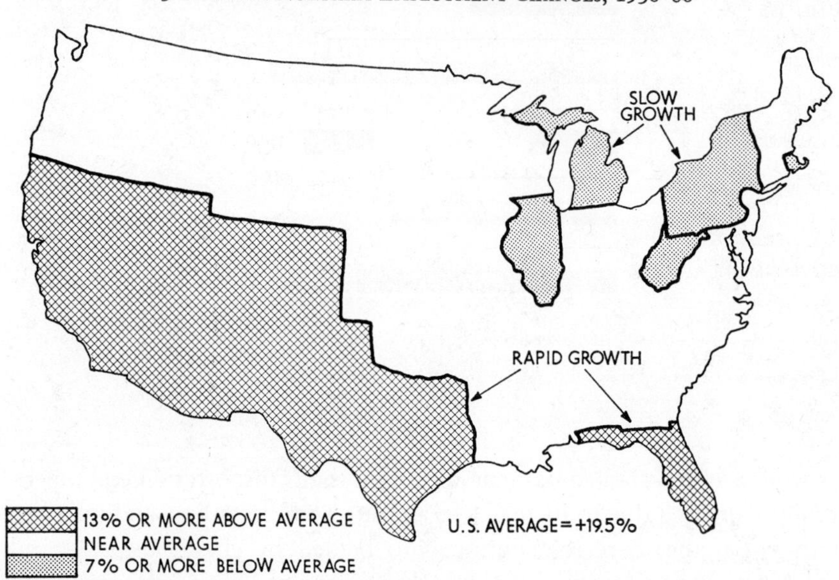

Source: U.S. Bureau of Labor Statistics, *Employment and Earnings* (Washington, D.C.: U.S. Government Printing Office, 1961).

western rim of the Nation experienced greater than average rates of growth.

At this point the question might be raised as to why some industries and people do not move out of old areas even faster. Some of our idle capacity in the steel industry, for example, is in older high-cost locations. Here the existence of fixed capital investment in plant and equipment acts as a dampening influence on the rate of change. With their capital already "sunk" in fixed equipment that cannot be sold out or used up quickly, the owners continue to operate this equipment even though it no longer is very profitable. In the same sense, many farmers and homeowners in depressed industrial cities are reluctant to move away from their homes, schools, and churches in which they already have much useful capital invested. Thus some so-called depressed areas have managed to adjust to loss of demand for older industry output by converting their export base to new products or retraining their labor for other work. Some of the New England towns, in particular have been successful in using old textile mill plants for new and diversified types of industry.

The industries with lower capital requirements and less dependence upon bulky mineral raw materials are more able to locate most anywhere. These so-called "footloose" industries are able to move to depressed areas where labor supply is in surplus, provided that the labor surplus also means lower wages and lower labor costs for these industries.

Southern rural areas especially have attracted such industries on the basis of their ample labor supply, low wages, and sometimes financial inducements in the form of low-interest or low-tax plants. Some of the newer depressed industrial areas recently have been competing for these footloose industries; and the new federal Economic Development Administration aims to aid both urban and rural depressed areas in obtaining such industry. The competition, however, is keen; and the number of jobs in such industries is limited in relation to the supply of surplus workers in depressed areas. Thus significant out-migration will have to continue in these areas.

Two other influences, however, have been favoring the southern half of the United States. One is the fact that with an increasing number of retired people, communities that have a warm or moderate climate and favorable recreational, cultural, and medical facilities are attracting older people to live there. In fact, some of the footloose industries are attracted, even if they have a relatively smaller requirement for unskilled labor and greater need for professional and skilled technicians. They find it easier to attract these key personnel to desirable living areas. Florida, Southern California, and the Southwest have the social and climatic amenities for desirable living which have helped them attract both people and industry.

Another influence has been the growing size of regional markets in the South and West. The limits of economies from large plants and from concentration in industrial centers apparently have been reached in many industries. Now many of them are locating branch plants in regions outside of the manufacturing belt in order to reduce transportation costs and provide quicker service. That is, as regions and regional centers grow larger, more and more industries find that they are large enough to support a new plant. Thus, the size of local markets has been a factor in encouraging regional decentralization of industry in the postwar period. This is in line with our earlier observation that the larger an economy, the more diversified and less dependent upon other economies it will be.

Expanding Metropolitan Areas

The pattern of urban growth and regional decentralization that has characterized the Nation's extensive growth has taken a new form since the 1920's. Regional decentralization is not a move back to rural areas and it is not a move toward ever larger central cities. Something is

15–7. Population by Residence

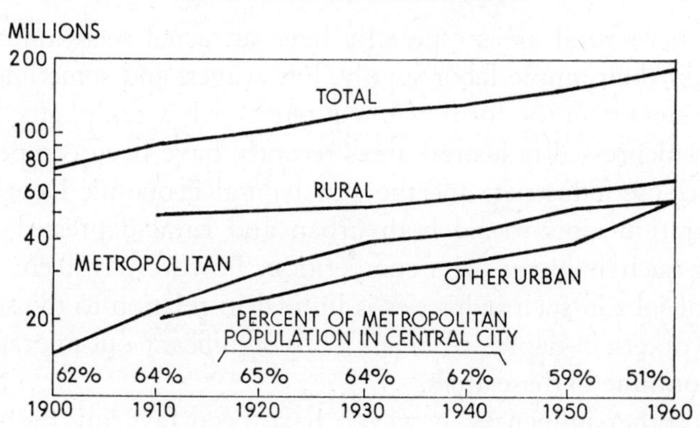

Source: U.S. Department of Commerce, *Statistical Abstract of the United States, 1962* (Washington, D.C.: U.S. Government Printing Office, 1963), p. 21.

happening to our metropolitan areas that is causing them to suffer major problems of readjustment. That something is the final culmination of the revolution in motorized transportation. Instead of causing our cities to get larger at the center, it is causing them to spread out. This is suggested by the data in 15–7. From 1900 to the end of the 1920's, metropolitan areas comprised the fastest growing population sector. Since 1950, other urban areas have suddenly shot up, further depressing growth in the metropolitan areas.

Within metropolitan areas (which are defined in census statistics to include a whole county or very often several counties), the percentage of the population in the central city itself has declined since the 1920–30 decade, especially since 1950. The population has used the automobile and better highways to move out to suburbs or rural nonfarm areas surrounding the cities. This "urban sprawl" has caused rising costs of sewer, water, streets, police, fire, and other public services, plus the costs of smog from a rising number of autos and industrial plants in each metropolitan area. It also has resulted in a decline in property values in the central cities as downtown stores feel the loss of business. And as poorer income groups crowd into the older dwellings abandoned by the middle classes moving outward, the social costs associated with high population density are intensified. Metropolitan decay has made the problem of adjustment worse in older industrial centers that are not expanding; but it is a major problem in all major cities.

Industry also has tended to move out of older multistoried plants in crowded city centers because of the transportation revolution. Trucks make movement of goods less dependent upon railroad marshalling yards; and workers are able to commute in private cars to outlying

15–8. Manufacturing Located in Metropolitan Areas, 1947 and 1958

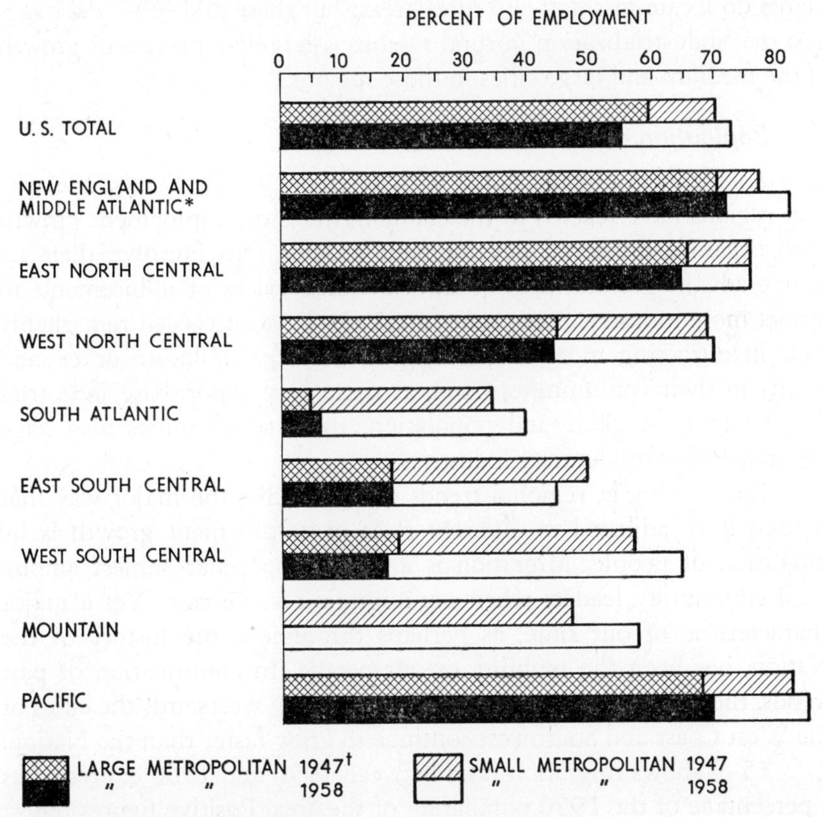

* Includes Maryland and Delaware.
† Over 40,000 industrial employment.
Source: Karl Fox, V. W. Ruttan, and L. W. Witt, *Farming, Farmers and Markets for Farm Goods*, Supplementary Paper No. 15 (New York: Committee for Economic Development, 1962), pp. 96–97.

plants or even plants in nearby cities. But the burden on transportation facilities at rush hours has partially offset any advantages of moving industry out, especially because crisscross traffic patterns are harder to provide for.

However, it would be misleading for rural areas to pin their hopes on the trend toward regional decentralization and movement out of the center of major cities. Manufacturing employment still tends to concentrate in cities and especially in metropolitan areas. The data in 15–8 show that, nationally, metropolitan areas have gained an increased share of all manufacturing employment. But the smaller metropolitan areas have gained at the expense of the larger ones. Additional data also might show that minor urban areas, especially the larger ones of this group have gained relatively. But only in the East South Central did nonmetropolitan areas gain a larger share of manufacturing employment in the postwar period. Small apparel, shoe, and light assembly plants do locate in small-city rural areas; but these and other data suggest that industrialization in rural regions is largely a process of growth of the medium and large cities in those regions.

Population and Income Changes

As we have already noted with reference to the South, one way that regions have reacted to the changing rates of employment growth is to organize industrial development programs to improve their resource advantages and provide information services or inducements to attract more industry. Some states and cities have succeeded remarkably well in attracting more manufacturing industry to locate or expand plants in their communities. And, as these new export-base industries support more workers and population, these communities also have expanded their residentiary industries.

But looking at regional trends quite broadly, the major way that regions have adjusted to different rates of employment growth is by migration of people. Migration is a rather unpopular subject among local community leaders when out-migration is the case. Yet a major characteristic of our time, as perhaps throughout the history of the Nation, has been the mobility of our people. In continuation of past trends, the U.S. population center is still moving westward; the cities of the West Coast and Southwest continue to grow faster than the Nation.

15–9 shows migration rates between 1950 and 1960 expressed as a percentage of the 1950 population of the area. Positive figures reflect in-migration, usually into cities, expressed as a percentage of the area they moved into. Negative figures reflect out-migration from the rural

15–9. Migration Rates, 1950–60
(Percent of 1950 Population)

	Total	*Urban*	*Rural*
New England			
Maine	−12	−12	−11
New Hampshire	− 4	− 2	− 6
Vermont	−14	− 9	−18
Massachusetts	− 8	− 9	− 2
Rhode Island	− 9	− 6	−24
Connecticut	9	10	5
Middle Atlantic			
New York	− 5	− 5	− 4
New Jersey	7	10	−11
Pennsylvania	−10	− 9	−14
East North Central			
Ohio	4	9	− 9
Indiana	1	5	− 7
Illinois	− 3	2	−18
Michigan	5	9	− 6
Wisconsin	− 3	9	−19
West North Central			
Minnesota	− 3	13	−23
Iowa	−12	− 1	−23
Missouri	− 9	0	−23
North Dakota	−16	18	−28
South Dakota	−14	6	−23
Nebraska	−11	5	−26
Kansas	− 4	16	−25
South Atlantic			
Delaware	22	28	10
Maryland	13	20	− 3
District of Columbia	−26	−26	None
Virginia	0	22	−20
West Virginia	−25	−16	−30
North Carolina	− 8	12	−18
South Carolina	− 9	6	−17
Georgia	− 6	19	−27
Florida	59	82	15
East South Central			
Kentucky	−15	6	−27
Tennessee	−11	9	−26
Alabama	−14	13	−35
Mississippi	−22	14	−36
West South Central			
Arkansas	−26	2	−40
Louisiana	1	20	−22
Oklahoma	−14	10	−39
Texas	5	30	−35
Mountain			
Montana	− 4	14	−17
Idaho	− 4	8	−14
Wyoming	− 4	12	−20
Colorado	15	38	−24
New Mexico	21	65	−23
Arizona	55	115	−20
Utah	12	31	−24
Nevada	60	101	5
Pacific			
Washington	2	11	−14
Oregon	− 1	17	−22
California	30	41	−13

Source: John M. Henderson, "Some General Aspects of Recent Regional Development in Melvin L. Greenhut and W. Tate Whitman, (eds.), *Essays in Southern Economic Development* (Chapel Hill, N.C.: University of North Carolina Press, 1964), p. 176.

areas of a state (or from the urban areas of the state as a whole); thus they are averages and net figures which do not quite reflect the size of the total movement.

The net migration figures, it should be noted, are not the same as total population changes; because the excess of births over deaths normally would cause population to grow in each area. In the United States between the same dates, total population increased by about 19 percent. In some areas the natural population growth would be higher.

15–10. State Income and Population Changes, 1950–60

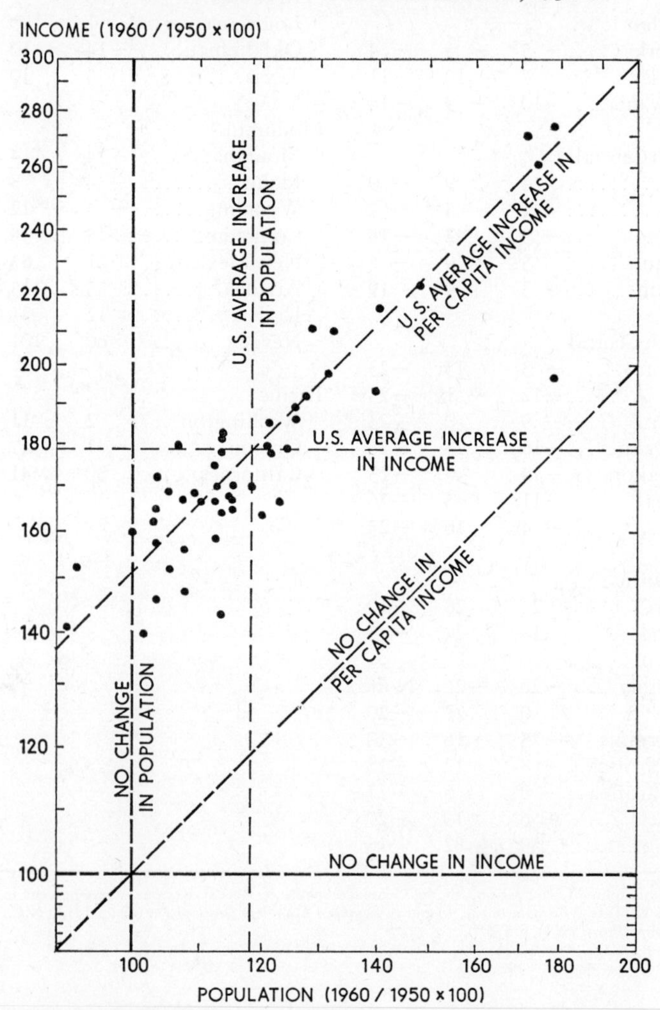

Source: U.S. Department of Commerce, *Statistical Abstract of the United States, 1962* (Washington, D.C.: U.S. Government Printing Office, 1963), pp. 11 and 322.

In Mississippi, for example, there was a net out-migration of 22 percent of the population, but the excess of births over deaths made up this loss so that total population remained unchanged. Arkansas and West Virginia were the only states which had absolute losses in population; but they were not unique in having a large flow of out-migration—any state that grew by less than 19 percent or so experienced out-migration.

15–10 provides a key to the significance of labor supply adjustment as the main regional means to adjust to different rates of industry growth. This chart shows changes from 1950 to 1960 as index numbers (1950 = 100) and plotted on a double-log scale. The vertical scale shows percent changes in income. The horizontal scale shows percent changes in population. The horizontal and vertical lines at 100 reflect the 1950 levels, or no change in either income or population.

The dashed diagonal line (from the intersection of 100 and 200 on the vertical and horizontal scales) reflects equal change in both income and population so that no change would occur in per capita income. The other diagonal line reflects the average per capita income line for the Nation. Along this line, if a state's population grew faster than in the United States, its income would have to have grown more to have equaled U.S. increase in per capita income. Of course, some states fell below and some above this line, although all increased their per capita incomes substantially over the decade.

The thing to note from these data is that those states which failed to have very large increases in total income still could have large per capita income increases if their population grew less. Thus a farm state which experienced a disappointingly slow rise in demand for its products and, therefore, in its income may have been able to achieve an above average increase in per capita income by heavy out-migration and, correspondingly, a slower growth in population. This is exemplified by Arkansas and West Virginia, the two states losing population (at the extreme left of the graph) and one of the lowest in overall gain in total personal income. However, ***primarily because of heavy out-migration,*** they were among the states that experienced the highest rates of per capita income gain.

It is chiefly because of the heavy migrations to the West and the heavy migrations out of the South, in fact, that regional per capita incomes have had a persistent trend toward coming closer to the national average. Thus, while each area cannot always grow at the same rate in total size, there is no reason why it cannot grow as fast or even catch up to the Nation in the individual incomes and living standards of its people. In our changing world, there are adjustments we can make to the changes occurring around us; but if we don't make these adjustments, there is no guarantee that our relative income levels will be protected.

AMERICA IN A GROWING WORLD

In the introduction to this chapter we pointed out that the larger a national economy becomes, the less will be its reliance upon exports to achieve efficiency and rapid growth. The development of the American economy has adhered to this principle. In the post-Revolution period the ascension of "King Cotton" raised the value of our export base and generated unprecedented gains in total and per capita income. In the period prior to the Civil War, the foreign sector of gross national product was as high as 13 percent of total production and a much more important part of the market sector.

But the very growth of cotton and its companion exports generated a series of secondary effects which caused the foreign sector to decline in importance. The sequence was something like this: export-base growth raised profits and wages which, in turn, attracted capital and labor. The inflow of capital and labor produced an extremely rapid absolute growth rate in the total economy. Extensive growth, i.e., growth of population, capital and land in use, increased the size and geographic density of our markets. Bigger and geographically more concentrated consumer and industrial markets made investment in the most modern and efficient transportation facilities practical. The combination of bigger markets and better transportation made possible capturing the economies of specialization and division of labor which had given European and British manufacturers competitive advantage over Americans. So manufacturing investment was encouraged at home and, thus, our dependence upon the rest of the world for manufactured products was reduced.

This chain of events which began with Eli Whitney's cotton gin set in motion a trend toward steadily declining importance of exports. This trend was well established by the Civil War. And by the post-World War II period, the foreign sector had fallen to less than 10 percent of GNP and currently is about 5 to 6 percent of total GNP.

Let us briefly review the changes that have occurred in America's world position over the latter portion of this period of growth and evolution. In doing so, we will contrast briefly the growth problems of Europe, Russia, the underdeveloped nations, and our own country.

U.S. Balance of Payments

Let us begin by bringing to a recent date the kind of balance-of-payments data that we have shown for previous historic periods. 15–11 and 15–12 show these data, this time in billions of dollars, for the period 1915 to 1957.

Considering each type of payment in turn, we can see a continuation of our positive balance of ***trade,*** the excess of exports over imports, with especially high levels during both World War I and World War II. During World War I and immediately afterwards, ***capital*** movement was the main way for other nations to pay for our surplus of

15–11. U.S. Balance of Payments—Balances of Trade and Specie, 1915–65

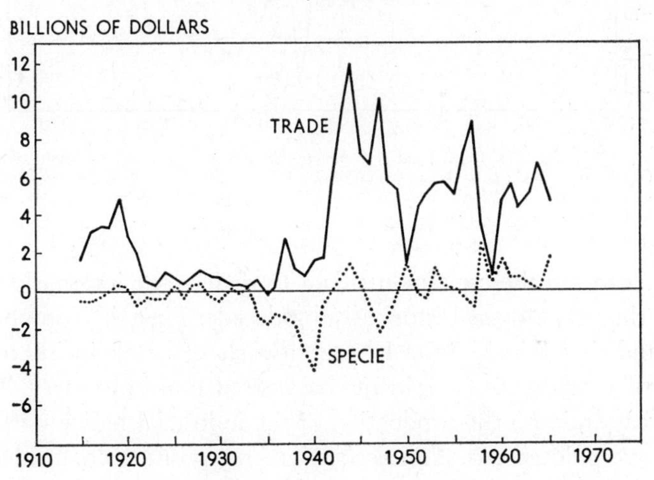

Source: U.S. Department of Commerce, *Historical Statistics of the United States* (Washington, D.C.: U.S. Government Printing Office, 1960), pp. 537–38, 563–64; and U.S. Department of Commerce, *Statistical Abstract of the United States, 1966* (Washington, D.C.: U.S. Government Printing Office, 1967), p. 814.

exports. During World War I, we changed from a debtor to a creditor nation, as other nations withdrew their investments to meet war needs and as Americans invested in Europe during the postwar recovery.

During World War II and the postwar period, ***invisible items*** were the main offsets to our export surplus. This was largely because of our payments for payrolls and supplies of troops stationed abroad. Some large capital movements went to aid European recovery immediately after World War II. ***Gold*** also flowed in during these years, when the rest of the world was experiencing a dollar shortage and was attempting to buy American goods and machinery to rebuild its own economies.

Since then gold flows have been reversed for several reasons: our governmental committments abroad have increased, our export surplus has declined, and, our capital movements have accelerated.

15-12. U.S. Balance of Payments—Balances of Invisible Items and Capital, 1915–65

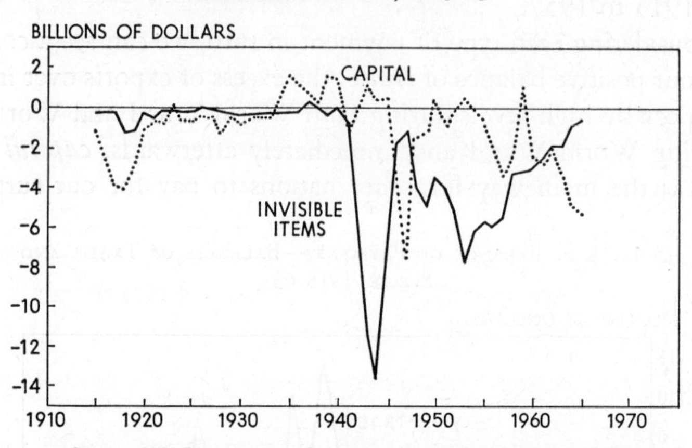

Source: U.S. Department of Commerce, *Historical Statistics of the United States* (Washington, D.C.: U.S. Government Printing Office, 1960), pp. 537–38, 563–64; and U.S. Department of Commerce, *Statistical Abstract of the United States, 1966* (Washington, D.C.: U.S. Government Printing Office, 1967), p. 814.

We can use these payments data to review our international relations as they developed historically by decade. First, it is important to understand that World War I brought a sharp break in international trading relations, as well as in the balance of political power. The war was a great drain on the production of the industrial nations of Europe. As we have pointed out, America's payments position changed without being fully recognized. No longer could the rest of the world pay for its excess of imports over exports from the United States with its earnings from its investments in American business and securities. For a while in the 1920's, our surplus exports were made possible by the flow abroad of American loan and investment capital. In other words, with the money we loaned or invested in other countries, those countries could buy our machinery to rebuild their production.

Our Nation, however, continued a policy of raising tariffs to excude foreign imports. The Emergency Tariff Act was passed in 1921, and the Fordney-McCumber Act in 1922 raised the rates even higher as a part of the "return to normalcy" program of President Harding. In 1930, under President Hoover, the Hawley-Smoot Tariff Act was passed in the midst of the depression decline.

America's Great Depression was part of a worldwide depression.

On just which side of the Atlantic the Great Depression began is an unsettled point. Nevertheless, America's Great Contraction had a severe impact on the other nations of the world. With the end of the 1929 boom, American investment abroad was reduced. Along with higher American tariffs, this made it increasingly difficult for other countries to pay for American goods. Other nations followed our example by pushing tariffs even higher. Just as our economy suffered a cumulative slowdown in the flow of income and production when everyone became pessimistic and tried to reduce investments and hold cash, so the nations of the world fell into a vicious circle of reducing imports and trying to expand their exports to others.

The depression was a shock to our confidence and led to reform measures. Other countries were equally shaken by the depression. With this calamity following so soon after the destruction of World War I, and with the example of Russia turning communist, the European industrial nations were ready for measures more desperate than social reforms. As the Communist and Socialist parties became stronger, the traditional upper classes were frightened into supporting military dictatorships. Where the Fascists did come to power a policy aimed at economic self-sufficiency followed with further restricted world trade.

The 1930's decade was one of conflicting actions on the international economic scene. Although he initially followed on isolationist line, Franklin D. Roosevelt in the late 1930's used the Reciprocal Trade Act to reduce tariffs and restore trade somewhat. But, the dictatorships and impending war in Europe caused flight of capital to America mostly in the form of gold flows to this country. Such capital movements were a source of embarrassment and a spur to financial restrictions among nations.

Thus, after more than a century of world peace, industrial expansion, and free trade, the international economy broke down. It broke on the rocks of war and depression. The aftermath consisted of dictatorships, attempts to be self-sufficient, rivalry for exclusive trade and resources, and further world war.

By joining the fight in World War II to remove the threat of world domination by Fascist dictatorship, America helped the free world take the first step toward restoring a worldwide market economy. During World War II, America had a very large volume of exports to its Allies. These were offset by large current payments in the form of spending on supplies and payrolls for our military forces abroad. Our lend-lease program also supplied both military and civilian goods to support our allies.

In the first few postwar years, foreigners withdrew funds and American investors supplied a large volume of capital funds to Europe to help them buy American machinery and materials to repair and restore their own productive capacity. Under the Marshall Plan, public loans and financial grants (included under current payments) were made by our government to help the European nations, including Greece and Turkey. An Organization for European Economic Cooperation was established to help direct the use of these aid funds.

The United States also took the leadership in establishing certain international organizations which included in their functions duties aimed at restoration of world trade. Chief among them was the United Nations. The International Bank for Reconstruction and Development which lends money for development purposes and the International Monetary Fund which assists balance of payments flows between nations were also both founded in this period.

During the Korean War period of the early 1950's, America's invisible items deficit and export surplus were even larger. Not only were expenditures on military forces abroad increased but a very large increase in foreign investment was largely responsible for supporting a further increase in our export surplus. After 1960 our foreign aid for development rather than military purposes was moderately increased, but in recent years its course was reversed and it remains in constant jeopardy as a consequence of congressional and public dissatisfaction.

The growth and evolution of the world and U.S. economies has put us in a paradoxical position in that foreign trade is a small part of our GNP, but a very large part of world trade. This paradox has been intensified by the post-World War II expansion of trade among nations.

Our exports are only 5 percent of our GNP, but they account for 18 percent of all free world exports and about the same is true of imports. We hold about 40 percent of the free world's gold stocks and foreign exchange reserves (although this is considerably reduced from the 71 percent in 1948), and we account for about 40 percent of the free world's industrial production. Therefore, whatever happens to the American economy has a major impact on the economies of most other nations. With a rise in our prosperity, our imports rise; so demand for the production of other countries rises and vice versa.

15–13 shows some of the deficits of trade relations among nations and underscores the complexity and multilateral nature of world trade. Inspection of 15–13 also highlights our dominant role in world economic affairs. The total exports of the countries on the left are distributed among destination countries as indicated by the columns on the

15–13. FREE WORLD TRADE, 1961
(In Billions of Dollars)

Origin	Total Exports	Destination					
		U.S.	Canada	Japan	EEC*	Other European	Rest of World
United States	18.7	...	3.6	1.7	3.5	2.7	7.2
Canada	5.6	3.2	...	.5	.5	1.1	.9
Japan	4.0	1.1	.1	...	.2	.3	2.3
Europe							
EEC	30.9	2.2	.3	.3	11.9†	8.9	7.3
Other	21.2	1.7	.7	.2	5.8	6.3†	6.5
Rest of free world	29.9	6.1	.6	2.2	7.2	6.1	7.7†
Totals	110.4	14.3	5.3	4.6	29.1	25.4	31.6

* European Economic Community
† Exports between nations in group.
SOURCE: Council of Economic Advisors, *Annual Report*, 1963, p. 100.

right. American exports were $18.7 billion, while our imports (totaled at the bottom of the destination column) were only $14.3 billion. Some of the U.S. export surplus to a particular country is made up by that country's exports to other countries, but most of it is balanced by transactions other than in physical goods.

One of the groups of countries in 15–13 was the European Economy Community (EEC), which includes three large countries—Germany, France, and Italy—and three small countries—Belgium, The Netherlands, and Luxemburg (the "Benelux" countries). These countries have set out to achieve an economic advantage for themselves that in potential our Nation started out with: a large domestic market of free trade among neighboring states. During the 1960's, they have scheduled a lowering of tariffs among their countries while gradually establishing a common schedule of tariffs with outside countries. Common tariffs involve lowering the particular commodity tariffs of some member countries while raising those of others.

This "Common Market" as it is called, is expected to strengthen the economies and speed the growth of these countries of Western Europe. It may create a problem, however, for the United States and other industrial nations. It may raise the tariffs we face and restrict our sales to member countries; and it may create stronger industrial competitors selling in our markets. In order not to be left out, Great Britain recently attempted to gain admission to the Common Market. Although it failed, Great Britain still may accomplish this in the future. If Britain does gain admission to the Common Market and if it does not raise its tariffs too high, formation of the Common Market may prove a step toward greater freedom of trade and a more efficient worldwide market.

Underdeveloped Nations

In addition to the rise of a stronger European economy, in the postwar period there also has been an effort among governments of underdeveloped nations to develop their economies. World War II started the breakup of the colonial empires of the European nations, and in the postwar period many nations were granted or won their freedom. These nations, however, have faced severe problems and obstacles to development of their economies at the same time that their people have adopted overoptimistic hopes that their incomes could be suddenly raised.

On the one hand, the governments of the new countries are unstable, and the people are poorly prepared for self-government. Thus, many are controlled by military dictators; and there is continual danger of revolt, especially near the borders of Russia and China. On the other hand, these countries are very poor, they have very unequal income distributions, they have relatively little capital, and they have few capable business leaders to build private industry. Thus they tend to seek to solve their problems through central planning and government direct production. Although this approach is no doubt more productive than unrestrained laissez-faire, given the absence of a large well-edu-

15–14. U.S. Foreign Aid
(Since World War II)

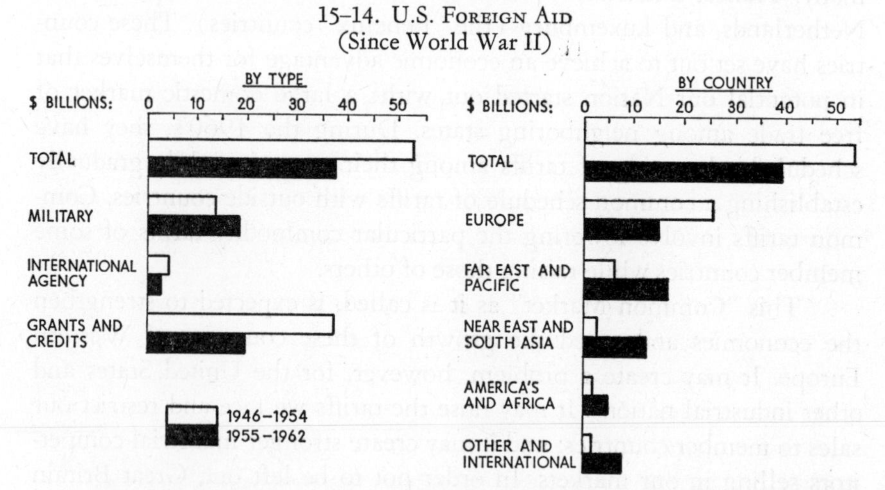

Source: Council of Economic Advisors, *Annual Report*, 1963, p. 264, and U.S. Department of Commerce, *Statistical Abstract of the United States, 1962* (Washington, D.C.: U.S. Government Printing Office, 1963), p. 865.

cated entrepreneurial class, the lack of entrepreneurial types is a serious impediment to a centrally planned economy also.

The United States has attempted to help the underdeveloped nations through loans, outright grants, and technical assistance. The amount of foreign aid extended by the United States, however, has been relatively small compared to the aid it gave to Europe during and after World War II. Yet, the needs of the underdeveloped nations are much greater than were those of Europe. Europe lost its capital and much of its manpower, but in its people it retained the knowledge necessary to operate a modern industrial economy—the underdeveloped nations have never had this advantage. 15–14 shows the total U.S. aid for two periods: 1946 through 1954 in the light bars, and 1955 through 1962 in the dark bars. The data on the left show the breakdown of this aid by type, and the data on the right show where the aid has gone. The importance of military aid increased, although in 1961 and 1962 military aid was decreased and other aid increased over the previous two years.

More important than aid is the ability of the underdeveloped nations to raise their exports and to attract foreign private capital on a continuing basis. These nations have a great opportunity to "transplant" the most advanced technology in developing their economies. But all modern technology tends to require large capital investment and entrepreneurs or their governmental equivalents to perform the transplant. Also machinery initially needs to be imported from modern industrial nations. This requires that more goods be exported to pay for machinery imports, or it requires that foreign governments give aid or that foreign private investors provide capital funds to buy machinery.

Historically the largest flow of capital funds to any country has been provided by exports or by private investors. But, the new nations are handicapped by an attitude of hostility toward Europeans and toward owners of capital, because their experience has been conditioned by the excesses of colonial rule. By design colonial policy was aimed at furthering the interests of the large plantation and mining firms. Such progress came at the expense, real or imagined, of "host" nation or colony. Also, the process of growth requires considerable saving and investing to build up future production rather than expansion of immediate consumption. The hopes of the people, however, are directed toward immediate gains in consumption. Superimposed on all this are very rapid population growth rates attributable to modern medicine and hygiene.

Thus the rendering of aid to develop these countries is a difficult task and one that may require considerable patience and tolerance of disappointments on the part of Americans. The alternative of abandoning any foreign aid effort, however, is made unpalatable by the danger of the underdeveloped parts of the world falling under the domination of what we consider an abiding threat to world security—the power of Russia on the one hand and mainland China on the other hand.

Growth of Russia

After World II, in the view of most Americans, Russia and mainland China took the place of the Fascist nations as the major threat to world peace. With the development of atomic and hydrogen bombs and of missile delivery systems, the direct military power struggle between the United States and Russia has resulted in a deadlock. Much of the struggle, therefore, has been transferred to the less developed nations. Russia is attempting to take over these countries by military intervention and internal revolt, while the United States has used similar tactics to help them strengthen their defenses and their economies in the hopes that they will fall in with us.

Recently, however, our leaders have been concerned by the rapid rate of growth of the Russian economy. Such growth generates concern not only because it adds to Russian military power, but because it greatly increases Russia's prestige with the underdeveloped nations. It is observed that the Russian economy has been growing faster than that of the United States in the postwar period. And it is claimed that Russia may soon catch up and overtake us in productive capacity.

While there is no denying the faster growth of Russia in the postwar period, there are three aspects of this growth that cast doubt upon its long continuance or the likelihood of Russia soon surpassing our production. One is the extent to which Russia's growth represents a temporary catch-up in its long-term growth trend—Russia was able, after all, to import an already developed technology. The second is the extent to which Russia has allocated its resources into production of investment goods. Eventually, political pressure will likely force a reallocation toward a relatively larger role for consumer goods. The third factor is the Russian bent for allocating resources in favor of known technologies and known products whereas market economies characteristically allocate increases in productivity in the more expensive direction of innovation in consumer and capital goods. Political pressure is likely to force Russia's planners in this same direction.

15–15 shows the long-term growth of industrial production in Russia and in the United States in the form of indexes with 1913 as 100.

These indexes ignore the higher level of American production and merely shows the trends.[1] Prior to 1913, Russian growth under the Czar was very similar to the American trend. World War I and the Communist revolution and subsequent war against the counterrevolution caused a severe drop in Russian production. By 1928, Communist Russia had recovered and begun its successive five-year plans, which caused Russia to grow rapidly while the United States was set back by the Great Depression. World War II stunted Russia's growth in industrial pro-

15–15. U.S. and Russian Growth in Industrial Production Per Capita

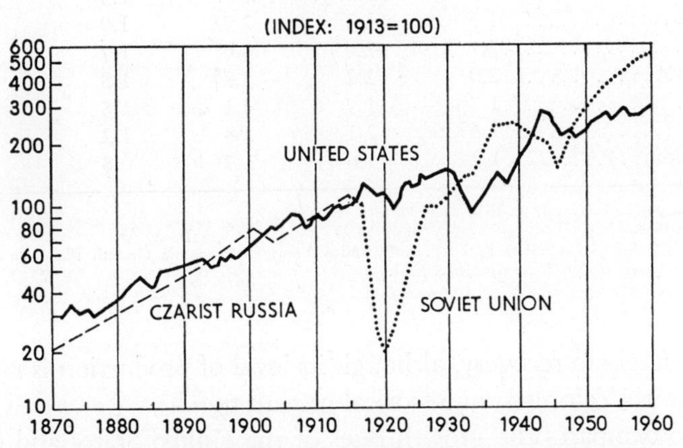

Source: Warren G. Nutter, "Measuring Production in the U.S.S.R.: Industrial Growth in the Soviet Union." *American Economic Review*, May, 1958, p. 406.

duction; then after postwar reconversion from military production, Russia began a period of rapid catch-up in its long-term growth trends. By the 1950's, however, Russia's more rapid growth probably cannot be

[1] At this point it is well to note that a single figure or index number for total national output requires a set of prices for different kinds of goods and services. Prices, however, reflect different patterns of resource supplies in different countries and especially different social values placed on various goods and services. In order to average together wheat production and steel production a set of prices for wheat and steel is required. Russian prices in rubles, however, are quite different from American prices in dollars—not because of the rate of exchange of rubles for dollars, but because commodities have quite different values compared with other commodities. Because of this difference in relative prices among commodities, Russian production has been estimated to be about 27 percent of American production if valued by Russian prices in rubles, compared with 53 percent of American production if valued by American prices in dollars. Some people have tried to split the difference between these two percentages and say that Russian production is one-third that of American; but these two types of measures cannot be averaged. You cannot meaningfully compare the production of two countries without choosing a relative price list by which to value that production in common units.

15–16. Productivity Growth Rates of Western Nations
(National Product per Man-Year)

	Annual Percent Rate of Growth				
	Long-Term (to 1959)*	*Pre-1913*	*Fastest 8 Years Before 1913*	*1913–59*	*1950–59*
Japan	2.9	3.4	4.7	2.6	6.1
Italy	1.2	0.7	2.3	1.7	4.7
Germany	1.5	1.5	3.5	1.4	4.5
France	1.5	1.5	n.a.	1.5	3.6
Netherlands	1.1	n.a.	n.a.	1.3	3.4
Norway	1.6	1.3	2.7	1.9	3.1
Sweden	2.1	2.4	4.6	1.7	2.8
United States	2.0	2.2	5.2†	1.8	2.2
Canada	1.7	1.9	4.1	1.5	2.0
Denmark	1.6	2.1	2.4	1.2	1.8
United Kingdom	1.2	1.6	2.7	0.8	1.7

* Starting points varying from 1855 to 1900.
† 1872 to 1880.
Source: Deborah C. Paige with F. T. Blackaby and S. Freund, "Economic Growth the Last Hundred Years," *National Institute Economic Review*, July, 1961.

attributed merely to recovery, although its level of production is not far out of line with its long-term historical growth trend.

15–16 compares the growth rates of the United States and other industrial nations. It shows that a similar catch-up of high growth occurred among other industrial nations after World War II. Few nations have had very high rates of growth for more than about eight years. The United States itself had one of the highest eight-year periods of growth early in its own past history, during the 1870's. Thus, we should be careful about jumping to conclusions about long-term trends on the basis of growth during short periods of years.

America's Challenge

Today the challenge that faces the United States is to adjust to the stronger trade rivalry of a stronger European economy while encouraging all industrial nations to move even further toward freer world trade and a worldwide market economy. Such a development undoubtedly would help stimulate the American economy and other economies—through increasing exports, more foreign investment, and cheaper goods available for all consumers—it also would bring with it adjustment problems. There seems to be no escape from the fact that changes which produce higher incomes also may require adjustments in the pattern in which our resources are allocated among industries and areas.

Meeting this long-term challenge has become increasingly difficult in recent years. We have exceeded our earnings of foreign exchange from investments and favorable trade balance by expansion of our military and nonmilitary foreign aid and private investment overseas. This has forced us to export gold in increasing amounts and caused us pesky if not insoluable problems.

We cannot here go deeply into the mechanics of foreign trade and payments. Suffice it to say at this point that we have been forced to make a long series of ad hoc adjustments which have had effects on virtually the entire domestic economy. Some of these adjustments have actually worked against the goal of expanded world trade. Why? Essentially because the post-World War II payments system adopted by the Western world has proved inflexible in the face of the drastically changed economic alignments that have been formed since 1946.

The growth of other nations is not cause for alarm—indeed our chances for sustained growth are enhanced by growth elsewhere. But, many say, America cannot afford to rest on its laurels. Europe is gaining new strength as an efficient competitor in world markets. Underdeveloped nations are looking to America for both aid and guidance in their development. However, rapid Russian growth is providing another kind of example and leadership. If we allow our own growth to falter, we may rapidly suffer loss of foreign markets and loss of world power and position.

If our goal is maintaining our position internationally, it means that domestically we must face and solve the problems of a high-production, high-consumption economy. We have a more interdependent economy which is sensitive to slight changes in spending. We have industries and regions that are lagging in their growth and adjustments to change. We have producer and labor groups that tend to turn to protective measures rather than adjustment measures when faced by changing conditions. We have a transportation and social revolution that is drastically altering the form of our metropolitan centers. The following and final section deals with the problem of maintaining or speeding our national growth while trying to cope with these growing pains.

MAINTAINING GROWTH: A POSTSCRIPT

Our subject has been economic growth—more specifically American economic growth. We have discussed the history of a process in operation, specifically the process of economic development. This concluding section will face the question, how do we maintain, or if it is our choice, speed the rate of economic growth? But, first it seems appropriate for us to raise the question, why is growth important?

Economic growth is a means to an end. That end is a higher level of economic welfare per capita. This means that growth is capable of bringing more goods, more services, and more leisure to the citizens of an economy.

But greater economic welfare is also a means to an end—it provides the material means and the time required for men to achieve more meaningful lives, to raise the quality of life. Historically, it was felt that this means was achieved once man had easy access to food, shelter, and clothing so that he no longer had to spend every waking hour, including some in which he should have been sleeping, grubbing for his livelihood.

As we have become more and more affluent we have learned that achieving the good life is not quite so simple. Man's material aspirations escalate along with the productivity of his economy. And, as we have remarked, both within and among economies, as some become increasingly rich others are left behind in poverty, relatively untouched by the fruits of economic growth and higher per capita income. As a consequence strife and warfare of one kind or another is carried on continuously between the haves and have nots. Yet, continued growth we feel will allow us to catch up with our rising aspirations and to bring high levels of economic welfare to all nations and their citizens.

Thus, as a policy matter, we are interested in at least maintaining growth and if possible raising the growth rate, both here in the United States and in the world as a whole. This, we caution, is not the economist's judgment—the Nation has made the value judgment that the growth rate is a concern of national policy. Let us now review our knowledge of the growth process by summarizing its important variables and then face the questions of how to maintain and accelerate the rate of economic development.

The Variables of Growth

The key variables which actively determine or modify the course of economic growth in a market economy are technology, resource inputs, methods of organizing production, and social goals including ways of sharing economic benefits. 15–17 is an outline of these variables and their most important subelements. With this outline in mind

15–17. MAINTAINING OR ACCELERATING ECONOMIC GROWTH IN A MARKET ECONOMY

1. Advance Knowledge
   a) research
   b) innovating enterprise
   c) education
2. Expand Inputs
   a) use of resources
   b) quality of labor
   c) incentives to invest
3. Organize Efficiently
   a) full use of resources
   b) flexible adjustment of resource allocation pattern
   c) resource allocation guided by free choice
4. Distribute Fairly
   a) broad participation
   b) security and opportunity

let us review the results of a study which analyzes the growth history of the United States between 1929 and 1957.[2] Note, however, that although the figures presented give an air of precision, this and similar studies rely on a great deal of subjectivity in making estimates and weighting specific variables. Tentative though such studies are, they are a great source of insight.

Over the 1929–57 period:

1. Increases in employment and rising average labor productivity resulting from shorter working hours accounted for 27 percent of the total increase in output.

2. Increases in the education level of the labor force so increased productivity that 23 percent of total growth is attributable to this factor.

3. The increase in the percentage of women in the labor force and the more efficient utilization of women accounted for 4 percent of total growth.

4. Increases in capital inputs contributed 15 percent toward the total increment in the rate of output.

[2] Edward F. Denison, *The Sources of Economic Growth in the United States and the Alternatives before Us* (New York: Committee for Economic Development, 1962).

5. Increases in knowledge and their application to production, marketing, and transportation and communication accounted for 20 percent of total growth.

6. Economies of scale realized through extensive growth of the economy produced 9 percent of the increase in total product.

7. The last 2 percent of the increment in output was accounted for by miscellaneous factors.

Note that increases in the quality of the labor force and the application of new knowledge to production accounted for 43 percent of the rise in the annual rate of production over the 1929–57 period. In contrast, increased physical capital yielded only 15 percent of the rise in GNP. This shows that having become the leading nation economically, we no longer can depend, as in the 19th century, upon extensive growth including the "importation" of capital and people that embodied the latest technology and knowledge. Growth must now come from learning more, developing new technologies, and building the capital and teaching the people that will embody it. With this in mind, let us investigate the problems of maintaining and accelerating growth in our market economy.

Influencing Growth Rates

Modern industrial society has been made possible by revolutionary advances in knowledge or methods of controlling our environment (physical and social) to serve our goals. Thus, if growth is our goal, primary attention should be given to ways to advance our knowledge. This requires more research, and perhaps more emphasis on research in business administration and methods of organizing our economic institutions. We need to find better ways to encourage inventions, and we need to encourage new and expanding business enterprise that is inventive in putting better methods into operation. Expanded education is an aid both to research into new areas of knowledge and to faster application of existing knowledge.

Greater output is in part a matter of expanded inputs, as we have seen; but the inputs need not be in the same proportions or the same quality. With out limited existing physical resources, we need to find better ways to utilize resources efficiently and utilize a greater variety of nature's resources, especially the more plentiful ones, to serve our purposes. Unless we find ways to speed up our output rate even more, we are going to need to limit our population growth sooner or later, both as a nation and as a world.

Part of our higher standard of living has resulted from reducing our labor input per person, especially the hard muscle effort and the long hours. As we have seen, this has been possible through education and improved skills. So, greater attention needs to be given to ways to make workers more productive. Our capital per worker still is increasing, but net capital formation has been slowing down. If we are to maintain full employment and maintain or speed our growth rate, we must not only encourage investment but find additional ways to increase the amount of capital each workingman can control.

Productive inputs also need to be organized efficiently to serve social goals. The first principle of efficiency is to fully utilize available resources; so every effort must be made to check and minimize repressions during which employment and equipment is partly idle.

At the same time, we must recognize the need for continual adjustments to change. There can be no guarantee to particular industries or producer groups that demand for their services will be maintained or that their income levels will be maintained without adjustment or change on their part. We must reexamine our economic institutions to see how flexible they are in adjustment to change and how well they contribute to encouraging more mobility of capital and labor resources.

We also should resist the incessant and often successful pressure of various producer and labor groups to use government agencies to force a resource allocation pattern that protects narrow vested interests rather than the public interest. Our market economy is consumer-oriented and requires a decentralization of production decisions among a multitude of individuals and firms. This preserves a maximum of freedom of individual choice in reaching a social consensus as to priorities among social goals.

Finally, our growth depends ultimately upon the consensus of American citizens as to how our resources are allocated and used; and this consensus, in turn, depends upon a feeling that growth's benefits are distributed fairly. In other words, it depends upon a continued wide distribution of benefits of our progress, with "middle-class" standards of consumption being enjoyed by the vast majority of our citizens. As we have seen, our standards of poverty are always rising; and we are increasingly enjoying high-level consumption on a mass-distribution basis. This has given our industries larger and larger markets, while we have a wider dispersion of decision making power and in our economy.

Fairness also involves a degree of protection against sudden or undue hardship, especially when the causes are beyond individual control. But fairness or equity does not require equality of income. Rather, it involves an expectation of equal opportunity to serve individual goals by saving, education, effort, and ability. It is mutually exclusive with discrimination in economic affairs along lines of race, religion, or gender.

One of the driving forces in our history of economic growth has been the range of opportunities afforded to the hard-working and unusual individual to try out ideas and to advance himself. Our market organization has provided the framework in which freedom of individuals has been relatively great, in spite of anticompetitive concentrations of business and labor groups, and in which individual energies have been harmonized to raise the standards of living for all.

Perhaps the best way to bring our study of growth into broad perspective is to address directly the problem of raising our long-term growth rate. Specifically, Denison, whose work was cited above, has calculated the changes necessary to raise the growth rate of total income by one percentage point over 20 years.[3] In other words, he asked the question, what must be done to cause total income to grow at an average yearly rate of 4⅓ percent rather than the 3⅓ percent he projected for the 20-year span. Modest as 1 percent sounds, note that it is more than 25 percent of the projected 3⅓ percent rate. To see just how formidable the job of spurring growth is, we need only take a cursory look at his catalog of changes. The most remarkable characteristic of his list is the very small gains that come from drastic changes in each of the various growth variables. Again we stress, Denison's work is groping and tentative, impressionistic in many respects, but it does highlight the fact that growth comes from many specific sources which individually make modest contributions to overall expansion.

To raise the growth rate by 1 percent per year, Denison suggests the following changes.

Increase inputs by:

1. doubling immigration—a gain of 0.10 percent;
2. adding 3 hours to the projected average work week—a gain of 0.28 percent;
3. adding 1 year to average length of schooling—a gain of 0.07 percent;
4. cutting structural unemployment and underemployment by one-half—a gain of 0.03 percent;
5. raising the increment in the capital stock by 10 percent—a gain of 0.20 percent;

[3] Edward F. Denison, "How to Raise the High-Employment Growth Rate by One Percentage Point," *American Economic Review* (May, 1962), No. 2, Vol. LII, pp. 67–75.

And increase output per unit of input by:

1. abolishing racial discrimination—a gain of 0.04 percent;
2. removing international trade barriers—a gain of 0.07 percent;
3. repealing "fair trade" laws—a gain of 0.05 percent;
4. eliminating union-enforced rigidities in the labor market—a gain of 0.02 percent;
5. adopting more widespread use of incentive pay systems—a gain of 0.05 percent;
6. consolidating the regulated industries such as railroads—a gain of 0.02 percent;
7. reducing the lag between development of new business methods and their adoption—a gain of 0.03 percent;
8. increasing research and development outlays—a gain of 0.04 percent.

Certainly the above list does not contain unachievable modifications of our system—each item has been subject to change and, indeed, altered in the past. How realistic it is to assume that all would be adopted is another question—especially in view of the fact that many of the variables are not directly subject to policy variation. Denison's exercise is perhaps less a guide to accelerating growth than it is a point-by-point enumeration of the difficulty of increasing the growth rate. This seems a fitting note on which to conclude this text.

STUDY QUESTIONS

1. Discuss the relationship between specialization, changes in world demand and technology, and a region's income. Use cotton as an illustrative example and contrast the 1850's with the 1950's.
2. Discuss the role of the city in regional development.
3. Discuss the relationship between per capita income and population changes. Is out-migration conducive to per capita income growth? How could in-migration cause the per capita growth rate to increase? "In the United States the states that grew the fastest in population, grew the fastest in income between 1950 and 1960;" evaluate this statement.
4. Trace the balance of payments history of the United States since World War I. With benefit of hindsight how would you have formulated international economic policy during the Great Depression? Since the gold losses began in the late 1950's?
5. Discuss the problems of transplanting our technology in underdeveloped countries.
6. Why is Russian growth likely to follow our lead in slowing down? How might added emphasis on consumer goods in Russia affect the growth rate?

7. Analyze this statement: "If Europe and/or Russia grows faster and larger we are going to suffer economically because that growth will come at the expense of our growth."
8. Analyze this statement: "To raise our growth rate by one percentage point should be rather easy—1 percent is a small increment and the government can readily influence our growth through monetary and fiscal policy."
9. Discuss the relationship between knowledge and growth. Do you see any similarity between education expenditures and purchases of machinery?
10. Why is growth important?

Index

INDEX

This book has been set in 12 point Garamond No. 3, leaded 1 point, and 10 point Garamond No. 3, leaded 2 points. Chapter numbers and part titles are in 18 point Spartan Medium italic; chapter titles and part numbers are in 18 point Spartan Medium. The size of the type page is 27 picas by 46 picas.